WINDOWS® 98
COMPLETE

SYBEX®

SAN FRANCISCO ► PARIS ► DÜSSELDORF ► SOEST

Associate Publisher: Gary Masters

Contracts and Licensing Manager: Kristine Plachy

Developmental Editor: Bonnie Bills

Compilation Editor: James A. Compton

Editors: Douglas Robert, Shelby Zimmerman, Pat Coleman, Ben Miller, Anamary Ehlen, Nancy Conner

Technical Editors: Rima Regas, Maryann Brown, Don Hergert, Peggy Brundy, Doug Smith, Doug Langston, Kim Wimpsett

Book Designer and Desktop Publisher: Maureen Forys, Happenstance Type-O-Rama

Interior Art: Chris Gillespie

Production Coordinators: Eryn Osterhaus, Amy Eoff

Proofreaders: Rebecca Rider, Duncan Watson

Indexer: Nancy Guenther

Cover Designer: DesignSite

Library of Congress Card Number: 98-84265
ISBN: 0-7821-2219-1

Manufactured in Canada

10 9 8 7 6 5 4 3 2

ACKNOWLEDGMENTS

This book incorporates the work of many people, inside and outside Sybex.

Gary Masters, Bonnie Bills, and Richard Mills hammered out the idea of an inexpensive showcase compilation including the widest possible range of topics for Windows 98 users. They defined the book's overall structure and contents.

A large team of editors, developmental editors, project editors, and technical editors helped to put together the various books from which *Windows 98 Complete* was compiled: Maureen Adams, Sherry Bonelli, Peter Kuhns, and Neil Edde handled developmental tasks; Kim Askew, Doug Robert, Ben Miller, Shelby Zimmerman, Kim Wimpsett, Anamary Ehlen, Vivian Perry, Peter Weverka, Bonnie Bills, Lee Ann Pickrell, Pat Coleman, and Michael Tom all contributed to editing or project editing; and the technical editors were Maryann Brown, Rima Regas, Don Hergert, Peggy Brundy, Doug Smith, and Doug Langston. Ms. Regas deserves particular thanks for helping to make sure the Internet and hardware chapters reflect Windows 98.

Jim Compton compiled and adapted all the material for publication in this book.

The *Windows 98 Complete* production team of designer and desktop publisher Maureen Forys, production coordinators Eryn Osterhaus and Amy Eoff, and proofreaders Rebecca Rider and Duncan Watson worked with speed and accuracy to turn the manuscript files and illustrations into the handsome book you're now reading. Liz Paulus, Dan Schiff, and Ina Ingenito also helped in various ways to keep the project moving.

Finally, our most important thanks go to the contributors who agreed to have their work excerpted into *Windows 98 Complete*: Sharon Crawford, Charlie Russel, and Neil J. Salkind; Robert Cowart; Mark Minasi, Eric Christiansen, and Kristina Shapar; Peter Dyson; Christian Crumlish; John Ross; Gene Weisskopf and Pat Coleman; Daniel A. Tauber, Brenda Kienan, and J. Tarin Towers; and the PC Novice/Smart Computing staff. Without their efforts, this book would not exist.

CONTENTS AT A GLANCE

Introduction   *xxxi*

Part I   Windows 98   **1**

Chapter 1   Introducing Windows 98   3
             From *Upgrading to Windows 98*

Chapter 2   Installing Windows 98 on Your Computer   19
             From *Mastering Windows 98*

Chapter 3   Visiting the Windows 98 Desktop   37
             From *The ABCs of Windows 98*

Chapter 4   Shortcuts Galore   57
             From *The ABCs of Windows 98*

Chapter 5   Windows Explorer and the Recycle Bin   71
             From *Windows 98: No Experience Required.*

Chapter 6   Installing and Running Programs   95
             From *Windows 98: No Experience Required.*

Chapter 7   Customizing with the Control Panel   111
             From *Mastering Windows 98*

Chapter 8   Printers and Printing   171
             From *Mastering Windows 98*

Chapter 9   Windows Multimedia   207
             From *Mastering Windows 98 Premium Edition*

Chapter 10   Hardware Mastery   253
             From *Windows 98: No Experience Required.*

Chapter 11   Maintaining the System   277
             From *Windows 98: No Experience Required.* and
             The ABCs of Windows 98

Chapter 12   System Troubleshooting   309
             From *Windows 98: No Experience Required.*

Chapter 13   Wired 98—Remote Access with Windows 98   319
             From *Expert Guide to Windows 98*

Chapter 14   Windows 98 Applets   363
             From *The ABCs of Windows 98*

Part II   The Internet and Windows 98   383

Chapter 15   Understanding Internet and World Wide Web Basics   385
From *The Internet: No Experience Required.*

Chapter 16   Communicating with E-mail   407
From *The Internet: No Experience Required.*

Chapter 17   Browsing the Web with Internet Explorer   443
From *ABCs of Microsoft Internet Explorer 4*

Chapter 18   Browsing with Sense and Security   483
From *Mastering Microsoft Internet Explorer 4*

Chapter 19   An Alternative to Internet Explorer: Netscape Navigator   521
From *Surfing the Internet with Netscape Communicator 4*

Chapter 20   Creating Web Pages with FrontPage Express   557
From *Mastering Microsoft Internet Explorer 4*

Chapter 21   Subscribing to Sites and Tuning in Channels   599
From *Mastering Microsoft Internet Explorer 4*

Part III   Your PC and Hardware   633

Chapter 22   A Buyer's Guide to PCs   635
From *The Complete PC Upgrade and Maintenance Guide*

Chapter 23   Avoiding Service: Preventive Maintenance   649
From *The Complete PC Upgrade and Maintenance Guide*

Chapter 24   Installing Random Access Memory   671
From *PC Upgrading & Maintenance: No Experience Required.*

Chapter 25   Upgrading to Multimedia   687
From *Mastering Windows 98*

Chapter 26   Installing External and Internal Modems   699
From *PC Upgrading & Maintenance: No Experience Required.*

Part IV   Windows 98 User's Reference   711

Appendix A   Windows 98 Command and Feature Reference   713
From *Windows 98 Instant Reference*

Appendix B   Windows 98 User's Glossary   791
From *The PC User's Essential Accessible Pocket Dictionary* and
The Internet Dictionary

Appendix C   Vendor's Guide   833
From *The Complete PC Upgrade and Maintenance Guide*

Appendix D   Finding and Downloading Windows Software Online   883
From *The Internet: No Experience Required.*

Index   906

TABLE OF CONTENTS

Introduction   *xxxi*

Part I ▶ Windows 98   1

Chapter 1 □ Introducing Windows 98   3

Must Be the Season of the Web   4
   The Big Difference   5
   Growing a New Shell   7
Find What You Need   7
   Shortcuts   8
   Seamless Web Connections   9
   What about My Mail?   10
   You're Not Connected Yet?   11
Getting It Delivered   11
   Channels   11
   Active Desktop   13
   Windows Update   13
Other Cool Stuff   14
What's Next?   16

Chapter 2 □ Installing Windows 98 on Your Computer   19

Easiest Approach: A Full Upgrade from an
   Earlier Version of Windows   22
Installing to a Fresh Disk or New Directory   28
Finding and Fixing Hard-Disk Problems during Installation   29
Reverting to the Previous Operating System   30
Removing Uninstall Files to Free Up Disk Space   32
Installing onto a Compressed Drive   32
How to Install Windows 98 to a Machine Running Windows NT   34
What's Next?   35

Chapter 3 □ Visiting the Windows 98 Desktop   37

The Start Button   38
Taskbars Galore   41
   Changing the Taskbar's Location and Size   42
   Making the Taskbar Disappear   42

Also on the Taskbar   42
Selecting the Taskbar's Toolbars   43
Quick Launch Toolbar   43
Desktop Toolbar   44
Address Toolbar   44
Links Toolbar   44
Creating a Toolbar   45
Making Room for All the Toolbars   45
Configuring Toolbars   46
What My Computer Can Do for You   46
Recycling Unwanted Files and Folders   47
The Windows 98 Properties Sheet   47
Setting Up Your Desktop   48
Background   50
Screen Saver   50
Appearance   50
Effects   51
Web   51
Settings   51
Getting All the Help You'll Ever Need   53
Using Offline Help   54
Using Web Help   55
What's Next?   55

Chapter 4 □ Shortcuts Galore   **57**
Creating Shortcuts   59
Creating a Shortcut When You Can See the Object   60
Creating a Shortcut When You Can't See the Object   60
Renaming a Shortcut   61
What to Name Shortcuts   61
Shortcut Settings   61
Finding the Target   62
Changing a Shortcut's Icon   62
Putting Shortcuts Where You Want Them   63
Putting a Start Menu Item on the Desktop   63
Adding a Program to the Start Menu   64
Adding a Shortcut to Send To   64
Starting a Program When Windows Starts   65
Starting a Program with a Keyboard Shortcut   66

Shortcuts to Other Places   67
   DOS Programs   67
   Disk Drives   67
Keyboard Shortcuts   67
What's Next?   69

Chapter 5 □ Windows Explorer and the Recycle Bin   71

Using Windows Explorer   72
   Viewing Extensions   73
Using Another Computer's Files   74
   Sharing a Drive or Folder   78
   Mapping a Drive   79
   Disconnecting from Mapped Drives or Folders 81
Exploring Floppy Disks   81
   Making Exact Copies   82
   Formatting Floppies   82
Using the Send To Option   84
   The Long...   84
   ...And the Short of It   84
Using the Recycle Bin   85
   What It Is   85
Sending Files to the Recycle Bin   86
   Sending a Floppy Disk's Files to the Recycle Bin   87
   Bypassing the Recycle Bin   87
   Files That Won't Go Willingly   88
Recovering a Deleted File   88
   More Than One File   89
Adjusting the Recycle Bin Settings   90
   How Much Space?   90
   Getting Rid of Confirmations   91
   Doing Away with the Recycle Bin   92
   Emptying the Recycle Bin   92
What's Next?   93

Chapter 6 □ Installing and Running Programs   95

Installing a Program   96
   Installing from a CD   96
   Installing from the Control Panel   99
Removing a Program   101
   Removing a Windows 3.1 Program   102

Removing a DOS Program 103

Finding a Program 103

Making Programs Easier to Find 105

Desktop Shortcuts 106

Programs Menu Shortcuts 106

Start Menu Shortcuts 107

Toolbar Shortcuts 107

Send-To Shortcuts 108

What's Next? 109

Chapter 7 ▫ Customizing with the Control Panel 111

Opening the Control Panel 112

Accessibility Options 116

Keyboard Accessibility Settings 117

Sound Accessibility Settings 119

Display Accessibility Settings 120

Mouse Accessibility Settings 121

Other Accessibility Settings 124

Adding New Hardware 125

Running the Install Hardware Wizard 126

When Your Hardware Isn't on the List 133

Adding and Removing Programs 134

Installing New Programs 134

Removing Existing Programs 136

Setting the Date and Time 137

Desktop Themes 138

Customizing Your Screen Display 138

Setting the Background and Wallpaper 139

Setting the Screen Saver 143

Adjusting the Appearance 147

Effects 152

Web 154

Driver Settings 154

Adjusting the Mouse 164

Switching the Buttons and Setting Double-Click Speed 164

Setting Your Pointers 166

Setting the Pointer Motion 167

General Mouse Settings 169

What's Next? 169

Chapter 8 □ Printers and Printing   171

A Print-Manager Primer   173
Adding a New Printer   174
  About Printer Installation   174
  About Adding Printers   176
  Running the Wizard to Add a New Printer   178
Altering the Details of a Printer's Setup—The Properties Box   187
Sharing a Printer for Network Use   189
Connecting to a Network Printer   190
How to Delete a Printer from Your Printers Folder   191
How to Print Out Documents from Your Programs   192
  About the Default Printer   192
  Printing from a Program   193
  Printing by Dragging Files onto a Printer Icon or
    into Its Window   194
  Printing by Right-Clicking on a Document   196
Working with the Print Queue   197
  Refreshing the Network Queue Information   198
  Deleting a File from the Queue   198
  Canceling All Pending Print Jobs on a Given Printer   199
  Pausing (and Resuming) the Printing Process   200
  Rearranging the Queue Order   201
Printing to a Disk File instead of a Printer   201
What's Next?   204

Chapter 9 □ Windows Multimedia   207

What Is Multimedia?   209
What's New in Windows 98 Multimedia   211
The Supplied Multimedia Applications and Utilities   213
  Doing It All with DVD Player   214
  Assigning Sounds with the Control Panel's Sound Utility   221
  Playing Multimedia Files with Media Player   226
  Recording and Editing Sounds with Sound Recorder   228
  Playing Tunes with CD Player   233
  TV Viewer   240
  Using TV Viewer   243
Managing Multimedia Drivers and Settings   249
What's Next?   250

Chapter 10 □ Hardware Mastery   253

Modems   254
  Installing a Modem   254
  Deleting a Modem   256
  Modem Settings   256
  Dialing Properties   259
  Troubleshooting   259
Scanners and Cameras   261
Adding and Configuring Printers   261
  Adding a Printer   262
  Uninstalling a Printer   264
  Printer Settings   264
  Troubleshooting   264
Changing a Mouse   265
Game Controllers   266
Using Infrared Devices   267
Setting the Display Adapter   268
  Changing a Video Card   269
  Changing a Video Driver   270
  Optimizing Video Settings   271
What's Next?   274

Chapter 11 □ Maintaining the System   277

Running ScanDisk   278
Fixing Disk Fragmentation   281
Disk Cleanup   283
Doing a System Tune-Up   286
Using Task Scheduler   287
Windows Update   287
Using Space Efficiently   289
  FAT32   290
  Compressing Hard Drives   293
Backing Up and Restoring Files   298
  Getting Started   298
  Tape Drive or Floppies   299
  Deciding on a Type of Backup   299
  Deciding What to Back Up   300
  Defining a File Set   301

Creating a Backup   301
Choosing Backup Options   305
Restoring Files   306
What's Next?   307

Chapter 12 □ System Troubleshooting   309

Using the System Information Utility   310
Meet Dr. Watson   311
Checking System Files   312
Using System Monitor   313
Using the Resource Meter   315
Troubleshooting Tools   316
What's Next?   317

Chapter 13 □ Wired 98—Remote Access with
Windows 98   319

What Is Remote Access?   321
So Near, and Yet So Far   321
What Are the Setup Options for Dial-Up Networking?   322
What Connection Protocols Are Supported by
Dial-Up Networking?   323
What Are the Different Combinations for Connection
Protocols and Network Protocols?   324
How Do I Install Dial-Up Networking?   325
Installing Dial-Up Networking on the Network   325
Configuring the DUN Network Connection   326
Installing Dial-Up Networking on the Client Machine   327
Configuring a DUN Client Connection   332
How Do I Test the DUN Connection?   337
Using the Internet Connection Wizard   339
Altering an Internet Connection   341
Sample ISP Information   343
Using WINS to Connect to an NT Domain over an
Existing Internet Connection   343
Troubleshooting a WINS Connection   348
Regular DUN vs. WINS vs. PPTP   350
Installing the Windows 98 Dial-Up Server   351

What about Security?   355
    Password Authentication Protocol (PAP)   355
    Challenge-Handshake Authentication Protocol (CHAP)   357
    Remote Access to Resources with DUN   357
What's Next?   360

Chapter 14 □ Windows 98 Applets   **363**

A World of Applets   364
Using Notepad   364
    What Notepad Has   364
Working with WordPad   364
    Opening WordPad   365
    Making and Formatting Documents   366
    Page Setup and Printing   367
What's on the Clipboard   367
    Taking a Look   367
    Saving the Clipboard's Contents   368
Drawing with Paint   368
    Creating Original Art   369
    Modifying the Work of Others   369
Entering New Characters   369
    Entering Characters   370
Phone Dialing for Fun   370
    Speed Dialing   371
    The Telephone Log   372
Using the Calculators   373
    Just the Basics   373
    Or One Step Beyond   374
    Pasting in the Numbers   374
Communicating with HyperTerminal   375
    How to Use It   376
    Sending Files   378
    And Receiving Them Too   379
    Saving a Session   380
    Using a Connection   380
Using the Briefcase   381
    How It Works   381
What's Next?   382

Part II ▶ The Internet and Windows 98 383

Chapter 15 □ Understanding Internet and World Wide Web Basics 385

Introducing the Internet 386
Communicating through E-mail or Discussion Groups 387
What's the Difference between the Web and the Internet? 388
Discovering What's New on the Net 392
Getting on the Internet 394
Cruising the Net at Work 394
Cruising the Net at Home 395
The Anatomy of an Internet Address 399
What You Can Do on the Net 401
Downloading Files from the Internet 402
Using Web Sites to Gather Information about the
Internet and the Web 403
What's Next? 404

Chapter 16 □ Communicating with E-mail 407

E-mail Basics 408
Running an E-mail Program 409
Sending Mail 409
Reading Mail 413
Replying to Mail 414
Deleting Mail 416
Using Proper E-mail Netiquette 416
Exiting an E-mail Program 418
Trying Out Microsoft Outlook Express and Netscape Messenger 418
Microsoft Outlook Express 418
Netscape Messenger 419
Using E-mail More Effectively 421
Sending Mail to More Than One Person 421
Sending Files via E-mail 422
Forwarding Mail to Someone Else 425
Enhancing Your E-mail with HTML Formatting 426
Writing E-mail with Your Word Processor 427
Checking Your Spelling 429
Attaching a Signature 430
Filing Your Messages 432

Filtering Messages as They Come In 434

Dealing with E-mail from Several Accounts 437

Managing an Address Book 438

Finding Internet E-mail Addresses 440

Use Search Tools on the Web 440

Say "Send Me E-mail" 440

Send Mail to Postmaster@ 441

What's Next? 441

Chapter 17 ▫ Browsing the Web with Internet Explorer 443

Starting Internet Explorer 444

The Internet Explorer Screen 444

Changing the Toolbars' Appearance 446

Creating Your Own Quick Links 447

Moving around the Web 449

Typing an Address 450

Using Hot Links 451

Returning to Sites You've Recently Visited 452

Explorer Bars 453

Moving Forward and Backward 457

Using More Than One Window at a Time 458

Home Pages 459

Choosing a Home Page 459

Changing Your Home Page 460

Using Internet Search Tools 461

Focusing Your Searches 464

Returning to Favorite Web Pages 464

Working with the Favorites List 465

Making Your Own Hot List 473

Creating and Using Web Shortcuts 474

Changing the Default Browser: A Warning 479

What's Next? 480

Chapter 18 ▫ Browsing with Sense and Security 483

Guarding Your Privacy on the Web 484

Staying Secure with Passwords 485

Saying No Thank You to Cookies 487

Retaining Your Privacy with the Profile Assistant 488

Keeping Transactions Secure with Microsoft Wallet 490

Filtering Sites with the Content Advisor   495
  Avoiding www.offensive   495
  The Content Advisor   496
  Cooperation between Web-Page Authors, Rating Systems,
    and Parents   497
  Determining the Ratings for Pages You Author   498
  Enabling the Content Advisor   499
  Setting the Ratings Criteria in the Content Advisor   501
  What to Do When a Page Is Disallowed   502
  Adding Another Rating System   504
Assigning Trust through Security Zones   507
  Dividing the Web into Security Zones   507
  Changing the Security Level for a Zone   508
  Assigning a Site to a Zone   510
Encrypting Transfers over a Secure Connection   512
Verifying Identity with Certificates   514
  Software Publisher Certificates   515
  Site Certificates   518
  Personal Certificates   519
What's Next?   519

**Chapter 19 □ An Alternative to Internet Explorer:
Netscape Navigator   521**

Launching Netscape Navigator   522
What You See: The Navigator Interface   524
Opening Your First Document   529
  Following Hot Links   529
  Opening a Document Using Its URL   531
Changing the Size and Color of Displayed Text   534
  Changing Fonts and Type Sizes   534
  Changing Colors   536
Saving Stuff to Your Local Machine   538
  Saving Stuff You Can See   539
  Saving Stuff That's Not in View   541
Viewing Documents You've Saved   542
Jumping Back and Forth While Viewing a Document   543
Getting Around in Frames   545
Caching and Reloading   547
Error Messages Demystified   550

Printing a Document or a Single Frame 552
Quitting Netscape Navigator 553
What's Next? 554

Chapter 20 □ Creating Web Pages with FrontPage Express **557**

Starting Out in FrontPage Express 558
Starting FrontPage 558
Navigating in FrontPage 559
Editing a Web Page 560
Inserting Line Breaks and Special Characters 561
Finding and Replacing Text 562
Adding Comments 563
Seeing the HTML Source Code 563
Previewing Your Work in Internet Explorer 565
Printing Your Work 565
Creating New Pages and Saving Your Work 567
Creating a New Page 567
Opening an Existing Page 569
Saving Your Work 571
Adding Structure to a Page 572
Separating Sections with a Horizontal Line 572
Creating Headings to Subdivide a Page 575
Organizing Data with Bulleted and Numbered Lists 575
Formatting Pages 577
Setting Character Properties 577
Setting Paragraph Properties 580
Setting Page Properties 582
Creating Meta Page Information 585
Creating Links 586
Creating a New Hyperlink 586
Revising and Deleting a Hyperlink 588
Working with Bookmarks 589
Working with Images 591
Getting the Picture 591
Creating an Inline Image 592
Setting Image Properties 593
What's Next? 597

Chapter 21 □ Subscribing to Sites and Tuning in Channels   599

Using Subscriptions to Stay in Touch	600
Signing Up for a Subscription	600
Subscribing to a Site	601
Browsing Your Updated Subscriptions	603
Canceling a Subscription	604
Viewing Your Current Subscriptions	605
Defining Your Subscriptions	606
Viewing Current Subscription Settings	607
Choosing How You Want to Be Notified	608
Choosing How Much Content Should Be Delivered	610
Setting a Subscription Schedule	613
Updating Your Subscriptions Manually	615
Choosing a Custom Schedule	616
Choosing a Custom Schedule for a New Subscription	617
Allowing Unattended Dial-Up Connections	617
Choosing a Custom Schedule for an Existing Subscription	618
Creating a New Custom Schedule	619
Editing an Existing Custom Schedule	620
Viewing and Subscribing to Active Channels	621
Viewing a Channel in Internet Explorer	622
Viewing a Channel in the Channel Viewer	622
Viewing a Channel from the Channel Bar	624
Subscribing to an Active Channel	624
Using a Channel on the Desktop or in the Channel Screen Saver	627
Setting a Channel's Options	629
What's Next?	631

Part III ▸ Your PC and Hardware   633

Chapter 22 □ A Buyer's Guide to PCs   635

Parts of a Generic PC	636
Problems with Proprietary PCs	637
Choosing a Market Niche	639
Choosing PC Parts	641
The CPU	641
The Bus	642

RAM   642
ROM BIOS   643
Motherboard/System Board   643
Hard Disks   643
Floppy Disks   643
Video Board   643
Video Monitor   644
Mouse   644
Printers   644
Serial Ports   644
Parallel Ports   645
From Whom Should You Buy?   645
What's Next?   646

Chapter 23 □ Avoiding Service: Preventive Maintenance   649

Heat and Thermal Shock   650
Removing Heat with a Fan   650
Good and Bad Box Designs   651
Dead Fans   651
Heat Sensor Devices   652
Safe Temperature Ranges for PCs   652
Duty Cycles   653
Thermal Shock   654
Sunbeams   654
Dealing with Dust   654
Magnetism   656
Stray Electromagnetism   657
Electromagnetic Interference   657
Power Noise   660
Electrostatic Discharge   663
Avoiding Water and Liquids   667
Corrosion   668
Making the Environment "PC Friendly"   668
What's Next?   669

Chapter 24 □ Installing Random Access Memory   671

The Fastest, Easiest Upgrade of All   672
Windows 98 Needs at Least 16MB   672
Choosing Memory Modules   673

Installing Additional RAM 674
Planning Ahead 675
How to Install RAM 676
What's Next? 684

Chapter 25 □ Upgrading to Multimedia 687

Three Ways to Upgrade 688
Features to Look For 691
Computer 692
CD-ROM Drive 692
CD Writer 693
DVD 694
Speakers 695
Sound Board 696
Video Card and Monitor 696
What's Next? 697

Chapter 26 □ Installing External and Internal Modems 699

Modem Basics 700
IRQ Nightmares 700
The External Modem 701
Connecting the Modem 702
Checking Your Work and Finishing Up 702
The Internal Modem 703
Choosing the Right Slot 703
Installing the Modem 704
Putting It All Together: Lines and Cables 705
Considerations for High-Speed Modems 706
Modem Configuration 707
Error-Checking 709
What's Next? 709

Part IV ▶ Windows 98 User's Reference 711

Appendix A □ Windows 98 Command and Feature Reference 713

Active Desktop 714
View As Web Page 714

Customize My Desktop	714
Update Now	715
Add New Hardware	715
Add/Remove Programs	716
Install/Uninstall Tab	716
Windows Setup Tab	717
Startup Disk Tab	717
Network Install Tab	718
Address Book	718
Importing an Existing Address Book	718
Creating a New Address Book Entry	719
Setting Up a New Group	720
Address Toolbar	720
Backup	720
Browse	720
CD Player	721
Chat	721
Clipboard	721
Closing Windows	721
Connection Wizard	722
Creating a New Connection to the Internet	723
Modifying an Existing Connection to the Internet	723
Control Panel	724
Copying Files and Folders	725
Using Drag-and-Drop	725
Using the Edit Menu	726
Using the Right Mouse Button	726
Creating New Folders	727
Date/Time	727
Deleting Files and Folders	728
Desktop	729
Disk Cleanup	729
Disk Space	729
Display	730
Documents	730
Drag-and-Drop	730
Entertainment	731
Explorer	731
Explorer Menus	731

Explorer Toolbar	733
Explorer Window	735
Customizing a Folder	735
Selecting a Drive and Choosing a File or a Folder	736
Favorites	736
Add to Favorites	737
Organize Favorites	737
Subscribing to a Web Site	737
Fax	737
Compose New Fax	738
Request a Fax	740
Find	740
Find Files or Folders	740
Find a Computer	742
Find on the Internet	742
Find People	743
Folder Options	743
General Tab	743
View Tab	744
File Types Tab	744
Fonts	745
Fonts Used in Windows 98	745
Adding a New Font to Your Computer	746
Displaying and Printing Font Samples	746
Formatting Disks	746
FrontPage Express	747
Games	747
Help	747
Windows Help System	747
Using the Built-In Troubleshooters	748
Getting Web Help	749
Help in a Dialog Box	749
Internet	749
General Tab	749
Security Tab	750
Content Tab	751
Connection Tab	752
Programs Tab	752
Advanced Tab	753

Internet Explorer 753
  Configuring Internet Explorer 754
  Browsing Offline 754
  Speeding Up Internet Explorer 754
Installing Applications 755
Keyboard 755
Log Off 756
Log On 757
Maximize/Minimize Buttons 757
Media Player 757
Modems 758
Mouse 758
  Buttons Tab 758
  Pointers Tab 758
  Motion Tab 758
Moving Files and Folders 759
  Using Drag-and-Drop 759
  Using the Edit Menu 759
  Using the Right Mouse Button 760
Moving and Arranging Icons 760
Multimedia 761
My Computer 761
  My Computer Folder 761
  Finding a File or Folder with My Computer 762
My Documents 762
Naming Disks 762
Naming Files and Folders 763
NetMeeting 763
Online Services 763
Outlook Express 764
  Reading the News 764
  Configuring Outlook Express 764
Paint 765
  Paint Toolbar 765
  Paint Menus 767
Passwords 767
  Enabling User Profiles 767
  Specifying a Password 768

Changing a Password   768
Allowing Remote Administration   770
Paste Command   770
Plug and Play   770
Printers   770
Programs   771
Adding a New Submenu to the Programs Menu   771
Properties   772
Recycle Bin   772
Regional Settings   772
Regional Tab   773
Number Tab   773
Currency Tab   774
Time Tab   774
Date Tab   775
Restore   775
Using the Restore Wizard   775
Using the Restore Tab   776
Run   776
ScanDisk   777
Screen Saver   777
Send To   777
Settings   778
Shortcuts   778
Shut Down   778
Sounds   779
Start   779
Startup   780
Taskbar   780
Switching with the Taskbar   781
Switching with Alt+Tab   781
Taskbar & Start Menu   782
Modifying the Taskbar Display   782
Adding Toolbars   783
Creating a Custom Toolbar   784
Task Scheduler   784
Undeleting Files   784
Uninstalling Applications   785

Users   785
Volume Control   786
    Varying the Recording Volume   787
Welcome to Windows   787
What's This   788
Windows Tune-Up   788
Windows Update   789

Appendix B □ Windows 98 User's Glossary   791

Appendix C □ Vendor's Guide   833

Manufacturers of Computers, Peripherals, and Components   834
Data Recovery Vendors   844
Memory Vendors   866
BIOS Upgrade Vendors   867
Storage Device Vendors   867
Miscellaneous Computer Products Vendors   868
Older PC Repair and Exchange   879
Computer Recycling Centers   881

Appendix D □ Finding and Downloading Windows
**   Software Online   883**

What's New with Searching?   884
Searching the Web   885
    Searching through a Directory   885
    Searching with a Search Engine   889
    Refining Your Search   892
    Visiting a Central Search Page   892
    Some Search Addresses   893
Downloading and Decompressing Files   893
Compression Programs   896
    Downloading WinZip   897
    Shareware.com   902
Buying Things Online   903

Index   *906*

INTRODUCTION

Windows *98 Complete* is a one-of-a-kind computer book—valuable both for the breadth of its content and for its low price. This thousand-page compilation of information from more than a dozen Sybex books provides comprehensive coverage of the Windows 98 operating environment and related Internet and PC hardware topics. This book, unique in the computer book world, was created with several goals in mind: first to offer a thorough guide covering all the important user-level features of Windows 98 at an affordable price; second to help you become familiar with the essential Windows 98 topics so you can choose your next Windows 98 book with confidence. The book's third goal is to acquaint you with some of our best authors—their writing styles and teaching skills, and the level of expertise they bring to their books—so you can easily find a match for your interests as you delve deeper into Windows 98 and the realms of software and hardware it opens up to you. *Windows 98 Complete* is designed to provide all the essential information you'll need to get the most from Windows 98 and your computer, while at the same time inviting you to explore the even greater depths and wider coverage of material in the original books.

If you've read other computer "how-to" books, you've seen that there are many possible approaches to the task of showing how to use software and hardware effectively. The books from which *Windows 98 Complete* was compiled represent a range of the approaches to teaching that Sybex and its authors have developed—from the quick, concise *No Experience Required* style to the wide-ranging, thoroughly detailed *Mastering* style. These books also address readers at different levels of computer experience, from *ABCs* to *Expert Guide*. As you read through various chapters of *Windows 98 Complete*, you'll see which approach works best for you. You'll also see what these books have in common: a commitment to clarity, accuracy, and practicality.

You'll find in these pages ample evidence of the high quality of Sybex's authors. Unlike publishers who produce "books by committee," Sybex authors are encouraged to write in individual voices that reflect their own experience with the software at hand and with the evolution of today's personal computers. Nearly every book represented here is the work of a single writer or a pair of close collaborators; when Mark Minasi, for example, says, "I once helped troubleshoot a network that had been installed...," you know you are getting the benefit of *his* direct experience. Likewise, all the Windows 98 chapters are based on their authors' firsthand testing of prerelease software and subsequent expertise with the final product.

In adapting the various source materials for inclusion in *Windows 98 Complete*, the compiler preserved these individual voices and perspectives. Chapters were edited only to minimize duplication, omit coverage of non-Windows tools, and update or add cross-references so that you can easily follow a topic across chapters. A few sections were also edited for length so that other important Windows 98 subjects could be included.

Who Can Benefit from This Book?

Windows 98 Complete is designed to meet the needs of a wide range of computer users working with the newest version of Microsoft's operating system. Windows 98 is an extraordinarily rich environment, with some elements that everyone uses, as well as features that may be essential to some users but of no interest to others. Therefore, while you could read this book from beginning to end—from installation through the features and on to expert tuning and tinkering—all of you may not need to read every chapter. The Table of Contents and the Index will guide you to the subjects you're looking for.

Beginners   Even if you have only a little familiarity with computers and their basic terminology, this book will start you working with Windows 98. You'll find step-by-step instructions for all the operations involved in running application programs and managing your computer system, along with clear explanations of essential concepts. You may want to start with chapters from the *ABCs* or *No Experience Required* titles.

Intermediate users   Chances are, you already know how to do routine tasks in Windows 3.1 or 95. You know your way around a few productivity applications, use e-mail extensively, browse the Web a little, and maybe have a favorite game or two. You also know there is always more to learn about working more effectively, and you want to get up to speed on the new Windows 98 features. Throughout this book you'll find instructions for just about anything you want to do. Nearly every chapter has nuggets of knowledge from which you can benefit.

Power users   Maybe you're a hardcore multimedia freak looking to upgrade your hardware to take advantage of Windows 98's expanded capabilities, or the unofficial guru of your office network, or an Internaut ready to try HTML authoring. There's plenty for you here, too; particularly in chapters from the *Mastering* books, *Expert Guide to Windows 98*, and the two *PC Upgrade and Maintenance* titles.

This book is for people using Windows 98 in any environment. You may be a "SOHO" (small-office/home-office) user, working with a stand-alone computer or a simple peer-to-peer network with no administrators or technical staff to rely on. In that case, you'll find plenty of information about maintaining, troubleshooting, and upgrading your computer and about sharing resources. Or you may be working within a larger network and simply want to get a leg up, quickly and inexpensively, as your office migrates to the new operating system. If you belong to both camps, with a home or laptop computer as well as one at work, you may be especially interested in Chapter 13's coverage of dial-up networking, a tool for telecommuting and for connecting via modem to the Internet.

How This Book Is Organized

Windows 98 Complete has four parts, consisting of 26 chapters and four appendices.

Part I: Windows 98   Not surprisingly, the biggest portion of the book is devoted to Windows 98 itself. The 14 chapters in Part I cover all the Windows essentials—installing Windows 98, touring the Desktop, creating shortcuts to programs and files you use frequently, using the Control Panel to customize your computer system, working with printers, and much more. You'll learn about Windows 98's extensive support for multimedia and about its tools for keeping your computer trouble-free. Anyone migrating from a previous Windows version (either 3.1 or 95) will want to start with Chapter 1's summary of the new features.

Part II: The Internet and Windows 98   One of the most significant features of Windows 98 is the integration of Internet Explorer with Windows Explorer and the Desktop. The extensive Sybex library of Internet books has already helped guide hundreds of thousands of users into cyberspace. Part II is an in-depth look at the Internet and the tools you've just acquired for browsing the Web, exchanging e-mail, subscribing to channels, and even building your own Web site. You'll also learn about Netscape Communicator, the most popular alternative to Internet Explorer, and about security issues such as screening inappropriate content and maintaining privacy for financial transactions.

Part III: PC and Hardware Tips for Windows 98 Users   If you're responsible for maintaining your own computer and for deciding what components to upgrade and when, you'll appreciate the last five chapters of this book. You'll learn how to protect your computer from physical hazards, and you'll get some guidelines for buying a new computer. If you don't want to spend thousands of dollars to get a system that's ready for Windows 98 and the Internet, check out the chapters on adding RAM, multimedia, and modems. With very little money and the expertise you'll gain here, you just might give your current PC another couple of years of useful life.

Part IV: Windows 98 User's References   The appendices here are designed for quick lookup—or casual browsing. There's an alphabetical reference to the essential commands and features of Windows 98, a glossary of Windows and Internet terminology you may encounter, a listing of Internet contact information for vendors of hardware and utility software, and a guide to downloading Windows software from the Web—finding it with search tools and "unzipping" it if necessary.

A Few Typographical Conventions

When a Windows operation requires a series of choices from menus or dialog boxes, the ➤ symbol is used to guide you through the instructions, like this: "Select Programs ➤ Accessories ➤ System Tools ➤ System Information." The items the ➤ symbol separates may be menu names, toolbar icons, check boxes, or other elements of the Windows interface—anyplace you can make a selection.

This typeface is used to identify Internet URLs and HTML code, and **boldface type** is used whenever you need to type something into a text box.

You'll find these types of special notes throughout the book:

TIP

You'll see a lot of these—quicker and smarter ways to accomplish a task, which the authors have based on many, many months spent testing and using Windows 98.

NOTE

You'll see these Notes, too. They usually represent alternate ways to accomplish a task or some additional information that needs to be highlighted.

WARNING

In a very few places you'll see a Warning like this one. There are few because it's hard to do irrevocable things in Windows 98 unless you work very hard at it. But when you see a warning, do pay attention to it.

YOU'LL ALSO SEE "SIDEBAR" BOXES LIKE THIS

These boxed sections provide added explanation of special topics that are noted briefly in the surrounding discussion, but that you may want to explore separately. For example, Chapter 9, on Windows 98's multimedia features, includes a look at the likely future of Web TV technology; and Chapter 18, on security issues for Internet users, includes a sidebar explaining how the SSL (Secured Sockets Layer) method of security works. Each sidebar has a heading that announces the topic so you can quickly decide whether it's something you need to know about.

For More Information...

See the Sybex Web site, www.sybex.com, to learn more about all the books that went into *Windows 98 Complete*. On the site's Catalog page, you'll find links to any book you're interested in. Also be sure to check the Sybex site for late-breaking developments about Windows 98 itself.

We hope you enjoy this book and find it useful. Happy computing!

PART I

WINDOWS 98

Chapter 1

INTRODUCING WINDOWS 98

Although the advance publicity for the release of Windows 98 may not have been quite up to the standard set by Windows 95, this newest version of the Windows operating system is indeed another big step forward—particularly if, like many users, you're making the transition from Windows 3.1.

Windows 98 offers substantial improvements in the user interface. Recognizing that the Internet and related technologies have become a vital part of what people do with desktop computers, Microsoft has designed Windows 98 to integrate seamlessly with the new version of its Internet Explorer browser. Windows 98 itself works more like Internet browsing, so that there is greater consistency between the online and offline worlds.

Adapted from *Upgrading to Windows 98* by Charlie Russel and Sharon Crawford

ISBN 0-7821-2190-x   432 pages $19.99

Windows 98 includes better multimedia and gaming support than its predecessors. In addition, it builds in support for lots of new hardware, such as Digital Versatile Disk (DVD) drives, multiple monitors, and Universal Serial Bus devices.

We aim to cut through the hype and hoopla about Windows 98 and explain what's really there. This book is a reliable guide to getting Windows 98 installed and working in the way that best suits you—whether you are upgrading from Windows 95 or making the big leap from Windows 3.1.

MUST BE THE SEASON OF THE WEB

Some of the most important changes in Windows 98 are right up front, on the Desktop and in the folders. They include simplified basic operations such as point-to-select and single-click-to-open, along with corresponding visual clues: underlined icon titles and a mouse pointer that changes to a pointing hand.

NOTE

You may not see these changes the first time you start Windows 98. The Windows 98 setup program attempts to keep options that you may have set under Windows 95, so the initial view is variable. For that reason, we will generally avoid talking about "default" conditions of the Desktop and folders; they are too variable. Instead, *Windows 98 Complete* shows how to achieve whatever look-and-feel you want; see Chapter 3 in particular.

Why the change? One of the main concepts pioneered by graphical user interfaces such as Apple's Macintosh is the consistent user interface. Microsoft has pushed the same idea in relation to Windows and programs written for Windows—as far as possible, they should all work the same way. Windows users have come to take it for granted that menus appear at the top, with File on the left and Help on the right. Toolbars have also become standard, and there is even a bit of consistency with regard to the images used on them.

But why do away with the venerable double-click as the way to open a document or launch a program? Because some of the most important

resources and programs now used on Windows computers are the Internet and World Wide Web browsers, and they work in a different way. If you've ever browsed the Net, you know that when you point to a link with your mouse, the link is automatically high-lighted. One click and the browser takes you there. Windows 98 can work the same way.

Notice that we say *can*. You don't *have* to use the new method. But Windows 98's setup process recommends it, and we agree: it only takes a bit of getting used to, and it really is easier. We expect that even users who don't spend much time online will see this and other changes as improvements.

The Big Difference

Even though millions more people now use computers than when Windows 95 was released, many are still intimidated when faced with using the Internet. Windows 95 helped make PCs easier to use, but the Internet remained a whole different world. The Internet's most popular features are those on the World Wide Web, accessible with browser software. The most popular browser over the last several years has been Netscape Navigator, although recently Microsoft Internet Explorer has gained in popularity. All browsers work with objects and links in ways that are different from the Windows 95 Desktop.

Windows 98, which includes Microsoft's latest version of Internet Explorer, aims to simplify Internet use in several ways. Some basic functions of the Windows 98 interface work like a Web browser, to simplify the transition between locally based and Internet-based work. These features can be easily configured to each user's preferences and level of comfort with the Internet. Figure 1.1 illustrates the seamlessness possible between the Desktop and the Internet.

One of the basic design objectives for Windows 95 was visual and functional consistency throughout the system. Windows 98 and Internet Explorer 4.0 extend this consistency of look-and-feel to the World Wide Web, while maintaining full compatibility with older software.

For example, in Windows 95 the Desktop windows in which folders are viewed are closely tied to Windows Explorer. It is no accident that folders and Windows Explorer offer similar options; they are simply different views of the same interface. Windows 98 extends this concept to the Internet. Type an Internet address (*URL*, for *Uniform Resource Locator*) in the address bar of any open folder or Windows Explorer, and the window turns into Internet Explorer to take you where you want to go. Likewise, you can enter the path to a folder (on your hard drive or local area network) in the address bar of Internet Explorer, and it will open the folder.

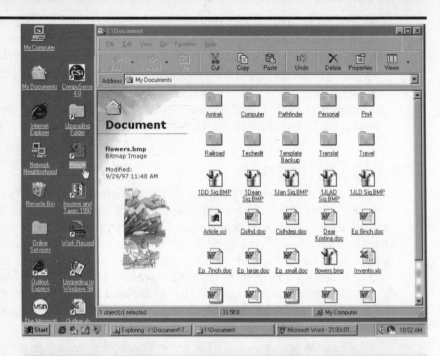

FIGURE 1.1:   The new Desktop can work like the Web: Point to select, and click to open.

Growing a New Shell

The change from Windows 3.1 to Windows 95 was a radical one. It wasn't just the exterior that changed; the plumbing and wiring were completely redone to give the system important new capabilities such as true multitasking.

The step up from Windows 95 to Windows 98 is less drastic. While the core operating system code has been tuned for better performance, it remains the same basic plumbing and wiring. A big part of the story this time is the exterior. Although Windows 98 doesn't shed the Windows 95 shell, it stretches it in a new direction and encourages the user to follow. The new direction is toward the Internet, and the range of new options points the user that way. At one end of the spectrum is full Web immersion, in which the user "lives" in Internet Explorer and never sees the Desktop. The suggested option is less radical: a Desktop that integrates smoothly with Web browsing. And it's even possible to stick with Windows 95–style behavior.

Windows 98 may have a greater impact on how people use computers than did Windows 95. If you have used Windows 95, you can think of Windows 98 as a former caterpillar emerging from the "shell" of its cocoon; genetically it's the same creature, but now it has brilliant colors, and it can explore a whole new world, because it can fly. Follow it, and you may find that you see with new eyes.

FOR WINDOWS 3.1 USERS

If you were one of the many who chose to stick with Windows 3.1 but now want to upgrade to Windows 98, you can take heart from two facts: Many millions of people have made the change to Windows 95, and you can benefit from their experience. In addition, you will get even more immediate benefits than did those who migrated to Windows 95 a couple of years ago.

FIND WHAT YOU NEED

Windows 95 introduced the concepts of folders and shortcuts. "Folder" is really just a new name for what used to be called a "directory"—a division of a hard drive or other storage device in which files and other folders can be stored. Though it took a while, the new name is catching on. Earlier versions of Windows, as well as other operating systems, have long used a file folder icon to represent a directory. Referring to directories as folders makes the name consistent with the image, and more accessible to users with little technical knowledge.

NOTE

Because folders and directories are the same thing, the various authors who have contributed to *Windows 98 Complete* use both terms interchangeably.

Shortcuts

Shortcuts were genuinely new with Windows 95, and they are unchanged in Windows 98. Many users, however, are still learning how to make the best use of them. Windows 98 makes a significant improvement in one of the shortcuts set up during installation. Microsoft's Office 95 and Office 97 suites attempt to force users to keep their work in a folder called My Documents, an approach that might not suit everyone. Windows 98 rescues the idea of a standard location for documents, without attempting to force the user to give it a particular name. The My Documents icon on the Windows 98 Desktop is a system icon, but you can modify it to point to any folder you wish.

FOR WINDOWS 3.1 USERS

Shortcuts are similar in some ways to the icons in a Program Manager group, but they are so much more flexible that the comparison could be misleading. Shortcuts are small files that serve as pointers. "Opening" a shortcut actually opens the object that the shortcut points to. That can be a program, as in Windows 3.1, but it can also be a document, a folder, or another resource available to your computer, such as a printer.

In addition, shortcuts can be placed anywhere you want them: on your Desktop, on the Start menu, or in any folder. Shortcuts are a big part of Windows 98's efficiency and ease of use. Details about shortcuts are in Chapter 4.

Seamless Web Connections

Windows 98 doesn't merely improve access to documents in folders on your hard drive or local area network. Where it really shines is with Internet or intranet access, which is quicker and more direct than in the past. You don't need to start your browser and make a connection before you open your Favorites list or type in an Internet address. Instead, you have two direct paths to the Internet available from any open folder or Windows Explorer. You can enter an Internet address (URL) in the address bar, or you can go to the View menu and open one of four Explorer bars shown in Figure 1.2.

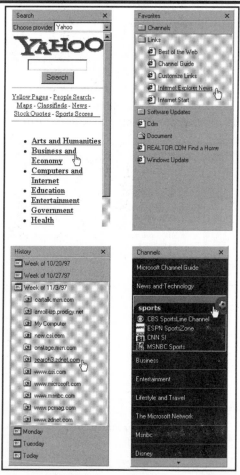

FIGURE 1.2: These Explorer bars give you direct access to Web sites and services.

The Explorer bars offer direct access to your favorite Web sites and to any site you have recently visited (as shown in the History bar). The new Internet channel technology has its own bar, explained in detail in Chapter 21. You also have a direct connection to a variety of Internet search engines.

Additionally, Windows 98 contains a completely new help system that integrates the built-in help files with online resources. System help files have been rewritten and are displayed in a window that looks like a simple browser. For more about your help options, see Chapter 3.

What about My Mail?

Windows 98 includes a new program for handling Internet email, called *Outlook Express* (see Figure 1.3). It's much less complex and easier to use than the Exchange/Windows Messaging system that was part of Windows 95. This is mostly good news for home users and those working in small offices that don't have their own email systems. Offices and companies that do have their own email system based on either a local area network or an intranet can, of course, continue to use it.

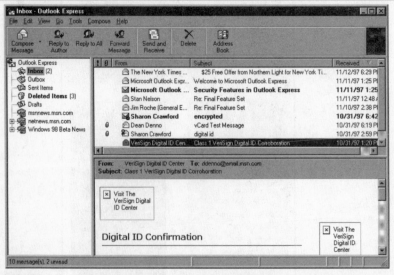

FIGURE 1.3: Outlook Express is excellent for handling Internet mail.

Besides handling Internet email, Outlook Express allows you to make use of Internet newsgroups. This is a big advance, as Windows 95 had no built-in access to newsgroups. Now you can sign on to an Internet news server and participate in discussions on any imaginable topic. The Internet has tens of thousands of newsgroups, with topics ranging from assassination conspiracies to software support. The uses of Outlook Express are described in Chapter 16.

WARNING

The switch from Exchange to Outlook Express has one big drawback: Windows 98 has no built-in fax capability. If that's important, you might want to continue using Exchange. To do that, you should install Windows 98 as an upgrade as discussed in Chapter 2.

You're Not Connected Yet?

Windows 98 can help you correct that lamentable situation! After installing Windows 98 you will find an Online services folder on your Desktop. Opening it will reveal shortcuts to setup programs for several major online services and Internet service providers. These include America Online, AT&T WorldNet, CompuServe, the Microsoft Network, and Prodigy Internet.

As long as your machine includes a modem, all you have to do is choose a service and Windows 98 will install the software and allow you to connect and set up an account.

GETTING IT DELIVERED

Some of the most important new features of Windows 98 and Internet Explorer 4.0 are the ones that automatically download Web sites so you can view them offline. These include channels, which are designed to provide easy access, and Active Desktop subscriptions, which download ordinary Web sites on a schedule, to be displayed on your Desktop. There is also an automated system for updating Windows 98 components over the Internet.

Channels

Windows 98 includes a mechanism for subscribing to channels. An Internet channel is a connection to a particular Web site. When you *subscribe* to a channel, content that you specify is delivered to your computer on a schedule that you can also specify. A wide variety of content providers such as PointCast, Disney, *The New York Times*, and *National Geographic* are designing channels. Many less-known companies and organizations are also setting up channels. The Windows 98 Desktop includes a channel bar for quick access to the channels you choose, and Microsoft's Web site even provides an online Channel Guide (Figure 1.4) to keep you aware of new channels.

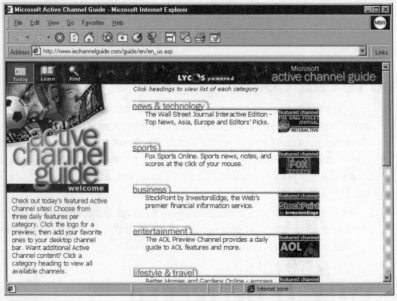

FIGURE 1.4: The Channel Guide tells you who is ready to push their material your way.

Part of the design of a channel is a recommended update schedule. This allows your computer to update the channel's content based on the provider's plans to update the site. Then you can view the channel content when you are ready, without having to go online. The channel content can be presented in several ways: in Internet Explorer, in a special full-screen window, on your Desktop, or as a screen saver. The full details on channels are in Chapter 21.

Active Desktop

The Windows 95 Desktop has a single layer to display all open windows, and the window in which you are working always comes to the foreground. The Windows 98 Active Desktop has two layers. Behind the windows where you work with your applications is an HTML layer that can display images of the Web sites of your choice. This HTML layer can also contain windows that display information from continuous-feed sources, such as a news wire or stock ticker, if you have a full-time Internet connection.

TIP

HTML stands for Hypertext Markup Language, the computer language in which Web pages are written. Windows 98 includes an HTML editor called FrontPage Express, which you can use to create documents for your Active Desktop or to create your own Web page. There's more about FrontPage Express in Chapter 20.

You can put any Web site you like on your Windows 98 Desktop, but to keep it current, it has to be updated. Windows 98 does this with subscriptions, which allow you to tell your computer when to go online and connect to a Web site to update it. Subscriptions and the Active Desktop are explained in detail in Chapter 21.

Windows Update

One of the big problems faced by many computer users is keeping the whole hardware/software system up-to-date. You may be one of the millions who have installed a new game or other video-intensive program, only to find it won't run because your system doesn't have the latest driver for the video display. Drivers for video, sound, and many other types of hardware are constantly being updated, but few companies send these updates out routinely, even if you have registered your hardware.

Microsoft has set the very ambitious goal of solving this problem with Windows 98. The Windows Update program is designed to compare the drivers and other system software you are using with a master database stored on Microsoft's Web site. When it finds that a newer version is available, it will offer you the option of upgrading.

OTHER COOL STUFF

The Windows 98 package has lots more new goodies, from system tools, to new hardware support, to a new file system that makes better use of large hard drives. Here are some of the most important ones:

Windows Tune-Up and System File Checker Windows 98 includes several new system tools to keep your computer running at its best and to help avoid problems. These are discussed in Chapter 11.

DVD support With Digital Versatile Disk drives and software finally coming on the market, Windows 98 is ready for them.

New buses for connecting peripheral devices Some Universal Serial Bus (USB) devices and Accelerated Graphics Port (AGP) graphics cards are already available. IEEE 1394 devices are still in the future, but Windows 98 includes support for all of these connections.

New types of input and output devices Details on such treats as digital cameras and force-feedback joysticks, among others, are in Chapter 10.

Power management functions Newer computers can go on standby, with greatly reduced power consumption, and still carry out scheduled tasks such as hard disk maintenance and the downloading of Web pages. The computer can restart quickly, with programs running just as you left them.

FAT32 This is a new method of storing information on hard drives that uses larger drives more efficiently. It is an important upgrade to the hard drive file system that came preinstalled on some Windows 95 computers, but it was "not available in stores" until Windows 98.

DirectX This feature provides improved playback of 3D graphics and other multimedia.

Desktop Themes These fun add-ons, some from the Windows 95 Plus Pack, are included in Windows 98.

FOR WINDOWS 3.1 USERS

The introduction of Windows 95 brought some major improvements over Windows 3.1. Here's a rundown of some of these features, which haven't changed in Windows 98.

One of the most crucial improvements is the change from a 16-bit operating system to one using 32-bit pieces of information. You don't really have to know anything about the jump to a 32-bit system other than the fact that it makes lots of good things possible.

Because this is a 32-bit system and built with today's computers in mind, other features and refinements are possible. One of the biggest is the switch to what's called 32-bit memory addressing, which is a way of identifying locations in memory. You probably know that computers work with information in the form of binary numbers—ones and zeroes. A binary number 32 digits (bits) wide can have 2^{32} possible values, so 32-bit addressing means that the computer can work with up to 2^{32} pieces of information in its memory.

Intel introduced a microprocessor that allowed 32-bit addressing back in 1988, but DOS and Windows 3.x were limited by a very peculiar system that managed to encompass a sort of 20-bit addressing. One result of this poor construct is that only 640 kilobytes are available for DOS programs. Another is that only 64 kilobytes were available for Windows 3.1 resources. This explains how you can have multi-megabytes of RAM and still run out of Windows resources.

With Windows 95 and 98 (let's call them 9x for short), we finally have full 32-bit addressing. This means, among other things, that a 32-bit application running in Windows 9x has access to essentially unlimited amounts of memory—in fact, up to 2 gigabytes.

Although Windows 3.1 could multitask—sort of—Windows 9x *really* can. This means the system makes decisions about priorities and doesn't depend on an application to release its hold on the CPU before taking care of other business.

In actual practice, it means that even if the hourglass is showing for one of your programs, you can usually switch to another program and do something useful. You can copy or format disks while printing a document. Or you can be downloading your email from the Internet while writing letters or entering information into a database.

CONTINUED ➡

You will also notice that multitasking works much better than it ever did in Windows 3.1. For one thing, it's faster; and most importantly, a disagreement between programs is much less likely to bring your whole system to a halt.

Another improvement is the introduction of long file names. Everyone coming from the world of DOS and Windows 3.1 has had to deal with the burden of the MS-DOS 8.3 file-naming restrictions. With only eight characters (often the extension was used by the program itself), your files ended up with names that were cryptic at best. What are you to make of a file called SSCRANRL.DOC? Six months down the road, were you likely to remember what it stood for?

Windows 95 brought relief in the form of long file names. Now instead of SSCRANRL.DOC, you can call the file Susan Stamberg's Cranberry Relish Recipe. File names can be up to 255 characters long, can include spaces, and can include both capital and lowercase letters.

WHAT'S NEXT?

Now that Charlie Russel and Sharon Crawford have given you an overview of Windows 98, they and the other contributors will start digging into just what you can do with it. The next chapter shows you how to install Windows 98.

Chapter 2

INSTALLING WINDOWS 98 ON YOUR COMPUTER

If you've just bought a new computer, chances are good that it came installed with Windows 98 already, in which case you don't need to read this chapter. On the other hand, if you are still using Windows 3.*x* or Windows 95, or have no version of Windows on your computer at all, you'll want to read this chapter.

NOTE

If at some point after you install Windows 98 you discover that you are missing some of the components discussed in this book, you can install them later from the Windows Control Panel's Add/Remove Programs applet, as explained in Chapter 7.

There are several basic scenarios when installing Windows 98:

▶ Installing on a new or newly formatted hard disk

▶ Installing over Windows 3.*x*

▶ Installing over Windows 95

Within each scenario, there are sub-scenarios, based on the source of the installation programs:

▶ Local CD-ROM or hard disk

▶ Local floppy disks

▶ Network CD-ROM or hard disk

In the vast majority of cases, you'll be installing from a local CD-ROM drive, over an existing Windows 3.*x* or Windows 95 installation.

NOTE

If you have a previous version of Windows on your computer, you can install from a DOS prompt, but Microsoft *recommends* installing from within Windows.

Although I don't recommend it, you can choose to install Windows into a directory other than the existing Windows directory. This lets you install a "clean" version of Windows 98, with no settings pulled in from the earlier installation. Although this assures you of having a fresh Registry, and might make you feel safer about trying out the new version, it will be a hassle in the long run. What I *do* recommend is upgrading *over* your existing Windows directory, by which I mean installing into the same directory; typically this would be C:\Windows. Besides, when you install over an existing version of Windows, you are offered the option of saving your old system files, so you can effortlessly revert to the old system if you want. (But be warned that if you're currently running Windows 95 it can take as much as 50 MB of additional space to perform this save, even though it is ultimately compressed to about 10 MB.)

When you opt to install over an existing Windows version (that is, 3.x or 95—see the note below about Windows NT), various important settings—such as program INI settings, file locations, program associations, program groups, and so forth—are transferred into your new version. The most important advantage of this approach is that you won't have to install all your applications (such as Microsoft Office) again for Windows 98. (If you install to a separate directory, things get pretty complicated, because with two separate versions of Windows on the same computer, the changes you make in one version don't carry over to the other.)

NOTE

If you are installing on a computer that has Windows NT on it, read the NT section at the end of this chapter. You cannot install *over* NT, though 98 can coexist *with* NT on the same drive.

Microsoft has done a laudable job of making the Windows 98 installation process pretty painless, thanks to the Setup Wizard, which provides a pleasant question-and-answer interface. It's been made even simpler than in Windows 95 by asking only a few questions up front, and then doing the rest of the work on its own without your intervention. Therefore, I'll spare you the boredom of walking you through *every* step here on paper. Instead, I'll get you going and discuss some of the decisions you'll have to make along the way.

TIP

Setup requires approximately 120 MB of hard disk space to complete. Of this, about 45 MB is temporary space used only during setup, and will be freed up again after the installation process is finished.

WARNING

Microsoft strongly suggests that you back up any important existing data and programs before you install Windows 98, just to be safe. Also, be sure to take Setup's advice about making a new Startup disk. Startup disks that you may have created with Windows 95 are not compatible with some features of Windows 98.

Easiest Approach: A Full Upgrade from an Earlier Version of Windows

First off, you'll need to decide whether you are going to install from floppy disks, CD-ROM, or your local area network. I highly recommend using a CD (or networked CD or hard disk if one is available) rather than floppies. It will save you a lot of time and disk swapping. With floppies you have to stay by the computer for close to an hour, plugging in disks (though there's a way to reduce the wait somewhat; see the following Tip). With the other options you can get things going, then take a coffee break while the necessary files are copied in.

Before beginning, make sure you have at least 120 MB of free hard-disk space on the target drive. You can use Windows Explorer or File Manager or the DOS **dir** command to check this.

TIP

If you must take the floppy-disk approach, here's a way to make it a little less onerous. If you have *more* than 120 MB of free disk space (this approach requires an additional 1.8 MB per floppy), you can copy all the disks into a directory on your hard disk and then run Setup from there. This will speed up the install-by-floppy version of the process considerably. Just make sure you still have the requisite 120 MB of free space after copying the floppies to the hard disk.

To begin the setup process:

1. Boot your computer into Windows.

2. Insert the CD into the CD-ROM drive, or, if you're going with the floppy approach, insert the first diskette into the appropriate floppy drive.

TIP

As I mentioned earlier, if you're using the CD, the CD-ROM drive needn't be on your local computer. You can install over a local-area network or dial-up connection from a shared directory or drive that has the CD in it, or contains all the files from the CD. You simply switch to that directory (via File Manager in Windows 3.*x* or Windows Explorer in Windows 95) and run Setup.exe.

3. I recommend you read through two text files that contain last-minute information about Windows 98. These files might provide special tips about your brand of computer or cards, printers, and other accessories. The files are called readme.txt and setup.txt. They can be found on Disk 1 of the floppy set or in the \Win98 directory on the CD-ROM. To read these files, just get to them via the File Manager or Windows Explorer, then double-click on them.

4. If you're in Windows 3.*x*, switch to the File Manager or Program Manager, open the File menu, and choose Run. If you're running Windows 95, go to Start ➤ Run. Then enter one of the following commands:

▸ If installing from a CD, enter **d:\win95\setup**

▸ If installing from a floppy, enter **a:setup**

(You may have to replace a: or d: in the above statements with the appropriate drive letter for your machine.) Alternatively, in File Manager or Windows Explorer you can look around for setup.exe and double-click on it. In a few seconds you'll be greeted with a fancy blue screen and some directions about installation (as in Figure 2.1).

NOTE

If you install from the DOS prompt instead of from Windows, you will have more questions to answer than the ones you're asked from this series of screens, relating to your choice for the destination directory for Windows and concerning which components to install. If you're interested in this approach, see the section below, "Installing to a Fresh Disk or New Directory."

5. Click on Continue to let Setup check out your computer. If you have too little disk space, you'll be alerted.

▸ You'll also be alerted to quit other programs if they are running. This is because Setup might bomb, in which case any work you have open in those programs could be lost. Switch to any program in which you have open work, save the work, close the program, and switch back to Setup.

6. Next, you'll see a license agreement. If you agree to the terms, click on Yes, then click on Next.

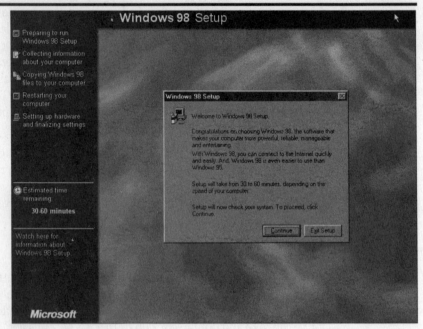

FIGURE 2.1: The first welcome screen when installing over an existing version of Windows

7. Setup now checks out what hardware is in your computer, and initializes the system's Registry file. It will check for installed components if you are upgrading from a previous version of Windows, and it will check to see that you have enough hard disk space. Assuming there is enough disk space (you checked for that earlier, didn't you?), you won't see any error messages about that. If you do, see the "Removing Uninstall Files to Free up Disk Space" section later in this chapter.

You'll also be asked at this point if you want to save your "system files." This is so that you can uninstall Windows 98 if it doesn't work, or if you decide you don't like it, or if for some other reason you want to be able to go back to your old operating system. (See the "Reverting to the Previous Operating System" section later in this chapter.) Click on Yes or No. If in doubt, click on Yes, then Next.

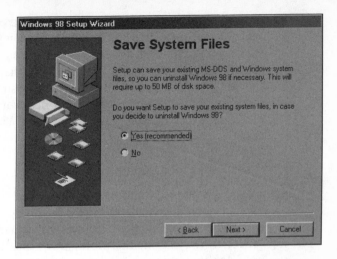

8. Your current system files will be backed up to a hidden, compressed file. If doing that would leave too little space for installation of Windows 98, you'll be alerted and given the option of skipping the backup in order to save disk space.

9. Next you're asked something about "channels," a question which pertains to using the Internet. For now, just click on the country you are in, and then click on Next. (Scroll the list if necessary.) Don't worry now about what this box is asking you; you'll learn about channels in Chapter 21.

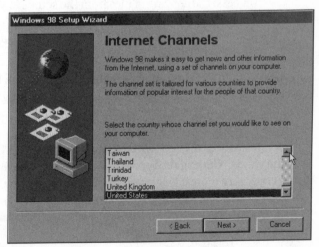

10. At this point Setup offers the opportunity to create an emergency startup disk. This is for starting your computer in case the hard disk is damaged or some system files get lost or corrupted. Since these are problems that could happen to even the best of machines, it's a good idea to make such a disk and keep it in a readily accessible drawer near your computer. This disk is also necessary for uninstalling Windows 98 in case the installation bombs. Just read the screen, then click on Next. Setup creates the list of files that will be put on the startup disk, but it doesn't make the disk yet.

11. You'll be prompted to insert a floppy disk in the disk drive and click on OK to make the disk. Anything on the floppy disk will be erased, so don't use one with something important on it. You can skip this procedure by clicking on Cancel, but I don't recommend it.

    ▶ For reasons given earlier, it's a very good idea to proceed with the creation of the startup disk now. However, if you don't have a floppy with you, you can cancel this process for now and continue with the rest of the installation. You can always return to Setup at some other time (even after you've been using Windows 98 for months) to make a startup disk later.

12. Now you'll move on to the main stage of the installation process: the copying of files from the source to your hard disk. This is the portion that takes the most time. Click on Next to start this process. A status bar keeps you abreast of the progress of the file copying operation.

At this point your computer will reboot. Remove the floppy disk, if you haven't already, and let the computer restart. If nothing happens for an extended period, you may have to turn the machine off and then on again. It will pick up where it left off.

Upon restarting, a Windows 98 screen appears with blue clouds on it, and the words "Getting ready to run Windows for the first time." This screen may stay there a *long time* (like 15 minutes or more) and your hard disk may sound like a garbage disposal (lots of activity), but that's okay. Really. Setup is doing some major housekeeping on your hard disk, possibly defragmenting it. Just sit tight.

NOTE

I've actually had to sit for 20 minutes while waiting for Windows to do its initial housecleaning. As long as the hard disk light is still lighting up, or you hear hard disk activity, all is well. Don't despair unless everything goes silent for multiple minutes.

Now you're in the phase in which hardware drivers are installed. Plug-and-Play devices are detected first, and then older, non Plug-and-Play hardware is detected.

Then the system may reboot again in order to load the hardware drivers it just set up. Devices such as PCMCIA cards should initialize. Again, if the system hangs (nothing happens for a long period of time), turn the computer off and on again using the power switch.

Next, a number of other things are adjusted:

▶ Control Panel options are set up.

▶ Programs on the Start menu are set up.

▶ Windows Help is installed.

▶ MS-DOS program settings are adjusted.

▶ Applications are set to start faster.

▶ Some system configuration is optimized.

The last activity, updating system settings, can take a bit of time, like five to ten minutes. But a progress bar lets you know how it's going. A few files may be copied from the CD at this time, so make sure the CD is still available.

Again the system restarts. The blue clouds will appear. It may take a couple of minutes for the Windows Desktop to appear. If you were updating from a previous version of Windows, you should see the same Desktop background or wallpaper you had before. You'll be prompted to enter your user name and password.

TIP

You may choose a user name and password now and enter it if you like. Remember the password for the next time you log into Windows 98.

After that, the computer may even restart one more time. Once it does, you're up and running.

Part i

INSTALLING TO A FRESH DISK OR NEW DIRECTORY

You may prefer to install Windows 98 into a new directory for one of three reasons:

▶ You have no version of Windows on the machine.

▶ *Or* you have an existing version of Windows on the machine, but want to keep that version and set up Windows 98 too. Then, by changing directory names or using some third-party utility program such as Partition Magic or BootCom, you can choose which version boots up. (This option is for confident, advanced users.)

▶ *Or* you want to control what components of Windows get installed. When you install to a new directory you have many more options than when upgrading over an existing installation.

To control the destination directory, you must (1) run Setup from a DOS prompt, and (2) boot in such a way as to have access to the CD-ROM drive, or, if you're installing across a network, to the network drive. If you have Windows 95 on the machine, the best way to do this is to create a Windows 95 emergency startup disk and boot from that. (To create this disk, go to Control Panel ➤ Add/Remove Programs ➤ Startup Disk.) If you had a CD-ROM drive available to you when you created the startup disk, it should have CD driver support files on them. Once you've booted to DOS, switch to the Setup source disk and run setup.exe.

When running Setup from DOS, ScanDisk runs first, checking the hard disk media. Assuming that all is okay (see the following section if it's not), exit ScanDisk by typing **X** (for Exit) when prompted. Setup will proceed, temporarily in character mode, then in a GUI mode with graphics, blue background, and mouse functionality.

After accepting the terms of the license agreement, you'll be given the option of choosing a hard disk directory for your Windows 98 installation. The default will be the existing Windows directory if there is one, but you can create a different directory at this point by typing a name for it. Next, you'll see a series of screens asking for your input or verification concerning the following tasks:

▶ Choose which set of Windows 98 components to install: Typical, Portable, Compact, or Custom (your choice).

- Provide your name and company name.

- Select specific components.

- Provide or verify your network ID: computer name, workgroup, and workstation description.

- Verify your computer settings: Keyboard, Language, Regional Variants, and User Interface (Windows 98 or 3.1).

- Choose your Internet Channels. (You can simply choose the country at this point.)

- Create a Windows 98 Emergency Startup disk.

The rest of the installation will go as explained in the previous section.

TIP

If you have a situation that requires additional setup options—for example, you may be a LAN administrator and want remote setup capabilities—refer to the Microsoft Windows 98 Resource Kit.

FINDING AND FIXING HARD-DISK PROBLEMS DURING INSTALLATION

The Setup program automatically runs ScanDisk to check for problems on your hard disk before proceeding. If it finds problems on your hard disk, the setup process won't continue until they are fixed. It's also possible that you'll see a message during a later stage of the setup process that says you have to run ScanDisk to fix the problems. This section offers a couple of approaches to run ScanDisk most effectively.

WARNING

The MS-DOS–based version of ScanDisk that Setup runs may detect long-filename errors, but it can't correct them. These errors will not prevent Setup from proceeding, but once it completes, you should run the new Windows version of ScanDisk from within Windows 98 to correct these errors.

1. Exit from the Setup program (and quit Windows if it's running).

2. Boot to a DOS prompt that offers access to the drive you're installing from.

3. Insert the CD (or floppy Setup Disk 1) into the drive, and from a DOS prompt, type the following:

    `d:scandisk.exe /all`

    (replacing the "d:" with the letter for the drive that contains the setup disk; for example, "a:" if you're working with a floppy).

4. Follow the instructions on your screen to fix any problems that ScanDisk finds.

5. Run Setup again (from Windows if it's available on your machine; otherwise, run it from a DOS prompt).

TIP

If you have problems or questions about Setup that are not covered in this chapter, check out the file called `setup.txt` on the CD or your floppy disks. On the CD you'll find it in the `readme` directory.

REVERTING TO THE PREVIOUS OPERATING SYSTEM

Assuming you opted during your Windows 98 setup to save your previous version's system files, you can revert to that version of Windows in case of a failed or unappreciated installation of Windows 98. (For exceptions to the "Saving System Files" scenario, see the sidebar nearby.)

To uninstall Windows 98 and completely restore your system to its previous versions of MS-DOS and Windows 3.x or Windows 95, follow these steps:

1. Choose Start ➤ Settings ➤ Control Panel.

2. Double-click Add/Remove Programs.

3. On the Install/Uninstall tab, click Windows 98, and then click Remove.

WHY YOU CAN'T ALWAYS SAVE YOUR SYSTEM FILES

The option of saving your system files for a future uninstall is not always offered during setup. Here are some situations where Setup does not offer the option:

▶ You are upgrading over an earlier version of Windows 98 itself (in which case your "system files" are the installed files themselves).

▶ *Or* you are installing to a new directory (in which case you don't need to *revert* to your previous version; instead, you can simply boot to the previous version's directory to run that version).

▶ *Or* you are running a version of MS-DOS earlier than 5.0 (in which case your system is automatically updated with the version of DOS that is used in Windows 98).

In most other situations, you are given the option to save your system files. When you choose this option, Setup saves your system files in a hidden, compressed file on your local hard drive. (They cannot be saved to a network drive or a floppy disk.) If you have multiple local drives, you will be able to select the one you want to use.

If you are not in one of the above exception situations but you see a message during setup about not being able to save your system files, refer to the "Setup Error Messages" section of the setup.txt file in the CD's readme directory or on the floppy installation disk.

Or, if at some point you have problems starting Windows 98, use your startup disk to start your computer. Simply insert the floppy startup disk, and, from a DOS prompt, type **a: UNINSTAL** and press Enter. Here are a few notes to be mindful of when running Uninstal.exe:

▶ The uninstall program needs to shut down Windows 98. If your computer starts to run Windows 98 again on reboot, try restarting it again, this time quickly pressing F8 when you see the message "Starting Windows 98." (Note, though, that you might only have a fraction of a second to do this, depending on how fast your machine is. Another approach is to hold down the Shift key while Windows is booting.) Then choose Command Prompt Only and run Uninstal from this command prompt.

▶ There should also be a copy of the Uninstal in your Windows directory on the hard disk. If you've misplaced your startup disk, you can run it from there instead.

▶ If you saved your files on a drive other than C, you can use the /w option to specify the drive where the files are located. For example, if your system files were saved to drive E during installation, type **Uninstal /w e:** to access them on that drive.

REMOVING UNINSTALL FILES TO FREE UP DISK SPACE

If you want to free up an additional 6 to 10 MB of disk space, you can remove the Uninstall files by following the steps below. Please note, however, that without the Uninstall files, you will no longer be able to uninstall Windows 98.

Here are the steps for removing the Uninstall files. Note that Windows 98 must be running to perform this operation.

1. Choose Start ➤ Settings ➤ Control Panel.

2. Double-click Add/Remove Programs.

3. On the Install/Uninstall tab, click Old Windows/MS-DOS System Files, and then click Remove.

INSTALLING ONTO A COMPRESSED DRIVE

If you have used compression software to compress your hard disk, or if a host drive or partition for your startup drive is compressed, you may get a message during setup that there is not enough space on the host partition of the compressed drive. If you get this message, you should free up some space on the specified drive, and then run Setup again. Note that if the drive was compressed with SuperStor or Stacker, you'll have to decompress the drive and remove the compression program before you can install Windows 98. If you used MS DriveSpace, you don't have to decompress. (Surprised?)

Here are some other steps to freeing up space for your installation:

▶ If you are setting up Windows on a compressed drive, try setting it up on an uncompressed drive if possible.

▶ Delete any unneeded files on your host partition.

▶ If you are running Windows 3.1 and have a permanent swap file, try making it smaller. In Control Panel, click the 386 Enhanced icon, and then click Virtual Memory. Then modify the size of your swap file.

▶ Use your disk compression software to free up some space on the host drive for the compressed drive.

And don't forget to check out the following subsections concerning particular compression programs.

WARNING

If you create a startup disk during setup, make sure you do not use a compressed disk for the startup disk.

SuperStor or Stacker Compressed Drive

If you have compressed your hard disk by using SuperStor, Setup may not be able to find your startup drive and install Windows 98. If you get a message about this during setup, uncompress your disk and then remove SuperStor, and then run Setup again.

Windows 98 will not run on a Stacker-compressed hard drive. If you currently have Stacker v. 4.1 installed on your computer, uninstall Stacker before you upgrade to Windows 98.

DriveSpace or DoubleSpace Compressed Drive

1. Quit Windows and get to a DOS prompt.

2. Run Drvspace.exe or Dblspace.exe (probably in your DOS or Windows directory).

3. Select the compressed drive on which you want to free up some space.

4. On the Drive menu, select Change Size.

NOTE

If you notice a discrepancy between the amount of free space reported by Setup and the amount of space you *think* is available on your host drive, it may be because Windows is reserving some space for a swap file.

XtraDrive Compression

If you have compressed your hard disk by using XtraDrive and you are upgrading over a previous version of Windows, you'll have to turn off XtraDrive's *write cache* before doing the install. Here's how to do that:

1. Exit Windows and get to DOS.

2. Run Vmu.exe (XtraDrive's Volume Maintenance Utility).

3. Click Advanced Options, and then press Enter.

4. Set the EMS cache size to **0**.

5. Set the Conventional cache size to **1** (the minimum).

6. Set Allow Write Caching to **No**.

7. At the confirmation prompt, click Yes. You will see a message saying that you must restart your computer for the changes to take effect.

8. Quit the Volume Maintenance Utility, and then restart your computer.

9. Start Windows, and then run Windows 98 Setup again.

HOW TO INSTALL WINDOWS 98 TO A MACHINE RUNNING WINDOWS NT

Although you can install Windows 98 to a machine that is already running Windows NT, you must install it to a separate partition—you cannot install 98 *over* NT, or vice versa. (You may remember that you could install NT over Windows 3.*x* and share settings, associations, and so forth; Windows 98 does not work this way.) As a result, though you can have NT and Windows 98 on the same computer and boot either operating system as you like, they won't share INI settings, installed applications, and other settings. This may change in the future, but in the meantime, it's simply an annoyance, because it means you'll have to install most applications twice—once for NT and once for Windows 98.

If you're configured to multi-boot MS-DOS and Windows NT
Boot to MS-DOS, and then run Windows 98 Setup from either MS-DOS or Windows 95. You will not be able to install Windows 98 to a partition with a shared Windows 95/Windows NT configuration; you will need to install Windows 98 to a different partition.

If you're not configured to multi-boot MS-DOS and Windows NT
You must first configure your computer to multi-boot MS-DOS and Windows NT, and then follow the instructions above.

If you were planning to boot to MS-DOS from a floppy disk and then run Windows 98 Setup   This approach permits you to install Windows 98 as you wish; however, you will no longer be able to boot to Windows NT. You can *restore* Windows NT, however, by booting from the Windows NT boot/repair disk and then selecting the Repair option.

NOTE

Windows 98 Setup will not run on OS/2. You need to boot to MS-DOS and then run Setup from the MS-DOS prompt. For more about installing over OS/2, see the setup.txt file on floppy disk 1 or in the Readme directory on the CD.

WHAT'S NEXT?

Now that you've installed Windows 98 and it's running successfully, in the next chapter you can take a quick tour of the Desktop with Sharon Crawford and Neil Salkind.

Chapter 3

VISITING THE WINDOWS 98 DESKTOP

In this chapter, we'll make a quick tour of the screen you see when Windows 98 first starts up. There'll be a description of each item you see on the Desktop as well as how to get more information on each item. Of course, everything can't be covered in detail here, so there are frequent references to later chapters—but we'll try not to bounce around any more than necessary.

Adapted from *The ABCs of Windows 98*, by Sharon Crawford and Neil J. Salkind

ISBN 0-7821-1953-0   384 pages $19.99

THE START BUTTON

The opening screen in Windows 98 (see Figure 3.1) is a mostly blank Desktop with a Taskbar running along the bottom of the screen and two or more icons located along the left-hand side of the screen. Fortunately, there's a clear signal where to begin in the form of a Start button in the lower-left corner.

FIGURE 3.1:   The Windows 98 Desktop displays the Taskbar and various icons.

NOTE

Your Desktop can contain many icons, depending upon how Windows 98 was originally configured when it was installed. If you purchased a computer with Windows 98 already installed on it, there are probably items on the Start menu, the Programs submenu, and the Desktop in addition to the items that appear on your Desktop by default.

 Click the Start button once to open a menu of choices. (To close the Start menu, click somewhere else on the

Desktop.) Initially there will be only a few items, but they're enough to get you going. Starting from the top, here's what you'll see:

Programs   Slide the mouse pointer to Programs and you'll get a cascading menu that includes all the programs currently installed plus access to a DOS prompt used to launch programs from a command line, the Internet Explorer used to browse the Internet (covered in Chapter 17), and the Windows Explorer used to work with files and folders (addressed in Chapter 5).

Favorites   Want to find out the score of the Yankees game? Where to have dinner in Cleveland? How about the latest reviews of a Disney movie? These are just some of the options that are available on the Favorites portion of the Start menu. Here you can use the Channels feature (Chapters 17 and 21) to arrange for information to be updated and to connect with various Internet sites.

Documents   Windows 98 remembers the files you recently worked on and puts them on this menu. To clear all the entries on the Documents menu:

1. Click the Start button.

2. Point to Settings and select Taskbar & Start Menu.

2. Select the Start Menu Programs tab.

3. ⁄Under the Documents menu, click the Clear button.

4. Click OK or Close.

There's no way to clear this menu selectively. It's all or nothing.

Settings   Branching off this item, you'll find the Control Panel folder, the Printers folder, the Taskbar & Start Menu settings, Folder Options, and an Active Desktop submenu. The Control Panel (explored in detail in Chapter 7) allows you to customize the way that Windows 98 looks and works. The Printers folder (refer to Chapter 8) is the place to go to add or modify the way a printer operates. You already know that the Taskbar & Start Menu option help you customize what appears on both the Programs menu and the Start menu. Folder Options allow you to determine which items you want on your Desktop and how you want them to appear; and Active Desktop allows you to switch the Desktop view, including whether you want to view the Desktop as a Web page, and to customize the Desktop appearance.

Part i

Find   This is a neat little program that will let you search for files (and folders) or even a particular piece of text within a file. You can search your whole computer, just a particular drive, or just selected drives. If you're on a network, you can search for a particular computer by name. You can even search for something on the Microsoft Network or the Internet, or e-mail a long-lost friend.

Select Find and then Files or Folders to begin a search for one of these items. Figure 3.2 shows the dialog box that appears if you select to find files.

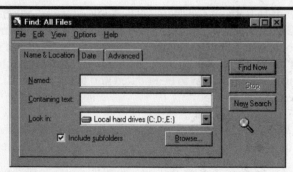

FIGURE 3.2:   The Find All Files dialog box

As you can see from the tabs, you can search by name and location and by the date a file was created or modified. The Advanced tab has an option for searching for a particular word or phrase. The menus include options to make your search case sensitive or to save the results of a search.

The really nice thing about Find is that once you locate the file or folder you want, you can just click to open it or you can drag it to another location. In other words, the file or list of files displayed at the end of a search is "live" and you can act on it accordingly.

TIP

To launch a search when the Desktop is visible, press the F3 key.

You can also use the Browse button on the Name & Location tab to look around for the file you want. And if you click the downward arrow on the Named box, you get a drop-down list of all the recent programs you've run from this box.

Help   The Help option on the Start menu is where you want to go to get help with anything and everything about Windows 98. When you click Help, you have the option of going to the help files that were installed along with Windows 98 or using the Internet to access help. Help is so important that we'll spend extra time on it later in this chapter in the section called "Getting All the Help You'll Ever Need."

Run   Those who loved the command-line option popular in earlier versions of Windows will be equally happy here. Select Run from the Start menu and you can type in the name of any program you want to launch. Or use the Browse button to go to the specific location. You can even enter an Internet site and Windows 98 will see to it that Internet Explorer takes you there.

Log Off   Log Off closes all programs, disconnects your computer from the network (if you're connected), and prepares your computer to be used by someone else. It does not shut the computer down.

Shut Down   This Start menu option is only used when you want to shut down your computer, restart it, or restart it in MS-DOS mode.

Taskbars Galore

The Taskbar appears at the bottom of your screen and contains the Start menu button and other helpful tools. Every open program has a button on the Taskbar associated with it. This is extremely handy because it means you don't have to close windows or move them aside to find other ones. Just click the button and the corresponding open item will become active.

You can modify the Taskbar's appearance and location to make its use even more convenient.

NOTE

While you can have many different buttons visible on the Taskbar, only one can be active. The active button is always the one that appears in a lighter shade of gray, as if it is depressed.

Changing the Taskbar's Location and Size

To change the location of the Taskbar, drag it to the top of the screen or to either side. (Make sure your cursor isn't over a button when you drag it.) To increase its size (so you can fit more buttons), position the mouse pointer at the edge of the Taskbar and when you see a double-headed arrow, drag the border to where you want it.

Making the Taskbar Disappear

If you have a smallish monitor, you may want the Taskbar to disappear except when you need it. This gives you more room on the Desktop. To try this look, follow these steps:

1. Click the Start button and select Settings ➤ Taskbar & Start Menu.

2. On the Taskbar Options page, click the Auto Hide box.

3. If you want to access the Taskbar even when you're running a full-screen program, select Always on Top as well.

4. Click Apply to preview the changes or OK to accept them and close the box.

Now the Taskbar will only appear as you move the mouse pointer toward the bottom of the screen. Once you move the mouse pointer away from the bottom, the Taskbar will no longer be visible. You can reverse this by deselecting the Auto Hide box in Taskbar Options.

TIP
You can also quickly get to the Taskbar Properties window by right-clicking between Taskbar buttons and selecting Properties.

Also on the Taskbar

The Taskbar contains the all-important Start menu and buttons for each open item, but it also contains other items to make your Windows 98 activities easier.

To the right of the Start button is the Quick Launch toolbar with buttons that can be used to access Internet Explorer (the Windows 98 Internet browser, discussed in Chapter 17), launch Outlook Express (the Windows 98 mail program, discussed in Chapter 16), change the view of the Desktop, and use Windows 98 Channels to access information.

The right corner of the Taskbar is interesting as well. That's where you'll find active bits of hardware. If you have a sound card and it's working, there'll be a little speaker icon on the Taskbar. Also, when you're printing or faxing, a miniature printer appears in the same area. Position the mouse pointer over the clock display and a box showing the day and date will pop open. To change this, either double-click, or right-click and select Adjust Date/Time. If you install software that opens when you start Windows 98 and remains available at all times, a corresponding icon will appear as well in this area of the Taskbar.

Selecting the Taskbar's Toolbars

The Taskbar can contain a series of different toolbars. To display a toolbar, point to a blank place on the Taskbar and click the right mouse button. Select Toolbars and then select the toolbar you want to use. The menu includes ready-made toolbars plus the opportunity to make your own.

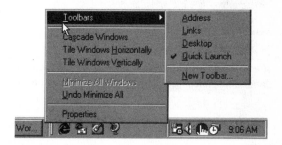

Quick Launch Toolbar

The Quick Launch toolbar is on the Taskbar by default. It consists of icons representing Internet Explorer, Outlook Express, the Desktop, and Channels.

A single click will open Internet Explorer or any of the other programs represented. When you have a bunch of windows open and you want to get at something on your Desktop, just click the Show Desktop icon to minimize the current windows. Click the icon again to return the open windows to their original positions.

Desktop Toolbar

Select the Desktop toolbar and every icon on your Desktop will be represented in the Taskbar. Click any of the icons to open the file or program it represents.

Address Toolbar

Select Address to open a toolbar that allows you to enter a Web address without having to open an Internet browser first. The address can be on your own computer, on your intranet, or on the Internet.

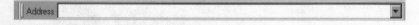

TIP

The Address and Links toolbars may not be available on your computer, depending on whether or not you have established an Internet connection.

Type in an address or click the drop-down arrow to select a recently visited site.

NOTE

For more on using Web addresses, see Chapter 17.

Links Toolbar

The Links toolbar is another Web-based toolbar. It contains all the shortcuts to Web sites that are listed in the folder WINDOWS\FAVORITES\LINKS (or in Start ➤ Favorites ➤ Links). You can add shortcuts and delete the ones you don't want (see Chapter 4).

Right-clicking on the Taskbar allows you to select the toolbars option and choose which toolbars are displayed on the Desktop.

Creating a Toolbar

After right-clicking on the Taskbar, select Toolbars ➤ New Toolbar to create a toolbar of your own design. In the New Toolbar window (see Figure 3.3), select a folder and then click the OK button. The items in the folder you selected will appear as a toolbar.

FIGURE 3.3: Selecting a folder that will become a toolbar

Making Room for All the Toolbars

Opening even two toolbars at the same time will surely overcrowd the Taskbar. To make more room for an individual toolbar, point to the top of the Taskbar so your cursor looks like this vertical bar. When your pointer grows two heads, click once and drag the vertical sizing bar to the position you want.

If you want even more room, point to the right or left edge of a toolbar and when the pointer turns to a double-headed arrow, click and drag to make it wider. Now you can have all the toolbars you want!

Configuring Toolbars

Are the icons on the toolbar too small? Right-click on a blank part of the toolbar and select View ➤ Large. You can make one toolbar large and leave the others at their default setting.

WARNING

It's a big help that each of the toolbars can be adjusted. It can be a challenge to find a truly blank spot to right-click on once you have several toolbars on the Taskbar.

To change the contents of a toolbar, right-click on it and select Open. In the window that opens, delete items you don't need and add shortcuts to files or programs you want. Below is the Quick Launch toolbar with the addition of a shortcut to Quicken. This program can now be opened by single-clicking on the Taskbar.

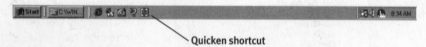

Quicken shortcut

WHAT MY COMPUTER CAN DO FOR YOU

The My Computer icon is on every Windows 98 Desktop. Single-click the icon to see icons for all your drives, plus a folder for the Control Panel and a Printers folder, as well as folders used in creating dial-up connections. My Computer is one of several ways to access information about the drives on your computer and your printer. It's the perfect place to go to highlight a hard drive and then right-click to find out about some of the drive's properties, such as how much space is available through its Properties option.

Right-click on the My Computer icon and select Properties for a look at your hardware.

Click on the My Computer icon and select Folder Options from the View menu. On the General tab, you can select whether you want Web

Style, Classic Style, or a combination of the two. Web Style is where only one window is displayed at a time, which is probably preferable unless you have a very large monitor. On the average monitor, having every click open a new window (with all the old ones remaining) can turn your Desktop into a crowded mess very quickly.

NOTE

If the name My Computer is just too cute for your tastes (and it is for ours), right-click the icon and select Rename from the menu. Then edit the existing name or type an entirely new one.

RECYCLING UNWANTED FILES AND FOLDERS

The Recycle Bin, as you might imagine, is where old, deleted files hang out until you may need them again, or until you send them to a quick and painless death (meaning they are no longer recoverable).

Despite the name, the deleted files aren't actually recycled unless you rescue them from the bin before they're deleted permanently. Nevertheless, the Recycle Bin gives you a nice margin of safety. When you delete a file, you have days or even weeks (depending on how you set things up) to change your mind and retrieve it.

There are two very important things to know about the Recycle Bin:

▶ The Recycle Bin icon cannot be renamed or deleted.

▶ Files that are deleted using DOS programs or any program that is not part of Windows 98 are not sent to the Recycle Bin. They're just deleted, so be careful.

THE WINDOWS 98 PROPERTIES SHEET

Sometimes it's important to have information about files, folders, and programs. For example, you might be having trouble running a certain program and need the size and location of a particular file. In Windows 98, it's a snap to use Properties sheets and find out about objects that appear on your Desktop. You can try it by right-clicking on the object you want to learn more about and selecting Properties.

When you select Properties, you open what's called a *Properties sheet* (shown in Figure 3.4). Properties sheets vary, of course. Some types of files will have multiple pages in the Properties sheet; others will have only one page and very few options. The one you see in Figure 3.4 is a simple Properties sheet for a file created using Microsoft Word.

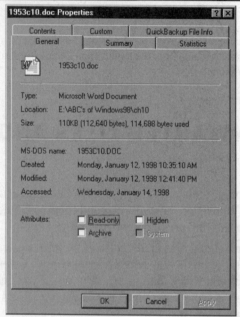

FIGURE 3.4:   A Properties sheet for a simple Microsoft Word file

Properties sheets contain valuable information about files, programs, devices, and virtually anything else that can be represented by an icon. So when you find yourself with a program or a piece of hardware that isn't working the way you want it to, right-click on it, select Properties, and then examine the contents of the Properties sheet.

Setting Up Your Desktop

The default Windows 98 Desktop screen you saw in Figure 3.1 probably does not elicit cries of joy on first glance. But this can be easily changed. One of the most convenient and friendly features that Windows 98 offers is that you can change the appearance of the Desktop and almost any of the elements it contains such as the color of the display or the resolution of the objects on the Desktop.

WARNING

When you begin changing default Windows 98 settings, it's a good idea to write down the old settings just in case you end up with something you like less than the original. This will make it fairly easy to switch back to the original settings should you need to.

Remember that you can use the entire area of your monitor's screen in Windows 98. You can have many folders, a few, or none at all. You can have all your programs on menus that fold out of the Start button's menus or you can have program icons on the Desktop where you can open them with a mouse click. You can also have colors, fonts, and Desktop wallpaper of many types. You can do just about anything you can imagine, so experiment until you find a setup that works the way you do. Here's how to get at all the settings that affect the Desktop.

To get to the Properties sheets that control the Desktop, move the pointer to a blank spot on the Desktop and right-click the mouse. Select Properties from the pop-up menu and you'll see the Display Properties dialog box (see Figure 3.5) with seven labeled tabs or pages.

Next, we'll explore the contents of each individual page that is part of the Display Properties sheet.

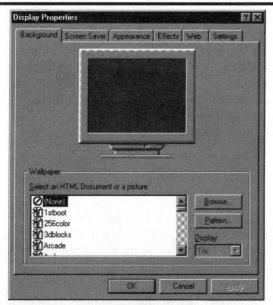

FIGURE 3.5: The Display Properties dialog box allows you to change the appearance of your Desktop.

Background

The wallpaper and background pattern is what appears as your Desktop. On the Background page, you can set both of these elements. If you have a special type of pattern, you can use the Browse button to locate that file and use it as your wallpaper. Any file that is in a bitmap format (.BMP) or device-independent bitmap file format (.DIB) can be used as wallpaper.

WARNING

When Windows 98 is installed, it uses the minimal amount of memory necessary to maintain the Desktop display. Changes, such as adding complex patterns to the Desktop, uses valuable memory. If you don't want to use memory resources, minimize the number of Desktop settings you change.

TIP

The Apply button lets you see how a setting will work without having to close the Display Properties box. It also allows you to try several different settings before you make a decision as to which one you want to use.

Screen Saver

When personal computers were relatively new, monitors could be damaged if the same image was left on the screen for an extended period of time. Screen savers, a constantly moving and repetitive display, came to the rescue. If you installed a screen saver—the one that comes with Windows 98 or some other one—you can adjust the settings on this page. All the installed screen savers are in the Screen Saver drop-down list. Click the Preview button to get a full-screen view of the selected screen saver. Move your mouse or press any key on the keyboard to return to the Display Properties screen.

Appearance

This page allows you to change the color scheme of the different Desktop elements, such as the title bar and how text will appear on the Desktop. Click any of the elements in the window at the top of the Appearance page, and the name of the element appears in the Item box as well as the colors and any other settings. Change the size or color, or both. If there's a font that can be changed, the current one will appear in the Font box.

And if you're just not in a very creative mood, select one of the many different color schemes ranging from Desert to Lilac. How pretty.

Effects

This page, a new addition to Windows 98, allows you to work with the various icons used to represent files and folders on the Windows 98 Desktop, and it even allows you to hide all the icons on the Desktop if you are viewing it as a Web page. You can also adjust visual effects such as the size of the icons on the Desktop, and even smooth the edges of those pesky fonts that refuse to cooperate.

Web

The Web tab gives you the opportunity to create different configurations of items on the Windows 98 Active Desktop, and to open a series of Channels or links, which you can go to using Internet Explorer (see Chapter 17), with a click. You can also place other active resources (links to other Internet sites) on your Desktop and change the way you click the Desktop icons using the Folder Options button.

Settings

Of all the pages in the Display Properties dialog box, this page offers the changes that have the most direct impact on your working environment. Here's where you can change how your screen actually looks (as well as what Windows 98 knows about your display hardware).

You can change the number of colors that are used (which is limited by the type of monitor you have and the capability of the video driver), the size of the fonts used on the Desktop (by clicking the Advanced button), and most important, the area of the Desktop that is used by Windows 98 (also limited by your hardware and software capabilities).

Changing Resolutions

Displays are described in terms of their resolution—that's the number of dots (or pixels) on the screen and the number of colors that can be displayed at the same time. The resolutions you can choose using the slider under the Screen Area are limited by the hardware and software you have. You can't make your monitor and video card display more than is built into them. As the resolution increases, objects become more defined, but they become smaller as well. Also, as the relocation increases, more of your computer's memory is devoted to appearance rather than performance.

Most computers and most people are happy with the 800×600 setting. Resolution choices are based on what you like to look at—constrained by the capabilities of your monitor and video card. At the lowest resolution, you may not be able to see all the elements of some programs, so try the next higher resolution. At the highest resolutions, screen elements are very small, so you may want to try Large Fonts from the Font Size box (by clicking the Advance button). That will make the icon captions on the Desktop easier to see.

Here are the most likely display settings:

▶ 640×480   A standard VGA display that's 640 pixels wide by 480 pixels high.

▶ 800×600   A typical SVGA display (super VGA).

▶ 1024×768   This is the upper limit of SVGA and the beginning of more advanced systems such as 8514/A and XGA. This is a very fine (that is, non-grainy) resolution; but if your monitor is 15 inches or smaller, you'd better have very good eyes.

▶ 1280×1024   A very fine resolution but one that requires a large monitor. Even with a 17-inch screen, you'll need good eyes.

You'll notice as you move the slider toward higher resolutions that the number of colors displayed in the Colors box changes. As resolution numbers go up, color numbers have to go down because they're both competing for the same video memory. That's why, if you want the most realistic color represented on your screen, you'll need a video card (also called a display adapter) with 2, 4, or more megabytes of its own memory.

As with many display changes, you'll have to restart your computer to see the effect of these changes.

NOTE

If you change your screen resolution, you may end up with some very peculiar arrangements of your icons. They may be way too far apart or so close together that they're difficult to use. The Appearance page has controls for the spacing of icons. Pull down the Item drop-down list and select one of the Icon Spacing choices, and then adjust the spacing using the Size box.

GETTING ALL THE HELP YOU'LL EVER NEED

Who needs Help with Windows 98? Sooner or later, almost everyone. Windows 98 provides extensive help that is easily accessible and easily understood.

The most direct way to get Windows 98 help is from the Start menu. Click the Start button and then click Help. The initial Windows 98 help screen shown in Figure 3.6 opens.

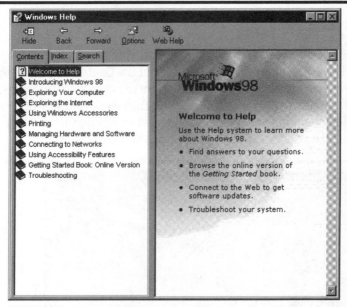

FIGURE 3.6: From the Help menu, you can select local Help or the Web Help button from the Internet browser.

You can elect to access offline help or access Web help through your Internet connection. Offline, Windows 98 will use the files stored on your computer to provide you with assistance on the topic of your choice. If you click the Web Help button, Windows 98 will use your Internet connection to make a direct connection to Microsoft and you can access help there.

Which help should you use? The offline option is great for most common problems, and you can probably find the help you need. But if you have a fast Internet connection and want to access all the help and services at your disposal, try the Web Help option. In a nutshell, offline is faster, but the Web Help option is more comprehensive.

TIP

Earlier versions of Windows allowed the user to press the F1 key and get help on the selected dialog box option. This easiest of help approaches is still alive and well. At any time in any Windows 98 dialog box, you can press F1 and get help on the Desktop or the current action you are undertaking. It's quick, it's handy, and it works.

Using Offline Help

Offline Help allows you to select from three different ways of getting help (see Figure 3.7). One is through a search of the Contents of Windows 98, which includes general help categories. Here you click the category in which you are interested (such as Printing) and then work your way through the selection of options until you find the topic on which you need help. Just follow the instructions provided to get the assistance you need.

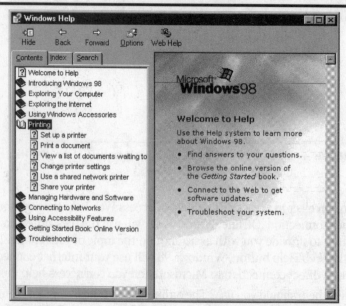

FIGURE 3.7: Use Local Help to find out about printing documents.

A second way to get help is through clicking the Index tab. This action produces a list of all the topics contained in Windows 98 Help; you can scroll through the list or type in a keyword or phrase to find the topic on which you need assistance.

The third way of using offline Help is to use the Search tab to look for a particular term or operation you want to perform. Windows 98 will find terms that relate to whatever you enter and provide you with help on that topic.

One of the nicer features of Windows 98 help is that you can continue performing those help steps without worrying about the help screen retreating to the background as you click a new Window or select a menu option. The help screen only disappears when you close out if it.

NOTE

Clicking in the right frame of help allows you to perform many different operations, including printing the contents of the help topic. You can then make up your own little book of special help tips. You can also save help screens as wallpaper, copy them as graphic files, or create a shortcut for a particular topic.

Using Web Help

Using the Web Help option allows you to use your browser and connect to Microsoft's Windows 98 Support Home Page. Here, you can get extensive help on almost any aspect of Windows 98.

There are just too many topics for which you can receive support to go through them all here, but when you use online help, you access an entire knowledge base of help topics. You can also submit a question to a Microsoft technician, find out phone numbers if you'd rather talk with someone, and get information about other support options.

WHAT'S NEXT?

Now that you've been at least casually introduced to Windows 98, we'll move to specifics. In the next chapter you'll learn about *shortcuts*—indispensable little tools that will make you a more efficient Windows 98 user. And they're also great fun! So, good work so far and let's move on.

Chapter 4

SHORTCUTS GALORE

There are many different ways to accomplish the same task in Windows 98. For example, you can open the Windows Explorer and click the application program you want to start. Or you can create a shortcut for that program, place it on the Desktop, and click it when you're ready to use it. Shortcuts introduce a new level of customization and ease of use to Windows. They're meant to be convenient ways to get at all the things on your computer or network: documents, applications, folders, printers, and so on. In this chapter, we'll cover all the ways to make and modify a shortcut and how to place the shortcuts you want in the places you want them to be.

Adapted from *The ABCs of Windows 98*, by Sharon Crawford and Neil J. Salkind

ISBN 0-7821-1953-0   384 pages $19.99

NOTE

At the end of the chapter you'll find a different type of shortcut—a set of keyboard combinations you can use to perform many of Windows 98's most important functions.

A shortcut is identified by the small arrow in its lower-left corner. The arrow isn't there just to be cute. It's important to know (particularly before a deletion) whether something is a shortcut or a real object. You can delete shortcuts at will. You're not deleting anything that you can't recreate in a second or two. But if you delete an actual file or folder, you'll have to reinstall it or rummage around in the Recycle Bin to retrieve it. And if it's a while before you notice it's missing, the Recycle Bin may have been emptied in the meantime, and the object may be gone.

Here's an example. Let's say that on your hard drive you have a folder called FrontPad (and you do, unless you've deleted it). On the Desktop, you can put a shortcut to that folder just like the shortcuts in Figure 4.1. You can get to the contents of the folder by clicking the shortcut. If you delete the shortcut folder on the Desktop, the folder on the hard drive remains untouched.

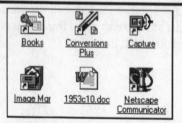

FIGURE 4.1: A sample of shortcuts representing various Windows 98 files and applications

If you delete the folder on the hard drive but not the shortcut on the Desktop, the shortcut will still be there, but it will be pointing to nothing. When you click the shortcut, you will get a dialog box telling you that Windows 98 is looking for the file to which the shortcut refers. But if you've deleted the file or folder it's looking for, Windows won't be able to locate it and neither will you. The best thing to do in this situation is delete the shortcut from the Desktop.

Shortcuts are an excellent tool for configuring your Desktop to suit you. You can create shortcuts to folders, to programs, and to individual files. In fact, you can create a shortcut to any Windows 98 object. Arrange them any way you want on the Desktop, inside other folders, or on menus.

CREATING SHORTCUTS

The Create Shortcut option can be found in many different places, including:

▶ An object's pop-up menu (see Figure 4.2)

▶ Various drop-down menus

▶ The Desktop pop-up menu, where it appears as New ➤ Shortcut

Open
Quick View
Add to Zip
Add to Imgmgr.zip

Backup Now
Restore Files

Send To   ▶

Cut
Copy

Create Shortcut
Delete
Rename

Properties

FIGURE 4.2:   Create Shortcut is an option almost every time you
use the right mouse button to click an object.

Shortcuts are pointers to objects. So you need to either find the object you want to create a shortcut to or be able to tell Windows 98 where the object is located.

The easiest way to create a shortcut is to use My Computer or the Windows 98 Explorer to locate the object for which you want to create the shortcut. Then, right-click the object and click Create Shortcut. A new icon named "Shortcut to..." will appear.

NOTE
There are some special circumstances you need to keep in mind depending upon where the original object is located. The next few sections address this issue.

Creating a Shortcut When You Can See the Object

To create a shortcut when you have the original object in view inside the Explorer or My Computer window, follow these steps:

1. Right-click the object for which you want to create a shortcut.

2. Click the Create Shortcut option on the pop-up menu.

The new shortcut is created with the name "Shortcut to *Name*" (where *Name* is the name of the program or file). For example, the shortcut shown here, when clicked, will open the Word for Windows program. You can now drag the shortcut to any location you choose, including another folder, the Start menu, or the Desktop.

Creating a Shortcut When You Can't See the Object

If the original object isn't handy or you can't remember where it is, you can still create a shortcut by following these steps:

1. Right-click on the Desktop and select New ➤ Shortcut.

2. In the dialog box that opens, type in the location and name of the original object. If you don't know the path (and who ever does?), click the Browse button.

3. Using the Browse window, mouse around until you find the file or object you want to link to. You may have to change the Files of Type item in the Browse window to the All Files option.

4. Highlight the file with the mouse (the name will appear in the File Name box) and click Open. The Command Line box will now contain the name and location of the object.

5. Click Next and either accept or change the name for the shortcut.

6. Click Finish and the shortcut appears on your Desktop.

RENAMING A SHORTCUT

To rename a shortcut from the default name assigned by Windows (for example, to change "Shortcut to Winword.exe" to simply "Word"), right-click the icon and select Rename from the menu that opens. Type in the name you want. Click a blank spot on the Desktop when you're through.

What to Name Shortcuts

When you name or rename a shortcut, take full advantage of the long file name feature (up to 255 characters) that Windows 98 makes available. No need to get carried away, but you might as well call a folder "March Budget Reports" rather than "MAR BUD."

As with naming any file, certain characters aren't allowed in shortcut names, including:

Backslash	\
Forward slash	/
Greater-than sign	<
Less-than sign	>
Pipe symbol	|
Colon	:
Double quotation mark	"
Question mark	?
Asterisk	*

Just be a bit creative, and learn to live without these characters in your shortcut names.

SHORTCUT SETTINGS

Like other Windows 98 objects, each shortcut has a Properties sheet associated with it that you can see by right-clicking the shortcut icon and selecting Properties from the pop-up menu. For shortcuts to Windows objects (as opposed to DOS programs), the most interesting page is the one labeled Shortcut (shown in Figure 4.3).

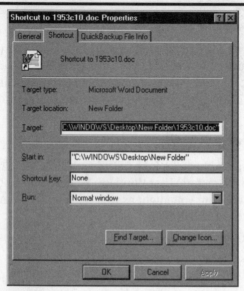

FIGURE 4.3:   The Shortcut page of the Properties sheet

Finding the Target

Forget what object is represented by the shortcut and where it's located? The path or address for the target, or the object from which the shortcut was created, can be found in the Target text box on the Shortcut page of the Properties sheet.

If you want to find out what the shortcut is pointing to and be delivered to that location, click the Find Target button. When you click this button, a window opens into the folder containing the application or file the shortcut is for. You can then click the file or application to open it.

Changing a Shortcut's Icon

Shortcuts to programs will usually display the icon associated with that program. You can, however, change the icon for any shortcut by following these steps:

1. Right-click the shortcut icon and select Properties from the pop-up menu.

2. Select the Shortcut tab and click the Change Icon button.

3. Use the Browse button to look in other files (WINDOWS\ MORICONS.DLL has a bunch). Click the icon you want to use.

4. Click OK twice and the new shortcut icon will be displayed, taking the place of the old shortcut icon.

TIP

Many icons are available from icon libraries that are distributed as shareware, and an especially great place to find them is on the Internet. Just use the Search tools found in Internet Explorer or any other browser. More about this in Chapter 17.

PUTTING SHORTCUTS WHERE YOU WANT THEM

The point of shortcuts is to save time and effort. Indiscriminately placing a bunch of shortcuts on the Desktop may help you, but it also may just clutter up the Desktop. There are a number of other ways and places shortcuts can be made useful, including placing them at locations other than the Desktop.

Putting a Start Menu Item on the Desktop

When you click the Start menu and follow the Programs arrow, you'll see a hierarchical display of programs installed on your system. All those menu items are just representations of shortcuts. To create the shortcuts you want on your Desktop, you'll need to (if you'll pardon the expression) go Exploring.

1. Right-click the Start button and select Open or Explore.

2. Click the Programs icon.

3. Find the programs you want here. (You may have to go down another level by clicking one of the folders.)

4. Right-click the shortcut you want and drag it to the Desktop, selecting Create Shortcut(s) Here from the menu that opens when you release the mouse button:

Part i

Adding a Program to the Start Menu

You undoubtedly have some objects that you'd like to get at without having to go through the menus or without searching around the Desktop.

To add a program to the top of the Start menu, just click a shortcut and drag and drop it on the Start button. Then when you click the Start button, the program will be instantly available.

You can remove programs from the Start menu by selecting Start ➤ Settings ➤ Taskbar. Click the Start Menu Programs tab and then the Remove button. Highlight the program you want to remove and then click the Remove button. Then select Close and OK. Once again, the shortcut (which appeared on the Start menu) is removed, but the actual program to which the shortcut refers remains.

Adding a Shortcut to *Send To*

When you right-click most things in Windows 98, one of the choices on the pop-up menu is Send To. By default, the Send To menu includes shortcuts to your floppy drive (or drives) and also may include (depending on your installation) shortcuts to mail and fax recipients.

A great example of using shortcuts effectively is to add one that represents a printer to the Send To folder. That way, all you need to do is right-click a file icon, then select the printer. The application associated with the icon will open and the document will print. Pretty nifty.

To add a shortcut to Send To, follow these steps:

1. Click the Start button and select Programs ➤ Windows Explorer.

2. Locate the Windows folder in the left pane of the Explorer and open it.

3. Locate the Send To folder and click it.

4. Now drag any item you want to appear on the Send To menu into the Send To folder.

You may have to open a second instance of the Explorer to get at other folders if the shortcuts you want are not on the Desktop.

TIP

When you use Send To, you're actually doing the equivalent of drag-and-drop. The item you highlighted will be dropped on the selection you make in Send To.

STARTING A PROGRAM WHEN WINDOWS STARTS

You may have programs you want to have ready to run when you start Windows—for example, your calendar or another application you want immediate access to. Windows 98 includes a StartUp folder for just such purposes.

To start a program when Windows 98 starts, you must first create a shortcut for that program and then place it in the Windows 98 StartUp folder. Here's how:

1. Right-click the Start button and select Open or Explore from the pop-up menu.

2. Click the Programs icon and then click the StartUp folder icon.

3. Drag whatever shortcuts you want to start to the StartUp folder.

NOTE

If you want to leave the original shortcut where it is, drag with the right mouse button and choose Copy Here from the menu that pops up when you release the button.

Now that you've got the shortcut in the StartUp folder, how do you want the window to appear when it starts? It can appear as minimized (on the Taskbar), normal (as it would if normally opened), or maximized (using the entire Desktop area).

To specify how you want programs to look when Windows 98 starts:

1. Right-click the shortcut and select Properties.

2. Click the Shortcut tab.

3. In the Run window, select Minimized (or Normal Window or Maximized).

4. Click OK when you're done.

Starting a Program with a Keyboard Shortcut

You can click a shortcut placed anywhere on the Desktop to work with a file, a folder, or an application. And you can also use a keystroke combination as a shortcut.

What's great about this Windows 98 feature? Imagine having a maximized window on your Desktop where all you can see is the document. You need to open another application. Even if you have a shortcut to what you need, you can't use it because you can't see it! A keystroke shortcut is just what you need. If you have a keyboard shortcut, you can use that to open the application without any other fuss.

To create a keyboard shortcut, follow these steps:

1. Right-click the shortcut and select Properties.

2. On the Shortcut page, click in the Shortcut Key field.

3. Type in a letter and Windows will add Ctrl+Alt. (So if you enter a W, the keyboard combination will be Ctrl+Alt+W.)

4. Click OK when you're finished.

Now whenever you want to use the shortcut to access the application, just use that key combination.

TIP

To remove a keyboard shortcut, you need to go to Properties again and click in the Shortcut Key field and press the Backspace key.

NOTE

It's best to limit keyboard shortcuts to just a few programs or folders because shortcuts assigned in Windows have precedence over those in Windows application programs. For example, Microsoft Word uses the Ctrl+Alt+T combination as a shortcut to insert the trademark (™) symbol; if you assign these keystrokes to a new Windows shortcut, you won't be able to use them for the Word shortcut.

SHORTCUTS TO OTHER PLACES

Shortcuts quickly become a normal way of accessing files and programs on your own computer, but they're a much more powerful tool than you'd first suspect.

DOS Programs

Shortcuts to DOS programs are made in the same way as other shortcuts. Find the program file in the Explorer and do a right-mouse drag to the Desktop.

WARNING

Windows 98 will always try to find the target for a shortcut, even if you move the target to another location. But you might not be so lucky with DOS programs. So if you move your game to another drive or rename a batch file, plan on making a new shortcut.

Disk Drives

Right-click a disk drive in the Explorer or My Computer and drag it to the Desktop to create a shortcut to the contents of a drive. When you click the shortcut, you'll see its contents almost instantly—it's much quicker than opening the entire Explorer.

KEYBOARD SHORTCUTS

The mouse is the mouse, but some people prefer to keep their hands on the keyboard and perform as many Windows 98 operations as possible from there. In fact, you can perform practically every Windows 98 function using either the mouse or the keyboard.

Of course, you probably can't be bothered memorizing all these keyboard combinations, but you may want to consider a few for your memory bank (the one in your head), particularly if there are actions that you do repeatedly and find the mouse too clumsy for. The more you use keyboard shortcuts that best fit your needs (such as Ctrl+S for Save or Ctrl+X for Cut), the easier they will be to remember, and the more proficient you'll be as a Windows 98 user.

The following table includes the most useful (and in many cases, undocumented) keyboard shortcuts:

Key	Action
Alt+Esc	Switch between open applications.
Alt+F4	Close the current application. If no application is open, it will activate the Shut Down window.
Alt+PrintScreen	Copy the active window to the Clipboard.
Alt+Tab	Cycle through open files and folders (see Figure 4.4).
Alt+Shift+Tab	Move the cursor through the open items in the opposite direction from Alt+Tab.
Alt+Spacebar	Open the Control menu (same as clicking the icon at the upper-left corner of the application or folder window).
Alt+Enter	View the selected Desktop item's properties.
Alt+hyphen	Open the Control menu (in Office applications).
Alt+underlined letter	Select the menu item.
Backspace	Move up one level in the folder hierarchy.
Ctrl+A	Select all.
Ctrl+X	Cut.
Ctrl+C	Copy.
Ctrl+V	Paste.
Ctrl+Z	Undo.
Ctrl+F4	Close the current window in programs that allow several windows to be open (like Word or Excel).
Ctrl+Esc	Open the Start menu.
F1	Get help.
F10 or Alt	Put the focus on the menu bar. To move between menus, use the left and right arrow keys ($\leftarrow$ and $\rightarrow$). The $\downarrow$ or $\uparrow$ key will open the menu.
F2	Rename the file or folder that's highlighted.
F3	Open Find.
F4	Open the drop-down list in the Address toolbar. Press F4 a second time and the drop-down list will close.
F5	Refresh the view in the active window.
Left arrow ($\leftarrow$)	Collapse the highlighted folder. If it's already collapsed, move up one level in the folder hierarchy.

Key	Action
Print Screen	Copy the current screen to the Clipboard, from which it can be pasted into Paint or another graphics application.
Right arrow (→)	Expand the highlighted folder. If the folder is already expanded, go to the subfolder.
Shift+Del	Delete immediately and do not place in the Recycle Bin.
Shift+F10	View the shortcut menu for the selected item.
Shift+Tab	Move the selection cursor in the opposite direction from Tab.
Tab or F6	In Explorer view, toggle the focus between the drop-down window in the left pane toolbar and the right pane.

NOTE

The Clipboard mentioned above is not an actual application; it's a special place in memory. However, there is a Clipboard Viewer (available under Programs ➢ Accessories ➢ System Tools) that can see whatever you copy. If it's not installed, go to Add/Remove Programs in the Control Panel. Select Windows Setup and then Accessories.

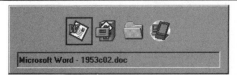

FIGURE 4.4: Use the Alt+Tab key to scroll through active programs. Here the program that will become active is Microsoft Word.

WHAT'S NEXT?

Shortcuts can really speed things up and make you a better and more efficient Windows 98 user. Whether you create shortcuts and place them on your Desktop or in a dedicated folder, they do their job very well. Next we'll move on to working with Explorer.

Chapter 5

WINDOWS EXPLORER AND THE RECYCLE BIN

At this point you've been introduced to Windows 98, seen how to install the system if necessary, toured the Desktop, and learned how to create and use shortcuts. That's a good start, but of course, there's more to the Windows interface.

In this chapter, we'll cover Windows Explorer, the Recycle Bin, and other Desktop elements. You'll also learn how to use important features such as the Send To menu, and you'll learn the basics of working with floppy disks. As you'll see, Windows Explorer is probably the single most important tool for any Windows user.

Adapted from *Windows 98: No Experience Required*, by Sharon Crawford

ISBN 0-7821-2128-4   576 pages $24.99

USING WINDOWS EXPLORER

Windows Explorer offers the easiest way of viewing folders, files, and other resources located on your machine (see Figure 5.1). The default Explorer is a two-pane window. When you click on an item in the left window pane, the right pane displays the contents. You can choose different viewing options from the View menu.

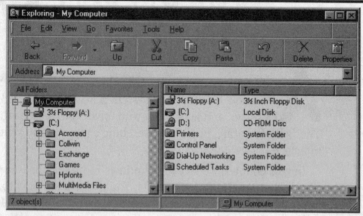

FIGURE 5.1: Windows Explorer at its most informative: the Details view

TIP

More than one Windows Explorer window can be opened at a time. In fact, that's often the easiest way to move files from one place to another.

The Explorer is always available from the Start menu. Click on the Start button, slide the pointer to Programs and then to Windows Explorer, and click.

If you use Windows Explorer a lot, as most people do, you may want to put a shortcut to the Windows Explorer on your desktop. Here's a quick way:

1. Begin as if you were opening Windows Explorer: Click Start and slide the mouse pointer to Programs, then Windows Explorer. Don't click just yet.

2. Using the right mouse button, drag the Windows Explorer shortcut icon out onto your desktop.

3. When you release the right mouse button, a pop-up menu appears. Choose Copy Here or Create Shortcut Here. (Since it's a shortcut you're dragging, the results are the same.)

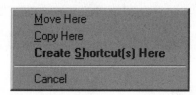

Inside Windows Explorer, folders are organized in a fashion that doesn't look all that different from Windows 3.1 or DOS, except that the top level folder/directory is called Desktop and the filenames look peculiar.

NOTE

Notice the plus and minus signs next to folders. A plus sign means there's at least one more layer of folders that you can see if you click on the plus icon. Click on the minus sign and the lower level will collapse into the upper level.

Viewing Extensions

You'll probably notice first that most files shown in Windows Explorer's right pane are missing their extensions. The thinking behind this is that these files are registered (in other words, the system knows what they are and where they came from) and can be activated by merely clicking on them—so why would you need to know the extension?

In a perfect world, of course, you wouldn't. But the Explorer screen shown in Figure 5.2 demonstrates how confusion can arise.

There are two files named CAPTURE, two called INSTALL, and *three* named IMGMGR. If you know what the icons mean or expand the window to show the file types, you can figure out which file does what. But if you prefer to see file extensions, here's how to do it:

1. Click the Start button, select Programs ➤ Windows Explorer, and click to Open Windows Explorer.

2. Click the View menu and select Folder Options.

3. In the dialog box that opens, click the View tab, then click the box next to *Hide file extensions for known file types* to remove the check mark. Click OK when you're done.

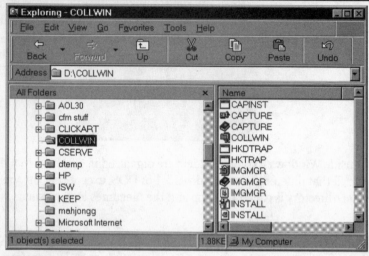

FIGURE 5.2:   The lack of extensions can prove confusing when there is more than one file with the same name.

TIP

If you really want to see everything, look under Hidden Files and select Show All Files, so even hidden and system files will show in Windows Explorer.

Of course, many, if not most, of the programs you'll be using will be started using the Start menu or from the desktop itself, so the file extensions are less important as time goes on.

USING ANOTHER COMPUTER'S FILES

If your computer is connected to others in a local area network (LAN), the Network Neighborhood icon will appear on your desktop and in the left window of the Windows Explorer. You can see a list of computers on your network when you click Network Neighborhood in the left window of Windows Explorer (or when you click the Network Neighborhood icon on the desktop). To see the contents of other computers' hard drives, the drives have to be *shared*. There are two steps to this. First the network itself has to be set up for file and printer sharing. See the accompanying box if you need to do that.

A QUICK GUIDE TO SETTING UP A NETWORK

Obviously, there's more to planning and setting up a peer-to-peer local area network (the type best suited to a small office of no more than about 10 computers) than we can summarize in a couple of pages. You'll need to decide on the network *topology*, or layout; the type of cabling; the type of network card; and the type of network connector. You'll also need to buy all of the network hardware. *Windows 98: No Experience Required* devotes most of a chapter to reviewing these choices, and there are many good books on networking.

Once you've decided what you're going to implement and have made the physical connections, here's what you'll need to do in Windows 98.

1. **The Add New Hardware Wizard** When you physically install the network card, Windows 98 will notice the change the next time it boots up, and it will run the Add New Hardware Wizard to configure it. This process should happen automatically, but you can do it manually if for some reason it doesn't happen by itself. Just click the Add New Hardware icon in the Control Panel.

   The Add New Hardware Wizard will walk you through the process of adding your new network card to your system. In addition, it will automatically install the minimal level of network support—adding the Microsoft client layer, so you can use files on someone else's Windows 95 or 98 computer—and both the NetBEUI protocol and the IPX/SPX compatible protocol. (NetBEUI is an older Microsoft protocol that still has merit in small network systems or where the primary access is over slower dial-up lines. IPX/SPX is the protocol used on Novell NetWare networks and is installed by default by Windows 98.)

CONTINUED ➡

2. **The Network Wizard**   If the Add New Hardware Wizard doesn't open the Network property pages shown here, then you can run it yourself. Just open the Control Panel and double-click the Network icon.

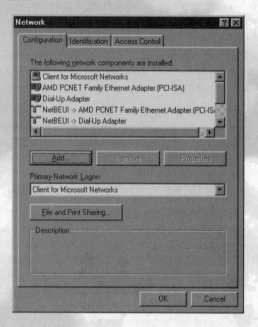

Some network components may have been added in already when you installed the new network card. Additional client protocols, hardware adapters, networking "stacks" or protocols, and networking services can be added here.

3. **Client Choices**   Network clients let you use the services being provided by another machine on your network. The default network configuration includes clients for both Microsoft Networks and Novell NetWare Networks. If you're just using Windows 98 as a peer-to-peer network, you can delete the Client for NetWare choice since you will only be using the built-in Microsoft networking. (To remove the NetWare client, just highlight it, and then click the Remove button. Don't worry, you can always add it back in later if you need to.)

CONTINUED ➡

Part i

If you don't see the Client for Microsoft Networks listed in the Network dialog box under the heading *The following network components are installed*, click the Add button, and then double-click the Client icon in the Select Network Component Type box:

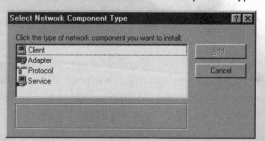

Clicking the Client icon opens the Select Network Client box. Highlight Microsoft, select Client for Microsoft Networks, and then click OK.

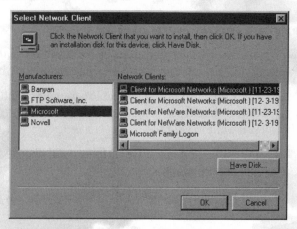

4. **Service Choices**   The default installation doesn't install any services at all, which is fine if you never want anyone else to be able to use the resources of your computer. If you were setting up your local network to have one main machine everyone else would share—the one with the fax modem, the big hard drive, the printer, and such—then you could leave this choice alone. But if you are going to distribute your resources across the network, you will need to add services to all the workstations to allow them to share their resources with others.

CONTINUED ➡

Double-click the Service icon in the Select Network Component Type box. Again, highlight Microsoft in the resulting **Select Network Service** dialog box, select *File and printer sharing for Microsoft Networks*, and click OK. This will add the necessary network services to allow others on the network to use your documents and folders as well as any printers or fax modems attached to your computer.

These steps should be enough to get your network configured and ready to go. You will need to reboot each machine when you get done adding the necessary hardware and software components, since these changes are more than Windows 98 can do on the fly.

Once this has been done, you can choose to share some or all of your files with others on the network and they can, in turn, share with you.

Sharing a Drive or Folder

How do you give others access to drives or folders on your computer? Once the network has been set up for file sharing, just follow these steps:

1. Click the Start button, select Programs ➢ Windows Explorer and click to Open Windows Explorer. Find the drive or folder you want to share.

2. Right-click on the drive or folder and choose Sharing from the pop-up menu.

3. On the Sharing page of the Properties sheet, select Shared As, as shown in Figure 5.3.

4. Accept the default Share Name or change it to something that others will understand. Share names are limited to 12 characters, but the shorter the better.

5. Indicate what type of access you want others to have, and enter a password if you want to limit access. Remember that if you grant full access, others will be able to change the files on your computer.

6. Click OK to accept the revised Properties sheet.

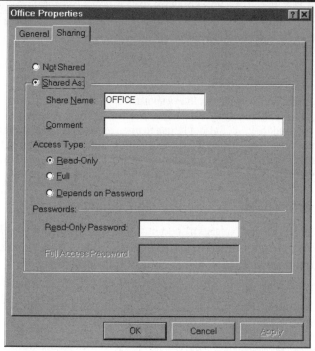

FIGURE 5.3: Sharing a drive with other users on your network

The drive or folder you have chosen to share will now appear under the name of your computer when others on your network open their Network Neighborhood. If you specified a password, they will need to know it to gain access.

TIP

If you don't want others to be able to make changes to your drive or folder, choose the Read-Only access type on the Sharing page of the Properties sheet. Read-Only also means that others will be unable to *add* any new files to the shared drive or folder. Use passwords for only the most sensitive files.

Mapping a Drive

If you find yourself often going through Network Neighborhood or Explorer to get to a particular drive, you may want to *map* it. You can make any shared drive or folder on another computer appear just as if it were a drive on *your* computer. A mapped drive will show up in Windows Explorer as another hard drive. For example, if you have a C drive plus a CD-ROM drive that uses the letter D, you can map a shared network drive as letter E.

TIP

A mapped drive is even better than a shortcut in one important respect: If you're using older programs, they're not going to recognize things like Network Neighborhood, and they will flat-out refuse to open or save files to anywhere other than your own computer. Map a drive, and the program will cooperate because now the drive on the other computer will appear (to the program at least) to be on your computer.

Here's how it's done:

1. Click Network Neighborhood in Windows Explorer or the Network Neighborhood icon on the desktop and find the folder or drive you want to show as one of your local drives.

2. Right-click on the object and select Map Network Drive from the pop-up menu. This will open the dialog box shown in Figure 5.4.

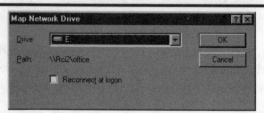

FIGURE 5.4:   Mapping the Office folder to be Drive E

3. Click OK when you're done. Open Explorer or My Computer and look. Figure 5.5 shows how the folder being mapped in Figure 5.4 ended up looking in Windows Explorer.

NOTE

The Reconnect at Logon box should be checked if you want the connection to the mapped drive to be made every time you start your computer. If the computer where the mapped drive resides is turned *off* when you log on, you'll get an error message.

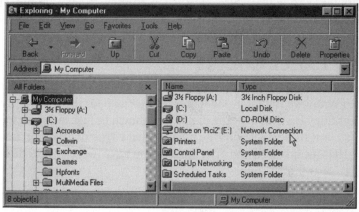

FIGURE 5.5: After being mapped, the folder on the other computer is listed as a drive among your own.

Disconnecting from Mapped Drives or Folders

To get rid of a mapped drive or folder, you can highlight it and right-click. Select Disconnect from the pop-up menu.

When you disconnect a mapped drive, you're just removing it from the list of drives shown on your computer. It has no other effect on the drive. You can always go back and remap it if you need to.

EXPLORING FLOPPY DISKS

Click the floppy drive icon in the Explorer's left window to see the contents of the diskette currently in the drive. Windows Explorer also provides the graphical interface for the care and maintenance of floppy disks. If you yearn for DOS, you can also open a DOS window to copy, format, and label a floppy disk.

Making Exact Copies

To make an exact copy of your floppy disk, put the disk in the drive and open Windows Explorer. Right-click on the icon for the floppy drive and select Copy Disk to open the dialog box shown in Figure 5.6. It doesn't say so, but these selections must be the same type of disk. For most people, that means the same drive (unless you have two identical diskette drives or two Zip drives).

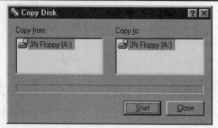

FIGURE 5.6:   Windows 98's direct route to copying a floppy disk

TIP

If you do much work with floppies, you may want to put a shortcut to the drive on your desktop. Just drag the floppy drive icon from the left window of the Explorer to your desktop.

Formatting Floppies

Here's how to format a floppy disk:

1.   Put the floppy disk you want to format into your A or B drive as appropriate.

2.   Click the Start button and select Programs ➤ Windows Explorer.

3.   In the left pane of the Explorer window, right-click once on the floppy drive icon. Do not open the floppy drive. A pop-up menu will appear.

4. Select Format from the menu.

5. Select the Format Type and Other options you want from the dialog box that appears:

     Quick   A quick format changes the names of any files on the disk so that they "disappear" as far as the operating system is concerned. This format is very fast (hence the name), but it doesn't check to make sure that the floppy disk is undamaged. It also doesn't work on new, unformatted disks.

     Full   A full format is necessary for new floppies and desirable for old ones because it checks for errors and defects on the disk. It's a lot slower, though.

     Copy system files only   This copies system files to a disk that's already formatted without removing any of the files already present. This allows you to turn any floppy into a bootable floppy—providing there's room available on the floppy disk for the system files.

     Label   This will let you provide a label for the floppy.

     Display summary when finished   This option is on by default. When the formatting is complete, it opens a sheet showing the details of the formatted disk. Clear the box if you don't want to be bothered with this information.

     Copy system files   Check this if you want system files copied to the disk to make the disk bootable.

6. When you're finished selecting options, click the Start button.

TIP

If Windows Explorer (or any open window) is showing the contents of the floppy disk, Windows 98 concludes that the floppy disk is in use and therefore can't be formatted. If you get that message, click on your C drive icon in the Explorer or close the desktop window showing the contents of the floppy. Then right-click once on the floppy icon and select Format from the pop-up menu.

USING THE *SEND TO* OPTION

When you're working in the Explorer (or any other folder for that matter) and you click on an object with the right mouse button, the menu that opens includes an option called Send To. When you first start using Windows 98, the system will put your floppy drive and other removable media such as a Zip drive on the Send To submenu automatically.

This is pretty handy, as you might guess. But it can be even handier. You can add any application or device you choose. So you can select a file and send it to your word processor or your printer.

The Long...

As an example, here's how to add the Notepad applet to the Send To menu:

1. Click the Start button and select Programs ➤ Windows Explorer.

2. Click on your Windows directory, then right-click the file Notepad. Select Create Shortcut from the pop-up menu. The shortcut will appear in Explorer.

3. Right-click on the shortcut you've just made and select Cut from the menu.

4. Scroll to the SendTo folder (it's a subfolder under the main Windows folder).

5. Right-click on the SendTo folder and select Paste.

...And the Short of It

If you want to be able to add stuff to the Send To menu without going through all the previous steps every time, just do the following once:

1. Click the Start button, select Programs ➤ Windows Explorer, and then click on the Windows folder.

2. Right-click on the SendTo folder and drag it to the desktop. Release the mouse button and select Create Shortcut Here from the pop-up menu.

3. Go back to the Explorer and open the SendTo folder under Windows.

4. Drag and drop the shortcut you just made to the SendTo folder.

Now when you highlight an object and open the Send To menu (the right mouse button menu), there's a shortcut to Send To as an option on the menu. Select that option and the item you've selected will be instantly added to the Send To menu.

When the menu gets too crowded, open the SendTo folder in the Explorer and delete any extra clutter.

TIP

For a quicker way to find the SendTo folder, click once on the Start button and select Run. In the Open box, type in **Sendto** (all one word) and press Enter. The SendTo folder will open on your desktop.

USING THE RECYCLE BIN

In the bad old days of computing, it was far too easy to accidentally delete a file from your system—and there was no going back. There were, of course, tools you could buy like the Norton Utilities. Norton included a program that could retrieve deleted files—providing you acted quickly enough. And DOS itself, starting with version 5, included a program to undelete files. The weakness of both approaches was if you didn't undelete right away, your file could easily be overwritten by another file, and then there was *no way* to recover.

The Recycle Bin, introduced in Windows 95, will retain all your deleted files for as long as you want, and you can adjust the amount of security from "just a little" to "all I can get" to match your own personal comfort level.

What It Is

The Recycle Bin is a reserved space on your hard drive. When you delete a file or drag it to the Recycle Bin icon:

Part i

the file is actually moved to that reserved space. If you have more than one hard drive, each drive has its own reserved space. There's an icon that represents the Recycle Bin on each drive—though the contents displayed when you click on any icon will be the same as the Recycle Bin on any other drive. If you want a deleted file back, you can click the Recycle Bin icon to open it and retrieve any file.

The Recycle Bin functions as a first-in, first-out system. That is, when the bin is full, the oldest files are the first ones deleted to make room for the newest ones.

As configurable as the rest of Windows 98 is, the Recycle Bin cannot be

- ▶ deleted
- ▶ renamed
- ▶ removed from the desktop

though there are a number of settings you can change to make the Recycle Bin suitable for your use.

NOTE

See "Adjusting the Recycle Bin Settings" later in this chapter for information on how to determine the amount of disk space used by the Recycle Bin as well as other settings.

SENDING FILES TO THE RECYCLE BIN

By default, Windows 98 is set up to deposit all deleted files into the Recycle Bin. When you right-click on a file and select delete, or highlight a file and press the Delete key, you'll be asked to confirm if you want to send the file to the Recycle Bin. After you click Yes, that's where the file is moved to. Deleted shortcuts are also sent to the Recycle Bin.

TIP

If you delete an empty folder, it's not sent to the Recycle Bin but you can recover it by immediately selecting Undo Delete from the Recycle Bin's Edit menu. If the folder came from the desktop, just right-click on a blank spot on the desktop and select Undo Delete from the pop-up menu.

Sending a Floppy Disk's Files to the Recycle Bin

Normally, files that you delete from a floppy drive are *not* sent to the Recycle Bin. They're just deleted. However, if that strikes you as just a little too impetuous, there's an easy way to make sure that the files on your floppy do go to the Recycle Bin.

1. Click the Start button and select Programs ➤ Windows Explorer.

2. Use the scroll bar for the left pane to move up so you can see the entry for your floppy drive.

3. Click (with the left mouse button) on the floppy drive icon. In the right pane, select the file(s) you want to delete but still want in the Recycle Bin.

4. Right-click on the file(s) and select Cut from the pop-up menu. Right-click on the desktop and select Paste.

5. Highlight the file on the desktop. (If there's more than one, hold down the Shift key while you click each one in turn.) Right-click on a highlighted file and select Delete. You'll be prompted to confirm that you want to send the file(s) to the Recycle Bin.

There's no more direct way to do this function because the Recycle Bin stubbornly refuses to accept any files that are sent directly from a floppy.

TIP

You can also use this method when you're deleting files from any external drive (such as a Zip drive) and you want the security of having the files safely stashed in the Recycle Bin for a while.

Bypassing the Recycle Bin

If you've got a file that you know for sure you want to delete and that you don't want taking up space in the Recycle Bin, just hold down the Shift key when you select Delete. But be sure that's what you want to do, because there's no way in Windows 98 to recover a deleted file that's bypassed the Recycle Bin.

NOTE

If you have the Norton Utilities for Windows, you can use their Unerase program to recover deleted files that are not in the Recycle Bin—again, you must do this very quickly before another file overwrites the one you want to recover.

Files That Won't Go Willingly

Some older programs (not written specifically for Windows 95 or later) allow you to delete files from within the program. Files deleted this way will not be sent to the Recycle Bin. Similarly, files you delete at the DOS prompt will also disappear into never-never land rather than into the Recycle Bin.

Therefore, you should make all your deletions through the Windows Explorer or My Computer or on the Desktop. If Windows 98 knows about the deletion, the file will automatically go to the Recycle Bin.

RECOVERING A DELETED FILE

Retrieving a file from the Recycle Bin is remarkably easy. Just click on the Recycle Bin icon. The Recycle Bin window can be set up in any of the choices on the View menu. The Large Icons view (see Figure 5.7) is useful because it lets you identify which programs made which files.

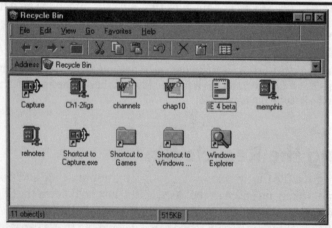

FIGURE 5.7:   In the Large Icons view, you can quickly identify files that were made by a particular program.

The Details view (see Figure 5.7) is the best view if you're looking for a file recently deleted. Just click on the Date Deleted bar to arrange the files in date order. A second click will reverse the order. Similarly, if you know the name of the file, a click on the Name bar will list the files in alphabetical order.

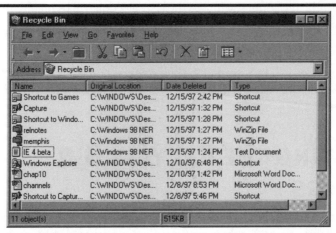

FIGURE 5.8: The Details view is useful if you're searching by date or name.

To retrieve a single file, click on it with either the left or the right button and drag it to a folder or the desktop. If you just want to send it back to its original location, right-click on the filename and select Restore from the pop-up menu.

More Than One File

To recover more than one file at a time, hold down the Ctrl key while selecting the filenames. Then right-click on one of the highlighted names and select Restore from the pop-up menu. Or use cut and paste to send the whole bunch to a different location. And of course, you can click (either the right or left button) and drag the files to your desktop or another open folder.

To retrieve a number of files all in a series, click on the first one and then hold down the Shift key while selecting the last one in the series.

Let's say you deleted a whole folder and the only thing all the items in the folder have in common is that all were deleted at the same time. Here's how to recover them:

1. Open the Recycle Bin by clicking the icon.

2. Select Details from the View menu.

3. Click the Date Deleted bar. Use the scroll bar to move through the list until you find the group of files you want to retrieve.

4. Click on the first one's name then, while holding down the Shift key, click on the name of the last one you want. All the files from the first to the last selection will be highlighted.

5. Right-click on one of the highlighted files and select Recover from the pop-up menu.

All the files will be returned to their original home, and although the original folder was not listed in the Recycle Bin, the files will be in their original folder.

ADJUSTING THE RECYCLE BIN SETTINGS

You can adjust the amount of space the Recycle Bin claims and change other settings that affect how the Recycle Bin works. Mostly you have to decide just how much safety you want and are comfortable with.

How Much Space?

Right-click on the Recycle Bin icon and select Properties from the pop-up menu. The Recycle Bin's Properties sheet will open, as shown in Figure 5.9.

As you can see, you can set the amount of space reserved for the Recycle Bin for each hard disk drive individually, or make a global setting. By default, 10 percent of each drive is set aside for the Recycle Bin. On a large drive, that's a lot of megabytes, so you may want to reduce the size a bit.

Click the radio button for *Configure drives independently* and then click each drive tab in turn. Click the sliding arrow and move it to the right or left until the space reserved is to your liking.

NOTE

There's also a field below the slider, showing the percentage of the drive that is reserved. If your drives are different sizes, you might want to make things easier for yourself by just reserving the same percentage on each drive.

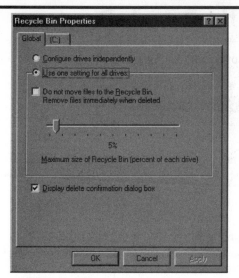

FIGURE 5.9:   The Recycle Bin's Properties sheet

Remember that the Recycle Bin is first-in, first-out, so if you make the reserved space very small, deleted files may pass into oblivion faster than you wish.

Getting Rid of Confirmations

On the Global tab of the Recycle Bin Properties sheet, a checkbox controls the confirmation notice that opens every time you delete a file or folder.

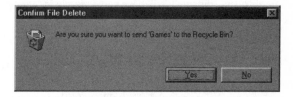

If you like the comfort of being consulted about every deletion, leave the check mark in the box. If you clear the check mark, files you choose to delete will move to the Recycle Bin without any further notice.

Doing Away with the Recycle Bin

You can't exactly do away with the Recycle Bin completely. As mentioned before, you can't delete it or remove it from the desktop. However, you can check this box:

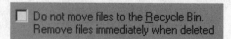

on the Recycle Bin Properties page. If you have the Recycle Bin space configured separately for each drive, you can pick which drives to apply this to.

WARNING

Bypassing the Recycle Bin is generally a very bad idea unless you have another program for undeleting files. Files that are deleted and not sent to the Recycle Bin are gone beyond recall.

Even if you do have a program that will rescue files deleted in error, it's still not a good idea to bypass the Recycle Bin completely. Most such programs are dependent on you getting to the deleted file before it is overwritten by something else. And that can easily happen in Windows 98, where there's usually something going on behind the scenes.

TIP

If you begrudge large portions of your hard drive, make the reserved space on the hard drive very small—maybe 5 or 10 MB. Check the box on the Properties sheet to disable the confirmation requests. Then the Recycle Bin will be quite unobtrusive, but you'll still have some margin for safety.

Emptying the Recycle Bin

To get rid of everything in the Recycle Bin, right-click on the Recycle Bin icon and select Empty Recycle Bin. There's also an option to Delete Recycle Bin under the File menu.

To remove just *some* of the items in the Recycle Bin, highlight the filenames, right-click on one of them, and select Delete from the pop-up menu. You'll be asked to confirm the deletion (assuming you have the confirmation option turned on), and when you say Yes, the files will be deleted permanently.

WHAT'S NEXT?

In the first five chapters, you've learned quite a bit about setting up and working with the Windows 98 interface. By now, you probably want to start doing something productive with your Windows 98 computer. In the next chapter, Sharon Crawford talks about installing and running programs.

Chapter 6

INSTALLING AND RUNNING PROGRAMS

Programs—also called applications—have become easier and easier to install in recent years, but there are still occasional pitfalls. In this chapter, we'll cover the steps for installing programs, whether or not the program is designed for Windows 98. Later in the chapter, you'll find information on how to set up the programs you use most so that they are available when you want them.

Adapted from *Windows 98: No Experience Required*, by Sharon Crawford
ISBN 0-7821-2128-4   576 pages $24.99

INSTALLING A PROGRAM

In general, computer programs are easy to install. If you're going to have a problem, it's most likely to happen when you try to *run* a program. Programs that are genuinely compatible with Windows 98 or Windows 95 are the easiest to install.

Installing from a CD

If the program is supplied on a CD-ROM, it may almost install itself. Some CDs are self-starting. Put the CD-ROM in the drive, and in a few seconds you'll see a window like the one shown in Figure 6.1.

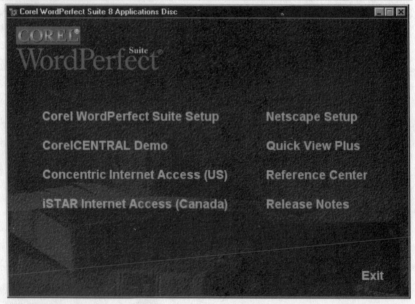

FIGURE 6.1: Corel's WordPerfect Suite on a CD-ROM automatically starts and lets you choose what to install.

In the window that opens, you choose what you want to install from the choices presented. After that, you answer the questions that are asked as you go along. You're often asked to supply your name, approve the location for files, and perhaps supply other information.

> ## TIP
>
> If you put the CD-ROM in the drive and nothing happens, go to "Installing from the Control Panel" later in this chapter.

Most applications will copy some files to your hard drive, and when the setup procedure is completed, you remove the CD-ROM. You won't need it again unless you need to reinstall or you later decide to install some piece of software on the CD that you skipped the first time.

Running from a CD

Some programs are so large that you may not be able to install all their data files for space reasons. Or you use them only infrequently and don't want to clutter your hard drive with a zillion graphics files. In that case, you can often *run* the program from the CD. For example, WordPerfect (see Figure 6.2) offers the option of running the program from the CD.

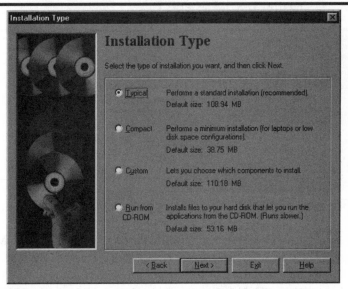

FIGURE 6.2: Selecting the installation type for WordPerfect

While this type of installation uses only minimal hard drive space, it will also cause the program to run much more slowly. For a word processing program, which you presumably use for extended periods, this will be both annoying and frustrating. Getting and using files from the hard drive is much faster than even the fastest CD-ROM drive. And you won't be able to run the program at all unless the CD is in the CD-ROM drive.

TIP

If your hard drive space is severely limited, try a laptop installation rather than running a frequently used application from the CD-ROM drive.

Many programs that are designed to be run from the CD-ROM don't give you any other option. These are often games and reference works (dictionaries, encyclopedias, catalogs of graphics, and the like). These programs will set up by copying some files to your hard drive, but they will still require the CD-ROM to be in the CD-ROM drive in order to work.

For example, The Encarta World Atlas copies about 10MB to your hard drive (see Figure 6.3). These are the files used, for the most part, to make accessing the CD-ROM faster.

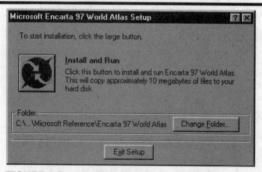

FIGURE 6.3: Installing files for a program to be run from the CD-ROM

The Encarta World Atlas runs speedily enough from the CD-ROM drive because you're looking at a series of maps with at least a second or two between each. This is a positively restful pace for acquiring images from a CD. In the case of games, where such delays would be unacceptable, perhaps 80MB or more will be copied to the hard drive. All the files necessary to keep the action moving will be on your hard drive, with only backgrounds or help files retrieved from the CD.

TIP

If you have plenty of space, you can copy the entire contents of a CD to your hard drive and run the program from there. For example, I speeded up searches through the Encyclopedia Britannica by copying all 601MB to my local hard drive. With hard drive space selling at an average of 4 cents per megabyte, that isn't as much of an extravagance as it might seem.

Installing from the Control Panel

All programs, whether on a CD or on floppy disks, can be installed using Add/Remove Programs in the Control Panel. Put the CD in the CD-ROM drive or the first floppy disk into the floppy drive and follow these steps:

1. Click the Start button and select Settings ➤ Control Panel.

2. In the Control Panel, click the Add/Remove Programs icon.

Add/Remove
Programs

3. In the Add/Remove Programs Properties box, click the Install button. Click Next.

4. The application will search for a setup program, first in the floppy drive and then in the CD-ROM drive. Usually it will find setup and proceed with the installation. If it doesn't, you'll see a dialog box like the one in Figure 6.4.

5. If you know exactly where the setup program is on the CD or the floppy disk, you can, of course, type the path into the Command Line text box. But more likely, you'll need to click the Browse button.

6. The Browse window opens showing your C drive. Use the Look In drop-down box to move to your floppy drive or CD-ROM drive.

7. Find the setup file (the program's documentation will be helpful here) and select it (see Figure 6.5). Click the Open button.

FIGURE 6.4:   Add/Remove Programs is unable to find the new program's setup file.

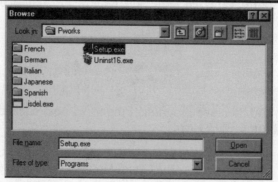

FIGURE 6.5:   This program's setup file is in a subdirectory on the CD-ROM.

8. You'll return to the installation process with the path for the setup file shown in the Command Line text box (see Figure 6.6). Click Finish.

9. The setup program will be run and the actual installation of the new program will start.

TIP

Programs downloaded from the Internet or other sources are installed in a similar fashion. You can use Add/Remove Programs, pointing to the setup file location on your hard drive. Or you can click the setup file directly to start the installation process.

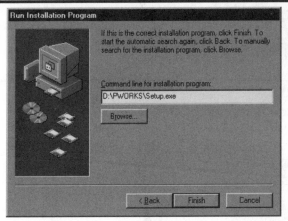

FIGURE 6.6: With the setup file located, you can click Finish to move on in the installation process.

REMOVING A PROGRAM

The process of removing a program (also called uninstalling) varies depending on whether the program is a true 32-bit program written for Windows 95 or Windows 98, or something older.

A software producer who wants the license to put a Windows 98 or 95 logo on a product is required to make sure the program can uninstall itself. This proviso is intended to correct a problem in Windows 3.1. When using Windows 3.1, it was very difficult to completely get rid of some programs because their files could be spread all over the hard drive. The average person has no way of knowing whether a file called, let's say, fxstl.dll is disposable because it belonged to a long gone program or whether deleting it will cause the entire system to fail!

A few programs that claim to have been written for Windows 95 or 98 can be uninstalled and still leave bits of themselves cluttering your hard disk. How the major programs written for Windows 98 or 95 handle Add/Remove varies widely. Some will just uninstall themselves without a fuss; others give you the option of removing all or just part of the program. *Nothing* will be uninstalled without your OK.

To remove a Windows 98 or Windows 95 program, follow these steps:

1. Click the Start button and select Settings ➢ Control Panel.

2. Click the Add/Remove Programs icon.

3. In the dialog box that opens (shown in Figure 6.7), you'll see a list of programs that can be automatically removed. If the program you want to uninstall is in the list, highlight it and then click the Add/Remove button.

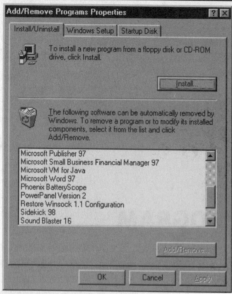

FIGURE 6.7: In this window, select a program to uninstall.

4. A dialog box will open, describing what will be removed by this step. Click Yes to continue.

5. The program will be uninstalled.

Sometimes after the removal, you'll get a message to the effect that not all parts of the program could be deleted. Since you're not told *which* parts, this is something less than helpful. For the ultimate in hard drive tidiness, look into one of the third-party programs like Uninstaller or WinDelete; these are very good at getting rid of stray files with safety.

Removing a Windows 3.1 Program

Programs written for Windows versions prior to Windows 95 don't have an uninstall capability. These programs aren't hard to get rid of—at least superficially. Just find the directory for the program and delete it. Delete shortcuts relating to the program. Unfortunately, these early Windows programs have an unhappy tendency to deposit files in the main Windows directory, the System subdirectory, and anywhere else that the program's designers thought appropriate.

Getting rid of every trace of such a program is very difficult unless you have a program like Uninstaller. Most of the time, however, it's not absolutely necessary to track down and delete every stray .dll file. You can survive quite well even if bits and pieces of a program remain.

Removing a DOS Program

Removing a DOS-based program is the easiest of all. Find the program's folder and delete it. DOS programs don't have roaming files, so if you delete the folder, you delete everything.

The only exception to the nonwandering file is if you have a shortcut to the program on the desktop or elsewhere. Delete the shortcuts at the same time you delete the program folder.

FINDING A PROGRAM

There are times when you've installed a program only to be abruptly returned to the desktop with your new application nowhere in sight. Or you inherit a computer that you know has certain programs on it—but they're likewise nowhere in sight.

Starting with the easiest method, here are some ways to find a program hiding on your system.

Program Menu   Your application may be in the easiest place of all. Click the Start button and select Programs. If it's not in the first menu, look for something that might be a "parent" to the one you want. For example, Figure 6.8 shows the Encarta World Atlas under the more general heading of Microsoft Reference.

Shortcuts   Look for a shortcut on your desktop. If all you want to do is launch the program, clicking on the shortcut should do the job. If you want to find the physical location for the program's files, right-click the shortcut and select Properties from the pop-up menu. In the Properties dialog box, click the Find Target button. The folder containing the program will open.

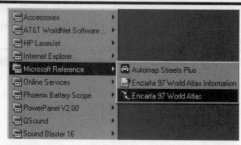

FIGURE 6.8: Finding the Encarta World Atlas program under a more general heading

Find   Knowing the name of the program is usually enough to use the Find feature. Click the Start button and select Find ➤ Files or Folders. In the Named text box, type in what you know. In Figure 6.9, I'm looking for a program made by Starfish. Sure enough, the search turns up a folder called Starfish, and inside is the program I'm looking for.

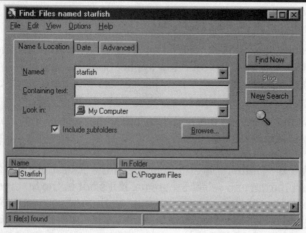

FIGURE 6.9: The Find function turns up a folder named Starfish.

I could just as easily search using a partial filename or program name. Sometimes it takes two or three tries to find what you're looking for.

Windows Explorer   When all else fails, you can simply open Windows Explorer and browse. Be sure to look in the Program Files folder as well as any Temp folders. The folder may be clearly named or it may not. In Figure 6.10, it's not hard to figure out what might be in Internet Mail and

News, but what about NAVHMI or the even more cryptically named NC? Once you get to this stage of searching, you'll just have to poke around.

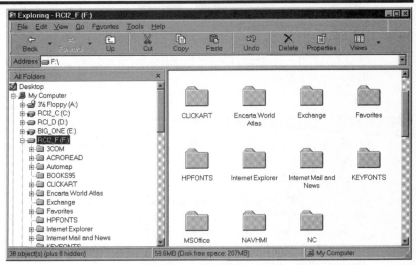

FIGURE 6.10: Searching for program files in Windows Explorer

TIP

If you're in an unhelpfully named folder looking at even more unhelpfully named files, look for a file that really might help (it'll have the .hlp extension) and click it. You'll be looking at a help file that—if its authors were at all thoughtful—should tell you what program you're dealing with.

MAKING PROGRAMS EASIER TO FIND

Once you've been through a few searches like the ones just described, you realize the importance of making your programs easy to find. In the next sections, you'll see how to put your programs in convenient locations. When you're deciding, do give some consideration to how often you use a given application. If you put shortcuts to all your programs on the Start menu or on the desktop, the resulting clutter will immediately cancel out any gain.

To make a shortcut to a program on the Programs menu, you need to first locate the program file. This is the program you click on to start running the program. In general, this file will have the extension .exe and will have the same name (or a shortened version) as that of the overall program. As an example, the program file for Word for Windows is Word.exe and that for WordPerfect 8 for Windows is wpwin8.exe. On the other hand, the program file for Quicken for Windows is qw.exe, and for InfoSelect it's is.exe.

Desktop Shortcuts

As described in Chapter 4, shortcuts are easily made. For a shortcut to a program, right-click the program file in Windows Explorer and select Send To ➢ Desktop As a Shortcut.

If you already have a shortcut on the desktop or in a folder, you can make a copy of it to use somewhere else. Even if you make a shortcut to a shortcut, the second shortcut will point back to the original file, *not* to the first shortcut. So you needn't worry that deleting a shortcut will somehow disrupt the connection.

Programs Menu Shortcuts

To put a shortcut on the Programs menu, follow these steps:

1. Right-click the Start button and select Open.

2. Click Programs. A window like the one in Figure 6.11 will open. Each item on this list corresponds to an entry on the Programs menu (shown on the left in Figure 6.11). Items that appear as a folder in the window are the items on the Programs menu with an arrow (➢) next to them—indicating that there are additional items to be found if you follow the arrow.

3. If the shortcut is to be at the first level of the Programs menu, drag and drop the shortcut you've made into the Programs window.

4. To put the shortcut at the next level down, drag it into one of the folders in the Programs window. For example, drag and drop a shortcut to a game in the Accessories folder.

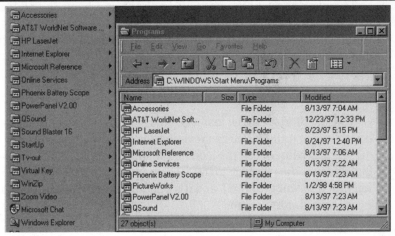

FIGURE 6.11: Comparing the Programs window to the Programs menu

You can also easily move a program that's a level or two down up to the first Programs menu level:

1. In the Programs window, find the shortcut you want to move.

2. Right-click on the shortcut and select Cut from the pop-up menu.

3. Click the Up icon on the Programs window toolbar to move up one level in the Programs menu.

4. Right-click in a blank area of the new window and select Paste from the pop-up menu.

The program shortcut will move to its new location.

Start Menu Shortcuts

Adding a shortcut to the Start menu is as easy as drag and drop. In fact, that's what you do. Drag the shortcut to the Start button and drop it. When you open the Start menu, your shortcut will be listed among the programs at the top.

Toolbar Shortcuts

Even quicker access to a program can be had if you add a shortcut to the Quick Launch toolbar. By default, the Quick Launch toolbar comes with shortcuts to Internet Explorer, Outlook Express, Channels, and the desktop already in place.

Add any shortcut to the toolbar by dragging the shortcut to the toolbar and dropping it there. You can remove shortcuts from the toolbar by reversing the procedure. Click the icon on the toolbar and, holding the mouse button down, drag the icon to the desktop. When you release the mouse button, the icon will be moved, and it's a simple matter to delete it using the right mouse button menu.

TIP

The Show Desktop icon on the Quick Launch toolbar is a great new addition in Windows 98. It acts as a "minimize all" button—minimizing all open windows to the Taskbar, even dialog boxes that won't ordinarily minimize. If you'd like to have other copies, right-click on the icon and drag it to the desktop (or to an open folder). Release the mouse button and select Copy Here from the pop-up menu.

Send-To Shortcuts

A right-click on a file or almost any other object will produce a menu that includes the option Send To ➤. When you follow the arrow, you'll see a list of shortcuts to possible file destinations such as the floppy drive, mail recipient, or My Briefcase.

To modify the Send To list, follow these steps:

1. Right-click the Start button and select Explore from the menu.

2. In the Windows Explorer window that opens, look for the SendTo folder in the left pane (see Figure 6.12).

3. Click the SendTo folder to open it.

4. Add to, delete, or rename any of the shortcuts. The changes will be shown as soon as they're made.

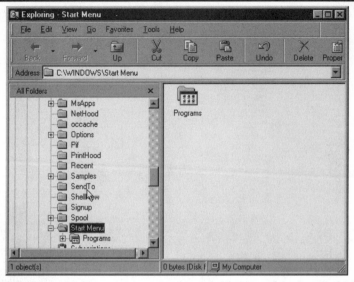

FIGURE 6.12: The mouse pointer shows the location of the SendTo folder.

NOTE

If a program—any program—doesn't want to run or hangs or crashes, see Chapter 12 for troubleshooting tips.

What's Next?

In the next three chapters, we'll call upon another Windows 98 expert, Bob Cowart, to take you through some topics related to hardware. First we'll look at customizing your configuration with the Control Panel, then we'll look at printers and printing, and finally (here's the fun stuff) at Windows 98's extensive support for multimedia.

Chapter 7

CUSTOMIZING WITH THE CONTROL PANEL

There are numerous alterations you can make to customize Windows to your liking—adjustments to screen colors, modems, mouse speed, passwords, key repeat rate, fonts, and networking options, to name just a few. Most of these adjustments are not necessities as much as they are niceties that make using Windows just a little easier. Others are more imperative, such as setting up Windows to work with your brand and model of printer, setting up Windows Messaging preferences for your e-mail, or getting your mouse pointer to slow down a bit so you can reasonably control it.

Adapted from Mastering Windows 98, by Robert Cowart
ISBN 0-7821-1961-1   1,184 pages $34.99
Order this book at www.masteringwindows.com

Preferences of this sort are made through Windows 98's Control Panel. Once you change a setting with the Control Panel, alterations are stored in the Windows configuration Registry. The settings are reloaded each time you run Windows and stay in effect until you change them again with the Control Panel.

This chapter discusses how you run and work with the Control Panel and delves into what the multifarious settings are good for.

OPENING THE CONTROL PANEL

You open the Control Panel by clicking on the Start button, choosing Settings, and choosing Control Panel. The Control Panel window then opens, as shown in Figure 7.1.

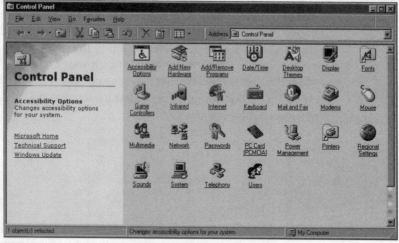

FIGURE 7.1: The Control Panel window. Each item opens a window from which you can make adjustments.

TIP

The Control Panel can also be reached from My Computer or from the Explorer. From the Explorer, scroll the left pane to the top and click on the My Computer icon. Then double-click on the Control Panel in the right pane.

In your Control Panel there will be as many as twenty or so items to choose from, depending on the hardware in your computer and which items you opted for during installation of Windows 98. As you add new software or hardware to your system, you'll occasionally see new options in your Control Panel, too.

Each icon in the Control Panel runs a little program (called an *applet*) when you double-click on it, typically bringing up one or more dialog boxes for you to make settings in. Below is a list of all the standard Control Panel applets and what they do.

Accessibility Options   Lets you set keyboard, mouse, sound, display, and other options that make a Windows 98 computer easier to use by those who are visually, aurally, or motor impaired.

Add New Hardware   Installs or removes sound, CD-ROM, video, MIDI, hard- and floppy-disk controllers, PCMCIA sockets, display adaptors, SCSI controllers, keyboard, mouse, printers, ports, and other device drivers.

Add/Remove Programs   You can add or remove modules of Windows 98 itself and sometimes add or remove other kinds of programs. Also lets you create a start-up disk to start your computer with in case the operating system on the hard disk gets trashed accidentally.

Date/Time   Sets the current date and time and which time zone you're in.

Desktop Themes   These combine custom sounds, color schemes, screen savers, and cursors into easily chosen settings groups.

Display   Sets the colors (or gray levels) and fonts of various parts of Windows' screens, title bars, scroll bars, and so forth. Sets the background pattern or picture for the Desktop. Also allows you to choose the screen saver, display driver, screen resolution, and energy-saving mode (if your display supports it).

Fonts   Adds and deletes typefaces for your screen display and printer output. Allows you to look at samples of each of your fonts.

Game Controllers   Adds, removes, and adjusts settings for "joysticks" and other types of game controllers.

Infrared   Configures and monitors infrared (wireless) communications.

Internet   Settings for all Internet-related activities such as Web, mail, newsgroups, your home page location, etc.

Keyboard   Sets the rate at which keys repeat when you hold them down, sets the cursor blink rate, determines the language your keyboard will be able to enter into documents, and lets you declare the type of keyboard you have.

Mail   As explained in Chapter 16, profiles are groups of settings that control how your faxing and e-mail are handled. This applet lets you manage these profiles.

Microsoft Mail Postoffice   If you are connected to a network that has a Microsoft Mail Postoffice, this applet lets you administer the postoffice or create a new postoffice. Postoffices are used as a central repository for mail on a network.

Modems   Lets you add, remove, and set the properties of the modem(s) connected to your system. Covered in Chapter 10.

Mouse   Sets the speed of the mouse pointer's motion relative to your hand motion and how fast a double-click has to be to have an effect. You can also reverse the functions of the right and left buttons, set the shape of the various Windows 98 pointers, and tell Windows 98 that you've changed the type of mouse you have. Covered in Chapter 10.

Multimedia   Changes the Audio, MIDI, CD music, and other multimedia device drivers, properties, and settings. See Chapter 9 for details.

Network   Function varies with the network type. Typically allows you to set the network configuration (network card/connector, protocols, and services), add and configure optional support for Novell, Banyan, Sun network support, and network backup hardware, change your identification (workgroup name, computer name), and determine the manner in which you control who gains access to resources you share over the network, such as printers, fax modems, and folders.

Passwords   Sets up or changes log-on passwords, allows remote administration of the computer, and sets up individual profiles that go into effect when each new user logs onto the local computer.

PCMCIA   Lets you stop PCMCIA cards before removing them, set the memory area for the card service shared memory (very unlikely to be needed), and disable/enable the beeps that indicate PCMCIA cards are activated when the computer boots up. This icon only appears on laptops or on desktop machines configured with PCMCIA slots.

Power Management   If you have a battery-powered portable computer or an energy-efficient desktop machine, this applet provides options for setting the Advanced Power Management details and viewing a scale indicating the current condition of the battery charge.

Printers   Displays the printers you have installed on your system, lets you modify the property settings for those printers, and lets you display and manage the print *queue* for each of those printers. Use this applet to install *printer drivers*. (Installing new printer drivers and managing the print queue are covered in Chapter 8.)

Regional Settings   Sets how Windows displays times, dates, numbers, and currency; see Appendix A.

Sounds   Turns off and on the computer's beep or adds sounds to various system events if your computer has built-in sound capability. Lets you set up sound *schemes*—preset collections of sounds that your system uses to alert you to specific events. Covered in Chapter 9.

System   Displays information about your system's internals—devices, amount of RAM, type of processor, and so forth. Also lets you add to, disable, and remove specific devices from your system, set up hardware profiles (for instance, to allow automatic optimization when using a docking station with a laptop), and optimize some parameters of system performance such as CD cache size and type. This applet also provides a number of system-troubleshooting tools, covered in Chapter 12.

Telephony   Lets you delete your location, your dialing prefixes for an outside line, and other attributes relating to telephone-dependent activities that rely on the TAPI interface.

Users Enables your computer to set up for use by other people, allowing each of them to have their own Desktop icons, background, color choices, and other settings.

I'll now discuss the Control Panel applets in detail. Aside from the Accessibility settings, the applets here are the ones you're most likely to want to adjust.

ACCESSIBILITY OPTIONS

Accessibility means increasing the ease of use or access to a computer for people who are physically challenged in one way or another. Many people have difficulty seeing characters on the screen when they are too small, for example. Others have a disability that prevents them from easily typing on the keyboard. Even those of us who hunt and peck at the keyboard have it easy compared to those who can barely move their hands, are limited to the use of a single hand, or who may be paralyzed from the neck down. These people have gotten the short end of the stick for some time when it came to using computers unless they had special data-entry and retrieval devices (such as speech boards) installed in their computers.

Microsoft has taken a big step in increasing computer accessibility to disabled people by including in Windows 98, features that allow many challenged people to use Windows 98 and Windows programs without major modification to their machines or software.

The Accessibility applet lets you make special use of the keyboard, display, mouse, sound board, and a few other aspects of your computer. To run the Accessibility option, double-click on its icon in the Control Panel. The resulting dialog box looks like Figure 7.2.

NOTE

As of Windows 98, several new accessibility features have been added, including support for screen readers, larger high-contrast font displays, screen magnification, and more. Most of these features are available via the Accessibility Wizard, which is an entry point and interface for the settings described in this section. To reach this wizard, click Start ➣ Programs ➣ Accessories ➣ Accessibility. For more information about Microsoft's ongoing advancements in accessibility support, and for API information, please see http://microsoft.com/enable.

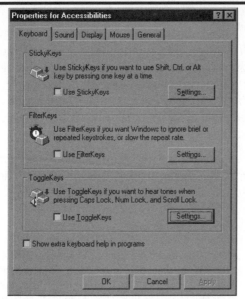

FIGURE 7.2:   The Accessibility dialog box

Keyboard Accessibility Settings

Probably all of us have some difficulty keeping multiple keys depressed at once. Settings here help with this problem and others.

1. Click on the Keyboard tab (if it's not already selected). There are three basic setting areas:

StickyKeys	Keys that in effect stay pressed down when you press them once. Good for controlling the Alt, Ctrl, and Shift keys.
FilterKeys	Lets you filter out quickly repeated keystrokes in case you have trouble pressing a key cleanly once and letting it up. This prevents multiple keystrokes from being typed.
ToggleKeys	Gives you the option of hearing tones that alert you to the Caps Lock, Scroll Lock, and Num Lock keys being activated.

2. Click on the box for the feature you want your Windows 98 machine to use.

3. Note that each feature has a Settings button from which you can make additional adjustments. To see the additional settings, click on the Settings button next to the feature, fine-tune the settings, and then click on OK. The most likely setting changes you'll make from these boxes are to turn on or off the shortcut keys.

4. After you have made all the keyboard changes you want, either move on to another tab in the Accessibility box or click on OK and return to the Control Panel.

TIP

You can turn on any of these keyboard features—StickyKeys, FilterKeys, or ToggleKeys—with shortcuts at any time while in Windows 98. To turn on Sticky-Keys, press either Shift key five times in a row. To turn on FilterKeys, press and hold the right Shift key for eight seconds (it might take longer). To turn on the ToggleKeys option, press the Num Lock key for five seconds.

When StickyKeys or FilterKeys are turned on, a symbol will appear on the right side of the Taskbar indicating what's currently activated. For example, here I have the StickyKeys and FilterKeys both set on. Sticky-Keys is indicated by the three small boxes, representative of the Ctrl, Alt, and Shift keys. FilterKeys is represented by the stopwatch representative of the different key timing that goes into effect when the option is working.

TIP

Turning on FilterKeys will make it seem that your keyboard has ceased working. You have to press a key and keep it down for several seconds for the key to register. If you activate this setting and want to turn it off, the easiest solution is to use the mouse or switch to Control Panel (via the Taskbar), run the Accessibility applet, turn off FilterKeys, and click on OK.

Unless you disable this feature from the Settings dialog box, you can turn off StickyKeys by pressing two of the three keys that are affected by this setting. For example, pressing Ctrl and Alt at the same time will turn StickyKeys off.

Sound Accessibility Settings

There are two Sound Accessibility settings—Sound Sentry and Show Sounds (see Figure 7.3). These two features are for the hearing impaired. What they do is simply cause some type of visual display to occur in lieu of the normal beep, ding, or other auditory alert that the program would typically produce. The visual display might be something such as a blinking window (in the case of Sound Sentry) or it might be some kind of text caption (in the case of ShowSounds). The Settings button for Sound Sentry lets you decide what will graphically happen on screen when a program is trying to warn you of something.

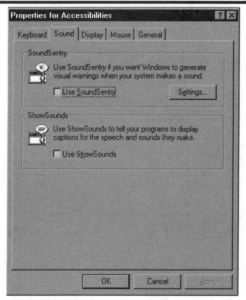

FIGURE 7.3: The two Sound Accessibility settings

NOTE

Not all programs will work cooperatively with these sound options. As more programs are written to take advantage of these settings, you'll see more *closed captioning*, for example, wherein sound messages are translated into useful captions on the screen.

Display Accessibility Settings

The Display Accessibility settings pertain to contrast. These settings let you set the display color scheme and font selection for easier reading. This can also be done from the normal Display setting, described below, but the advantage to setting it here is that you can preset your favorite high-contrast color scheme, then invoke it with the shortcut key combination when you most need it. Just press Left-Alt, Left-Shift, Prnt-Scrn. This might be when your eyes are tired, when someone who is sight impaired is using the computer, or when you're sitting in an adverse lighting situation. Figure 7.4 displays the dialog box:

1. Turn on the High Contrast option box if you want to improve the contrast between the background and the characters on your screen. When you click on Apply or OK, this will kick in a high-contrast color scheme (typically the Blue and Black) scheme, which will put black letters on a white work area. (You can't get much more contrast than that!)

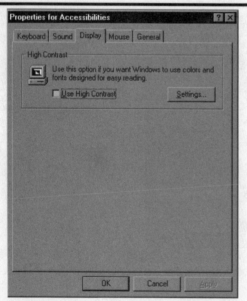

FIGURE 7.4: The dialog box for setting Display Accessibility

2. Click on the Settings button if you want to change the color scheme that'll be used for high contrast or if you want to

enable or disable shortcut-key activation of this feature. This option may come in handy because some of the schemes have larger fonts than others and some might show up better on your screen than will others.

TIP

The Display applet offers an easier way to experiment with the schemes. You can even create your own custom color scheme with large menus, title bar lettering, and dialog box lettering if you want. I explain how to do all this in the Display section.

3. Click on Apply if you want to keep making more settings from the other tab pages or on OK to return to the Control Panel.

Mouse Accessibility Settings

If you can't easily control mouse or trackball motion, or simply don't like using a mouse, this dialog box is for you. Of course, you can invoke most commands that apply to dialog boxes and menus throughout Windows and Windows programs using the Alt key in conjunction with the command's underlined letter. Still, some programs, such as those that work with graphics, require you to use a mouse. This Accessibility option turns your arrow keys into mouse-pointer control keys. You still have to use the mouse's clicker buttons to left- or right-click on things, though. Here's what to do:

TIP

This is a great feature for laptop users who are on the road and forgot the mouse. If you have to use a graphics program or other program requiring more than simple command choices and text entry, use the Mouse Accessibility tab to turn your arrow keys into mouse-pointer keys.

1. Click on the Mouse tab in the Accessibility dialog box. You'll see the box displayed in Figure 7.5.

2. Turn on the option if you want to use the arrow keys in place of the mouse. You'll probably want to adjust the speed settings for the arrow keys, though, so the pointer moves at a rate that works for you. The Settings button brings up the box you see in Figure 7.6. Note that you can also set a shortcut key sequence to activate MouseKeys.

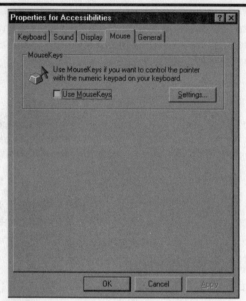

FIGURE 7.5: The Mouse Accessibility dialog box

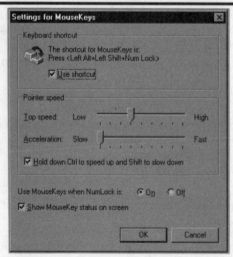

FIGURE 7.6: Additional Mouse Accessibility settings

3. Play with the settings until you like them. The Top Speed and Acceleration settings are going to be the most important. And note that you have to set them, click on OK, then click on Apply in the Mouse dialog box before you can experience the effect of your changes. Then go back and adjust your settings if necessary. Notice that one setting lets you change the tracking speed on the fly while using a program, by holding down the Shift key to slow down the pointer's motion or the Ctrl key to speed it up.

4. Click on Apply if you want to keep making more settings from the other tab pages or on OK to return to the Control Panel.

WHEEL MOUSE SUPPORT

One particularly crucial accessibility improvement in Windows 98 is the inclusion of support for the Microsoft "wheel mouse" (a.k.a. the Intellimouse™). That's a mouse with a little wheel sticking up between the mouse buttons. When you spin the wheel with some newer programs, it scrolls the contents of the active window; it relieves you of having to position the pointer on the scroll bar. Spinning the wheel one increment causes text to scroll several lines (default: three) per wheel detent.

Just because a window has a scroll bar doesn't mean it will work with the wheel. The program has to be "wheel aware." Some wheel-aware programs, including the programs in Office 97, will zoom in or out (cause the document to be displayed larger or smaller) if you rotate the wheel and hold down the Ctrl key at the same time.

Some wheel-aware applications (such as Internet Explorer or an Office 97 program) also offer "panning mode": you press down on the wheel to enter this special mode. When in panning mode, the mouse cursor changes to a special panning cursor, and just moving the mouse forward or backward will start the document scrolling in its window. The scroll speed is determined by how far you pull the mouse away from the position where you activated panning mode. When you want to exit the panning mode, simply press any mouse button.

TIP

The pointer keys that are used for mouse control are the ones on a standard desktop computer keyboard's number pad. These are the keys that have two modes—Num Lock on and Num Lock off. These keys usually have both an arrow and a number on them; for example, the 4 key also has a ← symbol on it. Most laptops don't have such keys because of size constraints. However, many laptops have a special arrangement that emulates these keys, providing a ten-key numeric keypad (and arrows when NumLock is off).

Other Accessibility Settings

The last tab in the Accessibility box is called General (Figure 7.7).

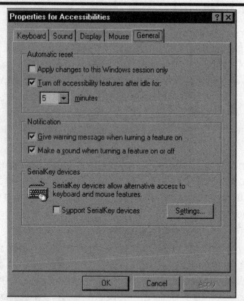

FIGURE 7.7:   The last of the Accessibility settings boxes

The box is divided into three sections pertaining to:

▶ When Accessibility functions are turned on and off. Notice that you can choose to have all the settings you've made during this Windows session apply only to this session (that means until you restart Windows).

▶ How you are alerted to a feature being turned on or off. You have the choice of a visual cue (a little dialog box will appear) and/or a sound.

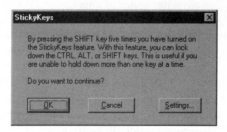

▶ Acceptance of alternative input devices through the serial (COM1 through COM4) ports on your computer.

ADDING NEW HARDWARE

If you have a computer that is Plug-and-Play compatible, this section won't be of a lot of use to you, and you should celebrate. That's because Plug and Play ensures that by simply plugging a new card or other device into your computer, it will work. The Plug-and-Play software in Windows 98—in concert with software coding in the computer and add-on cards and devices—takes care of installing the appropriate hardware device driver file and making the appropriate settings so your new device doesn't conflict with some other device in the system. That's the good news.

TIP

Of course, there are a limited number of IRQs, ports, and DMAs. Plug in enough Plug-and-Play cards, and one or more is guaranteed not to be installed by the system because Plug and Play will not enable a device unless resources are available for it.

The bad news is that there are a zillion non–Plug-and-Play PC cards and devices floating around in the world and just as many pre–Plug-and-Play PCs. This older hardware isn't designed to take advantage of Windows 98's Plug-and-Play capabilities. The upshot of this is that when you install such hardware into your system, many computers won't detect the change. This will result in disappointment when you've carefully installed some piece of new and exciting gear (such as a sound card) and it just doesn't work—or worse, it disables things that used to function just fine.

NOTE
If you're installing a new printer, please read Chapter 8 as well.

Microsoft has added a nifty feature that tries its best to install a new piece of hardware for you. All you have to do is declare your new addition and let Windows 98 run around and try to detect what you've done. Luckily, the Add Hardware applet is pretty savvy about interrogating the hardware you've installed—via its Install Hardware Wizard—and making things work right. You can also tell it exactly what you have in order to save a little time and ensure that Windows gets it right.

NOTE
Notice the applet is only for adding new hardware, not for removing hardware and associated driver files. Removing drivers is done through the System applet. Note that there are other locations throughout Windows for installing some devices, such as printers, which can be installed from the Printers folder via My Computer. However, the effect is the same as installing these devices from this applet.

TIP
Microsoft maintains a Windows 98 driver library that contains new, tested drivers as they are developed for printers, networks, screens, audio cards, and so forth. You can access these drivers through the Microsoft website, CompuServe, GEnie, or the Microsoft Download Service (MSDL). You can fax MSDL at (425) 936-6735. You can also order the entire library on disk by calling Microsoft at (800) 426-9400.

Running the Install Hardware Wizard

If you've purchased a board or other hardware add-in, first read the supplied manual for details about installation procedures. There may be installation tips and an install program supplied with the hardware. If there are no instructions, then install the hardware and follow the steps below (but *only* if there are no instructions).

NOTE

I suggest you install the hardware before you run the Wizard, or Windows 98 won't be able to validate that the hardware is present. Also, unless you follow these procedures, simply putting new hardware into your computer usually won't change anything. This is because Windows has to update the Registry containing the list of hardware in your system, it has to install the appropriate device-driver software for the added hardware, and it often has to reboot before the new hardware will work.

Part i

1. Close any programs you have running. You're probably going to be rebooting the machine, and it's possible that the detection process will hang up the computer, possibly trashing work files that are open.

2. Look up or otherwise discover the precise brand name and model number/name of the item you're installing. You'll need to know it somewhere during this process.

3. Run the Control Panel and double-click on the Add New Hardware applet. You'll see its dialog box, looking like the one in Figure 7.8.

FIGURE 7.8:   The Add Hardware Wizard makes installing new hardware pretty easy, usually.

4. There's nothing to do but click on Next. The wizard looks for any new Plug-and-Play hardware, and will list anything new that it finds. The next box, as shown in Figure 7.9, requires some action on your part, though.

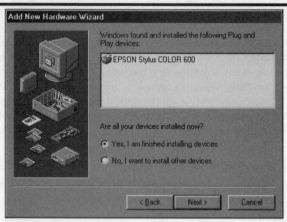

FIGURE 7.9:   Choose the type of hardware you want to install.

5. If the item(s) list looks complete, click Yes, I Am Finished and click Next. Follow instructions on screen. If you are not satisfied with the list and want some other stuff installed, click No, then Next, and move to step 6.

6. Now, if you want the Wizard to run around, look at what you have, and notice the new item you installed, just leave the top option button selected and click on Next. You'll be warned that this could take several minutes and be advised to close any open programs and documents. Keep in mind that the Wizard is doing quite a bit of sleuthing as it looks over your computer. Many add-in cards and devices don't have standardized ID markings, so identifying some hardware items isn't so easy. The Microsoft programmers had to devise some clever interrogation techniques to identify myriad hardware items. In fact, the results may even be erroneous in some cases. Regardless, while the hardware survey is underway, you'll see a gauge apprising you of the progress, and you'll hear a lot of hard-disk activity. In rare cases, the computer will hang during this process, and you'll have to reboot. If this happens repeatedly, you'll have to tell the Wizard what hardware you've added, as explained in the next section.

7. When the search is completed, you'll either be told that nothing new was found or you'll see a box listing the discovered items, asking for confirmation and/or some details. Respond as necessary. You may be prompted to insert one of your Windows 98 diskettes or the master CD-ROM so the appropriate driver file(s) can be loaded. If nothing new was found, click on Next, and the Wizard sends you on to step 2 in the section below.

Telling the Wizard What You've Got

If you're the more confident type (in your own abilities rather than the computer's), you might want to take the surer path to installing new hardware. Option two in the previous Wizard box lets *you* declare what the new hardware is. This option not only saves you time, but even lets you install the hardware later, should you want to. This is because the Wizard doesn't bother to authenticate the existence of the hardware: It simply installs the new driver.

1. Follow steps 1 through 5 above.

2. Now choose the second option button, *Install specific hardware.*

3. Scroll through the list to get an idea of all the classes of hardware you can install via this applet. Then click on the category you want to install. For this example, I'm going to install Creative Lab's Sound Blaster sound card because that's a popular add-in item.

TIP

If you don't know the class of the item you're installing, you're not sunk. Just choose Other Devices. Find and click on the manufacturer's brand name in the left-hand list; most popular items made by that manufacturer will be displayed in the right-hand list. Then choose your new hardware from this list.

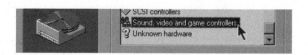

4. Click on Next. This brings up a list of all the relevant drivers in the class you've chosen. For example, Figure 7.10 lists the

sound cards from Creative Labs, the people who make the Sound Blaster cards.

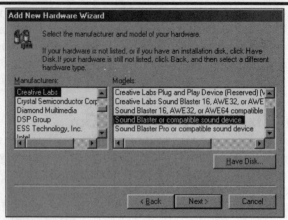

FIGURE 7.10: After choosing a class of hardware, you'll see a list of manufacturers and models.

5. First scroll the left list and click on the manufacturer. Then find the correct item in the Model list and click on that.

6. Click on Next. What happens at this point depends on the type of hardware you're installing:

   ▶ If the hardware is Plug-and-Play compatible, you'll be informed of it, and the Wizard will take care of the details.

   ▶ For some non–Plug-and-Play hardware, you'll be told to simply click on Finish, and the Wizard will take care of installing the necessary driver.

   ▶ In some cases, you'll be shown the settings that you should adjust your hardware to match. (Add-in cards often have switches or software adjustments that control the I/O port, DMA address, and other such geeky stuff.) For example, Figure 7.11 shows the message I got about the Sound Blaster card. Your job is to read the manual that came with the hardware and figure out how to adjust the switches, jumpers, or other doodads to match the settings the Wizard gives you.

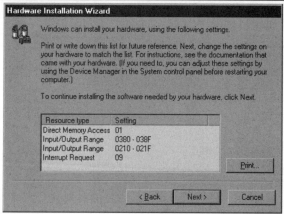

FIGURE 7.11: For hardware that has address or other adjustments on it, you may be told which setting to use to avoid conflicts with other hardware in the system.

TIP

If for some reason you don't want to use the settings suggested by the Wizard, you can set the board or device otherwise. Then you'll have to use the System applet's Device Manager to change the settings in the Windows Registry to match those on the card.

▶ In some cases, you'll be told there's a conflict between your new hardware and what's already in your computer (Figure 7.12). Despite the dialog box's message, you have *three* choices, not two. In addition to proceeding or canceling, you could also back up and choose a different piece of hardware, such as a different model number or a compatible make or model that might support a different port, DMA address, or whatnot. If you decide to continue, you'll have to resolve the conflict somehow, such as by removing or readdressing the conflicting board or device. In that case you'll be shown a dialog box that lets you run the *conflict troubleshooter*. This is a combination of a Help file and the System applet's Device Manager. The Help file walks you through a series of questions and answers.

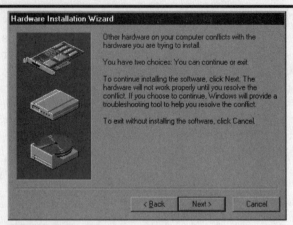

FIGURE 7.12: You have three options when the Wizard detects a conflict: the two choices offered and the Back button to try another piece of hardware.

7. Next, you may be prompted to insert a disk containing the appropriate software driver. Windows remembers the disk drive and directory you installed Windows 98 from, so it assumes the driver is in that location. This might be a network directory, your CD-ROM drive, or a floppy drive. In any case, just supply the requested disk. If the driver is already in your system, you will be asked if you want to use the existing driver. This is okay assuming the driver is up to date and you aren't trying to install a new one.

8. Finally, a box will announce that the necessary changes have been made and you can click on Finish. If you haven't physically installed the hardware already, you'll see this message:

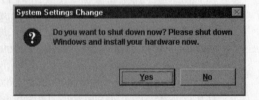

If the hardware is already installed, you'll probably see a message asking you to shut down and restart.

When Your Hardware Isn't on the List

Sometimes your new hardware won't be included in the list of items the Wizard displays. This means that Microsoft hasn't included a driver for that device on the disks that Windows 98 came on. This is probably because your hardware is newer than Windows 98, so it wasn't around when Windows 98 went out the door from Microsoft. Or it could be that the manufacturer didn't bother to get its product certified by Microsoft and earn the Windows "seal of approval." It's worth the few extra bucks to buy a product with the Windows 95 or 98 logo on the box rather than the cheapie clone product. As mentioned above, Microsoft makes new drivers available to users through several channels. However, manufacturers often supply drivers with their hardware, or you can get hold of a driver from a BBS, an information service such as CompuServe, or Microsoft Network.

If you're in this boat, you can just tell the Add New Hardware Wizard to use the driver on your disk. Here's how:

1. Run the Add New Hardware applet and choose the correct class of hardware, as explained above.

2. Click on the Have Disk button.

3. Enter the location of the driver (you can enter any path, such as a directory on the hard disk or network path) in this box.

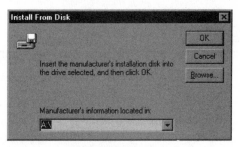

Typically, you'll be putting a disk in drive A, in which case you'd use the setting shown here. However, don't type the file name for the driver, just its path. Usually this will be just A:\ or B:\.

If the driver is on a hard disk or CD-ROM and you don't know which letter drive or which directory it is, use the Browse button and subsequent dialog box to select the source drive and directory. When the path is correct, click on OK.

4. Assuming the Wizard finds a suitable driver file (it must find a file called OEMSETUP.INF), choose the correct hardware item from the resulting dialog box and follow on-screen directions (they'll be the same as those I described above, beginning with step 6).

ADDING AND REMOVING PROGRAMS

The Add/Remove Programs applet has three functions:

- Installing and uninstalling programs that comply with Windows 98's API for these tasks. The API ensures that a program's file names and locations are recorded in a database, allowing them to be reliably erased without adversely impacting the operation of Windows 98.

- Installing and removing specific portions of Windows 98 itself, such as Windows Messaging.

- Creating a start-up disk that will start your computer in case the operating system gets trashed beyond functionality for some reason. With a start-up disk, you should still be able to gain access to your files and stand a chance of repairing the problem that prevents the machine from starting up.

Installing New Programs

The applet's first tab page is for installing new programs:

1. Run Control Panel, then the Add/Remove Software applet. You'll see the box shown in Figure 7.13.

2. Click on Install. Now a new box appears, telling you to insert a floppy disk or CD-ROM in the appropriate drive and click on Next. Assuming an appropriate program is found (it must be called *install* or *setup* and have a .bat, .pif, .com, or .exe extension), it'll be displayed as you see in Figure 7.14.

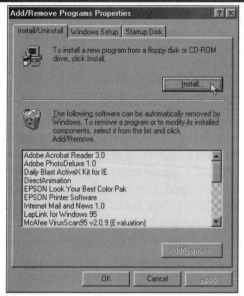

FIGURE 7.13: The Wizard for adding and removing software can be reached from the Add/Remove Programs applet (only programs that comply with Windows 98 installation standards).

FIGURE 7.14: The Wizard looks for a likely installation program on your CD-ROM or floppy, and displays the first one it finds.

3. Click on Finish to complete the task. The new software's installation or setup procedure will now run. Instructions will vary depending on the program. If your program's setup routine isn't compatible with the applet, you'll be advised of this. After installation, the new program will appear in the list of removable programs only if it's compatible with Windows 98's install/remove scheme.

Removing Existing Programs

With time, more programs will be removable via the Control Panel. This is because the PC software industry at large has heard much kvetching from users and critics about tenacious programs that once installed are hard to remove. Some ambitious programs spread themselves out all over your hard disk like olive oil in a hoagie, and there's no easy way of reversing the process to return your system to a pristine state. The result is often overall system slowdown, unexplained crashes, or other untoward effects.

To this end, aftermarket utilities such as Uninstaller have become quite popular. Uninstall utility programs monitor and record just exactly which files a new software package adds to your hard disk and which internal Windows settings it modifies. It can then undo the damage later, freeing up disk space and tidying your Windows system.

In typical fashion, Microsoft has incorporated such a scheme into Windows 98 itself. Time will tell if its mousetrap is as good as the competition's. Probably not, but it will be "close enough for jazz," as the saying goes. Programmers are beginning to write installation routines that work with Windows 9x's Add/Remove Software applet, so it looks like we're in luck.

Use of the uninstall feature of the applet is simple:

1. In the bottom pane, select the program(s) you want to uninstall.

2. Click on Remove.

3. Answer any warnings about removing an application as appropriate.

Once removed, you'll have to reinstall a program from its source disks to make it work again. You can't just copy things out of the Recycle Bin to their old directories because settings from the Start button—and possibly the Registry—will have been deleted.

Always check a program's disk or program group (from the Start button) for the possible existence of its own uninstall program. Such programs are frequently more thorough than the Windows Add/Remove Software approach.

TIP

See Chapter 6 if you want a more extensive discussion of adding and removing programs in Windows 98.

SETTING THE DATE AND TIME

NOTE

You can also adjust the time and date using the TIME and DATE commands from the DOS prompt, or by double-clicking the time in the System Tray on the end of the Taskbar.

The Date/Time icon lets you adjust the system's date and time. The system date and time are used for a number of purposes, including date- and time-stamping the files you create and modify, scheduling fax transmissions, and so on. All programs use these settings, regardless of whether they are Windows or non-Windows programs.

1. Double-click on the Date/Time applet. The dialog box in Figure 7.15 appears.

Set month from drop-down list

Click in desired area and use the little arrows to adjust

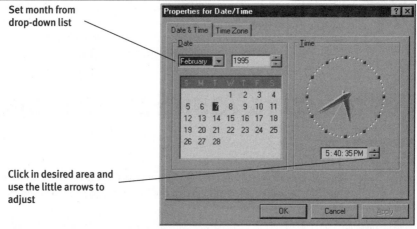

FIGURE 7.15: Adjust the date, time, and local time zone from this dialog box. A shortcut to this box is to double-click on the time in the Taskbar.

2.   Adjust the time and date by typing in the corrections or click-ing on the arrows. Note that you have to click directly on the hours, minutes, seconds, or am/pm area before the little arrows to the right of them will modify the correct value.

3.   Next, you can change the time zone you are in. Click on the Time Zone tab and you'll see a world map.

DESKTOP THEMES

The Desktop Themes applet combines sound schemes, color schemes, screen savers, and cursors for your Windows 98 system. It isn't much dif-ferent from what you can achieve using the Sounds, Display, and Mouse applets from the Control Panel. The advantage of Desktop Themes is that settings from these three areas are pulled into one applet called Desktop Themes, making it easy to recall many settings at once. If you've installed Desktop Themes (use Control Panel's Add/Remove Software applet, then choose Windows Setup), you'll have several preset themes to choose from, some of which are fairly artistic.

TIP

Because some of the visuals are actually photo-realistic, some of the schemes may look pretty bad on your monitor, even in 256 colors, if you don't switch to a high-color or true-color setting. High-color themes are marked as such. If you *don't* have a high-color video driver, you might as well remove these schemes; it will save a significant amount of disk space (about 9MB).

CUSTOMIZING YOUR SCREEN DISPLAY

TIP

The Display icon is accessible either from the Control Panel or from the Desk-top. Right-click on an empty area of the Desktop and choose Properties.

The Display applet packs a wallop under its hood. For starters, it incorpo-rates what in Windows 3.*x* were the separate Color and Desktop Control Panel applets for prettying up the general look of the Windows screen. Then, in addition, it includes the means for changing your screen driver and resolution—functions that in Windows 3.*x* were available only from the Setup program. If you were annoyed by getting at all these areas of display tweaking from disjunct venues, suffer no more. Microsoft has incorporated all display-related adjustments into the unified Display applet. If you are among the blessed, you will even have the option of changing screen resolution on the fly. If you've been using Windows 95, well, there's new stuff here for you, too.

Here are the functional and cosmetic adjustments you can make to your Windows 98 display from this applet:

- ▶ Set the background and wallpaper for the Desktop.
- ▶ Set the screen saver and energy conservation.
- ▶ Set the color scheme and fonts for Windows elements.
- ▶ Set the display device driver and adjust resolution, color depth, and font size.
- ▶ Change the icons you want to use for basic stuff on your Desktop such as My Computer and the Recycle Bin.
- ▶ Set color management compatibility so that your monitor and your printer output colors match.
- ▶ Decide which Web goodies you want alive on your Desktop, such as stock quotes, news, the Channel Bar, and so forth.

Let's take a look at this dialog box page by page. This is a fun one to experiment with and will come in handy if you know how to use it. First run the applet by double-clicking on it.

Setting the Background and Wallpaper

The pattern and wallpaper settings simply let you decorate the Desktop with something a little more festive than the default screen. Patterns are repetitive designs, such as the woven look of fabric. Wallpaper uses larger pictures that were created by artists with a drawing program. You can create your own patterns and wallpaper or use the ones supplied. Wallpapering can be done with a single copy of the picture placed in the center of the screen or by tiling, which gives you multiple identical pictures covering the whole screen. Some of the supplied wallpaper images cannot be used if you are low on memory. This is because the larger bit-mapped images take up too much RAM.

Loading a Pattern

Take these steps to load a new pattern:

1.   Click on the Background tab of the applet's dialog box.

2.   Scroll the Wallpaper list to a pattern you're interested in and
     highlight it. A minuscule version of your choice will show up
     in the little screen in the dialog box (Figure 7.16).

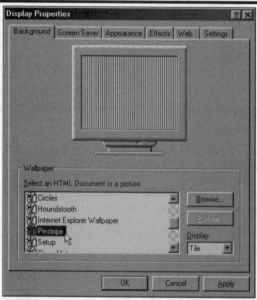

FIGURE 7.16:   Simply highlighting a pattern will display a facsimile
of it in the dialog box's tiny monitor screen.

3.   To see the effect on the whole screen, click on the Apply but-
     ton. This keeps the applet open and lets you easily try other
     patterns and settings. (If you want to leave it at that, click on
     OK. Then the applet will close, and you'll be returned to the
     Control Panel.)

Open the Display drop-down list and choose Center, Tile, or Stretch to
position the chosen item. If the picture is rather large, you'll want to use
Center. Tile repeats the graphic across the screen in a mosaic, so that every
inch is covered. Stretch will ensure that a single copy of the graphic fills the
entire screen. This can look pretty ghastly, since usually the dimensions of
the graphic become disproportional.

You can have a *pattern* on your Desktop rather than wallpaper, if you want. Patterns give the Desktop a nice texture rather than placing a whole picture there. And they easily fill up the whole Desktop if you use the Tile setting.

To choose a pattern, follow these steps:

1. Select None in the list on the left.

2. Click on Pattern.

3. From the resulting list, choose a pattern you like.

4. Click on OK.

NOTE

For a pattern to show up, wallpaper has to be set to None or be smaller than the full-screen size. This is because wallpaper always sits on top of the Desktop's pattern.

Editing a Pattern

If the supplied patterns don't thrill you, make up your own with the built-in bitmap editor. You can either change an existing one or design your own. If you want to design your own, choose None from the Name drop-down list before you begin. Otherwise, choose a pattern you want to play with:

1. Click on the Edit Pattern button. A new dialog box appears.

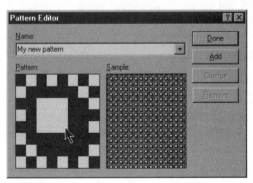

2. In the Name text box, type in a name for the new pattern.

3. Create the pattern by clicking in the box on the left. What you are doing is defining the smallest element of the repeated pattern (a cell). It is blown up in scale to make editing easier.

Each click reverses the color of one pixel. The effect when the pattern is applied across a larger area and in normal size is shown in the Sample section to the right.

4. When you like the pattern, click on Add and the pattern will be added to your list of patterns.

5. Click on Done when you're through creating new patterns.

If you later want to remove a pattern, select the pattern while in the editor and click on Remove. If you want to edit an existing pattern, get into the editor, select an existing pattern, make changes to it, and click on Change.

TIP

If you want to abandon changes you've made to a pattern, click on the Close button (X) and answer No to the question about saving the changes.

Loading a New Slice of Wallpaper

If you don't like the wallpaper you see, you can go hunting. Click on Browse, and look around for something else to use. A nice improvement over Windows 95 is that you can now use pictures other than BMP (Microsoft Paint) files. So in addition to BMP files, GIF and JPG files will work. HTML files (a.k.a. Web pages) will also display as wallpaper on your Desktop. Well, most of them will. They may not link properly or scroll correctly, but they'll show up. With all these file types accepted as Desktop wallpaper, the sky's the limit. For example, you could use a scanned color photograph of your favorite movie star, a pastoral setting, some computer art, a scanned Matisse painting, or a photo of your pet lemur. Figure 7.17 shows an example of a custom piece of wallpaper.

TIP

In Microsoft Paint's File menu there's a choice for setting the currently open bit-mapped file to Wallpaper. Chapter 14 covers the Paint program.

TIP

If you have some other form of picture file, such as a tif or pcx file that you want to use, you can, but you'll have to convert the file to bmp, jpg, or gif format first using another graphics program such as Collage Image Manager, Publisher's Paintbrush, Paintshop Pro, or other.

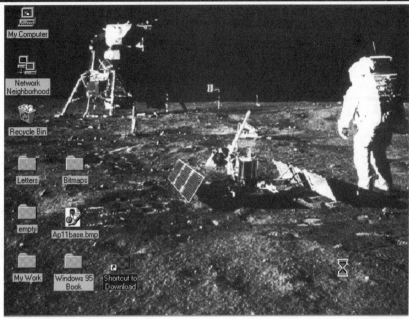

FIGURE 7.17: A custom piece of wallpaper. This is a .bmp file of the Apollo 11 base camp on the moon.

Setting the Screen Saver

A Screen Saver will blank your screen or display a moving image or pattern if you don't use the mouse or keyboard for a predetermined amount of time. Screen savers can prevent a static image from burning the delicate phosphors on the inside surface of the monitor, which can leave a ghost of the image on the screen for all time no matter what is being displayed. They can also just be fun.

Many modern computer monitors have an EPA Energy Star, VESA, or other kind of energy-saving strategy built into them. Because many people leave their computers on all the time, efforts have been made by power regulators and electronics manufacturers to devise computer–energy-conservation schemes. If your monitor has an Energy Star rating and your video board supports this feature, the screen saver in Windows 98 can power the monitor down after it senses you went out to lunch or got caught up at the water cooler for a longer-than-expected break.

The screen-saver options allow you to choose or create an entertaining video ditty that will greet you when you return to work. You also set how much time you have after your last keystroke or mouse skitter before the show begins. And a password can be set to keep prying eyes from toying with your work while you're away.

TIP

For an energy-saving screen saver to work properly, you'll have to set the Energy Star options from the Control Panel ➤ Display ➤ Settings ➤ Advanced Properties ➤ Monitor tab. Also, the monitor must adhere to the VESA Display Power Management Signaling (DPMS) specification or to another method of lowering power consumption. Some LCD screens on portable computers can do this. You can assume that if your monitor has an Energy Star emblem, it probably supports DPMS. Energy Star is a program administered by the U.S. Environmental Protection Agency (EPA) to reduce the amount of power used by personal computers and peripherals. If you notice that your screen freaks out or the display is garbled after your power-management screen saver turns on, you should turn off this check box.

Loading a Screen Saver

Here's how it's done:

1. Click on the Screen Saver tab. The page appears as you see in Figure 7.18.

2. Choose a name from the drop-down list. The saver will be shown in the little screen in the dialog box. (The 3-D Pipes are particularly dazzling.)

3. Want to see how it will look on your whole screen? Click on Preview. Your screen will go black and then begin its antics. The show continues until you hit any key or move your mouse.

4. If you want to change anything about the selected screen saver, click on Settings. You'll see a box of settings that apply to that particular screen saver. For example, for the Mystify Your Mind saver, this is the Settings box:

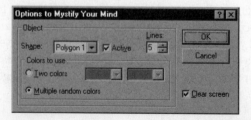

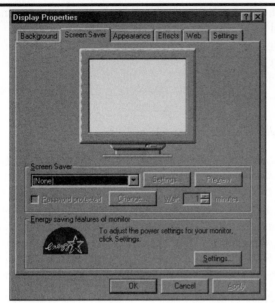

FIGURE 7.18:   Setting up a screen saver

Most of the option boxes have fun sliders and stuff you can play with to get an effect you like. Depending on which screen saver you chose, you'll have a few possible adjustments, such as speed, placement, and details pertinent to the graphic. Play with the settings until you're happy with the results and OK the Setting box.

5. Back at the Screen Saver page, the next choice you might want to consider is Password Options. If you set password protection on, every time your screen saver is activated you will have to type your password into a box to return to work. This is good if you don't want anyone else tampering with your files or seeing what you're doing. It can be a pain, though, if there's no particular need for privacy at your computer. Don't forget your password, either, or you'll have to reboot to get back to work. Of course, anyone could reboot your computer to get to your files, so this means of establishing security is somewhat bogus. Click on the Password Protected check box if you want protection and go on to the next two steps. Otherwise skip them.

6. Click on the Change button to define or change your password. In the dialog box that appears, type in your new password.

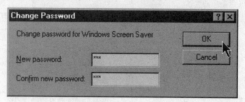

You won't see the letters, just an asterisk for each letter (to preserve confidentiality). For confirmation that you typed it correctly, type it again (don't copy the first one and paste it; a mistake in the first one can result in your being locked out of your computer) in the Confirm New Password text box. If there is a discrepancy between the two, you'll get an error message. Reenter the password. (If you're changing a password, the steps will be approximately the same. Enter your old password first, then the new one and its confirmation.) When it is correct, click on OK.

7. Back at the Desktop dialog box, set the number of minutes you want your computer to be idle before the screen saver springs into action. Next to Wait, either type in a number or use the up and down arrows to change the time incrementally.

8. Next you have the Energy Star options. Energy Star monitors need an Energy Star-compatible video card in the computer. If your screen setup supports this, the options will not be grayed out. Otherwise they will be. Assuming you can gain access to the settings, click on Configure. That will bring you to the Power Management dialog box, where you have two choices: when the low-power mode kicks in and when total power off kicks in. You don't want total power down to happen too quickly because the screen will take a few seconds (like about ten) to come back on when you move the mouse or press a key, which can be annoying. So make the two settings something reasonable, such as 15 minutes and 30 minutes.

9. When all the settings are correct, click on Apply or OK.

TIP

Some Energy Star displays require the "Blank Screen" screen saver in order to shut down.

Adjusting the Appearance

The Appearance page lets you change the way Windows assigns colors and fonts to various parts of the screen. If you're using a monochrome monitor (no color), altering the colors may still have some effect (the amount will depend on how you installed Windows).

Windows sets itself up using a default color scheme that's fine for most screens—and if you're happy with your colors as they are, you might not even want to futz around with them.

However, the color settings for Windows are very flexible and easy to modify. You can modify the color setting of just about any part of a Windows screen. For those of you who are very particular about color choices, this can be done manually, choosing colors from a palette or even mixing your own with the Custom Colors feature. Once created, custom colors and color setups can be saved on disk for later use or automatically loaded with each Windows session. For more expedient color reassignments, there's a number of supplied color schemes to choose from.

When you click on the Appearance tab, your dialog box will look like the one shown in Figure 7.19. The various parts of the Windows graphical environment that you can alter are shown in the top portion and named in the lower portion. As you select color schemes, these samples change so you can see what the effect will be without having to go back into Windows proper.

Loading an Existing Color Scheme

Before playing with the custom color palette, first try loading the supplied ones; you may find one you like:

1.   Click open the drop-down Color Schemes list box.

TIP

You can always toggle a drop-down list box open and closed from the keyboard by pressing Alt-↓ or Alt-↑.

FIGURE 7.19: The dialog box for setting the colors, font, and metrics of the Windows environment

2. Choose a selection whose name suits your fancy. The colors in the dialog box will change, showing the scheme. Try them out. Some are garish, others more subtle. Adjusting your monitor may make a difference, too. (You can cycle through the different supplied color schemes without selecting them from the drop-down list: with the Color Schemes space highlighted, just press the ↑ and ↓ keys. The sample screen elements will change to reflect each color scheme as its name appears in the Color Schemes box. There is an amazing variety!)

3. Click on Apply or OK to apply the settings to all Windows activities.

Microsoft has incorporated a few color schemes that may enhance the operation of your computer:

▶ On LCD screens that you'll be using in bright light, you might try the setting called High-Contrast White.

▶ If your eyes are weary, you may want to try one of the settings with the words Large or Extra Large in the name. These cause menus, dialog boxes, and title bars to appear in large letters.

Choosing Your Own Colors and Other Stuff

If you don't like the color schemes supplied, you can make up your own. It's most efficient to start with a scheme that's close to what you want and then modify it. Once you like the scheme, you may save it under a new name for later use. Here are the steps:

1. Select the color scheme you want to modify.

2. Click on the Windows element whose color you want to change. Its name should appear in the Item area. You can click on menu name, title bars, scroll bars, buttons—anything you see. You can also select a screen element from the Item drop-down list box rather than by clicking directly on the item.

3. Now click on the Color button to open up a series of colors you can choose from.

4. Click on the color you want. This assigns it to the item. Repeat the process for each color you want to change.

5. Want more colors? Click on the Other button. This pops up another 48 colors to choose from. Click on one of the 48 colors (or patterns and intensity levels, if you have a monochrome monitor) to assign it to the chosen element.

6. Once the color scheme suits your fancy, you can save it. (It will stay in force for future Windows sessions even if you don't save it, but you'll lose the settings next time you change colors or select another scheme.) Click on Save Scheme.

7. Type in a name for the color scheme and click on OK.

TIP

If you want to remove a scheme (such as one you never use), select it from the drop-down list and click on the Delete button.

Before I get into explaining custom colors, there are two other major adjustments you can make to your display—the fonts used for various screen elements, and Windows metrics, which affect how big or small some screen elements are.

You can choose the font for elements such as title bars, menus, and dialog boxes. For example, you can compensate for high-resolution monitors by making your menus more easily readable by using large point sizes in screen elements. In any case, you're no longer stuck with boring sans serif fonts such as Arial or MS Sans Serif.

1. On the Appearance page, simply click on the element whose font you want to change, such as the words "Message Box."

2. In the lowest line of the dialog box, the current font for that element appears. Just open the drop-down list box and choose another font if you want. You may also change the size, the color, and the style (bold or italic) of the font for that element.

3. Be sure to save the scheme if you want to keep it.

Finally, consider that many screen elements—such as the borders of windows—have a constant predetermined size. However, you might want to change these settings. If you have trouble grabbing the borders of windows, for example, you might want to make them larger. If you want icons on your desktop and in folders to line up closer or farther apart, you can do that, too.

1. Simply open the list and choose the item whose size you want to adjust. Some of the items are not represented in the upper section of the dialog box. They're things that appear in other parts of Windows 98, such as vertical icon spacing or selected items. You'll have to experiment a bit to see the effects of these items.

2. Click on the up or down size buttons to adjust.

3. Click on Apply to check out the effects of the changes. You might want to switch to another application via the Taskbar to see how things look.

4. If you don't like the effects of the changes you've made, just return to the Control Panel and click on Cancel. Or you can just select another color scheme, because the screen metrics are recorded on each color scheme.

Making Up Your Own Colors

If you don't like the colors that are available, you can create your own. There are 16 slots at the bottom of the larger color palette for storing colors you set using another fancy dialog box called the color refiner. Here's how:

1. Click on the Color button and then choose Other. This opens the enlarged color-selection box.

2. In that box, click on Define Custom Colors. Now the Color Refiner dialog box appears (see Figure 7.20).

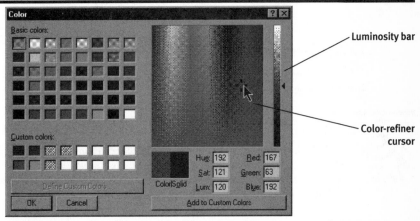

FIGURE 7.20: The custom color selector lets you create new colors.

There are two cursors that you work with here. One is the luminosity bar and the other is the color refiner cursor. To make a long story short, you simply drag these around one at a time until the color in the box at the lower left is the shade you want. As you do, the numbers in the boxes below the color refiner will change. Luminosity is the amount of brightness in the color. Hue is the actual shade or color. All colors are composed of red, green, and blue. Saturation is the degree of purity of the color; it is decreased by adding gray to the color and increased by subtracting it. You can also type in the numbers or click on the arrows next to the numbers if you want, but it's easier to use the cursors. When you like the color, click on Add Color to add the new color to the palette.

You can switch between a solid color and a color made up of various dots of several colors. Solid colors look less grainy on your screen but give you fewer choices. The Color|Solid box shows the difference between the two. If you click on this box before adding the color to the palette, the solid color closest to the actual color you chose will be added instead of the grainier composite color.

Once a color is added to the palette, you can modify it. Just click on it, move the cursors around, and then click on Add Color again. Click on Close to close the dialog box. Then continue to assign colors with the palette. When you are content with the color assignments, click on OK. If you decide after toying around that you don't want to implement the color changes, just click on Cancel.

Effects

The settings on this tab page were inherited from the Plus! program that used to be sold as an add-on for Windows 95. Among other creature comforts like font smoothing and full-window drag, Plus! lets you install what Microsoft calls Desktop "themes."

TIP

Full-window drag and font smoothing are included in Windows 98; they just aren't settable from the Display applet. Open any folder window, choose View ➤ Options ➤ Advanced, and look for the options *Smooth edges of screen fonts* and *Show windows contents while dragging*.

Themes were combinations of color settings, wallpaper, and icons designed for your Desktop. The fancy icons are what this option is about. Instead of being stuck with the same boring icons as everyone else, you can change them to something more your style.

1. Click on Effects from the Display Properties dialog box (see Figure 7.21).

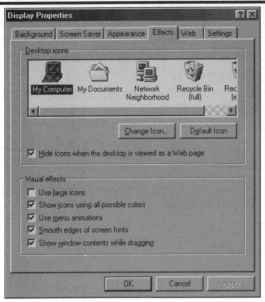

FIGURE 7.21:   Change the look of your Desktop icons from here.

2. Click on the icon you want to alter, then click Change Icon or Default Icon (to return to the factory setting). You'll get a resulting list of icons you can choose from, and you can also browse for icon replacements. (Where to look? Use the Browse box's "Files of type" selector to set the type of file as you're cruising. You can pick up an icon from an existing program (.exe), library (.dll), or icon (.ico) file.)

TIP

The Internet is a good source of icons. One way to find them is to do a search for the phrase *Icons* or *.ICO*.

TIP

The file Windows Explorer.exe (in the Windows directory) contains a bunch of icons. In fact, these are the old Windows 95 default icons, the ones you get if you click the Default Icon button when reassigning icons. To get back to the newer Windows 98 icons, use the file \windows\system\cool.dll.

The Visual Effects portion of the Effects tab page offers an assortment of other options. If you want your icons to be larger and more easily seen, set the *Large icons* check box on. You can click Apply to see the results. If you don't like them looking large on your Desktop horizon, just turn off the check box and click Apply again.

You can force Windows 98 to display icons in their full glory with the last checkbox, *Show icons using all possible colors*. This is normally on, so there typically isn't a problem.

In addition to the icon settings, this portion of the Effects tab also offers the following settings:

▸ **Use menu animations:** When this setting is on, menus will open up in a little more artistic manner. Instead of just popping up, they'll slide open.

▸ **Smooth edges of screen fonts:** Makes larger fonts look smoother on the screen.

▸ **Show window contents while dragging:** Keeps each window's contents visible while you are dragging or resizing it on screen.

Web

This tab page lets you set up your Active Desktop. Active Desktop is the feature in Windows 98 that lets you pull in stuff from the Web and have it display on the Desktop. This is discussed in Chapter 21 and Appendix A.

Driver Settings

The last tab page of the Display applet tweaks the video driver responsible for your video card's ability to display Windows. These settings are a little more substantial than those that adjust whether dialog boxes are mauve or chartreuse because they load a different driver or bump your video card up or down into a completely different resolution and color depth, changing the amount of information you can see on the screen at once (see Figure 7.22). Note that changing the color depth or palette on some systems requires rebooting before the changes take effect.

NOTE

This option is also the one to use for installing a Windows 3.*x* video driver for your video card just in case there isn't a Windows 98 driver for it.

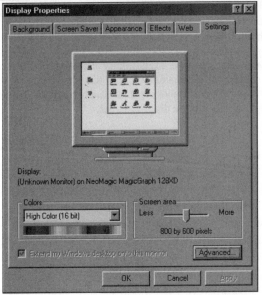

FIGURE 7.22:   The Settings page of the Display applet controls the video card's device driver. With most video systems, the slider lets you adjust the screen resolution on the fly.

Color Palette

Let's start with the color palette. Assuming your video card was properly identified when you installed Windows 98, this drop-down list box will include all the legitimate options your card is capable of. As you may know, different video cards are capable of displaying differing numbers of colors simultaneously. Your monitor is not the limiting factor here (with the exception of color LCD screens like those on laptops, which do have limitations); the limitations have to do with how much RAM is on your video card. All modern analog color monitors for PCs are capable of displaying 16 million colors, which is dubbed True Color.

It's possible that the drop-down list box will include color amounts (called depths) that exceed your video card's capabilities, in which case such a choice just won't have any effect. On the other hand, if your setting is currently 16 colors and your screen can support 256 or higher, Windows will look a lot prettier if you choose 256 and then choose one of the 256-color schemes from the Appearance tab page.

TIP

When you move the Desktop Area slider to the right, the resolution setting increases, right? True, but usually this will also lower the color palette setting to 256 or 16 colors (unless you have a really fancy display card). If after this you choose a lower resolution, such as 640 by 480, and you want to return to the richer color depth, you'll have to reset the color palette to a higher setting manually, by opening the color palette drop-down list.

Desktop Area

The Desktop Area setting is something avid Windows users have been wanting for for years. With Windows 3.*x*, changing this parameter (essentially the screen resolution) meant running Windows Setup, choosing a different video driver, and rebooting the machine and Windows. Windows 95 made this much easier. Now, with the right video card, you can change the resolution as you work. Some jobs—such as working with large spreadsheets, databases, CAD, or typesetting—are much more efficient with more data displayed on the screen. Because higher resolutions require a tradeoff in clarity and make on-screen objects smaller, eyestrain can be minimized by going to a lower resolution, such as 640-by-480 pixels (a pixel equals one dot on the screen). Note that there is a relationship between the color depth and the resolution that's available. This is because your video card can only have so much RAM on it. That RAM can be used to display extra colors or extra resolution, but not both. So, if you bump up the colors, you won't have as many resolution options. If you find the dialog box won't let you choose the resolution you want, try dropping the color palette setting to 16 colors.

To change the Desktop area:

1. Run Control Panel and run the Display applet.

2. Choose the Settings tab page.

3. Grab the slider and move it right or left. Notice how the little screen in the box indicates the additional room you're going to have on your real screen to do your work (and also how everything will get relatively smaller to make this happen, because your monitor doesn't get any larger!). Figure 7.23 illustrates.

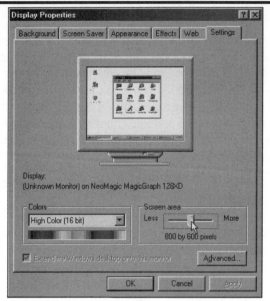

FIGURE 7.23: Change your screen resolution by dragging the slider. Here I've chosen 800 by 600.

4. Click on Apply. You'll now see this message:

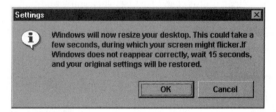

Go ahead and click on OK to try the setting. If your screen looks screwy and you can't read anything, don't worry. It will return to normal in about 15 seconds. If, on the other hand, you like what you see, there will be another dialog box asking you to confirm that you want to keep the current setting. Confirming that box makes the new setting permanent until you change it again.

Font Size

As you may know, some screen drivers use different size fonts for screen elements such as dialog boxes and menus. When you switch to a high

Desktop-area resolution, such as 1,280 by 1,024, these screen elements can get quite small, blurry, and difficult to read. For this reason, you can adjust the font size. Of course, you can do this via the Fonts settings on the Appearance page as discussed earlier. But doing it here is a little simpler. If you select a Desktop area above 640 by 480, you'll have the choice of Small Fonts or Large Fonts. Especially for resolutions of 1,024 by 768 or above, you might want to check out the Large Fonts selection from this drop-down list box. If you want, you can also choose a custom-sized font by clicking on the Custom button, which lets you declare the amount that you want the fonts scaled up. The range is from 100 to 200 percent.

Advanced Properties

Finally, the Advanced...button in the Settings box leads you to the Advanced Settings page, which allows you to actually change a bunch of nitty-gritty stuff like the type of video card and monitor that Windows thinks you have, the refresh rate, and some performance factors. If you install a new video card or monitor, you should update this information.

TIP

You may have noticed on the Advanced Settings page the option "Show settings icon on Taskbar." This is a very spiffy addition to Windows 98. Turn this checkbox on, and you'll get a little monitor icon next to the clock in the Taskbar. Click on the icon and you're able to immediately choose the color depth and Desktop area from a popup menu.

NOTE

If your screen is flickering, you'll want to check the refresh rate for sure!

WARNING

If you specify a refresh rating that is too high for your monitor, trying to expand the Desktop area to a larger size may not work. You'll just get a mess on the screen. If this happens, try using a setting with a lower refresh rate, such as 60 Hz or *interlaced*. The image may flicker a bit more, but at least it will be clearly visible.

TIP

If you have just received a new driver for your video adaptor card or monitor and want to use that instead of the one supplied with Windows 98 (Windows 95 doesn't include a driver), click on the Have Disk button and follow the directions.

Click on the Advanced Properties button, and you'll see something like Figure 7.24.

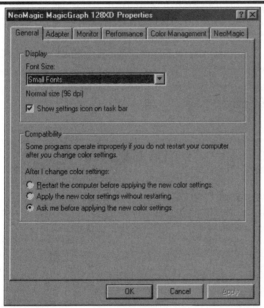

FIGURE 7.24:   You can make some hairy alterations to your monitor setup from here. You should investigate all the tab pages. If you're into monitors, you'll really like what's available from this box.

This stuff isn't for the novice, but if you're like me, you've waited a long time for settings like these to be easily available. Windows NT started the trend, and now it's migrated to Windows 98. The first tab page tells you more stuff about your display card than you may have wanted to know, such as the chipset and DAC (Digital to Analog Converter) type, which exact driver files are being used, and amount of RAM on your card. Useful, maybe. Boring, definitely. But the refresh rate, now that's a biggie in my book. In case you don't know, the refresh rate is how many times per second the screen is redrawn by the electron gun in the back of the monitor. Translation: It determines whether the screen appears to be flickering like an old-fashioned movie or not, and whether your eyes get tired looking at the screen for hours on end. Anything under 70Hz is too slow, say the experts, and I agree. In fact, I prefer 72Hz or above. But beware! Not all monitors can work that fast (that electron gun has to move really fast to paint all those dots on the screen), especially at resolutions above 800 by 600. Even if your display card can put out the right refresh signal, the monitor might not be able to handle it. And this can fry a monitor after some time. So if after setting the correct monitor on the Monitor tab page, you don't have the desired refresh available from the Refresh Rate drop-down list, take heed—your monitor probably can't cut the mustard, and Windows is trying to save you from damaging the monitor. Try living with a slower refresh like 70, or get a new monitor (or possibly just a new card). Or choose Optimum. The Adapter Default setting will accept whatever speed the display card is currently set to, or boots up in. This is more than likely not an optimal setting.

THINKING OF BUYING A NEW MONITOR OR DISPLAY CARD?

If you're thinking about purchasing a new monitor or card, check the specs on both the monitor *and* the card. For both the monitor and the card, you'll want to be ensured that you can:

- display at 72Hz or above, while

- displaying your favorite resolution (a.k.a. Desktop size, such as 1024 × 768), while

- displaying your favorite color depth (such as 64,000 colors or 16 million colors). At least 64,000 colors are necessary for photo-like display.

Make sure the monitor has a dot pitch value smaller than .28, preferably .26. If you have a big wallet, check out the new flat-panel displays just coming out from the likes of NEC and Viewsonic. These are *super* sharp and clear, and refresh isn't even an issue with them.

If you notice that the adapter setting for your computer is wrong, click on the Change button on the Adapter tab page. This will run a wizard. Depending on your choices here you may see a list of compatible boards. For example, on my computer the adapter is listed as S3. The S3 is a popular video chip, installed on my display adapter. But hey, my adapter is a Diamond Stealth 64 PCI. My guess is that the driver that Windows 98 assigned is some generic S3 chipset driver. When I clicked on Change, I saw this:

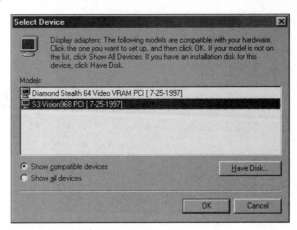

Looks like the Diamond Stealth is compatible, and there is a later date on the driver, so I think I'll try that. This driver was provided by the Diamond company and sent to Microsoft for inclusion in Windows 98.

If you want to see all the possible drivers to choose from (including ones that *won't* work with your card), click on Show All Devices. But typically this won't be useful unless you're planning to install another driver, power down, change display cards, and then boot up again.

Monitor Tab

Bought a new monitor? Here's the place to tell Windows 98 about it. Or at least to see what monitor it *thinks* you have. Click on the Monitor tab on the Advanced Display Properties dialog, and you'll see something like Figure 7.25.

Click on Change if the monitor is reported wrong. Then choose the correct monitor. You might have to use Show All Devices to see your brand. What's that? You say your monitor isn't listed, or you have a no-name monitor? If that's the case, choose Show All Devices, then select the topmost manufacturer type in the list ("Standard monitor types"), and choose the generic brand that most closely matches your monitor's maximum screen resolution and refresh rate at that resolution. You may have to look in your monitor's manual to figure this out.

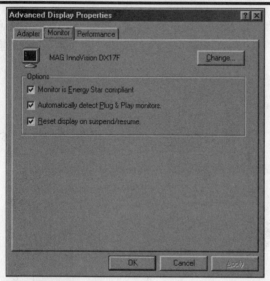

FIGURE 7.25:   The Monitor tab of the Advanced Display Properties box

NOTE

Notice there is a *Television* choice in the Standard monitor types. This may seem a little strange at first. But more and more computers are now equipped with a video output that can drive a TV set as your monitor.

The other options on this tab are also interesting:

▶ **Monitor is Energy Star compliant:** If yours fits this description, set this. It affects other Power Management settings in your computer.

▶ **Automatically detect Plug & Play monitors:** Windows runs around and detects Plug & Play hardware once in a while (when booting up, for example). In some cases this can cause PnP monitors to flash wildly. If yours does this, try turning off this checkbox.

▶ **Reset display on suspend/resume:** Does your computer have the ability to go into a suspended state (low power state)? I mean the whole computer, not just the screen. If it does, and your screen flickers or freaks out when your computer "wakes up," turn this checkbox off. It may help.

Performance

When you click the Performance tab, you'll see a dialog box that looks like Figure 7.26.

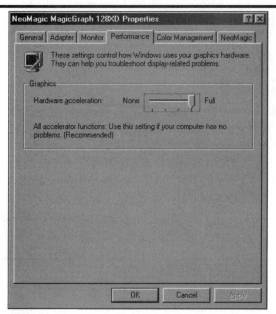

FIGURE 7.26: Tweaking the performance of your monitor/card duo can be achieved from this box.

If speed is your concern (and who isn't concerned with their computer's speed?), make sure the slider is set to Full. This is recommended for most computers. Occasionally a computer/card combo (the monitor has nothing to do with this) won't be able to take advantage of all the graphics speed-up routines that Windows is capable of for things like moving lots of graphics around the screen quickly ("bit blitting") and such. If you're seeing display anomalies, you might try slowing this setting down a bit, clicking OK, and closing the Display Properties box. Then see if anything improves.

ADJUSTING THE MOUSE

You can adjust six aspects of your mouse's operation:

- ▶ left-right button reversal
- ▶ double-click speed

- ▶ look of the pointers
- ▶ tracking speed
- ▶ mouse trails
- ▶ mouse type and driver

Switching the Buttons and Setting Double-Click Speed

If you're left-handed, you may want to switch the mouse around to use it on the left side of the computer and reverse the buttons. The main button then becomes the right button instead of the left one. If you use other programs outside of Windows that don't allow this, however, it might just add to the confusion. If you only use the mouse in Windows programs and you're left-handed, then it's worth a try.

1. Run the Control Panel and double-click on Mouse. Then click on the first tab page of the dialog box (Figure 7.27).

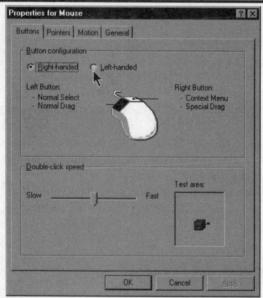

FIGURE 7.27:   First page of the Mouse setting. Here you can reverse the buttons for use by left-handed people. You can also adjust the double-click speed.

2. Click on the Left-handed button as shown in the figure. Then click on Apply to check it out. Don't like it? Revert to the original setting and click on Apply again.

On the same page, you have the double-click speed setting. Double-click speed determines how fast you have to double-click to make a double-click operation work (that is, to run a program from its icon, to open a document from its icon, or to select a word. If the double-click speed is too fast, it's difficult for your fingers to click fast enough. If it's too slow, you end up running programs or opening and closing windows unexpectedly. Double-click on the Jack-in-the-box to try out the new double-click speed. Jack will jump out or back into the box if the double-click registered. If you're not faring well, adjust the slider and try again.

NOTE
You don't have to click on Apply to test the slider settings. Just moving the slider instantly affects the mouse's double-click speed.

Setting Your Pointers

Your mouse pointer's shape changes depending on what you are pointing at and what Windows 98 is doing. If you are pointing to a window border, the pointer becomes a two-headed arrow. If Windows 98 is busy, it becomes a sandglass. When you are editing text, it becomes an I-beam, and so on.

You can customize your cursors for the fun of it or to increase visibility. You can even install animated cursors that look really cute and keep you amused while you wait for some process to complete.

To change the cursor settings:

1. Click on the Pointers tab page of the Mouse dialog box (see Figure 7.28).

2. The list shows which pointers are currently assigned to which activities. To change an assignment, click on an item in the list.

3. Next, if you've changed the shape and want to revert, click on Use Default to go back to the normal pointer shape that Windows 98 came shipped with. Otherwise, choose Browse and use the Browse box to load the cursor you want. When you click on a cursor in the Browse box, it will be displayed at the bottom of the box for you to examine in advance—a

thoughtful feature. Even animated cursors will do their thing right in the Browse box. (Cursors with the .ani extension are animated ones.)

4. Click on Open. The cursor will now be applied to the activity in question.

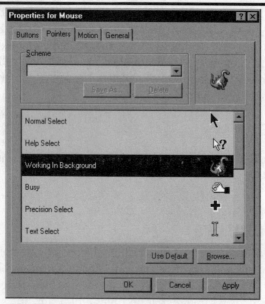

FIGURE 7.28:   Choose pointer shapes for various activities here.
As you can see, I have a couple of weird ones installed,
such as the walking dinosaur instead of the sandglass.

You can save pointer schemes just as you can colors. If you want to set up a number of different schemes (one for each person in the house, for example), just get the settings assigned the way you like, enter a name in the scheme area, and click on Save As. To later select a scheme, open the drop-down list box, select the scheme's name, and click on Apply or OK.

Setting the Pointer Motion

Two very useful adjustments can be made to the way the mouse responds to the motion of your hand—speed and trails (Figure 7.29).

Pointer speed is the speed at which the mouse pointer moves relative to the movement of the mouse. Believe it or not, mouse motion is actu- ally measured in *Mickeys*! (Somebody out there has a sense of humor.) A

Part i

Mickey equals 1/100 of an inch of mouse movement. The tracking-speed setting lets you adjust the relationship of Mickeys to pixels. If you want to be very exact in your cursor movement, you'll want to slow the tracking speed, requiring more Mickeys per pixel. However, this requires more hand motion for the same corresponding cursor motion. If your desk is crammed and your coordination is very good, then you can increase the speed (fewer Mickeys per pixel). If you use the mouse with MS-DOS programs that use their own mouse driver, you might want to adjust the Windows mouse speed to match that of your other programs so you won't need to mentally adjust when you use such non-Windows programs.

Incidentally, if you think the mouse runs too slowly in your non-Windows applications, there may be a fix. Contact your mouse's maker. For example, if you're using a Logitech mouse, a program called Click that is supplied with the Logitech mouse lets you easily control its tracking. See the Logitech manual for details.

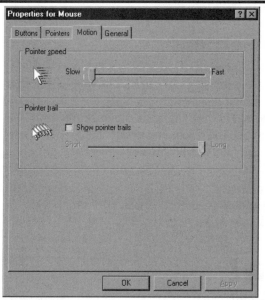

FIGURE 7.29:   You can adjust the speed at which the mouse pointer moves and whether you'll see trails.

The other setting—Mouse trails—creates a shadow of the mouse's path whenever you move it. Some people find it annoying, but for those who have trouble finding the pointer on the screen, it's a blessing. Mouse trails are particularly helpful when using Windows on passive-matrix or dual-scan laptop computers, where the pointer often disappears when you move it.

Here are the steps for changing these items:

1. Drag the speed slider one way or another to increase or decrease the motion of the pointer relative to your hand (or thumb in the case of a trackball) motion. Nothing may happen until you click on Apply. Adjust as necessary. Try aiming for some item on the screen and see how well you succeed. Having the motion too fast can result in straining your muscles and holding the mouse too tight. It's ergonomically more sound to use a little slower setting that requires more hand motion.

2. If you want trails, click the option box on and adjust the slider. You don't have to click on Apply to see the effects.

3. Click on OK or Apply to make it all official.

General Mouse Settings

The last tab page lets you change the mouse's software driver and possibly make changes that the driver has built in. The type of mouse is listed in the box. If this looks wrong or you're changing the mouse to another type, click on Change and choose the desired mouse type from the resulting Select Device box. See the discussion about changing the Display Adaptor, above, if in doubt about how to use the Select Device dialog box.

In some cases, you'll have an Options button on this tab page. The options will vary from mouse to mouse. They may include such things as choosing to have the mouse pointers be black rather than white or be transparent rather than opaque.

What's Next?

The next chapter continues our tour of Windows 98's hardware support with a detailed look at printers and printing.

Chapter 8

PRINTERS AND PRINTING

I f your printer is of the Plug-and-Play variety, your Windows system will probably have a so-called default printer driver already installed. This means you'll be able to print from any Windows program without worrying about anything more than turning on the printer, checking that it has paper, and choosing the File ➤ Print command from whatever programs you use. If your printer isn't Plug-and-Play compatible, wasn't plugged in at the time of installation, or you weren't upgrading over a previous version of Windows for which you had printers set up already, you'll have to manually set up your printer before you can print. This chapter tells you how to do that and how to manage the use of your printer to get your work done.

Adapted from *Mastering Windows 98*, by Robert Cowart

ISBN 0-7821-1961-1   1,184 pages $34.99

www.masteringwindows.com

As with Windows 3.1, Windows 95, and Windows NT, unless you specify otherwise, Windows programs hand off data to Windows 98, which in turn *spools* the data to a specified printer. Spooling means temporarily putting on the hard disk the information that's really headed for the printer. Your document then gets sent out to the printer at the slowest speed that the printer can receive it. This lets you get back to work with your program sooner. You can even print additional documents, stacking up a load of jobs for the printer to print. This stack is called a *queue*.

In Windows 3.*x*, a program called Print Manager was responsible for doing the spooling and managing the print jobs. Windows 98 nomenclature dispenses with the term "Print Manager," even though the same functionality is provided. Now you simply look at what's "inside" a printer by clicking on the printer's icon. This opens a window and displays the print queue for that printer. In reality, however, there *is* a spooler program and Print Manager-like thing in Windows 98, and that is how I'll refer to the window that displays and works with the print queue.

TIP

Unlike Windows NT, Windows 98 doesn't always prevent a program from writing directly to the printer port. (In Windows NT, any such attempt by programs to write directly to hardware, such as an LPT port, is trapped by the security manager.) Windows 98 offers less security in this regard. Applications can directly access a port. Also, if you shell out of Windows 98 and run MS-DOS mode, direct port access is allowed.

NOTE

MS-DOS programs can also be spooled so you can get back to work with your DOS or Windows programs while printing happens in the background.

When you print from a Windows program, Print Manager receives the data, queues up the jobs, routes them to the correct printer, and, when necessary, issues error or other appropriate messages to print-job originators. You can use the Print Manager user interface to manage your print jobs, making it easy to check out what's printing and see where your job(s) are in the print queue relative to other people's print jobs. You may also be permitted to rearrange the print queue, delete print jobs, or pause and resume a print job so you can reload or otherwise service the printer.

Each printer you've installed appears in the Printers folder, along with an additional icon called Add Printer that lets you set up new printers.

Printer icons in the folder appear and behave like any other object: You can delete them at will, create new ones, and set their properties. Double-clicking on a printer in the folder displays its print queue and lets you manipulate the queue. Commands on the menus let you install, configure, connect, disconnect, and remove printers and drivers.

This chapter explains these features, as well as procedures for local and network print-queue management. Some basics of print management also are discussed, providing a primer for the uninitiated or for those whose skills are a little rusty.

A PRINT-MANAGER PRIMER

Windows 98's Print Manager feature mix is quite rich. Here are some highlights:

- ▶ You can add, modify, and remove printers right from the Printers folder (available from My Computer, Explorer, the Start button, or Control Panel).

- ▶ An object-oriented interface using printer icons eliminates the abstraction of thinking about the relationship of printer drivers, connections, and physical printers. You simply add a printer and set its properties. Once added, it appears as a named printer in the Printers folder.

- ▶ Once set up, you can easily choose to share a printer on the network so others can print to it. You can give it a useful name such as *LaserJet in Fred's Office* so people on the network know what it is.

- ▶ If you're on a network, you can manage network-printer connections by displaying available printers, sharing your local printer, and connecting to and disconnecting from network printers.

- ▶ Because of Windows 98's multithreading and preemptive multitasking, you can start printing and immediately go back to work; you don't have to wait until spooling for Print Manager to finish. (This won't be true for older 16-bit programs.)

- ▶ While one document is printing out, other programs can start print jobs. Additional documents are simply added to the queue and will print in turn.

▸ You can easily rearrange the order of the print queue and delete print jobs.

▸ You can temporarily pause or resume printing without causing printer time-out problems.

ADDING A NEW PRINTER

If your printer is already installed and seems to be working fine, you probably can skip this section. In fact, if you're interested in nothing more than printing from one of your programs without viewing the queue, printing to a network printer, or making adjustments to your current printer's settings, just skip down to *Printing from a Program*, below. However, if you need to install a new printer, modify or customize your current installation, or add additional printers to your setup, read on to learn about how to:

▸ add a new printer

▸ select the printer port and make other connection settings

▸ set preferences for a printer

▸ install a printer driver that's not listed

▸ set the default printer

▸ select a printer when more than one is installed

▸ delete a printer from your system

About Printer Installation

As I mention in Chapter 2, before installing hardware, including printers, you should read any last-minute printed or on-screen material that comes with Windows 98. Often such material is full of useful information about specific types of hardware, including printers. Open the files Setup.txt and Printers.txt on your Windows 98 CD-ROM, then look through the files for information about your printer.

With that said, here is the overall game plan for adding a new printer. It's actually a really easy process thanks to the Add a Printer Wizard that walks you through it.

1. Run Add a Printer from the Printers folder.

2. Declare whether the printer is local (directly connected to your computer) or on the network.

3. Declare what kind of printer it is.

4. Select the printer's port and relevant port settings.

5. Give the printer a name.

6. Print a test page.

7. Check and possibly alter the default printer settings, such as the DPI (dots per inch) setting and memory settings.

After these steps are complete, your printer should work as expected. Once it's installed, you can customize each printer's setup by modifying its properties, such as:

▶ specifying the amount of time you want Windows to keep trying to print a document before alerting you to a printer problem

▶ specifying the share name for the printer so other network users can find it when they search the network for printers

▶ setting job defaults pertaining to paper tray, two-sided printing, and paper orientation

▶ stipulating a *separator file* (a file, usually one page long, that prints between each print job)

▶ selecting the default printer if you have more than one printer installed

▶ choosing whether your printer should substitute its own fonts for certain Windows TrueType fonts

▶ selecting printer settings relevant to page orientation, color matching, greyscaling, size scaling, type of paper feed, halftone imaging, and when file-header information (such as a PostScript "preamble") is sent to the printer

▶ set whether you want to share the printer for use by others on the network

▶ set whether documents will go directly to the printer or will go through the spooler

The good news is that normally you won't have to futz with any of these settings. The other good news is, unlike in Windows 3.*x*, getting to any one of these settings is now a piece of cake. You don't have to wind your way through a bevy of dialog boxes to target a given setting. The Properties dialog box has tab pages, so it's a cinch to find the one you want.

TIP

The Properties box has context-sensitive Help built in. Click on an element in a dialog box and press F1, or click on the ? button, then on the item. A relevant Help topic will appear.

About Adding Printers

Before running the Wizard, let's consider when you'd need to add a new printer to your Windows 98 configuration:

- ▶ You didn't tell Windows 98 what kind of printer you have when you first set up Windows.

- ▶ You're connecting a new printer directly to your computer.

- ▶ Someone has connected a new printer to the network and wants to use it from your computer.

- ▶ You want to print to disk files that can later be sent to a particular type of printer.

- ▶ You want to set up multiple printer configurations (preferences) for a single physical printer so you can switch between them without having to change your printer setup before each print job.

Notice that a great deal of flexibility exists here, especially in the case of the last item. Because of the modularity of Windows 98's internal design, even though you might have only one physical printer, you can create any number of printer definitions for it, each with different characteristics.

TIP

These definitions are actually *called* printers, but you can think of them as printer names, aliases, or named virtual devices.

For example, you might want one definition set up to print on legal-sized paper in landscape orientation while another prints with normal paper in portrait orientation. Each of these two "printers" would actually use the same physical printer to print out on. While you're working with

Part i

Windows 98's manual, online help, and this book, keep this terminology in mind. The word "printer" often doesn't really mean a physical printer. It usually means a printer setup that you've created with the Wizard. It's a collection of settings that typically points to a physical printer, but it could just as well create a print file instead.

About Printer Drivers

And finally, consider that a printer can't just connect to your computer and mysteriously print a fancy page of graphics or even a boring old page of text. You need a printer *driver.* The printer driver (actually a file on your hard disk) translates your text file to commands that tell your printer how to print your file. Because different brands and models of printer use different commands for such things as *move up a line, print a circle in the middle of the page, print the letter A*, and so on, a specialized printer driver is needed for each type of printer.

NOTE

Because some printers are actually functionally equivalent, a driver for a popular brand and model of printer (for example, an Epson or a Hewlett-Packard) often masquerades under different names for other printers.

TIP

DOS programs require a print driver for the application, too. For instance, Word-Perfect 5.1 running in a DOS session under Windows 98 will use a DOS printer driver *and* a Windows 98 printer driver to work under Windows 98.

When you add a printer, unless you're installing a Plug-and-Play–compatible printer, you're asked to choose the brand and model of printer. With Plug-and-Play printers, if the printer is attached and turned on, Windows queries the printer and the printer responds with its make and model number. Virtually all new printers are Plug-and-Play compatible, but if yours isn't, you'll have to tell Windows what printer you have so it will install the correct driver.

A good printer driver takes advantage of all your printer's capabilities, such as its built-in fonts and graphics features. A poor printer driver might succeed in printing only draft-quality text, even from a sophisticated printer.

If you're the proud owner of some offbeat brand of printer, you may be alarmed when you can't find your printer listed in the box when you run the wizard. But don't worry, the printer manufacturer might be able to supply one. The procedure for installing manufacturer-supplied drivers is covered later in this chapter.

NOTE

If your printer isn't included in the list, consult *"When You Don't Find Your Printer in the List,"* later in this chapter.

Running the Wizard to Add a New Printer

Microsoft has made the previously arduous chore of adding a printer something that's much more easily mastered by a majority of computer users. Here's what you have to do:

1. Open the Printers folder by clicking on the Start button and choosing Settings ➤ Printers. Two other paths are from My Computer and from Control Panel.

2. Double-click on Add Printer, as shown in Figure 8.1.

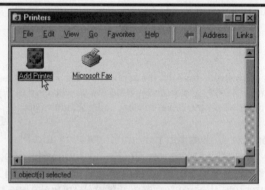

FIGURE 8.1: Run the Wizard to add a printer.

3. A dialog box like that in Figure 8.2 appears. Click on Next.

4. You're asked whether the printer is *local* or *network*. Because here I'm describing how to install a network printer, choose Network, then click on Next. (If you are setting up a local printer that is connected directly to your computer, at this point you should skip down to the next section, *Adding a Local Printer*.)

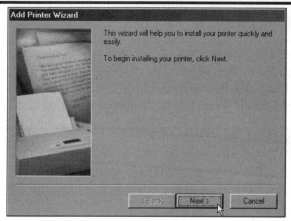

FIGURE 8.2:   Beginning the process of adding the printer

5. You'll now be asked two questions, as shown in Figure 8.3.

NOTE

For a printer to appear in the network listing, it has to have been added to the host computer's setup (the computer the printer is directly attached to) using the steps in *"Adding a Local Printer,"* below. It must also be shared for use on the network.

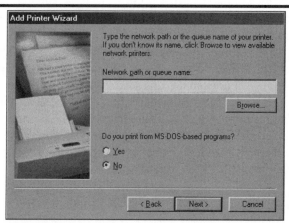

FIGURE 8.3:   When choosing a network printer, you have to specify the printer's path and declare whether you can print from DOS programs.

6. You don't have to type in the complicated path name for the location of the printer on the network. Just click on Browse, and up comes a list of the printers on the network. For example, in Figure 8.4 you see the network printer *Apple*. You may have to double-click on Entire Network or click on the + sign next to a computer to display the printer(s) attached to it. Either way, just highlight the printer you want to connect to and click on OK.

FIGURE 8.4: The Browse box graphically displays computers that have shared networked printers available for others to use.

If the network printer is currently *offline*, you'll be told that you have to wait until it comes back online before you can use it, but that you can go ahead and install it if you want. However, as long as it's offline, you'll be asked to specify the brand and model of the printer because the Wizard can't figure out what kind of printer it is when it is unavailable for your computer to question. If you can alert the owner of the printer to put it online (they have to right-click on the printer's icon at their computer and turn off the Work Offline setting), then you won't have to specify these settings. If this isn't possible, just select the brand name and model from the resulting list.

7. Back at the Wizard dialog box, decide whether you want to print from DOS applications or not.

    ▶ If you choose Yes, click on Next, and you'll be asked to choose a printer port to associate the output with (such as LPT1, LPT2, and so on). Usually this will be LPT1.

However, if you have a local printer attached to your computer using LPT1, you should choose a different port, such as LPT2. This doesn't mean the printer has to be connected to your LPT (parallel) port, it only tells Windows 98 how to fake the DOS program into thinking that it's printing to a normal parallel port. Click on Capture Printer Port, choose accordingly, and click on OK. Then click on Next.

▶ If you won't be printing from DOS applications to this new printer, choose No, and you won't be asked about the port. Just click on Next.

8. Now you're asked to name the printer (Figure 8.5). This is the name that will show up when you're setting up to print from a program such as a word processor, spreadsheet, or whatever. Type in a name for the printer; the maximum length is 32 characters. Typically, the type of printer, such as HP Desk Jet 320, goes here. There's also a description line in which you can be even more descriptive about the printer, accepting up to 255 characters. Specifying the location of the printer in this box is a good idea so network users can find a printer when browsing and will know where to pick up their hard copy when a print job is completed.

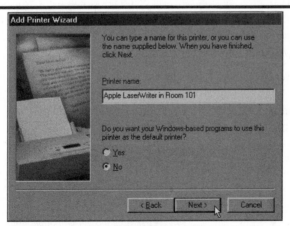

FIGURE 8.5: Name the printer and choose whether it's going to be your default printer.

9. In this same dialog box you'll have to decide whether you want the printer to be the *default* printer. The default printer

is the one that programs will assume you want to print to. Some programs don't let you choose which printer a document will print out on, so setting the default printer can be important. If you want this network printer to be the default printer, remember that the computer the printer is directly connected to (in the example here, that would be the computer called Samson) has to be up and running for the printer to work. So, if you have a local printer on your machine as well, it's better to make that the default printer.

10. Finally, you're asked if you want to print a test page. It's a good idea to do this. Turn on the printer, make sure it has paper in it, and click on Finish. You may be prompted to supply a printer driver for the printer, depending on the type of network you're connecting to and whether a driver is already on your machine. If you're told that a driver file for the printer is already on your machine, you'll be asked if you want to use it or load a new one from the Windows 98 CD-ROM or floppy disks. It's usually easier to use the existing driver. If the driver isn't on your hard disk, you'll be instructed to insert the disk containing the driver.

11. The test page will be sent to the printer; it should print out in a few minutes. Then you'll be asked if it printed OK. If it didn't print correctly, click on No, and you'll be shown some trouble-shooting information containing some questions and answers. The most likely fixes for the malady will be described. If the page printed OK, click on Yes, and you're done.

If all went well, you now have a network printer set up and ready to go. The new printer appears in your Printers folder. If there is a checkmark over the printer, this means you've set it as the default printer.

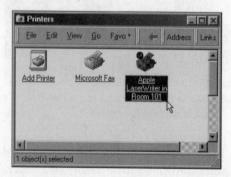

Adding a Local Printer

If you want to add a local printer rather than a networked printer, the steps are a little different from what I explained above.

1. Follow the first three steps in the section above.

2. In the box that asks whether the printer is local or networked, click on Local. Then click on Next.

3. You're presented with a list of brands and models. In the left column scroll the list, find the maker of your printer, and click on it. Then in the right column choose the model number or name that matches your printer. Be sure to select the exact printer model, not just the correct brand name. Consult your printer's manual if you're in doubt about the model. What you enter here determines which printer driver file is used for this printer's definition. Figure 8.6 shows an example for an HP LaserJet 4.

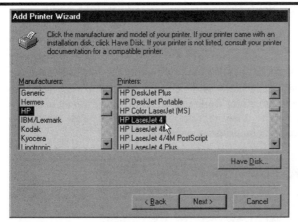

FIGURE 8.6:   Choosing the printer make and model: here I'm choosing a Hewlett-Packard LaserJet 4.

4. Click on Next. Now you'll see a list of ports. You have to tell Windows which port the printer is connected to. (A port usually refers to the connector on the computer—but see Table 8.1 for the "file" exception.)

   Most often the port will be the parallel printer port called LPT1 (Line Printer #1). Unless you know your printer is connected to another port, such as LPT2 or a serial port (such as COM1 or COM2), select LPT1 as in Figure 8.7.

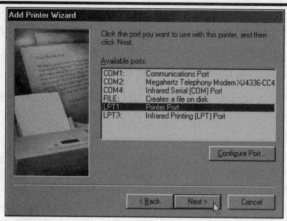

FIGURE 8.7: Choosing the port the printer's connected to is the second step in setting up a local printer.

5. Click on Next. Now you can give the printer a name (see Figure 8.8).

NOTE

If the printer will be shared with DOS and 16-bit Windows users (such as people running Windows for Workgroups 3.11), you might want to limit this name to 12 characters because that's the maximum length those users will see when they are browsing for printers.

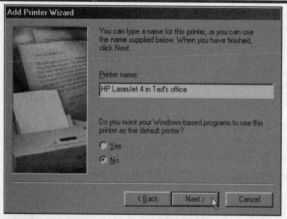

FIGURE 8.8: Give your new printer a name that tells you and other people something about it.

6. Also set whether the printer will be the default printer for Windows programs.

7. Finally, you're asked if you want to print a test page. It's a good idea to do this. Turn on the printer, make sure it has paper in it, and click on Finish. If the driver file for your printer is in the computer, you'll be asked if you want to use it or load a new one from the Windows 98 CD-ROM or floppy disks. It's usually easier to use the existing driver. If the driver isn't on your hard disk, you'll be instructed to insert the disk containing the driver.

TABLE 8.1: Printer Ports

PORT	NOTES
LPT1, LPT2, LPT3	The most common setting is LPT1 because most PC-type printers hook up to the LPT1 parallel port. Click on Configure Port if you want to turn off the ability to print to this printer from DOS programs.
LPT3 Infrared printing port	If your computer is equipped with an infrared port you may have this option.
COM1, COM2, COM3, COM4	If you know your printer is of the serial variety, it's probably connected to the COM1 port. If COM1 is tied up for use with some other device, such as a modem, use COM2. If you choose a COM port, click on Configure Port to check the communications settings in the resulting dialog box. Set the baud rate, data bit, parity, start and stop bits, and flow control to match those of the printer being attached. Refer to the printer's manual to determine what the settings should be.
File	This is for printing to a disk file instead of to the printer. Later, the file can be sent directly to the printer or sent to someone on floppy disk or over a modem. When you print to this printer name, you are prompted to enter a file name. (See the section in the chapter titled *Printing to a Disk File Instead of a Printer*.)

8. The test page will be sent to the printer. It should print out in a few minutes, then you'll be asked if it printed OK. If it didn't print correctly, click on No, and you'll be shown some troubleshooting information containing some questions and answers. The most likely fixes for the malady will be described. If the page printed OK, click on Yes, and you're done.

The new icon for your printer will show up in the Printers folder now.

When You Don't Find Your Printer in the List

When you're adding a local printer, you have to supply the brand name and model of the printer because Windows 98 needs to know which driver to load into your Windows 98 setup to use the printer correctly. (When you are adding a network printer, you aren't asked this question because the printer's host computer already knows what type of printer it is, and the driver is on that computer.)

What if your printer isn't on the list of Windows 98-recognized printers? Many off-brand printers are designed to be compatible with one of the popular printer types, such as the Apple LaserWriters, Hewlett-Packard Laser-Jets, or the Epson line of printers. Refer to the manual that came with your printer to see whether it's compatible with one of the printers that *is* listed. Some printers require that you set the printer in compatibility mode using switches or software. Again, check the printer's manual for instructions.

Finally, if it looks like there's no mention of compatibility anywhere, contact the manufacturer for their Windows 98-compatible driver. If you're lucky, they'll have one. It's also possible that Microsoft has a new driver for your printer that wasn't available when your copy of Windows was shipped. Contact Microsoft at (206) 882-8080 and ask for the Windows 98 Driver Library Disk, which contains all the latest drivers, or, better yet, check the Microsoft Web site www.microsoft.com/support/printing.

NOTE

All existing printer setups should actually have been migrated from Windows 95 to Windows 98 when you upgraded, so if it was working under Windows 95, it will probably work fine under Windows 98. This is true for other types of drivers, too, such as video display cards, sound boards, and so on.

Also remember that Windows 98 can use the 16-bit drivers that worked with Windows 3.x. So, if you had a fully functioning driver for your printer in Windows 3.x (that is, your printer worked fine before you upgraded from Windows 3.x to Windows 98), you should be able to use that driver in Windows 98.

Locate the Windows 3.x driver disk supplied with your printer or locate the driver file. (Sometimes font or other support files are also needed, incidentally, so it's not always as simple as finding a single file.)

Assuming you do obtain a printer driver, do the following to install it:

1. Follow the instructions above for running the Add a Printer Wizard.

2. Instead of selecting one of the printers in the Driver list (it isn't in the list, of course), click on the Have Disk button. You'll see this box:

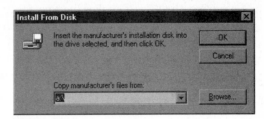

3. The Wizard is asking you to enter the path where the driver is located (typically a floppy disk). Insert the disk (or make sure the files are available somewhere), enter the path, and click on OK. Enter the correct source of the driver. Typically, it'll be in the A or B disk drive.

4. Click on OK.

5. You might have to choose a driver from a list if multiple options exist.

6. Continue with the Wizard dialog boxes as explained above.

TIP

If none of the drivers you can lay your hands on will work with your printer, try choosing the Generic *text-only* driver. This driver prints only text—no fancy formatting and no graphics. But it will work in a pinch with many printers. Make sure the printer is capable of or is set to an ASCII or ANSI text-only mode, otherwise your printout may be a mess. PostScript printers typically don't have such a text-only mode.

ALTERING THE DETAILS OF A PRINTER'S SETUP—THE PROPERTIES BOX

Each printer driver can be fine-tuned by changing settings in its Properties dialog box. This area is difficult to document because so many variations exist due to the number of printers supported. The following sections describe the gist of these options without going into too much detail about each printer type.

The settings pertaining to a printer are called *properties*. As I discussed earlier, properties abound in Windows 98. Almost every object in Windows 98 has properties that you can examine and change at will. When you add a printer, the Wizard makes life easy for you by giving it some default properties that usually work fine and needn't be tampered with. You can change them later, but only if you need to. It may be worth looking at the properties for your printer, especially if the printer's acting up in some way when you try to print from Windows 98.

1. Open the Printers folder.

2. Right-click on the printer's icon and choose Properties. A box such as the one in Figure 8.9 appears.

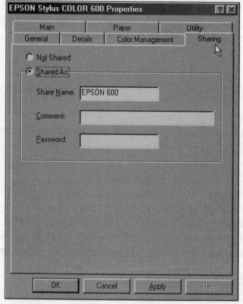

FIGURE 8.9:   Each printer has a Properties box such as this, with several tab pages. Options differ from printer to printer.

TIP

You can also type Alt-Enter to open the Properties box. This is true with many Windows 98 objects.

3. Notice that there is a place for a comment. This is normally blank after you add a printer. If you share the printer on the network, any text that you add to this box will be seen by other users who are browsing the network for a printer.

4. Click on the various tab pages of your printer's Properties box to view or alter the great variety of settings. These buttons are confusing in name, and there's no easy way to remember what's what. But remember that you can get help by clicking on the ? in the upper-right corner and then on the setting or button whose function you don't understand.

Sharing a Printer for Network Use

You have to *share* a printer before it becomes available to other network users. Sharing is pretty simple: First off, the printer must be a local printer. Then you share it by right-clicking on it and choosing Share, or via its Properties box. Here are the details:

1. Add the printer as described earlier in this chapter.

2. Right-click on the printer's icon and choose Properties or Sharing.

3. Now you'll see the box in Figure 8.9. Click on the Sharing tab if it's not selected.

4. On the Sharing page, click on Shared As.

5. A *share name* based on the Printer Name is automatically generated. You can leave the share name as is or give it another name. DOS-based network users see this name, which must conform to DOS file-naming rules. Other users will see this name, too, though some may see the other comments about the printer. The name can't be more than twelve characters long and mustn't contain spaces or characters not acceptable in DOS file names, such as ?, *, #, +, |, \, /, =, >, <, or %.

6. Fill in a comment about the printer, such as the location of the printer so users know where to pick up their printouts.

7. Fill in a password only if you want to restrict the use of the printer. If a password is entered here, other network users will be prompted to enter it at their machine before they can print to your printer. Make a list of people whom you want to give printer access to and tell them what the password is. This is one way to prevent overuse of a given printer. If you don't enter a password, protection is not in effect.

TIP

Another approach to preventing overuse of a given printer (at least temporarily) is to right-click on its icon and choose Pause Printing. Not a very elegant way to deter people from printing to your printer, but it *will* stop print jobs.

8. Click on OK. If you entered a password, you'll be prompted to verify it by reentering. Then click on OK, and your printer is shared! Its icon now has a hand under it. Pretty soon you'll start to see someone else's QMS-PS 810 print jobs rolling out of your printer.

To unshare your printer, open the Properties box again, choose the Sharing page, and click on Not Shared.

TIP

If you forget the password, don't worry. You can change it by simply entering a new password from the Share tab page.

CONNECTING TO A NETWORK PRINTER

Assuming your Windows 98 network system is successfully cabled and running, network printing should be possible. Before a network user can access a network printer, the following must be true:

▶ The printer must be cabled to the sharing computer.

▶ The printer must be created and working properly for local use.

▶ The printer must be shared.

▶ The printer's security settings and network users wishing access must match.

TIP

By default, new printer shares are given a security setting that gives all users access for printing. Only the creator and administrators can *manage* the printer, however. Managing the printer means rearranging the print-job queue: starting, stopping, and deleting print jobs.

Part i

HOW TO DELETE A PRINTER FROM YOUR PRINTERS FOLDER

You might want to decommission a printer after you've added it, for several reasons:

▶ You've connected a new type of printer to your computer and you want to delete the old setup and create a new one with the correct driver for the new printer.

▶ You want to disconnect from a network printer you're through using.

▶ You've created several slightly different setups for the same physical printer and you want to delete the ones you don't use.

In any of these cases, the trick is the same:

1. Open the Printers folder (the easiest way is using Start ➤ Settings ➤ Printers).

2. Right-click on the icon for the printer setup you want to delete and choose Delete (or just press Del). You will see at least one confirmation box before the printer is deleted. You may see another warning if there are print jobs in the queue for the printer.

NOTE

If you have stipulated that the computer can keep separate settings for each user (via Control Panel ➤ Passwords ➤ User Profiles), the removal process removes only the printer setup from Windows 98's Registry for the currently logged-in user. Also note that the related driver file and font files are not deleted from the disk. Therefore, if you want to re-create the printer, you don't have to insert disks, and you won't be prompted for the location of driver files. This is convenient, but if you're tight on disk space, you might want to remove the printer fonts and drivers. To remove fonts, use the Fonts applet in the Control Panel, as described in Chapter 7.

How to Print Out Documents from Your Programs

By now your printer(s) are added and ready to go. The procedure for printing in Windows 98 is simple. Typically, you just open a document, choose File ➤ Print, and make a few settings, such as which pages to print, and click OK. (You might have to set the print area first or make some other settings, depending on the program.) If you're already happy with the ways in which you print, you might want to skim over this section. However, there *are* a couple of conveniences you might not know about, such as using drag and drop to print or right-clicking on a document to print it without opening the program that created it.

About the Default Printer

Unless you choose otherwise, the output from both Windows and DOS programs are routed to the Print Manager for printing. If no particular printer has been chosen (perhaps because the program—for example, a DOS app or Notepad—doesn't give you a choice), the default printer is used.

NOTE

The default printer can be set by right-clicking on a printer icon and choosing Set as Default.

Exactly how your printed documents look varies somewhat from program to program because not all programs can take full advantage of the capabilities of your printer and the printer driver. For example, simple word-processing programs like Notepad don't let you change the font, while a full-blown word-processing program such as Ami Pro or Word can print out all kinds of fancy graphics, fonts, columns of text, and so forth.

WARNING

If you choose as a default a printer that your DOS programs can't work with, your print jobs could bomb. Suppose you're running WordPerfect 5.1 for DOS and have it installed to print to an HP LaserJet, but the default printer is a Postscript laser printer. This would cause your printouts to be nothing but a listing of PostScript commands, such as ERROR: undefined, OFFENDING COMMAND: |ume STACK {-pop-, and so on.

When you print from any program, the file is actually printed to a disk file instead of directly to the printer. Print Manager then spools the file to the assigned printer(s), coordinating the flow of data and keeping you informed of the progress. Jobs are queued up and listed in the Print Manager window, from which their status can be observed; they can be rearranged, deleted, and so forth.

Printing from a Program

To print from any program, including Windows 3.x and Windows 95 programs, follow these steps (which are exact for Windows programs but only approximate for other environments):

1. Check to see that the printer and page settings are correct. Some program's File menus provide a Printer Setup, Page Setup, or other option for this. Note that settings you make from such a box temporarily (sometimes permanently, depending on the program) override settings made from the Printer's Properties dialog box.

2. Select the Print command on the program's File menu and fill in whatever information is asked of you. For example, in WordPad, the Print dialog box looks like that in Figure 8.10.

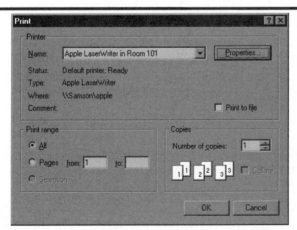

FIGURE 8.10: When you choose Print from a Windows program, you often see a dialog box such as this that allows you to choose some options before printing.

Some programs have rather elaborate dialog boxes for choosing which printer you want to print to, scaling or graphically altering the printout, and even adjusting the properties of the printer. Still, you can normally just make the most obvious settings and get away with it:

- ▶ correct printer

- ▶ correct number of copies

- ▶ correct print range (pages, spreadsheet cells, portion of graphic, etc.)

- ▶ for color printers, which ink cartridge you have in (black & white or color)

3. Click on OK (or otherwise confirm printing). Windows 98 intercepts the print data and writes it in a file, then begins printing it. If an error occurs—a port conflict, the printer is out of paper, or what have you—you'll see a message such as this:

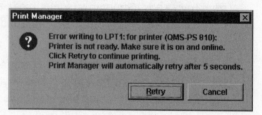

Check the paper supply, check to see that the printer is turned on, and make sure it's online (there may be a switch on the printer for this). If it's a network printer, make sure it's shared and that the computer it's connected to is booted up and has shared the printer for use.

TIP

When printing commences, a little printer icon will appear in the Taskbar next to the clock. You can double-click on this icon to see details of your pending print jobs.

Printing by Dragging Files onto a Printer Icon or into Its Window

You can quickly print Windows program document files by dragging them onto a printer's icon or window. You can drag from the Desktop, a folder, the Find box, the Windows Explorer, or a File Manager window. This will only work with documents that have an association with a particular program. To check if a document has an association, right-click on it. If the resulting menu has an Open command on it (not Open With), it has an association.

1. Arrange things on your screen so you can see the file(s) you want to print as well as either the printer's icon or its window (you open a printer's window by double-clicking on its icon).

TIP

You can drag a file into a shortcut of the Printer's icon. If you like this way of printing, keep a shortcut of your printer on the Desktop so you can drag documents to it without having to open up the Printers folder. Double-clicking on a shortcut provides an easy means of checking its print queue, too.

2. Drag the document file(s) onto the Print Manager icon or window. The file is loaded into the source program, the Print command is automatically executed, and the file is spooled to Print Manager. The document isn't actually moved out of its home folder, it just gets printed.

   If the document doesn't have an association, you'll see an error message:

Also, a nice feature of this approach is that you can drag multiple files onto a printer's icon or open window at once. They will all be queued up for printing, one after another, via their source programs. You'll see this message asking for confirmation before printing commences:

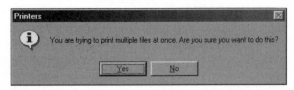

One caveat about this technique: as you know, some programs don't have a built-in facility for printing to a printer other than the default one. Notepad is a case in point: Try to drag a Notepad document to a printer that isn't currently your default printer, and you'll see this message:

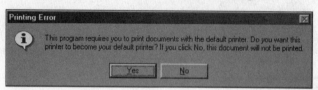

TIP

The drag-and-drop method can be used with shortcuts, too. You can drag shortcuts of documents to a printer or even to a shortcut of a printer, and the document will print.

Printing by Right-Clicking on a Document

Finally, you can print some documents using another shortcut that doesn't even require you to have a printer icon in view; instead, you use the right-click menu. Here's how:

1. Right-click on the icon of any document you want to print and notice whether the right-click menu has a Print command on it.

2. If there's no Print command, press Esc to cancel the menu. You can't print the document using this technique. If there is a Print command, choose it. The file will open in its source program and start printing right away. Once spooled to the Print Manager, the document will close automatically.

WORKING WITH THE PRINT QUEUE

If you print more than a few files at a time, or if you have your printer shared for network use, you'll sometimes want to check on the status of a printer's print jobs. You also might want to see how many jobs need to print before you turn off your local computer and printer if others are using it. Or you might want to know how many other jobs are ahead of yours.

You can check on these items by opening a printer's window. You'll then see:

Document Name   Name of the file being printed and possibly the source program

Status   Whether the job is printing, being deleted, or paused

Owner   Who sent each print job to the printer

Progress   How large each job is and how much of the current job has been printed

Start at   When each print job was sent to the print queue

Figure 8.11 shows a sample printer with a print queue and related information.

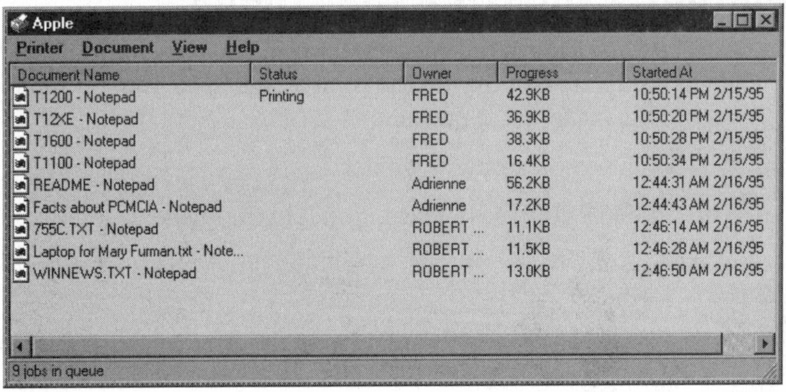

Document Name	Status	Owner	Progress	Started At
T1200 - Notepad	Printing	FRED	42.9KB	10:50:14 PM 2/15/95
T12XE - Notepad		FRED	36.9KB	10:50:20 PM 2/15/95
T1600 - Notepad		FRED	38.3KB	10:50:28 PM 2/15/95
T1100 - Notepad		FRED	16.4KB	10:50:34 PM 2/15/95
README - Notepad		Adrienne	56.2KB	12:44:31 AM 2/16/95
Facts about PCMCIA - Notepad		Adrienne	17.2KB	12:44:43 AM 2/16/95
755C.TXT - Notepad		ROBERT ...	11.1KB	12:46:14 AM 2/16/95
Laptop for Mary Furman.txt - Note...		ROBERT ...	11.5KB	12:46:28 AM 2/16/95
WINNEWS.TXT - Notepad		ROBERT ...	13.0KB	12:46:50 AM 2/16/95

9 jobs in queue

FIGURE 8.11: A printer's window with several print jobs pending

To see the queue on a printer:

1.   Open the Printers folder.

2.   Double-click on the printer in question.

3. Adjust the window size if necessary so you can see all the columns.

TIP

If the printer in question is a network printer, and the printer is offline for some reason, such as its computer isn't turned on, you'll be forced to work *offline*. An error message will alert you to this, and the top line of the printer's window will say *User intervention required—Work Offline*. Until the issue is resolved, you won't be able to view the queue for that printer. You can still print to it, however.

Refreshing the Network Queue Information

The network cabling connecting workstations and servers often is quite busy, so Windows usually doesn't bother to add even more traffic to the net by polling each workstation for printer-queue information. This is done when necessary, such as when a document is deleted from a queue. So, if you want to refresh the window for a printer to get the absolute latest information, just press F5. This immediately updates the queue information.

Deleting a File from the Queue

After sending a file to the queue, you might reconsider printing it, or you might want to re-edit the file and print it later. If so, you can simply remove the file from the queue.

1. Open the printer's window.

2. Select the file by clicking on it in the queue.

NOTE

I have found, especially with PostScript laser-type printers, that after deleting a file while printing, I'll have to reset the printer to clear its buffer or at least eject the current page (if you have a page-eject button). To reset, you'll typically have to push a button on the printer's front panel or turn the printer off for a few seconds, then on again.

3. Choose Document ➢ Cancel Printing, press Delete, or right-click and choose Cancel Printing. The document item is removed from the printer's window. If you're trying to delete

the job that's printing, you might have some trouble. At the very least, the system might take some time to respond.

NOTE

Pending print jobs will not be lost when computers are powered down. Any documents in the queue when the system goes down will reappear in the queue when you power up. When you turn on a computer that is the host for a shared printer that has an unfinished print queue, you will be alerted to the number of jobs in the queue and asked whether to delete or print them.

TIP

When an error occurs during a print job, Windows tries to determine the cause. For example, the printer might be out of paper, or the printer might be offline or unplugged from the AC outlet. You may be forced to work offline until the problem is resolved. Opening the printers queue should display an error message approximating the nature of the problem to the best of Print Manager's capabilities. Check the printer's File menu to see if the Work Offline setting has been activated. When you think the problem has been solved, turn this setting off to begin printing again.

Canceling All Pending Print Jobs on a Given Printer

Sometimes, because of a megalithic meltdown or some other catastrophe, you'll decide to bail out of all the print jobs that are stacked up for a printer. Normally you don't need to do this, even if the printer has gone wacky. You can just pause the queue and continue printing after the problem is solved. But sometimes you'll want to resend everything to another printer and kill the queue on the current one. It's easy:

1. Select the printer's icon or window.

2. Right-click and choose Purge Print Jobs, or from the printer's window choose Printer ➤ Purge Print Jobs. All queued jobs for the printer are canceled.

WARNING

Make sure you really want to cancel the jobs before you do this. This is a good way to make enemies if people on the network were counting on their print jobs being finished anytime soon.

Pausing (and Resuming) the Printing Process

If you're the administrator of a printer with a stack of jobs in the print queue, you can temporarily pause a single job or all jobs on a particular printer at any time. This can be useful for taking a minute to add paper, take a phone call, or have a conversation in your office without the noise of the printer in the background. The next several sections explain the techniques for pausing and resuming.

Pausing or Resuming a Specific Print Job

You can pause documents anywhere in the queue. Paused documents are skipped and subsequent documents in the list print ahead of them. You can achieve the same effect by rearranging the queue, as explained in the section titled *Rearranging the Queue Order*. When you feel the need to pause or resume a specific print job:

1. Click on the document's information line.

2. Choose Document ➢ Pause Printing (or right-click on the document and choose Pause Printing as you see in Figure 8.12). The current print job is temporarily suspended, and the word "Paused" appears in the status area. (The printing might not stop immediately because your printer might have a buffer that holds data in preparation for printing. The printing stops when the buffer is empty.)

3. To resume printing the document, repeat steps 1 and 2 to turn off the check mark next to Pause Printing.

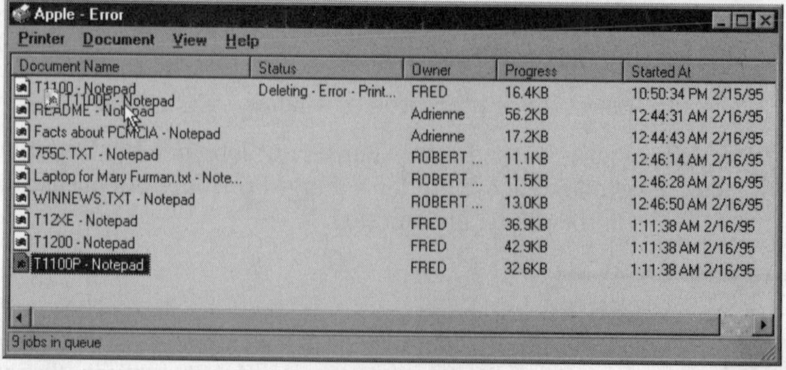

Document Name	Status	Owner	Progress	Started At
T1100 - Notepad	Deleting - Error - Print...	FRED	16.4KB	10:50:34 PM 2/15/95
T1100P - Notepad				
README - Notepad		Adrienne	56.2KB	12:44:31 AM 2/16/95
Facts about PCMCIA - Notepad		Adrienne	17.2KB	12:44:43 AM 2/16/95
755C.TXT - Notepad		ROBERT ...	11.1KB	12:46:14 AM 2/16/95
Laptop for Mary Furman.txt - Note...		ROBERT ...	11.5KB	12:46:28 AM 2/16/95
WINNEWS.TXT - Notepad		ROBERT ...	13.0KB	12:46:50 AM 2/16/95
T12XE - Notepad		FRED	36.9KB	1:11:38 AM 2/16/95
T1200 - Notepad		FRED	42.9KB	1:11:38 AM 2/16/95
T1100P - Notepad		FRED	32.6KB	1:11:38 AM 2/16/95

Apple - Error
Printer   Document   View   Help

9 jobs in queue

FIGURE 8.12: Pause the printing of a single document with the right-click menu. Other documents will continue to print.

Pausing or Resuming All Jobs on a Printer

In similar fashion, you can temporarily pause all jobs on a given printer. You might want to do this for a number of reasons including:

▶ to load paper or otherwise adjust the physical printer

▶ to alter printer settings from the printer's Properties dialog box

Follow these steps to pause or resume all jobs for a printer:

1. Deselect any documents in the printer's window; press the Spacebar if a document is selected.

2. Choose Printer ➤ Pause Printing. The printer window's title bar changes to say "Paused."

3. To resume all jobs on the printer, choose Printer ➤ Pause Printing again to turn off the check mark next to the command. The *Paused* indicator in the title bar disappears, and printing should resume where the queue left off.

Rearranging the Queue Order

When you have several items on the queue, you might want to rearrange the order in which they're slated for printing.

1. Click on the file you want to move and keep the mouse button depressed.

2. Drag the file to its new location. The name of the document moves to indicate where the document will be inserted when you release the mouse button.

3. When you release the mouse button, your file is inserted in the queue, pushing the other files down a notch (see Figure 8.13).

PRINTING TO A DISK FILE INSTEAD OF A PRINTER

There are times when you may want to print to a disk file rather than to the printer. What does this mean? When you print to a disk file, the codes and data that would normally be sent to the printer are shunted off to a

Document Name	Status	Owner	Progress	Started At
T1100 - Notepad	Deleting - Error - Print...	FRED	16.4KB	10:50:34 PM 2/15/95
T1100P - Notepad				
README - Notepad		Adrienne	56.2KB	12:44:31 AM 2/16/95
Facts about PCMCIA - Notepad		Adrienne	17.2KB	12:44:43 AM 2/16/95
755C.TXT - Notepad		ROBERT ...	11.1KB	12:46:14 AM 2/16/95
Laptop for Mary Furman.txt - Note...		ROBERT ...	11.5KB	12:46:28 AM 2/16/95
WINNEWS.TXT - Notepad		ROBERT ...	13.0KB	12:46:50 AM 2/16/95
T12XE - Notepad		FRED	36.9KB	1:11:38 AM 2/16/95
T1200 - Notepad		FRED	42.9KB	1:11:38 AM 2/16/95
T1100P - Notepad		FRED	32.6KB	1:11:38 AM 2/16/95

9 jobs in queue

FIGURE 8.13: You can shift the order of a document in the queue by dragging it to the desired position and dropping it.

disk file—either locally or on the network. The resulting file typically isn't just a copy of the file you were printing; it contains all the special formatting codes that control your printer. Codes that change fonts, print graphics, set margins, break pages, and add attributes such as underline, bold, and so on are all included in this type of file. Print files destined for PostScript printers typically include their PostScript preamble, too—a special file that prepares the printer to receive the instructions that are about to come and the fonts that are included in the document.

Why would you want to create a disk file instead of printing directly to the printer? Printing to a file gives you several options not available when you print directly to the printer:

▶ Print files are sometimes used by programs for specific purposes. For example, printing a database to a disk file might allow you to more easily work with it in another application. Or you might want to print an encapsulated PostScript graphics file to be imported into a desktop-publishing document.

▶ You can send the file to another person, either on floppy disk or over the phone lines, with a modem and a communications program such as Terminal. That person can then print the file directly to a printer (if it's compatible) with Windows or a utility such as the DOS **copy** command. The person doesn't need the program that created the file and doesn't have to worry about any of the printing details—formatting, setting up margins, and so forth. All that's in the file.

▶ It allows you to print the file later. Maybe your printer isn't hooked up, or there's so much stuff on the queue that you don't want to wait, or you don't want to slow down your computer or the network by printing now. Print to a file, which is significantly faster than printing on paper. Later, you can use the DOS **copy** command or a batch file with a command such as **copy *.prn lpt1 /b** to copy all files to the desired port. This way you can queue up as many files as you want, prepare the printer, and then print them without having to be around. Be sure to use the **/b** switch. If you don't, the first Ctrl+Z code the computer encounters will terminate the print job because the print files are binary files.

In some programs, printing to a disk file is a choice in the Print dialog box. If it isn't, you should modify the printer's configuration to print to a file rather than to a port. Then, whenever you use that printer, it uses all the usual settings for the driver but sends the data to a file of your choice instead of to the printer port.

1. In the Printers folder, right-click on the printer's icon and choose Properties.

2. Select the Details tab page.

3. Under *Print to the following port*, choose FILE:

4. OK the box. The printer's icon in the Printers folder will change to indicate that printing is routed to a disk file.

Epson LX-80

Now when you print a file from any program and choose this printer as the destination for the printout, you'll be prompted for a file name.

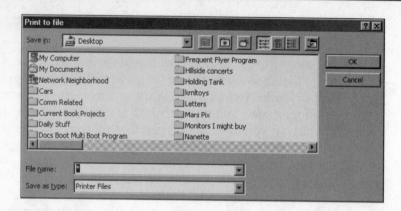

TIP

If you want to print the file as ASCII text only, with no special control codes, you should install the Generic/Text Only printer driver. Then select that as the destination printer.

TIP

If you want to print to an encapsulated PostScript file (. eps), print to a printer that uses a PostScript driver (the Apple LaserWriter or the QMS PS-810, for instance) or set up a phony printer that uses such a driver. (No physical printer is needed.) When prompted for a file name, specify an EPS extension.

WHAT'S NEXT?

In the next chapter we'll continue looking at Windows 98's extensive hardware support, digging into it's particularly rich multimedia features. You'll learn about working with everything from the simple Media Player to the latest-and-greatest gizmos like the DVD player and TV Tuner applications.

Chapter 9
WINDOWS MULTIMEDIA

Windows 98 is more *multimedia-ready* than any previous version of Windows. Gone are the days when upgrading your PC for multimedia meant days of intense hardware analysis. And because Windows 98 has built-in, high-performance, 32-bit support for digital video, digital audio, MIDI, game controllers, and even TV, developers and users no longer need to worry about installing special drivers and programs to squeeze maximum multimedia out of their Windows machines.

• •

Adapted from *Mastering Windows 98 Premium Edition*, by Robert Cowart

ISBN 0-7821-2186-1   1,584 pages
hardcover   2CDs $59.99

Order this book at www.masteringwindows.com

PC-based multimedia has grown dramatically in the last several years. Not only do practically all mainstream software packages (including Windows 98 itself) now come to us on CD-ROMs, many of them also have online multimedia tutorials to teach basic skills. These often include music, video or animation, as well as voice coaching. And that's just the tip of the multimedia iceberg. Internet-based multimedia games, music education programs, video telephone conferencing, 360-degree panoramic-view Web sites, streaming audio, and video Web sites are some of the nifty features that are becoming common.

Improvements in Plug-and-Play (PnP) technology have decreased the hassle of upgrading your system to add stuff like CD-ROMs, audio cards, microphones, and speakers. You're almost guaranteed nowadays that any new PnP multimedia device you add will install itself with little or no hassle. You're also more likely to meet with success when plugging in some older piece of gear, thanks to improved detection of "legacy" hardware by Windows 98.

With few exceptions, today's PCs are multimedia PCs, complying with standards that were primarily developed by Microsoft and a few other industry giants. The "multimedia PC standard" proposed a few years back has been widely adopted by PC makers partly by design and partly because of the popularity of specific pieces of hardware. (For example, most PC sound systems are "SoundBlaster" compatible. Manufactured by Creative Labs, Inc., SoundBlaster was one of the first add-in sound cards. Even without being endorsed by other hardware and software companies, it has become a de facto industry standard thanks to the sheer number of installed units in the field.) Windows 98 has helped solidify the standards for multimedia by adding multimedia APIs to Windows. By writing their code around the APIs, software developers only have to write one version of a program regardless of the hundreds of possible combinations of video, audio, MIDI, or other multimedia hardware that may be included in users' computer systems. Windows and the installed device drivers take care of the rest.

A multimedia PC equipped with Windows 98 can:

▶ Display cable and broadcast television in a resizable window or full-screen with better-than-TV quality, and even capture the closed-captioning text of a show to a text file for later perusal.

▶ Play DVD movies, complete with display of embedded textual or other material that the producer may add.

▶ Record, edit, and play sounds in a variety of formats from highly compressed monaural voice grade to CD-quality stereo.

▶ Play MIDI sequences on your synthesizer or other MIDI device.

▶ Play fancy CD-ROM titles such as interactive encyclopedias that talk or adventure games such as Myst.

▶ Display streaming video and audio from Web broadcasts such as live concerts or news shows.

▶ Display live video and audio teleconferencing over the Internet using NetMeeting or other compatible programs.

▶ Respond to voice commands (with the right third-party hardware).

All such capabilities and the hardware and software that make them work fall into the category of *Windows multimedia*. This chapter will answer your questions about Windows 98's multimedia abilities and how you can best take advantage of them.

WHAT IS MULTIMEDIA?

Multimedia—alias *interactive media* or *hypermedia*—is difficult to define, which accounts for much general confusion on the topic. The practical definition changes each time I write a book about Windows, and that's about every year or so. Actually, multimedia simply means two or more simultaneous types of display. Regular old TV is a good example—it's a multimedia device since it integrates audio and video. But computers are capable of more advanced levels of multimedia amalgamating animation, graphics, video, MIDI, digitally recorded sounds, and text—and can also interact with people while they view the presentation.

It's interesting to chronicle the breakneck rate of multimedia advancements. Just two years ago, updating a system to multimedia meant adding a CD-ROM drive. This year, any decent PC (even most laptops) have them built in, along with speakers, and even accelerated video display cards capable of 30 frame-per-second high-speed animation, and texture mapping.

Some multimedia programs are *interactive* and some are not. Interactivity means that through some input device such as keyboard, mouse, voice, or external controller—for example, a Musical Instrument Digital Interface (MIDI) keyboard—you interact with the system to control aspects of the presentation. Most of today's software is still primarily based on text display, though it's increasingly permeated with graphics, charts, and clip art. With the added capabilities of stereo sound, animation, and video, multimedia computing offers a much richer and more efficient means of conveying information.

As an example of a simple interactive program, consider the Windows tour, which demonstrates Windows fundamentals for the newcomer. (You launch it by choosing Start ➤ Programs ➤ Accessories ➤ System Tools ➤ Welcome to Windows. Then click on Discover Windows 98.) The tutorial demonstrates rudimentary multimedia, integrating animation, text, and voice. It does not incorporate live-action video clips. Now imagine expanding such a tutorial to include music, realistic 3-D animation, and moving video images just as if you were watching TV. As you probably know by now, animators, musicians, designers, writers, programmers, audio engineers, industry experts, and video producers have joined forces to create multimedia applications such as:

▶ A WordPerfect document that lets you paste in video clips (with audio) from a VCR tape you've made; instead of displaying just a still graphic, the document will be "alive" with sight and sound.

▶ A music-education program on a CD-ROM from Microsoft that plays Beethoven's Ninth Symphony while displaying informative and educational text about each passage and about the composer.

▶ A dictionary, thesaurus, book of quotations, and encyclopedia on a CD-ROM from Microsoft that not only contains a huge amount of textual information but actually pronounces the dictionary entries; reads quotations aloud in the voices of Robert Frost, Carl Sandburg, T.S. Eliot, e.e. cummings, Dylan Thomas, and John F. Kennedy; and illustrates scientific phenomena with animation.

▶ Programs that teach you how to play the piano using a MIDI keyboard connected to your PC. The computer senses whether you play the lesson correctly and responds accordingly with a recorded high-quality voice. Similar programs teach music theory.

▶ Interactive company annual reports, product demonstrations, presentations, or corporate training manuals for new employees.

▶ *Moving catalogs* from mail-order houses, displaying everything from cars to coats via high-quality video and audio.

▶ An interactive geography test used at the National Geographic Society Explorer's Hall in Washington, D.C.

▶ Interactive high-speed, random-access books, newspapers, or catalogs for the blind, using high-quality voice synthesis or recorded voices.

▶ Interactive training for hard-to-teach professions such as medical diagnosis, surgery, auto mechanics, and machine operation of various types.

▶ Complex interactive games and children's learning programs that incorporate stereo sound effects, flashy visuals, and the ability to move through synthetic virtual worlds.

In fact, most of these multimedia products already exist. The explosion of multimedia CD titles has been enormous in the last two years.

WHAT'S NEW IN WINDOWS 98 MULTIMEDIA

Windows 98 adds a number of new features as well as enhancing some of the better features of Windows 95 multimedia:

▶ Built-in support for compressed video allows playback of video files (such as AVI and QuickTime) without installation of additional licensed drivers.

▶ AutoPlay support lets users simply insert a CD and it will begin to run, eliminating the need to enter the correct command or find and click on the correct program icon in the CD's file directory.

▶ 2-D and 3-D graphics support is now provided through improved DirectX 5, a set of tools that help developers take advantage of new capabilities of Windows 98 such as multiple monitors, Intel Pentium MMX extensions, use of the USB (Universal Serial Bus) interface for gaming device input, faster texture mapping, and anti-aliasing.

▶ DirectShow, a streaming media player technology, allows Windows 98 to efficiently play back a variety of multimedia file types: AVI video, MPEG compressed video, Apple QuickTime video, and WAV audio. MPEG-compressed video can be played back on PCs that have no decompression hardware; Windows 98 can achieve decompression quickly enough.

▶ NetShow, a streaming media player, plays unicast and multicast streaming audio and video that comes over the Web. It's compatible with existing RealAudio and RealVideo formats as well as with Microsoft's own NetShow format.

▶ A DVD (Digital Video Disk) player program is included. If you have a (hardware) DVD player attached to your system, you can play DVD, CD-sized disks that contain huge amounts of data, such as audio, several hours of video, and optional text.

▶ Surround Video allows software developers an easy way to create programs that let users interact with objects, images, patterns, and live action video in a 360-degree view in a synthetic environment.

▶ CD-ROM support: Windows 98 includes 32-bit drivers for support of faster CD-ROM drives, while still supporting older drives and 16-bit Windows 3.x drivers (MSCDEX). Also supported is the new CD-PLUS specification developed by Sony and Phillips, which puts text (including biographies and music program notes), video, and other enhancements on the same CD with the usual audio material. These new CD titles can be played on a Windows 98 machine.

▶ Windows 98 "broadcast-enables" your computer. You can receive Web pages that contain video and audio content as well as view television programming from cable, over-the-air, and satellite networks.

▶ Smoother 32-bit multitasking and better codec (compression/decompression) software make it possible to display even full-screen video simultaneous with MIDI or audio playback—something not possible only a few years ago. Even modest-priced laptops have fast enough electronics to support this.

THE SUPPLIED MULTIMEDIA APPLICATIONS AND UTILITIES

Here's what you get in the way of multimedia programs and utilities with Windows 98:

Sound Settings   This Control Panel applet lets you assign specific sound files (stored in the .WAV format) to Windows system events such as error messages, information dialog boxes, and when starting and exiting Windows.

Media Player   This application, which you'll find in the Start ➤ Programs ➤ Accessories ➤ Multimedia folder, lets you play a variety of multimedia files on the target hardware. In the case of a device that contains data, such as a CD-ROM or video disk, Media Player sends commands to the hardware, playing back the sound or video therein. If the data is stored on your hard disk (as are MIDI sequences, animation, and sound files), Media Player will send them to the appropriate piece of hardware, such as a sound board, MIDI keyboard, or other device.

NOTE

The Media Player only works with MCI (Media Control Interface) devices and thus requires MCI device drivers.

Sound Recorder   This is a simple program for recording sounds from a microphone or auxiliary input and then editing them. Once recorded, sound files can be used with other programs through OLE or used to replace or augment the generic beeps your computer makes to alert you to dialog boxes, errors, and so forth. Sound Recorder is also the default program used to play back WAV files.

TIP

You can find more elaborate WAV file editors. For my CD recording projects I use a shareware program called Cool Edit, which you can find and download from the Web. Another capable shareware WAV file program is called WaveWorks.

CD Player   Assuming your computer's CD-ROM drive and controller card support it (most do), this accessory program lets you play back standard audio CDs. This can be a great boon on long winter nights when you're chained to your PC doing taxes or writing that boring report. On most computers, just inserting an audio CD will bring up the CD player program on your screen.

DVD Player   If the DVD drive you purchase, whether by upgrade or built-in, says it is Windows 98-compatible, then it will have a DVD player program supplied. Whether you choose to use that player or the one supplied with Windows 98 is up to you; they all work similarly. You just have to compare their respective features, as some have more bells and whistles than others. In this chapter I'll cover the player that comes with Windows 98.

Adding Drivers   The System and Add New hardware applets in the Control Panel let you install drivers for many add-in cards and devices such as CD-ROMs, MIDI interface cards, and video-disk controllers if they are not detected automatically once you plug them in. Drivers for most popular sound boards such as the SoundBlaster (from Creative Labs, Inc.) and Ad Lib (Ad Lib, Inc.) and popular MIDI boards such as the Roland MPU-401 (Roland Digital Group) are supplied. Other drivers can be installed from manufacturer-supplied disks using this option. Even if your hardware is physically installed, it won't work unless the proper driver is loaded.

Doing It All with DVD Player

As I just mentioned, Windows 98 includes support for DVD (Digital Versatile Disk / Digital Video Disk) drives. DVD and CD-ROM use very much the same technology (micro laser to read the disk), so besides being able to play DVD disks on your computer, you should be able to use a DVD drive to read your current CD-ROM and audio CD disks (this depends, however, on how early you buy; first-generation DVD drives could not read as many CD formats as the current generation). Pricewise, this will be an almost unnoticed transition, at least for new system buyers. A computer equipped with a DVD drive will probably cost only $100 to $200 more than one equipped with a CD-ROM drive instead. (If it weren't for the need for a decoder card to play DVD movies on your computer, the difference would be more like $100.) DVD drives will probably start to be offered as standard equipment in PCs by the end of 1998, as they begin to replace the now common CD-ROM drive.

Some DVD Specifics

I already sang the praises of DVD earlier in the chapter. However, as there is some confusion about different generations of DVDs, I want to make sure we have the basics understood before I discuss the DVD Player program supplied with Windows 98.

DVD is going to be the content-providing medium of choice over the next few years. The research group called IDC, from Framingham, Massachusetts, predicts that 13 percent of all PC software will be available on DVD by the end of this year (1998). Sure, CDs will still be around, but even with the CD's capacity of 650MB, some programs actually require multiple CDs! (Hard to believe, but true.) In addition, mega-databases such as national phone directories, the catalog of the Library of Congress, the complete Oxford English Dictionary, photo stock house collections, museum and gallery holdings photographed in high resolution, and fonts packages span multiple CD-ROMs. These are all prime candidates for appearing on DVD.

And then, of course, we've got movies—the hands-down winners of the disk-consumption sweepstakes. With a maximum capacity of 17GB (yes, gigabytes), an innocent DVD (which looks almost identical to a CD) can store two hours of video that displays more clearly (and has groovier options) than VHS, LaserDisk, or video CD-ROMs. DVD movies will boast multichannel surround sound, subtitles, multiple alternative audio tracks (for different languages), multiple video playback formats, and even, in some cases, user-selectable camera angles.

How does a DVD pack all that information onto a five-inch disk? Well, first, the optical pits on a DVD disk are stuffed in twice as close to one another as on a CD, and so are the tracks. Also, more of the surface is recorded on. *And* error correction is more rigorous! All this increases the data storage capacity from a CD's 650MB to a DVD's 4.3GB. But wait! That's only for one layer! DVDs can have *two* layers per side. By focusing the read laser carefully, a second layer can be used, adding another 4.3GB, for a one-side total of approximately 8.4GB. And there's more! DVDs can have data written on *both sides*, so by flipping the disk over, the 8.4GB is doubled.

Another compelling point about DVD is its versatility. CD-ROM suffers from a plethora of competing and often incompatible formats: multisession, Photo CD, Mode 1, Mode 2, Joliet, CD-I, and CD+, to name but a few. The DVD spec is, well, versatile (as the name implies: Digital Versatile Disk). A new disk file format that was devised for DVD, called Universal Disk

Format (UDF), ensures compatibility between disk and player, regardless of content. (Well, almost. As the saying goes, some limitations apply.) A single DVD drive should be able to read most existing CDs, as well as text, data, and video DVD formats. Even CD-R and CD-RW disks should be readable by most second-generation DVD drives.

Shop Carefully!

If you're thinking about buying a DVD, check the specs thoroughly, and ask around before you drop your cash. We're just beginning to see the third round of drives (Spring 1998), so you'll probably want to skip buying a first- or second-generation drive. The differences lie mostly in the formats they can read. Second-generation drives can read CD-R (recordable CDs) and CD-RW (recordable/eraseable CDs), whereas first-generation drives can't. Third-generation drives will probably read a greater variety of recordable and re-recordable formats, including (hopefully) the yet-to-be-standardized "writeable DVD" (DVD-RAM and DVD+RW) formats.

As for speed, don't worry. As long as they can play back a movie, you'll have speed to burn. The latest crop of DVD drives (2X DVD) played CDs at the equivalent speed of a 24X CD-ROM drive.

Installation of DVD can be tricky. I suggest you purchase a complete upgrade kit or purchase a computer with the DVD built in. I upgraded piece by piece. It cost me more, and was a hassle to get working. Read the requirements for an upgrade carefully. Typically you'll need at least a 166MHz Pentium with 16MB of RAM; you'll also need a bus-mastering PCI slot, an empty drive bay for the drive, and an open EIDE connector. (Although some DVDs are SCSI drives, most are EIDE. Besides, most motherboards support four EIDE drives, and you probably don't have four hard disks connected; so why buy a SCSI disk controller if you don't need it?) Most DVD drives don't care whether they are "slave" or "master" drives.

TIP

As a rule, just look for a kit or computer that is Windows 98-compatible, and follow the instructions supplied with the unit.

In addition, until you can buy a video card that is tailored to support DVD video playback, you'll need a *decoder card* to be able to watch DVD movies on your computer. (If you aren't planning to play video DVD disks, neither of these is necessary.) The decoder card plugs into the PCI bus (typically) and connects to your existing video card (via a ribbon cable) to translate the video data into the analog signals needed for display on your monitor. Among other things, such as decoding Dolby Surround-Sound audio, and handling copy-protection schemes, the decoder decompresses the MPEG-1 or MPEG-2 compressed video in real time. This takes some serious computing speed. Some DVD drives come with "software" decoders which they say can be used instead of a decoder card, but don't expect smooth performance from them, even on a fast Pentium 266 machine. The computer's CPU just can't keep up with the data stream very well, and ends up dropping frames to keep up.

Running the DVD Player

Typically the DVD player that comes with the drive will have all the basic controls found on a VCR, plus some number of additional bells and whistles, such as searching tools, audio controls for bass, treble, and volume, a viewing angle selector, child-proofing locks, video format selector, "chapter" and "title" features, and so on. Most of them are used in similar ways; you'll just have to compare the features of each. In this section, I'll provide the basic instructions for running the player that comes with Windows 98.

First, I'll assume that you've got your hardware installed (or someone at the factory did it for you), as discussed earlier. If your drive is in working order, then here are the basics of running the Microsoft DVD player:

1. Insert a DVD disk as you would insert a disk into any other drive, and shut the door. Windows will detect the disk; if the disk is a video disk, the DVD player will start; if it's an audio disk, the CD player will start (as discussed earlier in this chapter).

2. If a disk has been inserted and nothing happens, run the DVD player explicitly by choosing Start ➤ Programs ➤ Accessories ➤ Entertainment ➤ DVD Player. Then click the Options button and choose Select Disk. You'll see the following dialog box.

3. If you've set the option that prevents someone from running a movie without authorization (see the Tip following this step), you'll see a logon dialog box:

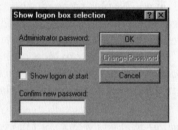

Enter your administrator password at this point and click on OK.

TIP

You can create a new logon password by choosing the Options button on the player. Typically, you might create a password to prevent children from playing your disks.

4. To start playing a disk, click on the ➤ button on the player toolbar. You should experiment with the other various controls by clicking on them as well, just as you might in the CD player application or on a VCR. You can play, stop, pause, fast forward, fast rewind, eject, etc. (There are also buttons here for "very fast forward" and "very fast rewind.") If you're better with words than icons, you can display a textual list of all of the commands available from the player toolbar by right-clicking on any one of the controls.

To see a full-screen view of the movie you are watching, click on the little icon of the television set in the toolbar. The toolbar disappears. You can access the tools again by right-clicking anywhere on the screen. That action pops up the following menu:

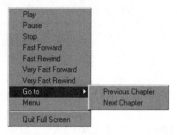

Choose the Quit Full Screen command to see the toolbar again, or choose any of the other commands as you wish. Alternatively, to cancel this menu and return to full-screen view, click anywhere outside of the menu.

Chapters and Titles   Typically you'll watch video DVDs just as you would a VHS tape; that is, you'll start it, pause it once in a while to get up for more popcorn, then sit down and click on Play to start it up again. But as more interesting DVDs start to hit the market, you may want to jump to specific *titles* and *chapters*. Think of a title as, say, one of several shows on the disk. A chapter, then, is a subset of a title: perhaps a lesson, a scene in the movie, a section of a tutorial, etc. Once a disk is inserted, you can quickly choose to search for sections by title or chapter by right-clicking on the display:

▶ If you choose Title, this handy little box lets you jump to a specific title and to any portion of the title track by entering its time value:

▶ If you choose Chapter, you'll see the following box, which also expects you to enter a time value:

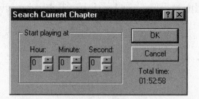

Just enter the hour, minute, and second of the spot you want to jump to (and if you're in the Title box, enter the title number), and click OK.

Selecting Language and Subtitles   Some disks will have subtitles (nice for when you're talking on the phone; that way nobody can hear what's distracting you), and some disks will have multiple languages (i.e., multiple alternative audio tracks), as I mentioned earlier. You can make choices for these features from the Options button:

The procedure is a no-brainer:

1.   Click Options.

2.   Choose SubTitles or Language.

3.   Set the subtitle or language option as desired, and click Close.

For example, suppose I wanted to see English subtitles (assuming my disk offered them). The Options ≻ SubTitles command might show the following choices:

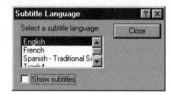

I'd just click on English, then on the Show Subtitles checkbox. For language choice, I might see the following little box. I'd just choose the audio language I'm interested in listening to:

Ending a DVD Session   When you're finished listening to, using, or viewing the disk, you can either press the Eject button on the front of the drive or click the Eject button on the DVD Player toolbar. Then close the DVD Player program.

Assigning Sounds with the Control Panel's Sound Utility

You can use the Control Panel's Sound utility for assigning sounds to system events, such as warning dialog boxes, error messages when you click in the wrong place, and so on. Once you've installed a sound board, you can personalize your computer's beep to something more exciting. If your computer had a sound card when you installed Windows 98, it's likely Windows established a default set of rather boring sounds for your system, most of which you're probably tired of already. Besides making life more interesting, having different sounds for different types of events is also more informative, because you can assign sounds to many more events than Windows does by default. You know when you've made an error as opposed to when an application is acknowledging your actions, for example.

Of course, to add basic sounds to your Windows setup, you need a Windows 98-compatible sound card. The sounds you can use must be stored on disk in the .WAV format. Most sounds you can download from BBSs or get on disk at the computer store are in this format. Also, the Sound Recorder program explained later in the chapter records sounds as WAV files. Windows 98 comes with more than a few sound files. In fact, just as with the color schemes you can create and save with the Control Panel's Display applet (covered in Chapter 7), you can set up and save personalized sound schemes to suit your mood. Microsoft has supplied us with several such schemes, running the gamut from happy nature sounds to futuristic, mechanistic robot utterances to the sonorities of classical musical instruments.

NOTE

You have to do a Custom installation to get all the sound schemes loaded into your computer. You can do this after the fact by running Control Panel ➢ Add/Remove Programs ➢ Windows Setup. Then click on Multimedia to select it and click on the Details button. The Multimedia Sound Schemes are located near the bottom of the list.

Despite this diverse selection, you may still want to make or acquire more interesting sounds yourself or collect them from other sources.

TIP

See Chapter 7 for a discussion of the Desktop Themes option. In addition to neat visual features, this adds some spiffy sounds to your system.

To record your own, you'll need a sound board that handles digital sampling. I have messages in my own voice, such as, "You made a stupid mistake, you fool," which—for a short time—seemed preferable to the mindless chime. If your system lets you play audio CDs, you should be able to directly sample bits and pieces from your favorite artists by popping the audio CD into the computer and tapping directly into it rather than by sticking a microphone up to your boom box and accidentally recording the telephone when it rings. Check out the Volume Control applet and adjust the slider on the mixer panel that controls the input volume of the CD. Then use the Sound Recorder applet to make the recording.

TIP

Any time your sound isn't working correctly (if there's no sound, for example), check the following: Are your speakers connected and turned on? Is the volume control on them (if they have it) turned down? Has the sound worked before? If so, it's probably the mixer settings that are wrong. Right-click on the speaker icon near the clock in the TaskBar and choose Open Volume Controls. Check the settings. Don't forget to choose Options ➤ Properties and poke around. Don't change the mixer device, but notice that you can choose to see the Recording mixer controls, and choose which sliders are on either the recording or playback controls. Make sure the source that isn't working properly isn't muted.

Like any good sound-o-phile, I'm always on the lookout for good WAV files. You'll find them everywhere if you just keep your eyes open: cheap CDs at the local Compu-Geek store, on the Internet, on CompuServe, even on other people's computers. Usually these sound files aren't copyrighted, so copying them isn't likely to be a legal issue. Most WAV files intended for system sounds aren't that big, either. But do check out the size, using the Explorer or by showing the Details view in a folder, before copying them. Sound files *can* be super large, especially if they are recorded in 16-bit stereo (about 172K bytes per second of CD-quality audio). As a rule you'll want to keep the size to a minimum for system sounds because it can take more than a few seconds for a larger sound file to load and begin to play.

Once you're set up for sound and have some WAV files, you assign them to specific Windows events. Here's how:

1. Open the Control Panel and run the Sounds applet. The dialog box shown in Figure 9.1 appears.

2. The top box lists the events that can have sounds associated with them. There will be at least two classes of events—one for Windows events and one for Explorer events. (Scroll to the bottom of the list to see the Explorer events.) As you purchase and install new programs in the future, those programs may add their own events to your list. An event with a speaker icon next to it already has a sound associated with it. You can click on it and then click on the Preview button to hear the sound. The sound file that's associated with the event is listed in the Name box.

3. Click on any event for which you want to assign a sound or change the assigned sound.

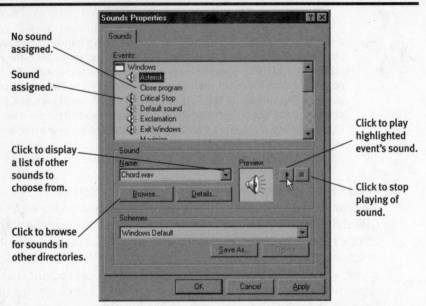

No sound assigned.

Sound assigned.

Click to display a list of other sounds to choose from.

Click to browse for sounds in other directories.

Click to play highlighted event's sound.

Click to stop playing of sound.

FIGURE 9.1: Use this dialog box to choose which sounds your computer makes when Windows events occur.

4. Open the drop-down Name list and choose the WAV file you want to use for that event. Some of the event names may not make sense to you, such as Asterisk, Critical Stop, or Exclamation. These are names for the various classes of dialog boxes that Windows displays from time to time. The sounds you're most likely to hear often will be Default sound, Menu Command, Menu Popup, Question, Open Program, Close Program, Minimize, Maximize, Start Windows, and Exit Windows.

TIP

The default directory for sounds is the \Windows\Media directory. That's where the WAV files that come with Windows 98 are stored. If you have WAV files stored somewhere else, you'll have to use the Browse button to find and assign them to an event. I find it's easier to copy all my WAV files into the \Windows\Media directory than to go browsing for them when I want to do a lot of reassigning of sounds.

5. At the top of the list of available sounds there is an option called <none> that has the obvious effect—no sound will

occur for that event. Assigning all events to <none> will effectively silence your computer for use in a library, church, and so forth. You can also quickly do this for all sounds by choosing the No Sounds scheme as explained below.

6. Repeat the process for other events to which you want to assign or reassign sounds.

7. Click on OK.

Keep in mind that different applications will use event sounds differently. You'll have to do some experimenting to see when your applications use the default beep, as opposed to the Asterisk, Question, or the Exclamation.

Clicking on the Details button displays information about the WAV file, such as its time length, data format, and copyright information (if any).

Loading and Saving Sound Schemes

Just as the Control Panel's Display applet lets you save color schemes, the Sounds applet lets you save sound schemes so you can set up goofy sounds for your humorous moods and somber ones for those gloomy days—or vice versa. The schemes supplied with Windows 98 are pretty nice even without modification.

To choose an existing sound scheme:

1. Click on the drop-down list button for schemes, down at the bottom of the box:

2. A list of existing schemes will appear. Choose a sound scheme. Now all the events in the upper part of the box will have the new sound scheme's sounds. Check out the sounds to see if you like them.

3. If you like the sound scheme, click on OK.

You can set up your own sound schemes by assigning or reassigning individual sounds, as I've already explained. But unless you *save* the scheme, it will be lost the next time you change to a new one. So, the moral is: once you get your favorite sounds assigned to system events, save the scheme. Then you can call it up any time you like. Here's how:

1. Set up the sounds the way you want. You can start with an existing scheme and modify it or start from scratch by choosing the No Sounds scheme and assigning sounds one by one.

2. Click on the Save As button:

3. In the resulting dialog box, enter a name for the scheme. For example, here's one I made up and saved:

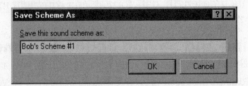

4. Click OK in the little dialog box, and your scheme is saved. Now you can create additional schemes and save them or just OK the large dialog box to activate the new scheme.

You can delete any existing sound schemes by choosing the doomed scheme from the list and then clicking on the Delete button. You'll be asked to confirm the deletion.

Playing Multimedia Files with Media Player

Media Player is a little application that plays multimedia files, such as digitized sounds, MIDI music files, and animated graphics. It can also send control information to multimedia devices such as audio CD players or video disk players, determining which tracks to play, when to pause, when to activate slow motion, and so on.

Obviously, you can only use Media Player on devices installed in your system and for which you've installed the correct device drivers, so first see to that task. Then follow these instructions for playing a multimedia file:

1. Run Media Player from the Start menu, by selecting Programs ➤ Accessories ➤ Entertainment ➤ Media Player. The Media Player's control panel appears.

2. Open the Device menu and choose the type of device that's going to receive the information.

3. If the type of device you've chosen has an ellipsis (...) after it, a File Open dialog box will appear, asking for the name of the file you want played and displaying the files with the correct extension for the selected device. This only happens with devices that play a file stored on hard disk (this type of device is called a *compound* device). Choose the file you want played. If the device you selected has no ellipsis after it, it's a *simple* device. This means the data to be played are already in the drive—as in the case of a CD-ROM or video disk—and don't have to be chosen (no File Open box will appear). When you load a file for a compound device, the Media Player's appearance will change slightly to display a scale and tick marks indicating the length of the item:

TIP

You can jump to a particular location in the piece by dragging the scroll bar, clicking at the desired point in the scroll bar, or using ↑, ↓, ←, →, PgUp, and PgDn. Also, check the Device menu for options pertaining to the device you are using.

4. Now you can use the buttons in the dialog box to begin playing the piece. The buttons work just as on a VCR or cassette deck; if in doubt, point to a button to see its pop-up description. The Eject button works for most devices with an Eject feature, like an audio CD player. However, not all devices respond to the Eject button.

5. If you want to open another file for the same device (in the case of compound devices), use the File ➤ Open command to do so. If you want to play a file intended for another device, you'll have to change the device type first from the Device menu, which will then bring up the File ➤ Open command for you to open a new file.

6. You can change the scale (tick marks) above the scroll bar to show *tracks* instead of time. Track display may be useful when you're playing audio CDs or video disks arranged by track. Do this from the Scale menu. Track tick marks will then replace the time tick marks. To change tracks, drag the scroll bar, click on the scroll buttons, or use →, ←, PgUp, and PgDn.

7. When you're done playing, close the application from the Exit menu.

NOTE
Compound devices will stop as soon as you quit Media Player; simple devices will continue to play.

Media Player has a few options worth noting. Check out the Edit ➤ Options and Device ➤ Configure options. Choose Device ➤ Volume control to bring up the volume control and mixer for your particular sound board.

Recording and Editing Sounds with Sound Recorder

Sound Recorder is a nifty little program that lets you record your own sounds and create WAV files. To make it work, you need a digital sampling card, such as the SoundBlaster, and some kind of input, such as a microphone. The program also lets you do some editing and manipulation of any WAV files you might have on disk, even if you don't have a microphone.

The resulting WAV files can be put to a variety of uses, including assigning them to system events or using them with other multimedia applications, such as Media Player. Once a file is recorded, you can edit it by removing portions of it. Unfortunately, you cannot edit from one arbitrary spot to another, only from one spot to either the beginning or the end of the file. You can also add an echo effect to a sample, play it backwards, change the playback speed (and resulting pitch), and alter the playback volume.

Playing a Sound File

Follow the steps below to play a sound file:

1. Make sure your sound board is working properly. If it's been playing sounds, such as the one that plays when Windows starts up, it probably is. If not, check that you've installed the correct driver and that your sound board works (Chapter 7 discusses how to add new hardware and drivers).

2. Run Sound Recorder by choosing Start ➤ Programs ➤ Accessories ➤ Entertainment ➤ Sound Recorder. The Sound Recorder window will appear, as shown here.

3. Choose File ➤ Open and choose the file you want to play. Notice that the length of the sound appears at the right of the window and the current position of the play head appears on the left.

4. Click on the Play button or press Enter to play the sound. As it plays, the wave box displays the sound, oscilloscope-style. The Status Bar also says Playing. When the sound is over, Sound Recorder stops and the Status Bar says Stopped. Press Enter again to replay the sound. You can click on Stop during a playback to pause the sound, and then click on Play to continue.

5. Drag the scroll button around (see below) and notice how the wave box displays a facsimile of the frequency and amplitude of the sample over time.

You can also click on the rewind and fast-forward buttons to move to the start and end of the sample or press the PgUp and PgDn keys to jump the play head forward or backward in longer increments.

Recording a New Sound

This is the fun part, so get your microphone (or line input) ready. Suppose you want to make up your own sounds, perhaps to put into an OLE-capable application document such as Wordpad or Word so that it talks when clicked on. Here's how:

1. Choose File ➤ New.

2. You may want to check the recording format before you begin. Choose File ➤ Properties. Select Recording Formats, then click on Convert Now. A dialog box appears, showing some details about the recording format. Click on the Convert Now button to see the dialog box shown in Figure 9.2. A combination of data-recording format (e.g., PCM, Microsoft's ADPCM, and so forth) and sampling rate (e.g., 8 KHz 4-bit mono) are shown. Together these comprise a format scheme.

Choose a preexisting format scheme here.

Choose a data format here.

Choose the sample rate here.

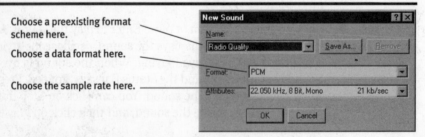

FIGURE 9.2: Choosing a data scheme for a new sound recording

NOTE

The Attributes list shows the amount of disk space consumed per second of recording. You'll want to consider this when making new files, as recording in high-fidelity stereo can suck up precious disk room, rendering sound files quite unwieldy. Also, for most purposes, you are best served by choosing one of the preexisting sound schemes—CD-Quality, Radio Quality, or Telephone Quality—for your recordings. All three use the PCM recording technique but employ different sample rates. If you are recording only voice, use either the Radio or Telephone setting. The CD-quality setting will only use up more disk space than you need to. If you are planning to record from an audio CD player, you'll probably want to choose the CD-quality setting unless you want to conserve disk space. If you accidentally record at a higher quality level than you wanted to, don't worry. You can convert to a lower quality and regain some hard disk space via the File > Properties > Convert Now button. You can save recording and playback settings with the Save As button in the dialog box.

Part i

3. Click on the Record button. The clock starts ticking, counting the passing time. Begin talking into the microphone that's plugged into your sound card, playing whatever is connected to your AUX input (aka *line in*) on the sound card, or playing the audio CD that's in the CD-ROM drive. You'll have to use the volume control applet to set the relative balance of the various devices. Typically you'll be able to mix these disparate audio sources into a single recording if you use the mixer deftly. The maximum recording time will vary, depending on your recording format. In the default setting (PCM, 22.050-KHz 8-bit mono) you can record for up to one minute. Be cautious about the length of your sounds, as they tend to take up a large amount of disk space. For example, a one-second sample at CD Quality in stereo consumes about 172K.

4. Click on Stop when you are finished recording.

5. Play back the file to see if you like it.

6. Save the file with File > Save As. You'll see the familiar File dialog box. Enter a name (you don't have to enter the WAV extension; the program does that for you).

When recording a voice narration, make sure to speak loudly and clearly, particularly if you notice that playback is muffled or buried in noise.

TIP

A simple way to create a new sound file is to right-click on the Desktop and choose New ➤ Sound File. Name the file, then double-click on it. Then click on the Record button.

Editing Sounds

You can edit sound files in several ways. For instance, you can:

▶ Add echo to a sample.

▶ Reverse a sample.

▶ Mix two samples together.

▶ Remove unwanted parts of a sample.

▶ Increase or decrease the volume.

▶ Increase or decrease the speed and pitch.

▶ Convert it to another format for use by a particular program.

NOTE

You may run out of memory if your file becomes very long because of inserting files into one another. The amount of free physical memory (not virtual memory) determines the maximum size of any sound file.

To edit a sound file:

1. Open the sound file from the File menu.

2. Open the Effects menu to add echo, reverse the sound, increase or decrease volume, or increase or decrease speed. All the settings except echo can be undone, so you can experiment without worry. You undo a setting by choosing its complementary setting from the menu (e.g., Increase Volume instead of Decrease Volume) or by choosing Reverse. Some sound quality can be lost by doing this repeatedly, however.

3. To cut out the beginning or ending of a sound—i.e., to eliminate the lag time it took you to get to the microphone or hit the Stop button—determine the beginning and ending points of the sound, get to the actual starting position of the sound, and choose Edit ➤ Delete Before Current Position. Then

move the scroll button to the end of the desired portion of the sample and choose Edit ➤ Delete After Current Position.

4. To mix two existing sounds, position the cursor where you'd like to begin the mix, choose Edit ➤ Mix with File, and choose the file name. This can create some very interesting effects that are much richer than single sounds.

5. To insert a file into a predetermined spot, move to the spot with the scroll bar, choose Edit ➤ Insert File, and choose the file name.

6. To put a sound on the Clipboard for pasting elsewhere, use Edit ➤ Copy.

7. To return your sound to its original, last-saved state, choose File ➤ Revert.

Note that not all sound boards have the same features. Some won't let you save a recording into certain types of sound files. Also, the quality of the sound differs from board to board. Some boards sound "grainy," others less so. This is determined by the sampling rate you've chosen, the quality of the digital-to-analog converters (DAC), and the analog amplifiers on the board.

Some programs require a particular sound file format to use sounds. For example, the Voxware plug-in for Web browsers (which lets you put sound clips on your Web pages) expects sound files in its proprietary Voxware format. You can convert an existing sound file by opening it in Sound Recorder. Then choose File ➤ Properties. Click on Convert Now and choose the correct setting from the Format list. Then click OK. Then save the file. It should be in the new format.

NOTE

Typically programs that require proprietary sound formats supply their own conversion tools, and it's often better to use those tools when they are available than a little accessory such as Sound Recorder.

Playing Tunes with CD Player

The CD Player accessory turns your computer's CD-ROM drive into a music machine: With it, you can play standard audio CDs with all the controls you'd expect on a "real" CD player, and then some. Of course, you'll need speakers (or at least a pair of headphones) to hear the music. Here's what CD Player looks like:

With CD Player, you can:

▶ Play any CD once through or continuously while you work with other programs.

▶ Play the tracks in sequential or random order, or play only the tracks you like.

▶ Move forward or in reverse to any desired track.

▶ Fast forward or rewind while a track is playing.

▶ Stop, pause, and resume playback, and (if your CD-ROM drive has the capability) eject the current CD.

▶ Control play volume if you're playing the CD through a sound card (this only works with some CD-ROM drives).

▶ Control the contents of the time display (you can display elapsed time, time remaining for the current track, or time remaining for the entire CD).

▶ Catalog your CDs (after you've typed in the title and track list for a CD, CD Player will recognize it when you load it again, displaying the titles of the disk and the current track).

Getting Started with CD Player

To run CD Player, begin from the Start menu and choose Programs ➤ Accessories ➤ Entertainment ➤ CD Player. Load your CD-ROM drive with an audio CD, turn on your sound system or plug in the headphones, and you're ready to go.

CD Player can tell when your CD-ROM drive is empty or doesn't contain a playable audio CD. In this case, it will display the message

```
Data or no disc loaded
Please insert an audio compact disc
```

in the Artist and Title areas in the middle of the window.

Basic Playing Controls

The CD Player window looks much like the front panel of a typical CD player in a sound system. The large black area at the top left displays track and time information. On the left, the faux LED readout tells you which track is currently playing, while on the right it keeps a running tally of how many

minutes and seconds have played in the track (you can change the contents of the time display as detailed below).

If you've ever worked a standard CD player, the control buttons (to the right of the track and time display) should be immediately familiar.

On the top row are the essential stop/start controls:

Play The largest button with the big arrow starts or resumes play.

Pause The button with the two vertical bars pauses play at the current point in the track.

Stop The button with the square stops play and returns you to the beginning of the current track.

On the second row, the first four buttons have double arrows pointing to the left or right. These let you move to other parts of the disc.

TIP

You can move directly to a specific track by choosing it from the list in the Track area near the bottom of the CD Player window. See "Playing Discs with the Play List" later in the chapter.

Previous and Next Track   At either end of this set of four
buttons, the buttons with the vertical bars move to the beginning of the previous or next track. The one at the left end—with
the left-pointing arrows—moves to the beginning of the previous track (or if a track is playing, to the beginning of the current track). The one at the right—with the right-pointing
arrows—moves to the beginning of the next track.

Skip Backward and Skip Forward   The two center buttons in
the set of four have double arrows only; these are for moving
quickly through the music while the disc plays in the reverse or
forward direction.

The *Eject* button is the last button at the far right of the second row,
with the upward-pointing arrow on top of a thin rectangle. Click here to
pop the current disc out of your CD-ROM drive. Of course, this will only
work if your drive is capable of ejecting automatically.

Display Options

Like other Windows programs, CD Player has a Toolbar with buttons for
other common commands (we'll cover these in a moment). The Toolbar
may not be visible when you first run the program; choose View ➤ Toolbar to turn it on and off. Here's how the CD Player window looks with
the Toolbar visible:

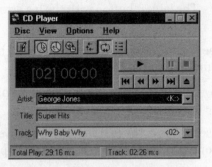

When the Toolbar is on, you can get a brief description of each button's function by placing the mouse pointer over the button.

Two other elements of the CD Player window can also be turned off
and on via the View menu. These are the Status Bar and the area displaying the artist and disc and track titles.

When visible, the Status Bar runs along the bottom of the window. It offers Help messages when the mouse pointer passes over a menu choice or rests over a button on the Toolbar for a few moments. Otherwise, it displays the total play time for the disc and current track. To turn the Status Bar off or on, choose View ➤ Status Bar.

Once you've cataloged a disc, CD Player displays the artist, disc title, and title of the current track in the middle of its window. If you want to hide this information, perhaps to make the window small enough to stay on your screen while you work with another program, choose View ➤ Disc/Track Info.

You can also control the display of time information in the main read-out of the CD Player window. The standard setting shows elapsed time for the track currently playing. If you prefer, you can instead see the time remaining for the current track or for the entire disc. To select among these options, open the View menu and choose one of the three relevant options: Track Time Elapsed, Track Time Remaining, or Disc Time Remaining. The currently active choice is checked on the View menu. Or, if the Toolbar is visible, you can click on the button corresponding to your time-display choice.

Other Play Options

You have several commands for determining the play order for a disc's tracks. Three of these are available as items on the Options menu or as buttons on the Toolbar:

Random order   Plays the tracks randomly. This is often called *shuffle* mode on audio-only CD players.

Continuous play   Plays the disc continuously rather than stopping after the last track.

Intro play   Plays only the first section of each track. You can set the length of this intro with the Preferences command.

NOTE

If you have a multiple-disc CD-ROM drive, you'll find an additional Multidisc Play choice on the Options menu. Select this if you want to hear all the discs loaded in the drive rather than just the currently active disc.

You can select these playback options in any combination. To turn them on or off, open the Options menu and choose the desired item; they are active when checked. Alternatively, click on the button for that command (the button appears pressed when the command is active). Here are the buttons you use:

If none of these commands are active, CD Player plays the tracks in full and in sequence, stopping after the last track.

Other play options include whether or not the current disc keeps playing when you close CD Player and playing a custom list of tracks, covered in the next section.

Cataloging Your CDs and Creating Play Lists

If you're willing to do a little typing, CD Player will keep a "smart" catalog of your disc collection. Once you've entered the catalog information, such as the disc title, the artist, and the track titles, CD Player automatically displays these details whenever you reload the disc:

Note that if you have a multidisc CD-ROM drive (or more than one unit), you can choose from the available drives by letter using the list in the Artist area.

Cataloging a Disc   When you load a disc that hasn't been cataloged, CD Player displays generic disc information. The Artist area reads *New Artist*, and the Title area says *New Title*. Tracks are titled by number (*Track 1*, *Track 2*, and so on).

To enter the actual information for the current disc, choose Disc ➤ Edit Play List, or, if the Toolbar is visible, click on the corresponding button (the one at the far left, shown here on the left). The dialog box shown in Figure 9.3 will appear.

The top area in this dialog box, labeled Drive, identifies the location of the disc being cataloged. If you have a multidisc player, you can double-check whether you're working with the correct disc here.

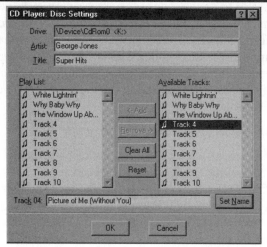

FIGURE 9.3: The Disc Settings dialog box

Type in the artist and title of the CD in the appropriate areas at the top of the dialog box. To type in track titles:

1. Select a track in the Available Tracks box (the one at the *right* of the dialog box).

2. Type in the track title in the Track area at the bottom of the dialog box.

3. Click on the Set Name button to change the current name.

You can change any of this information at any time. When you're satisfied with your entries, go on to create a play list as described below or click on OK to return to CD Player. The disc information will appear in the appropriate areas of the window.

Creating a Play List   The typical CD has some great songs, a few that are good to listen to but aren't favorites, and one or two that are just terrible. CD Player lets you set up a custom play list for each disc so you never have to hear those dog songs again. If you like, you can even play your favorites more often than the others (be careful, you might get sick of them).

Here's how to create a play list:

1. In the Disc Settings dialog box (Figure 9.3), the Play List box on the left side of the window displays the tracks in the play list. Initially, the box displays all the tracks on the disc in order.

2. If you just want to remove one or two tracks, drag each track off the list as follows: Point to the track's icon (the musical notes) in the Play List box, hold down the mouse button, and drag to the Available Tracks box. Alternatively, you can highlight each track in the Play List box and click on the Remove button. To remove all the tracks and start with an empty list, click on Clear All.

3. You can add tracks to the play list in two ways:

   ▶ Drag the track (or tracks) to the Play List box using the same technique for deleting tracks but in the reverse direction: Starting from the Available Tracks box, drag the track to the desired position in the play list. You can add a group of tracks by dragging across them to highlight them, releasing the mouse button, and then dragging from the icon area to the play list.

   ▶ Use the Add button: Highlight one or more tracks in the Available Tracks box and click on Add. In this case, the added track always appears at the end of the list.

4. If you want to start again, click on Reset. The Play List box will again show all the tracks in order.

5. Click on OK when you've finished your play list to return to the main CD Player window.

Playing Discs with the Play List   CD Player always selects the tracks it plays from the play list. Before you make any modifications, the play list contains all the tracks on the disc, and you'll hear every track when you play the disc. Once you've created your own play list, though, CD Player plays only the tracks on the list. If you select Random Order play, the program randomly selects tracks from the play list, not from all the tracks on the disc.

The play list tracks are accessible individually in the Track area near the bottom of the CD Player window. To move to a particular track, just select it in the list. If the disc is already playing, the selected track will start. Otherwise, click on the Play button to start it.

TV Viewer

One of my favorite multimedia applications in Windows 98 is the TV Viewer. It's probably not installed in your system, because it's an option.

To install it from the CD, run Control Panel ➤ Add/Remove Programs ➤ Windows Setup ➤ TV Viewer. You may be prompted to reboot the computer several times before the installation is complete, so close up any work in advance.

TV Viewer works in conjunction with special TV cards and video capture cards/drivers that are compatible with DirectShow 2.0 and WDM (drivers that are built into Windows 98). Even if you don't have a video capture card or TV display card, you can still take advantage of the program listing guide, which downloads TV listings from the Web and displays them in various formats that put *TV Guide* (even the online version) to shame. You can search for shows, times, show types (sci-fi, drama, specials, etc.), and set reminders so your computer reminds you not to miss a show.

With the appropriate hardware, you can select and tune among hundreds of analog (broadcast and cable) or digital satellite television programs, and navigate to Web channels and other information broadcast through these networks. For satellite reception, drivers specifically written for the Broadcast Architecture are required. Check with your satellite TV provider to see whether their service is compatible with TV Viewer.

You will need a PC system capable of running Microsoft Windows 98 or Windows NT Workstation 5.0, including:

▶ A Pentium-class PC with at least 16MB RAM

▶ Microsoft Windows 98 or Windows NT Workstation 5.0

▶ Television or standard VGA monitor (large screen monitor optional)

▶ Supported TV tuner and video card(s)

▶ Wireless remote control device (optional)

▶ Modem and Internet connection (optional)

TIP

For more information on supported hardware, search the Microsoft Web site for Broadcast Architecture. (When I wrote this chapter, the information was in a password-protected area of the site, for registered beta-testers, but it should be publicly accessible by the time you read this.) Visit http://www .microsoft.com/windows/tv/home.htm for the latest information about Microsoft's plans to integrate digital TV, the Web, and your PC.

What's So Cool about TV Viewer?

For starters, you watch TV either on the whole screen or in a window while you work, and the quality is very high. The picture is much sharper than on a standard TV; and some of the TV cards perform "line doubling," drawing twice as many lines on the screen as on a normal TV. This results in a better-looking picture, especially since you are typically watching from just a couple of feet from your screen. Most TV tuner cards decode stereo sound, so the sound will be good as well. Further, you also get the benefit of *enhanced TV* viewing. Here are some of the potential benefits of enhanced TV viewing (once this technology is more firmly developed):

▶ News and weather reports can be accompanied by local or other specialized information that satisfies the needs of limited audiences.

▶ Educational programs could spice things up with references and links to other programs, and locations on the Web.

▶ When watching sporting events, you could read statistics, or even create your own data sheets for personalized tracking of favorite players or teams. You could hear or read additional syndicated commentary.

▶ Shows can be enhanced by letting the viewer respond and interact. Viewers can then play along with game shows, enter contests, take quizzes, vote on issues presented in the show, express opinions, and take part in polls. Consumers using a back channel can actually investigate and purchase things from the comfort of their living rooms.

NOTE

Of course, your Internet connection must be correctly configured and working to download Program Guide information from the Web and to interact with shows.

How It Works

At its simplest, TV Viewer simply picks up TV signals from an antenna or cable TV input plugged into your TV tuner card and displays the result in a resizable window. Windows 98 provides the TV tuner program to make this happen. If your TV tuner card is supported, Windows 98 also supplies all the drivers. If not, you'll get them in the box with the card.

Going a step beyond that, if you're on a digital satellite system, you'll probably have to get a special accompanying card (either external or mounted inside the PC) that decodes the digital signals and then pumps them into the TV card.

You can download your program listings either from a broadcast channel or over the Web. It's much faster over the Web. The TV Viewer program is set up to decode the broadcast listings from StarSight and load them into the Program Guide.

Using TV Viewer

To run the program, first install it as I explained above. Then run it either by clicking on the TV set icon in the Quick Launch bar or choose Start ➤ Programs ➤ Accessories ➤ Entertainment ➤ TV Viewer. The first thing you'll notice upon running the program is that it takes a bit of time to load. You'll see the TV Viewer "splash screen" first and after a little wait you'll be walked through setting up the program the first time. There a man's voice telling you what to do. Just listen and follow the instructions.

If you're already hooked up to a good TV source (antenna, cable, satellite), have the wizard scan for channels. I have found that when I'm using a cheesy antenna, I have to input the channels manually or they don't get registered because the signals isn't strong enough. (I'll show you how to do that shortly.) And if you have a Web connection, choose that as the source for your Program Guide data, not the broadcast option, which can take hours to download, though you may be able to do this in the background. If you download from the Web, you'll have to answer a few questions about your zip code and perhaps specify what your source of TV signal is (which cable company, which local broadcast area), as in Figure 9.4.

After a few minutes of downloading, the Web page should tell you that the process is now complete. You can start using the program, and you'll see something like what I have in Figure 9.5. It looks totally unlike anything else in Windows 98, so get ready, since the interface is completely new and a little annoying at first. But it's pretty easy to learn, so don't worry.

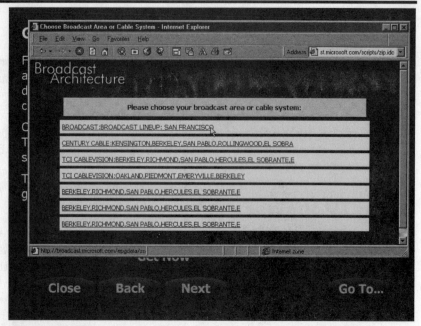

FIGURE 9.4: Specifying your broadcast medium when using the StarSight Program Guide Web download

NOTE

Only the shows displayed in green are being broadcast currently. Other times are displayed with a blue background. Clicking on them does nothing.

TIP

You may not have program listings, either because you aren't connected to the Web and therefore can't download them from the Net, or you don't live in an area that broadcasts the listings over the air. Not to worry. If you don't have program listings you can still watch TV. You just click on the TV channel number over to the left, or press the PageUp and PageDown keys to change channels. If you have no channels except 1 and 99 showing, you have to add your channels manually. See that section below.

Click here to see what is currently on this channel.

Preview appears here.

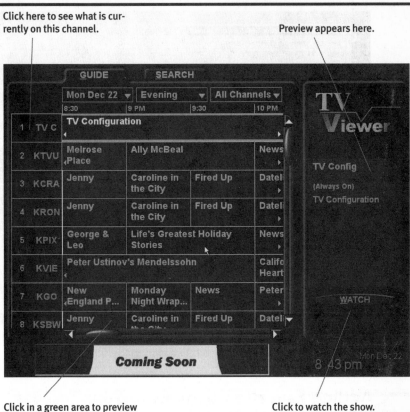

Click in a green area to preview
the show.

Click to watch the show.

FIGURE 9.5: Typical Program Guide appearance. Click on a green area to preview
a show on the right. Click on Watch to remove the guide from view.

Adding (and Removing) Channels Manually

Just like when you set up a new TV or VCR, the automatic scan option
can add channels you don't want, or can skip over weak channels and not
add them. To manually add or remove channels, do this:

1. With the TV Viewer window active (or full screen), press Alt
   or F10. This brings up a big toolbar with a few icons on it.

2. Click on Settings in the toolbar. In the resulting dialog box,
   click on Add Channels. Add and enter the number, as you
   see in Figure 9.6. To remove a channel, select it and click
   Remove.

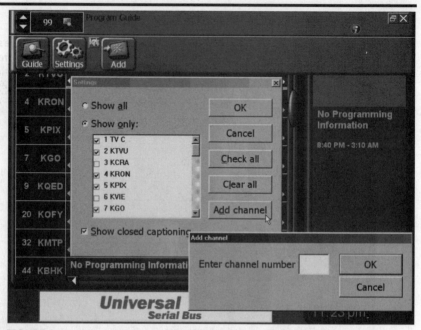

FIGURE 9.6:   You can add or remove channels using the Settings box. You also
choose which channels to display in the Program Guide.

Adding Favorite Channels to Your Toolbar

You can have up to five favorite channels in your toolbar, making it easy
to switch between favorite channels. If you have five and add another, the
oldest one disappears and is replaced by the new one.

1. Display the toolbar.

2. Select a channel you want, using one of the various techniques.

3. Click on Add:

The new channel appears on the toolbar. Click it now to switch to that
channel.

TIP

When you're viewing full-screen, just move the pointer to the top of the screen and wait a second. The toolbar will appear. If you then move it away from the top of the screen, the toolbar will disappear after a few seconds. Pressing Esc always makes the toolbar go away, too.

Remote Controls and Special Keys While Watching

The TV Viewer is designed to work with remote controls available (or to-be-available) from your computer manufacturer (not your standard TV remote!). If you don't have a computer remote control, you're not alone. As an alternative, you can use the keystrokes listed in Table 9.1 with the TV Viewer application: The most frequently used keys are listed first.

TIP

If you have a Gateway Destination entertainment system, your remote control will work with the TV Viewer. The only exception is that the Recall button on the Gateway remote control has no function.

TABLE 9.1: Keystroke Controls for TV Viewer

KEYSTROKE	ACTION
F10	Brings up toolbar menu (favorites, guide, logins, preferences, etc. are accessible from the toolbar).
F6	Toggles windowed/full screen mode. Windowed mode is useful for displaying video while using desktop applications.
0-9	Used for changing channels. Channels are three digits.
Enter	Confirms selection.
↑, ↓, ←, →	Scrolls up/down when viewing programming grid.
Win	Brings up Start menu.
Win+Ctrl+Shift+z	Shows the Program Guide (grid view).
Win+Ctrl+z	Brings up TV Viewer if not yet started, otherwise toggles between desktop and full screen.
Win+Ctrl+v	Volume Up (on Master Mixer)
Win+Shift+v	Volume Down (on Master Mixer)

TABLE 9.1 continued: Keystroke Controls for TV Viewer

KEYSTROKE	ACTION
Win+v	Toggle Mute (on Master Mixer)
Win+Ctrl+Alt+z	Channel Up
Win+Ctrl+Alt+Shift+z	Channel Down
Win+Ctrl+Alt+Shift+f	Arrow Left (some apps may interpret as REWIND)
Win+Ctrl+Alt+Shift+p	Arrow Up (some apps may interpret as PLAY)
Win+Ctrl+Alt+f	Arrow Right (some apps may interpret as FORWARD)
Win+Ctrl+Alt+Shift+g	Recall (some apps may interpret as EJECT)
Win+Ctrl+Alt+p	Arrow Down (some apps may interpret as STOP)
Win+Ctrl+Alt+g	PAUSE

* **"Win" means the Windows key on your keyboard if it has it. Older keyboards do not have this key.**

FUTURE PLANS FOR TV VIEWER, IE, AND WEBCAST RECEIVERS

A technology called Broadcast Architecture is built into Windows 98. It's both flexible and powerful, and it allows data to be broadcast to computers in a number of ways. The chapters on Internet Explorer and the Active Desktop talk about this as it pertains to the use of IE. However, Microsoft and others are working on ways to integrate TV broadcasts into the list of media through which Web-style information can be downloaded to your computer. One application that takes advantage of this "filter and store" architecture is the Webcast receiver.

Webcast receiver exists on channel 720 in the Program Guide. Through it you can subscribe to content which may be broadcast over your LAN, local TV stations, or Direct Broadcast satellites. Then again, you may not have this option in your area, in which case 720 won't appear as a station in your Program Guide listing.

The Webcast receiver application is also available through the Webcast Channel in the Internet Explorer Channel Bar, incidentally.

CONTINUED ➡

Here's how it works. Just as when you subscribe to a site or channel in Internet Explorer, the upshot is that Web pages are downloaded to your computer in the background. When you're ready to view pages, they are there for your viewing pleasure, even if you're not online. After you subscribe to a site, the Webcast filter constantly listens for content, and when received, will automatically store this content in your Internet Explorer cache. Unlike an Internet Explorer subscription, which "hits" the requested Web pages and downloads them semi-automatically, Channel 720 waits for this information to arrive through a broadcast interface.

As of this writing, the feature wasn't fully implemented, but was being tested through participating broadcast television networks in selected cities, as well as through direct broadcast satellite networks.

MANAGING MULTIMEDIA DRIVERS AND SETTINGS

When you add a new piece of hardware to your system, such as a sound board, CD-ROM controller, MIDI board, or other piece of paraphernalia, you'll have to alert Windows to this fact by installing the correct software device driver for the job. Some drivers simply control an external player as though you were pushing the buttons on the device's control panel by hand. These types of devices are called Media Control Interface (MCI) devices and include audio CD players, video disc players, MIDI instruments, and others. Other drivers actually send the sound or video data to the playback card or hardware, as well as control the playback speed and other parameters.

You use the Add New Hardware option in the Control Panel to install the device driver. Drivers for popular multimedia items are included with Windows and will often be detected when you've added the hardware, especially if the hardware is Plug-and-Play compatible.

TIP

As a rule, when you're purchasing new stuff, avoid non-Plug-and-Play hardware like the plague.

Chapter 7 covers the use of the Add New Hardware applet; refer to that chapter if you have added new multimedia hardware to your system and it isn't being recognized.

If you are having trouble running your multimedia hardware or need to make adjustments to it, you'll have to examine the Properties of the item and its driver. Device property dialog boxes can be reached from several locations. For example, the Edit menu in the Sound Recorder applet will take you to your sound card's Properties settings, though you could also use the System applet in the Control Panel to get there.

When in doubt, always contact the manufacturer of your multimedia hardware to obtain drivers and driver updates for use with Windows 98. You can often download new drivers over the Web, but not always. Sometimes a phone call is required.

WHAT'S NEXT?

In the next chapter you'll learn about Windows 98's features for installing and working with various types of hardware. As you'll see, Plug-and-Play technology and the New Hardware Wizard make adding new devices almost as easy as plugging them in.

Chapter 10

HARDWARE MASTERY

Imagine that you've bought a new kitchen appliance from Blenders 'R Us, and it turns out that different manufacturers are the sources for the glass container, push buttons, blade, and motor. Each piece comes with an instruction booklet and its own warranty card. After assembling all the pieces, you go to make yourself a milkshake, and a message pops out: "Sorry, the Framjit 34ExY894 blade isn't sharp enough to cut frozen products. You need to upgrade to the Framjit 34ExY894 Plus." (And incidentally, the new blade exerts additional torque, requiring a new shaft—but you don't find that out until after you've bought the blade upgrade and spent several fruitless hours trying to install it.)

Adapted from *Windows 98: No Experience Required*, by Sharon Crawford

ISBN 0-7821-2128-4   576 pages $24.99

Welcome to the world of computers! Except to actually resemble computers, the blender's new blade must not fit on the new shaft, and the manufacturers blame each other. But don't worry—a new blade-shaft adapter will be available by spring at the latest.

OK, so I exaggerate for effect. But not by much.

Fortunately, starting with Windows 95, sanity has begun to triumph in the world of computer hardware. The sanity goes by the name of the *Plug-and-Play* standard. Forget that the standard used to be called Plug and Pray—these days, "PnP" in Windows 98 really works. Nevertheless, there are so many manufacturers and so much new hardware, not everything will go perfectly. This skill addresses the possible problems and their solutions.

MODEMS

Installing and configuring a modem in Windows 98 is fairly simple (almost as simple as it should be). When you first install Windows 98, the modem that's physically installed in your computer or connected to it should be detected automatically. You'll only need to deal with the following steps if the modem wasn't detected or if you later change modems.

Installing a Modem

 NOTE

In the context of this chapter, "installing" a modem or other hardware means setting up the device to work with Windows 98 (and your other software) once it has been physically attached to your computer. See Chapter 26 if you need help with the modem hardware connection, and see Chapter 24 for general instructions about opening your computer case and adding hardware internally. Also, Chapter 7 describes another tool for telling Windows 98 about hardware that's not Plug-and-Play, the Add New Hardware applet.

Before starting any modem procedure, make sure the modem is plugged in and turned on (if it's an external modem) and that the telephone wire is plugged into the modem and into the wall receptacle (for both internal and external modems). To install a modem (where none has been before) follow these steps:

1. Click the Start button, then select Settings ➤ Control Panel.

2. Click the Modems icon in the Control Panel. This will start the Install New Modem Wizard (see Figure 10.1).

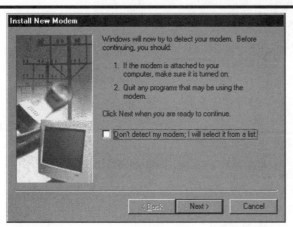

FIGURE 10.1: A Windows 98 Wizard steps you through the process of installing a modem.

3. You can let Windows 98 search for the modem, or you can select your modem directly. As a rule, let Windows try first—it's the easiest way. If Windows 98 has difficulty, you can always specify your particular modem on a second go-round. Windows will search around your communications ports and try to find a modem. When it finds one, you'll see a Verify Modem page. If the modem isn't correct, or the designation seems too generic, click on the Change button and continue with the next step.

4. If Windows 98 fails to find the modem (or if you click Change in the Verify Modem page), you'll be asked to get specific. Figure 10.2 shows the window where you select a manufacturer in the left box and the particular model in the right box. If your modem isn't listed, but you have an installation disk that came with it, click Have Disk.

5. Keep clicking OK, Next, or Finish until the installation is complete.

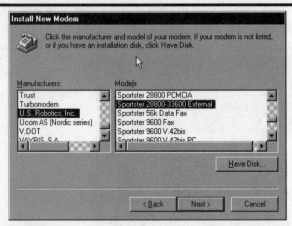

FIGURE 10.2: If Windows 98 doesn't find your modem, you can install a modem by selecting a particular manufacturer and model.

Deleting a Modem

If you change modems (or install the wrong one), it's easy to correct the situation:

1. Click Start ➢ Settings ➢ Control Panel.

2. Open the Modems icon in the Control Panel.

3. On the General page, highlight the modem name.

4. Click the Remove button, and it's gone!

Modem Settings

To find the hardware-type settings for your modem, click Start ➢ Settings ➢ Control Panel and click the Modems icon. Highlight your modem (if it isn't highlighted already) and select Properties. The modem's Properties sheet opens (see Figure 10.3).

The General Page

On the General page are:

- ▶ The full name of the modem
- ▶ The port it's connected to

- ▶ A slider for setting the volume of the modem speaker
- ▶ A drop-down box for setting the maximum speed

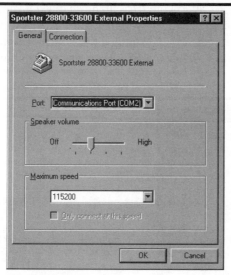

FIGURE 10.3: This is the place to check up on the settings for your modem.

NOTE

These settings (except for volume, which is strictly a matter of preference) rarely need to be fooled with. That's because they come from what Windows 98 knows about your specific modem. Only change the settings when you've had some difficulty with your modem being recognized and you're sure a particular setting is wrong.

INSTALLING A REPLACEMENT MODEM

When the time comes to replace your modem with something faster, the process is easy. Just delete the old modem using the procedure described above. Unplug the old modem and plug in the new one at the same location. Make sure the modem is turned on and that all connections—including the one to the phone line—are made; then follow the steps described under "Installing a Modem."

The Connection Page

More of the hardware settings are on the Connection page (see Figure 10.4). Again, unless you have a good reason for changing the Connection preferences, leave them alone. The Call Preferences can be changed if you find the default ones unsuitable. In particular, you may want to set a time to disconnect a call if the line is idle for an extended time. Although many online services will disconnect an inactive line, they may take quite a long time to do it.

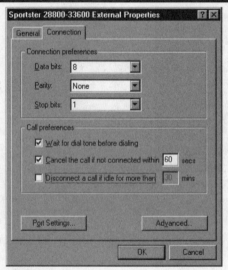

FIGURE 10.4:   The properties for the modem's connection

Advanced Settings

If you click the Advanced button on the Connection page, you'll see the page in Figure 10.5. These settings are rarely anything to be concerned about. They're just here for those odd and infrequent times when it might be necessary to force error correction or use software for error control. The one thing on this page that you might use more often is the log file. If you're troubleshooting a bad connection, click View Log to open a text file containing a log of the last connection (or attempt). Normally, this file is overwritten with the new log each time you connect. If you want to keep an ongoing log, check the Append to Log box.

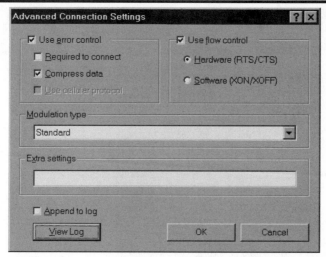

FIGURE 10.5: You might try these advanced settings with a connection that's otherwise difficult.

Dialing Properties

In addition to centralizing the modem's hardware and software settings, you also want to enter information about how you're dialing and where you're dialing from. Windows 98 allows for the configuring of multiple dialing locations, so if you travel with your computer, you can make calls from your branch office (or the condo in Maui where you take your vacations) without making complex changes every time you change locations.

Click the Modems icon in the Control Panel. Click Dialing Properties on the General page of the Modem Properties sheet and fill out the information for your location. Click the Add button to supply additional locations. When you change physical locations, you need only tell Windows 98 where you are (see Figure 10.6), and all your necessary dialing information will be loaded.

Troubleshooting

As a rule, when your modem is uncooperative, it's for obvious reasons:

- ▶ It's not plugged into a phone line.

- ▶ The modem's turned off or it's not plugged into an active electrical socket (external modems).

- ▶ One or more programs have confused the settings.

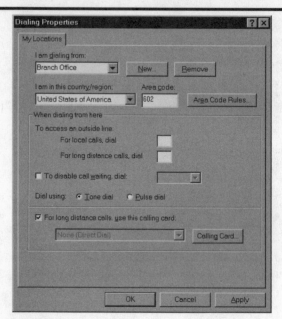

FIGURE 10.6: If you travel with your computer, you don't have to redo your communications settings when you change locations.

After you check the first two items, click on the Modems icon in the Control Panel. On the Diagnostics page, highlight the port your modem is connected to, and click More Info. The resulting page (see Figure 10.7) tells you that the system recognizes the modem and describes it in terms of speed, interrupt, memory address, and the modem's response to various internal commands.

If you receive a message that the system can't communicate with the modem, then the modem is either not plugged into a usable port, not turned on, or defective.

NOTE

ATI2 is a check of the modem's read-only memory (ROM); if the response isn't "OK," the modem may be defective. The other information in the More Info window is of little interest except to someone with an advanced degree in modemology. Depending on your modem, however, some actual information may filter through.

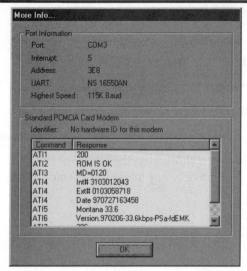

FIGURE 10.7: Here's where you verify that the system can find the modem and that the modem is responding correctly.

If your modem isn't recognized, go back to the main Modem Properties sheet and click the Remove button. After the modem's removed, close everything and reboot your system. Then go back to the Modems icon in the Control Panel and add your modem back.

SCANNERS AND CAMERAS

Most scanners and digital cameras come with their own installation programs. Windows 98 has added a Scanners and Cameras icon to the Control Panel to supply additional information and configuration options for these devices.

Click this icon to troubleshoot a problem with either a scanner or camera or to set logging options. Color profiles can also be added or removed. Color profiles are issues best addressed to the manufacturer or a photography expert.

ADDING AND CONFIGURING PRINTERS

Printing is generally a lot easier in Windows 98 than in any previous system. As in earlier versions of Windows, printers are set up to use a common set of drivers so you don't have to configure each program independently for printing. Adding or removing a printer is as easy as pointing and clicking, and sharing printers over a network is painless.

You can access your printers in any of the following ways:

▶ Click My Computer and select the Printers folder.

▶ Click Start ➤ Settings ➤ Printers.

▶ Click Start ➤ Settings ➤ Control Panel and select the Printers folder.

And of course, you can drag a shortcut to the folder (or to any of the printers in it) onto your desktop or to any folder where you'd like it.

Adding a Printer

You probably installed a printer when you installed Windows 98, but if you didn't or you want to add another or a network printer, it's very easy to do.

Adding a Local Printer

To add a printer that's connected directly to your computer, open the Printers folder as described above and follow these steps (clicking the Next button after each entry):

1. Select Add Printer.

2. When the Add Printer Wizard starts, click Next, and check the Local Printer entry.

3. Highlight the printer's manufacturer and the model name.

4. Select the port you want to use. Unless you know of some special circumstances, choose LPT1, the standard connection point for printers.

5. Type in the name you want to use for the printer and indicate whether it is the default printer for all your Windows programs. If this is the printer you plan to use practically all the time, select Yes. Otherwise say no—you'll still be able to select the printer when you want to use it. In the Printers folder, the default printer will have a checkmark by it.

6. Print a test page to verify all is well. Then click Finish.

Adding a Network Printer

A network printer is one that's plugged into someone else's computer—a

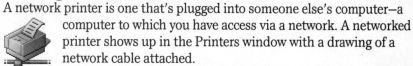

computer to which you have access via a network. A networked printer shows up in the Printers window with a drawing of a network cable attached.

To tell your computer about a network printer that you want to use, open the Printers folder as described above and follow these steps (clicking Next after each entry):

1. Open Add Printer. When the Add Printer Wizard starts, click Next, and then select Network Printer.

2. You'll need to tell the system the address of the printer. Click on the Browse button to look for available printers. Highlight the printer (as shown in Figure 10.8) and click OK.

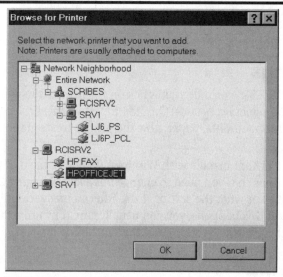

FIGURE 10.8: Here's where you select a printer on the network.

3. If you expect to print from DOS programs, click on Yes so the system can add the necessary information to the printer setup.

4. Enter the name you want to call the printer and check whether you want this printer to be the default printer. Only check Yes if you expect to be using the network printer for the majority of your printing.

5. Print a test page to make sure everything's running properly; then click Finish.

NOTE

To use a printer set up this way, the printer and the computer it's connected to must both be switched on.

Uninstalling a Printer

Sometimes you may need to uninstall a printer, which is quite easily done. Just right-click on the printer's icon in the Printers folder and select Delete. You'll be asked to confirm the deletion. You may also be asked if you want to delete files associated with this printer that won't be necessary if the printer is gone. If you're getting rid of the printer permanently, select Yes. If you're planning on reinstalling the same printer soon, select No.

Printer Settings

To get at the settings for a printer, right-click on the printer's icon in the Printers folder and select Properties. On the Properties sheet that opens, you can set details about fonts, paper, how the printer treats graphics, and so on.

The printer driver that installs with Windows 98 makes most of these settings. Change ones that you need to change but avoid changing settings if you're not clear what the setting does. You can inadvertently disable your printer. If this happens, you can usually cure it by uninstalling the printer (see the previous section) and then installing it again.

Troubleshooting

If you're not having any success getting your printer to print, or there appears to be something wrong with the printer, Windows 98 comes with excellent tools for troubleshooting the problem.

Select Help from the Start menu. On the Contents page, open Troubleshooting. Then open Windows 98 Troubleshooters and select Print. The guide is interactive: You select the problem you're having, and then you're stepped through the process of finding a solution.

TIP

For a more extensive discussion of installing and working with printers in Windows 98, see Chapter 8.

CHANGING A MOUSE

Usually, you can change the pointing device on your computer by simply turning the computer off, unplugging the old mouse, plugging in the new mouse, and then rebooting your computer.

Sometimes you'll see a window informing you that Windows 98 has found new hardware and is installing it, but more often than not, the new mouse will simply *work*. However, if your mouse needs a new (or different) driver, you can install it manually by following these steps (described in terms of keyboard commands because you can hardly use your mouse if the mouse isn't functional):

1. Use the Tab and arrow keys to move the highlight to the My Computer icon. Press Alt+Enter to open the System Properties dialog box. (The Tab key cycles from Start through any open program buttons and the last icon used, back to Start again. Once the focus is on an icon, the arrow keys can be used to move around the desktop icons.)

2. Press the Tab and arrow keys to move the focus to the Device Manager page.

3. Press the Tab key twice to move the focus to the list of devices, then use the down arrow to highlight Mouse.

4. Press the right arrow to display the devices under Mouse. Then press the down arrow to highlight the device (see Figure 10.9).

5. Press the Tab key once to move the focus to the Properties button; then press Enter. This will open the mouse's Properties sheet.

6. Press Tab again to move to the Driver page. On the Driver page, keep tabbing until the Update Driver button is selected, then press Enter. The Update Device Driver Wizard will start.

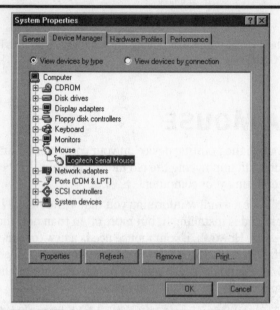

FIGURE 10.9: Selecting the mouse

From here on you can let the Wizard do the work. Use the default settings except when you get to the window shown in Figure 10.10. This window is where you specify the location for the new driver. It may have been supplied to you on floppy or CD; if not, it may be on a drive somewhere on your network. Or you can tell the Wizard to try the online Windows Update site, discussed in Chapter 11. You can check more than one box if you want to search in multiple locations.

GAME CONTROLLERS

Game controllers are what used to be called joysticks. It's possible that the name changed because not all game controllers are sticks, but I think it's because joystick sounds too much like fun.

Click on the Game Controller icon in the Control Panel to open a Properties sheet for adding a controller to the setup. Click Add to see a list of more than two dozen types that are ready to go (shown in Figure 10.11) or highlight Custom to specify another type altogether.

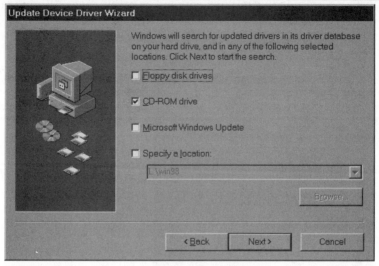

FIGURE 10.10: Telling Windows where to find the new device driver file

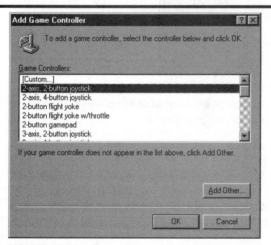

FIGURE 10.11: Game devices for all occasions

USING INFRARED DEVICES

Many new computers—particularly laptops—have infrared ports that allow for wireless communication. To communicate with a printer, for example, your computer needs an infrared port and the printer must have a corresponding infrared port and be within range. "Within range" means that the two ports must have an unobstructed "view" of each other. (Think of a television or VCR remote control.)

To set up the device, click the Infrared icon in the Control Panel.

On the Status page, you'll see what (if any) devices are in range (see Figure 10.12).

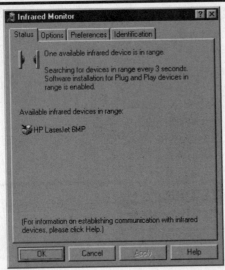

FIGURE 10.12:   Infrared devices are reported on this page of
the Infrared Monitor dialog box.

On the Options page, specify the port on which you wish to enable communications. It's important to understand that infrared communications are, shall we say, still developing. Depending on the devices involved, you may be able to communicate easily, or you may have to experiment with settings—at length—before you get results. Be prepared to call the manufacturer of the devices involved.

SETTING THE DISPLAY ADAPTER

The performance of the video system is absolutely critical to all versions of Windows. A slow video system makes your whole computer seem painfully slow—regardless of the processor or amount of RAM on your motherboard. Windows 95 increased the pressure on your video card and monitor, and Windows 98 continues to up the ante.

TIP

If your video card has 1MB of memory or less, you'll want to upgrade. You'll also have to consider whether your monitor can handle the increase in resolution and colors that the video card promises.

There are three video-related chores that you may have to deal with at some point in your Windows career. You may have to change a video card, change a video driver, or most commonly, optimize the appearance of the video system that you already have. All three are addressed in the next sections.

Changing a Video Card

Installing a new video card is one of the easiest computer chores—providing you're not completely averse to opening your computer box. Here are the steps:

1. Open the box with the new video card, make sure all the pieces are there, and read the instructions. Handle the card only by its edges. Don't handle the edge with the gold contacts.

2. With the computer turned off, unplug the monitor cable from the main computer box and then open the case.

3. Remove the screw holding in the video card (the one the monitor was plugged into). Save the screw.

4. Using a gentle rocking motion, remove the video card from the slot.

5. Put the new video card in the same slot—again, using the same gentle rocking motion. Make sure the card is firmly seated into the slot.

6. Replace the screw holding the card in place. Replace the monitor cable.

7. Close the computer case and restart the computer.

8. After the initial boot process, Windows 98 will start. The system will detect the new hardware and install it.

Video cards that are in production at the time Windows 98 is released will have drivers included with Windows 98. If you are installing a new card a year or more after the release of Windows 98, you may need to supply the floppy disk or CD that came with the new card to get the best driver.

Changing a Video Driver

Often the manufacturer of a video card will release new drivers sometime after the card has been in production. This may be to take advantage of a feature in a new operating system (like Windows 98) or to fix a bug that wasn't apparent at the time the card was manufactured.

To install a new video driver, just follow these steps:

1. Select Start ➤ Settings ➤ Control Panel and click the Display icon.

2. Click the Settings tab and then the Advanced button. This opens even more settings. Click the Adapter tab here.

3. The Adapter page (shown in Figure 10.13) shows the name of the video card and something about its features. Click the Change button.

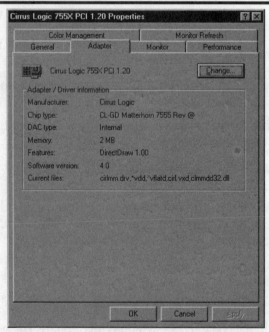

FIGURE 10.13:   The Adapter page describes the characteristics of the video card.

4. The Update Device Driver Wizard will launch and search for updated drivers.

Use the default settings except as shown in Figure 10.14, where you can be specific about the location of the new driver. As with other devices, you may have the driver file on floppy disk, CD-ROM, or a network drive; or you may want the Wizard to check the Windows Update site (Chapter 11). If you want, you can let the Wizard search all the locations.

FIGURE 10.14: Places the system should search for the new video driver.

NOTE

Deselect the floppy disk drive option if you don't have a floppy disk. Likewise, if you want the system to search the CD-ROM drive, make sure there's actually a CD in the drive. It won't do any harm, but you'll receive error messages that will slow the process.

Optimizing Video Settings

The video settings you can make are limited only by the capacity of your video card and monitor. Also, some settings—such as very high resolutions on small monitors—are aesthetically unappealing, not to mention rendering icons practically invisible. Feel free to experiment; you can't do any harm (except as noted below).

To modify your video settings, you need to open Display Properties. You can do this by clicking the Display icon in the Control Panel. Or you can right-click on a blank spot on the desktop and select Properties from the pop-up menu. Then click the Settings tab.

Changing Resolutions

Displays are described in terms of their resolution—the number of dots on the screen and the number of colors that can be displayed at the same time. The resolutions you can choose using the slider under Screen Area are determined by the hardware you have (see Figure 10.15). Resolution choices are based on what you like to look at—constrained by the capabilities of your monitor and video card. Chapter 3 describes the resolution options in detail.

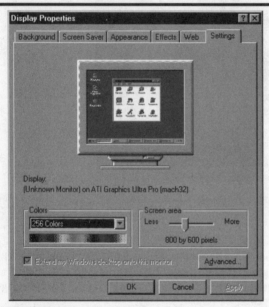

FIGURE 10.15:   Colors and resolution are configured on the Settings page.

Making Advanced Changes

Also on the Setting page is a button labeled Advanced. Click this button to get to additional pages for video configuration. Different types of video cards will have different effects on these pages. You may have other pages in addition to the ones described below. Consult the documentation for your video card and monitor for information on how these additional pages are to be used.

General   If you're using a very high resolution, the desktop elements can be very small. Try Large Fonts under Display to see if that works better for you. (Under the Display Properties' Effects page, you can also choose to use Large Icons.) This way you can preserve the higher resolution *and* have objects on the desktop that are legible.

The default setting under Compatibility is to be prompted whenever you make new color settings. While it's true that some programs require a reboot after colors and resolution have changed, most do not. If you don't have a problem program and you change color settings frequently, choose *Apply the new color settings without restarting.*

Likewise, if you change display settings often, put a checkmark next to *Show setting icon on task bar.* This will place a miniature Display icon on the Taskbar. Click the icon and you can change your display on the spot.

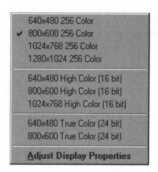

```
   640x480 256 Color
✓  800x600 256 Color
   1024x768 256 Color
   1280x1024 256 Color

   640x480 High Color (16 bit)
   800x600 High Color (16 bit)
   1024x768 High Color (16 bit)

   640x480 True Color (24 bit)
   800x600 True Color (24 bit)

   Adjust Display Properties
```

Monitor   If you change your monitor, you usually only need to plug it in and start Windows 98. The monitor will be detected and correctly installed. If the monitor isn't correctly detected, you'll have to provide the right information. Click the Change button and then supply the name of the manufacturer and the model.

NOTE

There's no reason to change settings if everything is functioning. Sometimes Windows will report "Unknown Monitor," and yet the monitor appears to work perfectly well.

Also on the Monitor page are several options relating to power management and Plug-and-Play. These are probably set correctly. However, if you have display problems such as a flashing screen after the monitor returns from Suspend mode, right-click on each option and read the description. Try checking or unchecking these options to see if your problem is solved. If you don't *have* a problem, leave the settings in their default state.

TIP

If weird things are happening to your screen—particularly a laptop screen—sometimes merely disabling the screen saver will set everything right. Screen savers often conflict with Power Management settings on laptops and computers with EnergyStar monitors.

Performance   The Performance page lets you adjust graphics acceleration. Again, if your display is working fine, leave the Hardware Acceleration set to Full. If your mouse pointer disappears frequently, try moving the slider down one notch.

Color Management   Many color profiles are included with Windows 98 and you can choose one or many. Click Add and select a profile. Add as many as you like. Highlight one and click Set As Default.

NOTE

See the previous section "Changing a Video Driver" for information on the Adapter page.

WHAT'S NEXT?

Windows 98 provides extensive tools for keeping your computer and its software running smoothly. In Chapter 11, Sharon Crawford and Neil Salkind show how to use ScanDisk, Disk Defragmenter, and other utility programs for system maintenance.

Chapter 11
MAINTAINING THE SYSTEM

Computers appear to be intelligent but, as we all know, they're only as smart as their software. Computers still have problems with internal errors—frequently caused by conflicts among programs—and require regular maintenance to operate at their best. This chapter covers the tools that perform that maintenance. In addition, you'll learn about the merits and demerits of FAT32, a newly developed Windows file system that can make efficient use of your available hard drive space.

Adapted from *Windows 98: No Experience Required*, by Sharon Crawford (ISBN 0-7821-2128-4   576 pages $24.99), and *The ABCs of Windows 98*, by Sharon Crawford and Neil J. Salkind (ISBN 0-7821-1953-0   384 pages $19.99)

RUNNING SCANDISK

Whenever a computer is turned on and operating, a lot of complicated tasks are going on inside. Fortunately, you're spared specific knowledge of these goings on, but you still have to deal with the consequences. As in most complex systems, errors are made, and, if not corrected, they tend to pile up into serious problems.

ScanDisk is protection against the accumulation of serious problems on your hard drive. It's a direct descendant of the CHKDSK utility in DOS, with many added features much like those in the justly famous Norton Disk Doctor.

You should run ScanDisk frequently—at least weekly. Once a month you should run its Thorough testing procedure, so the hard disk surface is checked for problems in addition to the standard checking of files and folders.

NOTE

You may have seen ScanDisk when you installed Windows 98, because part of the installation routine is to do a quick check of the hard drive to look for errors. Also, if you turn the computer off or reboot without the proper sign-off routine, ScanDisk runs automatically when the computer starts up again.

Starting ScanDisk

To run ScanDisk, follow these steps:

1. Click the Start button and select Programs ➤ Accessories ➤ System Tools ➤ ScanDisk. This will open the window shown in Figure 11.1.

2. Highlight the drive you want tested.

3. Select the type of test and whether you want ScanDisk to fix all errors automatically or prompt you.

4. Click Start to run.

NOTE

If the *Automatically fix errors* box is checked, ScanDisk will repair most errors without consulting you again. Such corrections are made based on the settings you can review by clicking the Advanced button.

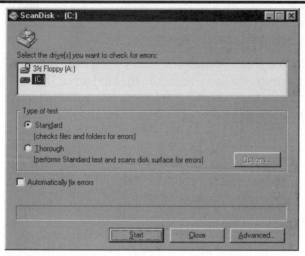

FIGURE 11.1: The basic ScanDisk window

Changing ScanDisk Settings

Click the Advanced button to see (and change) the settings that Scan-Disk uses.

> **Display summary**   This setting controls whether you see a summary of ScanDisk's findings after a check (see Figure 11.2).

FIGURE 11.2:   This is ScanDisk's summary report on the drive just scanned.

Log file By default, ScanDisk creates a new log detailing its activities every time it's run. If you want one long continuous log or no log at all, change the setting.

Cross-linked files A cross-link occurs when more than one file tries to use the same area (cluster) on the hard drive. The information in the cluster is probably correct only for one file (although it might not be correct for either of them). The Make Copies setting attempts to make some order out of the mess by copying the information in the cluster to both of the files that are contending for the space. This is the best of the three settings—it may not save your data, but the other two options definitely won't.

Lost file fragments File fragments are a fact of computer life. You can leave the default setting to convert them to files. (They'll be given names like FILE0001 and FILE0002 and deposited in your root directory.) The odds are very high that these fragments aren't useful, and they do take up valuable disk space. I always set this to Free, and I have never lost anything valuable—but you can be extra cautious and leave it at Convert to Files. (Just remember to go look at these files periodically and delete the junk.)

WHY SCANDISK RUNS AUTOMATICALLY

When you turn off your computer using the Start ➢ Shut Down procedure, Windows 98 goes through an orderly process of closing open files, deleting temporary files, and ending its own internal operations. That's what is going on between the time you order the shut down and the time you see the screen telling you it's OK to turn off the computer.

However, if you turn the computer off without going through the shut down procedure, when you start up again, ScanDisk will run automatically *before* Windows 98 is launched.

You may have turned the computer off by accident or because applications caused a lock-up; either way, the results will undoubtedly be file fragments, lost files, and other detritus left on the hard drive. It's even possible that a crash could produce errors that could prevent a normal reboot. ScanDisk finds and fixes those sorts of serious errors *and* minor problems that could accumulate and cause trouble in the future.

Check files for   The default is to look just for invalid names, although you can add dates, times, and duplicate filenames if you want. It will slow down ScanDisk's progress, but not dramatically.

Check host drive first   If you have a compressed drive, errors are sometimes caused by errors on the host drive. Leave this box checked so the host drive will be examined first.

Report MS-DOS mode name length errors   What with the mixture of long filenames and the eight-plus-three filenames used in MS-DOS mode, errors can result. Check this box for a report on name length errors.

FIXING DISK FRAGMENTATION

Windows 98 is like its Windows and DOS predecessors in that when it writes a file to your disk, it puts it anywhere it finds room. As you delete and create files, over time a single file can have a piece here, a piece there, another piece somewhere else. When a file is spread over multiple places, it's said to be *fragmented*.

This isn't a problem for Windows 98—it always knows where these pieces are. But it will tend to slow file access time because the system has to go to several locations to pick up one file. The Disk Defragmenter in Windows 98 addresses this problem, plus it can rearrange the files on your hard disk to improve the speed at which programs start up.

NOTE

If you are upgrading from a previous version of Windows, you'll notice that Disk Defragmenter no longer reports the fragmentation percentage of a drive. Some specific fragmentation of program files may be desirable for better performance, so the percentage of fragmented files is less important.

As a matter of good housekeeping, you should probably run Disk Defragmenter about once a month. Here's how it's done:

1. Click the Start button and select Programs ➢ Accessories ➢ System Tools ➢ Disk Defragmenter.

2. You'll be prompted to choose the drive you want to defragment; use the drop-down list to select one. You can also select All Hard Drives from the list.

3. Click OK to start Disk Defragmenter. Once the process starts, you can click Show Details to get a cluster-by-cluster view of the program's progress. Or you can just minimize Disk Defragmenter and do something else. If you write to the hard drive, Disk Defragmenter will start over—but in the background and without bothering you.

TIP

If you have Microsoft Office 95 or 97 installed, pause Find Fast while Disk Defragmenter runs. Do this by opening Find Fast in the Control Panel and clicking Find Fast Index ➤ Pause Indexing.

If you want to check out Disk Defragmenter options, click the Settings button rather than OK. The dialog box is shown in Figure 11.3. Here's what the options mean:

Rearrange program files so my programs start faster   Windows 98 keeps track of how often you start each program on your machine and what files are required. Disk Defragmenter can use this information to optimize the location of program files for faster startup. In the process, it deliberately fragments some program files, so you should not use a third-party disk defragmenter (such as Norton Utilities) if you use this option.

Check the drive for errors   Disk Defragmenter checks the drive before defragmenting. If it finds errors, you'll be advised of this fact, and Defragmenter won't continue.

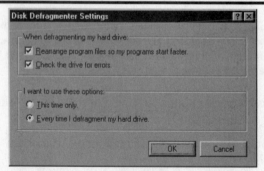

FIGURE 11.3:   The Disk Defragmenter options

NOTE

When Disk Defragmenter finds an error on your disk, run ScanDisk to repair the problem, and then run Defragmenter again.

Select whether these options are for this session only or should be saved for future sessions.

DISK CLEANUP

The Windows operating system creates a mass of temporary files and cached files—all designed to speed up the performance of the graphical interface. These files do a pretty good job of it, too, but there are too many of them, and they often don't get deleted when they should be. The result is a lot of files cluttering up your hard drive. Files that have inscrutable names and an unknown purpose.

Disk Cleanup is a new tool included with Windows 98 that is aptly represented as a small broom. When you run it, Disk Cleanup checks for files that can be safely deleted and then presents a listing of such files.

To start Disk Cleanup, click the Start button, then select Programs ➤ Accessories ➤ System Tools ➤ Disk Cleanup. The program will first run a check on the hard drive and then open a window like the one shown in Figure 11.4.

TIP

To run Disk Cleanup on a drive other than the C drive, open My Computer. Right-click on the drive you want to check and select Properties from the pop-up menu. Click the Disk Cleanup button on the Properties sheet.

Understand that just because a file *can* be deleted doesn't necessarily mean it *should* be deleted. It all depends on your needs. Some of the categories that Disk Cleanup finds are listed below. Options will vary in each Cleanup window.

Temporary Internet files   These are from various Web sites that you've visited, and they can make reconnecting to a Web site much faster. But there's no point in keeping them around forever. Click the View Files button. Choose Details from the View menu, then click Last Accessed (see Figure 11.5). Delete anything with a Last Accessed date of more than six months ago.

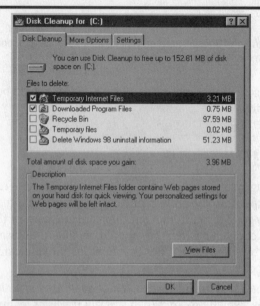

FIGURE 11.4: Disk Cleanup reports on files that can be deleted.

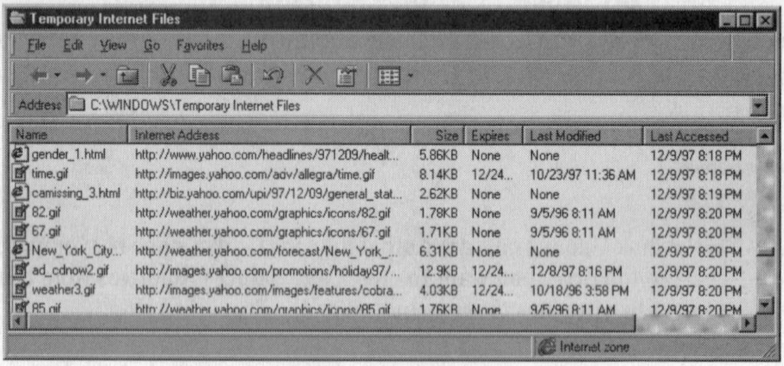

FIGURE 11.5: Select and delete Web files that you haven't used for a long time.

Downloaded program files   These are also files downloaded
from Web sites. They are ActiveX or Java applets that produce
effects on the Web pages you've visited.

Old ScanDisk files in the root folder   These are the recov-
ered file fragments converted into files described under "Running ScanDisk."

Part i

Recycle Bin   If the Recycle Bin settings are correctly configured, you shouldn't need to empty the bin to clear space on your hard drive. If the Recycle Bin is too large, reset it to some smaller size (see Chapter 5).

Temporary files   These are files created by Windows and Windows programs. In the normal course of events, these are routinely deleted by the operating system. Any that remain to be found by Disk Cleanup can be safely deleted. If you're at all unsure, use Windows Explorer to look at the files in the Temp folder inside your Windows folder. Any files older than a few days are strays and should be deleted.

Temporary setup files   Along with Windows setup files, these can be deleted, because a process long since finished created them.

Delete Windows 98 uninstall information   These are files you can obviously clear away once you have Windows 98 installed and running.

Put a check mark next to the categories you want to delete. The zealousness with which you delete whole categories of files is largely dependent on the amount of hard drive space you can afford to squander. If your available free space consistently hovers at 50MB or less, use Disk Cleanup with as much ruthlessness as you can muster. If you have a more recent multi-gigabyte hard drive, and you have hundreds and hundreds of megabytes of free space, run Disk Cleanup every two or three months just to get rid of the totally useless stuff.

TIP

Click the Settings tab to set Disk Cleanup to run automatically if the drive runs low on space.

NOTE

The More Options tab in Disk Cleanup just offers you alternate paths to the Adding/Removing Programs program in the Control Panel (see Chapter 7) and to FAT32 Drive Conversion (covered later in this chapter).

DOING A SYSTEM TUNE-UP

We're all fallible. We promise ourselves to faithfully do our computer maintenance tasks, and yet they often, in the press of events, don't get done. Fortunately, Windows 98 comes with a tune-up application called Maintenance Wizard that—run once—will set up Scan Disk, Disk Defragmenter, and Disk Cleanup to run automatically on a schedule you specify.

To start the Maintenance Wizard, follow these steps:

1. Click the Start button and select Programs ➤ Accessories ➤ System Tools ➤ Maintenance Wizard.

2. Select Express Setup and click Next. Choose one of three daily time slots for the tune-up process. The easiest, if you don't mind leaving your machine on all the time, is Nights. If it's an older machine that can't go to standby mode to conserve power, you may want to choose a different schedule.

3. Click Next, and the Wizard lists the three tasks to be performed, as shown in Figure 11.6.

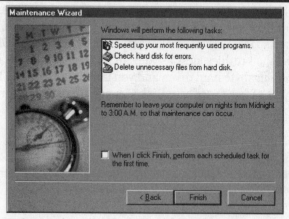

FIGURE 11.6:   Here's what the Maintenance Wizard can do for you.

Speed up your most frequently used programs   Disk Defragmenter will run weekly, processing all your hard drives with the option *Rearrange Program files so my programs start faster*.

Check hard disk for errors ScanDisk will run weekly with its default settings, checking all your hard drives.

Delete unnecessary files from hard disk Disk Cleanup will run at the beginning of each month. It will remove temporary Internet files, downloaded program files, old Scan-Disk files in the root directory, and temporary files.

4. Click the check box at the bottom of the dialog box if you want all the maintenance operations to run for the first time immediately after finishing the setup.

5. Click Finish. Now all you have to do is remember to leave the computer on at the appropriate times so that the programs can run.

You can also choose a custom setup which allows you to make very specific settings for when the programs will run and what their individual settings will be.

USING TASK SCHEDULER

The Task Scheduler icon appears in the System Tray at the end of the Taskbar on your desktop. Double-click the icon to open the Scheduled Tasks system folder. If you have already run the Windows Maintenance Wizard, you'll find a list of scheduled tasks already in the folder.

Click the Add Scheduled Task item to run the Scheduled Task Wizard, which will start any program on your computer according to a schedule you decide. The Wizard is simple and straightforward. You choose from a list of all the programs on your computer, then set the schedule. Schedule options include When My Computer Starts and When I Log On, so you can use Task Scheduler to start programs that you always want running when you work.

WINDOWS UPDATE

In years past, bugs or other problems in software were yours to live with until a new version of the software came out. If the maker of your printer or modem didn't produce satisfactory drivers for a particular operating system, you could even be forced to buy new hardware or do without. If you were very knowledgeable, you might be able to download bug fixes from the manufacturer's bulletin board system, or later, their site on the Internet. However, this was an avenue all but closed to the average user.

Windows Update is Microsoft's attempt to resolve this problem of keeping up-to-date by providing a single site for bug fixes, program patches, and hardware drivers.

Click the Start button and select Windows Update. This launches Internet Explorer and connects to the Windows Update Web site. To check for updated drivers or system files, click the Update Wizard link.

NOTE

If you haven't previously registered your copy of Windows 98, you'll be asked to now. Read the registration screens carefully. You only have to submit the system and software information, if you choose to do so.

The Update Wizard will start (see Figure 11.7).

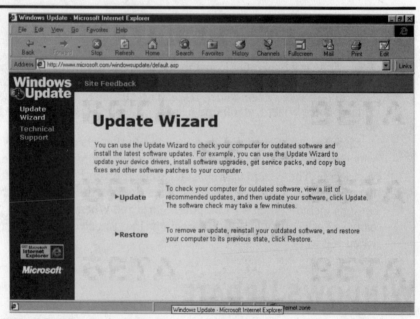

FIGURE 11.7: Running the system Update Wizard

The Update Wizard includes active components that must be downloaded and run by Internet Explorer on your system.

After the necessary components are downloaded, you will see a message that your system is being scanned to see what files need to be updated. When the scan is complete, the Update Wizard will present a list of available updates for your system. To install an update, click it and then click the Install button.

The Update Wizard also offers a restore function that allows you to return to your previous version of an updated file. You might need to do this if the update causes unexpected problems on your system.

TIP

A system update requires that the update site communicate with your computer. This means you may have to bypass some security warnings. You are not going to receive any viruses or Trojan horses or other vermin from a Microsoft Web site. However, if you're at all squeamish about letting an automated program scan your system, don't use Windows Update.

USING SPACE EFFICIENTLY

Windows 98 takes hundreds of megabytes of hard disk space, and some applications nearly reach that scale. Space can soon be at a premium, even on a large hard drive. Windows 98 includes two features that can effectively expand your hard drive by using the space on it more efficiently.

FAT32   Makes more efficient use of drives and partitions over 512MB by reducing wasted space.

DriveSpace 3   Compresses files so they take up less space.

The two systems are unrelated *and* mutually exclusive: You can't use DriveSpace on a FAT32 hard drive.

FAT32 is generally more useful on newer computers, which tend to have hard drives over one gigabyte (1000MB), often in the two to three gigabyte range. DriveSpace is more useful on machines with hard drives of about a gigabyte or less. It is essentially the same in Windows 98 as it was in Windows 95, except that it includes features that were part of the Plus! Pack for Windows 95.

NOTE

A *partition* is a section of a hard drive. When a hard drive is new, or if you are willing to wipe it clean, it can be divided into multiple partitions. Windows 98, like other operating systems, sees these partitions as separate drives, although they are located on the same physical hard drive. The drive sizes referred to in discussing FAT32 and DriveSpace actually refer to the size of individual partitions, not the whole physical drive. However, most computer manufacturers format hard drives as one giant partition, so it usually amounts to the same thing.

FAT32

FAT is an acronym for File Allocation Table. From their beginnings, MS-DOS and Windows have used the FAT system for keeping track of the contents of hard drives. Basically, the directory (or folder) tells the operating system where to look in the FAT, and the FAT stores the list of hard drive clusters, or allocation units, where the file is located.

The system used by DOS in the 1990s, and by the original version of Windows 95, is now called FAT16. It could divide a hard drive into, at most, 65,536 allocation units, which meant that as hard drives got bigger, allocation units also had to get bigger, and large allocation units waste space.

The FAT32 system allows for a much larger file allocation table, which means smaller allocation units and much less wasted space. On a drive in the one to two gigabyte size range, containing about 7500 files (which is typical for a Windows 98 machine), the saved space amounts to about 100MB.

Conversion Facts

Microsoft introduced FAT32 in 1996 as an interim improvement to Windows 95, but made it available only to computer manufacturers, to be installed on new machines. So although you couldn't buy the FAT32 version of Windows 95 in a store, the system has now been installed on millions of computers and is known to be reliable.

There are several limitations on the use of FAT32. The first is that it is not designed for use on hard drives smaller than 512MB, or about 537 million bytes, the units by which hard drive sizes are stated by the manufacturers.

The second important limitation has to do with the use of operating systems other than Windows 98. No other operating system (OS) can read a hard drive formatted with FAT32. If you run other operating systems on your computer (such as Windows NT, Windows 95, DOS, or Unix), they will have no access to drives that you have converted to FAT32. It also means that you cannot dual-boot Windows 98 and any other OS if your C drive is FAT32, nor will you be able to share removable hard drives unless all parties have FAT32.

About the only way to make effective use of FAT32 on a machine that needs to run multiple operating systems is to use a third-party utility, such as System Commander, to choose the OS at start-up time. In that case, you can use FAT32 on the drive where Windows 98 is installed, as long as you don't store any files on that drive that you need to get to when running another OS.

NOTE

If your computer is connected to a network, other machines on the network still have access to hard drives that you choose to share even if you're using FAT32 and they are not.

Another thing to think about before converting to FAT32 is third-party disk utilities. Most have now been upgraded to work with FAT32, but if you have older versions, you will not be able to use them.

Briefly put, if your hard drive is larger than 512MB, and you plan to run only Windows 98, you should convert to FAT32. Use only Windows 98's own disk utilities, or others that specify they are compatible with FAT32.

Converting to FAT32

If you install Windows 98 to a newly formatted (empty) hard drive, FAT32 can be part of the installation process. If you install Windows 98 over Windows 95 or Windows 3.1, FAT32 will not be used. After Windows 98 is installed and running, you can convert your hard drive to FAT32 by using the Drive Converter program.

TIP

If your computer came from the manufacturer with Windows 95 installed, it may already be using FAT32. To find out, open My Computer and right-click on the drive. Choose Properties. On the General page, you will see File System; it will show either FAT (meaning FAT16) or FAT32.

To convert a partition to FAT32, just follow these steps:

1. Start Drive Converter by clicking the Start button, then selecting Programs ≻ Accessories ≻ System Tools ≻ Drive Converter.

2. Click Next to see the dialog box shown in Figure 11.8. On many machines, this dialog box will show only drive C. Make your choice and click Next.

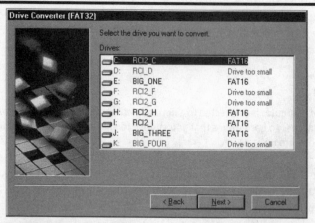

FIGURE 11.8: Choose the drive you want to convert to FAT32.

3. Windows 98 will then check your system for antivirus programs and disk utilities that are not compatible with FAT32. Once this is resolved, you can click Next.

4. The Wizard will now offer to start Backup so that you can back up your files before converting the drive.

WARNING

Although converting a drive to FAT32 is considered a safe operation, you should always back up important data before starting any task that tampers with your hard drive.

5. After creating the backup, click Next again to see the last dialog box before actual conversion of your drive. Be sure you have closed all running programs, and then click Next.

6. Your machine will reboot to MS-DOS mode and run the conversion. If you use System Commander or another multiboot system, make sure the machine reboots to your Windows 98 partition.

TIP

Although the dialog box in step 5 says the process might take a few hours, the basic conversion to FAT32 actually takes only a few minutes. What *may* take several hours is running Disk Defragmenter, which starts automatically after your drive is converted to FAT32. You can interrupt the defragmentation process if you wish. However, performance of the FAT32 drive will probably be poor until you run Disk Defragmenter and allow it to completely defragment the drive.

Returning to FAT16

Windows 98 does not include a converter for going from FAT32 to FAT16. If you find you need to do this, you have two options:

▶ Back up all your data files on the FAT32 drive. Run FDISK on the partition and choose No to the option to enable large disk support. Then format the drive and reinstall Windows 98 and any applications that were on the drive. For more details, see the installation appendices.

▶ Get a program called Partition Magic, which can convert FAT32 to FAT16 without losing the content. There has to be enough unused space on the drive to allow for the extra space the files will occupy using FAT16. If not, you can first use Partition Magic to change the partition size.

TIP

Not only can Partition Magic do FAT 32 to FAT16 conversion and resize partitions, it can also move programs from one partition to another without a reinstallation.

Compressing Hard Drives

Another way to make more efficient use of hard drive space is to use disk compression. Disk compression is helpful if you have a serious shortage of space—but in this era of super-cheap hard drives, it's a lot of trouble for a fairly modest return.

Windows 98 comes with DriveSpace 3. It will let you:

▶ Compress and uncompress a hard drive partition or a diskette.

▶ Upgrade a DoubleSpace or DriveSpace compressed drive to DriveSpace 3.

▶ Use your free space to create a new, empty, compressed partition.

Compressing an Existing Drive

To compress a drive, you need only follow these steps:

1. Click the Start button, then select Programs ➤ Accessories ➤ System Tools ➤ DriveSpace.

2. Highlight the drive you want to compress and select Compress from the Drive menu.

3. The next screen (shown in Figure 11.9) will show before-and-after pie charts for the selected drive.

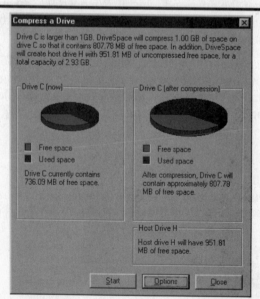

FIGURE 11.9: A drive before and after compression

4. Click Start. You'll be asked if you have an updated Windows 98 Startup disk. If you don't have a recent version of the Startup disk, make one now.

5. If you haven't backed up the files on the drive you want to compress, click the Back Up Files button and follow the instructions.

6. Click Compress Now.

7. The drive will be checked for errors, and then, if it's your C drive that's being compressed, you'll be advised that your computer needs to restart. Once you click Yes here, there's no stopping, so be sure you've done all the preparatory steps correctly, and you have something else to do during the time the compression is going on. This process can't be run in the background.

WARNING

If you're running more than one operating system, be sure the reboot is into Windows 98. This applies equally to reboots that are part of other DriveSpace conversion operations, such as uncompressing, creating a new partition, and adjusting free space.

The compression can take quite a while, especially on the older machines that are most likely to need it because of their limited hard disk space. For example, on a 75MHz 486 laptop with 16MB RAM, compressing 230MB of files took about 90 minutes. At the end of the compression cycle (an on-screen progress bar is displayed), you get a before-and-after report showing the previous space on the disk and new statistics on free space and used space.

How Compression Works

When you compress a drive—let's say your C drive—the whole thing ends up as one big file on a "new" drive called H (by default—though you can give it a later letter in the alphabet). The "new" drive H is called a host drive.

When you boot your machine, a DriveSpace command is loaded first. This tells the system to look for this big file and load it, so it looks to all the world like a regular boot into the C drive. Any other compressed drives present when you boot your machine are also recognized and interpreted.

On the Properties sheet for the host drive, there's an option to hide this drive from view. This is a good option to take, because there's not a thing you can do in a host drive. There's a little bit of free space, but this big compressed file that you can't read and mustn't fool with takes up the rest.

DriveSpace 3 Settings

Choose Advanced ➤ Settings in DriveSpace if you want to control how Drive-Space does its job. You can either set the degree of compression to be used when saving new files or limit the circumstances where compression is used. For a more complete description of each option, click the ? button in the top-right corner, then click the item for which you want more information.

TIP

To see the status of compression on a drive, right-click the drive in My Computer. Choose Properties, then look at the information on the Compression page.

Uncompressing a Drive

Providing you have room for the data once it's all uncompressed, you can get rid of the compression on a drive at any time. Just follow these steps:

1. Click Start ➤ Programs ➤ Accessories ➤ System Tools ➤ DriveSpace and highlight the drive you want to uncompress.

2. Select Uncompress from the Drive menu.

3. You'll see a window showing the drive as it is now and as it will be after uncompressing. Click Start to proceed.

4. You'll see a warning about backing up your files. If you haven't backed up the files on the compressed drive, click the Back Up Files button and follow the instructions.

5. Click Uncompress Now.

6. After a while, if this is the only compressed drive on your system, you'll be asked if you want to remove the compression driver at the end of the procedure. Choose:

   No If you're still going to be reading compressed removable media (that is, floppies or removable hard drives).

Yes If you're through using any compressed drives for the foreseeable future.

The drive will be checked for errors, and then the computer will restart. Uncompressing will be completed, and the computer will have to restart yet again (if drive C is involved).

NOTE

Uncompressing takes even longer than compressing. So it's not a task to undertake when you're in a hurry.

Creating a New Partition

DriveSpace can take the free space on your drive and make it into a new partition. This partition will be compressed and will provide more storage space than the amount of space it uses.

To make a new drive in this way, follow these steps:

1. Click Start ➤ Programs ➤ Accessories ➤ System Tools ➤ DriveSpace.

2. Highlight the drive that contains the free space you want to use, and select Create Empty from the Advanced menu.

3. Accept the suggested settings or make changes as you wish.

4. When you're finished, click Start.

Compression Agent

Compression Agent works with DriveSpace 3 to control and change the degree of compression used on your files. For example, you could improve performance on file save operations by telling DriveSpace to use No Compression (see Advanced ➤ Settings in DriveSpace). Then you can have Compression Agent compress these files when your computer is not in use.

Open Compression Agent from the System Tools menu. Click Settings to choose the compression options you want. The Overview button in Compression Agent takes you to the DriveSpace Help file, which explains all the options.

Changing the compression method used on files can take a substantial amount of time, so Compression Agent is best run on a regular basis by making use of the Task Scheduler, as described earlier in this chapter.

BACKING UP AND RESTORING FILES

Your hard disk has (or will soon have) a lot of material on it that's valuable to you. Even if it's not your doctoral dissertation or this year's most important sales presentation, you'll have software (including Windows 98) that you've set up and configured just so.

Hard disk crashes are really quite rare these days, but if you are unlucky enough to have a crash, not having a recent backup can change your whole perspective on life. So resolve now to do frequent backups of your important files. If you are lucky and/or cautious enough to have a tape drive or other high-capacity backup system, you should also make less-frequent backups of your entire system.

NOTE

Don't forget, there are two types of computer users. Those who have lost their data and those who back up their files! With Windows 98's Backup feature, you'll be able to tell Windows 98 what to back up, how to do it, where to back it up to, and when to do it. So make sure you are a computer user who backs up your files.

Getting Started

To start the Backup program, click the Start button, then select Programs ➤ Accessories ➤ System Tools ➤ Backup. Your first decision is whether you want Backup to create a set of emergency disks for you to use should your hard drive crash. Creating an emergency set takes lots of disks and will take some time, but it's well worth the effort. Click OK if you want to create a set of emergency disks, and follow the onscreen instructions. Click No if you do not want to create such a set, and continue with the backup.

NOTE

If the Backup program isn't on the menu, you'll need to install it. Go to Add/Remove Programs in the Control Panel and use Windows Setup to add Backup.

Figure 11.10 shows the opening window you'll see when you open Backup the first time.

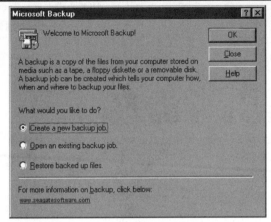

FIGURE 11.10:   Your introduction to Backup

Tape Drive or Floppies

If you have a tape drive and it's been installed properly, Backup will find it and prepare to back up to it.

WARNING
Not all tape drives are supported.

If Windows 98 doesn't find a tape drive, it will present you with a message telling you that if you really do have a tape drive, it isn't working and what to do about it. If you really don't have a tape drive, just click OK. You'll be backing up to floppies (which you already know about).

NOTE
If you have two hard drives, backing up from one to the other is as safe as any other method. But you must use two physically separate hard drives, not just different partitions on a single hard drive.

Deciding on a Type of Backup

When you decide that you need to make a backup, it's important to know what you need to back up and where you want the backup to be created.

There are three ways to perform a backup. In the Microsoft Backup dialog box, you can create a new backup job (if this is your first backup), open an existing backup job (which you created earlier), or restore files (previously backed up) that you no longer have immediate access to on your hard drive. Click OK when you're done.

Deciding What to Back Up

Before you create a backup, you should know that you don't have to back up your entire system at once. You can back up a set group of files or folders, or a specific drive on your computer.

NOTE

When you back up, don't select applications. You should have them on disk or CD anyway. If your computer came with the programs already installed, you may not have the original disks. Contact the manufacturer and ask for a set, or in that case, you may have to make a set for yourself. Better yet, if you can afford it, buy a CD-ROM player you can write to and make your backups there.

Backing Up Everything

You can back up all the files and folders on the local drive, or back up just selected files. This means that everything that is on your hard drive will be duplicated on a set of disks or on whatever medium you back up to.

TIP

If your hard disk suddenly sounds like it's full of little pebbles, there's nothing more comforting than having a Full System Backup on your shelf. You should make a Full System Backup when you first install Windows 98, after you install new applications, and occasionally thereafter. But keep in mind, if you do back up to floppy disks, the number of disks you use will be very large—possibly 30 or 40.

You need to tell Backup which folders need to be backed up every day or every week. Once you have a solid backup of your entire hard disk, you'll want to back up only certain folders on a regular basis.

Backing Up Selected Files

Regular backups involve less than the entire hard drive and will probably depend on how valuable certain files are, how difficult they would be to re-create (probably very difficult if it's a document like a college paper or a business plan), and how often they change.

Defining a File Set

If you want to back up all the files and folders on your computer, you need not specify anything else. Backup will back up everything. There's no need to define a set of files or folders. But, if you just want to back up selected files, Backup will create a *file set*.

What is a file set? Backup is based on the idea that you have a large hard disk with perhaps thousands of individual files and perhaps hundreds of different folders. You don't usually want to back up everything on the disk. Usually you'll be backing up a few folders—the folders containing your Corel drawings, your Excel spreadsheets, your WordPerfect documents, your appointment book, your customer database, and so on. A file set is a collection of files that is backed up as a unit and has a unique name. When you use Backup, you create such file sets.

TIP

You might want to make several file sets for backups of different depths. Back up really important folders at the end of every work day (or at lunch) and less important ones at the end of major projects. How to create a backup file set is covered in the following section.

Creating a Backup

In this section we'll create a backup to demonstrate how it's done. If Backup isn't running, start it now. (See the instructions in the "Getting Started" section earlier in this chapter.) Once you get through the initial dialog boxes, you should see the window shown in Figure 11.11.

Clicking the objects in the section on the left tells Backup which device, folders, or individual files you want to back up.

NOTE

Each of the drives shown in the Backup window has a tiny check box next to it. If you want to back up the entire device—every file and folder from the root to the farthest branch—click this box to automatically select everything. This, in itself, may take several minutes.

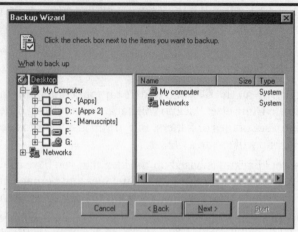

FIGURE 11.11: Designing your backup

Backing Up Particular Files or Folders

Here's how you can back up particular files or folders. For the sake of this example, we'll back up a single file, but the principle is the same for a larger selection.

1. Click your hard disk's name in the list. That will make all of the folders in the root folder of your hard disk appear in the list at the right.

NOTE

When you look at the Backup window, it looks like simply a list of folders. Where are the files? The folders appear at the top of the list, so they may be the only thing visible to you. If you use the scroll bar at the right edge of the list to move to the bottom of the list, you will see the files in the root folder of the selected device. We'll get down to the file level shortly.

2. Search through the list of folders to find your Windows 98 folder. If you want to back up every file and folder in Windows, you should click the box to the left of the Windows folder name. Instead, we are going to select a single file to back up.

3. Click the Windows folder. You'll see even more folders; scroll down until you start seeing individual files like those shown in Figure 11.12.

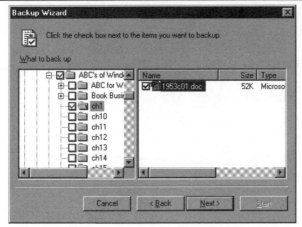

FIGURE 11.12: Individual files ready to be backed up

4. Scroll through the files in the folder until you locate the file called WIN. In the Type column, it will say Configuration Settings.

NOTE

If you have file extensions turned on, the file will be listed as WIN.INI.

5. If the files are not in alphabetical order, you can click the Name block at the top of the list to list them alphabetically. Or you might want to click the Type block and search through the configuration files for WIN.

6. When you have located the file, click the tiny box to the left of the file name in the list.

7. Click the Next button. You will now decide whether you want Windows 98 to back up all the files that you have selected or only files that are new and have been changed.

8. Click Next and select where you will back up the files that you have designated, as shown in Figure 11.13.

9. Select a media destination where the files will be backed up and click Start. For our example, we will pick the A drive.

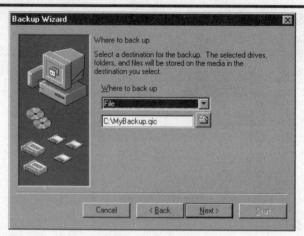

FIGURE 11.13: Selecting the files and folders you want to back up

10. Click Next and in the resulting dialog box, type the name WIN as the name of the file set. Here you can review the what, where, how, and when of the backup job. You can click the Back button to go back and change any decision you made earlier, but this is your last chance before the backup process begins.

11. Click Start and you'll see a progress report as Backup does its work. Once the backup is compete, click OK and then close the Backup dialog box.

TIP

If you want to keep this file set for future use, after you choose a destination for the backup, select Save from the File menu. Specify a name for your file set. When you next want to use it, start Backup and select Open File Set from the File menu.

Backing Up an Existing File Set

Let's do a backup of an existing file set. You'll do this once you've backed up files and folders and made changes that need to be backed up. Since we just created it, let's use the WIN file set. Here's what to do:

1. Begin by shutting down Backup. (You can do this by clicking the X icon at the extreme upper-right corner of the Backup window or by selecting Close from the File menu.)

2. Start Backup by following the instructions earlier in this chapter in the section "Creating a Backup."

3. When you get to the Backup window, pull down the Backup Job drop-down menu and click the icon WIN (or whatever you used as the name of the file set we just created). The file set will open.

4. Click Start. Make sure your backup medium (floppy disk or tape) is in the device selected, and then click OK to begin the backup process.

Choosing Backup Options

To use Backup's options, pull down the Job menu and select Options. This will display a dialog box showing six tabs: General, Password, Type, Exclude, Report, and Advanced.

Here is a description of each of the tabs:

General This tab is used to set verification of the backup to the original, determine if data will be compressed to save space or time, and to determine whether backup files will be appended or written over.

Password This tab is used to assign a password for any backup job.

Type This tab allows you to set whether you want all selected files or only new and changed files backed up.

Exclude This tab lets you set which files should be excluded from the backup. This is a very handy feature because it allows you to exclude hungry, space-eating files, such as those with a .GIF or .AVI extension.

Report This tab provides options for you to design how you want Backup to report the results.

Advanced This tab allows you to back up the Windows Registry.

Drag-and-Drop Backup

You can also drag-and-drop files that you want backed up by first placing Backup on your Desktop as an icon. You can then back up a file by dragging it to the Backup icon and dropping it. Here's how to place Backup on your Desktop as an icon:

1. Right-click the Start button and select Open.

2. In the window that opens, select Programs ➤ Accessories ➤ System Tools.

3. Right-click the Backup icon and drag it to the Desktop.

4. Release the mouse button and select Create Shortcut(s) Here from the pop-up menu.

When you're ready to back up a particular file, you can find it in the Explorer or My Computer and then drag-and-drop it on the Backup icon on the Desktop. Another way to back up a file is to make a folder called Backup. Put shortcuts to your file sets and to Backup inside the folder. If you want, put a shortcut to the folder on your Desktop. Then all you have to do is open the folder and drag the appropriate file to the Backup icon to start a backup.

TIP

Want some help backing up? Use the Backup Wizard on the Tools menu.

Restoring Files

Restoring is useful for more than recovering from disaster. It's a good way to restore large files that were backed up from your hard disk when they were no longer immediately needed. Now you can restore them and use them again.

Let's use Restore to restore the WIN configuration file we backed up earlier. (On the disk, it's called WIN.INI.) Specify where you want files restored from, what files you want restored, where you want the file restored to, and how you want the restore done. Here are the specific steps:

1. Start Backup.

2. When you get through all the introductory dialog boxes, click the tab at the top of the Backup window marked Restore.

3. In the Restore From drop-down menu, click From Here the Backup Will Be Made. In this case it is from a file. Then, select the location of the backup file. In this case, the location is A:\BACKUP.QIC.

4. Select the backup data set you want to restore.

5. Select where you want the data restored to and how you want it restored.

6. Click the Start button, and the restoration will begin.

Options for Restoring

Pull down the Job menu and select Options. You will see three tabs in the Restore dialog box (with names and functions similar to those listed in the "Choosing Backup Options" section earlier in this chapter). You can also click the Options button in the Restore dialog box to see the same set of tabs.

The tabs offer the following functions:

General   This tab lets you determine how and when you want files restored that already exist.

Report   This tab provides options for you to design how you want Restore to report the results of a restoration.

Advanced   This tab allows you to restore the Windows Registry.

WHAT'S NEXT?

As you've seen in this chapter, Windows 98 is well equipped with tools for automatically detecting and fixing problems with your computer. The preventive maintenance techniques you've learned here should keep your system running smoothly. But as we all know, "stuff happens." In the next chapter, you'll learn about using the tools that Windows 98 provides for troubleshooting.

Chapter 12
SYSTEM TROUBLESHOOTING

I n general, Windows 98 is pretty good at fixing itself. When a problem is detected, ScanDisk or some plug-and-play utility jumps into action, finds out the extent of the trouble, and notifies you what action needs to be taken. However, there are occasions when *you* must be the active party. Windows 98 includes enough system information and troubleshooting capability so that no fact about the system is hidden, if you're willing to look for it.

Adapted from *Windows 98: No Experience Required*, by Sharon Crawford
ISBN 0-7821-2128-4   576 pages $24.99

USING THE SYSTEM INFORMATION UTILITY

Support technicians require specific information about your computer when they are troubleshooting your configuration. Using the System Information utility, you can quickly find the data to answer their questions, so they can resolve your system problem.

System Information collects your system configuration information and provides a menu for displaying the associated system topics. To access System Information, click the Start button and select Programs ➢ Accessories ➢ System Tools ➢ System Information. The display is organized into three sections: resources, components, and software environment.

Resources   These are hardware-specific settings, namely DMA, IRQs, I/O addresses, and memory addresses. Click Conflicts/Sharing to see devices that are sharing resources or are in conflict (see Figure 12.1). This can help identify device problems.

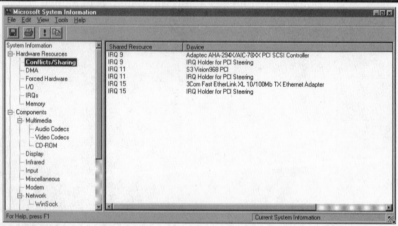

FIGURE 12.1:   Checking for IRQ conflicts

Components   Here you'll see information about the Windows configuration. You'll see the status of your device drivers, networking, and multimedia software. In addition, there is a comprehensive driver history, which shows changes made to your components over time.

Software Environment   This is a view of the software loaded in computer memory. This information can be used to see if a process is still running or to check version information.

Depending on the individual topic, you may be presented with a choice of basic, advanced, or historical system data.

Check the Tools menu for quick access to other diagnostic tools that a technician may ask you to run, such as Dr. Watson, the System File Checker, and the System Configuration Utility.

MEET DR. WATSON

Dr. Watson is a utility that runs in the background and keeps a log of errors that occur. The output of the log may not make much sense to the average user, but it can speak volumes to a service technician.

To run Dr. Watson, follow these steps:

1. Click the Start button and select Programs ➢ Accessories ➢ System Tools ➢ System Information.

2. Select Dr. Watson from the Tools menu. The Dr. Watson icon will be placed in the System Tray at the end of your Taskbar.

3. Right-click on the icon to open this menu:

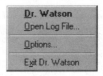

4. Choose Dr. Watson from the menu to get a snapshot of current conditions.

5. Choose Options to set how many error conditions Dr. Watson will record and to set the location of the log file (see Figure 12.2).

6. Choose Open Log File to see the incidents recorded by Dr. Watson.

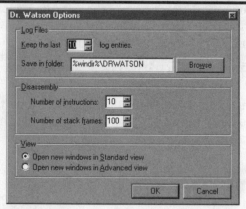

FIGURE 12.2:   Settings for Dr. Watson, the system detective

CHECKING SYSTEM FILES

System File Checker (available from the System Tools menu) is a new utility that scans the system files on your machine, checking for file corruption or other errors. System File Checker maintains a data file with characteristics of your installed system files, so it can recognize unexpected changes.

Run System File Checker only if you're having otherwise inexplicable errors. If a system file turns out to be corrupted, you can also use System File Checker to extract a clean version from the Windows 98 installation CD.

To open System File Checker, click the Start button and select Programs ➤ Accessories ➤ System Tools ➤ System File Checker (see Figure 12.3).

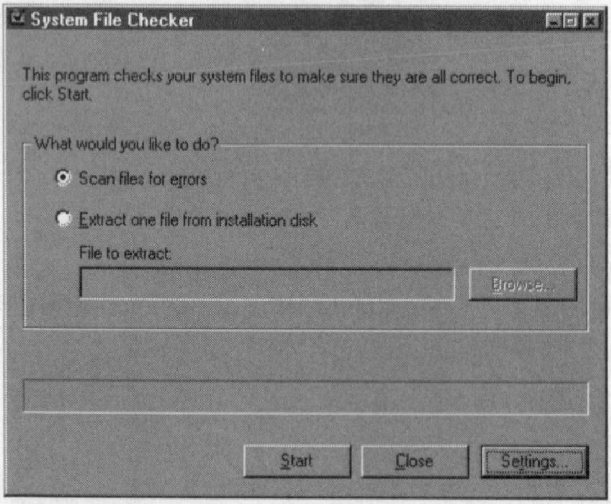

FIGURE 12.3:   System File Checker

Click the Settings button to make configuration settings for System File Checker. If a system file is corrupted or missing, you can extract that file directly from the Windows 98 CD. Click *Extract one file from installation disk.* Type in the name of the file or click the Browse button to locate the file. (Make sure the Windows 98 disk is in the CD-ROM drive.)

Click Start when you're ready to extract the file.

USING SYSTEM MONITOR

The System Monitor gives you a graphical representation of a number of processes going on inside your computer. If you know what you're looking for, sometimes the information can be helpful.

To open System Monitor, click the Start button and select Programs ➤ Accessories ➤ System Tools ➤ System Monitor.

In the initial window (shown in Figure 12.4), System Monitor tracks the processor usage.

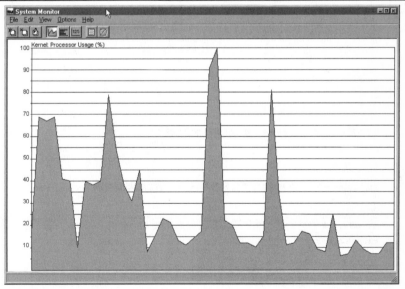

FIGURE 12.4: The System Monitor showing processor usage

To track use of other system components, select Add Item from the Edit menu. Highlight a category (see Figure 12.5), and then select the item you want to view.

Part i

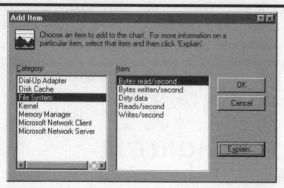

FIGURE 12.5:   Choosing the items you want to monitor

On the toolbar, click the Bar Chart button:

to display the data as a bar chart (see Figure 12.6).

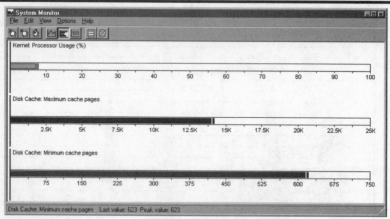

FIGURE 12.6:   Viewing three kinds of data in a bar chart

TIP

A numeric graph is also available. Click the Numeric Chart button next to the Bar Chart button to see one.

Using the Resource Meter

The Resource Meter offers visual feedback on the available Windows 98 resources. It's pretty hard to run out of resources in Windows 98, but you can get awfully low if you have enough windows open.

To put Resource Meter on the end of your Taskbar, take these steps:

1. Right-click on the Start button and select Open.

2. In the window that opens, double-click on Programs ➢ Accessories ➢ System Tools.

3. Right-click on Resource Meter and select Create Shortcut.

4. Right-click on the new shortcut and select Cut.

5. Next, go to the Windows Startup folder, using the Up icon on the toolbar at the top of the window. Click it twice to move up two levels to Programs.

6. Double-click on Startup. When the Startup window opens, right-click in an empty area and select Paste from the pop-up menu.

The next time you start up your computer, a small icon will be placed on your Taskbar. Place your pointer on the icon, and a flyover box will open, showing available resources. Or right-click on the icon and select Details. A window like the one in Figure 12.7 will open.

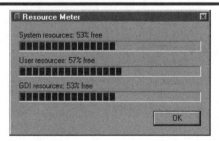

FIGURE 12.7: The Resource Meter in Details view

There's no point in trying to describe what the different resources mean, because the explanation would involve language like *memory heaps* and *device contexts*. Suffice it to say that if any of these numbers starts approaching zero, it's time to close some programs to give yourself more maneuvering room.

TIP

Sometimes, through no fault of your own, resources will dwindle dangerously, even though you have only one or two programs open. This is because one of those programs—or one you've had open recently—grabbed some resources and isn't letting them go. Blame it on bad programming practices, but the only practical solution is to reboot your computer (and then complain to the maker of the program).

TROUBLESHOOTING TOOLS

Windows 98 comes with its own set of relatively smart troubleshooting tools. If you run into a problem, try these troubleshooters first. They work very well, providing you observe some simple rules:

- ▶ Make sure you can see the Help window that contains the trouble-shooter text while you follow the instructions there.

- ▶ Resize the Help window and move it to one side of the screen so you can use the rest of the screen to follow the instructions.

- ▶ Always follow the troubleshooter steps *exactly*. If you don't, the troubleshooter can't do its job.

- ▶ After you complete a step in a troubleshooter, review the information in the Help window, and verify that you've followed the instructions.

To use a troubleshooter, click the Start button and select Help. In the left pane, click Troubleshooting, then Windows 98 Troubleshooters. The list shown in Figure 12.8 will open.

Select one that seems most appropriate to your problem. You may have to run more than one troubleshooting application to solve the problem.

TIP

After you start the troubleshooter, click the Hide icon at the top-left corner of the Windows Help window to close the left pane and make more room on the desktop.

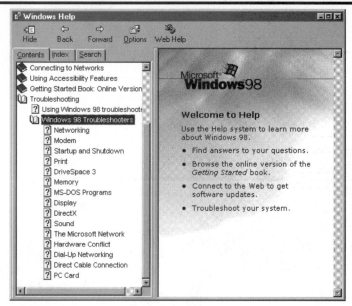

FIGURE 12.8: The list of built-in troubleshooting applications

WHAT'S NEXT?

With any luck, you will rarely, if ever, need to apply what you've just learned about Windows 98 troubleshooting.

In the next chapter, Windows expert Mark Minasi shows how you can use Dial-up Networking (also called Remote Access) to connect with your Internet Service Provider, and to log onto your office network from your home computer or on the road.

Chapter 13

WIRED 98 — REMOTE ACCESS WITH WINDOWS 98

One of the biggest features Microsoft introduced as an integral part of Windows 95 is *dial-up networking* (DUN): the ability to remotely attach to a major network, including the Internet, via a telephone or leased connection. Basically, you'll find that dial-up networking, which has been improved in Windows 98, has two main advantages:

- ▶ It can often replace whatever software you're using to dial into the Internet.

- ▶ It gives you the ability to connect from home to the office network to retrieve data or do remote network administration, and (new to 98) you can even connect to your office network over the Internet, *but in a secure fashion*.

Adapted from *The Expert Guide to Windows 98*, by Mark Minasi, Eric Christiansen, and Kristina Shapar
ISBN 0-7821-1974-3   1,008 pages $49.99

Dial-up networking also has many advantages for people who want to connect with their company's network from their home computers, while on the road, and from other places when they're not at their company's physical location.

One advantage is convenience. If you leave the office and decide to continue working on a project at home, often you'll discover that files you need were not saved to the floppy disk that you brought home with you. One option is to get in your car, drive back to work, and retrieve the files from the network. But wouldn't it be so much easier and more convenient to dial up your network from home and download the files? That's what's known as *telecommuting*.

Another advantage of DUN is remote administration. If you are a network administrator with a pager (and there are very few of you without pagers), you often get that dreaded page at 2:00 A.M. If a user locked himself out of the network (for example, he was having a bad typing day and mistyped his password three times), it becomes your job to either unlock his account or give him a new password. (If someone is actively working at 2:00 A.M., this must be a *very* important project.) Without dial-up networking, you must drive to the office and fix his user account. With dial-up networking, all you have to do is drag yourself to your computer at home, dial up the network, and perform the administrative task from home. Then—and most important—you get to go back to bed.

In addition to these advantages, dial-up networking is the way many business users and probably most home users connect with their Internet Service Provider (ISP) to access the Internet.

Now all of this probably sounds terrific, but you must be wondering, "How difficult is it to set up?" If you have ever worked with modems and telecommunications, you're probably fearing the adventure ahead of you. Good news! Once you get the terminology down, installing dial-up networking is not that difficult.

This chapter will consider:

▶ How to set up, configure, and test a DUN connection, including a PPTP connection

▶ Using the Internet Wizard to set up a DUN Internet connection

▶ Using WINS to connect to a remote network

▶ DUN vs. PPTP vs. WINS connections

▶ Installing a dial-up server

▶ Security concerns

▶ Remote access to resources via DUN

Let's begin by considering what remote access actually consists of.

NOTE

Unlike other books from which we've compiled *Windows 98 Complete*, Mark Minasi's *Expert Guide* is addressed to network administrators as well as to users. Most users will only need to read the sections of this chapter through "Using the Internet Wizard." If you need to connect to a Windows NT network, however, or if you have administrative responsibilities for a network, you should read the entire chapter.

What Is Remote Access?

Remote access (also known as *remote-node access*) makes the remote PC a node on the network, rather than the controller of a network PC. The remote PC does all the necessary processing. The remote PC should have on its hard drive all the applications that it will need, to keep the data transfer to a minimum.

So Near, and Yet So Far

Remote access to a network requires a modem, a phone line, a remote PC, and remote-access software on both ends of the connection. In effect, remote access makes the remote PC a node on the office LAN. The phone line acts as a cable that connects the remote PC to the network interface card at the office. To log on to the network, the remote user dials up the remote access server (which, depending on the type of network your company is running and how the servers are configured, may or may not be the same computer as the file server). Once connected, remote users must log on to the network just as they would if using one of the office PCs. (The security measures involved vary from product to product.)

Once logged on to the network, remote users can use the network just like any other user, according to their user rights. When a remote user accesses files, he works on them at the remote computer, only accessing the file server to save the file or to get a new one. Therefore, if the user is running Windows or other graphical user interface (GUI) applications, remote access is a faster option than remote control.

NOTE

Remote control is another form of dial-up networking, in which the remote user actually runs applications located on a network server or workstation. It has a number of disadvantages, however, the most important of which is that Windows 98 does not support it directly. Therefore, we've omitted coverage of it in adapting this material for *Windows 98 Complete*.

Of course, it will still take remote users longer to access files on the server than it will take local users, as remote users must use telephone lines for transmission instead of fast network cable. This is obviously more of a problem with bigger files. When accessing an 11K memo, it's no big deal. Accessing a 1MB *book*, however, will take significantly longer. Since the user is running the application on the remote PC, however, at least the GUI application screen needn't travel through the phone lines; only the data needs to make the trip.

WHAT ARE THE SETUP OPTIONS FOR DIAL-UP NETWORKING?

The most common method of implementing dial-up networking will be via a modem. I strongly recommend that you use a modem that follows a useful standard, for example Hayes compatibility. You definitely want to avoid modems that only talk to their evil twins, like the High Speed Transmission (HST) modems, which only talk to other HST modems.

Dial-up networking does not limit you to connecting via modem. You can use DUN to attach a cable between two machines, which turns them into a small network. DUN supports a direct connection via parallel cable or null modem cable.

Dial-up networking also supports *Integrated Services Digital Network* (ISDN) connections. In order to use ISDN for a dial-up connection, you must make sure that ISDN is supported in all the locations that you will be calling to and from.

NOTE

Dial-up networking is the same as *Remote Access Service* (RAS), with which you are familiar if you have used Windows for Workgroups 3.1x or Windows NT. Dial-up networking in Windows 98 is more powerful and flexible than WfW's RAS but not as complete as Windows NT's RAS.

What Connection Protocols Are Supported by Dial-Up Networking?

PPP   The protocol of choice for connecting with dial-up networking is the *Point-to-Point Protocol* (PPP). Microsoft has designed most of its remote access and dial-up connectivity around this protocol. At the speeds at which most of us will conduct our dial-up networking (128Kbps or less), the primary advantage of PPP is that the connection does error checking of data and data compression during the transmission process. This makes for faster and more secure data transfer. Another reason to consider using PPP is that it has pretty much become an industry-wide standard.

NOTE

If you are using PPP, you can connect to a network using IPX/SPX, TCP/IP, Net-BEUI, or any combination of the three. Because of its power and flexibility, PPP is the default protocol when installing dial-up networking.

PPTP   A variation on PPP, through *Point-to-Point Tunneling Protocol* (PPTP) multiprotocol virtual private networks can allow remote users to access a private network via a secure connection over the Internet or other public IP networks. For example, if a user wants to access his company's computer from his laptop while he's on the road, he can connect to the Internet—if he has a local access number, he'll even avoid long-distance charges—and then use this connection to access his company's network without having to dial into it directly. PPTP works by enclosing PPP packets within Internet Protocol (IP) packets and sending them out over the Internet or any IP network.

NetWare Connect   Novell uses software known as NetWare Connect to allow remote clients to dial up to the network. Windows 98 comes with a NetWare Connect client, which allows your Windows 98 machine to attach to a NetWare Connect server directly, without going through a Microsoft gateway of any type. Even though Windows 98 machines can connect to a NetWare Connect server, it is not a reciprocal relationship; NetWare Connect clients cannot dial in to a Windows 98 server.

RAS   Dial-up networking supports RAS as implemented by Windows for Workgroups 3.11 and Windows NT 3.1. (Windows NT 3.5x and 4.0 default to using PPP.) You may see this RAS option referred to as *asynchronous NetBEUI* in some systems' help files or in network documentation.

SLIP   An older protocol standard is the *Serial Line Interface Protocol* (SLIP). Unlike its PPP counterpart, SLIP does not perform error checking or data compression while transmitting data; the responsibility for performing these functions is placed on your hardware. This is not a bad thing, since most modern modems (14.4Kbps and 28.8Kbps, anyway) *do* perform these functions.

NOTE

Microsoft recommends against using SLIP except when dialing up a Unix network that is using a dial-up server with TCP/IP.

What Are the Different Combinations for Connection Protocols and Network Protocols?

There are two parts to dial-up networking: the dial-up *server* and the dial-up *client* (the remote user's machine). Let's take a look at the various combinations from that perspective. The information is summarized in Table 13.1.

TABLE 13.1: Various Combinations of Connection and Network Protocols

CLIENTS	SERVER
TCP/IP over SLIP	Unix remote server, Internet (SLIP Router)
IPX over NetWare Connect	NetWare Connect Server
IPX, NetBEUI, and/or TCP/IP over PPP	Internet (PPP Router), Windows 98, Windows 95, Windows NT RAS Server, and NetWare
NetBEUI over RAS (Asynchronous NetBEUI)	Windows 98, Windows 95, Windows NT, Windows for Workgroups 3.11, and LAN Manager Servers
TCP/IP over PPTP	Windows 98, Windows NT 4.0

How Do I Install Dial-Up Networking?

Installing dial-up networking is a two-step process:

1. You must install the dial-up networking software onto your client machine and onto your host PC or server.

2. You must configure the dial-up networking software as either client or server.

Installing Dial-Up Networking on the Network

Let's look at how to install the dial-up networking software on your company's host PC or server:

1. Click on Start ➤ Control Panel.

2. Select Add/Remove Programs.

3. Select the Windows Setup tab. You'll see the dialog box shown in Figure 13.1.

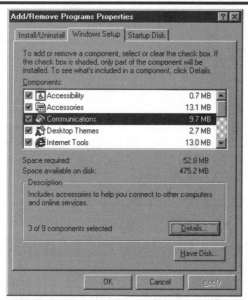

FIGURE 13.1: Going to Windows Setup to install DUN

4. Click the Communications option and then select Details.

5. Select Dial-Up Networking from the list, as illustrated in Figure 13.2. If you want your PC to act as a dial-up server, you'll want to check that box, as well. If you want to set up a Virtual Private Networking (VPN) connection, check the last box on the list to install the Microsoft VPN adapter. You can also do this through the Control Panel, as described later in this chapter.

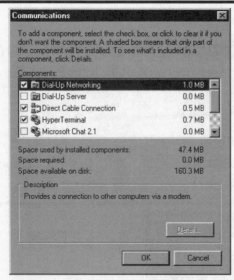

FIGURE 13.2: Adding DUN from Communications Details

6. Click OK to return to the main window to continue with the setup. Make sure your Windows 98 CD-ROM is in its drive, then click OK and wait for Setup to copy the necessary files from the CD to your hard drive.

Next you'll need to configure the DUN connection.

Configuring the DUN Network Connection

Good news! You do not have to restart your system in order to configure dial-up networking (although you will have to reboot your machine before you can use it). To configure the connection on a Windows 98 server, skip ahead in this chapter to the section on "Installing the Windows 98 Dial-Up Server." To configure the connection on a Windows 98 client machine, read on.

Installing Dial-Up Networking on the Client Machine

The first step to installing dial-up networking software on a remote machine is to install all the *protocols* the remote user might need and bind them to the *dial-up adapter*:

1. On the remote machine, go to Control Panel, choose Network, and select the dial-up adapter your remote machine will be using. Figure 13.3 shows the selection of component types for network services. You need to install an adapter for Dial-Up Networking, so click Adapter.

2. You'll get a listing of different companies whose adapters have been included in Windows 98. Figure 13.4 shows the adapters supplied by Microsoft. You'd choose the top one, Dial-Up Adapter, to set up most dial-up connections. But notice the third option, Microsoft Virtual Private Networking Adapter. If you want to set up a PPTP connection, you must select this option if you haven't set up the adapter in Add/Remove Programs in the Control Panel, as described earlier.

And while you're in Control Panel, if you want to set up a DUN connection to access an NT domain, you'll need to synchronize your Windows and Networking passwords using the Passwords applet and network identification (name of NT domain) in the Networking applet; you can read about this later in this chapter, in the section on setting up a WINS connection.

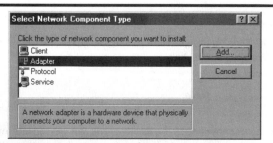

FIGURE 13.3: Different component types

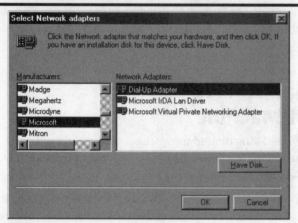

FIGURE 13.4: Microsoft network adapters

Creating a DUN Connection

The next step is to create a new dial-up networking connection:

1. Go, or have the remote user go, to the DUN folder in My Computer and, within the folder, choose the Make New Connection option. As you can see in Figure 13.5, you'll be asked what you want to call this connection (I have multiple ISPs and DUN connections, so I designate each with the name of the company or ISP I'm connecting to) and the device over which the connection is to be made, in most cases via your computer's modem.

2. Then you'll be asked (as shown in Figure 13.6) for the telephone number of the computer to which the connection is being made. Supply the necessary information and click OK. This creates a Connection icon in the Dial-Up Networking folder.

TIP

If you have Call Waiting, you might want to use the *70 prefix to turn off this feature when making the connection.

NOTE

If you want to set up a connection to the Internet, you can use the Internet Connection Wizard to set it up instead of following the steps detailed here. You can read about this Wizard later in this chapter.

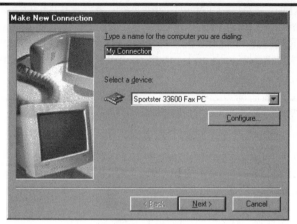

FIGURE 13.5: Setting up a DUN connection

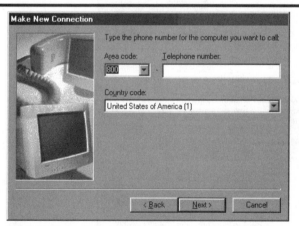

FIGURE 13.6: Entering the telephone number of the computer to be accessed

What about Setting Up a PPTP Connection?

The process is slightly different if you want to set up a PPTP DUN (ah, that acronymic alphabet soup) connection. (This assumes, of course, that the system administrator of the network you want to access via PPTP has installed a PPTP server. If in doubt, ask.) Remember that you first have to install the VPN adapter via Control Panel ➢ Add/Remove Programs ➢ Windows Setup ➢ Communications or via Control Panel Networking, as described earlier. After doing this and rebooting, go into

Dial-Up Networking ➤ Make a New Connection, and you'll have another choice of modem type, as shown in Figure 13.7. In the next dialog, enter the IP address RAS server of the domain you'll be connecting to via PPTP. Figure 13.8 shows such an IP address. Enter the correct address; then click Next.

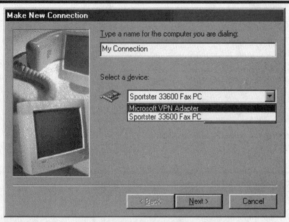

FIGURE 13.7: Setting up a PPTP connection

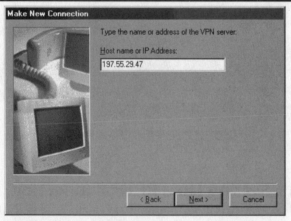

FIGURE 13.8: Specifying the IP address of the VPN server

Whether your new connection is a regular DUN or PPTP connection, the next screen, which you can see in Figure 13.9, will tell you that your new connection has been set up. If you're done, click Finish.

NOTE

Later, if you want to edit the properties of any DUN connection you've set up, you can do so by going to the Dial-Up Networking folder, right-clicking the connection you want to edit, and selecting Properties. See the section on configuring a dial-up connection for more info.

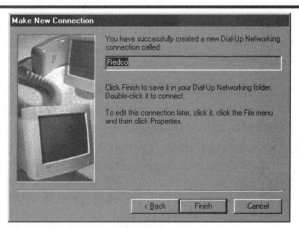

FIGURE 13.9: The connection has been set up.

TIP

If the DUN connection is to an NT domain, you must also specify the domain name in the Networking applet in Control Panel both in the Identification tab *and* under Properties for Client for Microsoft Networks. Otherwise, you may be able to connect, but you won't be able to "see" anything on the network.

Once you have created the DUN connection, you can double-click the Connection icon at any time to dial up to the network. The DUN setup program may ask for the name of the server or domain you want to log on to, as well as a password. DUN will then dial the location, verify the user name and the password, and if everything checks out, allow access to the server. At this point, you can now do anything you normally could if you were local to the network (only more slowly).

Use DUN to Access Data, Not Applications

I strongly recommend that remote users do *not* attempt to run applications across the DUN connection; they should only go DUN to get data files and information. For example, if you choose to start a network copy of Word for Windows from your remote DUN location, it could easily take over 45 minutes for the application to begin, because the entire program would have to be transported via modem to the memory of your remote DUN machine.

TIP
DUN is designed with data in mind. The best implementation of DUN would be a remote DUN machine that has its applications loaded locally and the data files on a network server.

Configuring a DUN Client Connection

To configure a DUN client connection, simply right-click the Connection icon that was created in the preceding section and select Properties.

Your first major decision here concerns the type of server you will be dialing up via this connection. If you typically dial to the same site, but you know that sometimes you'll want to connect via RAS (asynchronous NetBEUI) and other times you'll want to connect via NetWare Connect, use Make New Connection and create two separate connections. Then whenever you go to make your connection, you can choose from a pair of Connection icons.

You can see your choices for Type of Dial-Up Server in Figures 13.10 and 13.11.

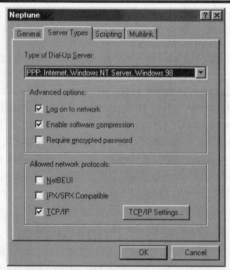

FIGURE 13.10:   Server Types tab

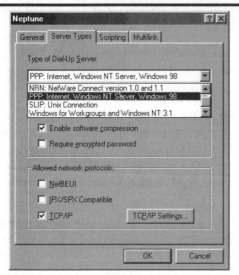

FIGURE 13.11: Types of dial-up servers

NOTE

Remember that *server* here refers to the computer you'll be connecting to, not a Windows 98 server you're setting up on your own machine.

Let's take a look at some of the options available on this screen:

PPP   This option is used for dialing into RAS servers that are using TCP/IP, IPX, NetBEUI, or any combination of the three. DUN will automatically detect which of the three to use, based on the protocols you select at the bottom of the screen. Use this option for dialing into a Windows 98 or 95 dial-up server or NT 4.0 RAS server.

NRN   This option is used for connecting to a NetWare Connect Server.

SLIP   This option is used for any implementation of SLIP of the TCP/IP protocol.

CSLIP   This option is used for any implementation of compressed SLIP connections. (Your network administrator should specify whether or not you need to use SLIP or CSLIP. The protocol must match what the dial-up server is using.)

The last connection   This option is used when dialing into a WfW RAS server or NT 3.1 server.

Advanced options:

Log on to network   This option, which is enabled by default, will dial up and log you into the network using the user name and password you typed in when you logged into Windows 98. If this option is deselected, it will ask you for a logon name and password every time you attempt a new connection.

Enable software compression   This option will compress the data before it is sent to the modem (or the like) for transmission.

Require Encrypted Passwords   This option enables a feature known as the Challenge Handshake Authentication Protocol (CHAP). CHAP is discussed in greater detail later in this chapter.

This screen is also where you specify the protocols that you want the DUN connection to support. If you want to configure a connection to the Internet, click the TCP/IP settings. This option, shown in Figure 13.12, will ask for information that you may need to get from your network administrator or your Internet service provider.

As you saw in Figure 13.11, there are other tabs with options you can select. The General tab, shown in Figure 13.13, contains pretty much the same options you chose when setting up the connection in the first place, giving you the chance to change them if necessary. The Scripting tab, shown in Figure 13.14, lets you specify the script to be run when this connection is made. The Multilink tab, shown in Figure 13.15, lets you add additional devices to make the connection. So, for example, if you want to increase the speed of the connection and you have two modems installed, you would use this tab to set up the second modem to be used in making this connection. Figure 13.16 shows how you can choose the second modem and configure it with the correct phone number for the connection.

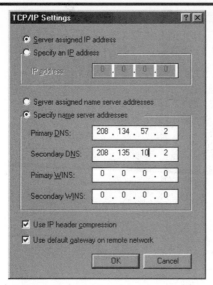

FIGURE 13.12: Specifying TCP/IP settings

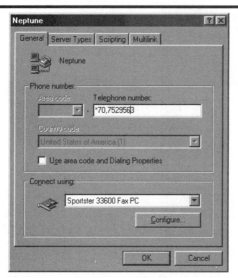

FIGURE 13.13: General DUN options

FIGURE 13.14: Specifying a DUN script

FIGURE 13.15: Setting up a multilink connection

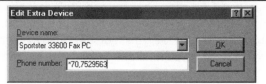

FIGURE 13.16:   Specifying additional modems and telephone numbers

How Do I Test the DUN Connection?

Once you have configured your DUN connection, just double-click and the connection will be made immediately. You should see the lights of your modem flashing, and, if you have enabled the modem speaker, you should hear the lovely and distinctive squelching noise that indicates that Windows 98 is negotiating a connection.

Whether you're using a regular dial-up connection or a VPN connection to connect to an NT domain, you'll see a User Logon box like the one shown in Figure 13.17. Once you've filled in the boxes, click OK to make the connection. If you're using DUN to connect to your ISP, if your Windows Networking password is the same as you use for this connection, and if you've checked the *Log on to network* box under Server Types in Properties for the connection, then you'll bypass this step when logging onto your ISP. Otherwise, you'll see the same screen but without the *Logon domain* line. Fill in your password, and you'll be connected.

You can then map network drives, see the other computers on the network via Network Neighborhood, and do whatever network functions you have permission to do.

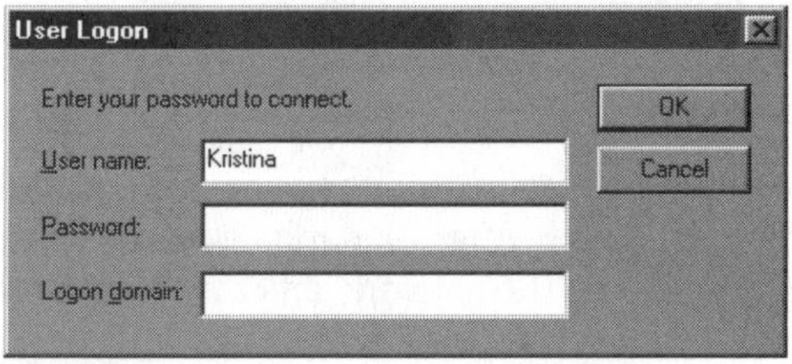

FIGURE 13.17:   Logging onto an NT domain

Part i

Using Microsoft's Universal Naming Convention (UNC), you should now be able to access any network resource for which you have permission. Or, if you're connecting to your ISP, you should be able to connect to any Internet service your ISP connection allows (e-mail, the World Wide Web, and so on).

TIP

When you are connected to a network, you can go to the *Connected To* window and see the number of packets sent, number of packets received, and the overall status of your connection.

Once you have established a connection for the first time, dial-up networking will be activated in any of the following circumstances:

- ▶ When you select a network resource that is not part of your network

- ▶ When a UNC directs you to a network resource (for example, \\server\public_)

- ▶ When an application calls for a network resource

SHORTCUTS TO POPULAR NETWORK INFORMATION

If you need to dial up to many different networks, shortcuts are a great way to organize all of your frequently visited sites. Shortcuts also get you quickly to the information on those networks that you use most frequently.

Without shortcuts, I have to take the following steps every time I want to connect to my home directory at work:

1. Open the My Computer folder.

2. Open the Dial-Up Networking folder.

3. Select my connection. (In my case, it's MMCO Office.)

4. Provide a password.

At this point the system starts to negotiate the connection and to authenticate me to the network. After validation, I map a network drive to my home directory on the network, and *then* I can access my files.

CONTINUED ➡

All this gets a little tiresome quickly, and this is where shortcuts come to the rescue. To create a shortcut to my home directory, I still follow the above steps the very first time I connect, but I let Windows 98 automatically create a shortcut to the directory by clicking and dragging my network home directory folder to the Desktop.

From that point on, if I want to get to my home directory I just double-click its shortcut. Windows 98 will now automatically call the network, validate me to the network (assuming my Windows 98 logon and network logon are identical), and take me to my home directory. If I am already connected to the network, the shortcut is still a useful way to fly directly to my home directory.

USING THE INTERNET CONNECTION WIZARD

If you want to set up a connection to the Internet, you can also use the Internet Connection Wizard (ICW) in Windows 98 to configure a connection to your ISP(s). Go to Start ≻ Programs ≻ Internet Explorer and click Connection Wizard (or go to Help and search for it in the Index). Start the Wizard, and you'll see a screen like the one shown in Figure 13.18.

Basically this screen gives you the chance to set up a new connection to the Internet via one of the ISPs listed with Microsoft, to reconfigure an existing connection (or to set up a new connection to an ISP not listed with Microsoft), or to do nothing. If you want to set up a new connection, you're asked for your phone number's area code and exchange, as shown in Figure 13.19. Then your computer will dial an 800 number to get a list of the ISPs in your area or, failing that, of national ISPs, and give you a listing. You can see more detailed info or sign up with an ISP you select here. If you select an ISP and click Sign Me Up, your computer will dial the ISP's computer to establish an account with them and set up the connection.

Some of the ISPs, like MSN, are also online services. You can set up an online service by opening the Online Services folder and clicking the icon for the service you want. This results in the same procedure: your computer will dial into the service's computer to set up the account and connection.

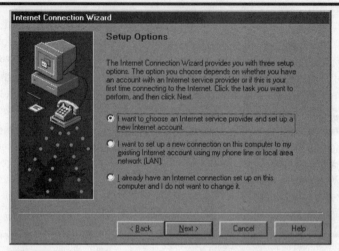

FIGURE 13.18: Using ICW to set up an Internet connection

FIGURE 13.19: Asking for your area code and exchange

This option is useful if you prefer to have your connection to the Internet set up "automatically." However, the ISP listing isn't very extensive—as of this writing, for instance, I saw no DC-area ISPs listed. Fortunately, setting up an Internet connection following your ISP's instructions for Dial-Up Networking and setting up your e-mail and other services is usually not difficult—many ISPs post instructions for doing this on their Web sites.

If you want to reconfigure an existing connection and you want to use Outlook Express as your e-mail, news, and Internet Directory client, you can change the details of your e-mail and news servers, and so on. (You can also change the telephone number you use to dial in with.) If you want to use other programs for these functions, such as Pegasus Mail or Netscape Navigator, don't use ICW to set them up—use the setup functions within these independent programs.

Altering an Internet Connection

If you want to alter the details of a preexisting connection, or if your ISP isn't on Microsoft's list and you want to use Outlook Express, click the second radio button of the initial ICW screen. You're then taken through a series of questions: Do you connect via a regular phone line or a LAN? Does your ISP's server use a proxy? Do you want to set up a new Internet mail account? A news service? and so on. You can also change the telephone number by which you connect to your ISP. You'll want to know the answers to these questions before you start.

For instance, say you want to create a new Internet mail account. You'll check the box next to that option in the dialog box and then fill in your name, e-mail address, and then the mail-server info asked for in Figure 13.20. You need to get this information from your ISP. (If Windows doesn't think you've typed in a valid server name, you'll get nagged.)

Next you'll be asked for your logon info (account name and password, and whether you log on using *Secure Password Authentication*, or SPA)

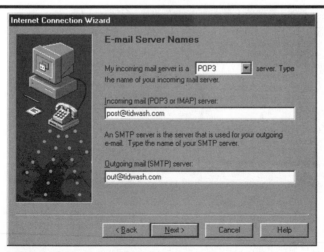

FIGURE 13.20: What type of mail server?

and to designate a "friendly" name (that is, one you'll easily remember) for this mail account. Then you'll be asked if you want to set up a news account, which involves roughly the same kind of questions.

The last part of the Wizard sets up any Internet directory (LDAP) services you may have accounts with. Figure 13.21 shows you some of the possible services. If you want to set up a new service or modify an existing one, you'll need the name and security information of the LDAP server in question, as shown in Figure 13.22.

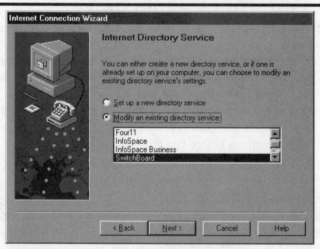

FIGURE 13.21: Some Internet directory services

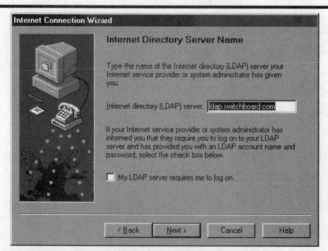

FIGURE 13.22: Specifying LDAP server info

Sample ISP Information

If you need to fill in this information manually for your ISP(s), Table 13.2 shows an example of the information your ISP must provide so that you can do so.

TABLE 13.2: Setup Information Taken from an Actual ISP and Modified

SERVER	LOCATION	FUNCTION
NNTP Server	newsdesk.worldwide.net	(News)
SMTP Server	postmaster.worldwide.net	(Outgoing Mail)
POP3 Server	postoffice.worldwide.net	(Incoming Mail)
FTP Host	ftp.worldwide.net	(Personal Sites)
FrontPage	ftp.worldwide.net	(FrontPage Sites)
Primary DNS	208.85.53.2	(Name Server #1)
Secondary DNS	198.85.50.2	(Name Server #2)

Only Enable Software Compression and TCP/IP should be checked in the Server Types tab.

NOTE

You set up the first options in each individual program, but this last set of options, namely, enabling software compression and TCP/IP, is set up by going to the Server Types tab in Properties of the connection in the Dial-Up Networking folder. You set the telephone number and name of the connection when setting it up initially as described in the earlier section "Creating a DUN Connection," but you can change the phone number and dialing and modem properties under the General tab.

USING WINS TO CONNECT TO AN NT DOMAIN OVER AN EXISTING INTERNET CONNECTION

If you have an existing connection to the Internet, there's another way to connect to (and log onto) a remote NT network: by exploiting that remote network's WINS servers. If you have the right information, it's a fairly simple matter to set up a WINS connection to an NT domain, say, between your home computer and your network at work. You need the machine name of the networked computer you want to access, and the information you need to access the network it's on: password, domain name, and WINS specification of the network's domain server.

TIP

If the network you're trying to access is behind a firewall, you won't be able to connect to it via WINS. Use PPTP (described earlier in this chapter) instead. Even with PPTP, however, the people administering the firewall must have opened the firewall to PPTP before you can PPTP to a network behind the firewall.

Here are the four steps to connecting to an NT domain via WINS:

1. Set your Windows and Windows Networking passwords to be identical to your password in the office. Your user name should also match the user name you employ in the office.

2. Point your TCP/IP software to the IP address of the WINS server in the office; this makes it easier for your computer to locate NT domain controllers in the office network. Alternatively, you can create an LMHOSTS file to achieve the same results—this often works where WINS fails.

3. Set the workgroup for your Windows 98 machine equal to the name of whatever NT domain your workstation at work uses.

4. Connect to the Internet, and you should be able to access the office network—again, assuming that the office doesn't use a firewall!

In step 1, you synchronize your Windows and Windows Networking passwords via the Password applet in Control Panel. If they differ, you won't be able to make the connection. First go to Control Panel ➤ Passwords. Since you'll probably need to change your Windows password, click the Change Windows Password button, fill in the old Windows password, then the password you need to use to access the NT domain and again to confirm the change, and click OK. You'll need to reboot for the change to take effect. (If you already have a Networking password as well, you can check a box to change it to the new password at the same time. Or, if your Windows password is correct but you need to change your Networking password, click Change Other Passwords and follow the instructions.)

WORKAROUND FOR POSSIBLE PROBLEM WITH CHANGING NETWORKING PASSWORDS

When writing this section, I was dutifully changing Networking and Windows passwords as necessary without trouble via the Passwords applet in Control Panel. But for some reason, one day I ran into major problems trying to change the Networking password when my machine was set up for connection to a domain in the Networking applet. I could change the Windows password without trouble, but I got an error message saying the Networking password couldn't be changed because the authenticating server for the new domain couldn't be found.

After at least an hour of trying to get this to work, I hit upon this workaround. The basic idea is to remove the domain references before changing the Windows password, then restore them after rebooting. In this way, the Windows and Microsoft Networking passwords will automatically be synchronized — without the problem of having an authenticating server validate the Networking password before it can be used.

Here's how to do it:

1. Go to Control Panel ➤ Networking ➤ Identification, and change the Workgroup.

2. Select Client for Microsoft Networks in the main Networking screen, and then click Properties.

3. Clear the check by Log On to NT Domain and clear out the name of the domain (for some reason, merely unchecking the box didn't work).

4. Go ahead and reboot.

5. When you're back up again, go to Control Panel ➤ Passwords and change the Windows password to whatever your new network requires.

6. Go to Networking and add the domain information in the same two places that you removed it above.

7. Reboot.

8. You'll be prompted for your Microsoft Networking password, which will be the same in this case as your Windows password. Enter it, and you should be fine.

Then you need to change your networking identification. Go to Control Panel ➢ Networking, and select Client for Microsoft Networks; then click Properties. You'll see a check box for Log On to NT Domain; click it to put a check there and fill in the name of the NT domain in the space provided. Then click OK and click the Identification tab at the top of the next window. In the resulting dialog box, fill in the name of the NT domain in the space for Workgroup. Click OK and reboot for the changes to take effect.

Next, enter the WINS address for the TCP/IP adapter by means of which you connect to the Internet. In my case, I access the Net via a cable modem, which means via a network card. So I go to Control Panel ➢ Networking, and find the TCP/IP adapter for my Net connection, which is the Ethernet card. This is shown in Figure 13.23.

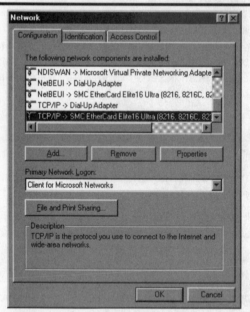

FIGURE 13.23: Changing the TCP/IP properties of the connection in Control Panel

Right-click Properties, then go to the WINS Configuration tab shown in Figure 13.24. Click the Enable WINS Resolution radio button, then enter the IP address in the WINS Server Search Order box. Click Add when finished; then click OK. You'll need to reboot before these changes take effect.

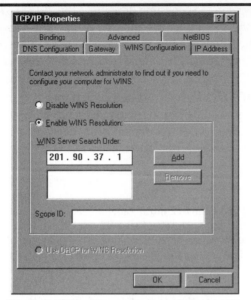

FIGURE 13.24: Specifying the WINS address

Creating an LMHOSTS File

If the network in your office doesn't have a WINS server, or if you try this entire procedure and can't get it to work, you can employ an older and simpler method than WINS: an LMHOSTS file.

To go the LMHOSTS route, you need to set up an ASCII file, lmhosts (no .TXT or other extension), in your \windows directory. This file, which can be as little as one line, must tell your machine how to locate the machine on the network you're trying to access. This means the server's DNS address, the machine name of the computer you're trying to access, and the name of the network domain. Although this only needs to be one line—for one machine—you can set it up to try other machines if the first one listed can't be reached. Here's a sample lmhosts file:

```
201.90.37.1 guava #dom:tropfruit #pre
201.90.37.2 mango #dom:tropfruit #pre
```

Here we have two different machines, *Guava* and *Mango*, both domain controllers in a domain called *Tropfruit*. The file gives the path of the signal between my home computer and my network at work. Guava can be found at the 201.90.37.1 address in the domain Tropfruit. But if Guava can't be reached, Mango can be reached in the same domain at the 201.90.37.2 address. Notice that Guava and Mango are the simple machine names for those PCs; don't enter the Internet name like guava.fruits.acme.com, just enter the up-to-15-character machine name (techies call it the *NetBIOS name*, by the way).

The #pre at the end of each line is for *preload*, which speeds things up by preloading the entries preceding it into the name cache. Without this enabled, the entries are parsed only after dynamic name resolution fails. (Translation: #pre makes the whole operation faster.)

TIP

Just a reminder: have you gone to Control Panel ➢ Networking and set the workgroup in the Identification tab equal to the NT domain that your network is a member of back at the office, as well as filling in the same domain information under Properties for Client for Microsoft Networks? If not, do so now and reboot.

OK, now it's time to connect to the Internet. Those of you with cable modems are already on the Internet as soon as you boot your machine, but those of you who use a dial-up Internet connection need to use that to dial into your ISP and get on the Internet. If all has gone well, you should also now be accessing your office network via your WINS connection. But if all *hasn't* gone well, read on.

Troubleshooting a WINS Connection

If you can't log onto the network after you've done these things and rebooted, you should wait a few minutes, since it takes a little time for the network master browser to update the browse list. But if the network still hasn't shown up in Network Neighborhood, or if you're unable to map a network drive after several minutes and you've checked to make sure you've entered the right password and domain name, you'll want to check into a few other things using the command line (sometimes GUI networking is a little flaky).

1. Go to Start ➢ Run and enter **winipcfg**. This results in a box like the one shown in Figure 13.25, which shows the details of your networking setup. If you click More Info, you'll see what WINS server, if any, you're attached to, along with the

host name, DNS servers, and so on. If you have more than one TCP/IP adapter installed and you don't see any WINS server info, click the drop-down list and select the adapter that you've set up for WINS. If you see the right numbers by Primary WINS Server (and Secondary if applicable), then go to Step 2. If not, go back to Networking and make sure your WINS information is correctly entered for the TCP/IP adapter you plan to use.

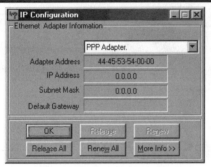

FIGURE 13.25: Using WINIPCFG to examine your networking setup

2. Go to a command prompt and type **net view \\servername**. If your server comes up, then go to Step 4. If that doesn't work, try typing **net view *ipaddress***, where *ipaddress* is the IP address of the server; for example, if NET VIEW \\GUAVA didn't work, I'd try NET VIEW \\201.90.37.1.

3. To connect to a share on the server, type **net use *driveletter*: *servername**sharename***, as shown in Figure 13.26. If NET VIEW with the NetBIOS name didn't work and NET VIEW with the IP address worked, then use the IP address in the NET USE command as well.

4. Sometimes you can also use Find from the Start menu to find your network. Click Start ➢ Find ➢ Computer, and fill in the IP address (for a WINS connection) or the server name with no backslash ("whack") characters (for a dial-up connection); then click Find Now. I've found that Find ➢ Computer with an IP address can work when nothing else does.

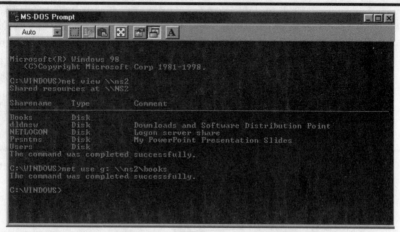

FIGURE 13.26: Connecting to a share via command prompts

Regular DUN vs. WINS vs. PPTP

What are the advantages and disadvantages of these three kinds of remote connections?

If you're going by speed, my testing showed the regular DUN and WINS connections to be faster; the regular DUN connection (over a 33.6 Kbps modem) was marginally faster than the WINS. In contrast, I found the PPTP connection to be extremely slow, even though I was using my one-megabit-plus cable connection to the Internet to make the connection.

Another issue is whether you want to tie up a phone line to make the connection (or indeed, whether your computer is connected to a phone line at all). A regular DUN connection requires that your computer be connected to a phone line; the other two connections don't (in my case, I just used my cable connection). However, if the network you want to access is behind a firewall, you won't be able to connect to it via WINS, but you can connect to it via a dial-up connection or via PPTP if the system administrator opens the PPTP port in the firewall for this purpose (it's port 1723 and Generic Routing Encapsulation (GRE) Protocol 47, by the way).

If security is your main concern, a PPTP connection offers encryption plus the usual RAS password protection, although this severely slows down the connection.

INSTALLING THE WINDOWS 98 DIAL-UP SERVER

Want outside users to be able to dial into your network, but you don't have an NT machine to act as an RAS server? No problem—a Windows 98 machine can be a dial-up server. Many users familiar with Windows NT Remote Access Server may be wondering, "What's the difference between NT's RAS and Windows 98's server?" The major difference comes down to how big or how simple the network being supported is. The Windows 98 server, which is designed for small LANs, supports one connection at a time. On the other hand, Windows NT is designed for much larger networks and can support up to 256 simultaneous connections. To install Windows 98 Server, do the following:

1. Make sure Dial-Up Server is included in your Windows 98 installation. Do this by going to the Add/Remove Programs applet in Control Panel, then Windows Setup ➢ Communications. Click Details, and see if there's a check in the box for Dial-Up Server (as shown in Figure 13.27). If there's not, you'll need to install the Dial-Up Server facility. With your Windows 98 CD in its drive, click the box by Dial-Up Server to put a check in it, then click OK twice and let your machine add the necessary files from the CD. Then reboot.

FIGURE 13.27: Looking for Dial-Up Server in Windows Setup

TIP

You can also see if you have Dial-Up Server installed on your system by going to Dial-Up Networking and seeing if there's a Dial-Up Server option in the Connections menu. If there isn't, you'll need to install one as described here.

2. Once Dial-Up Server is installed, go to Dial-Up Networking and open the Connections menu, which will have a new option, Dial-Up Server.

3. In the Dial-Up Server configuration window, shown in Figure 13.28, click *Allow caller access*. You can also describe the server if you like.

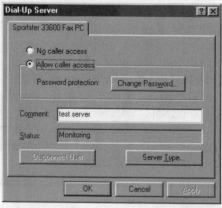

FIGURE 13.28:   Allowing caller access and describing the server

4. Set the Security option: you can define a password that anyone calling to this Windows 98 machine must provide in order to access the shared resources of the DUN server system. This is shown in Figure 13.29.

5. Alternatively, if you are implementing user-level security, you can specify the users who can access this machine. Figure 13.30 shows the Dial-Up Server screen set up for user-level security. Figure 13.31 shows adding a user from a list in a domain, and Figure 13.32 shows the results. (Note that the Status in all three figures is Idle instead of Monitoring, since I'm in the process of setting up a connection, not monitoring one that already exists.)

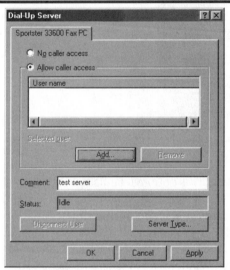

FIGURE 13.29: Setting a password

FIGURE 13.30: User-level security for Dial-Up Server

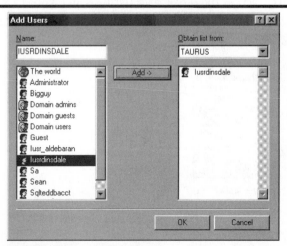

FIGURE 13.31: Adding a user

FIGURE 13.32: The user has been added

6. Click on Server Type. This option defaults to PPP, which supports TCP/IP, IPX, and NetBEUI. When you've selected this option, a determination is made during the negotiation of callers to this DUN server machine. If PPP cannot negotiate a viable connection, the DUN server will automatically switch to RAS for NT 3.1 and Windows for Workgroup clients. You can also enable software compression and require an encrypted password to access the server, as you can see in Figure 13.33.

FIGURE 13.33: Setting the server type

Once you click OK, your system is now waiting to receive calls. You'll see a little server icon in your system tray, like the one shown here:

 If you click it, you'll see a screen like the one shown in Figure 13.28, displaying the status of connections to your server.

WHAT ABOUT SECURITY?

I've discussed what it takes for DUN to work and to interact properly. But once you have DUN up and running, there are a few security concerns you might want to consider.

For example, Jennifer, dialing up from home, can locate another user—say Joe, who is currently logged into the DUN server—and kick him off. All she has to do is these four simple steps:

1. Go to My Computer.

2. Select Dial-Up Networking.

3. Select Dial-Up Server.

4. Click the Disconnect User button.

In the same vein, if Joe hasn't been kicked off yet, he can take a preemptive strike against everybody by remotely turning off the server! All he has to do is follow the first three of the steps above and then click No Caller Access.

Fortunately, once you have DUN working, there are a few security features you can enable.

Password Authentication Protocol (PAP)

The first level of security is established during the connection. If you have selected PPP as your server type on both the client and the server, then you can utilize a technology known as the *Password Authentication Protocol* (PAP). Before the invention of PAP, the server, client, and user would hold the following conversation:

Server (to client): *Do you use PAP?*

Client (to Server): *No.*

Server (to Client): *What is the user's name?*

Client (to User): *What is your logon name?*

User (to Client): *Frank.*

Client (to Server): *The user says his name is Frank.*

Server (to Client): *Great, what is the user's password?*

Client (to User): *What is your logon password?*

User (to Client): *Doghouse.*

Client (to Server): *The client says his password is Doghouse.*

Server (to Client): *Thank you.*

This conversation would take place every single time Frank wanted to log in to the network remotely. There was no encryption of information being sent back and forth. With some network servers, you might actually have had to create a script file so this conversation could be automated. In either case, it still required that the network administrator understand how to create the script file. In theory, scripts are very straightforward, but in practice the syntax can vary from hardware device to hardware device and from network operating system to network operating system.

If both your server and the client are using PAP, then the conversation goes something like this:

Server: *Do you use PAP?*

Client: *Yes.*

Server: *Great, then please send over the username.*

Client: *Frank.*

Server: *Great, please send over the password.*

Client: *Doghouse.*

Server: *Thank you.*

This entire conversation took place without any interaction on the part of the user. If it took any time at all, all Frank saw was the hourglass while this conversation took place in the background. Unfortunately, just as you saw the password *Doghouse* in the first conversation, the password was sent as a simple text string across the communication line. When I last looked in Webster's dictionary under the word *security*, this wasn't part of the definition. If you are looking for a secure validation, you want to use CHAP.

NOTE

Before we discuss CHAP, I would like to mention SPAP in passing. The makers of the Shiva modem have their own authentication protocol, known as *Shiva Password Authentication Protocol* (SPAP). Windows 98 supports SPAP for dialing into a Shiva server.

Challenge-Handshake Authentication Protocol (CHAP)

As I said previously, CHAP allows for secure validation. If the server and client have CHAP enabled, the following conversation takes place:

Server: *Do you do CHAP?*

Client: *Yes.*

Server: *47.*

Client (to itself): *Let me factor the password by 47 and send the encrypted version across the line.*

Client (to Server): *Kjsyao7r* (representing the password *Doghouse*).

Server: *Thank you.*

Now, since the server sent a *challenge code* (47 in the example), it knows that it will use the same number as the challenge factor to decrypt the password and then validate it. The power of CHAP is that when the first client logs in, the challenge code may be 47, but when the next client logs in, the challenge code dynamically changes. Since the challenge code is constantly changing, the passwords are encrypted using a different key every time.

To enable CHAP, just select Require Encrypted Password when configuring the client *and* when configuring the server. If Server Type is PPP, DUN will attempt a PAP conversation by default, unless Require Encrypted Passwords is selected.

Remote Access to Resources with DUN

DUN allows you to specify how people may gain access to the DUN server.

▶ The first option is *share-level security*. This permits you to assign passwords to each resource that you share. You can set a password

Part I

for read-only access and a different password for full-control access. The downside of this configuration is that a user may have to memorize many passwords. If you are looking for centralized control, you will want to set user-level permissions instead.

▶ When you set *user-level permissions*, Windows 98 will look for a Windows NT or NetWare server to validate a user. The user has to be a valid user of the Novell network or NT domain in order to gain access to your machine. Windows 98 still controls read-only or full-control access to the resource, but it enforces these security parameters by user, not by resource.

To set share-level or user-level security, go to the Network applet in Control Panel and click the Access Control tab, which you can see in Figure 13.34. If you want share-level security, make sure the first radio button is clicked. If you want user-level security, click the second radio button and fill in the name of the domain server for the network in question (*Pineapple* in the figure).

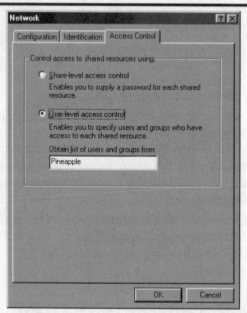

FIGURE 13.34:   Changing type of access in Control Panel

If you're not connected to this network at the time you're setting this up, Windows will tell you it can't find the security provider for this domain and ask if you want to proceed, as shown in Figure 13.35. If you do, click OK. Windows will ask you for the type of authenticator used by the network: choose between NetWare (bindery) and Windows NT domain, as shown in Figure 13.36. Select the right one, click OK, and reboot. Once you connect to the network after rebooting, your settings will take effect.

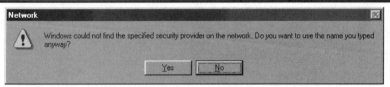

FIGURE 13.35: Can't find authenticator

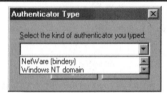

FIGURE 13.36: Choice of authenticator

HOW DO I CREATE A DIRECT SERIAL CONNECTION?

Users aren't limited to dialing in via a phone line to set up a network connection; they can connect their remote computer directly via a serial cable. To create a direct serial connection, the first thing that you need is an acceptable cable. Any of the following will do:

▶ Serial null modem cable

▶ LapLink cable

▶ InterLink cable

▶ 25-pin parallel cable (all wires must be present)

Of the four types of cables, the parallel cable will provide the fastest throughput between machines.

CONTINUED ➡

Once you have made a physical connection between the machines, take the following steps:

1. Choose *Add/Remove programs* in Control Panel.

2. Select Communications in the Components list.

3. Select Direct Cable Connection.

A new icon, Direct Cable Connection, will appear in the My Computer window. Please make sure this icon appears on both machines before attempting to establish a connection.

The first time you click Direct Cable Connection, the Direct Connect Wizard will appear and allow you to designate one machine as the host machine and the other machine as the guest machine.

WHAT'S NEXT?

In this chapter you've had a detailed look at setting up dial-up networking, the Windows tool for remote access to local area networks and for modem connections to Internet Service Providers.

In the next chapter, Sharon Crawford and Neil J. Salkind conclude our look at the features of Windows 98 with a survey of the applets, or accessory programs, supplied with the operating system. Then we'll move on to the Internet and the Windows 98 features that give you access to it, the subject of Part II.

Chapter 14

WINDOWS 98 APPLETS

From the first, graphical operating systems have come with a complement of smallish programs such as calculators and paint programs. Because of their usually limited capabilities, these programs are called *applets* rather than applications. In many cases, these programs are just as big as they need to be, so they actually *are* full applications. But the name applet has stuck and generally applies to programs that come with an operating system. This chapter looks at the Windows 98 applets.

Adapted from *The ABCs of Windows 98*, by Sharon Crawford and Neil J. Salkind

ISBN 0-7821-1953-0   384 pages $19.99

A World of Applets

The applets we'll try out in the following pages are Notepad, its "big sister" WordPad, the Clipboard Viewer, Paint, the Character Map, Phone Dialer, the Calculator, HyperTerminal, and the Briefcase—quite a selection. You'll be able to see which ones may be useful and which ones you can probably skip.

NOTE

Your computer may have more or fewer applets than what we've listed here already installed when you start using Windows 98. If you don't have the ones shown here, use the Add/Remove Programs icon in the Control Panel to add them to your system.

Using Notepad

Notepad is a simple text editor with very few charms except speed. Click any text file and it will immediately load into Notepad (unless it's associated with a word processing file installed on your system or it's bigger than 64K—in which case you'll be asked if you want to load it into Word-Pad instead).

To start Notepad, click Start ➤ Programs ➤ Accessories ➤ Notepad.

What Notepad Has

Notepad has the bare minimum of facilities on its menus. You can:

- ▶ Search for characters or words.

- ▶ Use Page Setup to set margins, paper orientation, customize the header and footer, and select a printer.

- ▶ Copy, cut, and paste text.

- ▶ Insert the time and date into a document.

Working with WordPad

WordPad, like Notepad, is a text editor, but it is more elaborate than Notepad. For one (important) thing, you can make format changes with

WordPad, but not with Notepad. However, WordPad still falls way short of being a real word processing program. WordPad will read Write, Notepad, and Word for Windows 97 documents, as well as Text and Rich Text formats.

To start WordPad, click Start ➤ Programs ➤ Accessories ➤ WordPad.

TIP

WordPad can be uninstalled using the Add/Remove Programs function in the Control Panel. However, if you use Microsoft Fax you'll need WordPad because it's the fax operation's text editor. If you use a different fax program such as WinFax or you don't fax from your computer at all, you can remove WordPad without worry.

Opening WordPad

When you open WordPad (see Figure 14.1), it looks like most other text editors. On the menus you'll find the usual things one associates with text editors. Pull down the menus to see the various options.

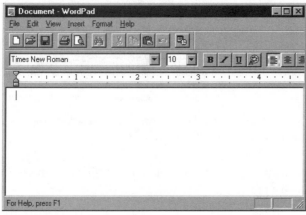

FIGURE 14.1: The opening screen for WordPad

WordPad is completely integrated into Windows 98. You can write messages in color and post them to the Microsoft Network so recipients see your messages just as you wrote them—fonts, colors, embedded objects, and all. WordPad also has the distinct advantage of being able to load really big files.

Making and Formatting Documents

You can always click on a document and drag it into WordPad. Documents made by Microsoft Word (.DOC) and Windows Write (.WRI), as well as those in text (.TXT) or Rich Text (.RTF) format, are all instantly recognized by WordPad. You can also just start typing away in the opening WordPad screen shown in Figure 14.1.

Formatting Tools

The toolbar (see Figure 14.2) and Format bar (see Figure 14.3) are displayed by default. You can turn either of them off by deselecting it from the list under the View menu.

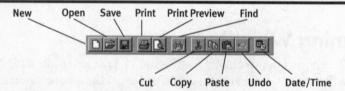

FIGURE 14.2:   Here are the various functions on the WordPad toolbar.

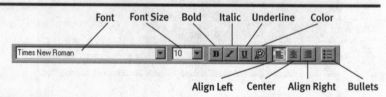

FIGURE 14.3:   The WordPad Format bar lets you manipulate text in all the
basic ways.

Tabs are set using the ruler. Click the ruler at the spot where you want a tab. To remove a tab, just click it and drag it off the ruler.

Other Options

Other formatting tools are under Options on the View menu. This is where you can set measurement units as well as Word Wrap and toolbars for each of the different file types that WordPad recognizes.

Page Setup and Printing

The File menu has the usual Print command, but there's also a Page Setup item that you can use to set margins as well as paper size and orientation. WordPad can be used to print envelopes as well as work with varying sizes of paper.

It may take some fooling around to get envelopes lined up correctly, but fortunately there's a Print Preview choice (on the toolbar and also on the File menu). There you can see how the envelope or paper is lining up with your text. Adjust the margin in the Page Setup dialog box until you get it the way you want.

TIP

To change printers, select Page Setup from the File menu. Click the Printer button and you can select any printer currently available to you.

What's on the Clipboard

The Clipboard Viewer is not much different than the one shipped with earlier versions of Windows. When you copy or cut something, Windows needs to have a place to store it until you decide what to do with it. This storage place is called the Clipboard. And if you look in the Clipboard, you will see the material that has just been cut or copied.

Sometimes you want to see what's on the Clipboard and maybe save its contents. Clipboard Viewer makes it possible for you to do this.

Taking a Look

To see the Viewer, click the Start button, then select Programs ➢ Accessories ➢ System Tools ➢ Clipboard Viewer. You'll see a window like the one shown in Figure 14.4.

NOTE

Immediately before snapping the screen shot of the Clipboard Viewer, we selected and copied the text you see in the figure. You can also press the PrintScreen key (which captures the entire screen to the Clipboard) or Alt+PrintScreen (which captures the active window to the Clipboard).

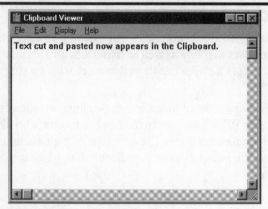

FIGURE 14.4: The Clipboard Viewer

Saving the Clipboard's Contents

To save the current contents of the Clipboard, pull down the File menu and select Save As. You can save files under a proprietary format identified by the .CLP extension. These files are (as far as we can tell) only used by the Windows Clipboard Viewer.

Once you've saved the contents, you can use the Clipboard to copy and paste other material, and later, you can reload what you saved by pulling down the File menu and selecting Open. Pull down the Display menu and you'll be able to see all your options for viewing the data on the Clipboard.

The most important thing to remember about the Clipboard is that it can only hold one thing at a time, which is always the most recently cut or copied material. So if you copy a section of text (which goes to the Clipboard) and then copy an image, the image will replace the text on the Clipboard.

DRAWING WITH PAINT

As a drawing and painting program, Paint has its limitations, but it's fine for creating and modifying simple graphics. To find Paint, select Start ➢ Programs ➢ Accessories ➢ Paint. It may not be installed by default, so if you don't see it, use the Add/Remove Programs function in the Control Panel. (It's under Accessories on the Windows Setup page.)

Creating Original Art

Open Paint and, using the tools down the left side of the window, create a drawing and/or a painting. When you're done, you can:

▶ Select File ➤ Save and give the picture a name. You can save it as one of several different kinds of bitmaps (see the Save as Type list).

▶ Select File ➤ Send, which will open Exchange and let you select an e-mail recipient worthy of receiving your work.

▶ Select File ➤ Save as Wallpaper. This will let you tile or center your work of art as the wallpaper on your screen. (You must save the file before you choose this option.)

Modifying the Work of Others

Any file with the extension .BMP, .PCX, or .DIB can be opened in Paint. Use the tools to make any modifications you want, and then do any of the things listed in the section above. Once a file is modified, it is saved as a bitmap (.BMP).

NOTE

For a really good painting program at a very reasonable price, check out the excellent shareware program Paint Shop Pro. It's available for download on the major online services at www.jasp.com. Just search for Paint Shop Pro, download the program, and install it.

ENTERING NEW CHARACTERS

The fonts that show up in your word processor are very nice, but they often don't go beyond the characters found on your keyboard. What about when you need a copyright sign (©) or an e with an umlaut (ë)? With the Character Map you have access to all kinds of symbols, including Greek letters and other special signs.

To start the Character Map, click Start ➤ Programs ➤ Accessories ➤ System Tools ➤ Character Map and you'll see the opening screen shown in Figure 14.5.

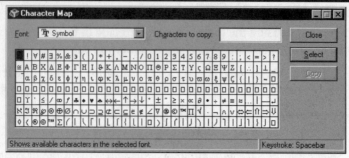

FIGURE 14.5: The Character Map shows all.

Entering Characters

Select the font you want to use by clicking the downward-pointing arrow at the right end of the Font list box. Each font represents a different set of symbols. To enter a character, double-click it in the window. It will appear in the text box at the top right of the window. Continue double-clicking until you have the entire string of characters you want in the text box. When you have all the characters you want in the text box, click the Copy button halfway down the right side of the window. Then return to your application using the Taskbar or by pressing Alt+Tab until your application is selected.

Position the cursor on the spot where you want to place the character, and select Paste from the Edit menu (or just press Ctrl+V).

PHONE DIALING FOR FUN

Do you frequently have to make a lot of telephone calls? Has your dialing finger ever felt as if it were going to fall off? If you have Windows 98, you can turn over the grief of dialing to its capable, virtual hands. Phone Dialer is a handy little program that doesn't do a lot, but if you need it, it's terrific to have.

To start the Phone Dialer, click Start ➤ Programs ➤ Accessories ➤ Communications ➤ Phone Dialer. You'll see the opening screen shown in Figure 14.6 (without a phone number in the Number to Dial box).

FIGURE 14.6:   The Phone Dialer window can help you put an end to the heartbreak of "Digititis."

NOTE

Windows uses your installed modem to dial your telephone. In order for this scheme to work, you need to have a telephone on the same line you're using for your modem. If you have a separate phone line for data, you'll need an actual telephone on that line to use Phone Dialer. You can pick up inexpensive couplers at Radio Shack that will allow all your available phone lines to work in conjunction with your data line.

The Phone Dialer gives you two simple ways to make phone calls:

Speed Dial   If you have a number you need in an emergency or one you call constantly, you can enter it in the Speed Dial list.

The Telephone Log   If you have a long list of numbers you call periodically, you can simply type those numbers into the Number to Dial text box and they will be added to a telephone log. You can access your log by clicking the downward-pointing arrow at the right end of the Number to Dial box.

Speed Dialing

To create a speed dial number, pull down the Edit menu and select Speed Dial. You will see the dialog box shown in Figure 14.7.

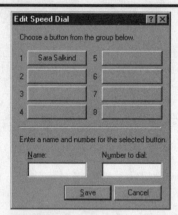

FIGURE 14.7:   Creating a Speed Dial number

Here's how to set it up:

1. Click the numbered speed dial button you want to assign.

2. In the Name text box, type the name of the person or place that you will dial with that button.

3. Type the number to dial in the Number to Dial text box.

4. Click Save. (You'll be returned to the Phone Dialer dialog box and the name you entered in the Edit Speed Dial dialog box will appear on the numbered speed dial button you selected.)

5. To speed-dial the number, just click the button and lift your telephone handset.

TIP

When you enter a phone number in the Phone Dialer, don't forget to enter any numbers that are needed before the number, such as 1 or 70. Also, numbers can be entered separated by a dash, a space, or nothing at all, such as 555-1212 or 555 1212 or 5551212.

The Telephone Log

As mentioned at the beginning of this section, there are two ways to use the Phone Dialer. The quick and easy way is to use the speed dialer, but as you may have noticed, the speed dialer is limited to a list of eight numbers.

If you have more than eight numbers that you call on a regular basis, you'll have to use your log. Here's how:

1. In the opening Phone Dialer screen, either type the number in the Number to Dial box or use the telephone keypad in the Phone Dialer dialog box to enter the number.

2. When the number is completely entered, click the Dial button and pick up your telephone. In a moment, you will be connected to the number you are calling.

3. If you need to call the number again, pull down the Tools menu and select Show Log. This displays a list of all the numbers you have called.

4. To redial one of these numbers, double-click its entry in the log.

You can see how the Phone Dialer can be a terrific convenience if you spend a lot of time making calls.

USING THE CALCULATORS

You actually have two calculators in Windows 98: a standard calculator, the likes of which you could buy for $4.95 at any drugstore counter, and a scientific calculator.

Just the Basics

To start the Calculator, click Start ➤ Programs ➤ Accessories ➤ Calculator and you'll see the opening screen shown in Figure 14.8.

FIGURE 14.8: The basic calculator

Using the mouse, click the numbers and functions just as if you were pressing the keys on a hand-held calculator. Or, if you have a numerical keypad on your keyboard, press NumLock and then use the keypad keys to enter numbers and basic math functions.

Or One Step Beyond

To access the scientific calculator, pull down the View menu on the Calculator and select Scientific. That displays the calculator in Figure 14.9.

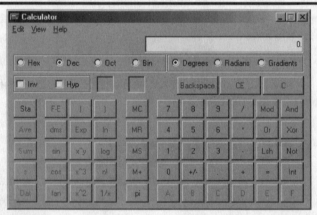

FIGURE 14.9:   The much more sophisticated scientific calculator

TIP

If you're unsure of the use for a function, right-click its button. You'll see a rectangle containing the words "What's This?" Click the text to see a short explanation of the function.

Pasting in the Numbers

Both calculators can be used in conjunction with the Clipboard. Type a number in any application, and select it. Press Ctrl+C (for Copy). Press Alt+Tab until the calculator is selected (or click it in the Taskbar) and then press Ctrl+V (for Paste). The number will appear in the number display of the calculator as if you had entered it from the calculator keypad.

Work your magic—adding, subtracting, multiplying, or deriving the inverse sine. You can pull down the Edit menu and select Copy, which places the contents of the display on the Clipboard, ready for you to paste into your document.

TIP

Here's a neat trick to transfer numbers from one calculator view to another. First, click the MS button to store the displayed number. Then, on the View menu, click the desired view. Finally, click the MR button to recall the stored number.

COMMUNICATING WITH HYPERTERMINAL

HyperTerminal is the Windows 98 applet that accesses other computers, bulletin boards, and online services through your modem. For the most part, all of HyperTerminal's work will be done for you by your Internet service provider or your online service. But there may be special occasions where you need HyperTerminal to make a connection.

To start HyperTerminal, click Start ➤ Programs ➤ Accessories ➤ Communications ➤ HyperTerminal. Then click the HyperTerminal icon (HYPERTRM.EXE) and you'll see the opening screen shown in Figure 14.10.

All you need to do to create a new connection is select File ➤ New Connection. The New Connection window will appear where you assign a name to the new connection and specify an icon (see Figure 14.10).

FIGURE 14.10: The HyperTerminal screen, where you begin the connection process

How to Use It

When you use HyperTerminal, each connection you make can be named and provided with an icon. That allows you to quickly identify connections so you can make them again. Once established, all it takes is a click on the icon to connect to where you want.

Let's create a fictional connection that will allow us to fill out the dialog box. Imagine you're a journalist working for a newspaper called *The Past Times* and you need to log on to the paper's BBS to file stories and columns.

1. Type **The Past Times** in the Name text box.

2. Scroll through the icons until you locate an icon that resembles a briefcase and an umbrella—what better icon for a reporter?

3. Click the OK button. You will see the Connect To dialog box shown here.

4. If the number you want to dial is located in a country other than the one listed in the Country Code list, click the downward-pointing arrow at the right end of the list box and select the correct country.

5. Enter the area code and phone number of the BBS in the appropriate text boxes. (For our example, enter 555-1212 as the number, and click the OK button.)

6. The Connect dialog box opens. Since this is the first time we've run this application, click the Dialing Properties button to confirm that the connection is made properly. Look over the options in this dialog box, and make sure that they're correctly set.

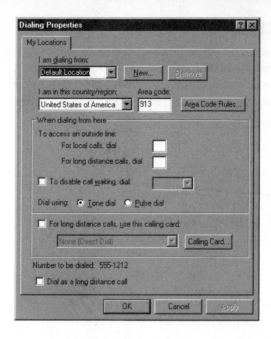

7. If you click the Calling Card button, a dialog box will open for you to enter your telephone credit card number.

8. If you have to dial a number to get out of your business or hotel phone system (typically 9 or 7), enter this number in the appropriate To Access an Outside Line text box and enter the number (or numbers) you dial for long distance access in the text box below it.

9. When you are through filling out this dialog box, click OK. You will see the Connect dialog box again.

10. At this point, all you need to do is click Dial to make the connection. If all the settings you made in the previous dialog boxes are correct, the call will go through, and you can use the BBS software to upload your story to the newspaper. (We'll cover file transfers in a moment.)

11. When you're through placing your call, pull down the Call menu and select Disconnect, or click the icon that looks like a handset being hung up and the connection will be broken.

12. When you close the window, you will be prompted to save the session.

Sending Files

Once you have connected with a remote computer, you will probably want to upload or download files. This is the principal reason for making this sort of connection. The file transfer protocols (which are the rules for transferring information) supported by HyperTerminal are:

- ▶ 1K Xmodem
- ▶ Xmodem
- ▶ Ymodem
- ▶ Ymodem-G
- ▶ Zmodem
- ▶ Zmodem with Crash Recovery
- ▶ Kermit

Binary Files

To send a binary file, follow these steps:

1. After the connection is made, pull down the Transfer menu.

2. Select Send File. A dialog box will open.

3. Using the options in this dialog box, specify the file to send. Click the Browse button to locate and identify the file to be sent.

4. Select the protocol for file transfer from the Protocol drop-down menu. Zmodem is the best choice because it combines speed and good error correction (see Figure 14.11).

5. Click the Send button. The file will be transferred.

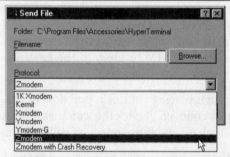

FIGURE 14.11: Here's where you select a binary file and the protocol for sending it.

Text Files

Text files are a little different from binary files. Most file transfer software distinguishes between binary files and text files—sending one in Binary mode and the other in ASCII mode or Text mode. HyperTerminal is no different.

To send a text file, follow the steps for a binary file, but choose Send Text File from the Transfer menu. When you specify the file to send and click the Open button, the file will be sent as if you had typed it into the terminal program.

TIP

Unless you're transferring files to a Unix system, you're usually better off sending every file as a binary file. Even a little bit of formatting in the file can cause a text file transfer to fail, while *any* file can be sent as a binary transfer.

And Receiving Them Too

To receive a file being sent from another computer:

1. Pull down the Transfer menu and select Receive File. That will open a dialog box like the one shown in Figure 14.12.

2. Click the Browse button to specify a file name and location for the received file.

3. Select a file transfer protocol.

4. Click the Receive button to start receiving the file from the remote location.

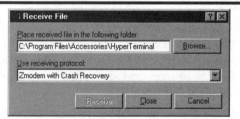

FIGURE 14.12: Receiving files using HyperTerminal

NOTE

Take the above steps when you hear the incoming call from the other computer. You have to do this yourself because HyperTerminal is not smart enough to answer the phone.

Saving a Session

To help you remember how to navigate the complexities of a service you don't use very often, terminal programs provide *logging*–a way to save everything you do in a particular session to disk and/or print it on paper.

To save everything to a file:

1. Pull down the Transfer menu and select Capture Text.

2. By default, all the screen information in a session will be saved in a file called CAPTURE.TXT in the HyperTerminal folder inside the Accessories folder. Of course, you can use the Browse button to save the file in a different location. Click Start when you're ready.

3. Pull down the Transfer menu again. Now you will note that there is a tiny triangle next to the Capture Text option. Select it and you will see a submenu with Stop, Pause, and Resume options to give you control over the capture.

4. If you prefer to send the session to the printer rather than to a file on your disk, pull down the Transfer menu and select Capture to Printer.

Using a Connection

As you may recall, when we started using HyperTerminal, we created a connection with a name and an icon. This connection appears in the HyperTerminal program group. Any time you want to use this connection in the future, simply double-click its icon, and all the settings (telephone number and so forth) will be in place for you.

Any time you want to change the settings in a particular connection, open the connection, pull down the File menu, and select Properties.

USING THE BRIEFCASE

The Briefcase is not an applet in the usual sense. You won't find it listed under Accessories, but Briefcase should be on your Desktop from the original installation of Windows 98. If you don't see it there, it's probably not installed. To install it, use the Add/Remove Programs option in the Control Panel (discussed in Chapter 6).

Briefcase is designed to help those with multiple computers keep a set of files synchronized. It may be your computer at work and your computer at home. Or maybe you have a desktop computer and a laptop where the same files are worked on. When two computers are involved, it's only a matter of time before things get confused as to which version of a memo or a speech is the most current one. Briefcase helps rectify that problem.

How It Works

When you open a Briefcase and copy a file into it, a link is made between the original and the copy in the Briefcase. This is called a *sync link*. After the link is made, you can work on the copy in the Briefcase or the original file and select Update All (from inside Briefcase), and the latest version will be copied over the earlier version, keeping both in sync.

To make use of Briefcase:

1. Drag the files that are important to the Briefcase folder on the Desktop of computer #1.

2. Copy the Briefcase to a floppy disk. Right-click and use the Send To command, which is particularly handy for this.

3. Take the floppy to computer #2. Open drive A either in Windows Explorer or My Computer.

4. Open the Briefcase. Work on the files inside the Briefcase on computer #2.

5. When you're finished, save and close the files on the floppy in the usual way.

6. Return the floppy to computer #1. Open the Briefcase on the floppy disk and select Update All from the Briefcase menu. Click the Update button.

WHAT'S NEXT?

You've now finished Part I of *Windows 98 Complete*, covering Windows 98 itself. Because one of the most important features of Windows 98 is its integration with the Internet Explorer browser, Part II of this book is an in-depth look at the Internet and the tools you've just acquired for browsing the Web, exchanging e-mail, and even building your own Web site. As an added bonus, you'll learn about Netscape Communicator, the most popular alternative to Internet Explorer, and about security issues such as screening inappropriate content and maintaining privacy for financial transactions.

PART ii
THE INTERNET AND
WINDOWS 98

Chapter 15

UNDERSTANDING INTERNET AND WORLD WIDE WEB BASICS

These days the Internet seems to be everywhere. Web addresses appear on television ads and billboards. There are TV shows and magazines devoted to the Internet. And virtually every new computer program that comes out has some Internet features. With the arrival of Windows 98, your computer desktop can now connect you just as easily to Internet resources as it does to the files on your hard drive.

I know, you're raring to go. You want to start sending and receiving e-mail, browsing the Web, and exploring the global library of fun stuff out on the Internet. Well, I don't want to hold you back. Feel free to skip to Chapter 16 and start right in on e-mail (or even jump to Chapter 17, to start messing around

Adapted from *The Internet: No Experience Required*, by Christian Crumlish
ISBN 0-7821-2168-3   528 pages $24.99

with the World Wide Web). However, if you're not clear on what the Net actually is, how you get access to it, and what you can do once you're there, I'll try to answer those questions here.

Notice that I just used the word *Net* and not *Internet*. For the most part, the words are synonymous, although some people will use the word Net to refer to just about any aspect of the global internetworking of computers. (Check out Appendix B—a glossary of Windows, Internet, and general computer terminology—to become more familiar with Internet jargon.)

NOTE

If you want a *really* thorough compendium of Internet jargon, terminology, and culture at your fingertips, try reading *The Internet Dictionary*, also written by Christian Crumlish and published by Sybex.

Introducing the Internet

Everybody talks about the Internet and the World Wide Web these days, but most people don't really know what the Internet is or what the differences between the Internet and the Web are. One reason for this is that the Internet looks different depending on how you come across it and what you do with it. Another reason is that everyone talks about it as if it's actually a network, like a local network in someone's office or even a large global network like CompuServe. Fact is, it's something different. A beast unto itself. The Internet is really a way for computers to communicate.

As long as a computer or smaller network can "speak" the Internet lingo (or *protocols*, to be extra formal about it) to other machines, then it's "on the Internet." Of course, the computer also needs a modem or a network connection and other hardware to make contact, too. Regardless of the hardware needs, if the Internet were a language, it wouldn't be French or Farsi or Tagalog or even English. It would be Esperanto.

Having said that, I might backtrack and allow that there's nothing wrong with thinking of the Internet as if it were a single network unto itself. It certainly behaves like one in a lot of important ways. But this can be misleading. No one "owns" the Internet. No one even really runs it. And no one can turn it off.

Communicating through E-mail or Discussion Groups

In addition to being a network of interconnected computers, the Internet is also a collection of different tools and devices for communicating and storing information in a retrievable form.

Take e-mail, for example. If you work in an office with a local-area network, then chances are you have an e-mail account and can communicate with people in your office by sending them messages through the company's internal system. (See Chapter 16 for an in-depth discussion of all the ins and outs of e-mail.) This is not the Internet.

Similarly, if you have an account at America Online and you send a message to someone else at AOL, you're still not using the Internet. But, if your office network has a *gateway* to the Internet, and you send e-mail to someone who does not work at your office, then you're sending mail over the Internet. Likewise, if you send a message from your AOL account to someone at CompuServe, or elsewhere, then again you are sending messages over the Internet (see Figure 15.1).

NOTE

A *gateway* is a computer, or the program running on it, that transfers files (or e-mail messages, or commands) from one network to another.

But from your point of view, the Internet is not just a collection of networks all talking to each other. A single computer can also participate in the Internet by connecting to a network or service provider that's connected to the Internet. And while the local office network I described and the big commercial online services are not themselves the Internet, they can and often do provide access through their gateways to the Internet. (I cover online services later in this chapter, in the section called "Cruising the Net at Home.")

All of this can be confusing to first-time Internet users (universally referred to as *newbies*). Say you have an AOL account and you join one of the *discussion groups* (bulletin boards) there. It may not be obvious to you right away whether you're talking in an internal venue—one only accessible to AOL members—or in a public Internet newsgroup. One of the benefits of an online service is the way various functions, including e-mail, Internet access, and online content, are brought together seamlessly so that they appear to be part of the same little program running on your computer.

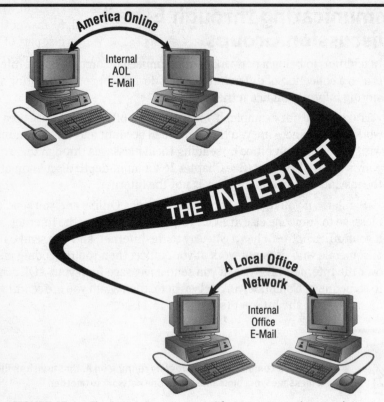

FIGURE 15.1: The Internet carries e-mail from one network to another.

NOTE

A *bulletin board* is a public discussion area where people can post messages—without sending them to anyone's individual e-mail address—that can be viewed by anyone who enters the area. Other people can then reply to posted messages, and ongoing discussions can ensue. On CompuServe, a bulletin board is called a *forum*. On the Internet, the equivalent areas are called *newsgroups*.

What's the Difference between the Web and the Internet?

Nowadays, most of the hype about the Internet is focused on the World Wide Web. It has existed for less than 10 years but it has been the fastest growing and most popular part of the Net for many of those years (except, perhaps, for the voluminous flow of e-mail around the globe). But what is the Web and is it the same thing as the Internet? Well, to answer the second question first: yes and no. Technically, the *Web* is just part of the Internet—or, more properly, a way of getting around part of the Internet. But it's a big part because a lot of the Internet that's not (strictly speaking) *part of* the Web can still be reached with a Web browser.

So the Web, on one level, is an *interface*. A window onto the Net. A way of getting to where you're going. Its appeal derives from three different benefits:

1. It disguises the gobbledygook that passes for Internet addresses and commands. (See "Getting On the Internet" later in this chapter.)

2. It wraps up most of the different features of the Internet into a single interface used by Web applications.

3. It allows you to see pictures, and even hear sounds or watch movies (if your computer can hack it), along with your helpings of text.

TIP

To play sounds, your computer needs a sound card, speakers, and some kind of software (such as Microsoft Sound Recorder for Windows, but there are many others). To play movies, your computer needs software (such as Media Player or QuickTime) and a lot of memory (or else the movies will look herky-jerky).

It helps to know a little bit about the history of the Net to understand why these three features of the Web have spurred on the Internet boom. First of all, before the Web existed, doing anything beyond simple e-mailing (and even that could be difficult, depending on your type of access) used to require knowing weird Unix commands and understanding the Internet's system for numbering and naming all the computers connected to it. If you've ever wrestled with DOS and lost, then you can appreciate the effort required to surmount this type of barrier.

Imagine it's 1991 and you've gotten yourself an Internet account, solved the problems of logging in with a communications program to a Unix computer somewhere out there, and mastered the Unix programs needed to send and receive e-mail, read newsgroups, download files, and so on. You'd still be looking at lots of plain text, screens and screens of words. No pictures. Well, if you were dying for pictures you could download enormous

Part ii

text files that had begun their lives as pictures and then were encoded as plain text so they could be squeezed through the text-only pipelines that constituted the Net. Next you'd have to decode the files, download them onto your PC, and then run some special program to look at them. Not quite as easy as flipping through a magazine.

The Web uses a coding method called *hypertext* to disguise the actual commands and addresses you use to navigate the Net. Instead of these commands and addresses, what you see in your *Web browser* (the program you use to travel the Web) is plain English keywords highlighted in some way. Simply click on the keywords, and your browser program talks the Internet talk, negotiates the transaction with the computer at the other end, and brings the picture, text, program, or activity you desire onto your computer screen. This is how all computer functions should work (and probably how they will work one day).

Early Unix-based Web browsers, such as Www (developed at CERN, the European particle physics laboratory where the Web was invented) and Lynx (developed at the University of Kansas), were not especially attractive to look at, but they did offer the "one-step" technique for jumping to a specific location on the Net or for downloading a file or piece of software.

The next advance on the Web was the development of graphical Web browsers that could run on a desktop PC (or Macintosh), permitting the user to employ the familiar point-and-click techniques of other software and incorporating text formatting and graphics into the browser screen. The first program of this type was NCSA Mosaic, which was developed at the National Center for Supercomputer Applications and distributed for free.

Furthermore, the various Web browsers can more or less substitute for a plethora of little specialty programs (such as Gopher clients, newsreaders, FTP programs, and so on) that you had to assemble and set up yourself "in the old days." The browsers all have their own little idiosyncrasies, but they're still remarkably uniform and consistent compared to the maze of different programs and rules you had to work your way through just a few years ago. These days, the most popular browser is Netscape Navigator, shown in Figure 15.2, which is now part of Communicator, Netscape's all-purpose network client program.

NOTE

"Just a few years ago" is the old days on the Internet. Changes happen so rapidly in the online world that time on the Internet is like "dog years"—something like seven years go by for each one in the real world.

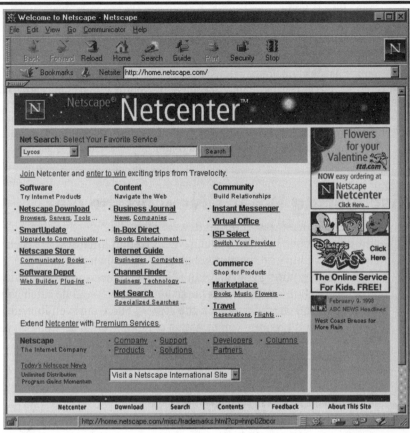

FIGURE 15.2: Netscape Navigator is hands-down the most popular World Wide Web browser program.

The Web has made it possible for browsers to display pictures right there in the midst of text, without your having to know how to decode files. A picture's worth a lot of words, and pictures look better in newspaper articles and on TV than scads of typewritten text. So this final ingredient made the Web seem both accessible and interesting to people who would never in a million years care to learn what a Unix "regular expression" is.

I have tried to answer the question that heads up this section: What's the difference between the Web and the Internet? Technically the Web and the Internet are not exactly the same, but for all intents and purposes they have a lot in common. Web browsers are the must-have programs that have made the Internet what it is today.

NOTE

You can use the Internet and the Web to find new friends and uncover fun facts and interesting Web sites. Individuals and groups all over the planet have gotten together on the Internet to explore mutual interests. Environmental and political causes, pets, sports, leisure activities, the arts, and the sciences are just some of the popular topics continually updated on the Internet.

Discovering What's New on the Net

These days, the latest Internet developments are mostly being driven by the access tools. Browser makers Netscape and Microsoft are each trying to develop all-in-one solutions that make their own products the "platform" for everything you do on the Net. New companies are offering free Internet accounts with a Web-based e-mail interface. The catch? You have to keep the ad window open on the screen. There are even Internet solutions that don't require you to have a computer, such as WebTV (your TV plus a modem plus a keyboard plus a remote), or a modem, such as DirectPC (your computer plus a special satellite hook up).

The Web on Your Desktop

From the user's point of view, the biggest changes planned for day-to-day Internet and World Wide Web use are in the way Internet access is being built directly into computer operating-system desktops (as well as directly into many new applications). Both Netscape and Microsoft are trying to turn their browsers into substitute desktops, more or less merging your view of the Internet (out there) and your own computer (in here). The integration of Windows 98 with Internet Explorer is by far the most ambitious step in this direction so far.

NOTE

The Internet has also become a great source of career information. Companies list jobs and freelance opportunities. You can research companies on the Internet and train yourself on a variety of topics that might come up in an interview. You can find business contacts and develop new ones through Internet e-mail, conferencing, and forums on particular subjects.

Netcasts Beamed onto Your Screen

The popularity of PointCast (see Figure 15.3), a program that displays news on your screen and automatically connects to the Internet for updates, has demonstrated a market for "netcasting" software (programs that "broadcast" over the Internet directly to your computer screen). This use of the Internet is more passive, more like TV than the interactive, Web-browsing model, but it's possible to do both. The new Internet Explorer will offer various netcasting "channels" and Microsoft has already made a special deal with PointCast to make their offerings one of those channels.

FIGURE 15.3: The PointCast Network (shown here in screen-saver mode) automatically downloads news from the Net and displays it on your computer screen.

NOTE

The type of news you can have netcasted to your desktop ranges from sports to headline and financial news, as well as more specialized topics (science and technology, fashion, arts and entertainment) that you define and refine with your netcasting software.

Applications with Internet Features

The growth of the Internet, coupled with the advent of smaller, local, company or organization intranets running on Internet principles, has led users to expect their everyday business software to help them deal with retrieving remote documents, collaborate with colleagues over network links, and save or publish documents to Web and intranet servers. To meet this demand, software publishers are adding Internet features to their programs left and right. You can expect your next upgrade of various programs to include the ability to transfer files (open them from and save them to remote computers) and probably to create documents and reports in HTML (hypertext Web format) as well. See Chapter 20 for more on how to make Web documents.

NOTE

Knowing how to use Internet features in common business applications is a great job skill, even if you don't work in a high-technology field. All kinds of companies are depending more on the Internet and the World Wide Web to find information and promote their services and products. Companies and organizations are also developing in-house intranets to store policies, manuals, and other information. Having knowledge of the Internet is certainly a big plus in today's competitive job market.

GETTING ON THE INTERNET

So what exactly does it mean to be "on the Internet"? Generally, if someone asks you, "Are you on the Net?" it means something like, "Do you have an Internet e-mail address?" That is, do you have e-mail and can your e-mail account be reached over the Internet? With the popularity of the Web being what it is, another common interpretation of what it means to be on the Net is, "Do you have the ability to browse the World Wide Web?" Often these two features—Internet e-mail and Web access—go hand in hand, but not always. We're also getting to a time when being on the Internet will also entail having your own home page, your own "place" on the Web where information about you is stored and where you can be found.

Cruising the Net at Work

More and more companies these days (as well as schools and other organizations) are installing internal networks and relying on e-mail as one of the ways to share information. E-mail messages are starting to replace interoffice memos, at least for some types of announcements, questions, and scheduling purposes. The logical next step for most of these organizations is to connect their internal network to the Internet through a gateway. When this happens, you may suddenly be on the Net. This doesn't mean that anything will necessarily change on your desktop. You'll probably still use the same e-mail program and still send and receive mail within your office in the same way you always have.

WARNING

Some companies use Internet-usage monitoring programs that tell them how long employees have been using the Internet and what type of sites they are visiting. Use good judgment when you surf the Internet at work and try to explore only those sites that have potentially important work-related information.

What will change at this point is that you'll be able to send e-mail to people on the Internet outside of your office, as long as you type the right kind of Internet address. (Generally, this means adding @ and then a series of words separated by periods to the username portion of an address, but I'll explain more about addresses at the end of this chapter.) Likewise, people out there in the great beyond will be able to send e-mail to you as well.

Depending on the type of Internet connection your company has, e-mail may be all you get. Then again, it might also be possible for you to run a Web browser on your computer and visit Internet sites while sitting at your desk. Of course, your company will only want you to do this if it's relevant to your job, but it works the same way whether you're researching a product your company uses or reading cartoons at the Dilbert site.

NOTE

Your ability to find information on the Internet that your company needs will become a highly prized career asset, especially as more and more organizations contribute to the growth of the Internet.

Cruising the Net at Home

If you're interested in exploring the Internet as a form of entertainment or for personal communication, then a work account is not really the way to do it. (An account minimally consists of a username and an e-mail Inbox; it may also provide storage space on a computer or access to a Web server.)

Part ii

You'll need your own personal account to really explore the Internet on your own time, without looking over your shoulder to make sure nobody's watching.

TIP

If your office is quite sophisticated, you may actually be able to dial into a company network from home via a modem to check your e-mail messages. Chapter 13 shows how to use Windows 98's features for remote access.

Your best bet is to sign up for an account from a commercial online service or a direct-access Internet service provider. What's the difference between those two choices? Well, an *online service* (such as CompuServe, America Online, Prodigy, Microsoft Network, and so on) is first and foremost a private, proprietary network, offering its own content and access to other network members, generally combined with Internet access. An *Internet service provider* (also called an *ISP*) offers just access to the Internet and no proprietary content (or only very limited local information and discussion groups). Figure 15.4 will help illustrate this distinction.

Online services have only recently begun offering full (or somewhat limited) Internet access. Because they are trying to do two things at once (sell you their own content and connect you to the Internet), they are usually an expensive way of exploring the Net. On the other hand, they tend to offer a single, simplified interface. I often recommend to people who just want to get their feet wet before plunging wholeheartedly into the Net, to sign up for a free trial account at one of the online services. If they like what the Internet has to offer or if they start using the Net so much they run up an expensive bill (after that first free month), then I recommend that they switch to a direct-access Internet service provider.

ISPs can be much cheaper than online services, especially if you can find one that offers a flat rate—a monthly charge that doesn't vary no matter how much time you spend connected to the Net. They also don't try to compete with the Internet by offering their own content and sponsors. Instead, they function as a gateway, getting you onto the Internet and letting you go wherever you want.

What Kinds of ISP Accounts Are There?

An ISP account generally includes, along with the e-mail address, storage space on a computer somewhere on the Net. You will be billed monthly,

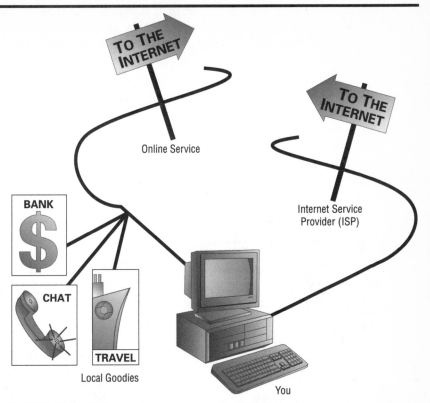

FIGURE 15.4: Online services connect you to the Internet but encourage you to explore their own offerings, whereas ISPs just connect you to the Internet and let you fend for yourself.

and depending on the provider, there may be a surcharge based on the amount of time you spent connected that month or the amount of space you used on their hard drive.

But how do you use an account? Well, you need a computer with a modem, and you need software that knows how to use that modem to call up (dial up) your provider and allows you to log in to your account. Fortunately, most modems come with their own software.

Your ISP will take care of all the technical details for you and will probably supply you with a setup disk and easy-to-use software for connecting to the Internet. Once you're set up, you won't have to think much about whether you have a PPP or SLIP account or any other kind of account, but I want to introduce the terminology now so you'll know what I'm talking about when I mention it again. If you want more than simply a connection to a Unix command-line and a plain text account (and I suspect that you do), then nowadays you need something called a *PPP* or *SLIP account*. (The other kind is usually called a *shell account* or sometimes a *Unix shell account*.)

A PPP (or SLIP) account lets your computer behave like it's connected directly to another computer on the Internet—when it's really connected over a phone line whenever you dial in—and it enables you to run software, such as graphical Web browsers like Microsoft Internet Explorer and Netscape Navigator, that functions in your computer's native environment (Windows) instead of forcing you to deal with plain-text programs like the text-only browsers Lynx and Unix (see Figure 15.5).

PPP-Type Internet Connection

Unix-Shell Type Internet Connection

FIGURE 15.5: With a PPP (or SLIP) account, your connection to the Internet is seamlessly integrated into your computer's normal environment.

WARNING

By the way, the speed of your modem—and that of the modem at the other end of the dial-up line, that is, your provider's modem—determines the speed of your Internet connection, and even the fastest modems these days are still slower than a direct network connection to the Net, such as you might enjoy at your office.

The Anatomy of an Internet Address

One of the confusing things to Internet newbies is that the word "address" is used to mean at least three different things on the Internet. The most basic meaning—but the one used least often—is the name of a computer, also called a *host* or *site*, on the Internet in the form something.something .something (to really use the lingo properly you have to pronounce the periods as "dot"—you'll get used to it and it saves a lot of time over the long haul). For example, I publish a magazine (or 'zine) on the Internet called *Enterzone*; it's stored on a machine at Vassar that is part of the American Arts and Letters Network. The address of that machine is

```
ezone.org
```

Reading from right to left, you first have the *domain,* org, which stands for (nonprofit) organization. Next you sometimes have a *subdomain*. Finally you have the *hostname*, ezone, which is the name (or a name) of the specific computer the magazine is stored on.

Another type of address is an e-mail address. An e-mail address consists of a *username* (also called a *login*, a *log-on name*, a *userID*, an *account name*, and so on), followed by an "at sign" (@) and then an Internet address of the type just described. So, for example, say you want to send mail to me in my capacity as editor of Enterzone. You could address that e-mail message to a special username created for that job (it will stay the same even if someone else takes over in the future):

```
editor@ezone.org
```

The third type of address is the kind you see everywhere these days, on billboards, on TV commercials, in the newspaper, and so on—a Web address, also called an *URL* (*Uniform Resource Locator*). You'll learn more about how to read (or ignore) URLs in Chapter 17. For now, it's enough just to know what one looks like. The Web address of that magazine I told you about is

```
http://ezone.org/ez
```

TIP

You can leave out the www portion of the address when using certain Web browsers. Some Internet addresses use the http:// designation, but leave out the www. portion, so try both ways if you have difficulty getting through.

Fortunately, you often can avoid typing in Web addresses yourself and can zip around the Web just by clicking pre-established *links*. Links are highlighted words or images that, when clicked-on or selected, take you directly to a new document, another part of the current document, or some other type of file entirely.

NOTE

The InterNIC committee attempting to govern the Internet has added some new domain name options. Now, in addition to .org for nonprofits, .com for commercial users, .net for service providers, and .edu for educational concerns; you may see .firm, .store, .web, .info, .rec, .arts, and .nom. The .mil designation is reserved for the military and .gov for government agencies.

USING THE NET WITH OTHER PLATFORMS

Of course, Windows 98 and Internet Explorer 4 integrate the Web and your computer Desktop more closely than any previous software. But if you sometimes work with other platforms, such as the Macintosh or Unix, you'll be glad to know that the Internet makes some of the seemingly important distinctions between types of computers a lot less important. The information out on the Internet, the public discussion areas, and the World Wide Web look and act more or less the same, no matter what kind of computer you use. In fact, the Web is quickly becoming a sort of universal computer platform now that certain types of programs and services are being designed to run on the Web, rather than to run on one specific type of computer.

Part of the elegance of the Internet is that much of the heavy duty processing power and storage of large programs and dense information takes place "out there," and not on your computer. Your computer—whether it's a PC, a Mac, or a Unix workstation—becomes just a convenient beanstalk to climb up to the land of the Internet giants. You'll sometimes refer to this common structure of Internet facilities as *client-server* (sorry for the jargon). In this scenario, you are the client (or your computer or the program running on it is) and the information source, or World Wide Web site, or mail-handling program is the server. Servers are centralized repositories of information or specialized handlers of certain kinds of traffic. All a client has to do is connect to the right server and a wealth of goodies are within your reach, without your having to overload your machine. This is a major reason why it doesn't matter what kind of computer you prefer.

WHAT YOU CAN DO ON THE NET

I've touched on the most popular facilities on the Internet—e-mail and the World Wide Web—but I'll run down some of the other useful features.

> **NOTE**
>
> Some of these Internet tools are covered elsewhere in *Windows 98 Complete*, but for others you'll need to consult books written specifically about the Internet. Current Sybex titles in this area include *The Internet: No Experience Required*, *Surfing the Internet with Netscape Communicator 4*, and others.

Search Engines   Once you start exploring the Web, you might get tired of its disorganization (imagine a library where every card-carrying member worked part-time as a librarian for one of the shelves, and each micro-librarian used their own system for organizing their section) or with not knowing for sure where anything is on the Internet. Fortunately, there are a lot of useful *search engines* available on the Net. A *search engine* is a program or Web page that enables you to search an Internet site (or the entire Internet) for a specific key word or words. Not as thorough as a card catalog, perhaps, but easier to use. (See Chapter 17 for more about search tools in Internet Explorer.)

Usenet   For many Internet users, the first step beyond e-mail and the Web is into the Internet's sometimes loosely organized system of public message boards called *Usenet* (or simply News). Here you'll find discussion groups (known as "newsgroups") on just about any area of interest imaginable. People "post" messages expressing opinions on topics related to the group or looking for information; other people reply with their own opinions or the requested information.

Usenet has a highly evolved subculture and a set of rules for good behavior known as "Netiquette." For example, if a newsgroup provides a FAQ (answers to Frequently Asked Questions), it's good Netiquette to read the FAQ before asking the whole group your question; someone may have already answered it. A good way to get started with newsgroups is to "lurk"— to read discussions without participating at first. Both Internet Explorer and Netscape Navigator provide access to News, directly and through search engines. You'll also find some Usenet terminology in this book's Glossary (Appendix B).

Chat   If you prefer the idea of communicating with people "live" rather than posting messages and waiting for people to reply later, then you'll want to know about the various chat facilities available on the Internet—particularly *IRC* (*Internet Relay Chat*). Briefly, if you're connected to another user via Chat, you can type messages back and forth. Each of you will see the other's response right away. It's like a telephone call, on your computer screen. And more than two people can participate, in conferences known as "chat rooms." A Chat program is part of Netscape Communicator, the larger suite that includes Navigator; Internet Explorer's NetMeeting tool also includes a Chat feature.

FTP   The File Transfer Protocol is one of the Internet's oldest and most reliable tools for exchanging ("uploading" and "downloading") files of any kind. FTP servers (known as "hosts") can make files available to specific users (who must provide a password) or to anyone (a technique called "anonymous FTP"); for example, software companies often provide updates or demonstration versions of their products for downloading via anonymous FTP. With both Internet Explorer and Netscape Navigator you can connect to FTP sites, either by clicking on links to them in some Web pages or by typing the server's URL in the browser's Address or Location field.

Building Your Own Web Page   Finally, if you want to join the ranks of people with their own home pages on the Web—to create a "presence" on the Net or publicize your favorite Internet sites—Chapter 20 of this book shows you how to do that as well.

Downloading Files from the Internet

Another aspect of the Internet that you will especially enjoy is the ability to download files from a vast selection of sample applications, digital art and music, and many other offerings. Software companies promote their new products by maintaining sites where their customers can obtain samples, updates, and related information. Entertainment conglomerates supply sound and video files for movies, bands, and video games. Some organizations just collect information relevant to their interests, such as schedules of upcoming activities, databases of similar organizations, and the like.

WARNING

Before you attempt to access files from the Internet, you should protect your computer (or your company's network) with anti-virus software. Computers downloading Internet files are the principal point of entry for computer viruses. You'll learn more about viruses and how to defend against them in Chapter 18.

The files obtained from the Internet can be quite large, so they often arrive compressed to a smaller size, and may also be coded for protection against unauthorized use or modifications. These files have to be decompressed and decoded before you can use them. Compression-decompression software and decoding applications are readily available, both as free Internet downloads (called freeware), and as commercial applications that you pay for.

Many Internet users are concerned about their privacy while using the Net, especially if they are filling out forms or making purchases with credit cards over the World Wide Web. Programming geniuses have given us applications that try to protect our good credit and our privacy. Some of these efforts are even given away free on the Internet. Chapter 18 will touch on some of the privacy precautions you can take on the Internet.

Using Web Sites to Gather Information about the Internet and the Web

You can visit the Internet itself to glean more details about its history, policies, and users. Use the Web sites listed below as the starting point for a journey through various interpretations of how to use the Internet, how it evolved, and how it should be regulated. These sites all contain links to even more sites that will take you surfing farther afield in your quest for knowledge about the Web.

The Internet Society `http://info.isoc.org` A simple site that includes Internet history and a timeline, as well as links to other technical organizations dealing with the Web and communication in general.

Electronic Frontier Foundation `http://www.eff.org` A mainly civil-rights oriented site with many pages on free speech, privacy, and policy. Also home of the (Extended) Guide to the Internet, a lengthy document containing everything you might ever want to know about the origins of the Internet.

Part ii

World Wide Web Consortium   http://www.w3.org   A site hosted by MIT, the European Union, and DARPA (the defense agency that developed the Internet). This site has everything from very technical and lengthy documents to press releases and policy statements.

Well, I think I've kept you waiting long enough. Are you ready for e-mail?

WHAT'S NEXT?

In the following chapters, Christian Crumlish and other *Windows 98 Complete* contributors will show how to use e-mail, browse the Web with Internet Explorer or with Netscape Navigator, make your Internet use more secure, use the new Channel bar, and build your own Web page.

Chapter 16

COMMUNICATING WITH E-MAIL

This is the real stuff. The reason why you're on the Net. E-mail! Instant (more or less) communication with people all over the globe. Once you can send and receive e-mail, you're wired.

When you get used to sending e-mail, you'll find that it's as useful a form of communication as the telephone, and it doesn't require the other person to drop whatever they're doing to answer your call. You can include a huge amount of specific information, and the person you sent mail to can reply in full in their own good time. And unlike the telephone, with e-mail you can write your message and edit it before you send it.

E-mail is the lifeblood of the Internet. Daily, millions of written messages course through the wires, enabling people all over the planet to communicate in seconds. One reason for the widespread use of the Internet as the international computer network is that it's a flexible enough system to allow just about any type

Adapted from *The Internet: No Experience Required*, by Christian Crumlish

ISBN 0-7821-2168-3   528 pages $24.99

of computer or network to participate. Of course, this book assumes you're using a PC with Windows 98 and either the Outlook Express mailer that's bundled with Internet Explorer or the Messenger mailer included in the Netscape Communicator suite. But it's important to remember that e-mail programs basically do the same things.

I'll start off by explaining the most common activities associated with e-mail, the kinds of things you'll want to know how to do no matter what program you have. I'll use generic terminology in this part of the lesson, such as Inbox and Outbox, even if some specific programs use different terms for the same ideas. Focus on the concepts and the standard features, not what they're called in one program or another. Then, I'll cover specific commands and tips for the e-mail programs you're most likely to use.

NOTE

Christian Crumlish wrote *The Internet: No Experience Required* for all new Internet users, no matter what operating system and software they are using; not just for Windows 98 users working with Internet Explorer or Netscape Communicator. In particular, its e-mail chapters include extensive coverage of other e-mail programs that we've omitted in adapting this material for *Windows 98 Complete*. If you have access to a Macintosh or Unix system, or a mailer such as Eudora or Pegasus, you may want to consult *The Internet: No Experience Required* for details.

E-MAIL BASICS

These are the things that you will do most often with e-mail:

- ▶ Run the mail program
- ▶ Send mail
- ▶ Read incoming mail
- ▶ Reply to mail
- ▶ Delete mail
- ▶ Exit the mail program

In the second half of this chapter, I'll show you some additional e-mail tricks you might find useful, such as how to forward mail and create an electronic address book.

Running an E-mail Program

You start most e-mail programs the way you do any program, usually by double-clicking an icon or by choosing a program name from a menu (the Start menu in Windows 98). If your Internet connection is not already up and running, your e-mail program may be able to start that process for you.

Your e-mail program will start and show you either the contents of your Inbox (the mailbox where your new messages arrive) or a list of all your mailboxes (in which case you'll want to open the Inbox).

NOTE

There are some new free Internet accounts (such as HotMail and Juno.com), that offer Web-based e-mail access. The accounts are paid for by advertising you have to keep on your screen while you're connected. To find out more about them, go to http://www.HotMail.com or http://www.Juno.com in your Internet browser.

In addition to an Inbox where just-arrived messages appear, you'll automatically have an Outbox in which copies of your outgoing messages can be saved (some programs will do this automatically), and usually a deleted-messages or Trash mailbox where discarded messages are held until they are completely purged.

Mailboxes generally list just the sender's name and the subject line of the message (and probably its date as well). When you double-click on a message in any of your mailboxes, the message will open up in a window of its own.

Sending Mail

All mail programs have a New Message or Compose E-mail command, often located on a message menu, and they usually have a keyboard shortcut for the command as well, such as Ctrl+N for New Message. When you start a new message, your program will open a new window. Figure 16.1 shows a new message window in Outlook Express.

TIP

You can also save addresses and then select them from an address book or list of names rather than type them in directly. See "Managing an Address Book" later in this chapter for more on this.

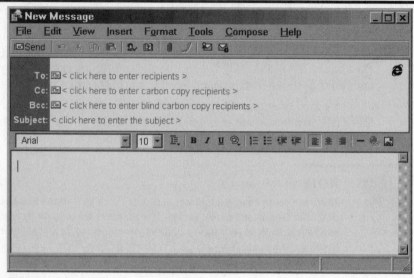

FIGURE 16.1: A blank New Message window

Type the address of the person to whom you wish to send the mail. The person's address must be of the form *username@address.domain*, where *username* is the person's identifier (the name they log in with); *address* is the identifier of the person's network or machine on the network (the address might consist of several words—the host and subdomain—separated by dots); and *domain* is the short code at the end indicating whether the address is a business (.com), a nonprofit (.org), a university (.edu), a branch of the government (.gov), a part of the military (.mi1), and so on. (Some e-mail programs require special text before or after the Internet e-mail address.) Would you rather write up your message ahead of time and then just paste it in when it comes time to send it? See "Writing E-mail with Your Word Processor," later in this chapter.

By the way, all the rules just mentioned apply only to sending mail over the Internet. Generally, if you're sending mail to someone on your own network (or another member of your online service or a subscriber of your service provider), you only have to specify the username, not any of the Internet information.

TIP

The easiest way to send mail to someone is to reply to mail that they've sent you. If you're not sure exactly how to form someone's e-mail address, ask them to send you some mail and then simply reply to it. That's what I always do.

One of my addresses is `xian@netcom.com` (you pronounce the "@" as "at," and the "." as "dot"). I log in as "xian," my service provider is Netcom, and Netcom is a commercial business.

Sending Mail to People on Other Networks

Many people have Internet addresses even though they are not, strictly speaking, on the Internet. Most other networks have gateways that send mail to and from the Internet. If you want to send mail to someone on another network, you'll need to know their identifier on that network and how their network address appears in Internet form. Here are examples of the most common Internet addresses:

Network	Username	Internet Address
America Online	Beebles	`Beebles@aol.com`
AT&T Mail	Beebles	`beebles@attmail.com`
CompuServe	75555,5555	`75555.5555@compuserve.com`
MCI Mail	555-7777	`555-7777@mcimail.com`
Microsoft Network	Beebles	`beebles@msn.com`
Prodigy	Beebles	`beebles@prodigy.com`

1. After entering the recipient's address in the Address box, press Tab and then type a subject in the Subject box (keep it short). This will be the first thing the recipient of your mail sees.

TIP

The subject you type in the subject line should be fairly short, but should be a good description of the contents of your message. Good subject lines can help recipients categorize their mail and respond more quickly to your messages.

2. If you want to send a copy of the e-mail message to more than one recipient, you can either:

    ▸ Type that person's address on the Cc: line.

    ▸ Type multiple addresses in either the To or Cc line, separating each address by a comma. In some e-mail programs, the addresses may appear on separate lines.

TIP

In both Internet Explorer and Netscape Messenger, you can press Tab to jump from box to box or from area to area when filling in an address and subject. You can also just click directly in the area you want to jump to.

3. Press Tab until the insertion point jumps into the blank message area.

4. When you are done, send the message or add it to a *queue*, a list of outgoing messages to be sent all at once. Press the Send button, or select File ➤ Send. Figure 16.2 shows a short e-mail message.

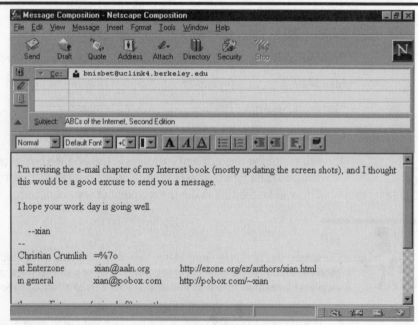

FIGURE 16.2: A short e-mail message to a friend

TIP

Both Outlook Express and Netscape Messenger can word-wrap your message, so you only have to press Enter when you want to start a new paragraph. I recommend leaving a blank line between paragraphs, to make them easier to read.

You can also filter messages, which is the same thing as sorting them according to some criteria as they come into your Inbox. The post office sorts mail according to zip code, and you can use your e-mail program to automatically sort messages according to who sent them, the subject, the date they were sent or received, or any other category that is useful to you from an organizational standpoint. And you can flag messages according to the urgency of the response needed, or other priorities. These options provide you with powerful organizational tools and transform your messages into valuable records that can be filed and retrieved for later reference. See "Filtering Messages as They Come In" later in this chapter for more on message filters.

Reading Mail

Whenever I connect to the Net, the first thing I do is check my e-mail. It's like checking your mailbox when you get home, except the contents are generally more interesting—and usually don't contain bills! Some mail programs (including Internet Explorer and Netscape Messenger) combine the process of sending queued messages with checking for new mail. Most also check for new mail when you first start them.

Unread (usually new) mail appears with some indicator that it's new, such as the Subject line appearing in bold, or a bullet or check mark appearing next to the new messages. This is supposed to help you pick out the messages you haven't read yet, so you don't miss any.

Here are the steps for reading an e-mail message:

1. Open your e-mail program by double-clicking on its shortcut icon or selecting it from the Start menu. Both Outlook Express and Netscape Messenger begin by displaying your Inbox contents automatically.

2. To view the contents of a mail message, highlight it in the Inbox window and press Enter (or double-click on it). The message will appear in its own window, much like an outgoing message. Figure 16.3 shows an incoming message in Outlook Express.

3. If the message continues beyond the bottom of the window, use the scroll bar to see the next screenful.

4. After reading the message, you can close or reply to the message.

Part ii

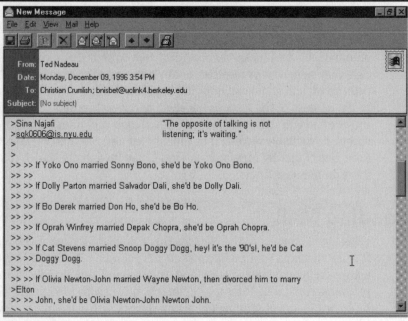

FIGURE 16.3: Here's an e-mail message I received.

TIP

I keep my mail around until I've replied to it. I could save it to a mailbox (as I'll explain later in this chapter) but then I might forget about it. When my Inbox gets too cluttered, I bite the bullet and reply to mail I've been putting off, and then delete most of it.

Replying to Mail

Both Outlook Express and Messenger offer menu options and toolbar buttons for replying to messages you've received. When you reply to an e-mail message, your new message is automatically addressed back to the sender, and you can easily quote the message you received.

TIP

If you start to reply by mistake, just close the message window and don't save the reply if prompted.

To reply to an e-mail message, follow these steps:

1. Highlight the received message in the Inbox or open the message, and then click the Reply (or Reply to Author) command.

2. Your program will create a new message automatically addressed to the sender of the message you're replying to. In Messenger, you can click the Quote button to include the original message. In Outlook Express, you'll need to choose Tools ➢ Options and, in the Send tab, click Include Message in Reply.

TIP

Any Web addresses mentioned in e-mail messages to you can function as clickable links in Messenger and Outlook Express. To use these links, click on the highlighted address, which will probably be underlined or depicted in a different color, such as blue. You will be transported to the Web site using that address. Outlook Express users can also add Web shortcuts as file attachments. Just click the Web icon to head for that site.

3. Sometimes, you'll want to reply to everyone who was sent a copy of the original message. Select Reply to All or a similar command to send your reply to everyone.

4. Tab to the subject line and type a new subject if the old one isn't very meaningful anymore. (People often fail to change the subject line of messages, even when the conversation has evolved its way onto a new topic.)

5. Add other recipients if necessary or tab your way into the message area to type your reply, and then choose the Send (or Queue) command when you are done.

TIP

E-mail tends to take on a life of its own, with people forwarding you messages from other people asking for help, information, you name it. Sometimes people send you long chains of related messages, often called *threads*. To avoid confusion when replying to a message forwarded to you, or when replying to many recipients, direct the mail program to "retain the original text," or however the command is worded, so that people reading the message will know what you are talking about and will know the history of the issue. However, if the thread starts getting too long, try to abbreviate it as described below in the "Using Proper E-mail Netiquette" section.

Deleting Mail

If you have read a piece of mail and you're positive that you have no need to save it, you should delete it so it doesn't clutter up your Inbox (and waste precious hard-disk storage space). To delete a message, highlight it and press Delete (or click the Delete button).

Using Proper E-mail Netiquette

Like any social system, the Internet has evolved to the point where its users observe a variety of informal rules for interacting politely. Collectively, these rules are known as *netiquette* and most of them can be inferred through the application of some common sense to various social situations.

For example, it's generally not considered good manners to misquote what someone said when talking to someone else, to take their words out of context, or to repeat something that was told to you in confidence (though the media and gossips often commit such acts!). Think of e-mail as a kind of online conversation. If people send you messages containing sensitive material, don't forward them on to others without the author's permission.

If you retain only part of the original text of messages in your replies (to keep the replies from becoming too long), be sure it is not misleadingly taken out of its full context (and likely to be misinterpreted). And please do not intersperse your own comments with the retained pieces of other people's messages so that it's not clear to the recipients who wrote what.

Keep Your Messages Brief and Tactful

When you write messages to business associates and colleagues, stick to the point and be informative. Break up large blocks of text into smaller paragraphs. Reread your messages and run a spell check before sending them—this will give you a chance to minimize mistakes, fix poorly organized sentences, and reconsider bad word choices.

If you are writing to friends (or potential friends in newsgroups or chat rooms), you can relax a little more, but still hold back on anything that could be considered offensive, even if you think it's funny and you are sure that your friends will, too. Seemingly innocuous statements in spoken conversation can take on a whole new meaning when written down. Figures of speech, jokes, and your own private way of referring to situations or people seem a lot more serious when viewed in writing.

WARNING

The old adage about never saying or putting anything in writing that you would not want to see in a headline the next day applies to e-mail and the Internet. Now you also have to worry about your words appearing on someone's Web page or showing up when someone searches the Web, a chat service, or a newsgroup. Journalists search the Web for juicy opinions every day. There's no law preventing potential employers from checking you out on the Web and uncovering some embarrassing thing you wrote or posted years ago.

When replying to messages, try to minimize the amount of quoted text that you keep in your return message. Leave enough so it's clear what you're replying to (people don't always remember exactly what they wrote to you). However, as mentioned at the beginning of this section, don't send abbreviated message bits attributed to other people that could be taken out of context. Just use your good common sense!

Don't Fly off the Handle

E-mail is a notoriously volatile medium. Because it is so easy to write out a reply and send it in the heat of the moment, and because text lacks many of the nuances of face-to-face communication—the expression and body cues that add emphasis, the tones of voice that indicate joking instead of insult, and so on—it has become a matter of course for many people to dash off ill-considered replies to perceived insults and therefore to fan the flames of invective.

This Internet habit, called *flaming*, is widespread and you will no doubt encounter it on one end or the other. All I can suggest is that you try to restrain yourself when you feel the urge to fly off the handle. (And I have discovered that apologies work wonders when people have misunderstood a friendly gibe or have mistaken sarcasm for idiocy.)

TIP

If you are the sort to flare up in an angry response, or if you find yourself getting emotional or agitated while composing a response to a message that upsets you, save your message as a draft rather than sending it right away. You can review the draft message later when you have calmed down, and you can decide then whether you want to send it, or you can send the draft to a disinterested third party and ask them if it is too harsh before you send it out.

Part ii

Exiting an E-mail Program

When you are finished sending, reading, and replying to mail, you can quit your program or leave it running to check your mail at regular intervals. You can quit Outlook Express or Messenger by selecting File ➢ Exit or File ➢ Quit.

TRYING OUT MICROSOFT OUTLOOK EXPRESS AND NETSCAPE MESSENGER

Well, now you know the basic e-mail moves no matter which program you're using. In the following sections, I'll detail the specific commands for our two e-mail programs. The second half of this chapter covers some of e-mail's more interesting possibilities. Jump to chapter 17 if you're impatient to get onto the World Wide Web.

Microsoft Outlook Express

Outlook Express is an Internet standards-based e-mail and news reader you can use to access Internet e-mail and news accounts. In this section, we'll look at how to use Outlook Express Mail.

Outlook Express can handle Internet mail, network mail, and mail from MSN. You can open Outlook Express by selecting Start ➢ Programs ➢ Internet Explorer ➢ Outlook Express, or by clicking on the miniature Launch Outlook Express icon in the QuickLaunch bar to the immediate right of the Start button.

You'll start off in a window showing two panes. The pane on the left shows the various features of the program that are available, with your Inbox first and foremost. The pane on the right shows you the contents of your Inbox (but you can click the large Inbox button at the top of the list of messages to choose another mailbox and Outlook will show its contents below).

NOTE

Outlook Express has a big Preview pane that shows you the contents of the highlighted message. You can turn this Preview on or off, and change its appearance and location with the View ➢ Layout menu selection.

Here's how to create a new Outlook e-mail message:

1. Select Compose ➤ New Mail Message (Ctrl+N). This will open up a new message window.

2. Type an address and press Tab to get down to the Subject box where you can type a subject.

3. Tab down to the message area and type your message. Click the Send button. If you are accumulating messages to send in bulk, select File ➤ Send Later, then click on the Send and Receive button in the main Outlook Express window when you are ready to send them all.

To read a message in your Inbox, just double-click its subject line. The message will appear in its own window. To reply to the message, select Reply to Author or Reply to All in Outlook Express (Ctrl+R). Outlook will supply the recipient's address. Proceed as if you were sending a new message.

To delete a message, just highlight it and click the Delete button or press the Delete key on your keyboard. It will be moved to the Deleted Items folder until you specifically open that folder and delete its contents (even then Exchange will warn you that you are permanently deleting the message).

TIP

To undelete a message, open the Deleted Items folder and select the message you want to restore. Then select File ➤ Move, choose the Inbox folder from the dialog box that appears, and click OK.

To exit Outlook Express, select File ➤ Exit.

Netscape Messenger

Netscape Communicator 4 (the successor to Navigator 3 and Navigator Gold) sports a full-featured mail program called Netscape Messenger. It's a redesigned version of Netscape Mail.

NOTE

You'll learn more about Netscape Communicator's Web capabilities in Chapter 19, *An Alternative to Internet Explorer: Netscape Navigator.*

Using Netscape Messenger for e-mail is a lot like using Outlook Express and many other mail programs. Here's how to create and send an e-mail message:

1. First select File ➤ Compose Message (or press Ctrl+M or click the Compose button).

2. Type an address in the To box. Press Tab and type a subject.

3. Press Tab again to enter the message area and type your message (see Figure 16.4).

4. When you're done, click the Send button.

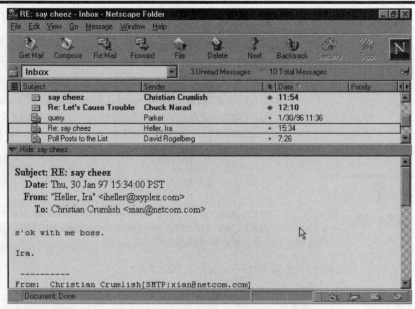

FIGURE 16.4: The Netscape Messenger window lists messages in the top pane and shows the contents of the current message in the hideable lower pane.

If you receive mail while working in Netscape (the little envelope in the lower-right corner of the Netscape window will alert you), select Window ➤ Inbox. (The first time you do this, Netscape may require you to enter your password.) Just highlight a message in the upper pane to see its contents in the lower pane.

TIP

Remember that any Web addresses mentioned in Netscape Messenger e-mail messages you receive will function as clickable links. That means when you finish reading, all you have to do is click on a highlighted word to go to that Web page and start surfing. For more information on the Web, see Chapter 17.

Here are some other Netscape Messenger commands you will find useful:

- ► To reply to a message, click the Reply button, press Ctrl+R, or select Message ➤ Reply ➤ To Sender.

- ► To delete a message, just highlight it and click the Delete button. Netscape will move the message to a Trash folder.

- ► To undelete a message, select the Trash folder in the drop-down folder list just above the top pane, select the message, and then choose Message ➤ File Message ➤ Inbox.

You can close the mail window and keep Netscape running if you want—in Windows 98, click the close button in the upper-right corner—or you can quit Netscape entirely by selecting File ➤ Exit.

USING E-MAIL MORE EFFECTIVELY

Now that you've learned the essentials of sending and receiving e-mail, we'll use the rest of this chapter to look at somewhat more advanced techniques that can help to streamline your work with either Internet Explorer or Netscape Messenger.

Sending Mail to More Than One Person

Sometimes you'll want to send a message to more than one recipient. You can do this in one of several ways. Both Outlook Express and Netscape Messenger (as well as most other programs) allow you to list multiple recipients in the To line, usually separated by commas (some programs require that you use a different character, such as a semicolon, to separate addresses).

Most programs also have a Cc line. As with traditional paper office memos, the Cc line in an e-mail message is for people who should receive a copy of the message, but who are not the primary recipient.

NOTE
When you reply to a message, if you select the Reply To Sender option, your reply will be sent only to the person in the To line. If you select Reply To All, your reply will be sent to everyone in the Cc list as well.

Some programs also offer a Bcc line, which lets you list one or more people to receive blind copies of that message. This means that the primary (and Cc) recipients will not see the names of people receiving blind copies.

WARNING
You can typically include as many names on the Cc: line as you want, but some mail servers will "choke" on a message if its headers are too long.

Sending Files via E-mail

It sounds too good to be true. Just "attach" a file to an e-mail message and it zips across the globe to your recipient, without having to be put on a disk and sent by mail or courier. Naturally, it's not that simple. Some files are just too big to send this way (anything close to a megabyte is probably too big). But even with files of a more appropriate size, you may encounter hitches. Most of the problem is in coordinating between computer types, file types, compression formats, and encoding formats. Getting all the elements to work out can be a little like trying a combination lock. But I'm getting ahead of myself. Let's start with what an attachment really is.

NOTE
Each Internet service provider is a little different, so you can experiment with the size of files you can send. Some services limit the size of files you may attach to messages, while others will take anything, but the transmission may become extremely slow. You can compress files to make them smaller and you can send each file in a group of files in separate messages to keep the size low.

How Attachments Are Created

One of the most important functions of e-mail is its ability to let you send files called *attachments* along with your messages. An attachment is a data file, in any form, that your program will send along with your e-mail message—it could be a word processor file, a picture, a spreadsheet, or any other kind of file. Each e-mail program is different in the way it handles file attachments, and some of the online services still don't let you send or receive files over the Internet. Also, because different programs have different ways of *encoding* attached files (translating the files into a form that can be shipped over the Internet), you may have to compare details with your sender or recipient to make sure that both of your programs can "speak" the same code. For example, a big part of writing *The Internet: No Experience Required* involved transferring files between a Macintosh, running one version of Eudora, and my PC, which was running another version. It took several file transfers before things worked seamlessly.

Internet mail generally consists of only straight text files, although there are some protocols for sending other forms of information. For example, some mail programs use *MIME* (*Multipurpose Internet Mail Extensions*) to send other kinds of data, including color pictures, sound files, and video clips. If you are sent e-mail with a MIME attachment, you may not be able to see the pictures, hear the music, or view the movies, but the text in the attachment should come through just fine. You'll be asked if you want to view the file or save it.

Working with Different File Formats

Quite aside from e-mail issues, you might be trying to send a file that your recipient doesn't have the right application for reading, so that's another thing you may have to work out in advance. For example, if you use Word for Windows and your recipient uses WordPerfect for DOS, then you may have to save your file in a format that your recipient's program can understand; this may involve both of you poking around your programs' Open and Save As commands to see what options are available.

When you receive a file attachment, your e-mail program will usually decode it and tell you where it's been placed (unless it doesn't recognize the coding format, in which case you'll get a bunch of garbage at the end of the message and no file attachment—if this happens, you'll need to negotiate with the sender as I just discussed).

Part ii

TIP

The Internet's FTP (file transfer protocol) offers another way to send and receive files. See Chapter 15 for a quick summary of using FTP.

Attaching Files to E-mail Messages in Outlook Express

In Outlook Express, use one of these options to attach files to your messages:

▶ Use Explorer or My Computer to open the window the file is in, click on the file, and drag it into the new message window.

▶ Select Insert ➤ File and choose the file you want from the Insert File dialog box that appears and then click OK. Figure 16.5 shows an attached file in an Outlook message. Your recipient will double-click on the icon to open the attached file.

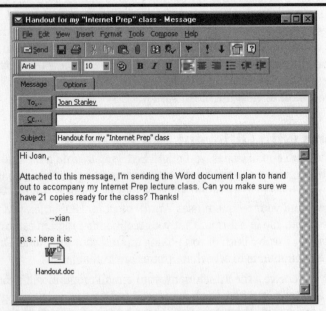

FIGURE 16.5: Outlook inserts an icon representing the attachment into your message at the insertion point.

Attaching Files to Messenger E-mail

Netscape Messenger's provisions for attaching files to e-mail are quite simple. You can also attach Web page links to your messages with these commands:

1. Select Message ➤ New Message to open the Composition window. Or you can click the New Message button in the Messenger toolbar or type Ctrl+M.

2. Address your message and type your message in the message body. To attach a file to the message, click the Attach button.

3. Choose File (as you can see, you can also attach Web pages, among other things).

4. In the dialog box that appears, choose the file you want to send, and then click on Open.

5. Click the Save button or the Send button to save a draft or send your message on its way.

FORWARDING MAIL TO SOMEONE ELSE

If someone sends you an e-mail message and you'd like to send a copy of it to someone else, most mail programs let you select a Forward command.

WARNING

Never send mail to a third party without the express permission of the original sender. Also, be sure to use a *reply separator*, such as a solid horizontal line, between all of the forwarded e-mail messages, to delineate where one person's response ends and another begins (most e-mail programs add reply separators automatically). This will avoid confusion about who wrote what and will avoid uncomfortable situations for both you and those who send you e-mail.

In both Outlook Express and Messenger, the Forward command is on the same menu or toolbar as the Reply command, and it works in almost the same way. The difference is that your mail program won't insert the original sender's e-mail address into the To line. Instead, the To line will be blank so you can fill in the address of the person you are forwarding the message to. The original message will automatically be included in the new message, often with some characters (like the standard ">" Internet e-mail quoting character) or other formatting to distinguish it from what you yourself write.

Here's how to forward e-mail messages:

1. Open your e-mail program and either highlight or open the message you want to forward.

2. Click on the Forward icon in the toolbar of your e-mail program, or use a command such as Compose ➤ Forward. A new message window will appear with the forwarded message included in the text area.

3. Type the recipient's e-mail address on the To line and then Tab your way down to the message area.

4. Edit the message if you want, or add your own note to the beginning, perhaps explaining why you are forwarding the message.

5. Then send the message as usual.

To forward a message in Microsoft Outlook Express, click the Forward Message button. You can also choose Compose ➤ Forward or press Ctrl+F and then proceed as you would with a new message.

To forward a message in Netscape Messenger, click the Forward button (or select Message ➤ Forward or press Ctrl+L). Then proceed as you would with a new message.

Enhancing Your E-mail with HTML Formatting

Internet mail has long been an "unformatted" medium, with only a guarantee that basic text would be transmitted from site to site. Formatted messages typically lose their formatting as soon as they pass through an e-mail gateway. Some mail programs can understand or create formatting that conforms to the Internet's MIME standard, but again, not all programs recognize MIME, so the point of the formatting may be lost.

Now, mail programs have appeared that are more closely integrated with Web browsers, such as Netscape Messenger, part of the same Netscape Communicator suite that contains Netscape Navigator. Microsoft Outlook Express, which is installed as part of Windows 98, is tightly meshed with Internet Explorer. These e-mail programs have become more "Web-savvy": able to recognize Web addresses (URLs), hyperlinks, and now most HTML formatting. (HTML is the coding language used to create Web documents.)

WARNING

Don't rely too heavily on any "brand" of formatting to make your point, because you can't be sure your audience will see the pulsing, blinking green text or other effects you may add. Your careful selection of just the right font may also backfire when the message arrives, because some programs substitute basic fonts for less common fonts, resulting in poorly aligned text at the message's destination.

Both Outlook Express and Messenger also let you create messages with HTML formatting. In fact, you can compose mail messages much the same way you can Web pages, inserting images and links to pages on the Web or other Internet resources. You don't need to "know the code" either, because the software makes it as easy to add HTML formatting as it is to change font styles with your word processor. See Chapter 20 for more on HTML and Web-style formatting.

Formatting an E-mail Message with HTML in Outlook Express

Your messages will resemble Web pages if you use Outlook Express HTML formatting to add colorful fonts and even graphics. Just the two steps here give you this capability:

1. Select Format ➤ HTML. A new formatting toolbar will appear at the top of your message.

2. Select the text to be formatted and use the buttons on the new toolbar to add HTML formatting, such as bold and italic, bulleted lists, alignment (center, flush left, or flush right), and text color.

Formatting an E-mail Message with HTML in Netscape Messenger

In Messenger, you can add any HTML formatting (or insert hyperlinks or even graphic images) to your message using the convenient toolbar in the Message Compose window. (Insert links and images with the Insert Object button furthest to the right.)

Writing E-mail with Your Word Processor

If you're more comfortable writing in a word processing program than you are writing in your e-mail program, you can write your message there, copy it using the Copy command, and then switch to your e-mail program and paste it into a new message window.

One problem with putting word-processed text into e-mail messages is that some e-mail programs substitute special characters for apostrophes and quotation marks. If they are not correctly interpreted by the receiving program, these special characters come out as garbage characters that make your mail harder to read. Also, there are sometimes problems with line breaks, either with lines being too long or with extraneous characters (weird stuff, such as ^M or =20) appearing at the end of each line.

Here's how to copy a message from your word processor to your e-mail:

1. In your word processor, create your message. When you are done, save it as a text file. (Figure 16.6 shows a text file I created in Word 97 for Windows.)

2. Close the file and open it again to ensure that none of the special (non-text) characters are still in the file. Look for odd characters that you would not see on a standard keyboard and delete them.

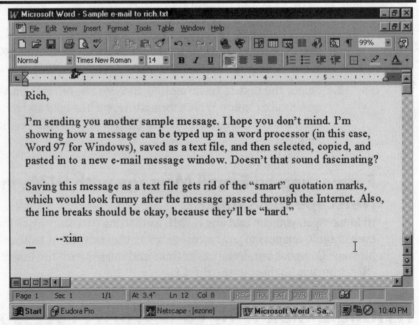

FIGURE 16.6: I created this file in Word 97 for Windows. Now I'm going to save it as a text file.

3. Select the entire document and copy it (Ctrl+C in Windows programs).

4. Then switch to your e-mail program.

5. Create a new message as usual, go to the message area, and paste the text you copied (Ctrl+V).

6. The text will appear in the e-mail program as if you had typed it there.

TIP

If you are a dedicated Word for Windows user and you have Microsoft Outlook Express installed, you can install WordMail (you have to re-run the Office setup program) to use Word *as* your e-mail program. Look up WordMail in Outlook's online help or in the Office Assistant to find out how to do so.

Checking Your Spelling

Most e-mail programs now offer spell-checking (so the traditional excuses for sloppily edited e-mail messages are vanishing fast!), but the specific techniques vary from program to program (as you might expect). It's a good idea to check the spelling in a message before sending it, especially if the message is long, formal, or for some business purpose.

If you write your messages ahead of time using a word processing program, then you can use your word processor's spelling checker to check the message. You may find this easier than working with two different spelling checkers.

Correcting Spelling Errors in Outlook Express

In the Outlook Express message window, select Tools ➤ Spelling (or press F7) to check the spelling of a message.

Outlook will start scanning the message for words it doesn't recognize. If you've ever used the spelling checker in Word or any other standard word processor, then you should be familiar with this drill:

▶ To skip the word in question, click on Ignore.

▶ To accept a suggested correction, click on Change.

- ▶ To make your own correction, type the correct word in the Change To box and click on Change.

- ▶ To add the word in question to the spelling checker's dictionary, click on Add.

Spell-checking in Netscape Messenger

To check the spelling of your e-mail message in Netscape Messenger, choose Tools ➤ Check Spelling in the Composition window.

ATTACHING A SIGNATURE

On the Internet, it's traditional to include a short *signature* at the end of each message. An e-mail signature is a few lines of text, usually including your name, sometimes your postal (*snail mail*) address, and perhaps your e-mail address. If you are including a signature in a business message, you might wish to include phone and fax numbers, and maybe the company Web page address. Many people also include quotations, jokes, gags, and so on. Signatures (also called *sig blocks*, *signature files*, *.signatures*, or *.sigs*) are a little like bumper stickers in this respect.

TIP

You can never be too careful when using company online resources, so consider adding a disclaimer to your signature block if you post to Usenet groups or mailing lists from a corporate e-mail address. The disclaimer can identify your views as solely your own and not those of the company.

Some e-mail programs do not support signature files, particularly those designed for local networks and those of some online services where signatures are less common, but many do and more are adding the feature all the time. Here's my current signature (I change it from time to time):

```
--
Christian Crumlish            http://www.pobox.com/~xian
Internet Systems Experts (SYX)  http://www.syx.com
Enterzone                     http://ezone.org/ez
```

It includes my name, the address of my home page on the Web, the name of my company and its home page address, and the name of my online magazine with its address.

WARNING

Test your signature block with various e-mail systems to see if it still looks good at the receiving end, especially if it uses unusual fonts, has a logo or other graphic, uses tabs, or is formatted in columns. Some of these features do not translate well to other programs, where monospaced fonts may be substituted for fancier proportional fonts.

I'll show you how to create your own signature when I discuss the specific programs that support them.

NOTE

Some e-mail programs let you include a graphic, such as a company logo, in your signature. For example, Microsoft Word and Outlook Express both have commands you can use to import graphics files into your signature file. Just be sure to format the signature in such a way that it looks good even for those who do not have graphics support in their e-mail setup, so that the absence of the logo or graphic will not detract from the appearance of your message. Logos are an easy way to cultivate a professional presence on the Internet.

Part ii

Using E-mail Signatures in Outlook Express

Microsoft Outlook Express supports signature files. These files retain your personal or professional information and add it to your messages according to your instructions. Here are the steps for creating a standard e-mail signature in:

1. Select Tools ➤ AutoSignature. This brings up the AutoSignature dialog box.

2. Type your signature and click Add to put this signature at the end of new messages. (You can also prevent the signature from being added to messages you reply to or forward.)

3. Then click OK.

Adding a Signature File to Messenger E-mail

Messenger's signature file feature does not include much formatting support, but you can create basic signature files and add them to your messages with a minimum amount of fuss. Here are the steps for creating and adding a signature file:

1. First, use a text editor or word processor to create and save a text file containing the signature you want to have at the end of your e-mail messages.

2. Then, in Netscape, select Edit ➤ Preferences. Double-click on the Mail & Groups item in the Category list in the Preferences dialog box.

3. Click on Identity in the Mail & Groups list item and type the full path and file name of your signature file in the Signature File box (or click on the Browse button to find and select the file, and click on OK).

4. When you're done, click OK.

TIP

If your signature exceeds the recommended four lines (this rubric is a widely accepted netiquette standard, though many people violate it), Netscape will warn you, but all you have to do is click on OK again to accept it.

Filing Your Messages

Even after you have deleted all the messages you've replied to or no longer need to leave lying around in your Inbox, your undeleted messages can start to pile up. When your Inbox gets too full, it's time to create new mailboxes to store those other messages.

NOTE

Your e-mail storage should conform to your general scheme of organization. I arrange mine alphabetically, chronologically, and/or by project, depending on the person involved. Think about the best system for yourself before you find your Inbox filled with 200 messages to sort. If your e-mail program allows you to save your own messages that you have sent to other people, you will also need to organize them before they accumulate and become unmanageable.

Different programs offer different commands for creating mailboxes and transferring messages into them, but the principles are more or less the same as those used for real-life filing. Don't create a new mailbox when an existing mailbox will suffice, but do file away as many messages as you can (even if you have to create a new mailbox to do so), to keep the number of messages in your Inbox manageable. When you find yourself scrolling up and down through screenfuls of message lists trying to find a particular message, you know that your Inbox has officially become disorganized.

TIP

You can also save your messages as text files or word processing files to move them outside of the e-mail program. This way you can store them with other files related to the same topic. Select File ➤ Save As in your message window and select a text file type. Or, select the message contents, press Ctrl+C to copy it to the Clipboard, open your word processor, paste the message into a document with Ctrl+V, and then save the new file.

Creating More Message Folders in Outlook Express

As you begin to accumulate messages, replies, and copies of original messages you sent to others, you will need additional folders to store them in for easy retrieval. Fortunately, creating new message folders isn't difficult.

In Outlook Express, it's quite easy to add new message folders to your set of personal folders:

1. Select File ➤ New Folder (or press Ctrl+Shift+E).

2. In the New Folder dialog box that appears, type a name for the folder and click on OK.

Once a folder is created in Outlook, moving a message into the folder is even easier—simply click on the message and drag it to the folder (in the left pane).

Creating New Folders for Filing Messenger E-mail

Messenger also allows you to create new folders for filing messages. Here's how you do it:

1. Press Backspace to get to your Message Center (your master mail folder).

2. Select the folder in which you want the new folder to appear (or select Mail to create an upper-level folder).

3. Then select File ➤ New Folder.

4. Type a name for the new folder in the dialog box that appears and then click on OK.

Filing Netscape Messenger Messages in Folders

Netscape Messenger (like the rest of the Communicator suite) has a re-vamped menu structure that gives toolbar buttons mini-menus of their own. This means that it really is even easier and faster to file messages in Messenger than it is in other e-mail programs, because you do not have to open a folder window or use a dialog box to find the folder where you want to put the message.

1. Highlight the message to be moved.

2. Click the File button (or select Message ➤ File Message).

3. Choose the destination folder from the menu that pops up (subfolders appear on submenus).

FILTERING MESSAGES AS THEY COME IN

When you start developing carpal-tunnel syndrome from "hand-filing" all your mail as it comes into your Inbox, it's time to start looking for an e-mail program with filters. The most basic use of a filter is to recognize a type of mail, usually by one of its headers (such as who it's from, who or what mailing list it was sent to, or what it's about), and to automatically transfer it out of your Inbox and into the appropriate folder (or mailbox, depending on what your program calls it). More sophisticated filters can send automatic replies, forward mail to other recipients, perform multiple actions (such as replying and saving a message in a specific folder), and so on.

NOTE

Your e-mail filters can also be used to automatically clear the old messages out of your Inbox. Depending on what type of functionality is built into your program, you can tell the filters to delete all of the messages older than a certain date. Even better, some programs (including Outlook Express) allow you to automatically archive old messages in a special file that you can move to a different directory or to storage media (tape cartridges, floppies, and so on).

Setting up a filter to work usually takes just a small investment of time compared to the donkey work you save yourself from doing in the long run. Once you start relying on filters to keep your mail manageable, you'll wonder how you ever got on without them (or you'll just up and subscribe to twelve more mailing lists!).

Sorting Outlook Express Messages with Filters

Microsoft Outlook Express has the simplest type of filtering possible: mail with specified text in one or more of four headers can be automatically filed in a specified folder.

These steps will get you started with the setup of an e-mail message filter in Outlook Express.

1. Select Mail ➢ Inbox Assistant, then click Add.

2. In the Properties dialog box that appears, type text in one (or more) of the top four boxes to single out the messages you want to filter. Any message that has the text you typed in its corresponding header field(s) will be moved where you specify.

3. Select the folder you want the e-mail transferred to in the Move To drop-down list (see Figure 16.7).

4. Click OK to save the filter and then add more filters if you wish.

Part ii

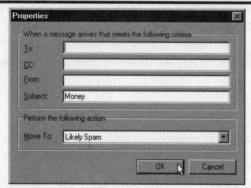

FIGURE 16.7: With Outlook Express you can sort
your messages as they arrive.

Filtering Netscape Messenger E-mail

Netscape Messenger's rules for filtering e-mail are quite specific and give
you more flexibility in organizing your mailbox than other mail filters.
Most of the time you can use the existing rules provided by Netscape. If
none of these rules are customized enough for you, you can construct
unique rules for your own mail management needs.

Here's how you create a new filter for incoming messages:

1. Select Edit ➢ Mail Filters.

2. Click the New button on the Mail Filters dialog box.

3. In the top half of the Filter Rules dialog box that appears,
   enter a name for your filter (see Figure 16.8).

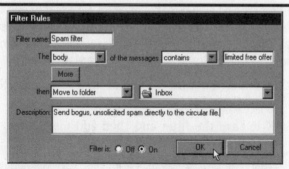

FIGURE 16.8: You can put together sophisticated filters
easily with Netscape Messenger.

4. Choose one of the nine different aspects of the message to base your filter on (such as the subject, the priority, or who's on the Cc list).

5. Choose one of the six different comparison criteria (Contains, Doesn't Contain, Is, Isn't, Begins With, and Ends With) and then enter the text that is to be looked for or avoided in the third box.

6. Click the More button if you want to add additional criteria.

7. Below the More button, choose from six actions (usually you'll want Move to Folder—some of the instructions are more suited for discussion groups than for private e-mail), and then choose a folder (if applicable).

8. Finally, you can enter a description if you wish, and click OK.

NOTE

Netscape Messenger has no provision, as of yet, for checking mail from multiple accounts. You can, however, have a number of User Profiles. Each profile can have a distinct e-mail address. This is very cumbersome since you have to switch profiles, but it works.

Dealing with E-mail from Several Accounts

You may find yourself with more than one e-mail account. It can happen more easily than you might think. All you need is to get a personal e-mail account and then get Internet access at work (or vice versa), and voilà! you've got multiple accounts to manage. How do you keep things straight?

There are several approaches. One is to try to keep any e-mail accounts you may have totally separate. This approach is ideal for keeping work and personal life separate or for keeping a public address and a private "back channel" for friends and emergencies.

On the other hand, some people get a personal account just to get access to an existing work account, in which case there's no reason to store the mail in separate places. Then the problem becomes how to consolidate all your mail and make sure you're not missing any of it. (A related problem is how to look at your mail when at home without deleting it from your main workspace.)

Consolidating mail from multiple accounts will make sure you get all your e-mail. You can set the secondary account (or all the accounts but one) to automatically forward mail to your primary address. However, this is not always possible. Even if it is, the methods vary from system to system, and you should check with your system administrator and ask about "automatic forwarding of e-mail."

When you want to check your work mail from your home computer, you need an e-mail application that supports remote mail connections. Microsoft Outlook 97 has this capability (but only if your company is using Microsoft Exchange Server), and even allows you to quickly download just the message headers from your work account. Then you can select the specific messages you want to download, to minimize connection time.

Managing an Address Book

Once you start using e-mail regularly, you will probably find yourself typing a few addresses over and over, or trying to remember some long and confusing ones. Fortunately, most e-mail programs enable you to create aliases (sometimes called nicknames) for these people. Aliases are shorter words that you type instead of the actual address. These lists of addresses and aliases are usually grouped together in something called an address book. Modeled on real-world address books, these windows or modules often have room for other vital information (such as street addresses, and phone and fax numbers).

Some e-mail and groupware programs share a single address box with other applications on your computer, so your contact information is available to various programs.

When you type an alias or choose a name from an address book, your e-mail program inserts the correct address into the To line of your message (some programs can also insert an address into the Cc line).

You can also set up an alias for a list of addresses, so you can send mail to a group of people all at once. I've got an alias for a group of people to whom I send silly stuff I find on the Net (no one's complained yet) and another one for contributors to my online magazine.

TIP

When you make up an address book entry or alias for an e-mail address, keep it short—the whole point is to save yourself some typing—and try to make it memorable (although you can always look it up if you forget).

Using the Outlook Address Book

Outlook's address book is useful for keeping track of all the e-mail addresses associated with your friends and business associates. Here's how to update the address book with new names:

1. To add a name to your address book, select Tools ➤ Address Book (or press Ctrl+Shift+B) and then select File ➤ New Entry (or press Ctrl+N).

2. In the New Entry dialog box that appears, choose Internet Mail Address and click on OK.

3. Type a name for the address, press Tab, and type the e-mail address.

4. When you're done, click on OK.

Using address book names in Outlook messages is even easier than adding them:

1. To send a message to someone in your address book, create a new message as usual, but instead of typing a recipient's address, click on the To button to the left of the To box.

2. Select a name from the address book list and click on the "To->" button.

3. Then choose OK to copy the address to the e-mail message.

Using the Netscape Messenger Address Book

You can add names to Netscape Messenger's address book by following these steps:

1. Select Communicator ➤ Address Book from any of the Messenger windows.

2. In the Address Book window that appears, click the New Card button.

3. Enter the name, e-mail address, and nickname, and then click OK.

4. Select File ➤ Close to close the Address Book window.

To use the addresses in your new messages, do one of the following, depending on how good your memory is:

▶ In the Message Composition window, type the nickname on the To line.

▶ If you don't remember the nickname you made up, click the Address button, select the name, click To, and then click OK.

FINDING INTERNET E-MAIL ADDRESSES

Because the Internet is such a large, nebulous entity, there's no single guaranteed way to find someone's e-mail address, even if you're fairly sure they have one. Still, if you're looking for an address, here are a few things you can try.

Use Search Tools on the Web

As discussed in the next chapter, Internet Explorer makes available a number of "search engines"—free services, based on the World Wide Web, that you can use to look up information. (Netscape Navigator also provides these services.) Most of them search for Web sites containing a word or phrase you specify, but some, described as "white pages," search for e-mail addresses. Two of the most common, included with both Internet Explorer and Navigator, are WhoWhere? and Four11. These services are quite easy to use. You just enter a name, optionally provide other information such as location or organization, and click a "Search" button. The program then reports any results it finds.

Say "Send Me E-mail"

If you're not sure how to send mail to someone but you know they're on the Net, give them a call and ask them to send you some mail. Once their mail comes through, you should have a working return address. Copy it and save it somewhere, or make an alias for it, or just keep their mail around and reply to it when you want to send them mail (try to remember to change the subject line if appropriate, not that I ever do).

TIP
The best way to collect e-mail addresses is from people directly. Many people now have their e-mail addresses on their business cards, so you can get people's addresses this way too.

Send Mail to Postmaster@

If you know someone's domain, such as the company where they work, or you know they're on one of the online services, you can try sending mail to postmaster@*address* and asking politely for the e-mail address. Internet standards require that every network assign a real person to postmaster@*address*, someone who can handle questions and complaints. So, for example, to find someone at Pipeline, you could send mail to postmaster@pipeline.com and ask for the person by name.

What's Next?

Whew! You have just completed a very thorough examination of the e-mail capabilities of some of our most celebrated Internet programs. Now that you are an e-mail "expert," it's time to push on and master the mysteries of the World Wide Web.

Chapter 17

BROWSING THE WEB WITH INTERNET EXPLORER

Installing and configuring Windows 98 to connect your computer to the Internet are essential steps that you must complete before you can explore the World Wide Web. Once you make your connection, you're ready to start looking around. In this chapter, you'll find the information you need to use Internet Explorer to display Web pages and other Internet resources. After you spend a little time working with the program, you'll probably stop noticing the details of Internet Explorer and devote your attention to the Web pages themselves.

Adapted from ABCs of *Microsoft Internet Explorer 4*,
by John Ross

ISBN 0-7821-2042-3   400 pages $19.99

Starting Internet Explorer

If you've chosen not to use the Active Desktop, you can start Internet Explorer by double-clicking the Internet icon, selecting Internet Explorer from your Start menu, or clicking on the Explorer icon in the Quick Launch bar. If you've decided to use the Active Desktop, look in Chapter 21 for information about this feature.

When Internet Explorer starts, it will look for an active connection to the Internet. If you use a modem and telephone line to make your connection, and there isn't an active connection, Internet Explorer will start Dial-Up Networking (unless you chose not to allow Explorer to automatically dial your service provider), take your telephone line off-hook, dial your ISP, and set up a new TCP/IP link. If you have more than one Dial-Up Networking Connection profile, Internet Explorer will choose the one you have designated as the default in the Connection tab of the Internet Properties dialog box.

You can use the same network connection with more than one application program at the same time. If you have other Internet tools (such as a telnet client or an e-mail reader), you can run them along with Internet Explorer through the same network connection. This can be especially convenient when you're using one program to download a large file while you're using another program to read your e-mail or participate in an online conference.

The Internet Explorer Screen

Figure 17.1 shows the main Internet Explorer screen, which includes these features and functions:

- ▶ **Title bar**   The title bar contains the name of the current Web page or other file on display in the Internet Explorer window, along with the familiar sizing buttons and the Close button.

- ▶ **Menu bar**   The menu bar contains a set of menus; each includes individual commands that you can use to control the way Internet Explorer works.

- ▶ **Toolbars**   The Internet Explorer toolbar has three parts: a set of standard command buttons that duplicate many of the most frequently used menu commands, an address field, and a group of Quick Links. When you move your cursor over a button, the icon changes from black and white to color. To enter a command from the toolbar or jump to a Quick Link site, click on a button. The

View ➤ Toolbar submenu includes an option that displays or hides text labels for the icons in the standard toolbar.

▶ **Activity indicator**   The Internet Explorer symbol to the right of the toolbar is animated when Internet Explorer sends and receives data from the network.

▶ **Main window**   The main portion of the Internet Explorer screen displays the text, images, and other graphic elements of the most recent Web page or other file.

NOTE

It's important to understand that the Web pages and other data you see in Internet Explorer are copies of files located on your own computer or LAN. Internet Explorer downloads files from distant servers, but it does not maintain a live connection to the server after the download is complete.

FIGURE 17.1:   The Internet Explorer screen uses many standard Windows conventions.

▶ **Status bar** At the bottom of the Internet Explorer window, the status bar supplies additional information about the current Web site. When you move your cursor to a link, the status bar shows the destination of that link. During a file transfer, the status bar displays a bar graph that shows the progress of the transfer. If a Web page includes multiple pictures, graphic elements, audio clips, or other files, the status bar will display the name of the specific file that is currently being transferred. Some Web pages also include a special script that places a scrolling message across the status bar.

▶ **Security zone** At the right side of the status bar, an icon and text identify the security zone assigned to the current Web page. You can assign Web sites to security zones from the View ➤ Options ➤ Security dialog box.

Changing the Toolbars' Appearance

You can use the View ➤ Toolbar submenu to hide or display one or more of the three toolbars (the Standard toolbar, the Address bar, and the Quick Links toolbar). It's also possible to combine the menu bar and two or more of the toolbars on a single line by dragging a toolbar up or down. When more than one toolbar occupies the same line, you can view the hidden toolbar by dragging left or right.

To move the menu bar or a toolbar, follow these steps:

1. Place your cursor over the vertical bar at the left side of the section you want to move. Notice that the cursor changes to a two-headed arrow.

2. Drag the toolbar or menu bar up to merge it with the toolbar immediately above, or down to place it on a separate line.

If two or three toolbars are on one line, you can open a hidden toolbar by double-clicking when the cursor is over the vertical bar.

To display the captions in the Standard Toolbar buttons, move your cursor to the thick bar under the toolbars and drag the bar down. To hide the captions, use the View ➤ Toolbar ➤ Text Labels command.

CREATING YOUR OWN QUICK LINKS

The Links toolbar contains five Quick Links to specific Web sites. When you install Internet Explorer, all five Quick Links are assigned to Microsoft sites, but you can assign each link to any other URL that you visit frequently.

The default Quick Links are:

Best of the Web Click on Best of the Web to jump to a page with links to a variety of online information sources, including financial services, telephone and address directories, home and garden information, and online reference books.

Microsoft Click on Microsoft to jump to a page with links to information about Windows and other Microsoft products and free downloads of programs, patches, and add-on software for Microsoft programs.

Product News Click on Product News to jump to a Microsoft page that contains information about the latest versions of Internet Explorer and links to file downloads.

Today's Links Click on Today's Links to jump to MSN's Link Central page, which contains links to a selection of new and timely Web sites, including pages devoted to current sports and news events, interesting new Web services, and recent movies and television shows.

Web Gallery Click on Web Gallery to jump to a collection of images, sounds, ActiveX controls, fonts and other elements that you can download and use to create your own Web pages.

All of these sites are fine if you want to spend all your online time looking at stuff from Microsoft. You don't. Trust me: you will find other sites that you visit a lot more often than these five.

Follow these steps to add items to your Quick Links toolbar:

1. Jump to the Web page or other site that you want to define as the destination of a Quick Link.

2. Open the Favorites menu and select the Add to Favorites command. The Add to Favorites dialog box will appear.

3. Click on the Create in button to display the list of folders shown in Figure 17.2, and select the Links folder.

Part ii

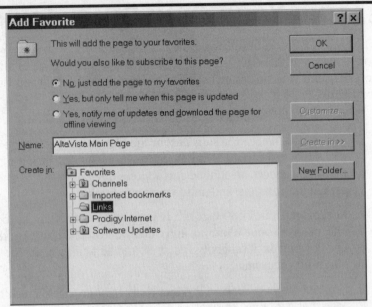

FIGURE 17.2: Select the Links folder to add a Web page to the Quick Links toolbar.

4. Type the name you want to use for this link in the toolbar in the Name field.

To change the order of the links, change the name of a link, or remove a link from the Quick Links toolbar, follow these steps:

1. Open the Favorites menu from the Menu bar. Don't use the Favorites command in the toolbar.

2. Select the Organize Favorites command.

3. Open the Links folder from the Organize Favorites dialog box, as shown in Figure 17.3.

4. Select the item you want to move, change, or remove and click on the button with that instruction.

5. After you have made all the changes you want, click on the Close button.

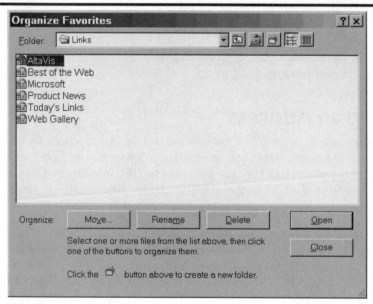

FIGURE 17.3: Use the Organize Favorites dialog box to change an existing Quick Link.

MOVING AROUND THE WEB

The whole World Wide Web is built around seamless links from one place on the Internet to another. Any Web page can include links to other files that may be physically stored on the same computer or on any other computer connected to the Internet. At its center, Internet Explorer is a tool for retrieving Web pages and following those links.

There are several ways to tell Internet Explorer which Web page or file you want to see next:

▶ Click on a link in the currently visible page.

▶ Type the URL of a new site in the address field.

▶ Choose a URL from a list of favorites.

▶ Choose a URL from a list of sites you've visited before.

▶ Use the Back and Forward buttons in the toolbar to return to a site you've recently seen.

- ▶ Click on one of the Quick Links.

- ▶ Select a link from one of the Explorer bars.

- ▶ Double-click on a shortcut to a Web site from the Windows Desktop or from the Start menu.

Typing an Address

When you discover a Web site address in a magazine article, on a TV show, in an online mention in e-mail or a newsgroup, or from some other source, you can visit that site by typing its URL into Internet Explorer. Simply type the URL of the Web site or other Internet file or service you want to see into the Address bar, and then press the Enter key.

Address | http://www.unitedmedia.com/comics/alleyoop/index.html

If you don't include the URL type, Internet Explorer assumes that you're trying to reach a Web page or other HTML document, and it will automatically add **http://** to the beginning of the URL. Therefore, you will reach exactly the same Web site if you type either **www.website.com** or **http://www.website.com**.

Internet Explorer's AutoComplete and AutoScan features can make it even easier to find a Web page. AutoComplete compares the address you're typing with addresses you've visited before, and automatically fills in the remaining characters. For example, when you start to type **www.website.com**, AutoComplete will add the remaining **w** and the dot (.) after you type the first two **w's.** When you start typing **website.com**, AutoComplete will offer to finish it for you. However, if you have previously visited www.webster.com and www.webb.com, AutoComplete won't know which one you want this time, so it will fill in **web**. To select from a menu of possible complete addresses, right-click the address field.

You may want to overtype some or all of the addresses that AutoComplete offers you. To jump forward or back to the next separation character (\ \ \ . , ? or +) within an address, hold down the Ctrl key and press the left or right arrow key.

AutoScan is another timesaver, especially when you aren't sure of the exact address of a Web site. When this option is active, it will try several variations of the address until it finds one that matches an address in the Domain Name Server's database. In other words, if you type *name*,

AutoScan will try *name*.com, www.*name*.com, *name*.org, www.*name*.org, *name*.edu, and www.*name*.edu. This won't do much good if the site's address is www.*name*.gov, or if you want *name*.edu. If none of those produce anything useful, AutoScan can offer to perform a search in one of the popular Internet search engines, such as Yahoo.

To turn AutoScan on or off, use the Advanced Options dialog box.

If you're trying to reach some other type of server, such as an FTP archive, a telnet host, or a gopher server, you must type the full URL address, including the type designator. For example, the URL for an FTP site might be ftp://ftp.archive.edu. If you leave out the type, Internet Explorer will try to reach an http server.

You can also use the address field to open up a file located on your own computer's hard drive, on a floppy disk, a CD-ROM, or on another computer connected to yours through a LAN. For example, to see a file called schedule.txt in your c:\calendar folder, type **c:\calendar\ schedule.txt** in the address field. You don't need to worry about a URL type identifier when you load a local file into Internet Explorer, but you should remember that DOS and Windows use the backslash (\) to separate folders in a path, instead of the forward slash (/) used by most Internet servers.

Using Hot Links

Except for a handful of Web sites that specialize in spicy sausages, like www.incrediblelink.com, hot links on the Internet are places on a Web page that contain jumps to other Web pages, files, and online services. A link may be a word or phrase in a block of text, a graphic image such as a picture of a push-button, or an image map that contains links to several different URLs, depending on the exact location within the image map. Web pages with links are illustrated throughout this chapter.

When you move your cursor over a link, the cursor changes to a pointing finger, and the destination of the link appears in the status bar at the bottom of the Internet Explorer window. If the "hover" option is turned on, the link also changes color. To jump to that URL, click on the link.

- Looking for Time Zones around the World - look no further!!! **NEW**
- Visit the historic town that is the centre of World Time - home of many English kings & queens
- See the preparations at Greenwich for the Millennium at the "Home of the Millennium"

Shortcut to http://greenwich2000.com/millennium.htm

Internet Explorer displays text links in a different color from other text. If an entire picture or other image is a link to another Web site, you may see a colored border around the image.

Returning to Sites You've Recently Visited

After you view a Web page, Internet Explorer stores a copy in a temporary folder, so you can return to that page without having to wait for another download. This is very convenient, because Internet Explorer can load and display a file from your hard drive a lot more quickly than it can transfer it from a distant server. However, there are two possible drawbacks to this technique: if the original Web page has changed since the original download, you won't see the changes, *and* you're filling up your hard drive with Web pages.

Fortunately, there are ways to work around both of these problems. The General Options dialog box includes a Temporary Internet Files settings button that opens the dialog box shown in Figure 17.4.

FIGURE 17.4: Use the Settings dialog box to control the way Internet Explorer uses temporary Internet files.

The Settings dialog box includes these options:

Check for Newer Versions of Stored Pages   When Every Visit to the Page is active, Internet Explorer will obtain a new (and possibly updated) copy of a Web page each time you view a Web page. When Every Time You Start Internet Explorer is active, the browser will go back to the server the first time during a session that you jump to a Web page, even if there's a copy of that page in the Temporary folder. When the Never option is active, Internet Explorer will always use the file in the Temporary folder. To check for a new version of a Web page you've already seen, click on the Refresh button in the command toolbar or the View menu.

Amount of Disk Space to Use   Move the slider to the left to reduce the maximum size of the Temporary Internet Files folder, or to the right to increase the maximum size of the folder.

Move Folder   Click on the Move Folder button to change the path of the folder that contains your temporary files.

View Files   Click on the View Files button to open your Temporary Internet Files folder. To view a file in a new Internet Explorer window, double-click on the name of that file.

Delete Files   Click on the Delete Files button to delete all the files in your Temporary Internet Files folder.

Explorer Bars

Explorer bars are a set of new features in Internet Explorer 4 that create a split-screen display in the browser window, with links to a list of Web pages that fit a specific category in the left-hand pane. Figure 17.5 shows the Internet Explorer window with an Explorer bar open.

The four types of Explorer bars are:

- ▶ Search bar
- ▶ Favorites bar
- ▶ History bar
- ▶ Channels bar

When you click on a link to a Web site or other file in an Explorer bar, Internet Explorer opens the target of that link in the right-hand pane, while the list of sites remains visible in the left pane. This makes it possible to move directly from one site on a list to the next, without the need to return to the Web page that contains the list. This is a major timesaver when you're trying to visit a series of sites, such as the result of a search.

Part ii

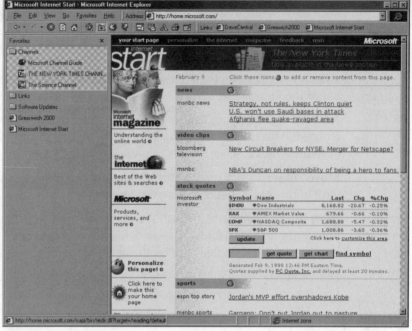

FIGURE 17.5: Explorer bars display links to Web sites and other files in a split-screen display.

Because most Web pages are designed to take up the full width of a browser window, the Explorer bars usually cut off the right side of the page. To see the full width of the page, click again on the icon button in the toolbar that you used to open the Explorer bar. Click again to reopen the Explorer bar with the same display that was visible when you hid it.

Using the Search Bar

The Search bar is a window that displays one of the major Internet search engines. When you click on a link displayed as the result of a search, the target Web page opens in the main Internet Explorer pane. For more detailed information about performing Internet searches, read the "Using Internet Search Tools" section later in this chapter.

Using the Favorites Bar

The Favorites bar contains your own list of Web pages and other files that you want to revisit more than once. Later in this chapter you'll find detailed information about creating and using Favorites.

Using the History Bar

Whenever you view a Web site, Internet Explorer adds a shortcut to that site to the History list. You can use these shortcuts to return to Web sites you've recently visited. To open the History bar as a separate pane in your browser window, either select View ➢ Explorer Bar ➢ History, or click on the History icon in the toolbar. Figure 17.6 shows the History bar.

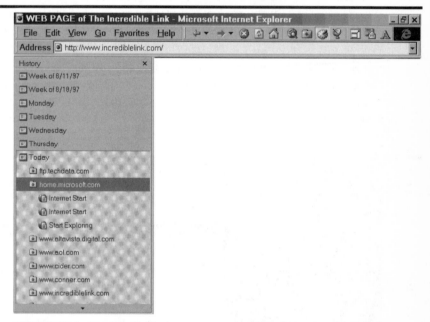

FIGURE 17.6: Use the History bar to return to a Web site you've visited before.

The subfolders in the History bar are organized by date—there's a separate folder for each day of the current week, and one for each of several previous weeks. Each of those folders contains a folder for each site you visited that day or week, with links to individual pages within the site folders. If you use the Single Explorer to view both Web sites and local files, the History bar will also include local files.

To return to a Web page or file listed in a History folder, click on the listing for that page or file. To hide the History bar and expand the current Web page click on the History icon in the toolbar.

Using the Channels Bar

Active Channels are a new feature of Windows 98 and Internet Explorer that connect you to content areas created and maintained by information providers such as newspapers, magazine publishers, and other sources of news, sports, financial information and feature material, including such diverse services as *Better Homes and Gardens*, the Mayo Clinic, and the *South China Morning Post*. As new information becomes available, the channel content provider automatically delivers it to your computer.

Unfortunately, many of the channel content providers are using this service as a new way to deliver their advertising to a targeted audience. It's one more step in the gradual commercial takeover of the Internet. But if you're selective about the channels you receive, they can be a convenient way to obtain the latest reports about topics that interest you.

Figure 17.7 shows a Channel bar in Internet Explorer. To view information received from an Active Channel, click on the channel icon. If the channel content provider offers information in more than one subtopic, select the subtopic from the list that appears when you click on the main channel icon.

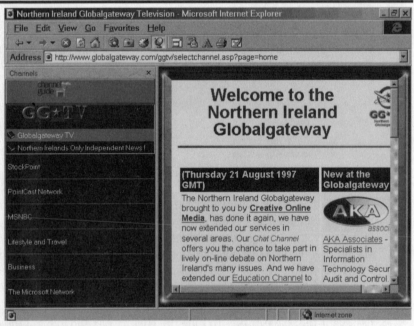

FIGURE 17.7: The Channel bar provides direct links to Active Channels.

The experience of viewing an Active Channel through the Internet Explorer browser is not much different from viewing information from any other Web site, but you can also view the contents of your Channel bar directly from your Windows desktop, or display the contents of a channel as a screen saver.

When you subscribe to an Active Channel, you can schedule automatic downloads of new information and read that information offline, without setting up a new connection to the Internet.

Adding New Channels   To add an Active Channel to the Channel bar, follow these steps:

1. Open the Channel bar by clicking on the Channels button in the Internet Explorer toolbar, or select View ➤ Explorer Bar ➤ Channels.

2. Click on the Channel Guide banner in the Channel bar. Microsoft's directory of Active Channels will appear in the right-hand side of the browser window.

3. Click on the "Start Here" button to see a list of available Active Channel categories.

4. Select a category and a channel content provider to see a preview of that channel.

5. Click on the Add to Channels button in the preview display to add this channel to your Channel bar.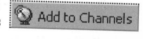

Removing Channels   To remove a channel from your Channel bar, follow these steps:

1. Open the Channel bar.

2. Right-click on the name of the channel you want to remove.

3. Select the Delete command from the right-click menu.

Moving Channel Icons   To change the order in which icons appear in your Channel bar, drag and drop the icon up or down to its new position.

Moving Forward and Backward

In addition to the History folders, which provide a long-term record of your visits to Web sites, Internet Explorer also keeps track of the Web pages you open during the current session, and the order in which you visited those pages.

Use the Back command in the toolbar or in the Go menu to return to the Web page from which you jumped to the current page. Use the Forward command in the toolbar or the Go menu to repeat the last jump you made from the current site. The Back and Forward buttons also have drop-down menus that list all the other sites you visited during the current session. To jump directly to one of those sites, select the description of that site from one of the menus.

TIP

The Back command is particularly useful when you try to follow a series of links, but you discover that you've reached a dead end—either a link to a site that's no longer available or a site that doesn't have any links that you want to follow. You can retrace your steps to return to a page with other links that you want to follow.

Using More Than One Window at a Time

In most cases, Internet Explorer loads the new page into the same window when you click on a link or enter a URL in the address bar. But sometimes it's convenient to keep the current page visible while you open a new page in a separate Internet Explorer window. For example, you might want to read the text in one window while you wait for the next one to load, or you might want to keep one eye on a page that automatically updates the score of the big game while you conduct other online business in a second window.

To open another copy of the current Web page in a new window, select the New command in the File menu, and select Window in the New submenu.

To jump to a new Web page and load it into a new window, follow these steps:

1. Move your cursor over the link to the Web site you want to visit.

2. Press your right mouse button to display the right-click menu.

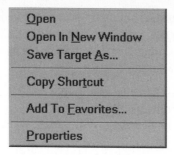

Part ii

3. Select the Open in New Window command.

The new window works exactly the same as the existing one. Once it's open, you can use the address field, the Favorites list, the History bar, and other navigation tools to move around the Web, while keeping an earlier page visible in the other window.

HOME PAGES

Every time you start Internet Explorer, the program will automatically load and display the page that you have specified as your Home Page.

Home page also has another meaning: it's a page that an individual or organization uses to provide pointers to other related pages or files. For example, many people have created home pages that contain links to information about their hobbies, favorite entertainers, and other interests. Businesses frequently have home pages with links to separate pages about each of their products or divisions. See Chapter 20 for information about creating this kind of home page.

Choosing a Home Page

Your Home Page is the first Web page you will see every time you open Internet Explorer, so it's a good idea to choose a page that contains information you can actually use, rather than one that has nothing but advertisements for products and services that you may not ever want. Most people never bother to change the default Microsoft page, but you may want to replace the Internet Explorer Start Page with one of these options:

▸ Microsoft's Custom MSN Start Page option.

▸ A home page from another online information provider, such as GNN's Whole Internet Catalog (http:www.gnn.com/wic/index.html) or PC/Computing's Web Map (http:www.zdnet.com/pccomp/java/webmap/).

▸ The front page of your favorite newspaper, weather, sports, or other Web site that contains information that you want to see every time you open the browser.

▸ Your own home page with links to your favorite sites, which you can create with an HTML editor, such as FrontPage Express.

Changing Your Home Page

To change the home page, follow these steps:

1. Jump to the page you want to use as your home page.

2. Open the View menu and select the Options command.

3. Click on the General tab to display the dialog box shown in Figure 17.8.

FIGURE 17.8: Use the General Options dialog box to change your home page.

4. Click on the Use Current button to define the current page as your home page.

To use some other page as your home page, type the URL of that page in the Address field.

USING INTERNET SEARCH TOOLS

The World Wide Web resembles a huge library where all the books are arranged on the shelves by size and color. You may stumble across a lot of interesting things by accident, but without a catalog to tell you exactly where to look for a specific item, the book you want is extremely difficult to find. In the library, you can search for a book by looking up the title or subject in a catalog or by asking a librarian for help. Internet search tools serve a similar purpose.

When you look for, say, a Hebrew dictionary in a library catalog, you will discover that the Dewey Decimal number is 492.43. Since the librarian places books on the shelves in numerical order, you'll find Hebrew books (492.4) between books about Balto-Slavic languages (491.8) and those about the Arabic language (492.7). Once you know where to look, that dictionary is easy to locate.

On the Internet, URLs serve the same purpose as the library's shelf numbers. And like the library catalog, the Internet's search tools can point you to the item you want to find.

Most Web search tools work in a similar manner: you type the words you want to search for and click on a Search button. The search engine looks for those words in a database and displays a list of URLs that match your request, with links to each one. To examine a possible match, click on the link. If that's not what you want, click on the Back button to return to the list and try another item.

There are about two dozen major general-purpose Internet search tools, and a couple hundred more specialized ones. Each uses a somewhat different set of rules to conduct its search, and each will give you a different list of URLs in response to a request. Some tools search for individual pages, others will take you to entire sites, and still others search through the text of each page rather than limiting their searches to titles or keywords. Some include subjective reviews or ratings of individual sites, while others list everything they find.

As a result, the same search through several different services can produce radically different results. For example, one search for the keywords "Joseph Conrad" produced 244 hits with Yahoo, 4,351 with Lycos, and about 30,000 with AltaVista. A search for "Andrew Jackson" produced 55 hits using Lycos, 231 with Open Text, and about 2000 matches with AltaVista. The exact numbers are not important, but they do illustrate the differences among search engines.

WARNING

The links that a search tool identifies are not always useful, especially when you enter more than one keyword, because some search engines include partial matches that include just one word in the search phrase. For example, a search for "Andrew Jackson" using the Magellan search engine produced 85 matching links. However, only one of the first ten had anything to do with the seventh President; the other nine were pointers to a Web page about the Jackson State University Computer Science Department, Steve Jackson Games, and singers named Alan Jackson, Michael Jackson, and Joe Jackson. See "Focusing Your Searches" later in this chapter.

If you're looking for a popular Web site, you can probably find it with almost any general-purpose search engine. But if you want everything related to a specific subject, you should perform the same search through several different services.

One of the best new features in Internet Explorer 4 is the Search bar (shown in Figure 17.9), which makes it possible to conduct a search in one pane of the browser window and follow search results in a separate pane. In other words, you don't have to return to the page that contains the results of your search, because it's visible on the side of your screen.

To use the Search bar, follow these steps:

1. Click on the Search button in the toolbar, or select View ➢ Explorer Bar ➢ Search from the menu to open the Search bar.

2. Choose the search engine you want to use from the Select Provider drop-down menu at the top of the Search bar.

3. Type the word or phrase you want to find into the search field, or select one of the other options offered by the search engine.

4. Click the Search button. The search engine will return a list of links to Web sites that match your request and display the list in the Search bar.

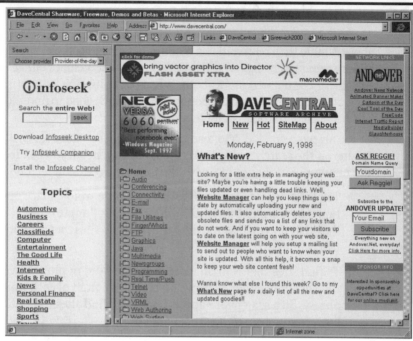

FIGURE 17.9:   The Search bar provides a direct link to one of the Web's major search engines.

5.   Click on the link to the first item you want to see. Internet Explorer will display that page in the main section of the browser window. To move to another item on the list in the Search bar, select the link to that item.

6.   If you want to hide the Search bar and expand the main window to fill the browser, click on the Search button in the toolbar. Click on the Search button again to reopen the Search bar.

The Search bar has connections to half a dozen different search engines, but it may not always open the particular engine you want to use. To select a different search engine, use the drop down Select Provider menu at the top of the Search bar. The default is "Pick-of-the-day" (which is really pick-of-the-moment, since it can change every time you open the Search bar), but it's simple enough to choose the search engine you really want to use.

For more specific searches, you might want to bypass the Search bar and use a specialized directory Web page instead. http://www.search.com is a good place to start. It includes links to more than 250 different directories, search engines and other interactive databases.

Focusing Your Searches

Each search engine handles search requests differently, especially if you include more than one word in a request. For example, if you enter **apple cider**, some search engines will list every page that includes either "apple" or "cider," but not necessarily both. When you're looking for information about fermented fruit juice, it doesn't do you much good to find thousands of sites related to Apple computers.

It's always a good idea to read the specific instructions for each search engine on the search service's Web site, but in general, you can reduce the number of irrelevant hits with the following common techniques:

▶ To search for a phrase rather than separate words, place quotation marks around the phrase. For example, **"apple cider"** (with the quotation marks) will limit the search to sites that contain the two words as a phrase.

▶ To find sites that contain more than one word or phrase, even if they're not together, place a plus sign (+) in front of each word or phrase. So a search for **+apple +cider** will find sites that include both words, even if they're separated.

▶ To exclude sites that contain a specific word or phrase, place a minus sign (−) in front of it. A search for **+apple +cider -recipes** will find sites that contain the words "apple" and "cider," but it will exclude pages where the word "recipes" appears.

RETURNING TO FAVORITE WEB PAGES

As you wander around the World Wide Web and other parts of the Internet, you will discover sites that you want to revisit later. You could write down the URL of each site on a notepad and then retype it into Internet Explorer's address field every time you want to return to that site, but that approach is both tedious and messy. There's an easier way—you can use shortcuts that take you directly to your favorite Web sites.

In fact, there are two easy ways. You can create a list of links to your favorite pages that you can open from within Internet Explorer, or you can place shortcuts to Web sites on your Desktop or Start menu, just like shortcuts to programs and files located on your own hard drive. In the rest of this chapter, we'll talk about using both of these techniques.

Working with the Favorites List

When you come across an interesting Web page, you can save a link to that page by adding it to your list of Favorites. Later, you can return to that page by opening the list and clicking the name of the page.

For example, if you're interested in finding online versions of newspapers from all over the world, you might want to add the AJR NewsLink directory (http://www.newslink.org/news.html), shown in Figure 17.10 to your list of favorites.

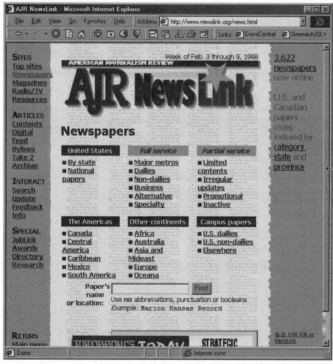

FIGURE 17.10: NewsLink offers an extensive directory of online newspapers.

NOTE

In Netscape and other Web browsers, the list of sites that you want to revisit is called a *bookmark* list. A note on a Web page that suggests you "bookmark this site" is encouraging you to add it to your Favorites list.

Favorites are not limited to Web sites. As part of the very close integration between Windows 98 and Internet Explorer, the Favorites list can also include files located on your own computer.

Viewing the Favorites List

You can open the Favorites list within Internet Explorer as either a conventional menu or a separate Favorites bar. Even if you choose not to use Windows 98's Active Desktop feature, your Favorites list is always available from the Start menu.

The Favorites Menu   The Favorites menu, shown in Figure 17.11, shows submenus and links as menu commands. If your list has too many entries, the bottom of the list might run off the screen. When that happens, you can display the whole list by clicking the arrowhead at the bottom of the menu.

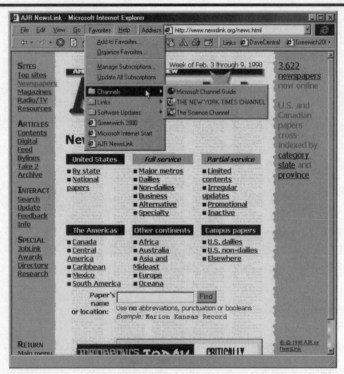

FIGURE 17.11:   Use the Favorites menu on the Internet Explorer menu bar to jump to a bookmarked site.

The Favorites Bar   The Favorites bar is a separate Explorer bar within the Internet Explorer window, as shown in Figure 17.12. Like the Search bar, the Channel bar, and the History bar, it can remain visible on your screen while you jump to the pages on the list. To open the Favorites bar, either click the Favorites icon on the toolbar or select View ➤ Explorer Bar ➤ Favorites.

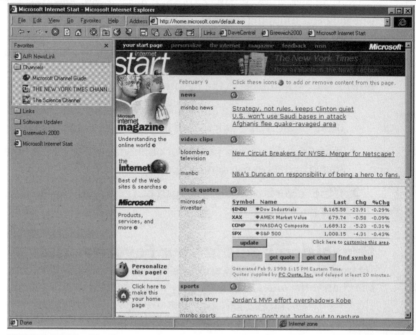

FIGURE 17.12: The Favorites bar displays your list of Favorites in a separate pane.

To jump to an item listed on the Favorites bar, click the name of that item. To hide the Favorites bar and allow the current page to fill the entire window, click the Favorites icon on the toolbar again, or click the x button in the upper-right corner of the Favorites bar.

Adding Items to the Favorites List

To add the current Web page to your Favorites list, follow these steps:

1. Jump to the page you want to add to the list.

2. Open the Favorites menu from the menu bar.

Part ii

3. Select the Add to Favorites command.

4. If you want to place this page in your top-level Favorites menu, click the OK button. If you want to add it to a submenu, click the Create In button and select the folder where you want this item to appear. Click the New Folder button to create a new submenu.

You can also add a link in the current page to your Favorites list by dragging and dropping the link to the Favorites icon on the toolbar, or you can use the Add to Favorites command in the right-click menu. When you use the right-click menu to add an item to your Favorites list, the exact location determines whether you will add the current page or a link on the current page to the Favorites list:

▶ If your cursor is over a link when you right-click, you will add the destination of that link to your list, rather than the current page.

▶ If you right-click on a picture or other graphic, you will add that image to the list without the rest of the current Web page.

▶ If the cursor is over any other part of a page, you will add the current page to your list.

Organizing Items in Your Favorites List

Internet Explorer normally arranges Favorites in alphabetical order. You can change the order in which items appear in the Favorites menu or on the Favorites bar by dragging an item to a new position in the list. You can also drag and drop items between submenus and the main Favorites menu.

TIP

Internet Explorer can open and display local files (including Windows 98 folders) just as easily as it downloads files from the Internet. In fact, all of the pages you see in Internet Explorer are really copies that you have downloaded to your own system. Therefore, the program treats the Favorites folder (which is a subfolder located within the top-level Windows folder, although the exact location doesn't matter) just like any other Web page. You can open this folder—or any other folder on your hard drive or LAN—by typing the path in the Internet Explorer address field.

The Organize Favorites command on the Favorites menu opens a dialog box that you can use to do most of the same things that you can do to files and subfolders from a Windows 98 folder:

▶ Open files, which are generally shortcuts to Web pages

▶ Change the way the program displays the files in the folder

▶ Add and delete files and subfolders

▶ Import files or shortcuts to files

▶ Move files to subfolders

▶ Change the names of files

▶ Change the icon assigned to a file

Changing the Appearance of the List   The Organize Favorites dialog box, shown in Figure 17.13, offers two view options: List and Details. To change views, use the buttons at the top of the dialog box.

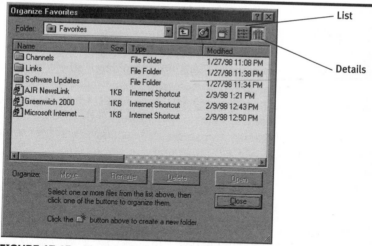

FIGURE 17.13:   The Favorites list can appear as either a list or a set of icons.

TIP

If you use List view (or if you just like messing around with your screen layout), you may want to assign a distinctive icon to each item on the list. See "Changing a Web Shortcut Icon" later in this chapter for more information.

Adding Other Items to Your Favorites List

The Favorites list is not limited to Web sites. It can also include shortcuts to any other program, data file, or folder on your own computer or on a computer connected to yours through a LAN. This feature can make Internet Explorer even more flexible.

Here are some of the things you might want to add to your Favorites list:

▶ Copies of HTML documents or text files stored on your hard drive.

▶ A shortcut to the Notepad program. When you want to extract text from a Web page, you can select and copy the text, open Notepad, paste the selected text, and save it as a text file.

▶ A shortcut to the Windows Desktop folder (c:\windows\desktop). If you keep shortcuts to frequently used files and programs on your Desktop, you can use the Favorites list to open them from within Internet Explorer. If you do create a shortcut to your Desktop, you should also use the Shortcut tab in the Properties dialog box to change the shortcut icon.

Creating New Subfolders

Once your list of Favorites reaches about a dozen entries, you should think about moving some of them into subfolders. If there are a few Web sites that you expect to revisit more often than others, you can leave shortcuts to those pages in the main Favorites list (or you could create Quick Links to those sites) and move less frequently used items to subfolders. You can organize your shortcuts in whatever way best suits your needs. For example, you can sort them:

▶ By topic

▶ In alphabetical groups (A through D, E through H, and so forth)

▶ In separate folders for particular types of Web sites, such as FTP archives or news summaries

Each folder listed on the Favorites bar has a folder icon. When you click on the name of a folder, the files and subfolders within that folder open as an indented list. In the Favorites menu, folders show up as subcommands; when you move your cursor over the name of a folder, the contents appears as a submenu.

To create a new folder, follow these steps:

1. Open the Favorites list from the Internet Explorer menu bar.

2. Click the Organize Favorites command.

3. When the Organize Favorites dialog box appears, click the Create New Folder button (that's the button at the top of the window with a folder and a star on it).

4. A new folder will appear at the bottom of the list, as shown in Figure 17.14.

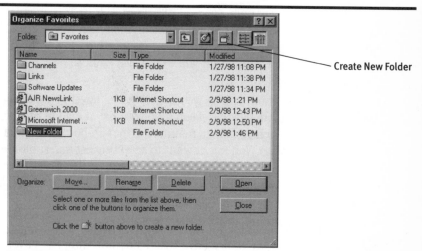

FIGURE 17.14: The new folder appears at the bottom of the list of Favorite pages.

5. Type the name you want to assign to this folder, and press the Enter key.

The next time you open the Favorites list, the name of the new folder will move to the top of the list, in alphabetical order relative to other folder names. To move an item from the main list or another subfolder to a new subfolder, follow these steps:

1. Select the name of the Web page or folder you want to move.

2. Click the Move button.

3. When the Browse for Folder dialog box appears, select the destination folder and click the OK button.

When your list gets even larger and more complicated, you might want to consider placing subfolders within subfolders. For example, you might want to create a folder called Travel, with separate subfolders called Airlines, Trains, and Hotels. Or you may want separate subfolders for each letter within an alphabetical list.

Cleaning Out Your List

So there you are, surfing your way around the World Wide Web, finding all kinds of amusing and interesting Web sites: "Add to Favorites." Click. Here's another good one. "Add to Favorites." Click. Click. Click.

The next time you open your list of Favorites, it has dozens of items, most of whose names you don't recognize. And when you select a site, you cannot imagine why you thought it was worth saving in the first place. Did you really think that you would ever want to return to the History of Corn Flakes home page?

It's time to do some serious weeding. If you're never going to use a link, there's no good reason to keep it on your list at all. On the other hand, it's entirely reasonable to maintain a "not-so-hot list" separate from the main folder. You might want to keep this list in a subfolder or in a separate folder with a shortcut from the Favorites list. This secondary list will be just a couple of mouse clicks away, but its contents will be out of the way when you're looking for your daily news updates.

To clean up your list, follow these steps:

1. Open the Organize Favorites dialog box from the Favorites menu.

2. Look through the list for links to items you don't recognize or that you don't think you want to keep on the list.

3. Double-click the entry or icon for the first doubtful item to take one more look at this Web page. This page will appear in a new browser window.

4. Take a look at the page in the new window and decide if you want to keep it on your list.

5. Close the new browser window.

6. If you decide to remove an item from your list, select it in the Organize Favorites list and click the Delete button, or move it to your "not-so-hot" list.

7. If you want to keep this item on your list, consider changing the name to something that identifies it more clearly. Click the Rename button to change the description of the currently selected item.

TIP

As a rule of thumb, your top-level Favorites list should have no more than about 16–18 items in it—maybe a few more if you have a larger screen. When the list gets bigger than that, it's time to start moving things to subfolders.

Making Your Own Hot List

The Favorites list is easy to use, but it doesn't tell you much about the Web sites that are listed. If you want to give yourself more information about each link, you might want to create a local Web page with a one- or two-sentence description of your favorite sites. If you create a Quick Link to your hot list page, you can jump to the hot list with a single mouse click.

Creating a Hot List Page

The easiest way to create a quick-and-dirty HTML page (and quick and dirty is all you need for your own hot list, since you're the only person who will see it) is to use FrontPage Express, the HTML editor supplied with Internet Explorer. (You'll learn more about FrontPage Express in Chapter 20.)

When you save your HTML hot list, name the file **my list.htm**. Figure 17.15 shows a sample hot list set up as a Web page. Each item on the list includes a link to another site and a description of the information or service that's offered at that site. To jump to a site, click the link, just as you would on any other Web page.

Adding the Hot Link Page to Your Favorites List

When the page is ready to use, follow these steps to add it to your Favorites list:

1. Open my list.htm.

2. Open the Favorites menu and select the Add to favorites command.

3. When the Add to Favorites dialog box appears, change the name to **A Better Hot List**.

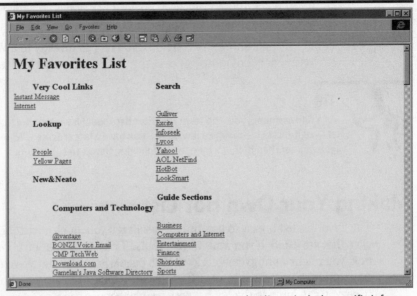

FIGURE 17.15:   Use a local HTML document as a hot list to include specific information about each page.

The next time you open your Favorites list, you should see a link to this page at or near the top of the alphabetical list of Web sites, but after all the folders. Click the link to open the page.

Creating and Using Web Shortcuts

The integration of Internet Explorer into Windows 98 extends the file-management features to files you download through the Internet. Even if you don't use Internet Explorer's Active Desktop features, you can set up shortcuts to Web pages in exactly the same way that you use shortcuts to programs, documents, and data files located on your own hard drive. In fact, the Favorites list and the History list in Internet Explorer are really just Windows 98 folders full of shortcuts to Web sites.

Like other shortcuts, a Web shortcut may be located on your Desktop, in any folder, or in your Start menu. When you click a shortcut to a Web site, three things happen:

▶ Internet Explorer starts.

▶ Dial-Up Networking connects your computer to the Internet.

▸ Internet Explorer downloads a copy of the Web page specified in the shortcut.

The benefit of using a shortcut is obvious: you can go directly to a Web page with just a couple of mouse clicks. You can create a shortcut to the current Web page, to a graphic file embedded in the current Web page, or to a link on the current page.

Creating a Shortcut to the Current Web Page

To create a shortcut to the current Web page, load the target page in Internet Explorer, and either select the Create Shortcut command in the File menu or move your cursor over a place on the page that is not a link or an image and select the Create Shortcut command from the right-click menu. When you create a shortcut, Internet Explorer places the shortcut icon on your Windows Desktop, as shown here. You can drag-and-drop the icon from the Desktop to any folder or to a floppy disk, network drive, or other destination, just like any other shortcut.

Changing a Web Shortcut Icon

Internet Explorer uses the same icon for all Web shortcuts, but it's easy to change the icon to something that's related to the contents of the target Web site.

TIP

You can download more extra icons than any rational person could ever want from the file archives at ftp://mjablecki.extern. ucsd.edu/archive/cica/win3/icons/ or ftp://ftp.cdrom.com/pub/cica/win3/icons/ (these are mirror sites that contain the same files). The index file contains descriptions of each of the files in this archive.

Here's the way to change icons:

1. Right-click on the item whose icon you want to change.

2. Select Properties from the right-click menu.

3. Click the Shortcut tab.

4.   Click the Change Icon button at the bottom of the dialog box.

5.   When the Change Icon dialog box appears, shown in Figure 17.16, choose an alternative from the Current Icon field, or click on the Browse button to find an icon in another file or folder.

FIGURE 17.16:   Use the Change Icon dialog box to assign a new icon to an item in your list of Favorites.

6.   Click the specific icon you want from the Current Icon field in the Change Icon dialog box. If necessary, use the slider bar at the bottom of the icon display to see additional choices.

7.   To use the currently selected icon, click the OK button.

8.   In the Properties dialog box, click the OK button.

Creating a Web Shortcuts Folder

If you have more than three or four Web shortcuts on your Desktop, you might want to place them in a separate Web Shortcuts folder, with a shortcut to the folder on the Desktop. Follow these steps to create a new folder:

1.   Move your cursor to a blank spot on your Desktop.

2.   Click the right mouse button and select the New ➤ Folder command. A folder icon similar to the one shown here will appear.

3. Enter **Web Shortcuts** as the new name for this folder.

4. Drag the icons for each of the Web shortcuts you want to place in this folder from the Desktop to the folder icon.

Unfortunately, Windows won't let you change a folder icon to something more interesting, so you're stuck with the boring old file folder.

Opening Shortcuts from the Keyboard

There's still another way to use a shortcut to start Internet Explorer and jump to a Web site. You can define a set of keystrokes as a keyboard shortcut. Keyboard shortcuts are especially convenient when you're using a word processor, spreadsheet, or other application, because you don't have to take your hands away from the keyboard.

Keyboard shortcuts are combinations of the Ctrl key, the Alt key, and almost any other key. When you press all three keys at the same time, Windows will automatically start Internet Explorer and open the Web page assigned to that combination.

To create a keyboard shortcut, follow these steps:

1. Right-click the Web shortcut icon for which you want to create a keyboard shortcut.

2. Select Properties from the right-click menu.

3. When the Properties window opens, click the Internet Shortcut tab to display the dialog box shown in Figure 17.17.

4. Move your cursor to the Shortcut Key field.

5. Hold down the Ctrl or Alt key and the letter or other key you want to assign to this shortcut. Even though you don't press both Ctrl and Alt, the keyboard shortcut will require both of those keys. If you plan to use this shortcut with Microsoft Word, don't use Ctrl + Alt + a number key, because those combinations are already assigned in Word.

6. While you have the Internet Shortcut dialog box open, make sure the Run field is set to Normal Window rather than Maximized. When you use the keyboard shortcut from a maximized application program, Internet Explorer will open in a less-than-full-screen window, so you will be able to switch back to the application more easily when you're finished with the Web browser.

7. Click the OK button.

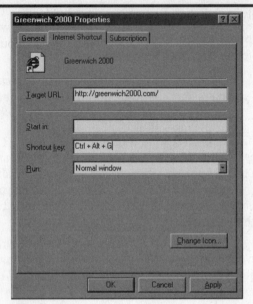

FIGURE 17.17: Use the Internet Shortcut tab to assign a keyboard shortcut.

Sending a Shortcut to Another User

Unlike shortcuts to programs and data files located on your own system, the target addresses of Web shortcuts are universal; you can point to a URL from anywhere on the Internet. Therefore, you can embed a Web shortcut into a document or copy it to a floppy disk and send it to another user. For example, you might want to send a daily or weekly "best of the Web" bulletin to friends and customers via e-mail, with shortcuts to new or otherwise important Web sites that you want them to see. The recipients can jump to the sites you describe by clicking the shortcuts within the bulletin. If you and the person receiving your messages are both using an e-mail client that can handle Rich Text Format (RTF), you can include your shortcuts in a message.

To attach a shortcut to an existing document, follow this procedure:

1. Open the document in a word processor such as WordPad or Word for Windows 98.

2. Drag and drop the shortcut icon into the open word processor application window.

3. Use the formatting tools in the application program to control the placement of the icon in the document.

In general, you can treat a Web shortcut just like any other embedded object in a Windows 98 application program. If you haven't worked with embedded objects before, consult the manual and online help for your application.

CHANGING THE DEFAULT BROWSER: A WARNING

If Internet Explorer is your only Web browser, you can skip this section. But if you have both Internet Explorer and Netscape Navigator or some other browser loaded on your computer, only one program at a time can be your default browser.

When you open a browser that is not your current default, it will display a message like the one shown below, asking if you want to change the default. As you read the rest of this section, you will understand why you should always make the current browser the default.

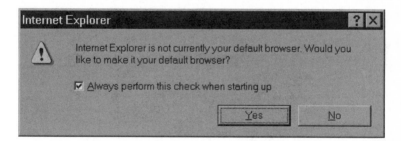

The default browser is the program that Windows associates with .HTM and .HTML files. In other words, the default program is the one that starts when you use a shortcut to a Web page. Just because you used Internet Explorer to create a shortcut doesn't mean Internet Explorer will automatically start when you select that shortcut—if that other browser is your default. To make things even more confusing, Windows uses the default browser to open Web sites in the Internet Explorer Favorites and History folders.

If the current browser is not the default when you start it, things can get extremely messy. If Internet Explorer is not the default, it will open the default browser when you try to jump to a new Web site. If you open the Favorites folder, you will see an icon for the current default browser next to each item. And in general, things won't always work the way you expect them to work.

The only way to avoid this confusion is to answer "Yes" whenever a browser asks if you want to make that program the default. Even if that browser is not your favorite, you should still make it the default, at least for the moment. This is really not a big deal because it's so easy to change defaults. Using a nondefault browser is just not worth the trouble.

What's Next?

In the next chapter, Gene Weisskopf and Pat Coleman discuss the security concerns that face every Internet user—maintaining privacy online, avoiding or restricting access to inappropriate Web content, securing financial transactions, and keeping viruses out of the computer—and they show how to use the tools that Internet Explorer provides in these areas.

Chapter 18

BROWSING WITH SENSE AND SECURITY

As we spend more of our daily lives on the Internet, we confront and must resolve new issues. One that has quickly become important is security, which we'll discuss in this chapter. Internet Explorer provides many features for ensuring that our time online is private when needed, free of inappropriate Web content, secure when we are making financial or confidential transactions, and safe from viruses or other malevolent programs.

Adapted from *Mastering Microsoft Internet Explorer 4*, by Gene Weisskopf and Pat Coleman

ISBN 0-7821-2133-0   960 pages $44.95

GUARDING YOUR PRIVACY ON THE WEB

Sitting at a keyboard and browsing the Web in your own home gives a wonderful *illusion* of privacy. As you've read before in this book, however, every bit of information you send or receive over the Internet passes through multiple computer servers and networks. Unlike our public phone system, the Internet was designed as an open, accessible system, and privacy was not a foundation of the architecture.

That lack of privacy is still one of the best features of the Internet. The coalition of Internet networks throughout the world can expand with ease, and new computers can hook into the Internet without seeking approval from any one company or government. From our perspective as users, we can simply enter a URL, and Internet Explorer fetches whatever it finds there. The password is "Welcome," and we're all invited. Whether you're visiting Web sites, sending e-mail, or participating in online chat sessions or newsgroups, you're taking advantage of the built-in openness of the Internet.

Privacy becomes an issue, however, when you're no longer just viewing mundane Web pages or sharing information with your peers on the Internet. What would you think if a business were collecting information about how much time you spend browsing the Web, the places you visit, and what you purchase? What if your government were tracking your spending habits via your online financial transactions or surreptitiously monitoring what you say in a newsgroup?

NOTE

This lack of privacy is why Internet Explorer displays a notice when you are about to send information over the Internet, such as when you click the Submit button in a form you have filled out. If that form contains your credit card number or other confidential information, you may not want to send it if you are not currently connected to a secure server, as discussed later in this chapter. Once you understand the reason for this notification message, you can disable it by clearing a check box.

Many of the potential security issues on the Internet are no different from the ones we already deal with. For example, how do you feel about talking on a telephone in a public place with people standing nearby? Or giving your credit card to a waiter in a crowded restaurant, and watching as the waiter disappears into the back room with it? Or taking cash from an ATM machine on a public street? You need to familiarize yourself with the issues and take precautions where pertinent, but learn to accept the others as minor sources of potential, but usually rare, problems.

Internet Explorer can maintain the security and privacy of your online sessions by allowing you to:

▶ Store your passwords securely on your own computer and offer them automatically when requested by a Web site, so you don't have to remember them.

▶ Limit how cookies collect information about you for a server.

▶ Control your personal information with the Profile Assistant, and send some or all of it when a server requests it.

▶ Keep financial transactions secure and reliable with Microsoft Wallet.

▶ Prevent Internet Explorer from opening Web sites that you may find offensive for yourself or for those in your care.

▶ Assign Web sites to security zones, in which all sites have the same set of restrictions.

▶ Connect to secure Web sites that encrypt all data transfers between you and the server, making them virtually impossible to decipher by anyone else.

▶ Limit the extent to which ActiveX and Java programs are allowed to run on your computer.

▶ Verify the validity of Web sites, and identify yourself to others, with certificates.

Staying Secure with Passwords

People used passwords to protect their private resources long before computers came along. Remember "Open, Sesame"? With the advent of computerized transactions, passwords have become an essential part of our daily routine. Have you ever counted how many different passwords you use? Can you even remember all the places where you've been issued a password?

Part ii

When you work on the Internet, you end up collecting a large number of passwords. Some will be for high-security sites such as your online bank or stockbroker, where the password plays a critical role in your online security. Other passwords will simply identify you as a registered user with rights to access a site, such as for many online newspapers.

Most Web sites give you the option of having them remember your password, just as Windows' Dial-Up Networking allows you to do. Once a site remembers your password, you don't have to enter it each time you visit the site. You may still be prompted with a dialog box, but your user name and password will already be filled in (the password will be displayed as asterisks), so you can simply press Enter or click OK.

Some passwords are stored in your password file (with the PWL file name extension) in your Windows folder, where they are encrypted and safe from prying eyes. Most Web sites store your password in their cookie files on your computer; in most cases the password portion of the file is encrypted.

You can develop several habits to ensure that your privacy (and perhaps your money) is protected to the fullest extent possible:

▶ Don't use a real word when you create a password. It is best to mix letters and numbers, and punctuation characters, too, when they are allowed by the server. Doing so makes it much more difficult for someone to crack your password.

▶ Use a minimum of six characters; the more you use, the more secure the password.

▶ Avoid the obvious passwords, such as your birthday or Social Security number.

▶ Change your password every month or two at sites that contain crucial personal or financial information. You can be more relaxed about changing other passwords, but it's still a good idea to do so every now and then.

▶ When changing a password, don't recycle an old password.

▶ Resist the temptation to keep a list of all your passwords in an easily accessible file on your computer.

Although you'd find it quite convenient to have a file for looking up a password, it would be equally convenient for someone who was surreptitiously using your computer, either in your office or in their getaway car.

A simple alternative is to keep a list of your passwords in a password-protected file, which most word processors allow you to do. You'd then have to memorize just one password. (But please, don't name that file My Passwords.)

Saying No Thank You to Cookies

A server at a Web site can have Internet Explorer (or Netscape Navigator) create a *cookie*, which is a file on your hard disk that contains information the server will need when you visit that site. For example, the Web sites that allow you to create customized pages usually store your preferences in cookies. When you return to one of those sites, the server will ask for its cookie file and set up your personal page appropriately.

When you are purchasing items at a Web site, you might put the items you want to buy into a virtual "shopping basket" until you're finished. That shopping basket is actually a cookie file on your computer that contains a list of the items you've selected to purchase. When you're finished shopping, the server uses that file to calculate your charges and draw up your bill.

It's easy to see how the cookie concept could be rife with security problems—another computer is having files created on your computer about your activity while you browse that site. In reality, however, cookies are typically used for mundane purposes. Because they are simple data files, they cannot "look" at your hard disk and report back to the server or run other programs on your computer.

But the potential for gathering personal information and sending it back to a server is the real issue. Although a server can't use a cookie to discover and store truly private information, such as your name, address, credit card number, and so on, would you still feel comfortable knowing that a market research company is collecting a list of all the pages you've visited at a site? Worse, we have no idea what type of data, or how much of it, is being collected while we're visiting a Web site.

You can adjust the settings for the Cookies option on the Advanced tab in Internet Explorer (choose View ➢ Internet Options). You can choose to be notified when a server wants to create a cookie, or you can choose to disallow all use of cookies (which would truncate your Web experience quite a bit). A new solution to the cookie conundrum is discussed in the next section.

Retaining Your Privacy with the Profile Assistant

Most of us understand that Web sites are much more valuable when they're allowed to know something about our preferences and who we are. But we would like to have a little control over just how well Web sites can get to know us! That's why Microsoft worked with the industry to develop a standard for Internet Explorer and other browsers that allows us to restrict "unverifiable transactions," such as when a server reads a cookie on our computer or creates one there.

When a server wants to transfer personal information between it and our computers, the Open Profiling Standard (OPS) allows us to choose whether to send any of that data. This not only lets us know what type of information the server is requesting, but also lets us control the process. Here's how OPS works:

▶ Each user of Internet Explorer can use the Profile Assistant to create a personal profile, which is a file that contains commonly used personal information, such as name, address, telephone number, e-mail address, and so on.

▶ When you visit a Web site and the server asks you for information from your profile, you can decide whether to give it all, some, or none of that information.

▶ When a server exchanges information with your profile, the transaction can be done through a secure (encrypted) connection (as discussed later in this chapter), so that your information will remain private during its travels over the Internet.

▶ The information in your profile need only appear in that one place to be available to any Web site that asks you for it, instead of being spread among many cookie files for different sites. If you move and get a new address, you can update your profile accordingly, and any Web site you visit will be able to access the most current information (if you choose to give it).

▶ While you're browsing a site, the server might want to store new information in your profile and will have to ask you for permission to do so. This is the type of data that would otherwise have ended up in yet another cookie file.

▶ Whenever you return to that site, the information the server stored in your profile will be available, but only with your permission. Once you get to know a Web site, you can tell Internet Explorer that this site no longer needs permission to access your Personal Profile.

Handling personal information is more sensible with personal profiles than with cookies. As we use the Web more and more, these issues will only grow in importance, so it's critical to establish a means for handling them now. Your profile is designed to be flexible. Although you set it up with a core of basic information, new types of information can be stored there as the industry adopts new standards.

To create your personal profile, follow these steps:

1. Choose View ➤ Internet Options and select the Content tab.

2. In the group of options labeled Personal Information, click the Edit Profile button. This opens the [*Your Name*] Properties dialog box, shown in Figure 18.1. If it looks familiar, then you must be using the Windows Address book, as they share the same tabs and fields.

3. Enter your information into the relevant fields. If you don't have a cell phone, for example, just leave that field blank (you can press Tab or Shift+Tab to move between fields).

NOTE

Keep in mind that filling in *any* of this information is optional. Its only purpose is to make your travels on the Web easier, more enriching, and more secure. You may want to limit the amount of data you include at first, until you see a pattern to how it is used by the Web sites you visit.

4. When you've filled in all the relevant fields, or at least those you want to fill in at this time, click OK.

Once you've created your profile, it will be available to any server that requests that information—with your permission, of course. When a server at a Web site makes that request, you'll be shown its URL for identification purposes, the type of information it is requesting, and how the information will be used. After you've visited sites that ask to tap into your profile, you'll begin to appreciate the security the profile provides, as well as the welcome relief from having to enter your name, e-mail address, mailing address, and so on for the wide variety of sites that request that information.

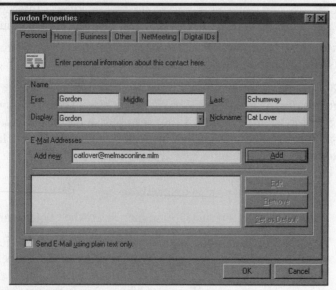

FIGURE 18.1:   You enter information about yourself into the [*Your Name*] Properties dialog box.

Keeping Transactions Secure with Microsoft Wallet

Along with the Profile Assistant, Internet Explorer offers Microsoft Wallet as a convenient and secure way for you to manage your credit card or other payment information (debit cards, ATM cards, and so on) and transmit it privately to Web sites. By storing that information on your computer, you avoid having to type it every time you make a purchase online. Of course, you can only take advantage of Wallet at those sites where the server has been configured to accommodate it.

Once you have set up Wallet with your relevant information, you can shop at a Wallet-enabled Web site and have that information just a click away. When you're ready to purchase items and you've gone to the page where you usually enter your credit card information, the site's server asks Internet Explorer to display your information to you. All you have to do is click the credit card you want to use, and the relevant information from it will be sent to the server over a secure connection.

To set up Wallet on your Internet Explorer, choose View ➤ Internet Options and select the Content tab. In the Personal Information group of options, you'll see the Microsoft Wallet buttons:

Addresses stores the mail and e-mail addresses and phone numbers that you'll want to be able to send over the Internet.

Payments stores the pertinent information for any credit cards you will use for online transactions. The information you enter is password-protected.

The next two sections will show you how to set up addresses and credit card information.

Entering Addresses

The addresses you enter into Microsoft Wallet will be available for sending to a site that supports Wallet and requests that type of information. For example, when you're making a purchase online, you can select a shipping address from those that are in Wallet. That's much faster than typing it yourself and much more accurate than trying to remember the ZIP code for your company's branch office in another state.

To enter a new address or revise an existing one, click the Addresses button in the Content tab in the Internet Options dialog box. This displays the Address Options dialog box, shown in Figure 18.2.

FIGURE 18.2:   Each address is represented by a friendly name in Wallet's Address Options dialog box.

Part ii

NOTE

The names and addresses you enter here will also be placed in your Windows Address Book. Note that if you delete a name from the Address Book, it will also be deleted from Wallet. On the other hand, you can delete a name from Wallet and the name will remain in the Address Book until you delete it there.

This example shows several addresses that have already been entered. Each is listed under a "friendly" name of your choice. You can delete an address or revise its information by clicking the Delete or Edit button, respectively.

To create a new address, click the Add button to display the Add a New Address dialog box, which is shown in Figure 18.3. Enter the necessary information for each field, or click the Address Book button and select a name from your Address Book.

FIGURE 18.3: The Add a New Address dialog box

You define an address either as home or business by clicking the appropriate button near the bottom of the dialog box. The one you choose will determine where the address will appear in this person's entry in the Address Book—either on the Home or the Business tab. You also enter a friendly, easy-to-identify name for this address, which will appear in the list in the Address Options dialog box.

When you're finished, click OK to save this name and address. You can then create another name by clicking the Add button, or click OK to return to the Internet Options dialog box.

Entering Credit Card Information

In the Content tab of the Internet Options dialog box, the Payments button opens the secure side of Microsoft Wallet, where you enter information about your payment transaction cards (credit, debit, and so on) that you'll want available for online purchases. Click that button to display the Payment Options dialog box, which looks similar to the Address Options dialog box shown in Figure 18.2.

To add a new payment type to the list, you'll need to enter information about the credit card and the billing address associated with that card. Remember, most merchants want to know the official billing address associated with a credit card. You'll then seal this information with a password (because each card has its own password, multiple users of a computer can all store their credit cards in Microsoft Wallet):

1. Click the Add button, which displays a list of credit cards or other payment methods that you can use in Microsoft Wallet.

2. Click the card you want in the list. You can limit the type of cards that are shown on the list by clicking the Methods button and deselecting any cards that you do not want to be made available.

3. When you've selected a card, a dialog box is displayed that explains how you create a new credit card entry; click Next to continue.

4. Now you'll see the Credit Card Information dialog box, shown in Figure 18.4. Enter the information for your credit card exactly as you would when you're making a purchase over the phone or on the Web. You can enter a friendly name in the Display Name field, one that you'll recognize in the Payment Options list.

NOTE

If you have an older Visa or MasterCard that has only 13 digits instead of 16, be sure to select the Only Display 13 Digits checkbox.

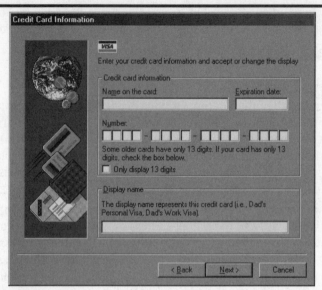

FIGURE 18.4: The Credit Card Information dialog box

5. When you're finished, click Next. If you have entered an invalid credit number or expiration date, or if the date has already passed, you will be prompted to fix the problem.

6. In the next dialog box, you select the billing address that is used for this credit card. You can either choose from a list of all the entries in the Address Options dialog box, or click the New Address button to create a new entry, as though you were doing so in the Address Options dialog box.

7. When you've completed the billing address for this card, click the Next button.

8. Finally, you'll be asked to enter a password that will be needed to send this credit card information over the Internet, or to revise the information on your computer. Enter the password into both the Password field and the Confirm Password field, and click the Finish button. The new credit card will appear in the list in the Payment Options dialog box.

FILTERING SITES WITH THE CONTENT ADVISOR

The free-flowing wealth of information on the Internet brings with it the need to filter out content that may not be appropriate. This is especially true for parents who are concerned about what their children might encounter on the Internet. It's also true for employers, teachers, librarians, and anyone else who wants to regulate the use of their computers. Of course, deciding what material is appropriate and who has the authority to block that type of content is the overwhelming question of the day. Are we being appropriately protective or acting like sinister Thought Police? The issue is definitely food for thought, and the answer will vary depending on whom you ask.

Avoiding www.offensive

Before you can view a Web page in Internet Explorer, you must specifically ask for that page from its server. It's important to remember this, as it means that objectionable Web sites can't come looking for you. You don't need to worry about nefarious Web pages lurking about your computer, just waiting to pop up when you least expect them. In order to be offended, you have to go to them. Nevertheless, it's possible to reach these sites by accident.

We once queried a search site on the Web, which returned a long list of links that the site thought relevant to the keywords we had entered. While quickly sampling some of those result links, we hit one that contained what is euphemistically called "adult material." We were certainly surprised and wondered how in the world this search site thought we were looking for this type of content.

The answer is simple enough: Search engines search and index the entire Web, without regard to content. The keywords we had used for the query happened to return the adult site near the top of the list. We're still not sure which keywords did the trick, but it really doesn't matter. There are probably thousands of everyday words that will rank some lascivious sites near the top of the list.

NOTE

The Web site for the Net Shepherd content-filtering software (www.netshepherd.com) offers a "filtered" search engine. You not only specify the keywords you want to find, but also specify the level of "maturity" for the result pages, such as Child, Pre-Teen, or Adult.

You can reduce the chances of this sort of close encounter if you:

▶ Read a link and its description before you click.

▶ Use Internet Explorer's Content Advisor to help filter out pages whose ratings don't meet your standards.

▶ Block individual objectionable sites that may be unrated by assigning them to the Restricted zone of sites (choose View ➤ Internet Options and select the Security tab). This is discussed later in this chapter.

▶ Be prepared to click the Stop or Back button when a site is being opened if that site seems to come from the wrong side of the ethical tracks.

If you exercise a little caution, you may rarely run into objectionable content on the Web. When you need to enforce some restrictions, however, you can limit the type of content that Internet Explorer will open, as discussed in the next section.

The Content Advisor

Should the responsibility fall into your lap, you can use Internet Explorer's Content Advisor to block Web pages whose content ratings exceed the limits you set. This system relies on Web authors to include a content rating in their pages, but as you'll see in the following discussion, it's to their own benefit to do so.

By default, Internet Explorer lets you set limits based on the Big Four issues that affect literature, art, movies, television, and advertising:

▶ Language

▶ Nudity

▶ Sex

▶ Violence

The Content Advisor is a powerful tool for parents who are concerned about their children's travels in the vast reaches of the Web. You can specify acceptable levels for each of the four categories, and Internet Explorer will not open pages that have content ratings that exceed those levels. Because you must have a password to set up or change the acceptance rules in Internet Explorer, you're assured that your standards will be upheld no matter who is using the computer.

NOTE

The Content Advisor performs some of the functions that are found in several "net watching" software products, such as SafeSurf, SurfWatch, Cyber Patrol, Cyber-Sitter, and Net Shepherd. If you want more control over how Internet Explorer is used on your computer, you can visit the Web sites for these products, most of which are listed in the Yahoo category Business: Companies: Computers: Software: Internet: Blocking and Filtering: Titles.

Internet Explorer makes use of the rating system pioneered by the Recreational Software Advisory Council, or RSAC. That system has been tuned to Internet content and goes by the acronym RSACi. It is based on the World Wide Web Consortium's (W3C) Platform for Internet Content Selection, or PICS.

The PICS standard was developed by the computer software industry to enable Web authors to include a standardized rating in their pages and to enable Web browsers to block inappropriate pages based on those ratings. When Internet Explorer begins to open a page, it first reads any PICS rating codes that it finds in the HTML code. If the PICS rating exceeds the limits set in the Content Provider, Internet Explorer will display a message explaining why it cannot open the page, as described a little later in this chapter. You can read more about how the PICS standard works at

```
www.w3.org/pub/WWW/PICS/
```

Other ratings systems based on the PICS standard are also available. A parent or other Web overseer can choose the rating systems that best fit their own way of judging the appropriateness of Web content. As you'll see a little later, a Web author can assign multiple ratings to a page, and you can add multiple rating systems to the Content Advisor in Internet Explorer, allowing you to make use of those that work best for you.

Cooperation between Web-Page Authors, Rating Systems, and Parents

Now that you understand the concept behind the Content Advisor, you may notice that there's a weak link in the chain. Internet Explorer can only judge the content of a Web page when the page's author has included the necessary HTML code that defines the various levels of smut, violence, profanity and the like. That may sound as workable as the proverbial lead balloon, but it can actually work quite well when authors are truly interested in their pages being seen by those who want to see them.

Another way a parent can filter undesirable Web content in Internet Explorer is with the help of a third-party reviewing service, which is a company that acts like a rating system by reviewing and vouching for the appropriateness of Web sites. For example, the Cyber Patrol filtering software from Microsystems Software, Inc. at

```
www.microsys.com
```

offers parents two lists of rated sites. One is called the CyberNOT Block List, which contains sites that would be inappropriate for children. The CyberYES Allowed Sites List contains sites that parents don't need to worry about. When a parent chooses to use the CyberNOT list, their children can visit any site on the Web *except* those in the list. When they use the CyberYES list, only the sites on that list can be visited.

As you can see, there are many ways for parents to control the type of sites their children visit on the Web. If Internet Explorer's filtering capabilities don't go far enough, you can look into buying one of the many third-party content-filtering software packages.

Determining the Ratings for Pages You Author

The RSACi rating standard, along with several others, helps authors rank their pages via an online questionnaire and checklist that asks the author very specific questions about the content of the Web page or site in question.

TIP

Even if you think the pages you've authored are quite innocuous, it can still be a good idea to include content ratings in them. A browser that uses a content filter like the Content Advisor will by default block any pages that aren't rated. It's the only way the filters can do their job, and your pages would be blocked if they didn't include a rating.

When an author completes the questionnaire at the RASCi site, for example, the site displays the RSACi ranking, or score, for the page in question. It also displays the necessary PICS code (in HTML) that the author can include in the page's header to establish its ranking.

If you'd like to rank Web pages you've authored or a site you manage, or if you simply want to learn more about these ratings systems, you can visit the RSAC home page at

```
www.rsac.org
```

Enabling the Content Advisor

By default, the Content Advisor is disabled in Internet Explorer, and is therefore *not* filtering pages, and Internet Explorer will open *any* Web page you or another user requests.

The first time you enable the Content Advisor in Internet Explorer, you'll be asked to create a supervisor's password. Thereafter, you or anyone else who wants to enable or disable the Content Advisor, or change any of its settings, must supply the password. Once you've created the password, it's up to you to decide who else should have it.

NOTE

You can change the password at any time by clicking the Change Password button, which you'll find on the General tab of the Content Advisor dialog box.

To access the Content Advisor in Internet Explorer, choose Tools ➤ Internet Options and select the Content tab. The group of options labeled Content Advisor contains two buttons (shown below). When you first access the Ratings options, the button on the left is labeled Enable. The Content Advisor is inactive until you click this button.

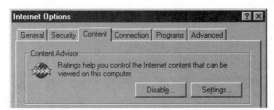

Here's how to sign yourself up as a content supervisor and the keeper of the password, prior to setting up any content-rating criteria. Remember, this procedure assumes that no one has yet created a password for the Content Advisor.

1. Choose View ➤ Internet Options and select the Content tab, where you'll see the Content Advisor buttons, as shown above.

2. Click the Enable button to open the Create Supervisor Password dialog box. Because this is the first time, you'll need to create a password before you can set any ratings.

3. In the first field, enter the password you want to use, and enter it again in the second field for confirmation. Then click OK.

4. You'll see a message telling you that the Content Advisor is enabled, and when you click OK you'll be returned to the Internet Options dialog box.

5. To see where you define the ratings, click the Settings button, enter your password, and click OK.

6. This opens the Content Advisor dialog box; its Ratings tab is shown in Figure 18.5.

7. You can click OK at this point to close the dialog box and return to the Internet Options dialog box.

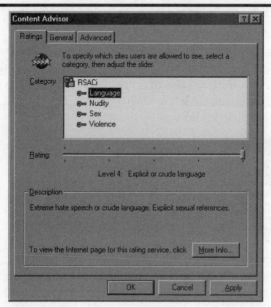

FIGURE 18.5:   You can apply ratings to various types of Web content with the Content Advisor.

Notice that the first Ratings button is now labeled Disable, indicating that the Content Advisor is now actively filtering Web pages that you open. When you want to turn off its filtering, click the Disable button and enter your password.

If you enable the Content Advisor without changing any of its settings, it will check the RASCi rating (its default rating system) for each page you open. It will also use its default filtering criteria, which are the strictest possible. In the next section, you'll see how to relax or fine-tune those criteria.

WARNING

Before you consider the job finished, you might want to disable (deselect) the "Users can see sites that have no rating" option, which you'll find on the General tab in the Content Advisor dialog box. Internet Explorer will then block (not open) any pages that have no PICS rating. Unfortunately, this means a lot of the Web will be inaccessible, but it ensures that your content filtering will work as you want it to. Then be sure to read the section named "What to Do When a Page Is Disallowed" a little later in this chapter.

Setting the Ratings Criteria in the Content Advisor

You can change the filter settings for the Content Advisor whether the Advisor is enabled or disabled, but you'll need the supervisor password to do so.

1. Choose View ➤ Internet Options and select the Content tab.

2. Click the Settings button in the Content Advisor options.

3. Enter the supervisor password and click OK. This displays the Content Advisor dialog box Ratings tab.

The Category list displays all the rating systems and their various filtering categories that are currently installed in Internet Explorer. In Figure 18.5, only the RSACi system is available, with its four categories of Language, Nudity, Sex, and Violence.

4. To read a short description of a rating system, select its name in the list. For example, in Figure 18.5, the RSACi rating system name was selected and you can see a description of it in the lower portion of the dialog box.

5. To adjust the filtering effects, select a category in the list, which displays a slider bar in the center of the dialog box. By default, each category will be set to level 0, which creates the most restrictive filter possible for that category. Any page you

try to open in Internet Explorer that has a RASCi PICS rating for that category that is higher than 0 will be disallowed by the Content Advisor.

6. Move the slider to the right to relax the filtering effect for this category. The stops on the slider bar are numbered, and a short description of the current selection appears in the lower portion of the dialog box.

7. Continue to select categories and set their rating levels. Remember, once you have enabled the Content Advisor, *all* the categories in the list will be applied when Internet Explorer checks the content rating of a Web page.

8. To see what happens when a page is disallowed, set the Nudity category to a level of **2** or less.

9. When you are finished, click OK to return to the Internet Options dialog box.

10. To test your settings, as we'll do in the next section, remember to enable the Content Advisor; otherwise, your filter settings will have no effect. Click OK to close the Internet Options dialog box and return to Internet Explorer.

What to Do When a Page Is Disallowed

When you have enabled the Content Advisor, it will check the PICS rating for each Web page that you or anyone else opens in Internet Explorer. If the page exceeds the rating levels you have specified, Internet Explorer will display a dialog box alerting you to the problem. You can experiment with the Content Advisor by going to the Web site

```
www.playboy.com
```

This is the home on the Web for *Playboy Magazine*, which is well known for its gauzy journeys into the uncharted and boundless seas of sex, nudity, and language. The Web site maintains PICS ratings for all its pages using both the RASCi and SafeSurf rating systems, so this is a great place to see how the Content Advisor works.

When you go to the Playboy Web site, the Content Advisor will read the PICS ratings for the home page and compare it with the settings in your Content Advisor. Unless you have increased those settings a great deal, the page will be disallowed, and you'll see the dialog box shown in Figure 18.6. It lists all the categories that exceed the content rating levels in the Content Advisor.

In this example, the dialog box offers two options:

▶ Click the Cancel button to close the dialog box and not open the page. This is the option that a child would need to choose.

▶ Enter the supervisor password and click the OK button to open the page. This allows you to make exceptions when you're around to do so, and lets you keep the Advisor enabled while you go to a site that you don't want your kids to visit.

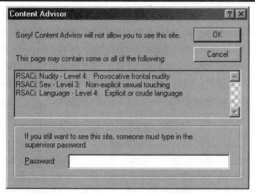

FIGURE 18.6: When any of the PICS ratings for a page exceeds the settings in the Content Advisor, Internet Explorer will not be allowed to open the page.

You can choose to disable this second option so that the password field is not displayed. In Internet Explorer, choose View ➤ Internet Options, select the Content tab, click the Settings button, enter your password, and then choose the General tab. There you can deselect the "Supervisor can type a password to allow users to view restricted content" option. If you have kept your password away from prying eyes, you can safely leave this option enabled.

The Content Advisor may disallow a page for several other reasons, even if that page would be quite acceptable to you:

▶ The rating in the page includes an optional expiration date, and that date has expired.

> ▶ The page includes PICS codes from a rating system that you do not have installed in the Content Advisor (see the next section about installing other systems).

> ▶ The page has no PICS rating.

This last possibility is an important one, because you, as the Content Advisor supervisor, can decide whether unrated pages can be opened in Internet Explorer.

As mentioned earlier, when in doubt, it's safer to block unrated pages by deselecting the "Users can see sites that have no rating" option. Although this will vastly restrict the amount of browsing that can be done in Internet Explorer, it will ensure that only pages that meet your rating levels will be seen.

You might choose to select this option and relax the restriction when you're going to be around to supervise the children you're responsible for (and to keep an eye on the computer screen too). But when you're not going to be around to watch over your charges, you should enable this option again so that the Content Advisor will have its full effect.

WARNING

It's important to understand that at this time only a small percentage of all the pages on the Web include a PICS rating, although that fraction is sure to grow as the Web matures. For now, no matter how restrictive you make the Content Advisor, it will only be effective with that small number of rated pages.

Adding Another Rating System

The Content Advisor in Internet Explorer comes equipped with the RASCi content-rating system, but there are other page-rating systems in use on the Web. When the Content Advisor is enabled and you attempt to open a page that uses a rating system that you do not have installed, the page will be blocked. You'll see a message similar to the one shown in Figure 18.7. Notice that the message includes the URL of the site where you can learn about this rating system. You can also download its rating vocabulary file from that site, which you should do if you want the Content Advisor to accept or reject pages that use this system.

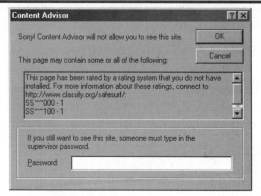

FIGURE 18.7: The Content Advisor will block a page that includes a PICS rating that you do not have installed.

NOTE

You can have more than one rating system installed, and each has its own criteria for content filtering. If a page uses just one PICS rating system that you have installed, your others will be ignored. If a page uses more than one system that you have installed, however, the settings in each will be used to determine whether the page is acceptable.

Anyone can download a rating file, but you'll need the content supervisor password to install it in Internet Explorer. Here's how to install the new rating system mentioned in Figure 18.7:

1. In Internet Explorer, go to the site listed in the dialog box:

   `www.classify.org/safesurf/`

2. Here you can see a description of the categories used by this system (the SafeSurf system in this case). To download its rating file, go up one folder to

   `www.classify.org`

   and then click the link that downloads the SafeSurf file, which is named SafeSurf.rat. (All rating vocabulary files have the file name extension RAT.)

3. Once you have downloaded the file, you can move it to your Windows\System folder, which is the default location where the Content Advisor looks for these files.

4. In Internet Explorer choose View ➤ Internet Options and select the Content tab.

5. Click the Settings button and enter your password to access the Content Advisor dialog box.

6. Select the Advanced tab and then click the Rating Systems button. This displays the Rating Systems dialog box, where you can see all of the rating files that are currently installed:

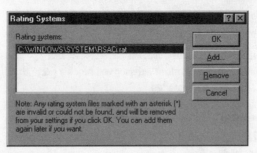

7. Click the Add button to add a new system. In the file-selection dialog box that is displayed, select the RAT file that you previously downloaded and stored in your Windows\System folder, and then click the Open button.

8. You'll see the name of the new file in the Rating Systems dialog box; click OK to continue.

9. Back in the Content Advisor dialog box, choose the Ratings tab.

10. You'll see that the Category list now includes the categories for the new rating system.

11. You'll need to set the rating criteria for each new category, as explained earlier in this chapter.

12. When you're finished, click OK to close the Content Advisor dialog box.

Setting and fine-tuning the rating levels for the categories in multiple rating systems can become a maintenance chore. If you find that you're really relying on the Content Advisor, you might want to look into purchasing separate filtering software for Internet Explorer.

ASSIGNING TRUST THROUGH SECURITY ZONES

One of the problems with life on the ever-evolving Internet is that it's a lot like a young man or woman moving from life on the farm to life in the big city—the pace is maddening and it's hard to know whom (or what) to trust.

We've already looked at how you can use Internet Explorer's Content Advisor to filter out potentially objectionable material. Now we'll look at how you can limit the amount of interaction a Web server has with Internet Explorer and your computer. The main issue is how Internet Explorer handles downloaded *active content* (programs), or *dynamic content* as it is also called. Dynamic content refers to programs that are downloaded by Internet Explorer from the server when you open a page. You'll commonly encounter two types of programs: ActiveX controls and Java applets.

The main concern with any unknown program that you run on your computer is that the program might be malicious, such as a computer virus. As you'll read a little later, Internet Explorer can notify you when a page contains active content and let you decide whether to accept it.

The problem with this is that more and more sites are using more and more active content to bring their pages to life. This means that not only will you be inundated with announcements from Internet Explorer about incoming programs, but you'll also be left scratching your head and wondering which sites are safe and which are questionable. In other words, you're not about to inspect the source code of every program a site wants to send you! Instead, you simply want to know if this site is trustworthy. That's where the security zones of Internet Explorer come into play.

Part ii

Dividing the Web into Security Zones

Internet Explorer lets you divide the Web into *security zones*. Each zone has its own set of security restrictions that determine how to handle active content, download files, run other applications on your computer, and more. There are four predefined zones:

Zone	Security	Description
Internet	Medium	All Web sites, except those URLs that you assign to other zones or are on your local intranet

Zone	Security	Description
Local Intranet	Medium	Sites that you access through your own private network; the URLs are defined by your system administrator
Trusted Sites	Low	Sites you are familiar with and trust to a high degree
Restricted Sites	High	Sites you visit but do not trust

When you first install Internet Explorer, all sites are assigned to the Internet zone. As you browse the Web and become familiar with a site you frequent, you can assign that site to any of the other three zones. This will apply the zone's security settings to that site. If you look on the right side of Internet Explorer's status bar, you'll see the zone to which the current page is assigned (as shown here to the left).

The three security levels—Low, Medium, and High—provide a simple way to apply a group of restrictions to a zone without having to adjust each individual setting. You can, however, choose the Custom security level for a zone and fine-tune each of the security options. Setting the security level is discussed in the next section.

NOTE

If you upgraded from Windows 95 with Internet Explorer 3, any security settings you were using were *not* brought into Internet Explorer 4, because they aren't really equivalent.

To change the security level for a zone or to assign sites to a zone, choose View ➤ Internet Options and select the Security tab, which is shown in Figure 18.8.

Changing the Security Level for a Zone

You can change the overall security setting for any of the four zones. For example, you might loosen the restrictions on the Local Intranet Zone by setting it to Low so that few restrictions would apply to sites in that zone. In Figure 18.8, you would choose Local Intranet Zone from the drop-down menu labeled Zone, and then select the Low radio button.

When you click OK, the security level for all sites assigned to that zone would now be Low.

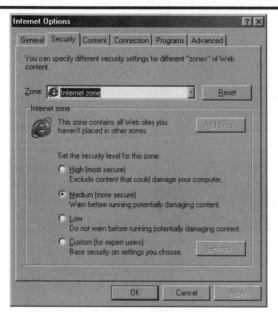

FIGURE 18.8:   In the Security tab, you assign sites to a security zone or adjust the security restrictions for a zone.

It is unlikely that you would ever want to relax the security level for the Internet zone, as the Medium setting offers a good balance of protection without overly restricting your freedom to browse.

When you have specific reasons for changing the security level of any of the zones, you can choose to set each individual security option, instead of relaxing or tightening the entire collection of options. In the Security tab in the Internet Options dialog box, select the zone you want, choose the Custom radio button, and then click the Settings button to the right of that option. This displays the Security Settings dialog box, shown in Figure 18.9. As you can see, most of the options offer three choices: Enable, Prompt, and Disable. For the Medium security level, most of the options are set either to Enable or Prompt so that either a task will happen automatically when needed, or you will be prompted and allowed to choose whether to proceed with that task.

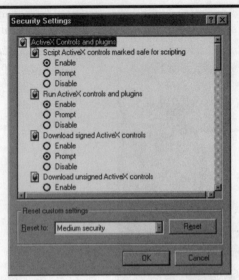

FIGURE 18.9: You can adjust each of the security settings in the
Security Settings dialog box.

WARNING

Avoid changing these individual settings unless you know exactly which settings you want to change and why you want to do so. On the other hand, looking over this list of options is a good way to familiarize yourself with the security
issues that confront you each time you browse the Web.

When you've made changes to the security options, you can always
return to one of the three security levels by choosing Low, Medium, or
High from the Reset drop-down menu near the bottom of the dialog box.

Assigning a Site to a Zone

As mentioned earlier, *all* Web sites are initially assigned to the Internet zone,
which by default has a security level of Medium. You can assign an individual site either to the Trusted Sites or Restricted Sites zone, which will give
that site either a Low or High security level, respectively (or whatever level is
currently assigned to the zone). Here's how to assign a site to a zone:

1. In the Security tab of the Internet Options dialog box, choose
    either the Trusted Sites or Restricted Sites zone from the drop-
    down menu.

2. Click the Add Sites button, which displays a dialog box similar to the one shown in Figure 18.10, which is for assigning a site to the Trusted Sites zone.

3. In the "Add this Web site to the zone" field, enter the URL of the site you want to assign to this zone, and click the Add button. You'll see the URL appear in the Web Sites list.

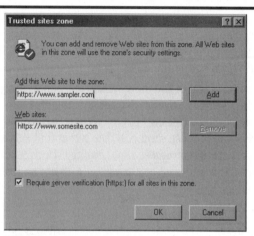

FIGURE 18.10: You can assign URLs either to the Trusted sites or Restricted sites security zone.

WARNING

Instead of typing the URL yourself, you can open the page in Internet Explorer, select its URL in the Address toolbar, and then copy and paste it into the zone-assignment dialog box.

4. You can continue to add other URLs, each of which will appear in the list of sites for this zone.

5. When you're finished, click OK to return to the Security tab in the Internet Options dialog box.

You can assign individual pages to a zone, but you can also assign entire sites by using the asterisk wildcard in the URL. For example, this URL:

```
*://sample.com
```

would assign all protocols for this site, such as HTTP and FTP, to the same zone.

ENCRYPTING TRANSFERS OVER A SECURE CONNECTION

The Internet is fast becoming a vital means for conducting our daily business, and security looms large in that context. Again, any data you send or receive on the Internet can be viewed at numerous points along the route it travels.

Internet Explorer can provide you with a great deal of online security when you connect to a Web site that uses data encryption when exchanging data with you. As you might think, encrypted data is encoded when sent and will be meaningless to anyone except the recipient.

Internet Explorer supports two of the more widely used encrypting protocols on the Web: Secured Sockets Layer (SSL, the most widely used one) and Private Communications Technology (PCT). When you connect to a secure Web site that uses one of these protocols, the server first sends a *certificate* to Internet Explorer that guarantees that the site is both secure and authentic. In other words, this site is what it says it is, and not an impostor.

WARNING

There are no absolutes in the field of encryption, and any code, no matter how sophisticated, can eventually be broken when there's a large and concerted effort. However, the amount of time and the number of people and computers required to do so can be astronomical when the code is a tough one. Therefore, code breaking is not something that can be done casually, and certainly not by an amateur cracker who has tapped into a server. At this point in history, we can consider the encryption technologies used on the Web safe and reliable.

You may first notice that you're connecting to a secure Web site that uses the SSL protocol when its URL begin with HTTPS, rather than HTTP. Whether you notice or not, Internet Explorer will make use of the security protocol automatically; there's nothing for you to do. However, it is important to know when you're connected securely and when you're not so that you don't send any sensitive information over an unsecure connection.

WARNING

By default, when you open a page in Internet Explorer, it is cached (saved) in your Temporary Internet Files folder. To keep your connection to secure sites completely private, you should choose View ➢ Internet Options and select the Advanced tab. In the Security group of options, select either "Do not save encrypted pages to disk" or "Delete saved pages when browser closed." Any secure pages you open will no longer be stored in the cache.

ABOUT SSL SECURITY

A computer works a lot harder when it has to encrypt data it sends or decrypt data it receives. That's why secure connections are usually reserved only for those pages that contain sensitive information. For example, you might spend hours browsing unsecure pages at an online shopping site, but when you click the button to purchase the items you've selected, the page in which you enter your credit card information will be a secure one. Out of dozens of pages on that site, only one secure page might be needed to protect your finances.

The same is true when you access a site for which you need a password. Only the page that actually prompts you for your name and password may be a secure one, while the other pages that follow will be unsecure.

Until mid-1997, a special export license was required when a company in the United States or Canada wanted to export any software that utilized security features stronger than what is known as 64-bit encryption (the more bits, or pieces of information, the stronger the encryption). Anything greater than that was considered a potential threat to national security if not regulated closely.

That's why the standard Internet Explorer software and other browsers did not use encryption stronger than 64-bit (in fact, the default encryption in Internet Explorer 3 was 40-bit). There was a stronger version of Internet Explorer available that used 128-bit encryption, which any citizen of the U.S. or Canada could use as long as they filled out a form asserting their citizenship.

But that changed in 1997, when the export laws were relaxed, so that we may soon find that the off-the-shelf version (or off-the-Net) of Internet Explorer has 128-bit encryption built in (as of this writing, it's still a separate version). This is an extremely tough level of security that has been used by banks and other financial institutions, so Internet Explorer now can offer you an extremely high level of safety when it comes to transferring encrypted data.

It may not be too long before you see a new encryption standard called Transport Layer Security (TLS) become common on the Web, which may eventually replace the current SSL technology. Microsoft plans to add support for TLS in Internet Explorer in future releases.

Part ii

That's why Internet Explorer displays a Security Alert message when you are about to open a secure site. It's a notice, not a warning, that your connection is going to be secure, and any information you send or receive will be safe from prying eyes on the Internet.

Other than the Security Alert, the only difference you'll notice when you're connected to a secure site is the small padlock security icon on the status bar (shown here). When you see that icon, you'll know that any data you receive or send will be encrypted and secure from prying eyes. If you point to the padlock, you'll see a ToolTip that shows the type of security currently in effect.

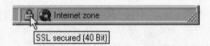

When you leave a secure site for an unsecure one, you'll see another Security Alert message. This time it advises you that the connection is going to be an open, unsecure one and that any data you send or receive is no longer safe from scrutiny by others. When you are no longer connected securely, the padlock icon on the status bar will no longer be displayed.

VERIFYING IDENTITY WITH CERTIFICATES

One of the most difficult security issues on the Internet is that of identities. How do we know that a Web site is really what it claims to be—that the company or organization whose name appears in the heading actually maintains the site—or that its active content is safe to download? For that matter, how do we prove to a Web site that we are who we claim to be?

Internet Explorer can help you deal with identities through the use of *certificates*, which are electronic assertions that guarantee the identity of a Web site, a downloaded program, or a person. These certificates of authenticity are issued by independent companies acting as third parties in the relationship between clients and servers. When using Internet Explorer, you'll encounter three types of certificates:

> **Publisher certificates** authenticate active content or other programs that are downloaded and run by Internet Explorer.

Site certificates authenticate a secure Web site, so you can exchange personal or other private information with the site, knowing it is the real McCoy.

Personal certificates authenticate you as a client and guarantee your identity to Web sites that request the certificate.

You're most likely to encounter publisher certificates as you open pages that include active content.

WARNING

Certificates add a substantial layer of security when browsing the Web, but they are only effective when they are actually implemented for a program, Web site, or person. Even then, they are not a fail-safe system. If you have any doubts about the veracity of a certificate or the object it claims to identify, stop and take the time to track down the owner or issuer of that certificate.

Software Publisher Certificates

We've all learned that people can create malicious software, which we often refer to as viruses (the software, not their creators). A potentially easy way to find malicious software is by downloading active content from the Web. Do we really feel comfortable downloading and running programs from any Web site that we visit?

To help avoid this problem and protect our computers, Microsoft introduced Authenticode technology. No, this isn't a new technology for miraculously detecting and eliminating viruses, but it goes a long way toward providing that same level of protection.

NOTE

Many of the popular antivirus programs can screen downloaded programs as they come to Internet Explorer. You can check out the Web sites of the publishers of these programs from the following category at Yahoo: Business and Economy: Companies: Computers: Software: System Utilities: Utilities: Virus Protection.

When you buy software from a store, you probably don't even think about viruses or other malicious problems because you're familiar with the company and its reputation, and the software has been safely shrink-wrapped by that company before it was shipped out.

Part ii

With the Internet, however, you really don't know where software comes from. An IP address isn't a physical address, so you can't even trace it to its country of origin. When you surf the Web and connect to a site that wants to send you active content with the page you requested, you simply don't know who's attempting to install that new program on your computer. This situation is bursting with potential hazards.

The solution proposed by Microsoft is to create *electronic packaging* for programs such as ActiveX controls (a popular form of active content), which is sometimes called a *digital signature*. This is an excellent method of molding the software manufacturer's identity onto the program itself and lets you know who is ultimately responsible for the software.

Downloading a Certificated Program

In a typical case, when you open a page that contains active content, such as an ActiveX control, Internet Explorer downloads that control but does not install or run it. That's because the default security setting for Web sites in the Internet security zone asks you if you want to download and install the active content.

NOTE

If a downloaded program has no certificate, Internet Explorer may reject it without even notifying you. Or, if your security settings for this page are relaxed, it may let you decide whether to download it. You'll read about certificate security settings in the next section.

The Security Warning message asks whether you want to install and run the downloaded program and shows you the name of the publisher and of the certificate provider. You have several choices:

Yes accepts the downloaded program. Internet Explorer will install it on your system and run it. If it's an ActiveX control, it will remain on your computer and may be used by this page or any other page that needs it in the future.

No rejects the program, so that Internet Explorer will not install or run it. Note that the page that sent you this program may be effectively "dead" without it, but it's your choice.

More Info displays a page from Internet Explorer's help system that explains certificates for downloaded software.

Company name displays the certificate properties for the publisher of this program.

Always trust software from always accepts the downloaded program. If you feel comfortable accepting programs from this publisher in the future, select this option. Thereafter, you won't be prompted when Internet Explorer downloads active content published by this company. You can view a list of publishers you've identified as trusted by clicking the Publishers button on the Content tab of the Internet Options dialog box. You can remove one from the list by selecting it and clicking the Remove button.

You might choose to reject the active content because you don't know the company that published the program, or simply because you're not interested in what that program will do.

NOTE

Downloaded ActiveX controls are stored by default in Windows\Downloaded Program Files. You can open that folder in the Internet Options dialog box by clicking the Settings button on the General tab, and then clicking the View Objects button. You'll see which controls are installed on your system. You can view the properties of a control to see what other programs or objects use it, and you can delete any control that you no longer want.

Setting Certificate Security Options

The download scenario you just read is typical, but the actual course of events depends on the security settings in Internet Explorer and the security zone to which you have assigned this page.

By default, all Web pages fall into the security zone called Internet in Internet Explorer, until you specifically assign a site either to the Trusted Sites or Restricted Sites zone. Each zone has its own group of security settings, which by default are grouped into three categories: Low, Medium, and High. By default, Internet Explorer handles active content in the following ways for each level of security:

Low   The program is assumed to come from a trusted publisher because it comes from a trusted site, and is automatically downloaded, installed, and run without your being prompted.

Medium   You are allowed to choose whether to download and run the program, as described in the example in the previous section.

High   The program is rejected without your being prompted, because no downloading of active content is allowed from pages given a High security setting.

You can see the actual security options that come into play by opening the Internet Options dialog box (choose View ➤ Internet Options) and choosing the Security tab. Then select the Custom security option and click the Settings button.

The first group of options in the Security Settings dialog box is ActiveX Controls and Plugins. Each option has three choices, Enable, Prompt, and Disable, which coincide with the three security settings discussed above. For example, when a zone's security level is Medium, the "Download signed ActiveX controls" option will be set to Prompt, while the option "Download unsigned ActiveX controls" will be set to Disable.

Of course, you can set the security level for any zone to Custom and adjust any of these options. But the initial settings used for the three default levels should be appropriate for most users.

Site Certificates

A certificate can also be issued to a secure Web site to authenticate its identity when you log on to that site. In fact, a certificate is required for sites that use the SSL security protocol. This ensures that when you log on to your bank's Web site, for example, you're not actually connecting to a counterfeit site that is just itching to get your password.

When you connect to a secure Web site, Internet Explorer will verify the IP address stored in the certificate, and check that the certificate's date has not expired. If this information is not valid, Internet Explorer can warn of the potential problem. If everything is correct, you'll connect to the site without a hitch.

You can view a list of the Web site certificate providers that Internet Explorer recognizes. Choose View ➤ Internet Options, select the Content tab, and click the Authorities button in the group of options labeled Certificates. To view the properties of a certificate provider, select it in the list and click the View Certificate button. To remove a provider, select it and click the Delete button.

Personal Certificates

Even though you know quite well who you are, your identity is not easy to prove when you're trying to connect to a Web site somewhere out on the Internet. One way of providing that proof is through a personal certificate that guarantees your identity. In fact, in order to send encrypted e-mail with Outlook Express, you'll first have to obtain a personal certificate.

One of the more well-known certificate providers that issues personal certificates is VeriSign, Inc. (which we mentioned earlier). You can apply for one at

```
digitalid.verisign.com/ms_client.htm
```

Although there's usually an annual fee involved with getting any certificate, VeriSign has been offering a free, Class 1 personal certificate for quite some time. You can use this type of certificate to send and receive secure e-mail through Outlook Express, and you won't need a password to log on to Web sites that support personal certificates.

Like all certificates, a personal certificate has an expiration date and must be renewed in order to remain valid.

WHAT'S NEXT?

In the next chapter you'll learn about the most popular alternative to Internet Explorer, Netscape Communicator. You can then decide which browser best meets your needs.

Chapter 19

AN ALTERNATIVE TO INTERNET EXPLORER: NETSCAPE NAVIGATOR

Although Internet Explorer is closely integrated into Windows 98, Netscape Navigator is such a popular alternative that *Windows 98 Complete* wouldn't live up to its name without a look at what you can do with this browser. In this chapter, you'll learn how to start Navigator, how to open and save Web documents, and how to switch between documents and other hypermedia (sound and video, for example) via hot links. You'll also get a good look at navigating through *frames*, which are like window panes within a document.

Adapted from *Surfing the Internet With Netscape Communicator 4*, by Daniel A. Tauber and Brenda Kienan with J. Tarin Powers

ISBN 0-7821-2055-5   496 pages $24.99

NOTE

This chapter assumes you already have an Internet connection and have installed Netscape on your PC. Once you're connected to an Internet service provider, you can use Internet Explorer to download Navigator (or the whole Communicator suite) from one of Netscape's dedicated FTP sites, ftp2.netscape.com through ftp8.netscape.com. On the Netscape FTP site, first select the pub directory and then follow the links to the version of Communicator or Navigator you want. By the time you read this, a Windows 98 version should be available for downloading. If you have an earlier version of Navigator, check the Netscape Web site for information about upgrading.

LAUNCHING NETSCAPE NAVIGATOR

Launching Netscape Navigator is easy. Once you have the software installed and set up you'll have a Netscape Communicator icon on your Desktop, and you'll have a new item in your Programs menu named Netscape Communicator. To start Navigator, follow these steps:

1. Start your Internet connection. How you do this depends on the sort of Internet service you have.

2. Now start up Navigator. You can do this in one of two ways:

   ▶ Double-click on the Desktop's Netscape Communicator icon, shown here. (Navigator will launch by default.)

   or

   ▶ From the Windows 98 Start menu, select Programs ≻ Netscape Communicator ≻ Netscape Navigator. Either way, Netscape Navigator, the central component of Communicator, will open.

NOTE

Depending on your connection speed, the traffic level of the Internet, and how fast-acting the server that holds the Web page is, it may take more than a few seconds for the entire thing to load. In current Net parlance, that's known as *cometizing*—named for what the N icon does while you wait (and wait, and wait...).

SLIP AND PPP: THE COMMUNICATOR CONNECTION

Before you can start using Communicator, you must start the connection software that you use to access the Internet. This may seem a bit more complicated than starting many other programs, but it's really no big deal.

Here's how it works: You start your connection software—by default, Windows 98 Dial-Up Networking—which then connects your computer to the Internet. This software "introduces" Communicator to the Internet; it is a vital link in your Internet connection. (At one time, this could be accomplished only through special SLIP/PPP software, but Windows 98 includes newer technologies that accomplish the same purpose.) Your connection software and your provider will then pass back and forth the TCP/IP packets that make it possible for you to run Communicator (which is on your machine). Voilà—your machine is accepted as a little network hooked into the bigger, more exciting network called the Internet, and you're on your way! If all goes well (and it surely will), the Netscape Navigator window will open, and the Netscape icon in the window's upper-right corner will become animated. This tells you that Navigator is transferring data, which will appear in a few seconds in the form of a Web page. Whenever Navigator is "working" (downloading a document, searching, and so on), the Netscape icon is animated. It stops when the action has been completed.

Part ii

When you first start Netscape Navigator, you'll see the Welcome to Netscape home page, with its sleek, colorful graphics. The home page is where you begin, where Navigator first lands you on your Internet voyage. Think of it as one of many ports of entry into the Web. The Web, you'll recall, doesn't just go from here to there—it's a *web*. It doesn't really matter where you start, because everything's interconnected.

You can return to the start-up home page (the one you see when you start a Netscape Navigator session) at any time simply by clicking on the Home icon on the Navigator Navigation toolbar.

TIP

You can always return to Netscape's own home page, no matter what else you've chosen as your start-up home page, just by clicking on the N icon in the upper-right corner of the Netscape Navigator window.

If you followed the steps just presented and have Navigator running now, try clicking on the Search button in the Navigation toolbar. This brief exercise will test your Internet connection. The N icon should become animated, and in a few seconds Netscape's Search page should appear. Now try clicking on the Back button. The N icon will again become animated, and Netscape's home page will reappear.

WHAT YOU SEE: THE NAVIGATOR INTERFACE

Let's look at the parts of the Navigator window. The interface shows the Document View window. Figure 19.1 shows you what's what.

NOTE

Via the View menu, you can display or hide any of the toolbars, including the Navigation toolbar, the Location toolbar, and the Personal toolbar. Or, you can click on the blue arrow buttons at the left of any toolbar to collapse it (and expand it again later). You may want to hide this stuff if you want the page display area to be larger.

Title Bar   In the title bar, you can see the name of the page you are currently viewing.

Menu Bar   The menu bar in Navigator is similar to menu bars in other Windows applications: It provides you with drop-down menus. When you move the mouse to the menu and click on a selection, choices appear.

Navigation Toolbar   The Navigation toolbar performs some common actions. It's like other Windows toolbars in that all you have to do is click on the button for the specified action to occur. (If you point at a tool for a few seconds, a ToolTip will appear, telling you what the tool does. The ToolTip is simply a text box that displays the name of the tool to which you are pointing.) Let's quickly go over the Navigator toolbar buttons.

Menu bar   Navigation toolbar   Personal toolbar   Location toolbar   N Icon (also known as the status indicator)

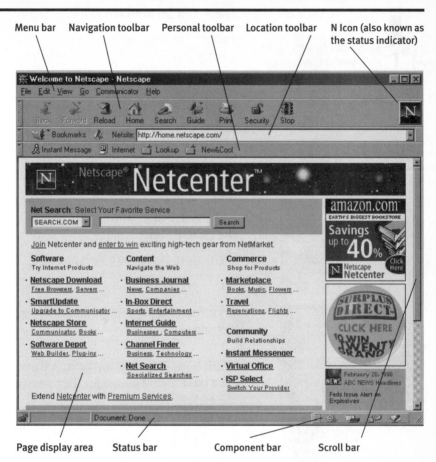

FIGURE 19.1: Here's the Navigator window with all its parts labeled so you can see what's what.

Page display area   Status bar   Component bar   Scroll bar

The Tool	What You Do with It
	Jump back to the previous page in your History list (that is, the page you were viewing just prior to the current page).
	Jump forward to the next page in your History List. (If you're on the last item in the History list, this button is dimmed—it looks grayed out.)

The Tool	What You Do with It
	Refresh the document in the page display area.
	Return to the start-up home page.
	Visit Netscape's Net Search page.
	When you have turned off image auto-loading, use this button to see images in the current Web page.
	Visit one of Netscape's Web pages.
	Print the Web page you're currently viewing.
	If this button is not grayed out, you can click on it to find out about the security of the current Web page.
	When a page is loading, click on Stop to cancel the process of loading an incoming document.

TIP

Images load automatically unless you tell Navigator to do otherwise. If you have a slow Internet connection and prefer to decide whether to view pictures on a Web page, you can turn off image auto-loading. To toggle image auto-loading from Navigator's menu bar, select Edit ➢ Preferences ➢ Advanced. A check mark will appear next to Automatically Load Images when auto-loading is turned on. When auto-loading is turned off, the Images button appears on Navigator's Navigation toolbar. You can click on this button to load images on a selected Web page.

NOTE

Security is a topic of great concern to many users who want to protect their personal information—such as credit card numbers and bank records—from theft. Netscape Communicator has encryption and security features that make it the preferred Web client for accessing all types of commercial Web servers. Check out "A Few Quick Words on Security" in this chapter for more on Communicator's security features. Or look at Netscape's Web Security Solutions page, at `http://home.netscape.com/info/security-doc.html`. Chapter 18 covers Internet Explorer's security tools.

Location Toolbar   On the left is a blue folder icon you can click on to access bookmarks (shortcuts to favorite sites; you create one by selecting Bookmarks ➤ Add Bookmark while viewing a page). The rest of this toolbar is occupied by the Location text box, where you'll find the *URL* (the Uniform Resource Locator) of the current document. We'll get to a discussion of URLs a little later in this chapter.

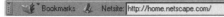

TIP

Here's a sneaky trick: Click on the arrow on the far-right end of the Location text box, and any URLs you typed into the box recently will pop up. Select any one of them to visit that site again. Even neater than that: if you're in the habit of typing URLs directly into the Location text box, you'll be pleased to see a type-ahead feature there: type the first several characters of an oft-used URL, and Navigator will guess the rest for you.

Personal Toolbar   Below the Location toolbar is a toolbar that you can customize by dragging and dropping URLs into it using the page icon.

Page Display Area   This is the main portion of the screen—it's where you'll see what you came to the Web to see.

Status Bar   The status bar is at the bottom of the screen. As you move the cursor about the viewing area and come across links, the cursor changes into the shape of a hand with one

Part ii

finger pointing, and the status bar displays the URL for the link you're pointing to. When content is being transferred to your machine, you'll see numbers in the status bar indicating the progress of the transfer.

Scroll Bars   These are just like regular Windows scroll bars: They appear on the side of the viewing area, and possibly at the bottom, when the page is too big to fit in the window. Click on the scroll bars to bring into view whatever's off-screen.

Component Bar   Netscape Communicator includes a task bar with which you can open Navigator (the browser), Messenger's Inbox (the e-mail program), Collabra (the newsgroup reader), or Composer (the HTML editor). This component bar can be *docked,* meaning that it appears at the bottom of the Navigator window as part of the status bar; or it can *float,* meaning that it appears as a tiny window with buttons that launch the various Netscape components.

To make the component bar float (see Figure 19.2) when it's currently docked on the Navigator status bar, click on the gray bars at the left side of the component bar. Once it floats, you can drag it to wherever you'd like it to live for the time being. To dock the component bar, click on the little N icon on the floating component bar. Alternatively, you can use the Navigator menu bar and select Communicator ➤ Show Component Bar to float the component bar, or Communicator ➤ Dock Component Bar to anchor the component bar to the Navigator window's status bar.

FIGURE 19.2:   Communicator's floating component bar lets you open Communicator programs while you work.

OPENING YOUR FIRST DOCUMENT

You actually opened your first document when you started Navigator and the home page appeared. But let's dig around a little further and see what else we can do.

TIP

The Netscape Assistance area, online documentation for Netscape Communicator, is at http://home.netscape.com/assist/.

Following Hot Links

Moving around the World Wide Web is a snap, thanks to hyperlinks. It's as easy as a mouse-click on the link—each link points to some other piece of the Internet, just as Windows 9*x* shortcuts point to something on your hard drive.

As we've said before, hypertext is nonlinear. (That means you don't have to follow a straight path from point A to point Z, but rather you can skip around from one place to another to another, back to the first, round to a fourth, and so on.) Hypertext is hypertext because it has links—*hot links*, they're often called—to other sources of information. You follow these links through a document, or from document to document, document to image, or perhaps from server to server, in any way you like as you navigate the Web. (You can think of hypertext as both the text and the links—it's the navigational means by which you traverse the Web.) The great thing about the Web is that you don't have to know whether the information you're looking at is in Paris, France, or Paris, Texas—all you need to do is follow a link.

NOTE

If you do want information about a link before you click on it, just check the status bar at the bottom of your screen. There you'll see a URL for anything from another site to a sound or video file, to an e-mail address. For example, if you drag your mouse over the linked word *Webmaster* on any given Web page, you might see the URL for the Webmaster's home page, an e-mail address provided by the Webmaster for feedback, or the URL for a Help page about the site you're viewing. Read on, and we'll tell you more about URLs later in this chapter.

How can you tell what is hypertext in a document? Words that are hyperlinks will usually be in a special color and underlined. On Netscape's home page, the special color is blue. A Webmaster (or producer) can choose any

Part ii

color at all to designate links, but in most cases the chosen color will be different from the color chosen for "ordinary" text. The words that stand out on a page are generally the links.

Images can also be links. Sometimes an image will have a border of color around it to designate it as a link, but in any case, the cursor will almost always turn into a pointing hand when you drag it over part of a Web page that is linked to something else.

Just as both text and images on a Web page can be hyperlinks, these hyperlinks can lead you to many different kinds of information. A link could lead you through a single document, off to a different Web page, across the world to a page on a different server, or to an FTP server, Gopher site, newsgroup, or e-mail address. Links can also lead you to images, sounds, movies, and multimedia files.

TO CLICK OR NOT TO CLICK?

When you click on a link on the Web, it may take a few seconds to access the information you requested. Don't click again; let Navigator do its job. Every time you click on a link, Navigator cancels the last order you gave it and starts a new one. So if you click on the same link four or five times, Navigator has to start all over again each time.

If we slowed this whole business down and showed you its underpinnings, you'd see that when you click on a hyperlink, Navigator contacts the machine (or machines) on the Internet that you told it to call. Then the dance between software and servers does one of these things:

- ▶ It gets and displays the document that the link specifies.

- ▶ It goes to another location in the current document.

- ▶ It gets a file, such as an image or a sound file, and through the use of a plug-in or an external viewer or player (another piece of software on your PC) displays the image or plays the sound.

- ▶ It gives you access to another Internet service, such as Gopher, FTP, Telnet, and so on.

If you still have the Netscape home page open now, click on a few links. Don't be shy—just click on anything that looks interesting. You'll soon see why they call it the Web. Try jumping back and forth a couple of times, too, by clicking on those tools on the Navigation bar. When you've had enough, simply click on the Home button or the N icon to get back to the Welcome to Netscape home page.

NOTE

When you look at a document that has a link to something you've already seen, the color of that link changes. These are called *visited links*, and this is Navigator's way of letting you know you've been to that place before.

Opening a Document Using Its URL

Sometimes you're going to want to go straight for the jugular—you know where the document is, and you just want to see it without starting on a home page and skipping through a lot of hot links. Maybe your pal just sent you the URL for the Exploratorium, a really wonderful interactive science museum in San Francisco.

To open a document using its URL, follow these steps:

1. From the Navigator menu bar, select File ➤ Open Page, or press Ctrl+O. The Open Page dialog box will appear.

2. In the Open Page dialog box (see Figure 19.3), type the URL of interest (in our example, `http://www.exploratorium.edu`).

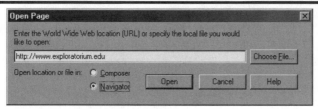

FIGURE 19.3: The Open Page dialog box

TIP

If you need a refresher on URLs, see Chapter 15 for a complete explanation. Always keep in mind that, unlike e-mail addresses, URLs are case-sensitive— capitalization matters! This is because lots of Web servers are Unix machines; in Unix, filenames in uppercase letters are not considered the same as filenames in lowercase letters. All the punctuation marks you see in some URLs are significant too—one misplaced hyphen, period, or tilde (~) will trip up the whole works. So if you're typing in a complex URL, look at it closely as you type. You can copy URLs from e-mail or other documents and paste them directly into either the Open Page dialog box or the Location text box.

3. Click on Open, and Navigator will find the document for this URL and display it on your screen. (See Figure 19.4.)

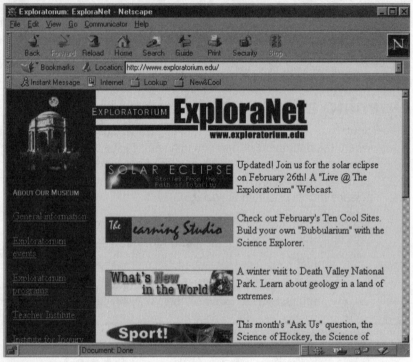

FIGURE 19.4: Here's the Exploratorium's home page. We found it using the URL a friend gave us.

TIP

You can also jump quickly to a document by typing or pasting its URL directly into Navigator's Location text box, if you have the Location toolbar displayed. And you don't even have to type **http://** every time you want to type in a URL. You can start with the next bit of the URL instead. Navigator assumes that the URLs you ask for are HTTP URLs (Web pages) unless you tell it otherwise. In fact, you can often type just one word. For example, typing **Ford** and pressing Enter will get you straight into that car maker's site.

The Web is very big. And it changes all the time. From time to time you might have difficulty locating or accessing content. The original may have been removed by its owner, the machine that holds the content may be unavailable or overworked when you try to access it, or the network path between your machine and the server might be down. If Navigator has been trying for a while to access a document without success, it will display a dialog box saying that it just plain cannot locate the document. (See "Error Messages Demystified" later in this chapter for the dish on error messages and what to do about them.) To go back to the document that was on-screen before you tried making the jump, just click on OK.

TIP

If you're waiting for a page to arrive, and you want to look at something else (another page, for example) while you're waiting, select File ➢ New Navigator Window from Navigator's menu bar. A second Navigator window will open, and you can use it to look at something other than what you were trying for in the first window. You can then use Alt+Tab or the Communicator menu to switch back and forth between the two open windows. Now who said attention spans are getting shorter?

A FEW QUICK WORDS ON SECURITY

Keeping the data that passes across the Internet safe and secure is an issue that bigwigs in both business and government are discussing now, and one that will soon become relevant even to the casual user.

You've probably noticed a lot of talk in newspapers and magazines and on TV about commercial ventures on the Web—merchants and malls all setting up shop and taking your credit card order, or banks offering home services through their sites. You can even use the Web to buy and sell stocks. If this data (your credit card number, your bank balance and access code, or your stock portfolio) is not safe, it can be read by some eavesdropper lurking in an electronic shadow. Well, you can surely see the concern!

Fortunately, the designers of Netscape Communicator had this issue in mind when they developed the software. Netscape Navigator was the first Web browser to allow secured transactions to take place (between your computer running Navigator and a Web server running Netscape's Netsite Commerce Server). In practical terms, this means that when you, running Navigator at home, connect to a home page on a special server that was purchased from Netscape Communications, the data sent back and forth can be secure from prying "eyes."

CONTINUED ➡

Part ii

By now you may have noticed the little blue lock icon on Navigator's command toolbar. Usually, if you click on the security lock, a Netscape window will pop up and tell you that "There Is No Security Info for This Page." If, however, you are connected to a secure page—one where such eavesdropping is not possible because the data is encrypted before it is transferred and decrypted upon arrival—clicking on the lock will open a similar window, but one that's filled with reassuring data that offers copious detail about the relative security of the Web page.

Netscape Communicator (and therefore Navigator 4) offers even more sophisticated security with the addition of certificates to its features. Certificates are meant to prove your identity to Web servers through a system of verification. Look for this technology to become an increasingly important security feature as Web producers upgrade their sites to take advantage of new versions of Netscape's server software using certificates.

You can find out more about security by selecting Help ➤ On Security from the Navigator menu bar. To get a directory of sites using Netsite Commerce Servers and other Netscape software, visit Netscape's Customer Showcase at http://home.netscape.com/home/netscape-galleria.html. To find out more about the current document on your screen, select View ➤ Page Info from Navigator's menu bar.

CHANGING THE SIZE AND COLOR OF DISPLAYED TEXT

If you've been working along with this chapter, you'll notice that text appears on your screen in different sizes. Usually, the text that makes up the substance of the page—the *body text*—is about the size you'd expect, while the title of the page is larger.

Changing Fonts and Type Sizes

Some folks are annoyed by gigantic titles all over the page that necessitate scrolling around a lot, while others can deal with big headlines in order to make the main text of the page larger and easier to read. Whichever you prefer, you can change the font and size of displayed text in Navigator.

Here's how you do it:

1. From Navigator's menu bar, select Edit ➢ Preferences. The Preferences dialog box will appear.

2. In the Category column along the left of the Preferences dialog box, double-click on Appearance (or click on the plus sign next to that word). The Preferences dialog box will be updated to reflect your choice.

3. Indented below the word *Appearance,* you'll see the word *Fonts.* Click on that word, and once again, the Preferences dialog box will change to reflect your last click.

4. Now, in the Fonts and Encodings area, you can set either a variable-width or a fixed font. Just click on the menu boxes for either the font face or the font size to choose any font and size available on your machine.

5. When you're finished making your selections, click on OK to return to the Navigator window.

The variable-width or proportional font is the one used for most of the text—body, head, and lists. The fixed font is the one used for preformatted text, which is a rarely used HTML element, but it also happens to be the font that appears when you type stuff in to the forms that some pages offer; for example, when responding to surveys.

NOTE

Leave the Preferences dialog box's "encoding" set to Western. Western is the proper setting for English and most European languages. Note, too, that while other choices are apparent in this dialog box, they aren't really available unless you have a version of Windows that's been localized to a specific language or country. Leave this stuff alone unless you know what to do with it.

TIP

As a shortcut, you can change font sizes without opening the Preferences dialog box at all. From Navigator's menu bar, select View ➢ Increase Font or View ➢ Decrease Font, depending on what you want to accomplish.

How does changing one font size change the style of more than one kind of text on a single page? Good question. Basically, Navigator displays different sizes of text (the title, headings, body text, and so on) in comparison to one "measure"—the basic font size. Navigator will display the title so-and-so many times larger than this base measure, and so forth. It is the base measure that you are changing in the procedure we just described.

TIP

A good rule of thumb is to select the font you find the most readable as your Proportional Font. A font such as Times New Roman or Bookman Old Style would be a sensible choice. For the Fixed Font, which is generally supposed to resemble a computer code look, Courier New or some other "typewriter" font will work well. A size of 12 or 14 for both fonts will make text readable on almost any screen.

Changing Colors

In Navigator, you have the option of changing the color of text. To do so, follow these steps:

1. From Navigator's menu bar, select Edit ➤ Preferences. The Preferences dialog box will appear.

2. If the word *Colors* is not already visible in the Category column along the left of the Preferences dialog box, double-click on Appearance (or click on the plus sign next to that word). The Preferences dialog box will be updated to reflect your choice.

3. Indented below the word *Appearance,* you'll see the word *Colors.* Click on that word, and the Preferences dialog box will show Navigator's true colors (see Figure 19.5).

4. To make your upcoming color choices override any other settings, select the checkbox Always Use My Colors, Overriding Document. To allow the settings that exist in a given document to override the color choices you are about to make, deselect this checkbox.

5. As you can see in Figure 19.5, you can set the color for Text, Background, Unvisited Links, or Visited Links. Click on any of these buttons to adjust the color choice for that option. The Color dialog box will appear.

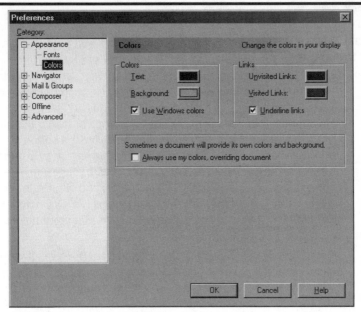

FIGURE 19.5: The Preferences dialog box displaying color information

6. In this dialog box, you can select any of a number of predefined colors by clicking on one in the Basic Colors area, or you can define a custom color by clicking on the Define Custom Colors button. You can also choose here to use the default Windows color scheme.

7. Click on OK to close the Color dialog box. The Preferences dialog box will reappear, with the color(s) you've chosen appearing in place of the default Netscape colors that were there before.

8. You can repeat steps 4–6 for all four elements (text, background, unvisited links, and visited links), if you like.

9. When you are done specifying Navigator's colors, click on OK. The Preferences dialog box will close, and you will once again see the Netscape window.

The changes you've made will take place immediately. If you don't like the results, you can always go back and repeat the whole color-changing process, selecting something new and different.

Part ii

GUESTBOOKS, SURVEYS, AND FORMS—GEE WHIZ!

When you see a box on a Web page that lets you type stuff in it, that's often what's called a *form*. Forms are used by Web site producers to let users participate in Internet surveys, order merchandise, "sign" guestbooks, and give feedback, among other fun things. The purpose of a form is usually obvious, as is the way you use it. You'll type some words in a text box, then perhaps click on a few radio buttons and check boxes, and finally press a button at the bottom of the page that whisks that information on its way. You may be invited at some sites to fill in a guestbook with your name, e-mail address, and a message to tell the Webmaster and other Web users what you think about the Web page you just visited. Or you may be asked to fill out a survey or registration form as a prerequisite to seeing the rest of a site.

This process is usually quick, simple, and free. However, if you're not sure exactly who might be receiving personal information, and if you don't want your e-mail box cluttered with junk from strangers, you may want to think twice about filling out every survey or questionnaire you run across. Watch for sites that do not sell their mailing lists—they usually tell you as much, and they usually stick to their word.

SAVING STUFF TO YOUR LOCAL MACHINE

Let's say you've been skipping around the Internet and looking at a lot of stuff, and you've found something really nifty you want to hold on to.

Saving takes up valuable disk space. This means you don't want to save *everything*. You do want to save things you want to keep for reference or access quickly in the future. For alternatives to saving, see Chapter 4's discussions of Bookmarks and Internet shortcuts.

You can save a document to your local hard drive in three ways. We'll get to those in a second; first, a word or two on naming files in general and hypertext files in particular.

WHICH BROWSER SHOULD I USE?

If you're running Navigator with Windows 98, you have the option of viewing any Web page with either Navigator or Internet Explorer. Generally both of these browsers can handle any kind of Web content, including fancy things such as special colors and the use of columns, frames, and tables, as well as audio and animation. Older Web browsers might not be able to display that stuff as it was intended to appear, and so you will occasionally see messages like "Use Netscape for best viewing" or "Netscape not required." A few pages, including some (not surprisingly) on the Microsoft Web site, seem to work only with Internet Explorer. In any case, if you have problems viewing a site with one of your browsers, you can always try the other one.

Saving Stuff You Can See

Saving documents and images to your hard drive can be a good idea if you want to look at them later without paying for connect time. You can also use your store of saved documents as a library to jog ideas in constructing your own home page—this may be an easier process if the page is on your hard drive. See Chapter 20 for more on creating your own Web pages.

Saving Web Pages

Here's how to save the page you are viewing at the moment to your hard disk:

1. From the Navigator menu bar, select File ➤ Save As. The Save As dialog box will appear (see Figure 19.6). This is much like a Save As dialog box you'd see in any other Windows application.

2. In the File Name text box, type a filename. Navigator will usually assign either .htm or .html as the extension automatically—these are the extensions for hypertext files. (If you want to be sure the program is assigning one of those extensions, just take a look at the bottom of the dialog box, where the Save As Type drop-down list appears.)

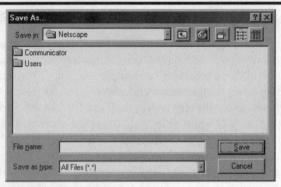

FIGURE 19.6: The Save As dialog box

NOTE

Some files on the Web don't end in .html or .htm—they end in trailing slashes, as in http://www.webpage.com/ (rather than http://www.webpage.com/home.htm), or they end in some sort of goop given them by a CGI or other interactive script. Generally, Navigator rolls with the punches and gives the file a name ending in .html, but you may want to double-check your filenames before you save them anyway.

TIP

If you want to save just the page's text, and not the HTML format, you can select Plain Text as the file type.

3. Pull down the Save In list by clicking on its down arrow. From the list, select the drive to which you want to save the file. Below the Save In drop-down list, the contents of the drive you selected will appear as a list of folders and icons.

4. In that list, double-click on the directory into which you want to save the file.

NOTE

If you want to place the file in a subdirectory (within a directory), first double-click on the directory that contains that subdirectory so you can see it. For sub-subdirectories, repeat this process as needed until you find the target subdirectory.

5. Click on the Save As dialog box's Save button.

Perhaps this is obvious, but you won't see the document you've saved on-screen when you save it. You'll know it's been saved when you check the Directory list and see the filename there.

Saving Images

You might want to save one special image to your hard drive instead of a whole Web page. What for? Well, you can use that image as desktop wallpaper for your computer, send it as a map to a friend who's coming to town, or print it to hang over your desk at work. If the image is clip art (or otherwise in the public domain), you can also use it on your own home page. (See Chapter 20 for more on creating Web documents.)

Saving an image to your hard drive is easy. Just do this:

1. Using your right mouse button, click on the image of interest. A pop-up menu will appear asking you what you want to do.

NOTE

Your other choices from this menu include viewing the image on a separate page, or if the image is a link, creating a Bookmark or Internet Shortcut to the page it's pointing to. See "Pop-Up Menus and You," later in this chapter, for more on how to use your handy right-mouse-button tool.

2. From the pop-up menu, select Save Image As. The Save As dialog box will appear.

3. Now follow steps 2 through 5 in the "Saving Web Pages" procedure just shown. Navigator will automatically detect and choose the correct file format (usually either GIF or JPEG) for the image.

4. To verify that the save was successful, you can use Windows Explorer to look in the directory to which you just saved the file. You should see the file listed.

Saving Stuff That's Not in View

Let's say the page you are viewing at the moment includes a link to something (maybe to a sound or to an image) that you want to save to disk to check out later. You can save the stuff at the other end of the link without first having to travel that link. Just follow these steps:

1. Pointing to the link that goes to the stuff you want to save, click the right mouse button. A pop-up menu will appear.

2. From the menu, select Save Link As. The Save As dialog box will appear.

3. Now follow steps 2 through 5 in the section titled "Saving Web Pages," earlier in this chapter.

To verify that the save was successful, you can use Windows Explorer to look in the directory to which you just saved the file. You should see the file listed.

NOTE

When you save an HTML document to your hard drive, what you get is the HTML code and the text—not the images. When you load the page later into Navigator, the images won't be there. This is because HTML documents tell Navigator where to find images, but they don't actually contain any pictures. An image in a Web page is really a link to a picture located on the Internet—but Navigator loads the pictures onto the page instead of just linking to them.

VIEWING DOCUMENTS YOU'VE SAVED

You can view a document you've saved to your local hard drive by selecting File ➤ Open Page from Navigator's menu bar.

TIP

You don't have to be running your Internet connection to use Navigator to look at files on your computer.

The Open Page dialog box will appear; to open a file on your local drive, click on Choose File, and the standard Open dialog box will appear. Again this is a standard Windows dialog box. Select and open the HTML file of interest by double-clicking on it. Once you're back at the Open Page dialog box, click on the Open button to display the file in the Navigator window.

By the way, saving a file and then viewing it this way is a lot faster than accessing and viewing it when it's somewhere else in the world; the drawback is that if the owner of the document has made changes to it, you won't know about them. A really cool aspect of this, though, is that when you view a document that's been saved to your local machine, the links have been saved with it, and you can simply click on those links and start up your Web travels again—assuming you're dialed in for the clicking part.

POP-UP MENUS AND YOU

Netscape Navigator offers a lot of handy shortcuts that are no further away than your right mouse button. The available shortcuts change depending on where you point your cursor when you click. Try these:

▶ Point at some white space or nonlinked text and click the right mouse button. A pop-up menu will appear offering options for going back or forward and for adding a bookmark or Internet shortcut for the page you're currently viewing, among other things.

▶ Point your mouse at a link and click with your right mouse button. A pop-up menu will appear offering options to copy the link's URL to the Clipboard, to add a bookmark or an Internet shortcut, to save the document behind the link to your hard drive, to open the link in Netscape Communicator's HTML Editor, or to open the link in a new window instead of the one the link is in.

▶ Point at an image and click with the right mouse button. A pop-up menu will appear offering options for saving the image to your hard drive, copying the image's URL, or viewing the image in a separate window.

JUMPING BACK AND FORTH WHILE VIEWING A DOCUMENT

The Back and Forward buttons on the toolbar provide a convenient way to jump back and forth among the hot links you've followed. This is because Navigator tracks the documents you visit in a History list. The Back and Forward buttons actually let you travel through the History list. If you have Navigator running, try clicking on the Back button to jump backward along the links you just followed, and then try clicking on Forward to jump forward.

TIP

In addition to going back and forward one page at a time, try clicking on the Back button and holding down the left mouse button for a second or two. A small pop-up menu will appear, listing the last five pages you've visited. You can do the same thing with the Forward button; the menu will list the next five pages in your History list.

There is an end to this—if you jump back to the first document you viewed in a session, or forward to the last one, you reach the end of the History list. The Back or Forward button, depending on which end of the history you reach, will be grayed out. (You can, as always, create more history—click on another hypertext link to explore further.)

NOTHING'S SHOWING UP! WHAT TO DO?

Sometimes the N icon will be animated, its comets flying along, and either nothing shows up, or the text arrives sans any images. What's going on?

When a Web server is busy, overloaded, or just plain slow, you'll get the text and basic HTML from it first and the images last. Images are a lot bigger (file-size-wise) than text, so they take longer to load. You can try any of these ways to address this:

Stop: Click on the Stop button. Often, the images that were trying to load are mostly there, and hitting Stop will say, "Hey images! Hurry up and load!" Many times, they will.

Reload: If that doesn't work, click on the Reload button. In fact, if a Web page ever looks funny or incomplete in some way, try reloading it.

View Image: If a single image hasn't shown up, but the rest of them have, click the right mouse button over the placeholder (that funny-looking picture that represents an image that should be there, but isn't). When the pop-up menu appears, select View Image. Navigator will then try to retrieve that single image and load it onto the page you're viewing.

Give up: Sometimes Webmasters goof up, and sometimes, particularly if the Web server you're trying to access is halfway around the world, the connection is just too danged slow. Oh, well. If you really want to see that picture of Joe Namath as a baby, try your luck again some other time.

NOTE

At the bottom of many documents, you'll find a hot link that says something like *Go Back*. If you click on this link, you won't necessarily go back to where you came from; instead, you'll visit the page that the Webmaster assumed you just came from (usually another page at the same site). If you want to go back to where you were before, click on the Back button on the Navigator toolbar.

GETTING AROUND IN FRAMES

Frames are popping up all over, ever since they became a design option in version 2 of Netscape Navigator. Frames appear on a Web page looking like a bunch of panes within the larger viewing area window; these "panes in the window" each hold some piece of the larger whole. Like everything else in life, frames are good when used purposefully, and not so good when they're used gratuitously. In Figure 19.7, you can see News of the Day, a Web page that uses frames to enhance the organization of the page by offering a navigation frame on the left and a larger frame in which various news sources appear on the right.

Having too many frames in a Web site is like putting too many bows on a dress—too much. Frames are best used when no other option will do. To be fair, many sites use frames quite well—one of the most practical applications of frames are pages that offer a table of contents in one of the frames. That index stays put (in some form or other) the whole time you're navigating the rest of the site.

NOTE

Many frames-based sites are quite apparent—there are solid lines of one sort or another, and maybe even scroll bars, that make it clear that the Navigator viewing area is being divided into little window panes. Recently, however, it's become possible to create a site that uses *borderless frames*—the usual, obvious gray lines and bars that divide the window are invisible. You may not even notice that a site uses frames until you start navigating through it and notice that only part of the page is changing while you click.

Whatever their purpose in a Web site, each individual frame has its own URL. They also can have their own scroll bars, various background colors, images, text, Java or JavaScript elements—anything, in short, that a nonframe Web page can have.

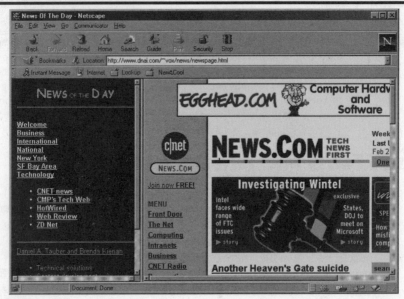

FIGURE 19.7:   The News of the Day page uses frames to enhance the navigation of its contents.

When you click on a link in one frame, often another frame on the page will change to reflect that click. That means you can easily get lost trying to find some information that was in a frame you saw five clicks ago.

Still, using frames, you can easily get back to where you once belonged. The easiest way is to use the Back button—in Navigator 4, the Back button sends you back one frame at a time until you reach the beginning of a framed-up site. You can also use the right mouse button to navigate backward—click, and when the handy pop-up menu appears, select Back. You'll navigate backward one frame at a time.

NOTE

You can bookmark a document or a frame; this is much like putting a bookmark in a book in the sense that it helps you find where you've been without having to retrace your steps.

CACHING AND RELOADING

Navigator stores the pages you visit in what's called the *cache* (pronounced "cash"). A cache is just a chunk of storage—it can be RAM or the disk drive—on your computer that's been set aside as a temporary storage place. Your PC stores parts of the programs that you're running in its cache to make them run faster. Similarly, Navigator caches the Web pages you look at, so when you go back and forth between pages, you don't have to access the Internet anew every single time you look at the same page. Instead, your machine accesses the copy of the page that's in the cache. As you continue to visit new sites on the Web, old stuff in the cache is flushed out, and the newer stuff you visit in your travels is added.

NOTE

Navigator actually maintains two caches of documents—one in your computer's memory that goes away when you end your Netscape session, and another on disk that it uses between sessions. When you access a Web page, Navigator first checks to see if you have a current copy of the page either in the memory cache or in the disk cache. If a copy of the current page is located in either of these places, that copy is displayed instead of a fresh copy, relieving Navigator of the slow process of downloading the page from the Internet anew. (This is also true of images, sounds, video—in short, anything on the Net you access via Navigator.)

When you click around from page to page, you may not be seeing the most current version of a Web page; you may instead be seeing the cached version. This can be a drag if the page changes a lot and you want the fresher version. Certain pages, like weather maps, newsfeeds, and live camera links, for example, change minute by minute, and you want the freshest view of them. If you ever doubt that you're seeing the most current version of a page, just click on the Reload button and the page will appear from scratch, rather than from the cache.

Specifying How Often to Check the Cache

You can specify how you want Navigator to approach this matter by checking the cache Every Time, Once per Session, or Never settings in the Network Preferences dialog box. The default is Once per Session. It's best not to mess with this unless you have some compelling reason and know what you're up to, because it'll slow down other operations. But here are the details:

1. From Navigator's menu bar, select Edit ➤ Preferences. The Preferences dialog box will appear.

2. In the Category area of the Preferences dialog box, double-click on the word *Advanced.* The Preferences dialog box will change to reflect this choice, and some other options should become visible.

3. Click on the word *Cache,* and the Preferences dialog box will be updated once again (see Figure 19.8.).

4. Locate the label marked "Document in cache is compared to document on network." Below the label you'll see three radio buttons, one for each option:

   Once per Session   Navigator will go looking for each page once (the first time you access this particular Web page in this particular session). This is the default setting, and it's the best for most of your usual activities.

   Every Time   Navigator will not look at your disk cache and will always retrieve from the Internet instead of locally. This setting is good when you're viewing lots of pages that change frequently, and especially if you're on a high-speed line.

   Never   Navigator will always go for the copy in your disk cache unless it becomes unavailable (or unless you click on the Reload button). Choose this when you're not dialed in to the Net, and you want to look at pages in the cache.

   Click on the button of choice. Then click on OK to close the dialog box. Navigator will hereafter comply with your choice.

Increasing the Size of Your Disk Cache

As a default, Communicator sets the disk cache at 7680K unless it picked up your Preferences from a previous version of Navigator. This is a good minimum, but you may want to increase it, depending on how much disk space you want to dedicate to Net surfing. The more disk space you allocate to Navigator's cache, the more stuff it will hold.

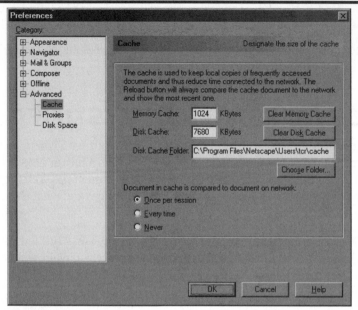

FIGURE 19.8: The Preferences dialog box displaying information about the cache

WARNING

It makes a lot less sense to increase the size of the memory cache than to increase the size of the disk cache. The other programs you're running, including Windows 98, need all the memory they can get. Don't shortchange Windows for the sake of Navigator or other applications that rely on Windows.

To increase your disk cache, follow this simple procedure:

1. Follow steps 1–3 in the "Specifying How Often to Check the Cache" section to display the Cache area of the Preferences dialog box, as seen in Figure 19.8.

2. In the Disk Cache text box, type the number of kilobytes (K) you want to reserve for Navigator's disk cache. The default is 7680K (or 7.7MB); 20000K (20MB) is a better choice if you have that much disk space to spare.

3. Click on OK. The dialog box will close, and you'll find yourself in the familiar Navigator window.

From this moment forward, you should find accessing the pages you visit most often a lot faster than it was before.

ERROR MESSAGES DEMYSTIFIED

The Internet works really well most of the time, but both computers and humans are fallible, and sometimes you'll click on a link or enter a URL and get an unhappy message from Netscape instead of the Web page you wanted. See Table 19.1 for a listing of error messages and what they mean.

A few general tips:

▶ Most errors aren't permanent. If you get an error, try a few minutes, hours, or even days later, and the page you want will usually come back.

▶ You're more likely to get Busy or Connection Refused messages during peak hours, like lunchtime and right after the workday ends. Try accessing busy pages during off-peak hours.

▶ Good Webmasters do routine maintenance on Web pages fairly often, and this can increase the chances of certain parts of a server being off-limits. If you try accessing the site a day or two later, you'll usually be able to access the page you want, or you'll be given a pointer that says the site has moved.

▶ If a page disappears inexplicably or permanently, check your favorite search engine to see if it can locate an alternate address for the page.

▶ There are probably lots of other error messages you could get, and a good rule of thumb is to try the page again later, especially if you know you've been there before, or to check the spelling and format of the URL.

NOTE

As always, when in doubt, click on Reload and see what happens.

TABLE 19.1: Navigator Error Messages We Know and Love

ERROR MESSAGE	WHAT IT MEANS	WHAT TO DO
Too Many Users	This Web site may restrict the number of accesses allowed per day or per hour.	Try again later.
A Network Error Occurred. Unable to Connect to Server	Either the host is busy, the URL is spelled wrong, or something else is funny.	Make sure you actually put the forward slashes in after `http:`. If that doesn't work, just try again later.
Broken Pipe	Something went wrong en route and some data got lost.	Click on the Reload button, or try again later.
Connection Refused	The line is "busy," and this is the Web's busy signal.	Try again later.
Document Contains No Data	The Web page you tried to link to is there, but there's nothing on it.	Forget about it. Whoever pointed you there made a mistake.
The Location (URL) Is Not Recognized.	You asked for a type of URL that doesn't exist.	Look for typos in the URL you entered, especially the `http://` part.
The Server Does Not Have a DNS entry.	This server doesn't exist right now, at least not the way you spelled it.	Check your spelling of the domain name. If it's spelled correctly, try again later.
Netscape Is Out of Memory	Boy, you've been looking at a lot of huge Web pages today!	Quit Navigator, and then launch it again.
403 Forbidden	The part of the Web server you're trying to access is off limits right now.	Try it again tomorrow or next week. If that doesn't work, forget about it. Someone doesn't want any visitors.
Please Enter Username and Password	If you don't have an account on this server, it won't let you in.	Try visiting the site's home page to see if they require you to complete a registration process.
404 Not Found	The page you tried to link to may be gone forever, or there may be a typo in the URL you entered.	Try it again tomorrow or next week. If that doesn't work, the thing's probably gone.

PRINTING A DOCUMENT OR A SINGLE FRAME

To print a Web document, you must first have it open. Then, follow the usual printing procedure:

1. From the Navigator menu bar, select File ➤ Print. The Print dialog box will appear.

2. Fiddle with the dialog box to specify what you want exactly, and click on OK.

The whole document will pop out of your printer. Note, however, that the document probably will not be a single page long (unless it's a very brief home page, for example). This, of course, is because Web pages do not have the same physical boundaries as paper pages. So a single Web page may be several paper pages long.

TIP

It may be helpful to print out a page at less than 100 percent scale. If your printer dialog box has options for printing a page at 75 percent of its normal size (or some other likely ratio), give that a try.

Also, perhaps obviously, if you want to print other pages linked within a single site, you'll have to go to those pages and print them separately. (Of course, you can't click on a printed-out Web page. But you already knew that, right?)

With frames, the matter gets a little stickier. You can't print out an entire Web page full of frames, because each pane in the window is technically a distinct document. To select the frame you want to print, again with the page (with frames) open:

1. Click on some blank space within the frame, and that frame will appear highlighted.

NOTE

To see how this works, try clicking from frame to frame in a site that uses frames. Try News of the Day, which is located at http://www.dnai.com/~vox/news. You can see how each individual frame gets highlighted as you go from frame to frame. Keep in mind, though, that the highlight may not be apparent in sites that use borderless frames.

2. From Navigator's menu bar, select File ➤ Print Frame. The Print dialog box will appear.

3. Fiddle with the dialog box to specify what you want, and click on OK.

TIP

To make sure you're printing the frame you want, you can select File ➤ Print Preview from Navigator's menu bar before you print. A window will appear showing you what you're printing, how many pages long it is, and other nifty things about the page. To exit Print Preview and return to the Navigator window, click on Close from Print Preview's toolbar. To go ahead and print, click on the Print Frame button.

The frame you selected will pop out of your printer. Now, the thing to remember is that it's one frame that you've printed, and a whole Web page can be made up of several frames. If you want to print an entire Web page with all its frames, you'll unfortunately have to print each frame individually.

QUITTING NETSCAPE NAVIGATOR

You can quit Navigator any ol' time—even when the N icon is animated. To leave Navigator, simply do the following:

1. If the N icon is animated, click on the Stop button on the toolbar. This will cancel whatever Navigator is trying to do at the moment. (If the N icon is not animated, skip this step.)

2. To actually quit the program, click on the Control button in the upper-left corner of the screen, or select File ➤ Exit from the menu bar. The Windows Desktop will reappear.

3. Remember, even if you aren't running Navigator, you are still connected to your Internet service provider, and you must break this connection, using whatever techniques are appropriate. (Check with your Internet service provider to find out about that.)

WARNING

If you have more than one Navigator window open, or another Communicator component running, such as Messenger, you can exit all Netscape windows at once by selecting File ➤ Exit from any Communicator menu bar. A dialog box will appear asking if you wish to close all windows and exit Netscape Communicator. Click on Yes to close all the windows. Click on No to continue Communicator.

Keeping Track

Now, with your basic skills in place for navigating the Web via Netscape Navigator, let's take a look at how you can more closely track where you've been by using Internet shortcuts and bookmarks, and how you can manage your bookmark list as it grows and grows.

TIP

Want to be hip to what's happening on the Net? Find out what's new on the Net at http://www.yahoo.com/new/. And you can get advance information about new versions of Netscape and other Web browsers via the Browser Watch site at http://browserwatch.internet.com/.

WHAT'S NEXT?

For many Internauts, the next logical step beyond browsing the Web is building one's own site. Individuals, organizations, and businesses of all sizes are taking advantage of easy-to-use Web authoring tools to publish their messages to the world. One of the best authoring tools for new Webmasters is bundled with Internet Explorer and Windows 98—FrontPage Express. In the next chapter, Gene Weisskopf and Pat Coleman guide you through the process of building your own site.

Chapter 20

CREATING WEB PAGES WITH FRONTPAGE EXPRESS

The common language for creating content on the Web is the HyperText Markup Language, or HTML. You can use any text editor, such as Notepad, to create a Web page in HTML, but the job is greatly simplified if you use a dedicated HTML editor that displays your page as it will appear in a browser. FrontPage Express, a worthy HTML editor, is part of the Internet Explorer suite of applications, and it can make the job of creating Web pages as simple as creating documents in your word processor. The more you learn about HTML, the more you'll appreciate that simplicity. With FrontPage, anyone can create Web pages that include a variety of HTML features.

Adapted from *Mastering Microsoft Internet Explorer 4*, by Gene Weisskopf and Pat Coleman
ISBN 0-7821-2133-0   960 pages $44.95

NOTE

FrontPage Express is the slightly trimmed down HTML editor component included with Windows 98. FrontPage 98, the full-blown version, has even more advanced features, and if you're planning to create Web pages and put together Web sites, it could be a worthy addition to your software arsenal. Any mention in this chapter of the full-featured product will include the "98" to differentiate it from FrontPage Express.

STARTING OUT IN FRONTPAGE EXPRESS

No matter how complicated HTML coding can look, if you think of Front-Page in the same way that you do your word processor, you'll be up to speed in no time. The only difference is that when you save a file in FrontPage, the result is a pure HTML file in plain text, ready to be opened in a Web browser.

Starting FrontPage

You can start FrontPage from the Start menu, as you would any other program; choose Start ➤ Programs ➤ Internet Explorer ➤ FrontPage Express. The program opens in its own Window with a new blank document, ready for you to get to work.

When you install FrontPage, it becomes the default editor for HTML files. When you right-click a Web page in Windows Explorer and choose Edit, that document opens in FrontPage.

NOTE

If you install some other HTML-enabled program after FrontPage is installed, that program might then become the one associated with editing HTML documents. You can change the association back to FrontPage for the file type Internet Document (HTML) by going to the File Types tab in the Options dialog box in Windows Explorer.

When you're viewing a page in Internet Explorer, you can choose View ➤ Source to open the underlying HTML code in Notepad. When FrontPage is installed, you can choose Edit ➤ Page or click the Edit button on the toolbar to open the current page for editing in FrontPage.

As you create Web pages in FrontPage, be sure to save your work regularly, as you would in your word processor. (You'll read about file operations later in this chapter.) When you're finished with FrontPage, you can close it by choosing File ➢ Exit.

Navigating in FrontPage

FrontPage looks much like a typical WYSIWYG word processor, where "what you see is what you get." In this case, what you see in FrontPage is what the rest of the world will see when they view this page in their Web browsers. Figure 20.1 shows FrontPage with an open document.

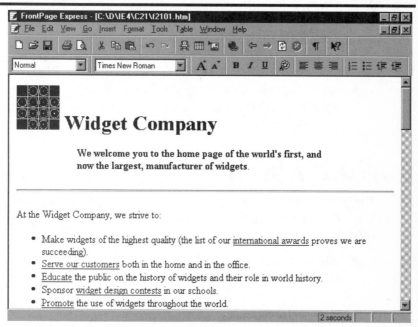

FIGURE 20.1:   You create Web pages in FrontPage in a WYSIWYG environment.

Let's take a quick look at some of the features you'll find when you're creating Web pages in FrontPage:

▶ At the top of the screen is the title bar, where you'll see the current page's HTML title (if you opened that page via a Web server) or the file name (if you opened the page from your local disk).

▶ Beneath the title bar are the menu, the Standard toolbar, and the Format toolbar. When you're creating an HTML form page, you can also display a Forms toolbar. You can turn on or off the display of a toolbar by selecting it from the View menu, and you can move a toolbar simply by dragging it to a new location.

▶ At the bottom of the screen is the status bar, which behaves much like the status bar in Internet Explorer. For example, the left side of the status bar displays a description of the currently selected command on the menu, and it displays the target address of a hyperlink when you point to a link in the page.

▶ The document (Web page) that you're editing appears in the window beneath the toolbars. You can open multiple documents (pages) and switch between them in the standard ways, such as by selecting a document name from the Window menu or by pressing Ctrl+F6.

▶ The horizontal and vertical scroll bars offer one way to scroll through your document; you can also use the expected keyboard keys, such as PgUp and PgDn.

EDITING A WEB PAGE

The best way to familiarize yourself with FrontPage is to start typing. You'll find that most of the basic procedures you've already learned in your word processor are applicable here as well:

▶ Enter text just as you would with your word processor; press Enter only to create a new paragraph.

▶ Press Del to delete the character to the right of the insertion point; press Backspace to delete the character to its left. Press Ctrl+Del to delete the word to the right of the insertion point; press Ctrl+Backspace to delete the word to its left.

▶ Press Ctrl+Home to go to the top of the document, and press Ctrl+End to go to the bottom.

▶ Using the standard Windows commands, you can change the size of the active document's window, minimize it to an icon, or maximize it so it's as large as possible (like the document you saw in Figure 20.1).

- ► Select text or graphic images by dragging over them with your mouse or by pressing the Shift key while you use a keyboard arrow key to select the material.

- ► Once you select a portion of the document, you can invoke a command from the menu or toolbar to act on that material. For example, choose Edit ➤ Cut or click that button on the toolbar to remove the selection from the document and place it in the Clipboard.

- ► You can transfer text or images between FrontPage and other programs in the usual ways, such as with Edit ➤ Copy in FrontPage and then with Edit ➤ Paste in the other program.

- ► Choose Edit ➤ Undo (Ctrl+Z) or click that button on the toolbar to undo your most recent action in the document. You can "undo an undo" by choosing Edit ➤ Redo or by clicking that button.

- ► To change the properties of an object in a page, such as selected text or a horizontal line, select the object and choose Edit ➤ Object Properties (such as Font Properties when you have selected text) or press Alt+Enter. You can also right-click the object and choose Object Properties from the shortcut menu.

Inserting Line Breaks and Special Characters

In most browsers, a paragraph in an HTML Web page (designated by the <P> tag) has a blank line above and below it, which may not always be appropriate for the format you want. For example, a name and address will appear on multiple lines, but you won't want extra paragraph spaces between them.

Use the Insert ➤ Break command, and the text that follows will appear on a new line without starting a new paragraph. This saves the new line from having to appear with a blank line above and below it. Another advantage of using the line break is that any paragraph formatting continues on the new line, whereas it won't if you create a new paragraph (you can read about formatting text and paragraphs later in this chapter).

FrontPage also offers a way for you to insert characters into your document that you cannot normally enter from the keyboard, such as the degree symbol (100°), the copyright symbol (© 1998), and the trademark symbol (™).

Place the insertion point where you want the character or characters to appear, and choose Insert ➤ Symbol. In the Symbol dialog box, click the character you want, and then click the Insert button to place it in the document. You can continue to insert characters as needed; click the Close button when you're finished.

TIP

Some symbols require special encoding in HTML in order to be displayed in a browser; FrontPage will do this for you. For example, the HTML code for the trademark symbol is &trade. In fact, a few characters you can type from the keyboard must be specially encoded because they have special meaning within HTML code. Such is the case with the ampersand, which precedes a variety of character codes in HTML. When you type an ampersand in FrontPage, it actually enters the special code &amp. Likewise, the less-than and greater-than symbols are part of HTML tags. When you enter those characters in a page, FrontPage encodes them as &lt and > this way, the browser software that eventually displays your page will interpret them as characters and not tags.

Finding and Replacing Text

You can use the Edit ➤ Find command to find all occurrences of text you specify in the current page. In the Find dialog box, enter the characters you want to find. You can also choose to find those characters only when they are a complete word or when the case exactly matches what you entered. You can also choose to search up or down the page, starting from the insertion point.

To begin the search, choose the Find Next button. The first occurrence of the specified text is selected in the page. At this point you can:

▶ Choose Find Next to find the next occurrence.

▶ Click Cancel to close the Find dialog box.

▶ Click within the page so that you can continue to work in it, perhaps to edit the text that was found. The Find dialog box remains open.

TIP

You can only search for text that is displayed in FrontPage, which means you can't search for HTML tags or other encoded characters that are hidden behind the scene. For example, you might want to search for a URL that is targeted in a link somewhere in the page. To do that, open the current page in WordPad or another text editor, where you'll see the HTML code itself. Now when you search, you'll be looking through everything that's in the file, including any URLs referenced in a link.

For the Edit ➤ Replace command, you specify the text to search for as well as the text with which to replace it. If you leave the Replace With field empty, the text that is found will effectively be deleted.

Adding Comments

You can add comments in a page with the Insert ➤ Comment command. You can use a comment to explain an area in the page, serve as a reminder to you or another author, or provide a more detailed explanation of a task that needs to be completed. The text you enter is displayed in FrontPage, but not when the page is viewed in a browser, because the text is enclosed in the HTML comment tags:

```
<!-- This text is a comment. -->
```

Actually, FrontPage adds a bit more to the comment tag, so that the previous comment would actually look like this in FrontPage:

```
<!-- webbot bot="PurpleText" preview="This text is a comment." -->
```

In case you're wondering, the WebBot is a FrontPage tool for adding non-standard HTML features to a page. In this case, the WebBot tells FrontPage not only to display the comment text, but to display it in purple. Again, in Internet Explorer this comment would not be shown at all.

Seeing the HTML Source Code

When you want to see the HTML code on which the current page is based, choose View ➤ HTML. A window will open that displays the actual HTML code for your page, the same code that will be saved to disk when you save your page.

Figure 20.2 shows the View or Edit HTML window for the page that was displayed in Figure 20.1. Use caution when you make changes to the HTML code, as they will be reflected in the page when you return to the Editor. If you accidentally delete one of the angle brackets for an HTML tag, you'll immediately see the result in the Editor.

If you're just viewing the code and do not want to make any changes to it, you can close the window by clicking the Cancel button or pressing Esc (a good way to negate any accidental changes you might have made). If you make changes to the code and want to keep them, click the OK button to close the window.

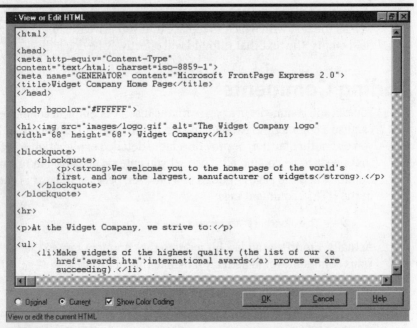

FIGURE 20.2: Choose View ➤ HTML to view or edit the underlying HTML code for a page.

NOTE

Although the Editor's menus are not active while you are in the HTML window, you can still cut or copy text to or paste text from the Clipboard—just use the standard shortcut keys for those commands (they are shown on the FrontPage menu).

The HTML window also helps you interpret the code by color-coding it:

▶ The text you have entered is in black.

▶ HTML tags are in purple.

▶ The attribute or argument names within tags are in red.

▶ The actual attributes that you have entered (via the formatting or other choices you make in FrontPage) are in blue.

The colors help make sense of the code as you scroll through it, and viewing the code is always a good exercise that will help you get a feel for the ins and outs of HTML.

Previewing Your Work in Internet Explorer

The ultimate destination for your work in FrontPage is a browser, possibly any browser on the planet if you post your work to the World Wide Web. Keep in mind that a lot of variables affect the way your page appears in a browser, and it's important that you preview your work outside FrontPage and inside Internet Explorer regularly as you're building the page.

NOTE

If you are creating pages for the Web, consider previewing your work in several browsers and on different computers as well. Try viewing the page at different screen resolutions (640×480 or 800×600) and at different color depths (256 colors or 16 million colors). You need to keep your page design somewhat flexible to accommodate the various combinations of computer hardware and software that may visit your site.

While you're working in FrontPage, open the current page in Internet Explorer to view it there, such as with the File ➣ Open command. If your page includes any animated GIF images, scrolling marquees, or active content such as ActiveX controls or Java applets, you'll see them go into action inside Internet Explorer.

You can switch back to FrontPage to continue working on the page. Whenever you want to preview the file, just save it, switch to Internet Explorer, click the Refresh button on the toolbar or press F5, and there it will be.

Printing Your Work

You can print the current page in the same way that you print a document in your word processor (or just about any other Windows program, for that matter). Of course, the need to do so may arise only rarely, because a page is meant to reside on a Web site and be viewed by a browser. None- theless, you may want to print pages in order to edit them for correctness outside the computer or to show them to others who may not have access to a computer.

Choose File ➣ Print to display the standard Print dialog box, in which you can specify the number of copies to print, the range of pages to print, and the printer to which the job should be sent.

NOTE

As in Internet Explorer, the document you view in FrontPage is not literally divided into pages. After all, it's formatted not to be printed, but to be viewed in a browser. If you want to print just a few pages of a large document, first choose File ➤ Print Preview to view on-screen what would be printed. This will also show you the pages and their numbers so that you can make a note of the pages you want to print.

Before you print, you can modify the page layout via the File ➤ Page Setup command; its dialog box is shown here. You can specify the margins for the printout, as well as the text that should appear in the header and footer on each page.

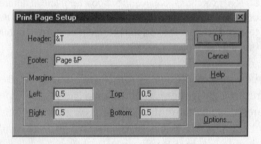

You can include two special codes in the header and footer, each of which begins with the ampersand (&). Use &T to display the page's title (this is the same title you specify with the File ➤ Page Properties command); use &P to display the page number in the printout.

NOTE

Unlike your word processor, the settings in the Page Setup dialog box affect all the pages (files) you print within FrontPage, and they remain in effect until you change them.

Before you print a page, take a few seconds to preview on the screen what your printout will look like on paper by choosing File ➤ Print Preview or by clicking the Print Preview button on the toolbar. The preview screen displays the page as it would appear when printed on paper. You can use the buttons on the toolbar to navigate through the page. When you're satisfied that you're ready to print, click the Print button. Click Close to return to your document in FrontPage.

CREATING NEW PAGES AND SAVING YOUR WORK

FrontPage offers you a variety of ways to work with Web pages, whether they're from your local disk or directly from your Web site. You'll find that its templates and Wizards give you a real boost when creating new pages. If you want to bring in non-HTML files from other sources, you can import a variety of file types.

Creating a New Page

To create a new page, choose File ➤ New (Ctrl+N). This displays the New Page dialog box (shown in Figure 20.3), which lists the available templates and Wizards that you can use to create a new page (a Wizard includes that word in its name).

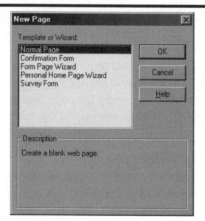

FIGURE 20.3: The New Page dialog box

Creating a Page from a Template

A *template* is simply a ready-made page that you can use as a starting point for a new page. A template makes it easier to get a page going and also provides a consistent look when you create several pages from the same template.

Part ii

If you choose the template named Normal in the New Page dialog box, you'll create a new, blank page that's basically the same page you see when you start FrontPage. Use this when you want to start a new page from scratch. You can also create a new page based on the Normal template by clicking the New button on the FrontPage toolbar.

You'll find several other templates in the New Page dialog box, including Confirmation Form and Survey Form, which let you create form pages without having to start from scratch.

NOTE

The Confirmation and Survey templates include FrontPage WebBots that will work only on a Web site where the server has the FrontPage Server Extensions installed. These add-ons for servers are available for free from the Microsoft Web site, and allow a server to interact with the pages you create using FrontPage WebBots. Some WebBots require no server interaction and can be used in any pages you create.

At first glance, each template looks like a completed page, with titles, sections, bulleted lists, names, and dates. At second glance, you'll see that some of the text consists of instructional comments that help you fill in your own information on the page. Other text is generic, such as a title that simply says Company Name, and you should replace it with your own text. Be sure to read the comments for tips on using the page, and be sure to delete any information in the page that is not relevant to your purposes.

Creating a Page with a Wizard

A Wizard helps you create a new page by asking you a series of questions about the content or layout of the page. It then builds the page based on your responses, and you get to work on the result.

For example, the Personal Home Page Wizard helps you customize a home page for your own use. The number of steps in this Wizard depends on the choices you make in the first step. There can be well over a dozen steps in all, each of which lets you fine-tune the page to your own needs. When you choose this Wizard from the New Page dialog box, you'll see the first dialog box of the Personal Home Page Wizard, as shown in Figure 20.4. You can select the main sections for your personal home page, which will appear as main headings, with relevant information beneath each one.

As you proceed through the steps of this Wizard, you'll specify a URL for the page you're creating if it's going to a Web site, or you'll specify a file name if it's staying on your local disk. You can make many choices for each of the categories you chose in the first step. When you finally click the Finish button, the page appears in FrontPage, containing the sections and information you specified. You are now free to modify the page as you would any other page.

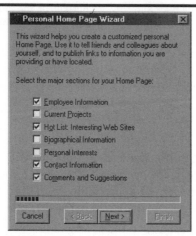

FIGURE 20.4: The first step of the Personal Home Page Wizard

Opening an Existing Page

To open an existing Web page or another type of file, choose File ➤ Open (Ctrl+O), or click the Open button on the toolbar. This displays the Open File dialog box, from which you can open a file from your local disk, or

 open a page from a Web site by supplying the URL. Instead of using the Open command, you can select a name of a recently opened file from the bottom of the File menu.

To open a page from disk, select the From File radio button and enter the path and file name in that field. If you don't know the path and file name, click the Browse button.

To open a page by specifying its URL, select the From Location radio button and enter the URL in that field. Using this method, you can open any page from any Web site to which you have access, just as you do in Internet Explorer. Once the page is open, you are free to save it to your local disk or another Web site.

Free, that is, within the constraints of upright behavior and copyright law. But this is a handy way to bring a page from one Web site into FrontPage, where you can revise it as necessary and then save it to a different location.

TIP

You can navigate through the hyperlinks in your Web pages from inside Front-Page—hold down the Ctrl key and click the link. When multiple pages are open in the Editor, you can switch between them in the usual ways, such as by pressing Ctrl+F6. You can also use the Back and Forward buttons on the toolbar to move from one page to another, just as you do in Internet Explorer. In this case, the pages must already be open.

You can open many types of files besides standard HTML Web pages. FrontPage will convert an incoming file from its native format into an equivalent-looking HTML file. You can then save it as an HTML Web page in the usual way.

To make it easier to find a file, and to see the types of files that Front-Page can convert, use the Browse button and look at the Files of Type drop-down menu in the Open File dialog box. When you choose one of the file types on the list, only files with the appropriate file name extension for that type, such as DOC or XLS, are displayed in the dialog box.

You will find a wide variety of file types in the list, including several versions of Microsoft Word, Excel, and Works and also WordPerfect. The more generic Rich Text Format (RTF) and plain text (TXT) file types are also on the list.

TIP

If you can't open a certain file type in FrontPage, you may be able to save that file in the HTML format in the program that created the file. You could then open the HTML file directly into FrontPage.

If the incoming file contains any graphic images, FrontPage will attempt to place them in the document where they belong. Because images are always separate files from the pages in which they appear, you will be asked if you also want to save the images as separate files when you later save this document as an HTML page (see the next section). By saving the images, you are making them available the next time you open this page, either in FrontPage or in a browser on your Web site.

You can bring another file into the current page by choosing Insert ≻ File. The contents of the other file appears at the insertion point's position within the page. Choose Insert ≻ Image or Insert ≻ Video to display an image or video file in your page.

Saving Your Work

When you have opened an existing page, you can save it back to its original location under the same file name by choosing File ➤ Save (Ctrl+S) or by clicking the Save button on the toolbar. The page is saved immediately, and you can continue with your work.

When you are working on a new page that you have not yet named, choosing File ➤ Save displays the Save As dialog box. This is the same dialog box you will see when you choose File ➤ Save As to save an existing page under a new name or to a different location.

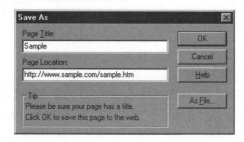

If you have not yet done so, enter a page title; you can also specify a page title at any time in the Page Properties dialog box, which you'll read about later in this chapter. In the Page Location field, you can enter the URL where you want to store the page and then click OK. With the help of the Web Publishing Wizard, the file will be saved at the location you specified. To save the page as a file on your local disk, click the As File button and enter a path and file name for the file.

If you added one or more graphic images to this page from an outside source (such as from the Web or by copying the image from another program), you will be asked if you want to save those images when you save the page. In the dialog box shown here, you can enter a new name for the image file if you choose, and then click the Yes or Yes to All button if there is more than one image. If you don't want to save the image, click the No button.

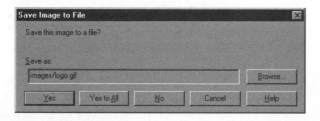

ADDING STRUCTURE TO A PAGE

HTML offers several elements for creating structure or hierarchy within a page, including horizontal lines, headings, and bulleted or numbered lists. These features can make your Web page more attractive and easier for someone to browse.

TIP

Tables offer another way to organize a page, into columns and rows. To begin creating a table, place the cursor where you want the table to appear and choose Tables ➢ Insert Table. This displays a dialog box where you can define the size and look of the table. A toolbar button is also available but offers less control in defining the table.

Separating Sections with a Horizontal Line

You can use the Insert ➢ Horizontal Line command to do just that—place a horizontal line in the page. The line is built on the HTML tag <HR> and is often referred to as a horizontal rule. By default, the line spans the entire width of the page in FrontPage or in a browser. It is a simple but effective way to delineate one section from another.

Changing the Look of a Line

To modify the look of a horizontal line in FrontPage, open its Properties dialog box (shown here) by right-clicking the line and choosing Horizontal Line Properties from the shortcut menu.

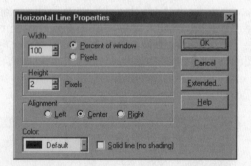

You can change the width, height, alignment, and color of the line:

Width   The width of a default line is 100 percent of the width of the window in which it is displayed. Change the percentage to

50 for a line that is half the width of the window. Choose Pixels to specify an exact width for the line, no matter how wide the window may be. If the resulting line is longer than the width of the window, you'll have to scroll to the right in Internet Explorer to see the rest of the line.

Height   The default height (thickness) of the line is 2 pixels; increase or decrease the height as needed.

Alignment   If you specify a width for the line other than 100 percent, you can choose to align the line to the left or right side of the window, or you can center it within the window.

Color   Select a color for the line. You can also choose to display the line with a shadow effect or as a solid line.

When you have modified several of these attributes, the HTML tag will reflect your choices, such as:

```
<HR ALIGN="left" WIDTH="50%" COLOR="#FF0000">
```

for a red line that is left-aligned, with a width that is 50 percent of the width of the current window.

INSERTING YOUR OWN ATTRIBUTES FOR AN HTML TAG

The changes you make to the properties of a horizontal line appear as attributes in the HTML tag that creates the line. You're not limited to the options that FrontPage offers, however. If there are other accepted attributes for a tag that FrontPage doesn't provide, you can include new attributes at any time. FrontPage will ignore those it doesn't recognize, but they will be in the page when a browser later views it.

Look for a button labeled "Extended" in the properties or options dialog box for a component in the page, such as a horizontal line, a hyperlink, a marquee, and selected text (Paragraph Properties).

Click that button to open the Extended Attributes dialog box, where you can click the Add button to create a new attribute. You enter the name of the attribute in the Name field and the value of that attribute in the Value field. For example, to create the alignment attribute shown earlier for the horizontal line, you'd enter **align** as the name and **left** as the value. Click OK, and the attribute is added to the list in the Extended Attributes dialog box. You can repeat this process for other attributes, each of which would appear within the tag.

Using Images of Lines

Another way to create a dividing line in a page, which you'll find on many Web sites, is with a linear graphic image. An image can add multiple colors, patterns, or a picture to a page to liven it up. (Working with other kinds of images is discussed in the next chapter.)

NOTE

One small disadvantage of using a graphic image is that it takes time to download. But most line image files are quite small, and if you reuse that image as a horizontal line elsewhere in the page or in the Web site, the browser only needs to download it once.

One easy way to find suitable line images for your pages is to visit the Microsoft Web Gallery at

```
www.microsoft.com/gallery/
```

You'll find a variety of multimedia components here, including images that can serve as lines (called *rules* at the site, as in *horizontal rule*). You just click one of the names in the list to display that image, then right-click the image, choose Save Picture As from the shortcut menu, and save the image to your local disk. (You'll read more about this great resource and others later in this chapter.)

You can then choose the Insert ➢ Image command in FrontPage to bring that image into a Web page. Several examples of images from Microsoft's gallery that can serve as horizontal dividing lines are shown here.

TIP

Besides Microsoft's Web Gallery, dozens of other sites offer graphic images suitable for Web pages (lots of them are free, too). You can read about these resources and others later in this chapter in "Getting the Picture."

Creating Headings to Subdivide a Page

There are six HTML heading tags, <H1> through <H6>, which you can use to create six levels of headings in a page. The look of each heading depends on the browser in which it is displayed, but what you see in FrontPage is exactly what you'll see in Internet Explorer.

To create a heading for an existing paragraph, click within that text, and then choose one of the six headings from the Change Style drop-down menu on the Format toolbar. You can also select a heading from the list of paragraph styles with the Format ➤ Paragraph command.

To create a new heading before typing any text, move the insertion point to a blank line, choose the heading style you want, and then start typing. When you end the paragraph by pressing Enter, the heading style will not be applied to the next line.

You can align a heading at the left or right side of the window, or you can center it. You can choose the alignment (left is the default) in the Paragraph Properties dialog box, or you can simply click one of the three alignment buttons on the toolbar. The HTML tag for a right-aligned heading looks like this:

```
<H1 ALIGN="right">This is the Heading Text</H1>
```

Organizing Data with Bulleted and Numbered Lists

You can create several types of lists in HTML, such as the ordered, or numbered, list with the <OL> tag, and the unordered, or bulleted, list with the <UL> tag. It's easy to create these types of lists in FrontPage—just click a button and the job is done. To change existing paragraphs in a page into a bulleted list, simply select them all, such as by dragging over them with your mouse, and then click the Bulleted List button on the Format toolbar (or select Bulleted List from the Change Style drop-down menu on the Format toolbar). The process is the same for a numbered list.

NOTE

To create a new list, click the appropriate list button and type the first item in the list. Press Enter to create the next item in the list, and so on. When you're finished, press Enter twice or press Ctrl+Enter to end the list and return to the normal paragraph formatting.

While the text in this example is still selected, you can click the Numbered List button on the Format toolbar to change the paragraphs to that type of list. You can switch back and forth between the two list styles at any time.

The four items in the left column are shown as they would appear as a bulleted list (center) and as a numbered list (right).

Table of Contents	Table of Contents	Table of Contents
International awards	• International awards	1. International awards
	• Corporate history	2. Corporate history
Corporate history	• Public education	3. Public education
	• Widget hotline	4. Widget hotline
Public education		
Widget hotline		

You can nest one list with another so that the second is a subordinate of the first. This allows you to create outlines or tables of contents with indented subheadings. Shown here is the bulleted list from the previous example, this time with a second list nested within it:

Table of Contents

- International awards
- Corporate history
- Public education
  - Kidz Widget Magazine
  - Public television Widget Night
  - Widgets at Home pamphlet
- Widget hotline

NOTE
Although FrontPage displays a different type of bullet in the nested list, not every browser will bother to do so.

Here is how you would create the nested list shown above:

1. At the end of the Public education line, press Enter to create a new item in the primary list.

2. With the insertion point still on the new line, click the Increase Indent button on the Format toolbar:

3. Now click the Bulleted List button to turn this new line into an item in a bulleted list (you could make it a numbered list by clicking the Numbered List button).

4. Enter the text for this line and then press Enter, which will create the next item in this nested bulleted list.

5. Continue to create new items until you're finished with the nested list. Then simply move the insertion point to another location in the page or click the Decrease Indent button twice to create a new bullet in the primary list.

NOTE

You can change the look of a bulleted or numbered list by selecting the list (or only some of the items in it) and choosing Format ➤ Bullets and Numbering or by right-clicking the list and choosing List Properties from the shortcut menu. Then select the list style in the List Properties dialog box.

FORMATTING PAGES

This section deals with the way things look on a page and the way a page looks behind the text and images it displays. You'll learn how to change the formatting of text, paragraphs, and the page itself.

The first thing to remember about formatting your pages in HTML is that it is the *browser* that ultimately determines how your pages are displayed. You can play with page formatting all you want, but once it's out on your Web site, all your design work and artistry may be lost on an older browser that can't support the features you've included. With that said, you are reasonably safe formatting your pages in FrontPage because most of its features are mainstream and part of the HTML specification.

Setting Character Properties

Most of the formatting you can apply to characters in a page—text—is found in the Font dialog box, shown in Figure 20.5. To display it, choose Format ➤ Font or right-click selected text and choose Font Properties from the shortcut menu. The properties, or attributes, that are associated with text include the familiar ones such as bold, italic, underline, subscript, and superscript. You can apply some of these from their buttons on the Format toolbar.

TIP

You can return selected text to its default style (for that paragraph) by choosing Format ≻ Remove Formatting or by pressing Ctrl+spacebar. This is a quick way to eliminate any changes you've applied to that text, such as a font, font size, or font style.

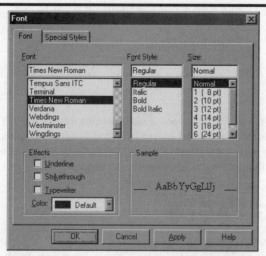

FIGURE 20.5: Choose Format ≻ Font to change the look of selected text with the options in the Font dialog box.

The Font dialog box shown in Figure 20.5 displays the default settings for text in FrontPage. Because we haven't applied any special formatting to the selected text, a browser will display the text in its own default style.

Incidentally, Internet Explorer uses a 12-point Times New Roman font as its default, the same as FrontPage (as shown in the Font dialog box). Nonetheless, you can change that default font in Internet Explorer, as well as the screen magnification (making all fonts larger or smaller than their actual size). What you create in FrontPage may often be displayed quite differently in a browser.

Changing the Font

In the Font dialog box, you can select a specific font from the list of all the fonts available to Windows on your computer. You can also choose a font from the Change Font list on the Format toolbar. Again, keep your eye on the Sample pane in the dialog box to see the effect of your font changes.

The font you choose will appear in the FACE attribute for the <FONT> tag in the HTML code, such as:

```
<FONT FACE="Arial">This is not the default font.</FONT>
```

Now comes the big caveat. Any font you apply must also be available to the browser that opens this page from your Web site. If the font you choose isn't on the browser's computer, the browser will display the text in its default font. The result may or may not be to your liking, but those are the breaks when you're publishing on the Web! To play it safe, stay away from the more obscure fonts that other computers aren't likely to have.

When you become more experienced and confident as an HTML author, you can use the View ➤ HTML command and then include multiple font names in the FACE attribute. If a browser doesn't have the first font, it will try the second, and so on until it finds one it does have. Otherwise, it will use its default font. Here's how the previous code looks with alternative fonts included:

```
<FONT FACE="Arial,Helvetica,Humana">This is…</FONT>
```

Changing the Font Style

The choices in the Font Style list give you the expected options of Bold, Italic, and Bold Italic (you can also press Ctrl+B and Ctrl+I as shortcuts for those styles). The Regular choice removes any bold or italic formatting from the selected text. You can also use the Bold and Italic buttons on

the Format toolbar to turn those text styles on or off for the selected text.

Changing the Font Size

To change the size of the font, select one of the seven sizes from the Size list. The other choice, Normal, specifies no size so that a browser will use its default font size, whatever that might be.

You can also change the font size from the Format toolbar with either the Increase Text Size or the Decrease Text Size button. Click a button once to change to the next size.

The choices in the Size list range from 1 through 7. A point size is shown in parentheses next to each of those numbers, but use that only as a guide. The font-size choices are HTML-related, and each number represents a *relative* font size that is either bigger or smaller than the default font that a browser is using. Size 3 is assumed to be the default size in any HTML page. If you choose a size bigger than that, the browser will display that text in a font larger than its default font. The resulting HTML code will look like this:

```
<FONT SIZE="5">
```

which displays the text two sizes larger than the default text in a browser. Obviously, specifying a smaller number gives a smaller font.

Setting Paragraph Properties

You can apply a variety of styles that affect entire paragraphs, not just some text within a paragraph. You've already seen some of them, such as the heading tags <H1> through <H6> and the list tags which separate each item in the list into a separate paragraph.

First, select the paragraphs whose style you want to change. To change only the current paragraph, you don't need to select anything; the format will automatically apply to the entire paragraph. Access the paragraph styles either in the Change Style list on the Format toolbar or via the Format ➤ Paragraph command:

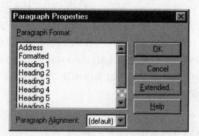

The opening and closing tags for each of these styles surround entire paragraphs. In fact, by definition these tags create paragraphs, so you may not see the regular paragraph tag, <P>, when these paragraph-related format tags are present.

NOTE

The Normal style is a special case that removes any paragraph formatting and resets the paragraph to its default style.

When you create a new paragraph, you can choose whether it should have the same formatting as the preceding paragraph:

▶ To begin a paragraph in the same style as the current paragraph, position the insertion point just after the last character in the paragraph and press Enter.

▶ To split a paragraph in two and retain the formatting of the original paragraph for both, position the insertion point where you want the split and press Enter.

▶ To create a new paragraph after the last paragraph in the page that uses the default style, move to the last line of the paragraph and press ↓ to create a new line and a new paragraph.

The Address style is represented by italicized text in Internet Explorer and most other browsers. It is typically used for paragraphs that contain an address or other contact information, such as an e-mail address or a URL.

NOTE
You can include text formatting, such as <STRONG> or <EM>, within a paragraph format, such as <H3> or <PRE>. However, only one *paragraph* format can be applied to a paragraph.

The Formatted paragraph style in FrontPage is particularly useful. It uses the <PRE> tag (for *preformatted*). Internet Explorer and other browsers display text in this style in a monospace (fixed-width) font; each character takes up exactly the same amount of space. It is the one instance in HTML when multiple spaces or hard returns are displayed exactly as they appear in the code. You can use the Formatted style to align text in columns or with indentions, and the characters will fall exactly where you expect them. The HTML table obviates some of the need for the Formatted style, but the style is still quite practical and easy to apply when you need to align text.

By default, paragraphs are aligned along the left side of the window, both in FrontPage and Internet Explorer. You can change the alignment of the current paragraph or the selected paragraphs by clicking the appropriate button on the Format toolbar:

You can also choose an alignment from the drop-down menu in the Paragraph Properties dialog box.

You can indent the current paragraph or selected paragraphs from both the left and the right with the Increase Indent button on the Format toolbar. Click the button multiple times to increase the amount of indention. Click the Decrease Indent button to remove indention one level at a time.

Setting Page Properties

A Web page has its own set of properties that you can access by choosing File ➤ Page Properties or by right-clicking anywhere on the page and choosing Page Properties from the shortcut menu. The Page Properties dialog box has four tabs: General, Background, Margins, and Custom.

Changing the Title and Other General Options

In the General tab of the Page Properties dialog box, shown in Figure 20.6, you can view or revise the title for the current page. You usually create a title the first time you save a page. You'll find the <TITLE> tag appearing within the <HEAD> tag near the top of the page's HTML code. You should make the title descriptive of the page, not only for readers of the page, but also because it is often used by Web searching and indexing sites to name your page.

The Location field shows the page's complete URL or file name. To change a page's name or location, either choose the File ➤ Save As command or rename or move the source file.

You can specify the name of a sound file in the Background Sound options, such as a WAV or MIDI file, that Internet Explorer will play when it opens this page. By default, the sound file is played once, as specified in the Loop field in the Page Properties dialog box; you can increase the number if you want to play the file more than once. Select the Forever checkbox to have the sound play continuously while this page is open in a browser.

WARNING

Visitors to your page may enjoy hearing a short, welcoming sound, but they may be annoyed when that sound plays over and over. Use discretion with the background sound; probably you should never use the Forever option.

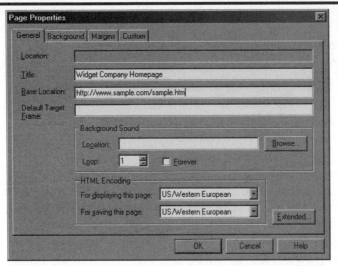

FIGURE 20.6:   The General tab of the Page Properties dialog box

Changing the Background Color

Use the options in the Background tab of the Page Properties dialog box (shown here) to set the look of the page's background. You can also access these settings via the Format ➤ Background command. You can specify either a color or an image file that a browser will display as a page's background. These settings are attributes of the page's <BODY> tag.

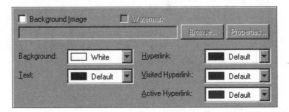

The default setting for the page's background color is white. The setting for text is called Default, in that no color is specified. In other words, a browser will be told to display this page with a white background, but to use its own default color for the text.

You have three options for specifying the colors of hyperlinks. They are all set to Default so that no specific color is specified (the color shown next to each one is the default color in Internet Explorer). It's generally best to leave them this way, unless they conflict with the page's background color; using your own colors may make it difficult for a reader of this page to recognize text as links.

Specifying a Background Image

You can specify an image file that will serve as the page's background instead of a color. Select the Background Image option in the Background tab and enter the file name of the image, or click the Browse button to select an image.

A browser normally tiles a small image to fill the background completely, so you need not specify a large image. In fact, the smaller the image file, the faster it will load into a browser. Many visitors to a Web site will simply skip over a page if it takes too long to load.

Another aspect of the image file is how well it serves as a background. For example, dropping a stunning M.C. Escher picture into the back of a page of text may make the page almost jump out of the screen at you, but it may also make the text mostly unreadable. You'll find that most background images in use are small and textured, and can be easily tiled together into a seamless background. They provide a muted and comfortable backdrop that will not dominate the page.

Again, you'll find plenty of suitable background images at the Microsoft Web Gallery.

NOTE

When a background image is tiled to fill a page, Internet Explorer scrolls the background as you scroll the page. If you choose the Watermark option in the Background tab, Internet Explorer leaves the background image stationary while you scroll the page.

Setting Page Margins

You can use the options on the Margins tab of the Page Properties dialog box to specify a top or left margin for the page. By default, they are set to zero so that no margins are specified. You define the margin in pixels, so the actual width of the blank area at the top or left side of the page in a browser depends on the screen resolution for that computer. For this reason and because not all browsers support the MARGINS attribute for the <BODY> tag, avoid setting margins for your pages.

Creating Meta Page Information

You can use the <META> tag to include information in a page that can be read by the server that sends out that page or by the browser that receives it. When included in a page, the <META> tag normally appears within the page's <HEAD> tag. You'll find that this tag is used in many ways. For example, the following tag (shown on two lines) tells the browser to use the Japanese character set:

```
<META HTTP-EQUIV="Content-type"
CONTENT="text/html; charset=x-sjis">
```

Other <META> tags could include a description and keywords to be used by search spiders that come to your site, or rating information so that a browser such as Internet Explorer can determine if the page meets its rating criteria (see Chapter 18 for more about site ratings).

You can create these types of page-definition tags in FrontPage via the Custom tab in the Page Properties dialog box. You can add, modify, or remove what FrontPage refers to as *variables*, which appear within the <META> tag for a page. Creating a variable is much like creating an extended attribute for an HTML tag, as discussed earlier in this chapter.

By default, FrontPage creates two variables for a page. The single system variable tells a browser or server what type of document this is and the character set to use for it. The user variable simply lets the world know which program generated this page.

To create a description that a search engine could use, go to the Custom tab and click the Add button next to the User Variables list. In the dialog box (shown here), enter the attribute **Description** in the Name field and the text that you want to describe the page in the Value field. Click OK, and you'll see this new variable in the list.

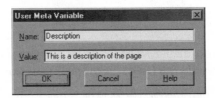

When you click OK to return to the page, choose View ➤ HTML and look for your new tag near the top of the page. It will look something like this:

```
<META NAME="description" CONTENT="This is a description of the page">
```

Any system variables you create will appear as part of the HTTP-EQUIV attribute for the <META> tag.

CREATING LINKS

You can make a hyperlink in a Web page from either a graphic image or text (which will be displayed in a different color and underlined); click the hyperlink in Internet Explorer to open the link's target resource. You can easily create a document that links to several other documents anywhere on the Web. A hyperlink always contains at least two components:

▶ The text or image you click to open the link's target file

▶ The URL of that file (which can be a relative reference or an absolute one)

FrontPage makes it easy to create links because you see the clickable link in the WYSIWYG editing environment, and you create the link in a straightforward dialog box where it's easy to specify the URL of the target.

Creating a New Hyperlink

You can create a link from either text or an image in several ways, but here's the most common way:

1. Select the text or image you want to serve as a hyperlink (either click an image or use the Shift+drag method you would use to select text).

2. Choose Edit ➤ Hyperlink (Ctrl+K) or click the Create or Edit Hyperlink button on the toolbar.

This displays the Create Hyperlink dialog box, where you specify the target file of the link in one of its three tabs:

Open Pages   Select the target from a list of all the pages currently open in FrontPage.

Word Wide Web   Choose the type of hyperlink to create—such as HTTP, Mailto, or FTP—and then enter the URL of the target.

New Page   Enter a page title and a URL to create a new Web page in FrontPage that will serve as the target for the link.

3. When you are finished defining the hyperlink, click the OK button.

If the hyperlink is textual, the selected text is now underlined and displayed in blue. You can edit the text that serves as the link just as you would edit any other text in the page. When you move your mouse over the text or image hyperlink, you'll see the URL of the target displayed on the left side of the status bar.

NOTE

A *frameset* is one page that displays multiple pages, each in its own frame or window. When the link you're defining will be in a page in a frameset, you can use the Target Frame option to specify the name of the frame in which the target should be displayed.

Creating a Link Automatically

Once you understand how links work, you can take advantage of these other methods to create links:

▶ Type the URL of the target file (it must begin with a valid protocol, such as HTTP) and press the spacebar; FrontPage automatically defines that text as a link to the URL. You can then revise the text so that it no longer looks like a URL, but the target URL would remain.

▶ Drag the icon in the Address toolbar in Internet Explorer into your document in FrontPage to create a link to that page. The title of the page will appear as the text of the link, and its URL will be the target.

▶ Drag a hyperlink from a page in Internet Explorer into your document in FrontPage to create the same link.

▶ Drag an Internet shortcut (a URL file) into your document in FrontPage to create a link to that URL. For example, choose Favorites ➤ Organize Favorites in Internet Explorer and drag a link from the dialog box.

Linking to a Bookmark

A *bookmark* is simply the FrontPage name for a specific, named location within one page that can serve as the target for a link (you'll read about creating bookmarks a little later in this chapter). You'll also hear the term *destination* or *named target* to describe this HTML feature. When you define a hyperlink by targeting a page listed on the Open Pages tab in the Create Hyperlink dialog box, you can include a bookmark from the page in the URL by selecting it from the Bookmarks drop-down menu.

NOTE

To create a link to a bookmark in the current page (the page in which you're creating the link), just select that page in the Open Pages tab, and then choose a bookmark from the drop-down menu.

For example, suppose you create a link to a page named GUIDE.HTM that's open in FrontPage, and you select the bookmark in that page named Section 1.0. In HTML, a reference to a bookmark name is preceded by a pound sign (#), so the complete reference for this link is

```
guide.htm#Section 1.0
```

When a reader later clicks the text or the image for this link in a browser, the page GUIDE.HTM will open, and the browser will display the bookmark named Section 1.0 at the top of the screen.

Revising and Deleting a Hyperlink

You can change the text of a hyperlink (the text you click to activate the link) simply by editing it as you would any other text. As long as the text you revise is still underlined, you'll know it's still a link.

You can also change the image for an image hyperlink. Simply right-click the image and choose Image Properties from the shortcut menu. In the Image Properties dialog box, specify the new image in the Image Source field.

To modify the target URL of a hyperlink, select the image (click it) or position the insertion point anywhere within the link text (you need not select any of the text), and choose Edit ➤ Hyperlink or click the Create or Edit Hyperlink button on the toolbar.

You can delete a link from a page in several ways:

▶ Delete the image or all of the text for the link, and the link to the target file (but not the actual file, of course) will be deleted as well. Keep that in mind when you're simply revising the text of a link, and be careful not to accidentally delete all the text (if you do, remember Undo).

▶ To delete a link without deleting the link text or link image from the page, select the link image or position the insertion point anywhere within the link text, and then choose Edit ➤ Unlink.

▶ To remove the link definition from just some of the link text, select that text and choose Edit ➤ Unlink.

▶ When you're working in the Create Link or Edit Link dialog box, click the Clear button to delete the link definition.

Working with Bookmarks

Creating a bookmark is essentially naming a location in the page so you can then refer to that location by that name in the target of a link. Here's how to do it:

1. Move the insertion point to the line where you want to create the new name.

2. Although you can create a name there without selecting any text, it's a good idea to select the text you want the name to define. That way, if you add more text to the paragraph, the bookmark will still be attached to the text you selected.

3. Choose Edit ➤ Bookmark, which displays the Bookmark dialog box (shown here).

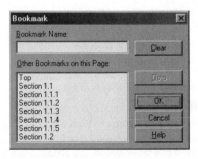

4. Enter the text for the new name in the Bookmark Name field. If you selected some text before invoking the command, you'll find that text already in the field, which you can revise as necessary.

5. When you're finished, click OK.

NOTE

The name you create for a bookmark should clearly describe the location you're naming so that you or another author can easily find it in the list of bookmarks when you are creating a hyperlink to its page. Try to keep your bookmarks reasonably short, perhaps just a word or two in most cases (spaces are allowed).

The HTML tag for a bookmark is the NAME attribute of the anchor tag. If you selected the text Section 1.2 Production Cycles and then created the bookmark name Section 1.2, here's how the code would look:

```
<A NAME="Section 1.2">Section 1.2 Production Cycles</A>
```

In FrontPage, any text within the opening and closing anchor tags will be underlined with a dashed blue line, as long as the View ➤ Format Marks command is enabled. You can also click the Show/Hide button to toggle this command on or off. Internet Explorer, however, does not indicate

 any bookmarks within a page (nor does any other browser); it simply uses them as reference points when they are included in hyperlinks.

Within FrontPage, you can jump to any bookmark in a page by selecting it in the Bookmark dialog box (Edit ➤ Bookmark) and clicking the Goto button. If you want to remove this bookmark name (but not the text it defines), click the Clear button.

To revise the name of a bookmark, click anywhere within the text defined as the bookmark, or use the Goto command to get there. In the Bookmark dialog box, you should see the name of that bookmark in the Bookmark Name field. Edit the name as needed, and, when you're done, click the OK button.

WARNING

If the current page is part of a Web site, changing a bookmark name would affect any links that reference it—those links would no longer target the bookmark. This type of operation requires a little planning and note taking.

WORKING WITH IMAGES

Most images you'll encounter on the Web are either GIF or JPEG files. Both file types compress the image to shrink the file size and, therefore, the time required to download the image. The GIF format can handle images with as many as 256 colors (8-bit). The JPEG format, on the other hand, can handle true-color images (24-bit), making it better suited for photographs or other richly colored images. FrontPage can display either type of image in a page, and you can import many other types of images, but FrontPage will translate them into either the GIF or the JPEG format.

Getting the Picture

Even if you aren't an artist, you can add interesting and lively pictures to your Web pages in lots of ways. Some may already be at your fingertips, and others are just waiting for you to access them.

The first thing to remember is that you can right-click any image in any Web page you're viewing in Internet Explorer and choose Save Picture As to save that picture to your local disk. Instant art—although common courtesy and copyright laws usually dictate that you aren't allowed to borrow someone else's work if you plan to use it for commercial purposes.

NOTE

You might want to create an archive of useful images on your own disk so that you can reuse them in the future. You could follow the lead of many Web sites that supply images by placing them in relevant folders, such as Buttons, Lines, Backgrounds, Photographs, and the like. When you're collecting GIF and JPEG images, there's no need to fuss with compressing these files to save disk space, because those file formats are already compressed about as small as they can be.

You may already have thousands of pictures scattered among the disks and CDs you own. Many software packages, including the major office suites, come with a collection of clip art. You'll generally want to use only GIF and JPEG images in your Web pages, but you can convert other image types in many ways, such as by inserting them into a FrontPage document and saving them to disk.

The Web is burgeoning with an ever-growing number of sources of great drawings, clip art, photographs, animations, and so on. You can even keep your credit card safely ensconced in your wallet, because many of these images are free. The first place to visit is the Microsoft Web Gallery, where you'll find a great collection of images that you can use as buttons, icons, page backgrounds, lines, and more. Another site is Andy's Art Attack at:

```
www.andyart.com
```

where you can find loads of art for your Web pages. Then pay a visit to the Yahoo category:

```
Computers and Internet: Graphics
```

for a long list of sites you might want to visit.

Don't forget that you can use a scanner to create an image from any drawings or photographs you have, and inexpensive video capture devices are available, as well. When the output from your scanning will be displayed on the screen at a modest resolution, just about any scanner will do. This is especially true when you consider that a small file size is the ultimate goal for any art you include in a Web page, because that file must be downloaded (often at modem speeds) to be viewed.

Creating an Inline Image

Inline images are those displayed as part of a page, without requiring the user to click on a link. Because HTML pages are always just plain text, an inline image is actually stored as a separate image file, which is then opened and displayed along with the page in a browser. Of course, you can also specify an image file as the target of a hyperlink, so a browser will open and display only that image when you activate its hyperlink. To bring an image file into a page:

1. Position the insertion point where you want the image to appear (although you can move the image later).

2. Choose Insert ➤ Image to open the Image dialog box. (To insert a video clip, choose Insert ➤ Video.)

3. Enter the name and location of an image file, either a location on disk or a URL. You can click the Browse button to select a file from disk in a standard Windows files dialog box. To display only files of a certain type, such as Bitmap (BMP) or TIFF (TIF), select that type from the Files of Type drop-down menu.

4. When you click OK to close the Image dialog box, the image you selected is inserted into the page.

NOTE

When you insert an animated GIF image into your document, it will appear to be static. You won't see its animations until you open the page and image in Internet Explorer.

In addition to using the Insert ➤ Image command, you can bring an image into a page in the usual Windows way. Select the image in another program and choose Edit ➤ Copy, then switch to FrontPage and choose Edit ➤ Paste. You can also drag an image from another program into FrontPage, assuming that both programs are visible on the screen at the same time.

In Internet Explorer, you can also save the image to disk by right-clicking the image and choosing Save Picture As. In FrontPage, you can then choose Insert ➤ Image to bring that image into your document.

NOTE

As we mentioned earlier in this chapter, when you save a page that contains new images that are not available locally, you will be asked if you want to save the images to disk. This ensures that you have a local copy of each image always available, and it lets you make changes to those images without affecting their source files.

The HTML code FrontPage uses for an image in a page includes the name of the image (ARROW.GIF in this case) and its size, such as:

```
<IMG SRC="images/arrow.gif" WIDTH="40" HEIGHT="38">
```

In the next section, you'll read about adjusting the look of an inline image.

Setting Image Properties

When you click an image to select it, you'll see selection handles appear at each corner and in the middle of each side. You can move the selected image by dragging it, or you can change its size by dragging any of its selection handles (you'll read about changing image sizes later in the chapter).

You can also choose Edit ➤ Image Properties or right-click the image and choose Image Properties from the shortcut menu, to display the Image Properties dialog box, shown in Figure 20.7. In the General tab, you can specify a different source file for the image. All the other settings will now apply to the new image. The alternative is to delete the image and start over (select the image and choose Edit ➤ Clear or press Del).

FIGURE 20.7: You can adjust the settings for an image in the Image Properties dialog box.

Choosing the Image Type

If the image you inserted into the page is a GIF or JPEG file, that option will already be selected in the Type group of options in the Image Properties dialog box. If the image is any other type of file, choose either the GIF or the JPEG option, which is how the image will be saved when you save this page.

With the GIF option, you can also choose to make the image Interlaced. When the image is displayed in a browser, it will seem to fill its allotted space faster, sort of "coming into focus," instead of appearing line by line from the top down. Of course, you'll only notice this effect when the image file is fairly large and it takes more than a second or two to download and display.

When you select the JPEG option, the image is saved in that format when you save the page. You can specify the amount of compression to apply when the image is saved by adjusting the value in the Quality field—the higher the number, the lower the compression, so lower the Quality setting if you want to shrink the file size.

Specifying an Alternative to the Image

The Image Properties dialog box lets you specify two alternatives to an image. If the image is large and will take some time to download to a browser, you can specify a second, smaller image (smaller in file size) in the Low-Res option (low resolution). Internet Explorer will download and display this image first, so the person viewing the page can see the image relatively quickly, even if it is a low-resolution version of the larger, primary image.

The second alternative is the Text option. Any text you enter here will be available to browsers to display, such as when the image is not available or when the browser is not accepting images. In Internet Explorer, you'll see this text in a ToolTip when the mouse pointer is over the image.

The Default Hyperlink option is relevant only when the image is being used as an image map. It allows you to define the target that will be opened when a viewer clicks outside a defined hotspot in the image map.

TIP

If you need to create image maps, you'll probably want to get a copy of Front-Page 98 or a similar full-featured Web publishing package.

Specifying Image Alignment

If you place an inline image within the text of a paragraph, it appears in that same position in Internet Explorer. For example, the following code

```
<P>This text is before the image<IMG
SRC="images\rightarrow.gif"> and this text is after it.</P>
```

would look something like this in Internet Explorer:

This text is before the image ➡ and this text is after it.

The bottom of the image is aligned with the baseline of the text. If you were to type more text to the left of the image, that text would then appear to the left of the image in Internet Explorer. You can change alignment and size of an image with the options in the Appearance tab in the Image Properties dialog box:

If you choose Right for the Alignment option, the image will now align with the right side of the window in Internet Explorer and look something like this:

This text is before the image and this text is after it.

Of course, if you maximized the Internet Explorer window, there could be a lot of blank space between this short line of text and the image to its right.

In the Horizontal Spacing option, you can specify the amount of space (in pixels) between the image and any text, image, or window edge to its left or right. The Vertical Spacing option determines the amount of space above or below the image. Finally, to enclose the image in a border, specify its thickness (in pixels) in the Border Thickness field. The default is zero, so no border is displayed.

Specifying Image Size

By default, an image is displayed in its actual size, so an image that is 200×200 pixels will take up that amount of room on the screen. You can change the size of an image in two ways.

The easiest but less precise way is simply to select the image in the page and then drag one of its selection handles to expand or contract the image. If you drag a corner handle, the image's width and height will both be changed and the image's original proportions will be maintained. If you drag a handle from the center of one of the sides, you can shrink or enlarge just one dimension of the image.

The more precise way to change the size of an image is with the Size options on the Appearance tab in the Image Properties dialog box:

1. First select the Specify Size checkbox, enabling the sizing options to its right.

2. Now choose how to define the image's width and height. To specify an exact size, select the In Pixels checkbox. To size the image in relation to the window in which it is displayed, choose In Percent.

3. Finally, enter a number in the Width and Height fields. If you have chosen In Percent, the largest number you can enter is 100.

When you change the size of an image, you are also changing the way it looks. If you stretch an image in only one dimension, the image may end up looking silly. If you enlarge an image to three or four times its original size, it may end up looking "grainy."

Some examples of changing an image's size are shown here. The image on the left is its original size, 40 pixels wide by 38 pixels tall. The size of the second image has been doubled in both directions (80 by 76 pixels); the graininess is one effect of that enlargement. The width of the third image and the height of the fourth image have been doubled, and you can see the "fun-house mirror" effect taking hold.

WHAT'S NEXT?

This chapter has given you a wide-ranging tour of many of the everyday features you'll use in FrontPage Express. It's a great program that makes the perfect complement to Internet Explorer. In the next chapter, we'll conclude our discussion of Windows 98's Internet features with a look at channels and subscriptions.

Chapter 21

SUBSCRIBING TO SITES AND TUNING IN CHANNELS

The one constant to the World Wide Web is that it seems to grow faster every day. This is a great boon for all of us, but it also introduces some rather hefty problems: How do we stay in touch with a Web site so we know when it has new information, without having to go back and visit it on a regular basis?

This chapter will offer two answers: subscriptions and channels. Subscriptions are a way for you to let Internet Explorer check Web sites for new content without your involvement. Channels are Windows 98's way of implementing *Webcasting*, a technology by which content from a Web site seems to be *pushed* to you, instead of your having to go and get it. In fact, channels are really just a more sophisticated form of subscriptions, in which the parameters for a subscription are set by the Web site and are, therefore, tuned specifically for that site.

Adapted from *Mastering Microsoft Internet Explorer 4*, by Gene Weisskopf and Pat Coleman
ISBN 0-7821-2133-0   960 pages $44.95

USING SUBSCRIPTIONS TO STAY IN TOUCH

Traditionally, when you *subscribe* to something, such as a magazine or a newspaper, it regularly arrives on your doorstep or in your mailbox—daily, weekly, or monthly.

In the new world of the Internet, the concept of needing a traditional subscription no longer exists—if you want to see what's happening on the London Times Web site, just go look at it! There's no need to wait by your mailbox for the next edition.

NOTE

Because of the ease with which a Web site can be updated, many online news-papers add content to their site several times throughout the day. If this sounds totally modern and high-tech, don't forget that back in the old days, big-city newspapers printed several updated editions throughout the day. Extra! Extra!

But the ease with which you can access data on the Internet creates substantial hurdles. We tend to access not just a few sites, but dozens or hundreds. It's not just the *London Times*, but the *New York Times*, the *Los Angeles Times*, and who knows how many other *Times* throughout the world? The list goes on and on. How do you find out if a site has new content without actually going there, and how do you then find the time to download it all at the less-than-thrilling speeds of our normal Internet connections?

Signing Up for a Subscription

The answer is the *subscription*, which is the Active Desktop's way of keeping you up-to-date with your chosen Web sites. When you subscribe to one of the sites on your Favorites menu, you're telling Windows 98, and subsequently Internet Explorer, that you want to keep in touch with that site, be notified when it has new material, and, optionally, have that material delivered to you.

NOTE

In spite of Windows 98's integrated Desktop, it's useful to remember that Internet Explorer and Windows 98 are actually separate applications.

The term *subscription* is a little misleading, because traditionally we subscribe to something by contacting the owners or publishers. But a site subscription is internal to Internet Explorer; it does not involve the publishers of a Web site. It's just a convenient term that describes an important part of the traditional subscription terminology: getting information regularly.

Subscribing to a site in Internet Explorer saves you time and effort in several ways:

▶ Internet Explorer will automatically check each subscribed site to see if it has any content that is new since the last time you visited that site. And you can have it do its checking at any time of the day or night. Imagine how much time it would otherwise take you to trudge manually from site to site, wondering if new material might be there.

▶ When a subscribed site changes or has new material, Internet Explorer notifies you and can automatically download all the new content.

▶ When Internet Explorer updates the content from a subscribed site, it stores the new content on your local drive. You can then access that new content *without* being connected to the Internet and downloading that content over your Internet connection. This means that you can do without that wire that binds you to the Net and that you can access the data from your hard disk, many times faster than you could access it from the Internet.

The bottom line is that you can come into work Monday morning and find that Internet Explorer has updated all your subscribed sites with their new content.

Subscribing to a Site

When you're adding a site to your Favorites menu, you choose whether to subscribe to that site in the Add Favorite dialog box, as shown in Figure 21.1. There are three subscription choices (the site is added to your Favorites menu no matter which one you choose):

No is the default choice, so that no subscription is set up.

Yes, but only tell me will have you notified when the site has new content.

Yes, and download will have you notified when there is new content, and that new content will also be downloaded to your local disk.

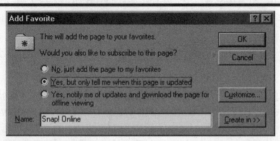

FIGURE 21.1:   Subscribing to a Web site as you add it to your Favorites menu

If you want to subscribe to this site, pick either of the Yes options and then click the OK button to accept the default subscription settings. You can instead click the Customize button, which starts the Subscription Wizard. It will take you through the steps of defining the subscription in the following main categories (you'll read about all of these later in the chapter):

Notification   The manner in which you will be notified when Internet Explorer finds new data on the site. By default, the item's icon in the Favorites menu displays a starlike gleam.

Download   How much of any new data will be downloaded.

Schedule   The schedule Internet Explorer will follow to check the site for new content. By default, if you have a LAN connection to the Internet, the site is checked automatically without your intervention. If you have a dial-up (modem) connection, by default you'll have to update the subscription manually, although you can choose to have the site checked automatically. You can also specify a custom schedule or choose to manually update this subscription no matter how you connect to the Internet.

You can also subscribe to a site that's already on your Favorites menu. The easiest way to do so is to find the site on your Favorites menu in the usual way, but don't open it. Instead, right-click on that item in the menu and choose Subscribe from the shortcut menu. You can also use the Favorites ➤ Organize Favorites command, find the folder that contains the item you want to subscribe to (remember that each submenu on the Favorites menu is actually a folder within the Favorites folder), right-click the item, and choose Subscribe. You'll also find a Subscribe Now button in the item's Properties dialog box.

Choosing Subscribe displays the Subscribe Favorite dialog box, which is similar to the Add Favorite dialog box shown earlier in Figure 21.1. Choose to be notified when the site has new content or to have that content downloaded, as well. Then click OK to accept the default settings, or click Customize to adjust them.

Whether you subscribe to a new or existing site on the Favorites menu, the result is the same. In the next section, you'll see how to browse a subscribed site without actually going there.

Browsing Your Updated Subscriptions

Let's take a short tour of how subscriptions work to give you a feel for why subscriptions can be so important. You'll learn about all these steps later in the discussion of subscriptions.

When you subscribe to a Web site, Internet Explorer automatically checks that site for new content, either when you specifically ask it to (a manual update) or according to the schedule you've chosen. If the site has new content, Internet Explorer downloads as much of the new material as you specified in the subscription settings (none, by default) and then notifies you by the method you chose, such as by displaying a star on the item's icon on the Favorites menu.

NOTE

When you highlight a subscription on the Favorites menu that has new content available, you'll see a ToolTip that displays the date and time when you last accessed the site and when Internet Explorer last updated it (checked it for new content).

To view all your subscriptions, choose Favorites ➤ Manage Subscriptions. An Explorer window then displays a list of your subscriptions. You can see which ones have been updated recently, open one as you would any Internet shortcut, or right-click a subscription to view or revise its properties.

Here's where the second half of the subscription trick kicks in. If you chose to have Internet Explorer download a subscription's new content, you can browse that updated Web site while offline—you don't need to be connected to the Internet. Internet Explorer has already downloaded all the new material from that site, and it is waiting for you on your local hard disk.

BROWSING YOUR SUBSCRIPTIONS WHILE OFFLINE

When trying to browse files offline, you may sometimes see an error message indicating that the file you requested is not available offline. The amount of offline browsing you can do for any subscribed Web site depends on how much of that Web site is already on your computer in the Temporary Internet Files folder (the cache folder for Internet Explorer).

If you browse to a site regularly or have that site's new content downloaded frequently via a subscription, just about all of that site's content should now be available, because Internet Explorer has already downloaded any new material.

If, however, you click a link that targets a file you don't have on your local computer, Internet Explorer must connect to the Internet to get that file. At this point, you'll see a dialog box in which you can choose to continue browsing offline and do without that file or let Internet Explorer try to connect and go get it.

Being able to browse without being connected to the Internet means that you might let Internet Explorer update your subscriptions on your portable computer the night before you plan to travel. The next morning, you can unplug your portable from the network or telephone line and head for the airport. Once you've settled into your seat on the plane, you can browse those updated Web sites as though you were connected to them over the Internet. Not only are you free of a network connection, but Internet Explorer opens Web sites at hard-drive speeds. You will have to wait barely a second for a site to open.

Canceling a Subscription

A subscription remains in effect until you revise or cancel it completely. You'll learn how to revise one in the sections that follow; here's how to cancel one. Find the item on the Favorites menu, right-click it, and then choose Unsubscribe from the shortcut menu. You'll be prompted about the impending removal of the subscription. Choose Yes to remove the subscription, or choose No to leave it as is.

You can also cancel a subscription in the Organize Favorites dialog box in the same way. If you're going to be canceling or otherwise revising several subscriptions, it might be more convenient to do this within the Subscriptions dialog box (choose Favorites ➢ Manage Subscriptions). Right-click the site you want, and choose Properties from the shortcut menu (there is no Unsubscribe command). Choose the Subscription tab, and then click its Unsubscribe button.

When you unsubscribe to a site, you're only canceling the subscription. The site remains on the Favorites menu as before, but Internet Explorer does not check it for new content.

VIEWING YOUR CURRENT SUBSCRIPTIONS

To open a list of all your subscriptions at any time, choose Favorites ➢ Manage Subscriptions. This opens an Explorer window that lists all your subscriptions, as shown in Figure 21.2. Notice the icons to the left of each item in the list. Some are Web pages (the icon shown here on the left), others are channels (shown here in the middle), and still others are channels that have their own unique icon (shown here on the right). The channels you subscribe to are essentially special Web sites that define their own subscription download schedule, but they are nonetheless subscriptions. You'll read about channels later in this chapter.

TIP

You can also view or modify the same list of subscriptions by Exploring to the Subscriptions folder in your Windows folder.

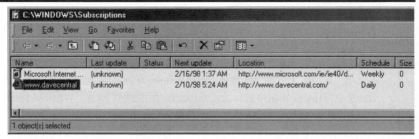

FIGURE 21.2: To view or modify your current subscriptions, choose Favorites ➢ Manage Subscriptions.

The columns of information in the list of Subscriptions are mostly from the various settings in each subscription's Properties dialog box, and they allow you to see these settings at a glance. You can easily see which subscriptions have new content, how many of them are updated daily, weekly, or manually, or which ones were updated most recently. To change the settings for a subscription, right-click it and choose Properties from its shortcut menu.

TIP

Click a column title to sort the list of Subscriptions by that column. For example, click the Last Updated column title to sort the list by the dates in that column. Click the column title again to sort in the opposite order (ascending or descending).

The Subscriptions list (or folder) is the place to go when you want to update a few, but not all, of your subscriptions. Simply select the subscriptions you want to update, and choose File ➤ Update Now, or right-click a selected subscription and choose Update Now.

When you want to go offline to browse the downloaded content of your subscriptions, you could look for each subscribed site that has the "gleam" on its icon in your Favorites menu, which indicates new content. But browsing through all the menus could be quite tedious, and the gleam doesn't tell you if a subscription includes downloading the content to your disk.

It's much easier to open your Subscriptions folder, where you'll have access to all your subscriptions with no other sites in the way.

DEFINING YOUR SUBSCRIPTIONS

As mentioned earlier, when you subscribe to a new site, you can choose to have Internet Explorer notify you when that site has new content, or download that content, as well. You'll be notified that there's new material at a site by the gleam on the item's icon in the Favorites menu. You can either choose the default schedule for that site or set your own custom schedule. In the sections that follow, you'll learn how to modify all these settings for any existing subscriptions on your Favorites menu or when you create a new subscription.

When creating a subscription for a new site on your Favorites menu, click the Customize button in the Add Favorite dialog box (look back at Figure 21.1), which starts the Subscription Wizard. Here's how to change the settings for an existing site subscription on the Favorites menu:

1. Find the site on your Favorites menu (or in the Organize Favorites dialog box or in the Subscription folder).

2. Right-click the site and choose Properties.

3. In the Properties dialog box, you'll find three subscription-related tabs with which you can view or revise the subscription settings.

   Subscription displays the current settings for the subscription.

   Receiving lets you choose how to be notified when Internet Explorer finds new content on the subscribed site and whether that new content should be downloaded. You can also limit how much content is downloaded so that you don't end up being surprised by who knows how many megabytes of new material!

   Schedule lets you choose the schedule that Internet Explorer will follow when checking the site for new content.

4. Make any changes you want to the subscription and click OK when finished.

The following sections will show you how to adjust all the subscription options so that you'll be able to tune any subscription to fit your need for updated content from that site.

Viewing Current Subscription Settings

To look at the current subscription settings for an Internet shortcut, open its Properties dialog box and select the Subscription tab, as shown in Figure 21.3. Here you'll see the name of the item as it appears on the Favorites menu, its URL, the type of subscription (notification only or notification and download), the update schedule, and the date and time when the site was last updated and when it will be updated next.

Part ii

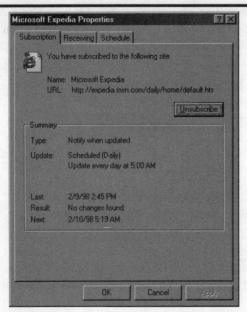

FIGURE 21.3: The Subscription tab in the Properties dialog box shows you the current settings and status of a subscription.

On this tab you'll also find the Unsubscribe button, which you can click to remove the subscription from this site.

Choosing How You Want to Be Notified

When you are subscribing to a new Web site and choose only to be notified, clicking the Customize button in the Add Favorite dialog box (refer to Figure 21.1) opens the first dialog box of the Subscription Wizard, which is shown in Figure 21.4. (When you have chosen to download pages, this step of the Wizard comes a little later in the process.)

Here you choose whether you want an e-mail message sent to you when Internet Explorer finds new content at this site. By default, the No option is selected.

If you choose Yes, Internet Explorer notifies you by e-mail when it finds new content at this site. If you normally use an HTML-enabled mail program, such as Outlook Express, the e-mail message will actually contain the Web page. Otherwise, you will receive a plain text message that includes the URL of the subscribed site.

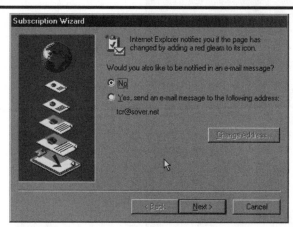

FIGURE 21.4: In this step of the Subscription Wizard, you choose whether to be notified by e-mail when new content is found at this site.

If you then click Change Address, you can enter a different e-mail address and mail server that Internet Explorer should use. If you're traveling, you could have Internet Explorer check your subscriptions from your desktop computer and then notify you by e-mail when a subscription has new content.

With either choice, when this site has new content, you'll be notified by a starlike gleam on this item's icon on the Favorites menu (shown here   as the icon on the right; the normal icon is on the left). This simply lets you know that there's something new at this site.

When you're revising the settings for an existing subscription, look on the Receiving tab in the Properties dialog box for the Notification options; it's shown in Figure 21.5. If you want to be e-mailed when this site has new content, select that checkbox. If you need to change the e-mail address, click the Change Address button. In the next section we'll discuss how you can have Internet Explorer download any new content it finds at a subscribed site.

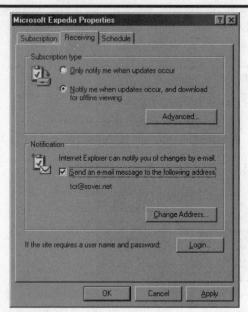

FIGURE 21.5: The Receiving tab of the Properties dialog box

Choosing How Much Content Should Be Delivered

When you're defining a new subscription or revising the settings for an existing one, you can limit how much new content Internet Explorer will download. As mentioned earlier, if you have chosen only to be notified, Internet Explorer simply checks the site for new content but does not download any. You can browse to the site in the usual fashion and see the new content that way. Let's look at the ways you can have Internet Explorer download that content for you—automatically and even while you're not at your computer.

When you're creating a new subscription, you have two options for downloading new content, as shown in Figure 21.6:

- ▶ Download this page.
- ▶ Download this page and pages linked to it.

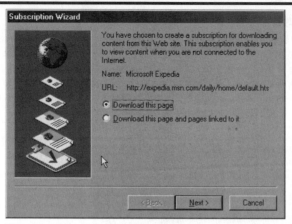

FIGURE 21.6: The Subscription Wizard lets you choose how much new content to download.

If you choose "Download this page," Internet Explorer downloads only the one page that is the target for this item on the Favorites menu. For example, if the URL for this item on the Favorites menu is:

```
www.widget.com/default.htm
```

only the page named DEFAULT.HTM is checked and, if there is new content, downloaded to your computer.

If you choose "Download this page and pages linked to it," the targets of any links on this page are also downloaded. In other words, if there are ten links on this page, you'll receive 11 downloaded pages, or whatever files are the targets for those links. Obviously, unless you know a site well, you really have no idea how many pages might be downloaded.

When you choose this second option and click the Next button, you'll see the dialog box shown in Figure 21.7, which asks you how many links "deep" you'd like to have downloaded. The default is 1 (the maximum is 3), so that only the target of each link is downloaded. If you set this option to 2, not only is the target of each link downloaded, but so are all the targets of all the links found on any of those pages.

WARNING

When you specify a certain number of pages deep, you're creating a potential situation that is not unlike the family tree of fruit flies multiplying in a biology classroom. If the site has lots of good links, you might be committing to a lifetime's supply of pages! Use caution even when specifying a depth of one page. Once you're very familiar with a site and how many links it tends to have, you can increase the depth as needed.

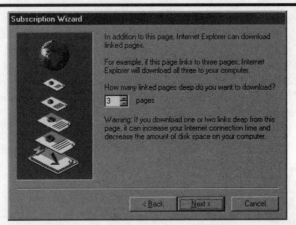

FIGURE 21.7:   Internet Explorer will follow links and download their targets as many levels deep as you specify.

You have even more download options when you revise the settings for an existing subscription. As you saw in Figure 21.5, the Receiving tab in the Properties dialog box has a group of options labeled Subscription Type. If you choose the "Notify and download" option, you can then click the Advanced button to access the Advanced Download Options dialog box, shown in Figure 21.8.

This dialog box gives you a wide range of options for limiting the amount of data that Internet Explorer downloads from this site.

As you can when you're specifying a new subscription, you can choose to download the pages targeted by the links on this page. Again, use caution with this option until you are familiar with this site. Use even more caution when you choose the option to download linked pages even when they reside outside the subscribed page's Web site. This is definitely an option to leave disabled until you are familiar with a site and the links it contains. You wouldn't want Internet Explorer to attempt to download the entire World Wide Web!

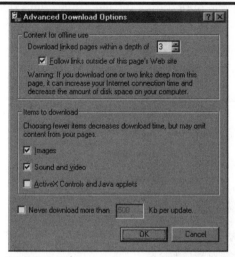

FIGURE 21.8:   In the Advanced Download Options dialog box, you can specify how much content to download from a subscribed site.

In the next group of options, Items to Download, you can choose the type of content to include or exclude from the download. To avoid lengthy downloads, deselect some or all of these options. If a page contains a deselected item, such as a video or an audio clip, you'll have to do without that content. When you select any of these data types, download times could increase drastically.

The last option lets you limit the amount of data that is downloaded when Internet Explorer updates this site. By default, there is no limit, so if you want to specify one, select this option and enter the maximum number of kilobytes that should be downloaded (remember that 1000 kilobytes (KB) is 1 megabyte (MB)).

Setting a Subscription Schedule

When you are subscribing to a new Web site and have chosen to download new content, one of the last dialog boxes in the Subscription Wizard, shown

Part ii

in Figure 21.9, lets you specify the schedule by which this site will be updated. You have two choices:

Scheduled   You can set the precise schedule, such as at a specific time each day, every hour during the nighttime hours, once each Monday, once a month, and so on.

Manually   You must specifically choose to update one or more sites, which you can do at any time.

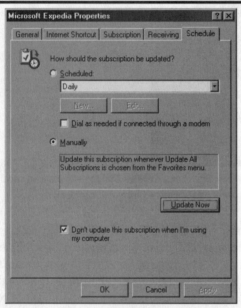

FIGURE 21.9:   You can specify a schedule for a new subscription or choose to update it manually.

Let's look at two disparate scenarios for scheduling the updating of your subscriptions. Suppose you have a network connection to the Internet that is always live and available and that you tend to leave your computer on 24 hours a day. In this case, you can set just about any schedule you want (you'll read about custom schedules a little later in this chapter).

Whenever the scheduled time rolls around, Internet Explorer automatically connects with the Internet, goes to each subscribed site, and downloads whatever content you specified. You can schedule these updates for the evenings or weekends when they won't get in the way of your daily work routine and when the Internet and your network may be less busy, as well.

At the opposite end of the spectrum, suppose that you connect to the Internet with a modem, that you pay for your connection by the hour, and that you tend to turn your computer off at the end of the day. In this case, you'll probably want to update your subscriptions manually while you're working at the computer, as described in the next section.

Updating Your Subscriptions Manually

You can update any or all of your subscriptions at any time by doing so manually. If a subscription is set to be manually updated, this is the only way you can have this site checked for new content. But even if a site has a custom schedule, you can still choose to update it manually at any time.

You can manually update sites in several ways:

▶ To update all your subscriptions, in any Explorer window choose Favorites ➤ Update All Subscriptions.

▶ To update a single subscribed site, right-click that site's item on the Favorites menu and choose Update Now. Or if you have already opened that site's Properties dialog box, choose the Schedule tab, and click the Update Now button.

▶ To update multiple subscriptions, open your Subscriptions folder in an Explorer window by choosing Favorites ➤ Manage Subscriptions. Select one or more subscriptions and choose File ➤ Update Now; or right-click one and choose Update Now.

When the update begins, you'll see a "progress" dialog box like the one shown here. Click the Details button to see a list of all the sites being checked and the status of each one. To cancel the updating, click the Stop button. To cancel it for just one site, select that site in the details list and click the Skip button. You can also minimize this dialog box or just ignore it while it does its job.

With the Manual Update schedule, there are no schedule options to set. With a custom schedule, however, there are many, which we'll look at in the next section.

CHOOSING A CUSTOM SCHEDULE

You can create a Custom schedule for a subscription that will update a site on just about any schedule you can imagine—many times each day, once each day, one day a week or a month, and so on. The Custom schedule choices are the same whether you're creating a new subscription or revising an existing one.

HOW OFTEN IS OFTEN ENOUGH?

The schedule you set for a subscription depends on several factors. First, decide how important the site is to you. Is it critical that you know as soon as possible when the site has new information, or would a day or two not really matter?

Consider how often you expect this site to get new content. Does it contain breaking news that may be updated several times a day? Have you noticed changes to the site every time you've visited it, or is it fairly static?

Don't forget that the type of connection you have to the Internet can drastically affect the process of updating subscriptions. If you have a fast, direct network connection that gives you almost instant access to the Web, checking a site for new content might happen in the blink of an eye. With a slower, dial-up connection, however, the process of connecting to the Web, checking each site for new content, and then downloading that content might take more time than you can spare for all your subscriptions.

When possible, assign each subscription to manual updating, or perhaps to the Weekly schedule, so that you can have Internet Explorer do the updating at night, when you're away from your computer and the Internet may run more briskly.

Use the Daily schedule for those sites that you really want to stay in touch with, and, when necessary, create a custom schedule for each site that requires its own schedule.

Choosing a Custom Schedule for a New Subscription

When you're creating a new subscription and choose to download content from the site, you can then choose to modify the schedule by clicking the Customize button, as shown here.

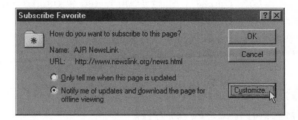

If you then select the Scheduled option (see Figure 21.9 again), you can select one of the existing named schedules from the drop-down menu. By default, you'll find the three schedules—Daily, Weekly, and Monthly. The actual schedule that is defined for the selected schedule is shown beneath the drop-down menu. If one of the defined schedules suits your needs, choose it from the menu and click the Next button. To change the settings for any of the named schedules, click the Edit button. To create a brand-new named schedule, click the New button. You'll read about both of these choices a little later.

WARNING

Revising the definition of any named schedule, such as Daily or Weekly, changes that schedule for all subscriptions that use it. If you want to change the settings for only the current subscription, create a new schedule for it.

Allowing Unattended Dial-Up Connections

If you have a network connection to the Internet that is always active and available, you can set a schedule for any day of the week or time of day, and Internet Explorer will be able to go out and check your subscribed sites for new content.

If you have a dial-up connection to the Internet with a modem, you'll have to decide whether you want Internet Explorer updating your subscriptions automatically on a schedule. If your modem's telephone line is available 24 hours a day for its own use, there may not be a problem. But if you also use the modem phone line for voice calls, you'll have to decide when it would be appropriate for Internet Explorer to dial out automatically to update your subscriptions.

By default, no automatic updates are allowed when you connect to the Internet with a modem, and you must do a manual update, as described earlier in this chapter. You can enable automatic updates, however, by choosing the "Dial as needed if connected through a modem" option, as shown earlier in Figure 21.9. You'll have to do some planning if you share the phone line with your modem, so that the various subscription schedules don't interfere with your use of the phone.

Choosing a Custom Schedule for an Existing Subscription

To change the schedule for an existing subscription, right-click that subscription's shortcut, choose Properties, and then select the Schedule tab, which is shown in Figure 21.10. As you can see, it gives you the same two schedule options that you are offered when creating a new subscription. For the custom schedule, there's the drop-down menu with the Daily, Weekly, and Monthly choices.

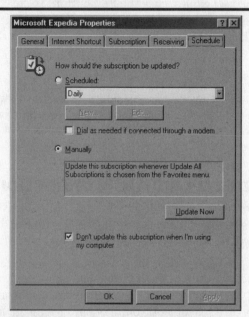

FIGURE 21.10: To revise the schedule for an existing subscription, open its Properties dialog box and choose the Schedule tab.

Creating a New Custom Schedule

When you are creating a new subscription or revising an existing one, you can click the New button to create a new custom schedule (see Figures 21.9 and 21.10). The name you specify for this new schedule will appear on the drop-down menu, along with the Daily, Weekly, and Monthly schedules.

Figure 21.11 shows the Custom Schedule dialog box that you see when you click the New button to create a new schedule. The options shown are for setting a daily schedule. When you select one of the other choices in the Days group, the options to the right change accordingly.

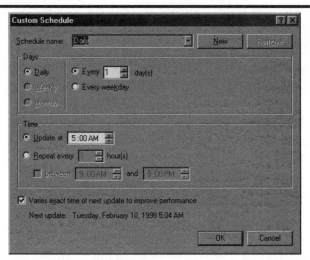

FIGURE 21.11:   You can create a new schedule in the Custom Schedule dialog box.

Creating a new schedule is a breeze. Simply select from the choices in the Custom Schedule dialog box:

1. Start by entering a name for this new schedule at the top of the dialog box, which will later appear on the drop-down menu of custom schedules. By default, a new schedule is named Custom Schedule.

2. Choose Daily, Weekly, or Monthly from the Days options, which will display the appropriate options for setting that schedule.

3. Choose the options you want for the type of schedule you're creating. For a Daily schedule, set the number of days to 1 to

run the schedule every day; to 2 to run it every other day, and so on. You can choose to run it every weekday instead.

4. Select the time of day for the updating by choosing from the Time group of options. If you choose 12:00 AM, the updating starts at the stroke of midnight for all subscriptions that use this schedule.

5. Choose the Repeat Every option if you want the updating to repeat throughout the day. Specify how often you want the update to occur and between what hours.

6. Choose the Varies Exact Time option to allow Internet Explorer to shift the update time in an attempt to improve network performance.

Near the bottom of the dialog box you can see when the next scheduled update will occur. This will change as you alter the schedule, so keep your eye on it.

When you're finished, click OK, and you'll be returned to the dialog box that displays the drop-down menu of schedules, where you'll find your new schedule listed.

Editing an Existing Custom Schedule

You can revise any existing custom schedule by clicking the Edit button on its Properties ➤ Schedule tab. You'll also find the Edit button in the Web Site Subscription Wizard dialog box when you're creating a new subscription. This displays the Custom Schedule dialog box, which looks much like the one shown earlier in Figure 21.11. The only difference is that here you must select a predefined schedule name from the drop-down menu at the top of the dialog box. The schedule options will change to match those for that schedule.

Make any changes to the options that you want, and when you're finished, click the OK button. The new settings will now apply to that named schedule and will therefore affect all subscriptions that use that schedule.

NOTE

The Custom Schedule dialog box has a Remove button, which allows you to delete any of the named schedules except the defaults: Daily, Weekly, and Monthly. It also has a New button that allows you to create a new schedule name instead of revising an existing one.

VIEWING AND SUBSCRIBING TO ACTIVE CHANNELS

So far we've looked at two ways to retrieve information from the Web:

► By explicitly visiting a Web site, such as by entering a URL into the Address toolbar or by following a hyperlink

► By subscribing to a Web site

Now we'll look at a third technique, which builds on the concept of subscriptions. This major new feature of the Active Desktop is called Active Channels, and you access it from the Channels Bar that appears on the desktop when Windows 98 is started. It can deliver just the information you want and on a timely basis, where *timely* is defined by the publisher of that information.

The term *channel* suggests TV quality or TV attributes, but the technology is not quite there at this point (for which we may yet give thanks). A channel is not a site that broadcasts information (thus, the term *channel* is confusing, to say the least). It is actually a regular Web site that provides information through regular Web pages. In fact, you can view a channel just as you would view any Web site; the trick becomes evident when you choose to subscribe to a channel.

When you subscribe to a Web page, Internet Explorer visits that site from time to time and checks that site's content to see whether it has changed. You can subscribe to any site, even if it was created prior to the release of Windows 98. A channel is similar, but you can only subscribe to a channel when that site has been configured as a channel.

You subscribe to a channel simply by linking to a file that contains the site's Channel Definition Format (a CDF file). This file is provided by the publisher of the site and automatically defines the subscription to this channel in Internet Explorer. You'll see how all this works in the sections that follow.

You can also customizes channels. Besides viewing a channel, either online or offline (if you have chosen to download its contents), you can make a channel an item on your Active Desktop, part of the Channel screen saver, or your desktop wallpaper.

Before we get into the details, let's see how channels are used. By looking at a few examples, you will be able to better understand the differences between channels and subscriptions, as well as the advantages of channels over plain browsing.

Part ii

Viewing a Channel in Internet Explorer

As mentioned earlier, you can view a channel in several ways. First, you can simply go to a Web site that happens to be a channel, in any of the usual ways, such as by entering its URL in the Address toolbar. In fact, you may often encounter Web sites quite by accident that are set up to be used as channels; whether you subscribe to a channel is your decision.

When you installed Windows 98, links to a variety of channels were also installed, which you can access in a number of ways. In Internet Explorer, or from the Task Bar if you have selected the option, choose Favorites ➤ Channels. To select a channel in the Explorer bar, choose View ➤ Explorer Bar ➤ Channels, or click the Channels button on the toolbar, and your list of channels will be displayed in the Explorer bar. To close the Explorer bar, click that button again.

NOTE

The Channel Guide channel is a Microsoft site at which you will find additional channels. You'll see shortly how to visit a channel so you can subscribe to it.

You can also access the list of channels with the Favorites ➤ Channels command on the Windows 98 Start menu. Selecting a channel in this way opens the channel in an Internet Explorer window.

Viewing a Channel in the Channel Viewer

 From the Quick Launch toolbar, you can click the View Channels button to open Internet Explorer in a full-screen mode known as the Channel Viewer, which is shown in Figure 21.12. The Explorer bar is displayed on the left side of the screen, as shown in the figure.

NOTE

The channels you'll see in your own Explorer bar will probably vary from those shown in Figure 21.12, in the same way that we can each have our own list of favorite Web sites. As Windows 98 is used by more and more people, you'll undoubtedly find that many Web sites will now offer you the option to subscribe to their channels from within their home page.

You can also launch a channel in the Channel Viewer by selecting it from the Channel bar on the desktop, as discussed in the next section. To

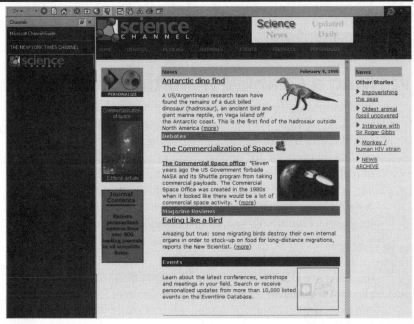

FIGURE 21.12:   The Channel Viewer is Internet Explorer's special full-screen mode for the maximum viewing area.

display the Quick Launch toolbar, right-click the taskbar and choose Toolbars ➤ Quick Launch. In Chapter 3, you can find more about displaying other toolbars on the Windows 98 Desktop.

You can close the Explorer bar by clicking the Channels button on the toolbar, but in the Channel Viewer, the Explorer bar will automatically slide out of the way when your mouse is not over it. Simply point to the left side of the screen to have the Explorer bar slide open again. To prevent the Explorer bar from hiding, click the pushpin button that you'll find on the right side of the Explorer bar's title bar.

When you're using Internet Explorer in Channel Viewer mode, almost all the tools in Internet Explorer are hidden, by default, leaving as much room as possible for the Web page. Only the standard toolbar is displayed, and you can even hide that by choosing the Auto Hide command from the shortcut menu when you right-click the toolbar. The other toolbars, the status bar, and even the menu bar are hidden! This really is a full-screen mode, because even the Windows Taskbar is hidden.

You can turn on these features in the usual ways. For example, right-click the toolbar and choose Menu Bar to display the menus, or use the

View menu to turn on the status bar or the other toolbars. To return to the normal view in Internet Explorer, choose View ➤ Full Screen, or click that button on the toolbar.

Viewing a Channel from the Channel Bar

Yet another way to access a channel is from the Channel bar, shown at right, which can be displayed on the Active Desktop. It offers the same choices that you'll find on the Channels menu or in the list of channels in the Explorer bar, only they're conveniently placed as icons in the Channel bar, which you can access from the desktop. When you open a channel in this way, it is displayed in Internet Explorer's Channel Viewer, as discussed in the previous section.

If you don't see the Channel bar, you need to add it to the Active Desktop. From the Windows Start menu, choose Programs ➤ Active Desktop ➤ Channel Bar. You can also turn on or off the Channel bar or other items on the Active Desktop in the following way:

1. Right-click the desktop and choose Properties to open the Display Properties dialog box.

2. Select the Web tab, which is shown in Figure 21.13.

3. In the list of items, select the Internet Explorer Channel Bar by clicking its checkbox.

4. Click OK to close the Display Properties dialog box.

The Channel Bar should now appear on your desktop.

Subscribing to an Active Channel

In most cases, the first time you access a channel, such as by clicking its button in the Channel bar, an introductory screen at that site invites you to subscribe to the channel. Unless you're informed otherwise, no cost is involved, and most channels don't even require a registration. You simply answer a few questions for Internet Explorer's Subscribe Wizard.

Internet Explorer organizes many channels into categories. For example, when you are viewing the Channel bar on the desktop or in the Explorer

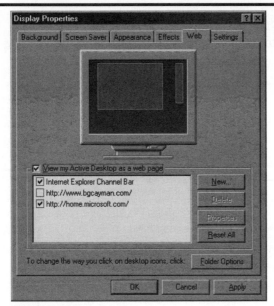

FIGURE 21.13:   The Web tab in the Display Properties dialog box, where you can add items to the Active Desktop

bar in Internet Explorer and click the News & Technology button, you will see the names of the channels in that category:

- ▶ CMPNet
- ▶ Live Wired
- ▶ The CNET Channel
- ▶ The New York Times
- ▶ ZDNet

These channels are all related to the news and technology category. In the right pane of the Internet Explorer window, you will see the icons that correspond to these channels. To subscribe to the CNET channel, for example, click its button to access that site. The Explorer bar with its list of channels slides to the left and is hidden (unless you leave the mouse pointer resting on it), and CNET's opening screen appears and invites you to subscribe, as shown in Figure 21.14.

To subscribe to the CNET channel, click the Click Here to Subscribe button (most channels will have a similar way to subscribe). This button

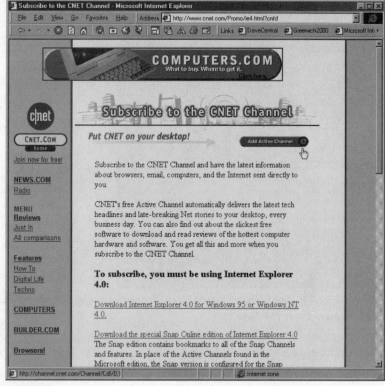

FIGURE 21.14: CNET invites you to subscribe to its channel.

links to a Channel Definition Format file (CDF), which will trigger Internet Explorer's Subscribe Wizard.

As you can see in Figure 21.15, the Wizard for adding a channel is just about the same as the one you see when you subscribe to regular Web sites, with the following differences:

▶ The new channel is added to your Channel bar, not to your Favorites menu.

▶ The default update schedule is specified by the channel's publisher via the CDF file at the Web site.

You can modify the default update schedule by clicking the Customize button in the Wizard's dialog box. If you choose the option to have content downloaded, you can then choose to have only the channel's home page downloaded, or all the channel content prescribed by the CDF file.

One component provided by many channels becomes part of the Channel screen saver, which you'll read about in the next section.

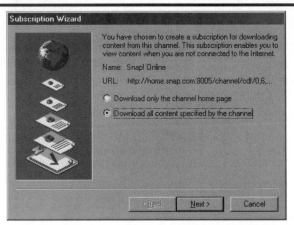

FIGURE 21.15: Subscribing to a channel is similar to subscribing to a Web site.

After completing the subscription process for the CNET channel, you will see the CNET home page, and a new icon for the channel will appear in the Channel bar on your desktop. In essence, you have subscribed to another site, except that this one is directed by its CDF file.

Using a Channel on the Desktop or in the Channel Screen Saver

As we mentioned earlier, you can also display channels as part of the Channel screen saver or as an item on the Active Desktop. Some sites will have a separate button for each display option, so you can choose to install the channel's screen saver component, its Active Desktop component, or all the content that the channel has to offer. Other sites might let you make that decision while you're subscribing to the channel, so you'll be able to choose the type of content while you're going through the Wizard.

When you configure this screen saver, you can choose which available channel to display when the screen saver is activated. Here are the steps in a nutshell:

1. Right-click the desktop and choose Properties.

2. In the Display Properties dialog box, select the Screen Saver tab.

3. On the Screen Saver drop-down menu, choose Channel Screen Saver.

4. Now click the Settings button to open the Screen Saver Properties dialog box, which is shown in Figure 21.16.

5. Select the names of the channels you want displayed when the screen saver is activated, and then click OK. Remember, you'll only see the channels that you specifically chose to include in the Channel screen saver when you first subscribed to the channels.

6. Now click OK to close the Display Properties dialog box.

When your computer is idle and the Channel screen saver starts up, it will connect to the Internet as needed and display the channels you have selected.

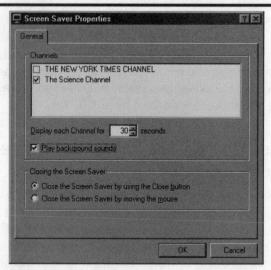

FIGURE 21.16: The Screen Saver Properties dialog box, in which you select the channels to include in the Channel screen saver

You can display pictures, Web pages, and other Web-related items on your Active Desktop, and that includes channel content, as well. When a Web site offers content designed for your desktop, it will most likely have a button to let you install just that content. When you click the button, the Subscribe Wizard takes you through the steps of downloading and installing the new item for your Active Desktop, as shown below. When you're finished and the new content is downloaded, you'll see the new item displayed on the Active Desktop.

Setting a Channel's Options

You can view or revise the settings for a channel subscription from its shortcut menu:

- ▶ Right-click the channel's icon on the Channel bar or within the Explorer bar in Internet Explorer.

- ▶ Choose Favorites ➤ Manage Subscriptions to open a list of all your subscriptions, including those that are channels (refer back to Figure 21.2 to see the Subscriptions window). Then right-click the one you want.

- ▶ Choose Favorites ➤ Channels in Internet Explorer, and right-click the channel you want.

The shortcut menu offers several choices related to channels and subscriptions. Choose Update Now, and Internet Explorer will connect to that Web site to see if there is any new content, just as you can do with any subscription. This command updates the contents of a channel on your disk, regardless of the update schedule that is specified in the channel's subscription.

When a channel has the Refresh command on its shortcut menu, you can choose that command to download the titles of the pages that make up the channel. These are displayed as hyperlinks that appear below the channel's icon.

Choose Properties to open the Properties dialog box for a channel subscription, which is shown in Figure 21.17. It should look familiar if you've read the earlier sections in this chapter on subscriptions (see Figure 21.3).

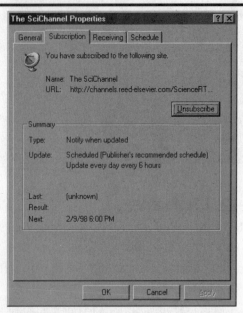

FIGURE 21.17: A channel's Properties dialog box displays the subscription settings for that channel.

The Subscription tab gives you an overview of the current settings. You can unsubscribe to this channel or change the login parameters, if the site requires that you log in with a user name and password.

On the Receiving tab you can specify the notification method and whether Internet Explorer will merely check the site to see if anything is new or will actually download any new pages. On the Schedule tab you can specify how often the channel will be updated.

WHAT'S NEXT?

The future of the Web may depend in part on our having tools such as subscriptions and channels. They allow us to maintain an ongoing relationship with the sites we value, while protecting us from the wild chaos of unlimited choices. Time will tell. But the beauty of both these tools is that they are optional—you can still browse the Web in any fashion you prefer.

With this chapter, we've now completed our look at Windows 98's Internet features, and at Windows 98 itself. Part III offers an in-depth look at maintaining and upgrading the hardware side of your computer system.

Part ii

PART iii

YOUR PC AND HARDWARE

Chapter 22

A BUYER'S GUIDE TO PCs

I f you're the kind of person who fixes your own or someone else's PC, then you're likely to be the kind of person who's often looking to the *next* PC, the latest-and-greatest machine. Perhaps your palms itch when you see that someone else owns a dual processor Pentium II system, when all you can afford is a Pentium 133. You eye 9GB hard drives the way teenage boys eye Corvettes.

Adapted from *The Complete PC Upgrade and Maintenance Guide*, by Mark Minasi

ISBN 0-7821-2151-9   1,520 pages $59.99

Or maybe you're not that way. Maybe computers are just a tool for you, a platform upon which to get some work done. But you've found that your current platform just isn't strong enough to support today's software: Windows 98 requires at least 16MB of RAM and a Pentium 120 in order to be useful; for most purposes you'll want at least 32MB and a faster processor. And you need to know how to either upgrade your existing machines, or buy new ones that won't offer as much trouble when it's time to upgrade again in a year or two.

It's a good time to upgrade; with prices these days, everybody can own some of the fastest PCs on the planet. Buyers with tons of money don't have much advantage over the rest of us now. (Unless, of course, you've *got* to have a 200 MHz Pentium-based notebook with the active matrix screen and 2-gig 1.75-inch drive.) And cheap Pentiums come *just* in time for those of us who are Windows users: Windows 98 is the best excuse that I know of for buying a new Pentium II.

But *which* one to buy? Well, I'm not going to tell you *that*: there are zillions of honest vendors out there that deserve your money. I'd just like to give you some advice on how to make sure that your vendor is one of the good ones.

I tell my clients that when they're going to buy a PC, they should consider four things: compatibility, serviceability, upgradability (I know, it's not a word), and price/performance.

Because I'm concerned about those things, I recommend that people avoid many of the big names in the PC business and buy a *generic* computer, rather than a *proprietary* computer.

Parts of a Generic PC

Before I go any further, let me clarify what I mean when I say "generic" and "proprietary." *Generic* refers to the majority of machines available today. Generic machines are PCs consisting of a few separate industry standard parts. Those parts include:

A standard case   If you buy a computer with an unusually shaped case, as you'd see in the "slimline" PCs or some of the more interesting offerings from large vendors, then you'll find that all of the boards inside the computer may be unusually-shaped as well. That means that you won't be able to easily locate replacement parts, should you need them. It also means

that you can't put an industry-standard ("generic") power supply in your system. That's undesirable because there are some
very nice power supply alternatives these days, such as super-
quiet fans or power supplies with built-in battery backup.

A motherboard   The circuit board inside the case that contains
the PC's CPU chip, its memory, and its expansion slots. On that
motherboard there should be *eight* expansion slots, rather than
the three that you find on some computers these days, so that you
can add expansion boards to your PC now and in the future. Be
aware that the vendor may have filled a number of them already.
You have a sound card, a video accelerator, a drive controller, and/
or something like a wave table for your Sound Blaster 16 or a 3D
Accelerator card for your 2D video card.

An I/O board   A board that acts as an interface—an "ambas-
sador," essentially—between the motherboard and your hard
disk, your floppy disks, two serial ports, and a parallel port.
The disks are, of course, the essential storage devices that you
keep your data on. A PC also contains the hard disk and floppy
disk drive or drives. You'll use serial ports for your mouse and
modem—the device that lets your PC communicate with other
computers over the phone—and the parallel port will let you
attach your PC to a printer.

A video adapter board   This allows your PC to display images
on a video monitor. It will probably be an SVGA board. SVGA is
Super Video Graphics Array, a common video standard. I'll recommend SVGA accelerators a bit later.

That's just a generic overview. I'll zoom in on particular features you
should be looking for in a few pages.

PROBLEMS WITH PROPRIETARY PCs

How is one of these generic PCs different from a proprietary PC? Well,
you find most of the same functions in a proprietary PC, but you find all
of them on a single circuit board, a kind of "workaholic" motherboard.
The big problem with proprietary computers is that you can't upgrade
them easily, nor can you fix them for a reasonable price. Proprietary computer motherboards are typically shaped differently from each other, and
from generic motherboards, making it impossible for you to replace an

Part iii

old or damaged proprietary motherboard with anything but another motherboard of the exact same make and model. As motherboards of that particular make and model are only available from that particular vendor (by definition, since the motherboard is proprietary), it may be expensive or impossible to get a replacement. Likewise, it's almost certainly impossible to get an upgrade.

For more specific problems with proprietary designs, let's return to my four criteria.

Compatibility is at stake because if the vendor did anything wrong—for example, if the company chose a mildly incompatible video chip, as AT&T did for some of their systems—there's nothing you can do but either throw away the computer or hope that the designer was far-sighted enough to allow you to disable the built-in video function so you can go out and spend more money on a separate video board.

Upgradability is a concern because the one-board design is "all or nothing." It's not shaped like other one-board designs—for example, Compaq's one-board design looks nothing like IBM's one-board design—so you can't replace the board with a better third-party offering.

Serviceability is a problem for reasons touched on above. A generic design like a Gateway 2000 is a safe buy in many ways, not the least of which is that even if Gateway goes bankrupt tomorrow (very unlikely), the entire machine is composed of generic parts that can be bought at *thousands* of clone houses around the country. And this isn't brain surgery; you've seen in this book that you can break down and rebuild a PC in about 30 minutes, and, in some cases, leaving it better than when you started.

And what about *price/performance*? First of all, notice that I put this last. That's because compared to what computers used to cost, *any* PC is a bargain, even if you pay list price for one made by IBM. As regards the proprietary computers: in theory, a single-board design can be faster and cheaper for many reasons. You don't see that in actual fact because single-board designs tend to be used primarily for notebook computers, an environment which, by available space alone, disallows expansions cards.

You don't need to buy a big name to get big performance, reliability, or flexibility. Look in your local paper's business section for the names of companies near you that can sell generic PCs. It couldn't hurt if your company offers service through a national service company like GTE, Wang, or TRW. Then choose that fire-breathing 333 MHz Pentium II you've always wanted and put it to work for you—and smile, knowing that you've bought the security of easy upgrades and independence from any single vendor.

CHOOSING A MARKET NICHE

Where will you buy your PC? People in some companies are only allowed to buy from IBM or Compaq; others put machines together from parts. Computer dealers basically fall into three categories.

▸ **First tier:** IBM and Compaq. The *definitions* of compatibility. Price/performance tends to be fairly low, innovation minimal or gimmicky. Despite past reputations, these two, and others that fall into this category, have been forced into the future by the smaller "screwdriver" shops. Their unlikely competition, which sold better, cheaper, upgradeable, and more compatible systems, chewed away the profit margins. This means that IBM, Compaq, Gateway 2000, Hewlett Packard, and Packard Bell all use a mostly industry-standard modular approach to system design. This is great for compatibility and upgradability, but you still pay an inflated premium for the name. You will most likely be offered the option of a 3-year service contract in addtion to the 1-year on-site service contract that's often included; and, if you have to ship it out for service, you can expect it back in a reasonable time period.

▸ **Second tier**: Micron, Acer, Sony, Digital, Quantex, and others. These companies tended toward the "modular generic" architectures for years, generating the competition from the first tier companies. Pros: better price/performance than first tier. Upgrade hardware (e.g. more RAM, better video, faster modem) will be more available, although this won't be true with the "small footprint" machines, which tend to be much less expandable. Cons: There is no storefront to take a broken machine to. Sure, there is that 1-year on-site service contract, but you spend at least an hour on the phone convincing technical support that your problem should be seen to be believed. You'll also typically have a 3–7 day wait for a service person to contact you and make arrangements to come to your home or office. Dead-On-Arrival hardware is somewhat common.

▸ **Third tier**: also known as "Screwdriver," "box shovers," or "Three Guys and a Goat PCs." This group gets a scary reputation that's really not deserved. Yes, some of them are sleazy, deceptive, and unreliable, but then those are adjectives that have been aptly applied to some of the *big* names in the business, too. On the positive side, these companies are always aware of the fact that every sale is a significant portion of their total business, and they'll do just about anything to get a multiple-machine contract with a large company or government client. You usually needn't worry about shoddy parts, as they're putting together pieces made by fairly big U.S., Taiwanese, Korean, and Japanese vendors. If you look at the sum total of all third-tier vendors, you'll see that between them, they use only about three or four suppliers for any given part (drives, motherboards, controllers, etc.). That means that if you really look at the companies that are *supplying* those parts—Micronics, DTK, AMI, Chips & Technologies, Adaptec, G2, and others—you'll see that they're pretty large and reliable companies. The absolute best part about these machines is that they're the simplest to upgrade and maintain. They also have the best price/performance in the group, and compatibility is usually as good as the second-tier machines.

AND THE WINNER IS...

Surprise! The biggest winner in this highly competitive climate is you, the consumer. There has not always been competition in the personal computer market. Back in the golden days of the first personal computers, IBM and Apple Computer were the big players, and they held all the cards. Apple had immense success with the Apple II+ and IIe, while IBM monopolized the business market with its rather uninteresting, but usable IBM PC XT. When IBM finally licensed their platform to other manufacturers, there was a small explosion in the personal computer market.

These computers, however, had some proprietary technology that varied from clone-maker to clone-maker. Most machines of the time were not 100% compatible with each other. IBM readjusted their license a few years later and coined the term "PC compatible," making possible the systems we are most familiar with today. The smart companies that heeded IBM's ominous, and powerful, license agreement still exist today. The others dropped like flies on a cold winter day. As the PC compatible platform slowly came to dominate the market, it also became a battleground.

CONTINUED ➡

Each clone-maker developed and introduced new "standards" for each basic technology. One of the most topsy-turvy skirmishes was over video. MDA, Hercules, CGA, EGA, VGA, XGA, XGA-2, SVGA, VESA SVGA, and UVGA are all so-called video standards, each very different from the other and all coined by different companies. Technically, SVGA isn't even a standard. It's a term that describes a *range* of resolutions and color depths that a video card and monitor *may* support. Fun, eh?

Many other battles like the last one are waged every day, to the benefit of every consumer, but the big rough and tumble in today's market is who can get to line cheaper and faster. They fight for supremacy in the sub-$1000 PC market, and you can buy a fully loaded Gateway 2000 300MHz Pentium II computer with a 17″ monitor for around $2000, among many others. It's hard to feel bad about that.

CHOOSING PC PARTS

In the process of choosing a PC, I look at what it's made of in order to decide if it's the kind of machine that I'm looking for. Let's look at the important parts of a PC and summarize what you should consider when buying one.

The CPU

If you're buying today, buy 200 MHz Pentium MMX or faster computers. The Pentium is a well-built fast chip that offers 100 percent compatibility with earlier chips as well as terrific speed. Are you missing much buying one of these rather than a Pentium II? Not really. The Pentium II is a faster CPU by all means, but the Pentium MMX is no slowpoke.

The fact of the matter today is that the CPUs are leveling out in speed, despite what the benchmarks say. What's *not* getting faster, however, are the peripherals. Today's CPUs are hundreds of times faster than XT-level CPUs were; modern peripherals, however, are only dozens of times faster than XT-era peripherals. Take the money you're saving by not buying the latest and greatest CPU and spend that on a faster bus and faster peripherals. (There are exceptions; some processes are very CPU-intensive and will benefit from a faster processor.)

The Bus

The *bus* is what brings the CPU and all the peripherals together and communicating efficiently. There are ISA, MCA, EISA, VESA, and finally, SCSI and PCI, the common adapter bus formats today. Then there's AGP, or Advanced Graphics Port. All systems today come with a mix of PCI and E/ISA slots on the motherboard, and most new Pentium II motherboards come with an AGP slot for the special video accelerator card. Watch out for older VESA Local Bus implementations, which are no longer supported and do not support Plug-and-Play.

Which brings me to my next bus requirement: Plug-and-Play. Make absolutely sure that your new machine will support Plug-and-Play as implemented by Windows 9*x*; that's an important qualification, because a good number of vendors have a loose interpretation of what Plug-and-Play means. The simplest hard-and-fast test is, "Does it work with Windows 98?" This problem, however, is dwindling swiftly as vendors realize the benefits of fully supporting the PnP API from Microsoft.

Not every board needs to be a PCI board, although that is preferable. You should be pretty sure, however, that the following adapters are PCI:

- ▶ The video adapter
- ▶ The SCSI host adapter or EIDE/ATAPI host adapter
- ▶ Any LAN cards
- ▶ Any video capture or sound capture hardware

RAM

Windows 98 runs best in a 32MB environment, but 16MB will do if your budget doesn't allow. Make sure you get a motherboard with *processor cache,* more commonly known as L2 Cache, of at least 512K, with the ability to increase that to 1MB. The option used to be very expensive, but it's now quite reasonable.

ROM BIOS

The BIOS is an important part of compatibility. Buy from one of the big three—Phoenix, Award, or AMI. That way, it's easy to get upgrades. Nice BIOS features:

- ▶ User-definable drive types
- ▶ Bus speeds that can be set in the setup
- ▶ Fast A20 gate that speeds up Windows
- ▶ Processor cache enable/disable

Motherboard/System Board

This is the board that contains the above items. If you're buying from a first- or second-tier company, you'll end up with their board. From a third-tier place, look for motherboards from Micronics, DTK, Mylex, Chips & Technologies, and AMI.

Hard Disks

You're probably going to end up buying ATAPI or Enhanced IDE-type drives, mainly because they're so amazingly cheap, fast, and reliable. Just back the silly things up *regularly*, because there's only a limited array of repair options open to you. Best buys these days are probably the 2.1GB drives (Seagate, Maxtor, and Conner make them) for about $230.

Floppy Disks

I've seen too many problems with Mitsubishi drives to recommend them; TEACs seem the most trouble-free. Don't bother with the 2.88MB floppies; nobody else uses them, but you might want to look into getting a Zip drive for easily expandable storage of 100MB per disk.

Video Board

Get a bit-blitting video accelerator board to support modern graphical operating systems. (Also called *bit-block transfer*, bit-blitting is a graphics function that copies a rectangular array of bits from memory to the screen.)

Part iii

Any accelerator based on the S3 chip set will be easy to support, as S3 drivers are common for any operating system. Alternatively, look at one of the two market leaders: either an accelerator card from Diamond or one from ATI. If you're into computer games, look at any card that takes 8MB of RAM and supports the 3Dfx accelerator API.

Video Monitor

Buy a monitor based on the resolution at which you'll use it. If you're doing regular old VGA (with a resolution of 640 dots across the screen by 480 dots down the screen), buy a 14-inch VGA monitor; it'll cost around $120. For the SVGA 800 × 600 resolution, get a 15-inch multisyncing monitor that can handle that resolution. For 1024 × 768, buy a monitor that's at least 17 inches diagonally. And *do not* buy interlaced 1024 × 768: sure it's cheaper, but the lawsuits from your employees going blind will be expensive. Buy noninterlaced. And only worry about it at 1024 × 768: nobody I know of tries to interlace 640 × 480 or 800 × 600. My favorite for a 17-inch monitor is the Viewsonic 17G.

Mouse

Although I hate to put more money in Microsoft's pocket, the Microsoft mouse seems the best of all the ones I've worked with. But $30 for a mouse? Arggh.

Printers

Well, they cost a little more, but it's hard to go wrong with HP laser printers. The series 6 produces beautiful output. If you need only an ink-jet printer, Epson makes the most incredible ones—you know, the ones that can print color art like a photograph. All that for starting around $199. Simply amazing!

Serial Ports

Look for serial ports based on the 16550 UART chip. It's built for multi-tasking, and you won't get any better than 33.600 out of your 56K modem without one.

Parallel Ports

Make sure that your parallel ports are Enhanced Parallel Port (EPP) interfaces. They're faster, and they're bidirectional. Bidirectional parallel ports are essential for modern printers, which send status information back to the PC over those ports.

FROM WHOM SHOULD YOU BUY?

When I ask this question, I don't mean whether you should buy from Dell, IBM, or Jeff and Akbar's House of Clones; instead, I mean, "Should you buy direct from the manufacturer, via mail order, or at a store?"

Well, if you're a really large company, then it probably makes sense to go straight to Compaq or whomever and negotiate a specific deal. But if you're a hobbyist or a SOHO (small office/home office) shop, then you'll have to examine your strategies.

You can probably buy cheapest from mail order. *But* if you do that, then returning defective merchandise involves shipping things around, getting RMA (Return Merchandise Authorization) numbers, and the like. That can be a hassle.

Going to a big computer retailer is just a fast way to waste money, so I'm not intending to shove you into the arms of Computerland or the like. But there are many small businesses whose main line of work is to sell computer parts, software, supplies, and systems at a reasonable price. These local vendors often offer prices that aren't that much more expensive than mail order. (Besides, the nice thing about local stores is that I like my vendors within choking distance....) And patronizing your local PC store means that when you need that disk drive on Saturday, you need only run down the street to get it, rather than waiting a week for it to ship.

That's not to say that mail order doesn't make sense. Mail order firms are more likely to have the latest and greatest software and hardware. Their prices will, again, be lower than the local store's. They may even know more about the product than a local vendor might. But take it from a veteran—there are a few things to be sure of.

- ▶ First, use a credit card. It's your line of defense when mail order companies get nasty. If you didn't get what you wanted, then just box it up, ship it back, and cancel the charge. Years ago, Dell used to charge a 15 percent "restocking fee." (They may still, but I refuse to do business with them, so I wouldn't know.) They sent me a hard disk that had clearly been dropped. When it worked, it registered seek times in the hundreds of milliseconds, despite what their ad promised. They tried to convince me that the drive was just what I wanted, but I knew better, and sent it back. They tried to charge me a restocking fee, so I just complained to Citibank, and Dell backed off.

▸ Second, find out who you're talking to. If the person responds, "operator 22," (I suppose his friends call him "2") ask to speak with a supervisor. You're about to give this guy your name, address, phone, and credit card number, and he won't even tell you who he is? Write the name down. Also get a confirmation number or order number.

▸ Third, only buy the product if it's in stock. Back-ordered things can take months to arrive, and by the time they do, you'll be charged the older (and higher) price. Get the salesperson to check that it can ship today. If not, don't make the order.

▸ Ship it overnight or second-day. By default, mail order companies use UPS ground, which can take anywhere from one week to a millennium to arrive. Second day is usually only a few dollars more, and then you can get a guaranteed delivery date out of the salesperson.

▸ Once you have the product, keep the carton that it came in for 30 days. That way, if a problem arises, then it's easy to ship it back. And if you do have to ship something back, then by all means insure it.

Just follow those rules, and you'll have some great luck getting things through the mail.

What's Next?

In the next chapter, Mark Minasi offers valuable guidance on preventive maintenance—simple things you can do to keep your computer hardware running smoothly and to protect it from physical hazards ranging from dust and static electricity to flooding. Everyone should read Chapter 23; even old pros may find new tips there.

Chapter 23

AVOIDING SERVICE: PREVENTIVE MAINTENANCE

The most effective way to cut down your repair bills is by good preventive maintenance. There are things in the PC environment—some external, some created in ignorance by you through inattention—that can drastically shorten your PC's life. Now, some of these are common-sense things; I don't really imagine that I've got to tell you not to spill soft drinks (or, for that matter, *hard* drinks) into the keyboard. But other PC gremlin sources aren't quite so obvious; so, obvious or not, we'll get to all the environmental hazards in this chapter. A few factors endanger your PC's health:

- ► Excessive heat
- ► Dust
- ► Magnetism
- ► Stray electromagnetism
- ► Power surges, incorrect line voltage, and power outages
- ► Water and corrosive agents

Adapted from *The Complete PC Upgrade and Maintenance Guide*, by Mark Minasi

ISBN 0-7821-2151-9   1,520 pages $59.99

HEAT AND THERMAL SHOCK

Every electronic device carries within it the seeds of its own destruction. More than half of the power given to chips is wasted as heat—but heat destroys chips. One of an electronic designer's main concerns is to see that a device can dissipate heat as quickly as it can generate it. If not, heat slowly builds up until the device fails. You can help your PC's heat problem in two ways.

▶ You can install an adequate fan in the power supply, or add an auxiliary fan.

▶ Run the PC in a safe temperature range.

Removing Heat with a Fan

Some computers, like most laptops, don't require a fan, as enough heat dissipates from the main circuit board all by itself. But most desktop and tower PCs will surely fail without a fan.

When designing a fan, engineers must trade off noise for cooling power. Years ago, power supplies were quite expensive, running in the $300 range for the cheapest power supply, and great care was exercised in choosing the right fan. Nowadays, power supplies cost under $25, and I doubt that most engineers at PC companies could even tell you what kind of fan is sitting in their machines, any more than they could tell you who makes the case screws. Now, that's a terrible shame, because the $3 fan that's sitting in most PC power supplies is a vital part. If it dies, your PC will cook itself in just a few hours. And they *do* die.

The more stuff that's in your PC, the hotter it runs. The things that make PCs hot inside include:

▶ Chips, memory chips, and CPUs in particular, as they have the most transistors inside them.

▶ Drive motors in hard disks, floppies, and CD-ROMs. Some CD-ROMs run quite warm, like the Plexor 4-Plex models. Large hard disks run *extremely* hot. It seems that the full-height 5.25-inch drives run at a temperature that will almost burn your fingers; I've seen that on old Maxtor 660MB ESDI drives, and more recently on my 1.7GB Fujitsu drive. Newer drives in the 3.5-inch, half-height or third-height format run much cooler.

▶ Some circuit boards can run quite hot, depending on how they're designed (or misdesigned).

In general, heat buildup inside a PC is much less of a problem than it was in the mid-80s.

Good and Bad Box Designs

It's frustrating how totally unaware of heat problems many computer manufacturers are. The first tower computer I purchased was from a company named ACMA, and they put together an impressive machine. There were two fans in the case—a very nice touch—as well as a CPU fan. I've got to say that they spoiled me. A much more recent purchase, from an outfit called Systems Dynamics Group, has been somewhat less enjoyable. The back of the PC chassis has room for two fans, but there's only one fan in the system. There's nothing intrinsically wrong with that, except that the cutout for the second fan—which is right next to the first fan—is left empty. The result is that the fan just sucks in air from the cutout a few inches away from it, and blows it back out.

I noticed this pointless ventilation system pretty quickly, so I took some tape and covered up the extraneous cutout. Within seconds, the air being pumped out the back of the Pentium got 10 degrees warmer. If I'd left the extra cutout uncovered, then the only ventilation that my Pentium system would have gotten was just the simple convection from the heated boards and drives. Even at that, however, the Pentium system—which includes a 1GB drive, 80MB of RAM, a CD-ROM, video capture board, video board, SCSI host adapter, and Ethernet card—only runs 10 degrees hotter inside the box than outside the box.

Things could have been a bit worse if the case was like some I've seen, with the fan *on the bottom of the tower*! This case—it's not too common, fortunately, but it's worth asking so you can avoid it when purchasing a PC—puts the circuit boards on the top of the tower, and the fan on the bottom. I have no idea who designed this case, but it's nice to know that the banjo player kid from *Deliverance* finally has someone to look down upon.

Dead Fans

The point I'm making here is, take a minute and look at the airflow in the box. Of course, even if you have a good box, you can still run into heat problems.

I recently installed Freelance Graphics on my system. Pulling the first floppy out of my A: drive, I noticed that the floppy was warm. My memory flashed back to 1982, when something similar had happened—so I knew what was going on. My system's fan had died. Fortunately, I found the problem early and shut down the computer. I had to travel to Europe for a few weeks to teach classes and consult, but I figured, no problem; I'll just leave the computer off. Unfortunately, while I was gone, one of my employees helpfully started up the computer—reasoning that I always leave my computers on all the time, so what the hey?—and so, despite the "do not turn it on" sign I'd left on it, the computer merrily melted itself down while I lectured in Amsterdam. By the time I returned, the hard disk had self-destructed, as had the Ethernet card in it.

It's actually pretty amazing what *didn't* die in the system. The CPU (a 50 MHz 486DX) still runs to this day, as does the Adaptec 1742 SCSI host adapter. The machine still sees service as a "test" machine, but it stays nice and cool. How? Simple. Other than the memory, CPU, SCSI host adapter, and display board, there's nothing in it. The hard disk and CD-ROM are external devices, with their own fans. It's not a bad idea to do this to help your computer keep its cool.

Heat Sensor Devices

Now, I could have avoided this problem altogether with a 110 Twinalert from a company called PC Power and Cooling Systems. They're a name to know when you're buying power supplies. The 110 Twinalert is a circuit board about the size of a business card that plugs into a floppy power connector. When the PC's internal temperature gets to 110 degrees F, it starts squealing, making an annoying noise. At 118 degrees F, it just shuts the computer down. The device is under $50, and every network server should have one.

While I'm on the subject of PC Power and Cooling, I should mention that the company also makes an interesting variety of power products for the PC, including power supplies with very quiet fans, power supplies with built-in battery backup, and high-quality PC cases. I use their stuff when I want to be 100 percent sure that my PC will be running when I need it.

Safe Temperature Ranges for PCs

Electronic components have a temperature range within which they are built to work. IBM suggests that its PC, for instance, is built to work in the range of 60–85 degrees F. This is because the circuit boards can run as hot as 125 degrees, but a typical machine may, again, be as much as 40 degrees hotter *inside* than outside. And 125 minus 40 yields 85 degrees, the suggested maximum temperature.

Obviously, if you've got a good fan, the acceptable range of room temperatures expands considerably. If you had a really good fan, the inside of the machine would be the same temperature as the outside. You don't want the inside of the PC to get any higher than 110 degrees—hard disks fail at that point, although, again, circuit boards can function in higher temperatures than that (so my old floppy-only laptops could function in the Gobi Desert, although I've had neither the chance nor the inclination to try it yet).

Since the temperature inside the PC is ambient plus some constant, there are two ways to cool the inside of the PC—lower the constant with a good fan, or lower the ambient temperature. Keep the room cooler and the PC will be cooler.

Heat aids the corrosion process. Corrosion is a chemical process, and chemical processes roughly *double* in speed when the temperature of the process is raised by 18 degrees F (about 10 degrees C). Chips slowly deteriorate, the hotter the faster.

How do you measure temperature and temperature changes in your PC? Simple—get a digital temperature probe. (Try Radio Shack or Edmund Scientific Corp., whose address is in Appendix C.) The easy way to use the probe is to tape it over the exit vents by the fan's power supply. An indoor/outdoor switch lets you quickly view the PC's inside temperature and ambient temperature.

Part iii

Duty Cycles

We said before that a device should get rid of heat as quickly as it creates it. Not every device is that good, however. Devices are said to have a *duty cycle*. This number—expressed as a percentage—is the proportion of the time that a device can work without burning up. For example, a powerful motor may have a 50 percent duty cycle. This means that it should be active only 50 percent of the time.

Duty cycle is used to describe active versus inactive time for many kinds of devices, although it is (strictly speaking) not correct. Some desktop laser printers, for example, will not run well if required to print continuously.

Thermal Shock

Because a PC is warmer inside than outside, changes in room temperature can become multiplied inside a PC.

This leads to a problem called *thermal shock*. Thermal shock comes from subjecting components to rapid and large changes in temperature. It can disable your computer due to expansion/contraction damage. The most common scenario for thermal shock occurs when the PC is turned on Monday morning after a winter's weekend. Many commercial buildings turn the temperature down to 55 degrees over the weekend: your office may contain some of that residual chill early Monday morning. Inside the PC, though, it may still be 55. Then you turn the machine on. Inside 30 minutes some PCs can warm up to 120 degrees. This rapid 65 degree rise in temperature over a half hour brings on thermal shock.

This is an argument for leaving the PC on 24 hours/day, seven days/week. (We'll see some more reasons to do this soon.) The temperature inside the PC will be better modulated. By the way, you can't leave portable PCs on all the time, but you should be extra careful with portables to avoid thermal shock. If your laptop has been sitting in the trunk on a cold February day, be sure to give it some time to warm up before trying to use it. And give it some time in a *dry* place, or water vapor will condense on the cold platters of your hard drive. Water on the platters is a surefire way to reduce your drive's life.

Sunbeams

Another heat effect is caused by sunbeams. Direct sunlight isn't a good thing for electronic equipment. A warm sunbeam feels nice for a few minutes, but sit in one for an hour and you'll understand why PCs don't like them. Direct sunlight is also, of course, terrible for floppy disks. Find a shadowy area, or use drapes.

Dealing with Dust

Dust is everywhere. It is responsible for several evils.

First, it sticks to the circuit boards inside your computer. As dust builds up, the entire board can become coated with a fine insulating sheath. That would be fine if the dust were insulating your house, but thermal insulation is definitely a bad thing for computers. You seek, as we have seen, to minimize impediments to thermal radiation from your computer components. To combat this, remove dust from inside the computer and from circuit boards periodically. A good period between cleaning is a year in a house and six months in an office. A simpler approach is to use the "while I'm at it" algorithm—when you need to disassemble the machine for some other reason, clean the insides while you're at it. A tool that can assist you is a can of "compressed air." Just as effective for the case and bracket assemblies is a dust-free cloth wetted with a little water and ammonia (just a few drops). Don't use the cloth on circuit boards—get a can of "compressed air" and blow the dust off.

Actually, the "compressed air" isn't compressed air, but some kind of compressed gas. Take a second look when you buy this stuff: a lot of it's freon or some other chlorinated fluorocarbon (CFC), which enlarges the hole in the ozone layer. There are a number of "ozone-friendly" alternatives. One is marketed by Chemtronics.

This should be obvious, but when you blow dust off boards, be aware of where it is going: if you can, have the vacuum cleaner nearby, or take the board to another area; then you'll have better luck. *Please* don't hold the board over the PC's chassis and blow off the dust with compressed air—all it does is move the dust, not *remove* the dust.

The second dust evil is that dust can clog spaces, like the air intake area to your power supply or hard disk or the space between the floppy disk drive head and the disk.

To combat the floppy drive problem, some manufacturers offer a floppy dust cover which you put in place when the machine is off. Unfortunately, you really need the cover when the machine is on. The reason: CRT displays attract dust. Turn your screen on, and all of the dust in the area heads straight for the display. Some of the particles get sidetracked and end up in the floppy drives. Some vendors say that the way to cut down on dust in floppy drives is to close the drive doors. This is wrong because the door *isn't* dust-tight.

A place which creates and collects paper dust is, of course, the printer. Printers should be vacuumed or blown out periodically, *away* from the computer (remember, dust goes somewhere when blown away).

Another fertile source of dust is ash particles. Most of us don't burn things indoors, *unless* we are smokers. If you smoke, fine: just don't do it near the computer. Years ago, I ran across a study by the U.S. Government Occupation Safety and Hazard Administration (OSHA) which estimated that smoke at a computer workstation cuts its life by 40 percent. That's $1200 on a $3000 workstation.

MAGNETISM

Magnets—both the permanent and electromagnetic type—can cause permanent loss of data on hard or floppy disks. The most common magnetism found in the office environment is produced by electric motors and electromagnets. A commonly overlooked electromagnet is the one in older phones that ring or chirp (rather than beep). The clapper is forced against the bell (or buzzer, if the phone has one of those) in the phone by powering an electromagnet. If you absent-mindedly put such a phone on top of a stack of floppy disks, and the phone rings, you will have unrecoverable data errors on at least the top one. Your stereo speakers can do the same thing to floppies.

Don't think you have magnets around? How about:

- Magnets to put notes on a file cabinet
- A paper clip holder with a magnet
- A word processing copy stand with a magnetic clip

Another source of magnetism is, believe it or not, a video monitor. I have seen disk drives refuse to function because they were situated inches from a monitor. X-ray machines in airports similarly produce some magnetism, although there is some controversy here. Some folks say, "Don't run floppies through the X-ray—walk them through." Others say the X-ray is okay, but the metal detector zaps floppies. Some people claim to have been burned at both. Personally, I walk through an average of three to four metal detectors per week carrying 3.5-inch floppy disks, and have never (knock wood) had a problem. My laptops have been through X-ray machines everywhere, and I've never lost a byte on the hard disk.

Airport metal detectors should be sufficiently gentle for floppies. Magnetism is measured in a unit called *gauss*—a power of 25 gauss is required to affect a 360K floppy, more for more higher-density floppies. Metal detectors *in the U.S.* (notice the stress) emit no more than 1 gauss. I'm not sure about Canada and Europe, but I notice that the fillings in my teeth seem to set off the metal detectors in the Ottawa airport.

What about preventive maintenance? For starters, get a beeping phone to minimize the chance of erasing data inadvertently. Another large source of magnetism is the motor in the printer—generally, it is not shielded (the motors on the drives don't produce very much magnetism, in case you're wondering).

Do you (or someone in your office) do a lot of word processing? Many word processors (the people kind, not the machine kind) use a copy stand that consists of a flexible metal arm and a magnet. The magnet holds the copy to be typed on the metal arm. The problem arises when it's time to change the copy. I watched a word processing operator remove the magnet (so as to change the copy), and slap the magnet on the side of the computer. It really made perfect sense—the case was iron, and held the magnet in a place that was easy to access. The only bad part was that the hard disk on that particular PC chassis was mounted on the extreme right-hand side of the case, right next to the magnet. You can start to see why I hate magnets...

Oh, and by the way, *speakers* have magnets in them. Years ago, a friend purchased a "home entertainment system," a VCR, stereo, and some monster speakers. That's when I noticed that he had stacked his videotapes on top of the speakers. I almost didn't have the heart to tell him, but I eventually advised him that his videos were history—and, sad to say, they *were*. Modern multimedia PCs all have speakers that claim to have shielded magnets; but I've got a Sony woofer/satellite speaker system that makes my monitor's image get wobbly when I put the speakers too near the monitor. No matter what the manual says, I think I'll just keep the floppies away from there.

My advice is to go on an anti-magnet crusade. Magnets near magnetic media are disasters waiting to happen.

Stray Electromagnetism

Stray electromagnetism can cause problems for your PC and, in particular, for your network. Here, I'm just referring to any electromagnetism that you don't want. It comes in several varieties.

- Radiated Electromagnetic Interference (EMI)
- Power noise and interruptions
- Electrostatic Discharge (ESD)—static electricity

Electromagnetic Interference

EMI is caused when electromagnetism is radiated or conducted somewhere that we don't want it to be. I discuss two common types—crosstalk and RFI—in the next two sections.

Part iii

Crosstalk

When two wires are physically close to each other, they can transmit interference between themselves. We're not talking about short circuits here: the insulation can be completely intact. The problem is that the interfering wire contains electronic pulses. Electronic pulses produce magnetic fields as a side effect. The wire being interfered with is touched or crossed by the magnetic fields. Magnetic fields crossing or touching a wire produce electronic pulses as a side effect. (Nature is, unfortunately, amazingly symmetrical at times like this.) The electronic pulses created in the second wire are faint copies of the pulses, i.e. the signal, from the first wire. This interferes with the signal that we're trying to send on the second wire.

Crosstalk can be a problem when bundles of wires are stored in close quarters, and the wires are data cables. There are four solutions to crosstalk:

- ▶ Move the wires farther apart (not always feasible).

- ▶ Use twisted-pair (varying the number of twists reduces crosstalk).

- ▶ Use shielded cable (the shield reduces crosstalk—don't even think of running ribbon cables for distances over six feet).

- ▶ Use fiber optic cable—it's not electromagnetic; it's photonic (is that a great word, or what?), so there's no crosstalk.

- ▶ Don't run cables over the fluorescent lights. The lights are noise emitters.

I once helped troubleshoot a network that had been installed in a classroom. The contractor had run the wires through the ceiling, but the network seemed to not work. (Ever notice how often the words "network" and "not work" end up in the same sentence? A Russian friend calls them "nyet-works.") I pushed aside the ceiling tiles and found that the cable installer had saved himself some time and money by forgoing cable trays, instead wrapping the cables around the occasional fluorescent lamp. So, on a hunch, I said to the people that I was working with, "Start the network up again," and I turned off the lights. Sure enough, it worked.

Radio Frequency Interference

Radio Frequency Interference (RFI) is high (10 KHz+) frequency radiation. It's a bad thing. Sources are:

- ▶ High-speed digital circuits, like the ones in your computer

- ▶ Nearby radio sources

▶ Cordless telephones, keyboards

▶ Power-line intercoms

▶ Motors

Worse yet, your PC can be a *source* of RFI.

RFI is bad because it can interfere with high-speed digital circuits. Your computer is composed of digital circuits. RFI can seem sinister because it seems to come and go mysteriously. Like all noise, it is an unwanted signal. How would we go about receiving a *wanted* RF signal? Simple—construct an antenna. Suppose we want to receive a signal of a given frequency? We design an antenna of a particular length. (Basically, the best length is one quarter of the wavelength.) Now suppose there is some kind of RFI floating around. We're safe as long as we can't receive it. But suppose the computer is connected to the printer with a cable that, through bad luck, happens to be the correct length to receive that RFI? The result: printer gremlins. Fortunately, the answer is simple: shorten the cable.

Electric motors are common RFI-producing culprits. I recently saw a workstation in Washington where the operator had put an electric fan (to cool *herself*, not the workstation) on top of the workstation. When the fan was on, it warped the top of the CRT's image slightly. Electric can openers, hair dryers, electric razors, electric pencil sharpeners, and printers are candidates. Sometimes it's hard to determine whether the device is messing up the PC simply by feeding back noise onto the power line (the answer there is to put the devices on separate power lines), or whether it is troubling the PC with RFI.

Your PC also *emits* RFI which can impair the functioning of other PCs, televisions, and various sensitive pieces of equipment. By law, a desktop computer cannot be sold unless it meets "Class B" specifications. The FCC requires that a device 3 meters from the PC must receive no more than the following RFI:

FREQUENCY	MAXIMUM FIELD STRENGTH (microvolts/meter)
30–88 MHz	100
89–216 MHz	150
217–1000 MHz	200

Protecting your PC from the devices around it and protecting the devices from your PC are done in the same way. If the PC doesn't leak

RFI, then it's less likely to pick up any stray RFI in the area. Any holes in the case provide entry/exit points. Use the brackets which come with the machine to plug any unused expansion slots. To prevent unplanned air circulation paths it is also a good idea to plug unused expansion slots. Ensure that the case fits together snugly and correctly. If the case includes cutouts for interface connectors, find plates to cover the cutouts or simply use metal tape.

A simple AM radio can be used to monitor RFI field strength. A portable Walkman-type radio is ideal, as it has light headphones and a small enough enclosure to allow fairly local signal strength monitoring. A cheap model is best—you don't want sophisticated noise filtering. Tune it to an area of the dial as far as possible from a strong station. Lower frequencies seem to work best. You'll hear the various devices produce noises.

The PC sounds different, depending on what it is doing. When I type, I hear a machine gun-like sound. When I ask for a text search, the fairly regular search makes a "dee-dee-dee" sound.

I've also used the radio in a number of other ways. Once, I received a new motherboard, a 486 that I was going to use to upgrade a 286 system. I installed it, and nothing happened. No beeps, no blinking cursor, nothing but the fan. So I removed the motherboard and placed it on a cardboard box (no electrical short fears with a cardboard box). Then I placed a power supply next to it, plugged in the P8/P9 connectors, and powered up. I ran the radio over the motherboard and got no response, just a constant hum. Placing the radio right over the CPU got nothing. I reasoned that what I was hearing was just the clock circuit. I felt even more certain of my guess when I noticed that the CPU had been inserted backwards into its socket. One dead motherboard, back to the manufacturer.

Power Noise

Your wall socket is a source of lots of problems. They basically fall into a few categories:

- ▶ Overvoltage and undervoltage
- ▶ No voltage at all—a power blackout
- ▶ Transients—spikes and surges

We'll look briefly at those issues in a moment. First let's look at the fourth kind of power noise, the one that *you* cause:

- ▶ Power-up power surges

In the process of discussing how to fix this, I'll have to weigh in on The Great PC Power Switch Debate.

Leave Your Machines On 24 Hours/Day

I'd like to discuss one power-related item here: user-induced power surges. What user-induced power surges, you say? Simple: every time you turn on an electrical device you get a power surge through it. Some of the greatest stresses that electrical devices receive is when turned on or turned off. When do light bulbs burn out? Think about it—they generally burn out when you first turn them on or off. One study showed that when a device is first turned on, it draws up to four to six times its normal power for less than a second. For that brief time, your PC may be pulling 600 to 900 watts—not a prescription for long PC life.

The answer? Leave your PCs on 24 hours/day, seven days/week. We've done it at my company for years. Turn the monitor off, or turn the screen intensity down, or use one of those annoying automatic screen blankers so the monitor doesn't get an image burned into it. Turn the printer off, also. Leaving the machines on also modulates temperature.

What? You're still not convinced? I know, it seems nonintuitive—most people react that way. But it really does make sense. First of all, consider the things that you keep on all the time, like:

▶ Digital clocks, which obviously run continuously, incorporate some of the same digital technology as microcomputers, and they're pretty reliable.

▶ Calculators—I've seen accountants with calculators that are on all the time.

▶ TVs (part of the TV is powered up all the time so that it can "warm up" instantly, unlike older sets).

▶ Thermostats—the temperature regulating device in your home or business is a circuit that works all the time.

Most of the things that I just named are some of the most reliable, never-think-about-them devices that you work with.

In addition to the things I've already said, consider the hard disk. Every hard disk mechanism incorporates a motor, spinning the disk at speeds between 3600 and 7200 rpm. You know from real life that it's a lot harder to start something moving than it is to keep it moving. (Ever push a car?) The cost, then, of turning hard disk motors on and off is that sometimes they just won't be able to get started.

Leaving your computer on all the time heads off thermal shock, yet another reason to leave it on. Machines should never be power cycled quickly. I've seen people fry their power supplies by turning their computers on and off several times in a 30-second period "to clear problems" and end up creating bigger problems.

A final word of caution. Leaving the machine on all the time is only a good idea if:

▶ Your machine is cooled adequately. If your machine is 100 degrees inside when the room is 70 degrees, it'll overheat when the room goes to 90 degrees on summer weekends when the building management turns off the cooling in your building. Make sure your machine has a good enough fan to handle higher temperatures.

▶ You have adequate surge protection. Actually, you shouldn't run the machine at all unless you have adequate surge protection.

▶ You have fairly reliable power. If you lose power three times a week, there's no point in leaving the machines on all the time— the power company is turning them off and on for you. Even worse, the power just after a power outage is noise-filled.

Before moving on, let's take a quick peek at the other kinds of power problems.

Transients

A transient is any brief change in power that doesn't repeat itself. It can be an undervoltage or an overvoltage. Sags (momentary undervoltage) and surges (momentary overvoltage) are transients. Being brief, the transient may be of a high enough frequency that it slips right past the protective capacitors, and whatever is in your power supply, and punches holes in your chips. (No, they're not holes you can see, at least not without some very good equipment.) Transients have a cumulative effect—the first 100 may do nothing. Eventually, however, enough chickens come home to roost that your machine decides, one day, to go on vacation. Permanently.

Overvoltage

We say that we have an "overvoltage condition" when we get more than the rated voltage for a period greater than 2.5 seconds. Such a voltage measurement is done as a moving average over several seconds. Chronic overvoltage is just as bad for your system as transient overvoltage: the chips can fail as a result of it.

Undervoltage

Summer in much of the country means air conditioners are running full blast, and the power company is working feverishly to meet the power demands that they bring. Sometimes it can't meet the full needs, however, and so announces a reduction in voltage called a brownout.

Brownouts are bad for large motors, such as you'd find in a compressor for refrigeration. They make your TV screen look shrunken. And they confuse power supplies. A power supply tries to provide continuous power to the PC. Power equals voltage times current. If the voltage drops and you want constant power, what do you do? Simple: draw more current. But drawing more current through a given conductor heats up the conductor. The power supply and the chips get hot, and may overheat.

Surge protectors can't help you here. A power conditioner can—it uses a transformer to compensate for the sagging voltage.

NOTE

In *The Complete PC Upgrade and Maintenance Guide*, Mark Minasi devotes an entire chapter to the topic of power supplies and power protection. There he evaluates the three most common types of protective devices: surge protectors; power conditioners; and backup power supplies, such as Standby Power Supply (SPS) and Universal Power Supply (UPS) devices. For most home and small-office users, a power conditioner may be the best compromise.

Part iii

Electrostatic Discharge

Electrostatic discharge—ESD, or, as you probably know it, static electricity—is annoyingly familiar to anyone who has lived through a winter indoors. The air is very dry (winter and forced hot-air ducts bring relative humidity to around 20 percent in my house, for example), and is an excellent insulator. You build up a static charge, and keep it. In the summer, when relative humidity can be close to 100 percent (I live in a suburb of Washington, D.C., a city built over a swamp), you build up static charges also, but they leak away quickly due to the humidity of the air. Skin resistance has a lot to do with dissipating charges, also. The resistance of your skin can be as little as 1,000 ohms when wet and 500,000 ohms when dry.

You know how static electricity is built up. Static can damage chips if it creates a charge of 200 volts or more. If a static discharge is sufficient for the average person to notice it, it is 2000 volts.

Scuffing across a shag rug in February can build up 50,000 volts. This is an electron "debt" which must be paid. The next metal item (metal gives up electrons easily) pays the debt with an electric shock. If it's 50,000 volts, why aren't you electrocuted when you touch the metal? Simple. Fortunately, the amperage—and the power—is tiny. Different materials generate more or less static. Many people think that certain materials are static-prone, while others are not. As it turns out, materials have a triboelectric value. Two materials rubbed together will generate static in direct proportion to how far apart their triboelectric values are.

Some common materials, in order of their triboelectric values, are:

► Air

► Human skin

► Glass

► Human hair

► Silk

► Paper

► Cotton

► Hard rubber

► Nickel and copper

► Polyester

► Silicon

► Teflon

Once an item is charged, the voltage potential between it and another object is proportional to the distance between it and the other item on the scale. For instance, suppose I charge a glass rod with a cotton cloth. The glass will attract things below it on the scale, like paper, but will attract more strongly things below paper.

Why does static damage PC components? The chips which largely comprise circuit boards are devices that can be damaged by high voltage, even if at low current. The two most common families of chips are CMOS (Complementary Metal Oxide Semiconductor) and TTL (Transistor-Transistor

Logic). TTLs are an older family. TTLs are faster switching—potentially faster chips (memories, CPUs and such) could be designed with TTL—but TTL has a fatal flaw: it draws a lot of juice. TTL chips need much more electricity than CMOS chips, so they create more heat.

CPUs and memories are all CMOS. This has a lower theoretical maximum speed, but it runs on a lot less power. Sadly, that also means that it is more subject to static electricity problems. TTL chips can withstand considerably more static than CMOS chips. CMOS chips can be destroyed by as little as 250 volts.

Even if static doesn't destroy a chip, it can shorten its life. Static is, then, something to be avoided if possible. Another effect occurs when the static is discharged. When the fat blue spark jumps from your finger to the doorknob, a small ElectroMagnetic Pulse (EMP) is created. This isn't too good for chips, either. (It's the thing you've heard about that could cause a single nuclear explosion to destroy every computer in the country, except a lot smaller.) The easiest way I get rid of my static is to discharge the static buildup on something metal that is not the computer's case. A metal desk or table leg is good, and it's a good idea to leave the power supply plugged in when disassembling a PC; touch the power supply, and you drain off your charges.

For your firm, however, you may want something a trifle more automatic. The options are:

- ▶ Raise the humidity with a humidifier (evaporative, not ultrasonic—ultrasonic creates dust).

- ▶ Raise the humidity with plants, or perhaps an aquarium.

- ▶ Install static-free carpet.

- ▶ Put anti-static "touch me" mats under the PCs.

- ▶ Make your own anti-static spray (see below).

From the point of view of comfort, I recommend the first option strongly. Your employees don't feel dried-out, and the static problem disappears. Raise humidity to just 50 percent and the problem will go away.

You can make inexpensive, homemade anti-static spray. Just get a spray pump bottle and put about an inch of fabric softener in it. Fill it the rest of the way with water, shake it up, and you've got a spray for your carpets to reduce static. Just spritz it on the rug, and the rug will smell nice, and everyone will know that you've been busy. (I hear you asking, "How long does it last?" You'll know.)

In a similar vein, a person from a temporary services agency once told me that they tell their word processing operators to put a sheet of Bounce under the keyboard to reduce static.

Technicians who must work with semiconductors all of the time use a ground strap to minimize ESD. The idea with a ground strap is that you never create a spark—and therefore EMP—because you've always got a nice ground connection that's draining off your charges. A good ground strap is an elastic wristband with a metal plate built into it to provide good electrical connection, attached to a wire with an alligator clip. You put the clip on something grounded—the power supply case is the most common place—and put the strap around your wrist. As you're connected to a ground, you continuously drain off your charges.

When you must handle electronic components, take these precautions:

▶ Get an anti-static strap.

▶ If you don't have an anti-static strap, just leave the power supply plugged in and touch the power supply case before touching any component.

▶ Reduce the amount of static that you transfer to a chip with a ground strap, or remember the high-tech equivalent of knocking wood—touch unpainted metal periodically.

▶ Don't handle components in areas having high static potential. For example, avoid carpets unless they are anti-static or low humidity environments. Don't wear an acrylic sweater when changing chips. Get leather-soled shoes. If your work environment allows it, you can really avoid static by removing your shoes and socks.

▶ Don't handle chips any more than is necessary. If you don't touch them, you won't hurt them.

▶ Use the anti-static protective tubes and bags to transport and store chips.

▶ If possible, pick up components by their bodies. Don't touch the pins any more than necessary.

▶ Use an anti-static mat.

Use the proper precautions, and your PC won't get a big "charge" out of being touched by you.

AVOIDING WATER AND LIQUIDS

Water is an easier hazard to detect and avoid. You don't need any sophisticated detection devices. Shielding is unnecessary—you just keep the computer away from water. Water and liquids are introduced into a computer system in one of several ways:

- Operator spills
- Leaks
- Flooding

Spills generally threaten the keyboard. One remedy—the one recommended by every article and book I've ever read on maintenance—is to forbid liquids near the computer. For most of us, this is unrealistic. Some people use clear flexible plastic covers on the keyboard, kind of like what Burger King uses on their cash registers. With one of these keyboard "skins," you might say that you can "practice safe typing."

SafeSkin is offered by Merritt Computer Products in Dallas. Their address is in the Vendor's Guide appendix. They offer versions for the various odd keyboards in the PC world.

On the other hand, should someone spill a Coke in a keyboard without one of these covers, all is not lost, so long as you act quickly! Disconnect the keyboard and flush it out at a nearby sink. Let it dry thoroughly and it'll be good as new. The correct way to do this is to use deionized, filtered water. In actuality, the tap water that you find in most parts of North America is clean enough that you'll end up doing more good than harm by simply using the water out of the tap. If, on the other hand, the smell of rotten eggs lingers in your bathroom after every shower, then I'd think about using some cleaner water for component flushing.

A similar disaster, flooding, sometimes occurs. Don't assume that flooded components are destroyed components. Disassemble the computer and clean the boards by cleaning the contacts and edge connectors: you can buy connector cleaner fluids, or some people use a hard white artist's eraser—do not use pencil erasers! (A Texas Instruments study showed that they contain acids that do more harm than good to connectors.) Blow out crevices with compressed air.

Avoid floods by thinking ahead. Don't store any electrical devices directly on the floor; they'll be damaged when the floor is cleaned. Generally, flooding indoors is under six inches. Be aware of flooding from improper roofing; when installing PCs, don't put one in just under the suspicious stain on the ceiling. ("Oh, that—it was fixed two years ago. No problem now.")

Corrosion

Liquids (and gases) can accelerate corrosion of PCs and PC components. Corrosive agents include:

- Salt sweat in skin oils
- Water
- Airborne sulfuric acid, salt spray, carbonic acid

Your fear here is not that the PC will fall away to rust; the largest problem that corrosion causes is oxidation of circuit contacts. When a device's connector becomes oxidized, it doesn't conduct as well, and so the device does not function, or—worse—malfunctions sporadically. Salt in sweat can do this, so be careful when handling circuit boards; don't touch edge connectors unless you have to. This is why some firms advertise that they use gold edge connectors; gold is resistant to corrosion.

Carbonated liquids include carbonic acid, and coffee and tea contain tannic acids. The sugar in soda is eaten by bacteria who leave behind conductive excrement—like hiring some germs to put new traces on your circuit board. Generally, try to be very careful with drinks around computers.

Don't forget cleaning fluids. Be careful with that window cleaner you're using to keep the display clean. If your PC is on a pedestal on the floor, and the floor is mopped each day, some of the mopping liquid gets into the PC. Cleaning fluids are very corrosive.

You can clean edge connectors with either hard white erasers or connector cleaner products. One of the best-known vendors of these products is Texwipe. You can get a catalog of their products by writing to them at their address in Appendix C.

MAKING THE ENVIRONMENT "PC FRIENDLY"

Let's sum up what we've seen in this chapter. Protect your PC by doing the following:

- Check power considerations:
    - No heating elements (Mr. Coffee, portable heaters) in the same outlet as a PC

- ▶ No large electric motors (refrigerators, air conditioners) on the same line as the PC

- ▶ Some kind of power noise protection

▶ Check temperature ranges:

- ▶ Maximum 110 degrees F (43 degrees C)

- ▶ Minimum 65 degrees F (18 degrees C)

The minimum temperature can be considerably lower so long as the computer remains *on* all of the time.

- ▶ Heavy dust—you can buy (from PC Power and Cooling) power supplies with a filtered fan that suck air in through the *back* rather than the usual approach of pulling it in through the front.

- ▶ Make sure there isn't a vibration source like an impact printer on the same table as the hard disk.

- ▶ Make sure you're familiar with or (if you're a support person) teach your users about:

  - ▶ Leaving the machines on all the time

  - ▶ Keeping cables screwed in and out of the way

  - ▶ Basic "don't do this" things in DOS, like formatting the hard disk

▶ Protect against static electricity.

WHAT'S NEXT?

Now that Mark Minasi has shown you how to protect your computer hardware against the most common environmental hazards, in the next three chapters the PC Novice/Smart Computing staff and Robert Cowart will show you how to install RAM, multimedia devices, and modems.

Part iii

Chapter 24

INSTALLING RANDOM ACCESS MEMORY

In the old days of computing with DOS, PC users didn't need to know much about memory. If a problem with memory developed, they could adjust the settings in the AUTOEXEC.BAT and CONFIG.SYS files and reboot the computer. If they wanted more memory, they installed a memory card and ran a memory management program. That's not the case now. Almost nobody runs just DOS anymore.

In fact, most people are using at least Windows 95, and you either plan to install Windows 98 or already own it. Needless to say, Windows 98 is a far cry from Windows 3.*x* in the memory management arena, but there are still things to keep in mind. Of course, there's the universal truth in computing, "Lack of RAM means lack of productivity," especially in an older system. If you don't have enough memory, your computer will run sluggishly, even with a fast Pentium processor.

Adapted from *PC Upgrading & Maintenance: No Experience Required*, by the staff of PC Novice/Smart Computing.
ISBN 0-7821-2137-3   544 pages $24.99

THE FASTEST, EASIEST UPGRADE OF ALL

So, if you want to improve your computer's operation, feed it a healthy diet of more memory. No other upgrade will better enhance your computer's performance, whether it is an older system or a blazing new 333 megahertz (MHz) Pentium II. With Windows 3.1x, you needed 4MB of random access memory (RAM). Although that was a big jump in memory needs compared to the 640KB required by the early DOS-based computers, Windows limped along on 4MB. Pop another 4MB and Windows 3.1 ran much better. With Windows 95, you needed at least 8MB of RAM to handle all the advanced graphical tasks and to run one or two programs at a time.

Windows 98 Needs at Least 16MB

To get satisfactory performance from Windows 98, your computer needs at least 16MB of RAM, and probably 32 (of course, if you're a graphics, multimedia, or video professional you'll most likely opt for 128MB of RAM, or more!). Windows manages available memory by sharing what it needs to run multiple programs, print files, operate the diskette drives and monitor, and so on. When it runs low on memory, Windows converts the overflowing data into a temporary file, called a *Windows swap file*, in space it reserves on the hard drive. As you can imagine, offloading data to and then retrieving it from the hard drive takes a toll on the computer's efficiency because getting data from the hard drive is a considerably slower process than retrieving something from RAM. When there is a large supply of RAM, however, Windows can bypass the swap file on the hard drive and maintain its speed.

Many computing novices confuse the capacity of the hard drive and the amount of RAM a computer has. Aside from electricity, memory is what drives your computer. The size of the hard drive only limits how many programs and how much data you can save to it. Having an overly large hard drive for storage won't help much if your computer is starving for memory.

It is relatively easy to install more memory. Even if you've never ventured inside a computer, you can slip more RAM chips into the waiting slots on the motherboard.

TIP

The Section "Steps to Installing RAM" walks you through the process of installing RAM.

Choosing Memory Modules

Memory is a vital component in all computers, but all memory isn't the same. Before you can upgrade memory, you must find out which type of memory chips your computer uses. You also must decide which kind of memory you want to upgrade.

Memory chips are measured by their RAM speed, which is the rate at which the modules work. RAM speed is expressed in nanoseconds (ns); rather than bog yourself down in technical definitions, remember simply that the smaller the number of nanoseconds, the faster the chip. You can install slower RAM than the other chips in your computer if you are adding to what's already there. But you cannot install a faster chip than your computer is rated to use. Check your computer's documentation to see which type and memory speed the system needs. You'll have to buy chips in multiples equal to the total memory you want. For instance, if you have 4MB now and need to upgrade to 16MB, see how many vacant memory slots there are. If the existing 4MB module is in one slot and there is only one slot remaining, you have to remove the existing module and buy two 8MB modules, one for each socket.

Here are the RAM types you'll encounter:

▶ **DRAM**   Dynamic random access memory. This is the most common and cheapest type of memory chip. This is also the slowest type of memory because it is made up of capacitors. The computer must constantly refresh its memory by recharging the capacitors. Usually DRAM chips are hard-wired to the motherboard and can't be removed without an expert's help. You can only add more chips in the available accessory slot.

▶ **SRAM**   Static random access memory. This memory chip is made of transistors, which do not need refreshing. Because it doesn't need constant refreshing, SRAM is about four times faster than DRAM. SRAM chips are larger than other types of memory so they are used to meet only some of the memory needs in a computer.

Part iii

▶ **EDO RAM**   Extended data out random access memory. This is the fastest, but is not necessarily the most expensive memory chip anymore. It handles memory access about 30 times faster than SRAM because it can move data in and out from different addresses at the same time.

▶ **VRAM**   Video random access memory. VRAM is used on video boards. It is much like DRAM but has a second port to speed up the access time. Adding more video memory speeds up the time it takes the motherboard to place colors, images, and text on-screen. If the video board is slow (meaning it only has 1MB of memory), the computer's motherboard has to spend too much time creating the image on-screen. The result is a slower response to programs and other functions.

When you upgrade RAM, you must add more of the same type of memory modules. For example, if your computer has DRAM, you cannot replace it with faster SRAM or EDO RAM chips because the electronic circuits can't handle this kind of design change. However, if your video card will accept more VRAM chips, adding them will measurably speed up the computer's performance even if you don't increase the overall RAM on the motherboard.

Installing Additional RAM

Computers use three types of RAM chips, depending upon their design. Older computers used dual inline chips (DIPs) that had to be pushed directly in their sockets. DIP chips were the most difficult to install, and fortunately you will almost never encounter them in today's computers. These chips had two rows of eight "legs" called contacts. You installed them by pushing them into available receptacles. This had to be done with extreme care; if even one contact was bent during installation, your computer would not start.

The next type of computer memory to come along was the single inline memory module (SIMM), which has a single row of chips soldered to a narrow circuit card with contacts on the bottom edge. SIMMs come in several varieties: 30-pin, 72-pin, and 168-pin. To install them, hold the SIMM at an angle to match the plane of the holder in the socket. Then align the plastic pin in the socket with the hole at one end of the SIMM; SIMMs only fit in the socket one way. Push the metal contacts at the bottom of the SIMM into the socket. Finally, press the SIMM firmly into the socket, and press the SIMM back until the tabs on either side slide into position.

The more common type of memory now is the dual inline memory module (DIMM), but if you have an older PC that doesn't meet the latest design standards, you won't have this type. DIMMs are installed the same way as SIMMs, but are thicker than SIMMs because the chips are stacked one atop another. The advantage is that DIMMs can provide more memory per module at only a slightly higher cost than SIMMs.

WARNING

Before you touch the inside of the computer or handle the memory chips, make sure you discharge static electricity. If you don't, even a tiny static charge (unnoticeable to you) can permanently zap the electronic components. If you walk across a carpet while working on your computer, always reground yourself. Better yet, buy a grounding cord, inexpensively available at most Radio Shacks and other electronics stores. The cord attaches one end to the interior of your computer and the other end to your wrist; this provides an equal ground and protects your new equipment.

Planning Ahead

Upgrading computer memory is one of the best ways to give your system a longer, more useful life. Spending a few hundred dollars for memory is much better than buying a new computer. Memory slots are limited, though, so buy a module with enough memory to handle your future needs. Otherwise, you'll waste what you spend now if you decide to upgrade again later. Also, buy memory from a reliable dealer. Bargain basement deals can cost you big bucks if the memory chip goes bad or if it isn't the right type of memory for your computer.

As a guide, Table 24.1 summarizes the memory demands of common applications and activities. Although each category is demarcated with minimum and maximum amounts, any of the tasks discussed here can be run on less RAM than is specified. However, running these applications at or near the recommended maximum amounts helps ensure optimum performance.

Part iii

TABLE 24.1: How Much RAM Is Enough?

AMOUNT OF RAM	APPLICATIONS
16MB to 24MB	Light word processing, e-mail, and database use with one or two open applications
24MB to 32MB	Medium administrative uses such as word processing, e-mail, fax and communications, spreadsheets, and business graphics, with one or two open applications
32MB to 48MB	Light number crunching involving spreadsheets, e-mail, and accounting software, one or two open applications
48MB to 64MB	Heavy number crunching involving spreadsheet and statistical applications, large research databases, and more than three applications open at once
64MB to 96MB	Light graphics involving word processing, page layout, and illustration or graphics software with one to two applications open at once
96MB to 128MB	Medium graphics involving basic photo editing, presentation software, font packages, multimedia, word processing, page layout, illustration/graphics software, and more than three applications open at once

How to Install RAM

Here are two reasons to perform a memory upgrade. First, memory takes less than 10 minutes to install. And second, it can help even a weak computer immensely. That's because random access memory (RAM) is like a large library where the CPU comes to gather the data it needs to make the applications run. As mentioned above, the more RAM your PC has, the less time the CPU has to spend searching for data in the swap file, which switches some of the data from RAM to the hard drive. The less swapping you do, the faster the CPU works.

A few years ago, the average PC was equipped with 4MB of RAM. That standard was upped to 8MB, and then to 16MB. A good number of new machines today come with 32 or more Megabytes of RAM. Users who play computer games or work with desktop publishing programs might need as much as 128MB of RAM, though. Along with the progression of RAM size, chip technology has changed to the point where it's become fairly difficult to know what type of RAM is needed. "EDO," "parity," "non-parity," "single inline memory modules," and "dual inline memory modules" are some of the phrases you'll need to understand. The irony is that it's actually more difficult and time-consuming to become familiar with these terms than it is to install RAM on your PC.

NOTE

Parity RAM is a type of memory that included an extra bit (a small piece of data) to every byte to "verify" the data as it was moved around. Since RAM has been greatly improved and is much more reliable, Parity RAM is very difficult to find and not really necessary. If someone tells you that you need Parity RAM, tell them you know what's what.

Finding the Current Amount of RAM

There are three ways to discover how much memory is now in your computer.

▶ Type **mem** at the DOS prompt. Look under the Total column for the amount of memory you have. The amount will be listed in kilobytes (KB); eliminate the numbers after the comma to convert it to megabytes. For example, if the amount is 16,192KB, remove the 192 and add MB to the 16. You have 16MB of RAM.

▶ Right-click the My Computer icon on the Windows 95 Desktop. From the menu that appears, click Properties. The amount of memory your PC has will appear on-screen.

TIP

In the old days you could watch the screen as the PC booted up. The BIOS, which is built into a computer's circuitry, controls the start-up routines for peripheral devices, such as the keyboard, display, and disk drives, and runs a diagnostic test on the PC's peripheral hardware. In the process, it told you how much RAM you had. This is still true today, but if you have anything over a 100 MHz Pentium computer you probably can't read it. Why? It flashes by too fast to read!

Part iii

NOTE

Adding memory will help a computer only so much. For example, we upgraded from 32MB to 64MB of RAM. After the upgrade, we saw improved performance but only by about an additional 5% (compared to the 30% increase when we jumped from 16MB to 32MB). Despite the infusion of RAM, performance was limited by the 133 megahertz (MHz) CPU installed in our PC. Therefore, you may be better off saving the money to invest in a newer computer.

Regardless of the limitations inherent in increasing your PC's RAM, there are obvious benefits to this type of upgrade RAM. For example, tests show that a 133MHz Intel Pentium processor with 32MB of RAM will easily outperform a 166MHz Pentium with 8MB of RAM. (Of course, a 166Mhz Pentium system with 8MB of RAM is practically worthless anyway.)

First Step: Open Up

There's an easy way and a hard way to know what kind of RAM you need to buy for your upgrade. The easy way is to go to the computer manual and research what kind of memory is already inside the PC. The more complicated way is to open your computer's case and determine what type of memory you need by investigating the chips that are already there.

Since the easy way needs little explanation, let's focus on the difficult path. The first step in locating your RAM is to close all open applications and turn off the power to your PC. Also, as an extra precaution, you should unplug the computer and all its peripherals. (You can leave the plugs connected to the back of your computer and devices, but remove all the plugs from their electrical sockets. This will eliminate the possibility of your getting zapped by an electrical surge.) Then remove the case to prepare for installation.

Try to determine which screws (if any) you need to unscrew in order to remove the case. Most systems will have screws running along the very edge of their cases. These are the screws you need to remove. On the system we upgraded, we didn't have to remove any screws; the case slid off after pinching two tabs in front. Your computer might be configured similarly. Make sure you don't remove any screws near your computer's fan, electrical connection, or ports—all of which can be found at the rear of the system. After the screws are removed, slide the cover toward the front or back to remove it. Ground yourself by touching the computer's metal case or power supply box or by using a grounding strap (available at your local Radio Shack).

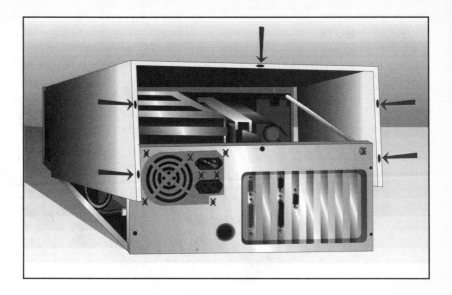

Finding the RAM

Now we can begin to explain what you might be looking for. The first items to locate are single or double inline memory modules (SIMMs or DIMMs), which are slender circuit boards dedicated to storing RAM. They're usually green with a row of rectangular, gray chips attached to them. SIMMs fit into sockets that have metal clips on either end. The sockets are usually located near the CPU on the motherboard (see Figure 24.1). We had to remove the power supply on our computer to access the SIMMs. Other computers may allow straight access to the SIMMs.

NOTE

If your computer is less than a year old you will most likely find DIMMs, but the majority of computers out there still use SIMMs. For this reason, we will use SIMMs in all the descriptions here. Just keep in mind that RAM installation works on the same principles, regardless of type, so if you have a 80386 DX33 with 30-pin SIMMs you would install new RAM in the same way as with a day-old Pentium II 333MHz machine.

If you have a newer computer (that is one powered by a Pentium or an IBM PowerPC microprocessor), it will have dual inline memory modules (DIMMs) instead of SIMMs.

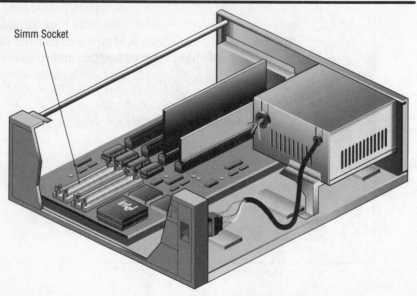

FIGURE 24.1: The SIMM Sockets are usually long, white parallel channels.

You'll be able to tell the difference between the SIMMs and DIMMs by the number of pins on each type of module. The two types of SIMMs are 30- and 72-pin modules (see Figure 24.2). DIMMs for desktop PCs come in a 168-pin variety and currently are slightly more expensive than regular 72-pin SIMMs.

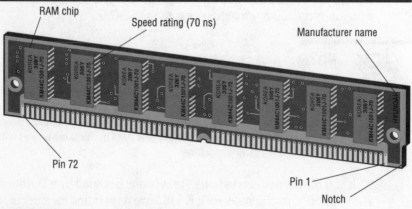

FIGURE 24.2: A typical 4MB 72-pin SIMM

A pin is a metal attachment on the module that allows data to pass from the PC to the rows of memory chips. Pins look like little fingers running along the bottom of the module. The number of pins is crucial because 30-, 72-, and 168-pin modules will be different lengths, and consequently are incompatible with one another. In short, you must have the correct number of pins on your module or the RAM won't fit into your computer's sockets.

No Room for More Modules

When you find the RAM sockets in your system, you may discover that the PC has no memory modules. In this case, your computer is hard-wired with a small amount of RAM on the motherboard, and you'll have to look in the user's manual to determine the type of RAM your system requires. On the other hand, you may find that your system doesn't have any empty sockets. This doesn't necessarily mean that you can't add more RAM. You'll just have to take out some of the modules already in place.

Before you do this, we need to issue one caveat. Some computers require sockets to work in tandem, meaning that two sockets must have memory modules in place in order to function. This requirement is called a *bank*. A bank of RAM could be one socket, two sockets, or four sockets. If a computer requires a two-socket bank, but only has one socket filled with SIMMs, it will fail to boot up.

Solving a RAM Space Crunch

How can you tell which type of banks your computer requires? Here's a shortcut: If you have an older computer—one with an early-model 486 CPU—it probably has a four-socket bank of 30-pin modules. Late-model 486s require one socket of 72-pin modules. Computers equipped with Pentium chips require two sockets of 72-pin modules.

NOTE

DIMMs can be installed individually, but to take full advantage of interleaving (a technology that reduces the amount of time the microprocessor must wait to access RAM), they must be installed in tandem.

Another shortcut is to deduce what kind of module you have by what is already in the PC. Assuming that you've never upgraded your RAM before, if your computer has two sockets of memory modules, it's likely that your computer has a two-socket bank. If all four of the sockets are

Part iii

filled, the PC probably has a four-socket bank. If only one is filled, the PC has a single-socket bank. To be absolutely safe, call the manufacturer, ask a salesperson, or consult the user's manual.

OKAY, NOW FOR A MATH QUIZ

Let's say you have a Pentium-equipped computer, and you want to add 16MB of RAM to it. You could buy one module of 16MB, but you would be making a mistake. Why? Because one module will fill only one socket, and from our discussion here, we know that Pentium-equipped computers must have two sockets filled. Thus, we must buy two modules of 8MB, which equals the 16MB we desire.

Proper Identification

Here are four other things that you'll need to know when buying memory for your computer.

Access Speed The speed rating of the memory chip is measured in nanoseconds. For the CPU and RAM to communicate, they have to have matching speeds. Memory chips are rated at 60, 70, and 80 nanoseconds (ns).

To find the access speed of your system, find the tiny numbers and letters printed on the side of your memory chips. There's usually a series of characters followed by a dash and then a number. The number will be the chip's access speed. If there's only a one-digit number, such as a six, seven, or eight, that's okay; these numbers represent 60, 70, or 80.

NOTE

It's okay to add faster chips but not slower ones. And in this case, the lower number is faster (that is, 60ns is faster than 70ns)

EDO or Non-EDO This is something that mainly applies to owners of Pentium-equipped computers. EDO stands for extended data out, which is a shortcut designed in some RAM chips to decrease the amount of time the CPU and memory interact. Putting EDO chips in a non-EDO computer won't do any harm. Putting non-EDO chips in an EDO computer won't hurt anything either; however, the computer won't boot up, or it will operate more slowly than if you used the proper EDO chips.

Tin or Gold Pins are composed of one or the other of these elements. You'll want to be consistent with the materials in your computer. Mainly, it's the high-end PCs that have modules with pins made of gold. A failure to match metals properly will deteriorate the connections in a computer.

Time to Change

After you've purchased the RAM, it's time to install it. Here are the steps you'll need to follow:

1. Ground yourself again by touching the computer's metal case or power supply box (you bought a grounding strap, didn't you?). Remove the module from its antistatic bag, being careful not to touch any metal parts on the chip. Try to hold the module from the sides.

2. One end of the module has a small notch so you know which way to align it in the socket. The socket has two posts, one on each side. One of these posts has a small plastic tab at its base that will just fit the notch of the module. Depending on the socket type, you'll need to bring the module in either horizontally or at an angle, then lift it to an upright position. On our computer, we pushed the module into the socket at a 45-degree angle, then moved it to a vertical position (see Figure 24.3). You shouldn't have to push very hard to get the module into the socket.

3. When the module is in place, two metal prongs attached to the plastic posts should fit evenly into the slot; one end should not be higher than the other. If everything looks okay, replace whatever components you had to move to install the RAM. You might want to test the machine before replacing the cover.

You'll possibly receive some sort of error message from the BIOS as your computer boots up. All BIOS setup programs are a little different, so you should follow the directions on-screen or in the user's manual. The bottom line is that your computer needs you to update the amount of memory it now has. The setup program might detect the amount of new RAM automatically or you might have to enter the new value yourself.

Part iii

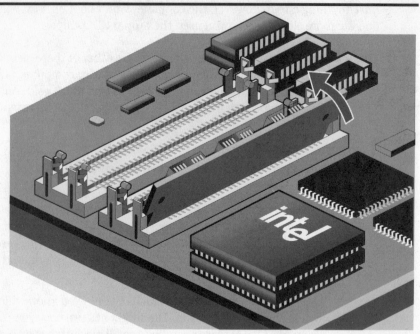

FIGURE 24.3: SIMMs are installed at an angle, then snapped into the metal clip holders.

If you try to boot your PC and nothing happens or your computer recognizes an amount of memory less than you installed, go back over the checklists above to ensure that you are using the right type of memory for your system. If that doesn't shed some light on the problem, try to reseat each of the modules following the steps above.

Once everything is working correctly, you should find that your applications run faster, and your computer generally performs better. And if nothing else, at least you won't have to worry about RAM prices for a while.

What's Next?

In the next chapter, best-selling Windows author (and self-confessed gadget freak) Robert Cowart offers tips for upgrading your hardware to take advantage of the extensive support that Windows 98 provides for multimedia. You'll get a quick look at the hardware involved, and you'll evaluate which of the three basic approaches to upgrading makes sense for you—buying a whole new computer, buying an integrated upgrade kit, or buying components separately.

Chapter 25

UPGRADING TO MULTIMEDIA

With Windows 3.*x*, working with multimedia required purchasing Microsoft's Multimedia upgrade kit or buying an expensive and hard-to-find MPC (multimedia PC). MPCs were manufactured by only a few vendors and were not generally available on the clone market. Whether upgrading an existing computer or buying an MPC, the results were about the same: you got the Microsoft multimedia extensions (drivers), a CD-ROM drive, audio card, and a good VGA video card. Either solution was pricey, often amounting to thousands of dollars, and in the end you didn't have much to write home about.

Beginning in Windows 95, Microsoft started to bundle multimedia drivers with their operating systems and to include related utility programs (such as Sound Recorder) in the hope that this would accelerate the development of multimedia Windows applications. Setting up the MPC specification helped set some

Adapted from *Mastering Windows 98*, by Robert Cowart
ISBN 0-7821-1961-1   1,184 pages $34.99
Order this book at www.masteringwindows.com

standards for what a multimedia PC should look and act like, and the PC add-on market did the rest. A vast profusion of multimedia hardware, applications, and utilities have subsequently become prevalent, many of which are now incorporated into Windows 98.

The magazines now inundate us with ads for newer and faster CD-ROM drives, 128-bit coprocessed video cards, high-resolution energy-efficient monitors, and fancy sound cards—some even have samples of real orchestral instruments built in. The MPC moniker has fallen by the wayside, and now what's really more important is whether a system is fully Windows 9x-compatible or not. After that, the rest is icing on the cake: How big is the screen, how good do the speakers sound, how clear is the image, and overall, how fast does the *whole system* (not just the CPU chip) perform? You'll have to rely on the magazines for these kinds of test comparisons. Don't rely on the guys in the store. One brand of 166-MHz Pentium machine might actually be faster than another one that's got a 233-MHz Pentium under the hood, because of the vagaries of hard-disk controllers, type of internal bus, memory caching, or speed of the video card.

If you already own a multimedia-ready machine with a couple of speakers and a CD-ROM drive, you could actually skip this chapter and go back to Chapter 9, particularly the section "Supplied Multimedia Applications and Utilities." But if you don't have such a machine, and you're thinking about endowing your machine with the gift of gab, some fancy video graphics capabilities, and the ability to watch TV or play DVDs, stay on track here.

THREE WAYS TO UPGRADE

There are three basic ways to upgrade your computer: buy a whole new computer, buy an "upgrade-in-a-box," or mix and match new components that exactly fit your needs. As of this writing, there were about twenty upgrade-in-a-box products to choose from. You'll typically get a CD-ROM drive, speakers, a sound card, a microphone, and maybe some CDs in the package. The sound card has the SCSI (Small Computer Systems Interface, pronounced "scuzzy") connector that hooks the CD-ROM drive to the computer. Mixing and matching is for us total control-freak geeks who must have the best or who don't like the idea of other people controlling our purchase decisions. The obvious downside is that sorting through the sea of components in the marketplace is a big waste of time. I've spent too many hours testing video boards, trying to get a SCSI upgrade to my sound card to work with my CD-ROM drive, or running around listening to speakers. In any case, here are a few points about the pros and cons of the three upgrade routes.

In your shopping, you may wonder what the minimal requirements of a multimedia system should be. With the technology changing so quickly, it's hard to predict what the pickings will look like a year from now and what the latest and greatest version of Riven (or some other multimedia game you'll want) will crave in the way of MM nuts and bolts. Still, here's Bob's rule of thumb about buying new computer stuff:

> **The best balance between price and performance lies just in the wake of the technology wave.**

That is, if price is an issue, eschew the cutting edge! State-of-the-art gear is too expensive and usually still has some bugs to be worked out or ends up becoming an "industry standard" with a half-life of about nine months before being dropped like a hot potato. When a product hits the mainstream, that's the time to buy; prices usually take a nosedive at that point, often by about 50 percent.

APPROACHES TO MULTIMEDIA UPGRADING

Here's a quick summary of your options in multimedia upgrading.

NEW COMPUTER

What is it? A whole computer system that is designed for multimedia Windows 98 from the ground up and includes a fairly zippy computer, color screen, speakers, microphone, sound card, fast video display card capable of TV tuning and video capture, built-in Zip drive, and a CD-ROM drive. Options will be CD writers and DVD players.

Who should buy? Any owner of an older computer who has already decided to purchase a new computer either because the existing computer isn't worth upgrading to a faster CPU and larger hard disk, or because an additional computer is needed.

How much hassle? No hassle. Everything is installed and working. Get the system with Windows 98 installed and working if you can, and you're really set.

Advantages? Low hassle factor. You can start getting work done instead of poring over magazines and manuals. Your church (or kid) gets your old computer (which means you get an easy tax write-off), you get more sleep, and you have only one vendor to deal with at service time.

CONTINUED ➡

Part iii

Disadvantages?   You have to buy a whole new system. You'll probably be compromising somewhat on the components for the low hassle factor.

Price?   Less than $2000 for most systems, which is not much more for a multimedia system than for those without multimedia. A few hundred additional dollars is typical. Tricked-out systems with all options and lots of memory and a large hard disk will be between $3000 and $4000.

KIT IN A BOX

What is it?   A box of stuff you get at a computer store or by mail order. Everything works together and costs less than $200. Includes a sound card, CD-ROM drive, microphone, and speakers. (For more money you can get a DVD drive instead of a CD-ROM drive. Most DVD drives can play normal CDs as well as DVD disks.)

Who should buy?   The average owner of a nonmultimedia computer that's acceptably endowed in terms of the CPU and hard disk (e.g., a Pentium and 1GB hard disk or larger) but needs multimedia capability to run multimedia games and standard productivity applications.

How much hassle?   You'll have to remove the cover to the computer, remove some screws, insert a couple of cards, hook up some cables and the CD-ROM drive (if the drive is the internal type), and then hook up the speakers. If the cards and computer are not Plug-and-Play compatible, you'll have to make IRQ and DMA settings. This may take some homework. You might have conflicts with existing hardware; if so you should have Windows 98 detect and install drivers for the new hardware, or use supplied drivers.

Disadvantages?   Installing it will take some work, unless it comes from the same people who made your computer (e.g., a Dell upgrade to a Dell computer). Again, some compromise on the components is likely. You may not have the best-sounding speakers, fastest video, greatest color depth, or CD-ROM drive.

Price?   Typically between $150 and $300 for fast CD-ROM drive, 16-bit sound card, speakers, and a few extras.

CONTINUED ➡

MIX AND MATCH COMPONENTS

What is it? CD-ROM drive, optional DVD drive, sound board, speakers, microphone, cabling, and possibly necessary software drivers. Purchase parts separately. $300-$500. Add an additional $300 minimum for a CD writer.

Who should buy? A power user who wants the best selection of components—or who already has one or two essential components, such as a CD-ROM drive, and now wants the rest. May be a professional (such as a musician, application developer, or graphic artist) who needs one element of the multimedia upgrade to be of very high quality.

How much hassle? About the same amount of hassle as a box upgrade, but you'll have to deal with separate documentation for each component and figure out how to get everything working together, unless they are Plug-and-Play components. IRQ and DMA conflicts are likely otherwise.

Advantages? You can have exactly what you want. 24-bit True-Color graphics, direct video capturing, video conferencing, great sound, superfast display at 1,600 by 1,280—you name it.

Disadvantages? Price and installation hassle can be high, but PnP is making things much easier. Multiple dealers to reckon with at service time.

Price? Difficult to predict. Bottom-of-the-line but functional clone parts could run you as little as a few hundred dollars. Or you could pay well into the thousands for the best brands.

Part iii

FEATURES TO LOOK FOR

What do these guidelines mean in the current market? Well the now old and crusty MPC specification requires at least a machine with 4 MB of RAM, a 130-MB hard disk, and a fast processor such as a 486 or Pentium. But that's now a joke. You'll be hard pressed to find a PC with that little RAM these days. Here are my thoughts about shopping for multimedia components and systems.

Computer

I'd suggest at least a 486DX2/50 CPU, a local bus video card, and a 500-MB hard disk (EIDE or SCSI), with 16 MB (preferably 32 MB) of RAM. A SCSI hardware interface is even better because you can also hook up as many as seven devices to most SCSI controllers, not just hard disks, and they run faster. But the bulk of machines these days have EIDE hard disks, and they are fast enough for most purposes short of doing real-time video capture. Remember, this is a minimum configuration.

Of course, if you're buying a new computer, you're probably going to get at least a Pentium 133 with a 1.6GB hard disk. For any serious work (or play) I'd recommend that kind of speed or faster.

CD-ROM Drive

Get at least an 8x speed drive. (The x means how many times faster the data can be read from the disk relative to the first CD drives, which are considered 1x.) As of this writing, affordable 24x drives are common. Windows 98 caches your CD-ROM drive data, so that it will help slower drives keep up with the data-hungry demands of applications that display video, for example.

If you want to be able to connect to a laptop or move the drive between computers, get a lightweight portable external job, maybe even a Zip or Jaz drive. You'll pay a little more for it, but prices are plummeting anyway, so the difference won't be that much. Make sure the drive supports multi-session Kodak photo format. This lets you not only view photographs in CD-ROM format on your computer but also take an existing photo CD-ROM to your photo developer and have them add new pictures to it. You might want up-front manual controls on the player so you can listen to audio CDs without running the CD Player program that comes with Windows.

PHOTOS AND WINDOWS 98

If you're among the gadget-happy, you'll probably be procuring yourself a digital camera soon, or at least want your photos on disk or in your computer somehow. That way, you can futz with your pictures using nifty software such as Adobe PhotoShop, Goo Power Tools, or other programs that let you make art out of common photographs. Or maybe you just want to e-mail pictures of Horny, your pet iguana, to your friends back home.

CONTINUED ➡

If you already have a CD-ROM drive in your computer, the easiest way to get your pix into the computer is to take your next roll of film down to the photo finisher's and request your snaps back on disk as well as on paper. Though some will give them to you on floppies, most services will provide the shots on CD. The standard format is the Kodak CD format.

Once you get the CD, check it for the info that tells you how to view the pictures. If all else fails, you may be able to simply click on the picture files using Windows Explorer, but it's better to use some software front-end to do it. The pictures usually show up as JPG or GIF files, and there may be numerous resolutions for each picture (thus, a set of files for each picture).

Digital cameras always come with Windows software that you can load up, and instructions for getting your pictures from the camera into your computer. I like using the cameras that have a pop-out memory card that I can plug into the PC card slot on my laptop. Then I don't have to hassle with wires (and thus the relatively slow download speed of the pictures over a wire). Two of the cameras I've tested (Panasonic Cool Shot and Kodak DC 210) used these cards, and they were interchangeable. I just took some pictures and then popped the card out of the camera and then into the computer. Windows 98 recognizes the card automatically and treats it like a disk drive, which makes it easy to display the contents in Windows Explorer or in a Browse box from a photo display program or other imaging program.

Part iii

NOTE

There are two flavors of Photo CD you should know about: *single-session* and *multi-session*. With a multi-session Photo CD, you can just bring in your existing CD to your photo finisher's shop and ask them to add your new pictures to the same disk. Single-session doesn't let you do that; it's a write-once format.

CD Writer

Among the latest goodies in the CD-ROM drive market are the now-affordable writers that will "burn" (record) a custom CD for you. These used to cost thousands of bucks, and only recording and software magnates could afford them. Now, creating your own music CDs or backing up tons of data on CDs is something anyone can do, if they have a CD-R (CD Recording) drive. The blank disks cost only a few dollars, and you can put 650 MB on one. But the drives that record them are about three times the price of a standard CD-ROM reader. I bought a CD-R kit recently (called the "Smart and Friendly" kit) for just a few hundred dollars at Costco/Price Club. Such a deal. It installed with only a little hassle, and the bundled Adaptec Easy CD Pro software was simple to use. Check the magazines and get a kit that has everything you might need, right in the box. You might be buying more than you need, but you'll be avoiding headaches in the long run. For example, I paid for the extra SCSI card they bundle with the drive (I already have a faster one), just so I knew I had a complete one-stop solution. Also note that CD-R drives tend to be slower at reading CD-ROMs than the fancy 24x drives are. Mine reads at only 6x and writes at a measly 2x. So I have two CD-drives: a regular 24x and the CD-R at 2x/6x. Many CD-Rs require a SCSI interface, but not all do. Many EIDE units are also available. Most of the SCSI units come with a simple SCSI adapter card. It doesn't have to be a fancy fast SCSI card (fast/wide/ultra or any of that), since speed isn't an issue. If you already have a SCSI card, it will likely work with a CD-R drive.

NOTE

The CD-R format allows you to record once, and that's all. Once a CD is written, it can't be erased and rewritten. With some formats you can add more data later, until the disk is full, but you can't erase. Another format, CD-RW (rewritable) uses *much* more expensive media to allow you to write and rewrite disks again and again.

DVD

DVD drives are the new hot item on the market. However, DVD is a technology in such an emerging state that manufacturers can't even agree what DVD stands for. (Some say Digital Video Disk, others say Digital Versatile Disk.) Regardless, we're going to see a lot more of them in the next few years. Many households in the US will have DVD players in their computers and on their TV set tops even before this book goes to print. As of this writing, set-top DVD players run about $500 and support lots of nifty features such as:

- ▶ 500 lines of horizontal resolution (more than twice as sharp as standard TV)

- ▶ 8 sound tracks (for different languages, instruction, etc.)

- ▶ 32 sets of subtitles

- ▶ Multiple movie viewing formats (standard, letterbox) and angles

- ▶ Theater sound

- ▶ 2 hours of video per side (up to 4 hours max)

- ▶ Dolby digital sound

Adding a DVD drive to your PC lets you view movies and educational titles on the PC, with the superior resolution of your computer's monitor (instead of the pretty funky resolution of a standard TV). In addition, you'll be able to interact with DVD titles designed for computers. Windows 98 supports DVD drives and has a DVD player program (similar to its CD player program) for playing DVD titles.

A few DVD add-in kits are available today for your PC. We'll see more and more PCs with DVD as an option or standard fare very soon. And writable DVDs will appear after that. Currently they are very expensive. But once those appear, editing your own homebrew movies will be a snap.

Speakers

The larger the better, usually. Little speakers will sound tinny, by definition. Listen before you buy if possible. Listen to a normal, speaking human voice—the most difficult instrument to reproduce. Does it sound natural? Then hear something with some bass. If you're going to listen to audio CDs, bring one with you to the store and play it. Speakers that are separate (not built into the monitor) will allow a nicer stereo effect. Separate tweeter and woofer will probably sound better, but not always. It depends on the electronics in the speaker. Magnetic shielding is important if the speakers are going to be within a foot or so of your screen; otherwise, the colors and alignment of the image on the screen will be adversely affected. (Not permanently damaged, though. The effect stops when you move the speakers away.) Of course, instead of buying speakers you can use your stereo or even a boom box if it has high-level (sometimes called *auxiliary*) input. Some boom boxes and virtually all stereos do have such an input. Then it's just a matter of using the correct wire to attach your sound card's *line* output to the stereo's or boom box's Aux input and setting the volume appropriately. The easiest solution is to purchase a pair of amplified speakers designed for small recording studios, apartments, or computers. For about $150 you can find a good pair of smaller-sized shielded speakers (4- or 5-inch woofer, separate tweeter) with volume, bass, and treble controls. For $300 you can get some that sound very good. If you like real bass, shell out a little more for a set that comes with a separate larger subwoofer you put under your desk.

Sound Board

This should have 16-bit, 44.1-KHz sound capability for CD-quality sound. Some newer boards (also called "cards") boast "20-bit sampling." (Above 16-bit, the audible advantages are debatable, in my opinion.) You'll want line-in, line-out, and microphone-in jacks at least. Typical cards also have a joystick port for your game controller. The card should be compatible with Windows 9x, with the General MIDI specification, and with SoundBlaster so it will work with popular games. This means it should have protected-mode 32-bit drivers for Windows 9x, supplied either with Windows 98 or with the card. If it doesn't, you'll be stuck using 16-bit drivers that take up too much conventional memory space, preventing many DOS-based games and educational programs from running. I've seen this problem with cards, such as the SoundBlaster Pro, that prevent a number of games such as the Eagle-Eye Mystery series from running. Fancy cards such as those from Turtle Beach don't sound like cheesy synthesizers when they play MIDI music because they use samples of real instruments stored in *wave tables* instead of using synthesizer chips, but you'll pay more for them. Wavetable cards are easy to find now. Even Turtle Beach makes one for $49.

VIDEO CARD AND MONITOR

The video card goes inside the computer and produces the signals needed to create a display on the monitor. A cable runs between the video card and the monitor. For high-performance multimedia, you'll want a *local bus* video card (typically VLB or PCI) capable of at least 256 colors at the resolution you desire. VLB has fallen from grace, so if you're looking for a new computer, don't get one with a VLB bus. Go for the current industry standard local bus format called PCI, a standard developed by Intel.

TIP

Local bus cards only work in computers that have a local bus connector slot, so check out which kind of slots your computer has before purchasing a video card upgrade.

Standard resolution (number of dots on the screen at one time, comprising the picture) for a PC is 640 (horizontal) by 480 (vertical). Most new video cards these days will support that resolution at 256 colors. If you have a very sharp 15-inch screen or a 17-inch screen, you may opt for a higher resolution, such as 800 by 600 or 1,024 by 768. When shopping for a video card, make sure it displays at least 256 colors (and preferably in the thousands of colors) at the resolution you want *and has at least a 70-Hz noninterlaced refresh rate at that resolution and color depth.* The correct refresh rate prevents screens from flickering, which can cause headaches and/or eye fatigue. Video cards with graphics coprocessor chips on them will run faster than those that don't. High speed is necessary when you move objects around on the screen or display video clips. Make sure the board will work well with Windows 98, preferably with the 32-bit video driver that comes with Windows 95 or 98, not an old driver designed for Windows 3.*x.* You don't have to worry about any monitor's ability to display colors, because any color monitor will display all the colors your card can produce. What you *do* have to check on are a monitor's dot pitch, controls, and refresh rate. The monitor should ideally have a dot pitch of .25 or .26, be at least 17 inches (though 15 inches will do), and run all your desired resolutions at 70-Hz refresh or higher to avoid flicker. Beware of the refresh-rate issue: False or misleading advertising is rampant. Many monitors and video cards advertise 72-Hz or higher refresh rates, but the fine print reveals that this is only at a low resolution such as 640 by 480. Bump up the resolution, and the refresh on cheaper cards or monitors drops to a noticeably slow 60 Hz. Get a monitor that has low radiation emissions, powers down automatically when it isn't being used (a so-called green monitor), and has a wide variety of controls for size, picture position, brightness, contrast, color, and so forth.

TIP

If you expect to view lots of TV or play the latest games, get a video card with 2D and 3D acceleration, video capture, a TV tuner, and video in and out. The ATI All-In Wonder card is currently my card of choice. It works well with Windows 98's TV tuner programs, and has a slew of video resolutions, and works right out of the box with Windows 98. It's about $150, street price.

WHAT'S NEXT?

If you're upgrading an older computer for use with Windows 98, you may need to install a modem—an essential tool for connecting to the Internet and going online. In Chapter 26, the PC Novice/Smart Computing staff show how to add a modem if you need to do that.

Chapter 26

INSTALLING EXTERNAL AND INTERNAL MODEMS

While internal modems traditionally have ranked among the most difficult pieces of hardware to install, people who use a modem to go online will testify that the toils are worth the frustration. A modem-equipped computer opens a whole new world of possibilities; for home users, a modem provides the connection to the Internet. Most newer computers for the home market already contain internal modems; and if that's your case, you can skip this chapter. But if you don't have one, and you're ready to get connected, read on. Here we'll provide step-by-step instructions for installing external and internal modems and provide advice for dealing with installation headaches.

Adapted from *PC Upgrading & Maintenance: No Experience Required*, by PC Novice/Smart Computing

ISBN 0-7821-2137-3   544 pages $24.99

NOTE

Although most external and internal modems connect to the PC in the same manner, the location and setting of COM ports and IRQs usually differ. We'll explain a common installation scenario, but you may encounter some different situations.

MODEM BASICS

A modem, or modulator/demodulator, lets your computer exchange information across telephone lines with another modem. It does this by converting a computer's digital signal to an analog signal that can travel over phone lines, and then converting the signal back to a digital form a computer can understand. Some modems can exchange data only; others, called fax/modems, can send and receive fax messages. Other modems add voice capabilities, letting you record messages on your computer.

Modems are available in internal and external versions. An external modem, the easiest to install, connects to a port on the back of your computer and sits on your desk. If you'd rather save the port (and desk space), you can install an internal modem, which is contained on an expansion card. (An expansion card provides additional features for your computer and plugs into a narrow socket inside the computer, called an expansion slot.

IRQ Nightmares

Making your computer communicate with a modem, especially if it's an internal model, can be a nightmare because of conflicts with IRQ settings and COM ports. An *interrupt request line* (IRQ), is the hardware line over which devices send interrupts, or requests, for service to the microprocessor. IRQs are assigned different levels of priority, allowing the microprocessor to determine the importance of each request. Unless each hardware device has a different IRQ setting, conflicts may occur. A *COM port* is a serial communications port. Different hardware devices connect to the serial ports, and the operating system uses different COM port designations (such as COM1, COM2, COM3, and COM4) to identify the connections. Two hardware devices cannot use the same COM port.

External modems, used in tandem with software, take care of the settings for you, making them simple to install. Although internal modems have become easier to install, you may still encounter some IRQ or COM port conflicts. Many times the modem's factory settings will prevent these conflicts, but, if they don't, you'll have to correct the settings manually. The ease-of-use that comes with external modems isn't free; such modems cost $20 to $50 more than their internal counterparts.

CHANGING MODEM SETTINGS

COM1 sometimes isn't available for a modem because it may host the mouse connection. And if your modem won't work on COM2, you'll have to change the modem's settings.

Most newer modems, and those from major manufacturers, use DIP (dual inline package) switches to configure the COM port and IRQ settings. Rocker DIP switches simply need to be flipped on or off (like an electric light switch), while Slide DIP switches are slid into the on or off position. The configuration of the DIP switches—which you'll find in groups of two, four, or six, depending upon your type of modem—determines the COM port and IRQ settings.

The DIP switches can be located in various places on the expansion board. Many times, the factory settings will suffice for installation of your modem. If not, you'll need to adjust the DIP switches. The modem's documentation should show the correct settings for your modem. If your modem contains no such documentation, you have two choices: Use a trial-and-error approach or call technical support.

Some modems contain pins with a plastic jumper switch. You must move the jumper switch to cover various pins to change the COM port settings. Mainstream modems usually don't use these pins. If you *must* change the COM port setting of your mouse or network connection, though, you probably will find this configuration on the expansion board.

THE EXTERNAL MODEM

To install an external modem, you only need a flat-head screwdriver and a modem cable. Many external modems don't include these cables in their packaging, so check the box or directions inside; if a cable isn't included, you can find one easily at a computer store. You will not need to open your computer's case to perform this upgrade.

Connecting the Modem

First, turn off the computer. Take all the components out of the box and follow these steps:

1. Plug one end of the modem cable into a vacant port on the back of your computer and the other into the back of the external modem. On our computer, the end with a nine-pin plug went into the computer while the 25-pin plug went into the modem. To firmly attach the plugs, you may need to turn the screws on either side of the plug into the port. The screws to the port on the back of the computer were easily fastened with our fingers, but those on the sides of the modem plug required a flat-head screwdriver.

NOTE

The port on the back of the computer that you plug your modem into will correspond to the COM port you'll be using. If you plug your modem into a serial port labeled *A*, this corresponds to COM1.

2. Locate the cord plugging into your phone line. Plug this cord into the back of the modem, at the port labeled *Line*. If you still want to use a phone on this line, take the gray phone cord that came with your new modem and plug one end into the port labeled *Phone* on the back of the modem and plug the other into the port on your phone.

3. Now, plug the small, round end of the power cord into the small, round port in back of the modem; on ours, it was labeled *AC*. Then plug the power supply into a wall outlet or into your surge protector.

You're ready to test your external modem.

Checking Your Work and Finishing Up

Next, we turned on our computer and the modem to check the connection. (On the Hayes Accura 28.8 V.34 + Fax we used, we turned the modem on by flipping a switch to the "1" position.) If the lights are working, you're ready to install the communications software.

If the lights on the modem are *not* working, there are four possible causes:

▶ You may not have securely connected the ports and plugs.

▶ You may have something plugged into the wrong port.

▶ There may be a problem with your modem.

▶ You may have the wrong kind of modem cable.

If all goes well to this point, you can turn on your computer and install the communications software. Follow the on-screen prompts. Eventually it will ask which COM port to use. We chose COM1 because we plugged the device into Port A. Since you are installing the modem in Windows 98, an Installation Wizard will walk you through the process, especially if your modem is a Plug-And-Play device, which most of them are.

THE INTERNAL MODEM

We installed a Hayes Accura fax/modem which, by virtue of being an internal device, was a little more difficult to install than the external model described earlier. A Phillips screwdriver is a necessity when installing an internal modem.

If you've never opened your computer case before, read the instructions in Chapter 24 for doing so.

Choosing the Right Slot

Internal modems can use either an 8-bit or a 16-bit expansion slot. (The expansion slots are at the back of the computer.) Most modem expansion cards have just one connector about 4 inches long. If your modem requires a 16-bit slot, the expansion card will have a second connector (about 2 inches long) behind the first. Your computer probably has a mixture of 8- and 16-bit expansion slots; the 8-bit slots are shorter and have room for only one connector. If possible, you'll want to install the modem in a slot that has empty slots on either side, which will help reduce electrical noise and interference that sometimes, although rarely, inhibits modem communications.

After you've selected an expansion slot, you'll need to remove the corresponding metal plate blocking the expansion slot's hole in the computer case. Remove the screw on top of the plate and lift the plate out from the top. Save the screw, which you'll need to fasten your modem card to the computer case. The metal plate you removed protects the inside of the computer from dust when no expansion card is installed in its corresponding slot. When you install your modem, the metal plate on the end of the card (containing the telephone line jacks) will replace the plate you just removed.

Installing the Modem

Remove the expansion card from its packaging, handling it by the edges as much as possible. Avoid touching the components on the card or the pins on the connector. Line up the connector on the expansion card with the empty expansion slot (see Figure 26.1). The connector should slide almost entirely into the expansion slot, leaving only the extreme top of the gold pins visible. It's a tight fit, so you might find it easier to roll the card into the slot by placing a corner in the expansion slot first and then fitting the remainder of the connector into the slot.

WARNING

Don't jam the expansion card into its slot; you could damage the components.

If you've properly installed the modem expansion card, the metal plate on the edge of the card will align with the empty slot in the back of the computer. You should be able to connect the metal plate of the expansion card easily to the computer's case with the screw you removed from the original plate. Don't use the screw to force the modem expansion card to line up properly; it should fit properly in the expansion slot with or without the screw in place.

TIP

One way to check the alignment of the modem expansion card is by connecting the telephone line to the modem. The telephone jacks are visible from the back of the computer. If your jacks are hidden, your board is incorrectly installed. You'll need to slide it out and start over again.

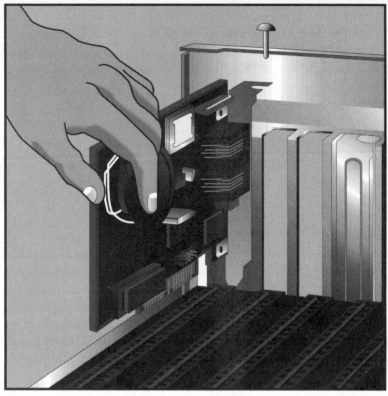

FIGURE 26.1: The connector is designed to fit into the expansion slot.

Putting It All Together: Lines and Cables

Now take the phone line (connected to the wall jack) and plug it into the jack on the back of the modem card labeled *Line*. Take the additional cable that came with your modem and plug one end into the modem jack labeled *Phone* and the other into the back of your phone (see Figure 26.2).

At this point, you can replace the computer case cover or wait until after testing the modem to ensure it is working properly.

Reconnect the cables and turn on your computer. You should notice no changes as it boots. The easiest and quickest way to check the status of your modem is the HyperTerminal application in Windows 98.

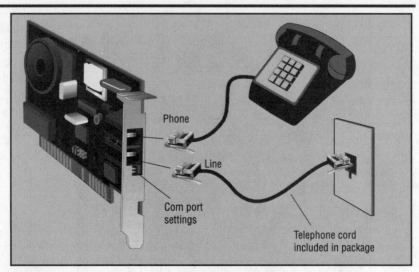

FIGURE 26.2:   The phone line is plugged into a jack on the modem card.

Go to Start ≻ Programs ≻ Accessories ≻ Communications and select HyperTerminal. (If HyperTerminal was not installed when you upgraded to Windows 98, you'll need to install it using Add/Remove Programs in Control Panel.) After the splash screen clears, you will be presented with a dialog box asking you to name the connection and select an icon. When you have done this, enter the connection information into the Connect To dialog box, which shows up next.

Windows 98 uses the information you entered into the Internet Control Panel to find the modem you have installed. The name of your modem will appear in the Connect To dialog box. You should not change this unless you have been directed to by your service provider. When you've entered the appropriate information and clicked OK, another dialog box, called Connect, will open. Click Dial to log on to your provider's system.

CONSIDERATIONS FOR HIGH-SPEED MODEMS

If you're installing a 33.6 kilobits per second (Kbps) or 56Kbps modem, make sure you have a 16550 UART. In the case of a 56K modem, it is crucial that you have purchased the format that is supported by your service provider. Ask your provider if they support either K56Flex or X2 modem technology. To take advantage of the higher throughput rates offered by these modems, you need a fast UART. The speed at which the computer can communicate with the modem may be as high as 115,200 bits per second (bps); on much older machines with a slower UART, such as an 8250 or a 16450, you will experience data loss at these higher speeds, though it is highly unlikely you have a computer with such outdated hardware. If you do have an older computer the presence of these chips is especially noticeable during file downloads, when you might experience an excessive number of retries that effectively slows or lowers the overall throughput.

NOTE

A chip with the strange name of UART (Universal Asynchronous Receiver/Transmitter) manages the data sent from your communications software to the modem and resides on your computer's motherboard.

If you buy an internal modem, an outdated UART won't be an issue because the new modem card will have an updated UART chip on it, which will override the one in your system. External modems are a different story; you will have to buy an input/output (I/O) port card, which will have new COM1 and COM2 ports and an updated UART. These cards cost about $30 and will disable the COM ports that came with your system.

Modem Configuration

Beyond hardware connections, there are other steps you can take to ensure good modem performance. One thing to remember: Once you install your modem, you generally shouldn't have to mess with it again.

Sam Knox, an online services engineer for Hayes Microcomputer Products, recommends picking your modem's exact name from a communications package's configuration list. If you don't see it, pick something similar. For example, if you have the external version of a company's modem, but your software only lists the internal version, try picking that; it's very likely they'll use the same initialization strings. Or pick the generic Hayes error-correcting setting, which won't slow down your modem transmissions or prevent you from getting online. What it will do, Knox says, is send out commands that most modems use and which should be enough to get you online. From there, he says, you can contact the manufacturer's World Wide Web site or bulletin board system to see if there's something else you can use.

I'VE GOT THE MODEM, NOW WHAT?

Many questions technical support staffs frequently hear are in one or more general, yet fairly obvious, categories. If you experience problems with your modem, run through this list. You could save yourself toll-call charges and/or technical support fees by being aware of the following:

▶ Are the power connections on your modem and the computer's power supply firmly placed? A not-so-tightly placed power cord can provide sporadic power supplies and confusing error messages.

▶ If you're using an internal modem, is the modem card seated properly in its expansion slot? If it's an external modem, is it securely connected in the proper port at the back of the computer?

▶ Is your connection to the telephone line secure?

▶ Have you properly configured the modem initialization strings in your communications software? (A common initialization string is AT&F&C1&D2S7=60, but if that fails try AT&F1, an old standby that works just fine.) Other things to check: dial-up procedures, special scripts, prefixes for outgoing calls (such as 9), and autologon settings for online services that let you bypass the usual sign-on process. (Initialization strings tell the software what to expect from the modem so they'll speak the same language during a transmission.) You can eliminate the need to enter AT strings if, during installation, you pick your modem model (or a generic one) from the software's install list.

▶ Most manuals have a section on frequently asked questions; check it before calling technical support.

▶ Have you disabled call waiting? If not, add *70, as a prefix to the phone number your modem will dial. Otherwise, you could be bumped offline by an incoming call.

Since you have Windows 98, expect relatively trouble-free installation, especially if you're using Plug-and-Play components. Some manufacturers don't intend for their products to support anything but Windows 98. Check the product's box; if you're still unsure, ask a salesperson or call the company.

Error-Checking

Unlike video cards, whose device drivers seem to be updated every 30 days, modems rarely have drivers.

If a modem requires a driver, it's called a "host-controlled" modem, which means error checking is done by the software, not the hardware. Because these modems use proprietary drivers, they can run into problems with operating systems; if you're not a techno-wizard, you may want to avoid these modems.

"If a product box says 'requires Windows,' it's a big tip off that error checking is done by the software," Knox says. When software does the error checking, it requires microprocessor time, which can slow down other operations; when the checking is done by the modem, it doesn't use the microprocessor. A majority of modems, though, conduct error checking within the hardware. Knowing industry buzzwords can save you grief later, so keep your eyes open and ask salespeople or the manufacturer to clarify catch phrases you don't understand.

Installing a modem can be one of the easiest hardware installations you'll perform. It also can be one of the toughest. Unless you know your computer's configuration inside and out, it's doubtful you'll know how difficult the installation will be until you're nearly finished. After you're done, though, your modem's obnoxious grinding, squealing, and whining noises will never have sounded so good. Not to worry though; Windows 98 will take care of the dirty work.

What's Next?

You've now read the last of the book's numbered chapters, so what you do next is entirely up to you. If you've decided to add a modem as described in this chapter (or any of the other hardware upgrades covered in Chapters 24 and 25), the Guide to Vendors in Appendix C would be a logical next step. If you haven't yet read the earlier coverage of Windows 98's support for multimedia and other hardware, you might want to go back to Chapters 9 and 10 now. Or dip into the Command and Feature Reference (Appendix A) or the Windows 98 User's Glossary (Appendix B). Finally, you might decide to put this book down and start exploring Windows 98 on your own. Happy Computing!

PART iV
WINDOWS 98
USER'S REFERENCE

Appendix A

Windows 98 Command and Feature Reference

Adapted from *Window's 98 Instant Reference*, by Peter Dyson, ISBN 0-7821-2191-8   352 pages $14.99

ACTIVE DESKTOP

 In Windows 98, you can use a conventional Windows interface similar to that in earlier versions of Windows, or you can use the Active Desktop. The Active Desktop brings the world of the Web right to the Windows 98 Desktop, allowing you to replace the static Windows wallpaper with a fully configurable, full-screen Web page. The Active Desktop can contain other Web pages, dynamic HTML; even Java components such as stock tickers and ActiveX controls, and you can add these elements to the Taskbar or to a folder.

NOTE
You can combine the Active Desktop and Internet Explorer's subscription capabilities to create your own personal push-content client, displaying data on your Desktop from whatever sources interest you. For example, you can display a continuously updating stock ticker or sports results right on your Desktop; assuming of course that you have continuous Internet access.

To set up your Active Desktop, choose Start ➤ Settings ➤ Active Desktop, and you will see three options: View As Web Page, Customize My Desktop, and Update Now. You can also right-click the Desktop and select Active Desktop from the menu.

View As Web Page

Turns on the Active Desktop interface. Selecting this option a second time removes the checkmark and turns the Active Desktop off again.

Customize My Desktop

Opens the Display Properties dialog box. You can also right-click the Desktop and select Properties, or if you prefer, choose Start ➤ Settings ➤ Control Panel and select the Display icon. The Display Properties dialog box contains six tabs, but we are only concerned with the following two:

Background Lets you choose an HTML document or a picture to use as your Desktop background. In the Wallpaper box, select the background you want to use, or click Pattern to choose or modify the background pattern. You can also click the Browse button to locate a file or to go directly to a Web site to find the

HTML document you are interested in using as a background. To cover your entire Desktop with a small wallpaper image, select Tile from the Display box, or choose Center if you prefer to see the image centered. Click the Apply button to see the effect of your changes before you exit the Display Properties dialog box, or click OK to accept the changes and close the dialog box.

TIP

You can also right-click any Web page graphic that takes your fancy and then click Set As Wallpaper.

Web   Lets you select and organize Active Desktop elements. At the top of the tab, you will see a representation of your Desktop, indicating the location of any Active Desktop elements. These same elements are listed in the box below. To add a new element such as a stock ticker or a weather map, click New to open the New Active Desktop Item dialog box. If you want to browse through Microsoft's Active Desktop Gallery on Microsoft's Web site for a component to add, click Yes. To select a different Web site, click No, and then enter the address or URL for the Web site, or click the Browse button to locate it. Be sure that the View my Active Desktop as a Web page box is checked if you want your Desktop to look like a Web page.

NOTE

You can also right-click any link on a Web page, drag it to your Desktop, and then click Create Active Desktop Item Here.

Update Now

Updates the Desktop contents right now to display any changes you have made.

ADD NEW HARDWARE

Guides you through the process of adding new hardware to your system using the New Hardware Wizard. This Wizard automatically makes the appropriate changes to the Registry and to the configuration files so that Windows 98 can recognize and support your new hardware. Be sure you have installed or connected your new hardware before you go any further.

→ *See* Chapter 7 for instructions on installing new hardware with the New Hardware Wizard.

ADD/REMOVE PROGRAMS

Installs or uninstalls individual elements of the Windows 98 operating system itself or certain application programs. Installing or removing application or system software components in this way enables Windows 98 to modify all the appropriate system and configuration files automatically so that the information in them stays current and correct.

To start Add/Remove Programs, choose Start ➢ Settings ➢ Control Panel, and then click the Add/Remove Programs icon to open the Add/Remove Programs Properties dialog box. This dialog box contains four tabs if you are connected to a local area network; otherwise, it contains three tabs.

Install/Uninstall Tab

To install a new program using the Add/Remove Programs applet, follow these steps:

1. Select the Install/Uninstall tab if it isn't already selected, and then click the Install button.

2. Put the application program CD or floppy disk in the appropriate drive, and click the Next button to display a setup or install message, describing the program to be installed.

3. To continue with the installation process, click the Finish button. To make any changes, click Back and repeat the procedure.

To uninstall a program previously installed under Windows 98, you must follow a different process. The programs that have uninstall capability (not all of them do) will be listed in the display box of the Install/Uninstall tab. Click the program you want to uninstall, and then click the Add/Remove button. You may see a warning message about removing the application. You will be to told when the uninstall is finished.

NOTE

Once you remove an application using Add/Remove Programs, you will have to reinstall it from the original program disks or CD if you decide to use it again.

Windows Setup Tab

Some components of the Windows 98 operating system are optional, and you can install or uninstall them as you wish; the Windows Clipboard Viewer is an example. Select the Windows Setup tab to display a list of such components with checkboxes on the left. If the box has a checkmark in it, the component is currently installed. If the checkbox is gray, only some elements of that component are installed; to see what is included in a component, click the Details button. Follow these steps to add a Windows 98 component:

1. Click the appropriate checkbox.

2. If the component consists of several elements, click the Details button to display a list of them, and check the boxes you want to install.

3. Click OK to display the Windows Setup tab.

4. Click the Apply button, and then click OK.

To remove a Windows 98 component from your system, follow these steps:

1. Click the Details button to see a complete list of the individual elements in the component you want to uninstall.

2. Clear the checkmark from the checkboxes of the elements you want to uninstall, and then click OK to open the Windows Setup tab.

3. Click the Apply button, and then click OK.

Startup Disk Tab

A startup disk is a floppy disk with which you can start, or "boot," your computer if something happens to your hard drive. When you originally installed Windows 98, you were asked if you wanted to create a startup disk. If you didn't do it at that time or if the disk you created then is not usable, you can create one now. Simply insert a disk with at least 1.2MB capacity in the appropriate drive, click Create Disk, and follow the instructions on the screen.

Network Install Tab

In some cases, you can also install a program directly from a network using the Network Install tab. If the Network Install tab is not present in the Add/Remove Programs Properties dialog box, this feature may not have been enabled on your computer or on your network; see your system administrator for more details.

If the Install/Uninstall tab is selected, your system is currently connected to the network, and you can click Install followed by Next to find the setup program for your network.

If the Network Install tab is selected, follow the instructions on the screen.

ADDRESS BOOK

Manages your e-mail addresses, as well as your voice, fax, modem, and cellular phone numbers. Once you enter an e-mail address in your Address Book, you can select it from a list rather than type it in every time. To open the Address Book, choose Start ➤ Programs ➤ Internet Explorer ➤ Address Book, or click the Address Book icon on the Outlook Express toolbar.

Importing an Existing Address Book

Address Book can import information from an existing address book in any of the following formats:

- ▶ Windows Address Book
- ▶ Microsoft Exchange Personal Address Book
- ▶ Microsoft Internet Mail for Windows 3.1 Address Book
- ▶ Netscape Address Book
- ▶ Netscape Communicator Address Book
- ▶ Eudora Pro or Lite Address Book

▶ Lightweight Directory Access Protocol (LDAP)

▶ Comma-separated text file

To import information from one of these address books, follow these steps:

1. Choose Start ➤ Programs ➤ Internet Explorer ➤ Address Book, or click the Address Book icon on the Outlook Express toolbar.

2. Choose File ➤ Import ➤ Address Book to open the Address Book Import Tool dialog box.

3. Select the file you want to import, and click Import.

Creating a New Address Book Entry

To add a new entry to your Address Book, click the New Contact button on the Address Book toolbar or choose File ➤ New Contact to open the Properties dialog box. This dialog box has six tabs:

Personal   Lets you enter personal information including the person's first, middle, and last names, a nickname, and an e-mail address. If the person has more than one e-mail address, click Add and continue entering addresses.

Home   Allows you to enter additional information about this contact; enter as much or as little information as makes sense here.

Business   Allows you to enter business-related information; again, enter as much or as little information as makes sense.

Other   Offers a chance to store additional information about this contact as a set of text notes.

NetMeeting   Lets you enter NetMeeting information such as a person's conferencing e-mail address and server name. If NetMeeting is not installed on your system, this tab will be called Conferencing.

Digital IDs   Allows you to specify a digital certificate for use with an e-mail address.

Setting Up a New Group

You can create groups of e-mail addresses to make it easy to send a message to all the members of the group. You can group people any way you like—by job title, musical taste, or sports team allegiance. When you want to send e-mail to everyone in the group, simply use the group name instead of selecting each e-mail address individually. To begin creating a new group, click the New Group icon on the Address Book toolbar or choose File ➤ New Group to open the Group Properties dialog box.

ADDRESS TOOLBAR

Shows the location of the page currently displayed in the main window; this may be a URL on the Internet or an intranet, or it may be a file or folder stored on your hard disk.

To go to another page, click the arrow at the right end of the Address toolbar to select the appropriate entry, or simply type a new location. When you start to type an address that you have previously entered, the Auto-Complete feature recognizes the address and completes the entry for you.

The Address toolbar is available in most Windows 98 applications, including the Explorer, Internet Explorer, My Computer, the Control Panel, and others.

BACKUP

Creates an archive copy of one or more files and folders on your hard disk and then restores them to your hard disk in the event of a disk or controller failure or some other unforeseen event.

➜ *See* Chapter 11 to learn about using the Windows 98 Backup Wizard, and about guidelines for deciding what and when to back up.

BROWSE

The Browse button is available in many common dialog boxes when you have to choose or enter a file name, find a folder, or specify a Web address or URL. Clicking the Browse button or the Find File button opens the Browse dialog box.

You can look through folders on any disk on any shared computer on the network to find the file you want. When you find the file, folder, computer, or Web site, double-click it to open, import, or enter it in a text box.

CD PLAYER

 Allows you to play audio compact discs on your CD-ROM drive. Choose Start ➤ Programs ➤ Accessories ➤ Multimedia ➤ CD Player to open the CD Player dialog box. ➡*See* Chapter 9 to learn more about using CD Player.

CHAT

➡*See* NetMeeting

CLIPBOARD

A temporary storage place for data. You can use the Cut and Copy commands as well as the Windows screen capture commands to place data on the Clipboard. The Paste command then copies the data from the Clipboard to a receiving document, perhaps in another application. You cannot edit the Clipboard contents; however, you can view and save the information stored in the Clipboard by using the Clipboard Viewer, or you can paste the contents of the Clipboard into Notepad.

WARNING
The Clipboard only holds one piece of information at a time, so cutting or copying onto the Clipboard overwrites any existing contents.

CLOSING WINDOWS

Closing an application program window terminates the operations of that program. In Windows 98, you can close windows in a number of ways:

► Click the Close button in the upper-right corner of the program title bar. ☒

- Choose Control ≻ Close (identified by the icon to the left of the program name in the title bar) or simply double-click the Control Menu icon.

- Choose File ≻ Close or File ≻ Exit within the application.

- If the application is minimized on the Taskbar, right-click the application's icon and choose Close or press Alt+F4.

CONNECTION WIZARD

Walks you through the steps of setting up your Internet connection. All you need is an account with an ISP (Internet Service Provider), and you're all set. You can start the Connection Wizard in several ways:

- Choose Start ≻ Programs ≻ Internet Explorer ≻ Connection Wizard.

- From the Windows 98 Help system, choose the Using the Internet Connection Wizard topic.

- Choose Start ≻ Settings ≻ Control Panel ≻ Internet to open the Internet Properties dialog box, and then select the Connection tab and click the Connect button.

- In Internet Explorer, choose View ≻ Internet Options to open the Internet Options dialog box, and then select the Connection tab and click the Connect button.

No matter which method you use, you first see the Welcome screen; click the Next button to continue. The Setup Options dialog box gives you three choices:

- Open a new account with an ISP. Select the first option if you do not have an account. The Wizard takes you through the steps of finding an ISP and starting an account and sets up the dial-up link for you.

- Establish a connection to an existing Internet account. Select the second option to set up a connection to your existing Internet account or to revise the settings for your current account.

- Make no change to your existing account. If you choose this option and click the Next button, the Wizard closes because there is nothing for it to do.

Creating a New Connection to the Internet

To create a new dial-up connection to the Internet, start the Connection Wizard, click Next at the Welcome screen, and then follow these steps:

1. In the Setup Options dialog box, choose the first option to select an ISP and set up a new Internet account, and then click Next.

2. The Connection Wizard now begins the automatic part of the setup by loading programs from your original Windows 98 CD. You may be asked to restart your computer; the Wizard will resume automatically. Be sure you complete all the steps; otherwise, the Wizard may not be able to set up your connection properly.

3. If you have a modem, the Wizard attempts to locate an ISP in your area and sets up the appropriate Dial-Up Networking software on your system. Follow the prompts on the screen to complete the setup.

Modifying an Existing Connection to the Internet

You can modify your existing Internet account settings at any time. Start the Connection Wizard, click Next at the Welcome screen, and then follow these steps:

1. In the Setup Options dialog box, select the second option to set up a new connection to an existing Internet account.

2. Choose the method you use to connect to the Internet, either by phone line or through your local area network, and click Next.

3. In the Dial-Up Connection dialog box, check the Use an Existing Dial-Up Connection box, select the connection from the list box, and click the Next button.

4. You'll then be asked if you want to modify the settings for this connection. Click Yes, and then click Next to open the Phone Number dialog box where you can enter the phone number to dial to make the connection.

5. In the next dialog box, enter your user name and password information, and click Next.

6. In the Advanced settings dialog box you are asked if you want to change any of the advanced settings for this connection, such as connection type, logon script filename, and IP address. You should only change these settings when your ISP or system administrator tells you to and provides the new information to use. Click Next.

7. You'll then be asked if you want to set up an Internet e-mail account; click Yes and then Next to specify whether you want to use an existing account or create a new one. If you opt to continue using an existing account, you will be asked to confirm your e-mail account settings; if you establish a new account, you will have to enter this information from scratch. Click Next.

8. Next, you'll be asked if you want to set up an Internet news account; follow the instructions on the screen.

9. Finally, click the Finish button to complete the configuration and close the Wizard.

CONTROL PANEL

Provides a way to establish settings and defaults for all sorts of important Windows features. To access the Control Panel, choose Start ➢ Settings ➢ Control Panel.

If you are using the conventional Windows interface, you will see a window that looks like this:

To open an applet, double-click it, or click once on its icon to select it and then choose File ➢ Open.

If you are using the Active Desktop and you have View As Web Page turned on, you will see a much different Control Panel:

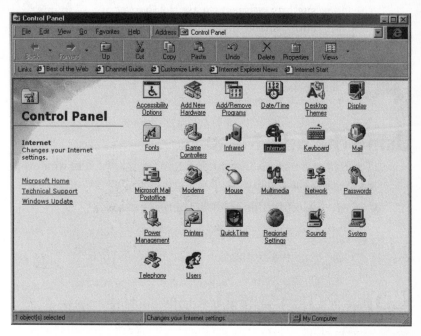

The Control Panel now looks and works like a Web page displayed in a browser. All the names of the applets are underlined, and the mouse pointer turns into a hand when you move the cursor over an icon. You will also see a short description of what each Control Panel applet does on the left side of the window. More important, it now takes only a single mouse-click to open an applet.

→ *See* Chapter 7 to learn more about using the Control Panel.

COPYING FILES AND FOLDERS

When you copy a file or a folder, you duplicate it in another location and leave the original in place. In Windows, you can copy files and folders in three ways. Let's take a look.

Using Drag-and-Drop

To use the drag-and-drop method, both the source and the destination folders must be open on the Desktop. Press and hold the Ctrl key while holding down the left mouse button, and drag the file or folder from one location to another. When the file or folder is in the correct place, release the mouse button and then release the Ctrl key.

WARNING

Be sure to hold down Ctrl. If you do not, the file or folder will be moved rather than copied.

Using the Edit Menu

The Edit menu in My Computer, Explorer, or any folder window provides a Copy and Paste feature. Follow these steps to use it:

1. Select the file or folder you want to copy.

2. Choose Edit ➤ Copy.

3. Find the destination file or folder and open it.

4. Choose Edit ➤ Paste.

You will see the name of the file in the destination folder.

TIP

You can select multiple files or folders to be copied by holding down Ctrl and clicking them. If the files are contiguous, you can also use Shift to select files.

Using the Right Mouse Button

Right-clicking a file or a folder opens a pop-up menu that you can use to perform a number of functions, including copying. To copy using the right mouse button, follow these steps:

1. Locate the file or folder you want to copy, and right-click to open the pop-up menu. Select Copy.

2. Open the destination folder, click the right mouse button, and select Paste.

You will see the name of the file in the destination folder.

CREATING NEW FOLDERS

Sooner or later you will want to add a new folder to a disk or to another folder, and you can do so in Explorer. Follow these steps:

1. In Explorer, select the disk or folder in which you want to place a new folder.

2. Choose File ➢ New ➢ Folder.

A new folder is added to the disk or the folder you indicated with the name "New Folder" highlighted.

3. Type a new folder name, something that will act as a reminder as to the files it contains, and press Enter.

You can also right-click in the blank part of the Windows Explorer file pane to open a pop-up menu from which you can choose New ➢ Folder.

TIP

If you would rather bypass Explorer altogether, you can create a new folder on the Desktop by clicking My Documents and then choosing File ➢ New ➢ Folder. Give the folder a new name, and then drag it to the Desktop.

DATE/TIME

The clock that appears in the right corner of the Taskbar displays the system clock, which not only tells you the time, but also indicates the time and date associated with any files you create or modify. At any time, you can place the mouse pointer on the time in the Taskbar to display the complete date. To vary the format of the date and time displayed in the Taskbar, select the Regional Settings applet in the Control Panel.

To set the clock, follow these steps:

1. Double-click the time in the Taskbar, or choose Start ➢ Settings ➢ Control Panel ➢Date/Time to open the Date/Time Properties dialog box.

2. Select the Date & Time tab to set the day, month, year, or current time.

3. To change the time, either drag across the numbers you want to change beneath the clock and type the new time, or highlight the numbers and click the up and down arrows to increase or decrease the values.

4. To change the date, click the drop-down arrow to select the month, use the up and down arrows to change the year, and click the appropriate day of the month.

DELETING FILES AND FOLDERS

You can delete a file or a folder in several ways. First, select the file or folder you want in My Computer or Windows Explorer, and then do one of the following:

▶ Choose File ➤ Delete. After you confirm that you want to delete the file or folder, Windows sends it to the Recycle Bin.

▶ Press the Delete key on the keyboard and verify that you want to delete the selected file or folder; Windows then sends it to the Recycle Bin.

▶ Right-click the file or folder to open the pop-up menu. Select Delete and then verify that you want to delete the selected file or folder. Off it goes to the Recycle Bin.

▶ Position the My Computer or Explorer window so that you can also see the Recycle Bin on the Desktop; then simply drag the selected file or folder to the Recycle Bin.

NOTE

If you accidentally delete a file or folder, you can choose Edit ➤ Undo Delete or retrieve the file or folder manually from the Recycle Bin. You cannot retrieve a deleted file or folder if the Recycle Bin has been emptied since your last deletion.

TIP

To delete a file without placing it in the Recycle Bin, select the file and then press Shift+Delete. You cannot recover the file if you do this. You will be asked to confirm the deletion.

DESKTOP

What you see on the screen when you first open Windows. If you are not using any of the Web-like features of the Active Desktop, you see the conventional Windows Desktop. Initially, it contains a set of icons arranged on the left, plus the Taskbar with the Start button across the bottom. As you work with Windows and load application programs, other objects such as dialog boxes and messages boxes are placed on the Desktop.

You can also change the appearance of the Desktop by right-clicking it and selecting Properties. This allows you to change display properties for the Desktop background and screen savers. You can also change the monitor type, as well as font types, sizes, and colors for objects on the screen.

DISK CLEANUP

A quick and convenient way to make more space available on your hard disk. Choose Start ➤ Programs ➤ Accessories ➤ System Tools ➤ Disk Cleanup to open the Disk Cleanup dialog box.

Alternatively, you can open Explorer or My Computer, right-click the disk you want to work with, and then choose Properties from the pop-up menu. On the General tab, click the Disk Cleanup button.

➟*See* Chapter 11 to learn more about using Disk Cleanup.

DISK SPACE

To find out how much disk space a file or folder occupies, select it (hold down the Ctrl key to select more than one) in My Computer or Explorer. The window's status bar will display the number of objects selected and the amount of disk space they occupy.

Alternately, you can choose File ➤ Properties or right-click a file or folder and select Properties. The General tab displays the amount of disk space or, in the case of a folder, its size plus the number of files or other folders it contains.

To see how much disk space remains on the entire disk, select the disk name in My Computer or Explorer and then choose File ➤ Properties or right-click and choose Properties. The Properties dialog box displays both the amount of used and the amount of free space. The status bar of My Computer also displays the free space and capacity of a disk drive.

DISPLAY

Controls how the objects on you screen—patterns, colors, fonts, sizes, and other elements—look. Choose Start ➤ Settings ➤ Control Panel ➤ Display (or simply right-click the Desktop and select properties) to open the Display Properties dialog box. It has six tabs: Background, Screen Saver, Appearance, Effects, Web, and Settings.

→*See* Chapter 7 to learn about setting and modifying display properties.

DOCUMENTS

Choosing Start ➤ Documents displays a list of all the documents you have created or edited recently. If you select a document from the list, Windows opens the document in the appropriate application, making this a quick way to continue working on an interrupted project.

Windows maintains this list of documents and preserves it between Windows sessions even if you shut down and restart your computer. The last 15 documents are preserved in this list, but some of them may look more like applications or folders than documents.

To clear the list of documents and start the list over, choose Start ➤ Settings ➤ Taskbar & Start Menu. Select the Start Menu Programs tab and click the Clear button. Once you do this, only one entry will remain in the list, the shortcut to the My Documents folder.

DRAG-AND-DROP

You can use drag-and-drop to move, copy, activate, or dispose of files and folders on the Desktop and in many accessory and application windows. Place the mouse pointer on a file, press the left button, and drag the file or folder to another disk or folder. Position the pointer over the destination and release the mouse button. The result depends on the file or folder being dragged and the destination:

▶ Dragging a file or folder to another folder on the same disk moves it (hold down the Ctrl key if you want to copy the file or folder).

▶ Dragging a file or folder to another disk copies it.

▶ Dragging a file to a shortcut printer icon on the Desktop prints the document.

▶ Dragging a file or folder to the Recycle Bin disposes of it.

ENTERTAINMENT

Menu used to access the Windows multimedia applications. Choose Start ➤ Programs ➤ Accessories ➤ Entertainment. This menu includes CD Player, Media Player, Sound Recorder, TV Viewer, and others.

EXPLORER

The Windows Explorer (to use its full name) is *the* place to go when working with files and folders in Windows 98. The Explorer lets you look at your disks, folders, and files, in a variety of ways and helps you perform such tasks as copying, moving, renaming, and deleting files and folders, formatting floppy disks, and so on.

Explorer Menus

To access Explorer, choose Start ➤ Programs ➤ Windows Explorer, or right-click the Start button and choose Explore. You may want to create a shortcut for it on the Desktop or in the Start menu itself since it is used so often.

The Explorer menus give you access to all common functions. However, for some menu selections to work, you may first have to select an appropriate object in the main Explorer window, and the type of object you select determines the available options. You may, therefore, not see all these options on any given menu, and you may see some options not listed here. You will also find similar menus in My Computer, the Recycle Bin, and Network Neighborhood.

File Menu

Displays basic file-management options. It allows you to do the following:

- ▶ Open a folder or file

- ▶ Explore the contents of a selected computer, disk, or folder

- ▶ Print a file or get a Quick View of the contents of a file (not shown on the menu unless it is available)

- ▶ Set parameters for sharing a folder with other users

- ▶ Send a file to a floppy disk, to an e-mail or fax correspondent (using Windows Messaging), to My Briefcase, or to another destination

▶ Create a new folder or a shortcut

▶ Make a shortcut to a file or folder

▶ Delete or rename a file or folder

▶ Display a file's properties

▶ Close a file or a folder

If you are working with the Printers folder, you will also see options to Capture Printer Port and to End Capture.

Edit Menu

Allows you to work with the contents of a folder or file. It allows you to do the following:

▶ Undo the previous action

▶ Cut, copy, and paste folders or files

▶ Paste a shortcut within a folder

▶ Select all files and folders

▶ Select all files except those already selected, which become deselected

View Menu

Allows you to change the window to include or exclude the toolbars, Status bar, and Explorer bar. You can choose how the files and folders are displayed:

▶ As a Web page

▶ With large icons or small icons

▶ In a list

▶ With details, describing the size and type of a file and the date modified

You can arrange icons by name, type of file or folder, size, or date created or last modified. You can also arrange icons into columns and rows. Refresh redisplays your screen. Folder Options lets you set defaults for how information is displayed in the main Explorer window, and Customize This Folder lets you change the appearance of the folder.

Go Menu

Lets you go back, forward, or up one level and gives fast access to certain Web sites and other Windows elements such as Mail, News, My Computer, Address Book, and Internet Call.

Favorites Menu

The Favorites menu is divided into two parts. You use the first part to manage your favorite Web sites with Add to Favorites and Organize Favorites, as well as those Web sites to which you subscribe with Manage Subscriptions and Update All Subscriptions. You use the second part for fast access to groups of Web sites with Channels, Links, and Software Updates.

Tools Menu

Gives you quick access to Find so that you can find Files or Folders, Computer, On the Internet, or People. You can also map a networked drive and disconnect a networked drive.

Help Menu

Provides access to the Windows Help system.

TIP

Some functions available from the Explorer menus are also available as buttons on the toolbar.

Explorer Toolbar

The following buttons are available on the standard Explorer toolbar:

Back　Displays the item you last displayed. Click the small down arrow just to the right of this button to see a list of all the items you have displayed in this Explorer session and click an item to go to it directly.

Forward　Displays the item you were viewing before you went back to the current item. Click the small down arrow just to the right of this button to display a list of items. Click an item to go to it directly.

Up   Moves up the directory tree in the left Explorer window, changing the contents displayed in the right window as it goes.

Cut   Moves the selected items to the Clipboard.

Copy   Duplicates selected items, placing their content on the Clipboard.

 Paste   Transfers the contents of the Clipboard to a file or folder. A destination folder must already exist and must be selected.

Undo   Cancels the previous action. The label changes depending on what you did last—for example, Undo Delete or Undo Copy.

Delete   Places the selected file or folder in the Recycle Bin.

 Properties   Opens the Properties dialog box for the selected disk, file, or folder.

Views   Changes the way information is displayed in the right-hand Explorer window. Click the small down arrow just to the right of this button to display a menu you can use to select the various displays. Alternatively, each time you click the Views button, the display cycles through these four views:

> **Large Icons**   Displays larger-sized icons representing the contents of the selected folder or disk.
>
> **Small Icons**   Displays smaller-sized icons in a horizontal, columnar list representing the contents of the selected folder or disk.
>
> **List**   Displays the contents as small icons, except in a vertical rather than horizontal orientation.
>
> **Details**   Displays the contents in a detailed list with additional information about the file size, file type, and modification date.

The Explorer also contains two other toolbars:

Address   Displays the location of the item currently displayed by the Explorer. The arrow at the right end of the Address toolbar opens a drop-down list of items; select one to open it.

Links   Displays a set of hyperlinks to various parts of Microsoft's Web site; you can also access these links from the Links selection in the Favorites menu.

You will also see a single status line across the bottom of the main Explorer window; it displays messages about your actions and lists information on disk storage space, including the number of items in a folder and the occupied and free disk space.

Explorer Window

When you run the Explorer, all items that make up your computer are listed in the left pane. Some objects have a plus sign (+) next to them, indicating that the object contains other objects that are not currently visible. To display the contents of such an item in the right pane, click the item, not the plus sign.

When you click the plus sign associated with an object, you display all the subelements, usually folders, in the left window, where they become part of the overall tree structure. The plus sign becomes a minus sign (−) if an object's contents are expanded. This tree structure is a graphical representation of how the files and folders on your system are related; the name of each folder appears just after its icon.

Customizing a Folder

Choose View ➢ Customize This Folder to open the Customize This Folder Wizard with these options:

Create or Edit an HTML Document   Lets you create an HTML (Hypertext Markup Language) document in three steps:

1. Open the editor and create the HTML document.
2. Save the document.
3. Close the editor.

Choose a Background Picture   Lets you select a picture that will be displayed as wallpaper when you open this folder.

Remove Customization   Lets you return this folder to its original look and feel.

Selecting a Drive and Choosing a File or a Folder

When you open the Explorer, all the disks and folders available on your computer are displayed in the left pane. The right pane displays the contents of the disk or folder you selected on the left. Follow these steps to find a file or a folder:

1. Scroll up and down using the left scroll bar. On the left, you can see all the disks on your computer, plus those that are shared on your network, and all the folders within each disk. On the right, you will see all the folders and files within the selected disk or folder.

2. If the drive you want is not visible, you may have to expand the My Computer icon by clicking its plus sign. Normally, you will be able to see a floppy disk and at least one hard disk.

3. Click a disk or folder in the left pane to display its contents in the right pane; when a folder is selected, its icon changes from a closed folder to an open one.

4. Once you find the file or folder you want, open it and get to work.

FAVORITES

Contains selections you can use to track your favorite Web sites. You can open your favorite Web sites from many places within Windows 98. You can choose Start ➤ Favorites, or you can use the Favorites menu in Windows Explorer, My Computer, Internet Explorer, Network Neighborhood, and Control Panel; even the Recycle Bin has a Favorites menu.

Add to Favorites

Choose Favorites ➤ Add to Favorites to bookmark a Web site so that you can find it again quickly and easily. Once you place the address, or URL, for the site in this list, you can revisit the site simply by selecting it from the Favorites menu; the result is the same as if you had typed the whole URL into the Address toolbar and pressed Enter. You can also display your Favorites menu from the Explorer Bar; choose View ➤ Explorer Bar ➤ Favorites.

Organize Favorites

Choose Favorites ➤ Organize Favorites to group your Web sites into an arrangement that makes sense to you; a single long list is certainly not the most efficient organization.

Subscribing to a Web Site

In addition to visiting Web sites in the normal way with Internet Explorer, you can also subscribe to a Web site. A subscription is a mechanism that Internet Explorer uses to check for new or updated content on a Web site without your involvement. Chapter 21 contains complete instructions for subscribing and managing subscriptions.

FAX

 Sends and receives faxes between computers or fax machines. You can send a fax in several ways:

- ▶ Drag a text or graphics file to the Microsoft Fax icon in the Printers folder.

- ▶ Right-click an icon and select the Send to Fax Recipient command.

- ▶ Select Microsoft Fax as the printer in any application program.

- ▶ Use Windows Messaging.

- ▶ Choose Start ➤ Programs ➤ Accessories ➤ Fax ➤ Compose New Fax.

No matter which of these techniques you use, the Compose New Fax Wizard will guide you through creating and sending a fax. Once you have a suitable profile set up under Start ➤ Programs ➤ Windows Messaging, the rest is a breeze.

TIP

To install Fax, you must have Microsoft Exchange, Windows Messaging, or Outlook already installed on your system.

Compose New Fax

Follow these steps to compose a new fax message:

1. Open the Compose New Fax dialog box using one of the techniques discussed earlier.

2. If you are using a laptop (and therefore may not always be calling from the same location), click Dialing Properties and review the methods used to dial an outside line. If you are not using a portable computer, you can click *I'm not using a portable computer, so don't show this to me again.* Click Next.

3. Complete the information on the person to whom you want to send the fax. Type a name, country, fax number, and a recipient list, if applicable.

4. Select whether to send a cover page and its type. Click Options to open the Send Options for This Message dialog box.

5. Specify the following settings for this fax:

   Time to Send   Specifies when the fax will actually be transmitted. Choose from As Soon as Possible, Discount Rates (click Set to specify the times when discount rates take effect), or a Specific Time (which you set using the up and down arrows).

   Message Format   Specifies whether the recipient can edit the fax message. You can send a message that is Editable, if Possible (the fax will be sent in the binary editable format; the recipient must also have Microsoft

Fax to be able to edit the fax), Editable Only (Microsoft Fax will try to send the fax as binary files and will refuse to send the message if the receiving system cannot accept that format), or Not Editable (the fax is sent as a bitmap).

Paper   Establishes the paper specifications, including size, orientation (landscape or portrait), and image quality—choose from Draft (200×100 dpi), Fine (200×200 dpi), 300dpi, or Best Available.

Cover Page   Confirms your choice of cover page.

Dialing   Specifies how fax numbers are dialed, how many times you want to retry a busy or unavailable number, and the waiting period between such retries. Click Dialing Properties to set the default location you normally dial from, the dialing prefix, and credit card information. Click Toll Prefixes to identify phone-number prefixes that are inside your default area code but which require you to use the area code.

Security   Specifies the security method to use with this fax. You can choose from None, Key-Encrypted (which uses a public-key encryption technique), and Password-Protected (the recipient must enter the same password you used when creating the fax to read the message).

6. When you have made your selections, click OK to return to the Compose New Fax dialog box. Click Next.

7. Type the subject of the fax, and in the Note box, type the contents of your fax message. Check the checkbox if you want the Note contents to be part of the cover page. Click Next.

8. If you want to send a file with this fax, click Add File to open the Open a File to Attach dialog box. Locate the file, and then click Open. The name will appear in the Files to Send text box. Click Next.

9. Your fax is now complete, and all you have to do to send it is click the Finish button. You will see two icons in the notification area of the Taskbar for the fax and dialing actions.

Request a Fax

You can also use Fax to call a remote computer, information service, or fax machine to retrieve a specific document; and you can retrieve all the documents available. Once the call is complete, the documents are placed in your Inbox. Follow these steps:

1. Choose Start ➢ Programs ➢ Accessories ➢ Fax ➢ Request a Fax to open the Request a Fax dialog box.

2. To retrieve all faxes stored at the remote site, click Retrieve Whatever Is Available. To retrieve one particular document, click Retrieve a Specific Document, and then type the name of the document and its password (if there is one) in the two boxes in the lower part of the dialog box. Click Next.

3. Type the name of the person to whom the retrieved fax will be routed in the To box. To retrieve a name from the Address Book, click that button, select a name, and then click Add. Verify the country, and type the fax number. Click Next.

4. To specify when you want to call, select from As Soon As Possible, When Phone Rates Are Discounted, or A Specific Time. Click Next.

5. Click Finish to complete the request.

TIP

To review the list of faxes scheduled to be sent, open Inbox and choose Tools ➢ Microsoft Fax Tools ➢ Show Outgoing Faxes to open the Outgoing Faxes dialog box. You'll see the sender, subject, size, recipients, and time to send.

FIND

Windows 98 adds several powerful items to the Find menu, which now includes options for finding files and folders, a computer, information on the Internet, or people. Choose Start ➢ Find and select an option, or choose Tools ➢ Find in Explorer.

Find Files or Folders

To find a file or folder, you can either use My Computer or Explorer to scan the disks yourself, or you can use the Find command to have

Windows 98 conduct the search for you. To use the Find command, choose Start ➤ Find ➤ Files or Folders, or in Explorer, choose Tools ➤ Find ➤ Files or Folders.

In the Find: All Files dialog box, you will see three tabs: Name & Location, Date Modified, and Advanced.

Name & Location Tab

Contains the following options:

Named   Displays the name of the file or folder for which you're searching. Click the down arrow to display a list of your most recent searches.

Containing Text   Lets you specify any text that you want to locate.

Look In   Tells Windows to search a specific path for the file or folder. Click the down arrow to display a list of the disks and folders on your computer.

Browse   Lets you look through the available disks and folders to find the one you want.

Include Subfolders   Searches sublevels of folders as well as the level you specified.

Date Tab

Contains the following options:

All Files   Searches all files in the specified path for the desired file or folder.

Find All Files   Restricts the search to files created, last accessed, or modified between two specified dates, during the previous number of months, or during the previous number of days.

Advanced Tab

Contains the following options:

Of Type   Searches for a specific type of file. Click the down arrow to display a list of registered types.

Size Is   Restricts the search for files to At Least or At Most (selected by the first down arrow) the number of kilobytes specified (typed or entered using the arrow keys).

Enter the Find specifications you want, and then select one of the following buttons:

Find Now   Starts the search.

Stop   Ends the search.

New Search   Allows you to enter new search criteria.

To save a search, including its parameters, choose File ➤ Save Search. To save the results of a search, choose Options ➤ Save Results. To make a search case-sensitive, choose Options ➤ Case Sensitive.

Find a Computer

To locate a computer on your network using the Find command in either the Start menu or Explorer, follow these steps:

1. Chose Start ➤ Find ➤ Computer, or in Explorer, choose Tools ➤ Find ➤ Computer to open the Find Computer dialog box.

2. Enter the computer name or select it from a list of previous searches by clicking the Named down arrow.

3. Click Find Now to activate the search. Stop terminates the search, and New Search allows you to enter the criteria for a new computer search.

Find on the Internet

The Find menu's On the Internet option uses Internet Explorer to connect to the Web site at home.microsoft.com/search/search.asp This site gives you access to some of the most powerful and popular search engines on the Internet, including Infoseek, AOL NetFind, Lycos, Excite, and Yahoo.

You can also use one of the other sites in the categories of General Search, Guides, White Pages, Newsgroups, Chat Guides, Specialty, or International. If you can't find what you are looking for using one of these search engines, what you are looking for doesn't want to be found.

Find People

The Find menu's People option lets you searches public LDAP (Lightweight Directory Access Protocol) directories on the Internet such as Bigfoot (www.bigfoot.com), Four11 (www.four11.com), and WhoWhere? (www.whowhere.com) for particular information. Here are the steps:

1. Choose Start ➤ Find ➤People, or in Explorer, choose Tools ➤ Find ➤People to open the Find People dialog box.

2. In the Look In list, select the name of the directory service you want to use

3. Type the information on the person you are looking for, usually just the first name followed by the last name, and then click Find Now.

The results of a search may vary depending on which of the services you use, but you will normally see a long list of names with different e-mail addresses. It is then up to you to decide which of those names is actually the person you want to contact.

FOLDER OPTIONS

In Explorer, choose View ➤ Folder Options (or Start ➤ Settings ➤ Folder Options) to open the Folder Options dialog box, in which you specify how your folders will look and work. The Folder Options dialog box contains three tabs: General, View, and File Types. When you open the Folder Options dialog box in My Computer, Network Neighborhood, and the Recycle Bin, you will see two tabs: General and View.

General Tab

Defines how the following systemwide settings work on your computer:

Web Style Specifies that your folders work with a single click just like the Web. Icon names will be underlined, and the normal arrow-shaped mouse pointer will turn into a hand as it passes over the icon.

Classic Style Specifies that your folders behave in the traditional Windows way. Click once to select an item; double-click to open or run an item.

Custom, Based on Settings You Choose   Specifies that you want to choose your own configuration. Click the Settings button to set these preferences.

View Tab

Controls advanced settings for files and folders. The Folder Views box contains two options you can use to make all the folders on your system look and work in the same way:

Like Current Folder   Uses the current settings in effect in the View menu (except for the toolbar settings) on all folders on your computer.

Reset All Folders   Uses the original View menu settings in effect when the program was first installed.

The Advanced Settings box contains a set of checkboxes for certain display options, such as how to treat hidden files, whether file attributes are shown in the Details view, and so on. Click the Restore Defaults button to put everything back into its original state.

File Types Tab

Displays all the file types currently registered with Windows; this is how Windows knows which program to use to open specific data files. When you select a file type in the list, the File Type Details box displays a short summary of which file name extension belongs to that type, its MIME content type, and the name of the program used to open it.

To change or delete one of the existing types, select it in the Registered File Types box, and then choose Edit or Remove. Click the New Type button to register a new file type with Windows. Here are the steps:

1. Click the New Type button to open the Add New File Type dialog box.

2. In the Description of Type field, enter a short text description along the lines of the other entries used, such as Active Streaming File Format.

3. Type the file name extension in the Associated Extension field.

4. Select an existing MIME Content_Type from the drop-down list, or enter a new MIME type.

5. Click the New button, and in the Actions field, enter the operation you want to perform; common operations are Open (to open the file) and Print. Then, in the Application Used to Perform Action field, enter the full path and file name of the application you want to associate with this file type. Click OK when you are done.

6. Click OK to return to the File Types tab in the Folder options dialog box.

FONTS

The styles of type used when Windows displays or prints text. Windows maintains a library of fonts that all applications that run under it use. Choose Start ➤ Settings ➤ Control Panel ➤ Fonts to open the Fonts folder, which displays all the fonts installed on your computer. Windows applications primarily use two types of fonts:

▶ TrueType fonts (represented by a pair of *T*s in the icon)

▶ Adobe fonts (represented by an *A* in the icon), which are bitmapped or vector fonts

The View menu of the Fonts folder offers two unique and quite useful views for fonts: List Fonts by Similarity, which groups fonts that are reasonably alike; and View ➤ Hide Variations, which hides bold, italics, and other variant forms of a typeface.

Fonts Used in Windows 98

The defaults for the size and type of fonts used in the Windows 98 windows and dialog boxes are set in the Display Properties dialog box. You can vary the font and size for text objects and in menus, message boxes, and title bars.

Right-click the Desktop and choose Properties from the pop-up menu to open the Display Properties dialog box, or choose Start ➤ Settings ➤ Control Panel ➤ Display. You use the Appearance and Settings tabs to control the size of fonts on the screen and the size and typeface of fonts for selected objects on the screen.

Adding a New Font to Your Computer

If you have acquired some new fonts, you can add them to those that come with Windows 98 by following these steps:

1. Choose Start ➤ Settings ➤ Control Panel ➤ Fonts to open the Fonts folder.

2. Choose File ➤ Install New Font to open the Add Fonts dialog box.

3. Select the drive and then select the folder that contains the new font.

4. Click the font you want to add. Hold down the Ctrl key and then click to select more than one font.

Displaying and Printing Font Samples

Once you have collected a large number of fonts, remembering what each one looks like can be difficult. Fortunately, the Windows 98 Font Viewer can help. To use it, follow these steps:

1. Open the Font folder.

2. Select any icon in the folder to open that font in the Font Viewer. Open additional Font Viewer windows if you want to compare two or more fonts.

3. To print an example of the font, click the Print button in the Font Viewer; alternatively, right-click the font in the Font folder and select Print from the pop-up menu.

FORMATTING DISKS

Format... Unless you purchase formatted disks, you must format a floppy disk before you can use it the first time. Formatting a new disk places information on the disk that Windows needs to be able to read and write files and folders to and from the disk. Formatting a used disk erases all the original information it contained and turns it into a blank disk, so be sure that you are formatting the right disk.

➔*See* Chapter 5 for instructions on formatting a floppy disk.

FRONTPAGE EXPRESS

A quick-and-easy Web-page editor you can use to create or customize your own Web pages without having to learn the details of Hypertext Markup Language (HTML). You can edit Web-page elements by selecting them in the main FrontPage Express window and then using a toolbar button or menu selection to apply formatting and alignment.

→*See* Chapter 20 for instructions on using FrontPage Express.

GAMES

Windows 98 includes four games: FreeCell, Hearts, Minesweeper, and that addictive time-waster, Solitaire. You can play Hearts over the network with other players. To get to the games, choose Start ➤ Programs ➤ Accessories ➤ Games, and then click the game you want to play. If you get stuck, click Help for instructions on how to play.

HELP

Windows 98 contains an extensive help system that provides you with online assistance at almost any time. You can use the main Windows 98 Help System to gain access to a huge amount of information, you can use Windows 98 Troubleshooters to diagnose and isolate a problem relating to specific hardware or software, and you can use Web Help to connect directly to Microsoft's Web site to look for program updates.

Windows Help System

Choose Start ➤ Help to open the main Windows 98 Help System dialog box, which has three tabs:

Contents   Lists the main categories in the Help system itself and a general overview of Windows 98.

Index   Lists all the subjects in the Help system in one giant alphabetic list. Type the first few letters of the word you're looking for in the text box at the top of this tab, and the list box will automatically scroll to the subject closest in spelling to what you have typed. Or you can scroll to it yourself by using the scroll bars on the right of the display box. When you get to the subject you want, select it and click Display.

Search   Allows you to find specific words or phrases contained within a Help topic. To do this, Windows 98 must create a database containing words used throughout the Help system. When you click the Search tab for the first time, the Search Setup Wizard creates this database. You can then use the Search tab to find the specific word or phrase you want.

When a Windows 98 Help topic is displayed, you may see a link icon. Click it to open the specific application, dialog box, or other element under discussion. When you close the application, you return to the same place in the Help system.

Using the Built-In Troubleshooters

Windows 98 extends the usual concepts of the Help system to include a set of built-in technical support troubleshooters you can use to help diagnose and isolate certain problems. There are two ways to find the right Troubleshooter and start it running on your system:

- ► You can choose Start ➤ Help to open the Windows 98 Help System. Select the Contents tab, select the Troubleshooting topic, and then open Windows 98 Troubleshooters. Choose the appropriate Troubleshooter from the list and follow the directions on the screen.

- ► Alternatively, you can start a Troubleshooter directly from a page of Help information. As you read through the information the page contains, you will come across a link to a Troubleshooter; click the link to start the Troubleshooter.

Once the Troubleshooter starts, click the Hide button on the Help toolbar to close the left pane. Be sure to follow all the steps the Troubleshooter suggests.

Troubleshooters are available for problems encountered with networking, printing, startup and shutdown, hardware such as modems, and procedures such as dial-up networking and connecting to the Microsoft Network.

Getting Web Help

Click the Web Help button on the Help System toolbar to connect to a
Microsoft site to look for updated versions of programs and device drivers.
You then select what you want to install; perhaps more important, you can
also uninstall a program or a device driver that is causing you problems.

Help in a Dialog Box

Context-sensitive Help is also available in certain dialog boxes and on
some property sheets in Windows 98. You may see a Help button on a
dialog box; click it to see information specific to that dialog box.

Other dialog boxes and many of the Windows 98 property sheets have
a Help button in the upper-right corner (look for the button with a question mark on it) next to the Close button. Click this Help button and the
question mark jumps onto the cursor; move the cursor to the entry on the
property sheet that you want help with and click again. A small window
containing the help text opens; click the mouse to close this window
when you are done.

INTERNET

 In Windows 98, you can view or change the configuration options
relating to the Internet in two ways:

▶ Via your connection to the Internet

▶ In Internet Explorer

To open the Internet Options dialog box, choose Start ➤ Connections ➤
Control Panel ➤ Internet, or open Internet Explorer and choose View ➤
Internet Options. The Internet Options dialog box has six tabs.

General Tab

The General tab contains these groups of settings:

Home Page   Lets you choose which Web page opens each
time you connect to the Internet. The home page is the first
Web page you see when you start Internet Explorer.

Temporary Internet Files   Lets you manage those Web pages
that are stored on your hard disk for fast offline access.

History   Contains a list of the links you have visited so that you can return to them quickly and easily. You can specify the number of days you want to keep pages in the History folder.

Colors   Lets you choose which colors are used as background, links, and text on those Web pages for which the original author did not specify colors. By default, the Use Windows Colors option is selected.

Fonts   Lets you specify the font style and text size to use on those Web pages for which the original author did not make a specification.

Languages   Lets you choose the character set to use on those Web pages that offer content in more than one language.

Accessibility   Lets you choose how certain information is displayed in Internet Explorer, including font styles, colors, and text size. You can also specify that your own style sheet is used.

Security Tab

Lets you specify the overall security level for each of four zones. Each zone has its own default security restrictions that tell Internet Explorer how to manage dynamic Web-page content such as ActiveX controls and Java applets. The zones are:

Local Intranet   Sites you can access on your corporate intranet; security is set to medium.

Trusted Sites   Web sites you have a high degree of confidence will not send you potentially damaging content; security is set to low.

Internet   Sites you visit that are not in one of the other categories; security is set to medium.

Restricted Sites   Sites that you visit but do not trust; security is set to high.

To change the current security level of a zone, select it from the list box, and then click the new security level you want to use:

High   Excludes any content capable of damaging your system. This is the most secure setting.

Medium   Opens a warning dialog box in Internet Explorer before running ActiveX or Java applets on your system. This is a moderately-secure setting that is good for everyday use.

Low   Does not issue any warning but runs the ActiveX or Java applet automatically. This is the least secure setting.

Custom   Lets you create your own security settings. To look at or change these advanced settings, click the Settings button to open the Security Setting dialog box. You can individually configure how you want to manage certain categories, such as ActiveX controls and plug-ins, Java applets, scripting, file and font downloads, and user authentication.

Content Tab

Contains settings you can use to restrict access to sites and specify how you want to manage digital certificates:

Content Adviser   Lets you control access to certain sites on the Internet and is particularly useful if children have access to the computer. Click Settings to establish a password, and then click OK to open the Content Advisor dialog box. Use the tabs in this dialog box to establish the level of content you will allow users to view:

> **Ratings**   Lets you use a set of ratings developed by the Recreational Software Advisory Council (RSAC) for language, nudity, sex, and violence. Select one of these categories, and then adjust the slider to specify the level of content you will allow.

> **General**   Specifies whether people using this computer can view material that has not been rated; users may see some objectionable material if the Web site has not used the RSAC rating system.

> **Advanced**   Lets you look at or modify the list of organizations providing ratings services.

Certificates   Lets you manage digital certificates used with certain client authentication servers. Click Personal to view the personal digital certificates installed on this system, click Authorities to list the security certificates installed on your system, or click

Publishers to designate a particular software publisher as a trustworthy publisher. This means that Windows 98 applications can download, install, and use software from these agencies without asking for your permission first.

Personal Information Lets you look at or change your own personal profile; this information is sent to any Web sites that request information when you visit their site. Click Edit Profile to review the current information.

Click Reset Sharing to clear the list of sites you previously allowed to access your personal information without asking your permission first. Microsoft Wallet gives you a secure place to store credit card and other information you might need for Internet shopping.

Connection Tab

Allows you to specify how your system connects to the Internet:

Connection Lets you specify whether your system will connect to the Internet via your corporate network or by modem. Click the Connect button to run the Connection Wizard and set up a connection to an Internet Service Provider (ISP). If you use a modem, click the Settings button to open the Dial-Up Settings dialog box where you can specify all aspects of the phone connection to your ISP.

Proxy Server Lets you access the Internet via a proxy server system connected to your corporate intranet. A proxy server is a security system designed to monitor and control the flow of information between your intranet and the Internet.

Automatic Configuration Lets you network system administrator configure your copy of Internet Explorer automatically.

Programs Tab

Lets you set your default program choices for e-mail, newsgroup reader, and so on and specify whether Internet Explorer should check to see if it is configured as the default browser:

Messaging Lets you choose which application programs are used for mail, news, and Internet calls.

Personal Information   Lets you choose which application programs are used for calendar functions and for your contact list.

Finally, you can specify that Internet Explorer check to see if it is configured as the default browser on your system each time it starts running.

Advanced Tab

Lets you look at or change a number of settings that control much of Internet Explorer's behavior, including accessibility, browsing, multimedia, security, the Java environment, printing and searching, and the Internet Explorer toolbar and how HTTP 1.1 settings are interpreted.

Changes you make here stay in effect until you change them again, until you download an automatic configuration file, or until you click the Restore Defaults button, which returns the settings on the Advanced tab to their original values.

INTERNET EXPLORER

The application that displays Web pages from the Internet or from your corporate intranet. In many ways, Internet Explorer resembles Windows Explorer; it is a *viewer* that presents information in a structured way. Internet Explorer is an easy-to-use program that hides a large part of the complexity of the Internet and Internet operations.

Help Menu

Gives you access to the Internet Explorer Help system through Contents and Index, lets you check for a newer version of Internet Explorer available through Product Updates, guides you through an online tutorial with Web Tutorial, and helps locate information on technical problems with Online Support.

When you choose Help ➢ Microsoft on the Web, the items on the submenu are actually links to different parts of the Microsoft Web site, including:

Free Stuff   Locates Internet Explorer program updates, free stuff, and add-on programs.

Get Faster Internet Access   Displays information about ISDN (Integrated Services Digital Network) service.

Frequently Asked Questions   Answers the most commonly asked questions about Internet Explorer.

Internet Start Page   Opens your home page.

Send Feedback   Lets you send your opinions right to Microsoft.

Best of the Web   Opens Microsoft's Exploring page, which contains a variety of links to useful and interesting sites. This is equivalent to clicking the Best of the Web button on the Internet Explorer Links toolbar.

Search the Web   Opens the same Web site as choosing Go ➢ Search the Web.

Microsoft Home Page   Opens Microsoft's Web site.

Configuring Internet Explorer

To view or set the many configuration options for Internet Explorer, choose View ➢ Internet Options to open the Internet Options dialog box. Or you can choose Start ➢ Connections ➢ Control Panel ➢ Internet. The Internet Options dialog box has six tabs. For a complete discussion of all the settings on these tabs, see the Internet entry earlier in this appendix.

Browsing Offline

You can browse the Web with Internet Explorer without being connected to the Internet. This is because many of the files that you open while browsing the Web are stored in the Temporary Internet Files folder on your hard disk. Choose File ➢ Work Offline, and Internet Explorer will not attempt to connect to the Internet when you select a resource, but will display the copy in the Temporary Internet Files folder instead. To go back to online browsing, choose File ➢ Work Offline a second time.

Speeding Up Internet Explorer

The text component of a Web page downloads quickly, but some of the other common elements, such as graphics, sound files, and animation clips, can take quite a long time to download.

Of course, there is nothing you can do to change the way a Web site is constructed, but you can stop certain types of files from being downloaded to Internet Explorer. You can essentially tell Internet Explorer to ignore all graphics files or all video clips and just collect the text. Here are the steps:

1. In Control Panel, click Internet, or choose View ➤ Internet Options within Internet Explorer to open the Internet Options dialog box.

2. Select the Advanced tab.

3. Scroll down the list box until you see the Multimedia settings, all of which are selected by default.

4. Deselect all the items you want to exclude from the Web pages you download to your system.

5. Click OK to close the Internet Options dialog box.

Remember that these options stay in effect for all subsequent Internet Explorer sessions until you turn them back on.

INSTALLING APPLICATIONS

You can install applications from floppy disks and CD-ROMs using the Add/Remove Programs applet in the Windows 98 Control Panel. You can also choose Start ➤ Run to invoke an individual Install or Setup program.

KEYBOARD

The Keyboard applet in the Control Panel allows you to set several important defaults for keyboard properties, such as the language displayed and at what speed a key must be pressed to be recognized as a repeat key.

To look at or change the keyboard properties, choose Start ➤ Settings ➤ Control Panel ➤ Keyboard to open the Keyboard Properties dialog box. It has two tabs: Speed and Language. The Speed tab contains the following options:

Repeat Delay   Sets the length of time you must hold down a key before the repeat feature kicks in.

Repeat Rate   Sets the speed at which a character is repeated while a key is held down.

Click Here and Hold Down a Key to Test Repeat Rate   Tests the repeat delay and repeat rate speeds that you have chosen.

Cursor Blink Rate   Sets the rate at which the cursor blinks, making the cursor easier to spot in some instances.

The Language tab contains the following options:

Language and Layout   Displays the language and keyboard layout loaded into memory when the computer is first started. Double-click the highlighted language or layout to open the Language Properties dialog box and select another keyboard layout.

Add   Adds a language and keyboard layout to those loaded into memory when the computer is booted.

Properties   Allows you to change the keyboard layout default.

Remove   Deletes the selected language and keyboard layout. It will no longer be loaded into memory when you boot the computer.

Set As Default with More Than One Language Installed Makes the currently selected language and keyboard layout the default to be used when the computer is started.

Switch Languages   Switches between two or more language and layout settings, as listed above. Click the key combination you want to use to switch the default.

Enable Indicator on Taskbar   Displays a language on the right of the Taskbar. Click this indicator to open a dialog box in which you can switch language defaults quickly.

LOG OFF

Windows 98 maintains a set of user profiles, each containing a different user name, password, Desktop preferences, and accessibility options. When you log on to Windows 98, your profile ensures that your Desktop settings—including elements such as your own desktop icons, background image, and other settings—are automatically available to you.

Windows 98 contains an option you can use to log off and log on again as another user quickly and easily. Click the Start button, and then click

Log Off *username.* In the Log Off Windows dialog box, click Yes. This closes all your programs, disconnects your system from the network, and prepares the system for use by other users.

Log On

When you log on to Windows 98 and are prompted to enter your user name and password, your user profile is loaded to ensure that your Desktop settings—including elements such as your own desktop icons, background image, and other settings—are automatically available to you.

Unfortunately, you can also press the Esc key to bypass this logon screen and completely circumvent all aspects of Windows logon security. This makes Windows 98 a particularly unsecure system.

If you are connected to a local area network and Windows 98 is configured for that network, you will also be prompted to enter your network password.

Maximize/Minimize Buttons

Allows you to change the size of an application window.

The Maximize button is in the upper-right corner of an application window, and when you click it, the window expands to full-screen size. Once the window has expanded, the Maximize button changes to the Restore button, which you can then use to shrink the window back to its original starting size.

You can also place the mouse pointer on the window border, and when the two-headed arrow appears, drag the border in the direction in which you want to change its size.

Use the Minimize button to place an open application on the Taskbar; click the Taskbar icon when you are ready to work with the application again.

Media Player

Allows you to play multimedia files, such as video, animation, and sound clips, depending on the hardware installed on your computer system. →*See* Chapter 9 for more information about using Media Player.

MODEMS

 Allows you to look at or change the settings Windows uses with your modem. Choose Start ➤ Settings ➤ Control Panel ➤ Modems to open the Modem Properties dialog box. ➡ *See* Chapter 10 for instructions on working with modem properties.

MOUSE

Changes your mouse settings. Choose Start ➤ Settings ➤ Control Panel ➤ Mouse to open the Mouse Properties dialog box, which contains three tabs. If you make changes to the settings in any of these tabs, click the Apply button to make sure your changes are implemented and then click OK.

Buttons Tab

Sets the mouse button configuration and speed with these options:

Button Configuration   Allows you to switch functions from the default right-handed use of the mouse buttons to left-handed.

Double-Click Speed   Allows you to set and then test the speed at which a double-click is recognized.

Pointers Tab

Allows you to change the appearance of the mouse pointer. For example, you can change the pointer used to indicate that Windows is busy from an hour-glass to a symbol or caricature of your choice.

The Scheme box contains the list of pointer schemes available in Windows. By selecting one, you'll see the set of pointers in the scheme displayed in the box below. You can create additional schemes by replacing the individual pointers.

Motion Tab

Controls the pointer speed and the presence of a pointer trail, which makes the mouse pointer much easier to see on LCD screens. If you select a pointer trail, you can also choose whether it is a long or a short trail.

MOVING FILES AND FOLDERS

In Windows, you can move files and folders in three ways:

- By dragging-and-dropping
- By choosing Edit ➤ Cut and Edit ➤ Paste
- By clicking the right mouse button

When you move a file or folder, you move the original to another location—no duplicate is made.

Using Drag-and-Drop

To use drag-and-drop, both the source and the destination folders must be visible, for example, in Explorer or on the Desktop. Hold down the left mouse button and drag the file or folder from one location to the other. When the file or folder reaches the correct destination folder, release the mouse button. The source and destination folders must be on the same drive. If you drag a file or a folder to a different drive, it will be copied rather than moved. If you want to move a file or folder to a different drive, you must drag using the right mouse button.

Using the Edit Menu

The Edit menu in My Computer, Explorer, or any folder window provides a Cut and Paste feature. Here are the steps to follow:

1. Select the file or folder you want to move.

2. Choose Edit ➤ Cut, or click the Cut button on the toolbar.

3. Find the destination file or folder and open it.

4. Choose Edit ➤ Paste, or click the Paste button on the toolbar.

TIP

You can select multiple contiguous files or folders to move by holding down Shift and clicking the first and last file or folder. To select noncontiguous files or folders, hold down Ctrl and click the files or folders your want.

Using the Right Mouse Button

Right-clicking a file or folder opens the pop-up menu, which you can use to perform a variety of functions, including moving. Follow these steps:

1. Right-click the file or folder you want to move and select Cut from the pop-up menu.

2. Open the destination folder, right-click, and then select Paste.

TIP

If you drag a folder or a file with the right mouse button, a pop-up menu opens when you release the button, allowing you to copy the object, move it, or create a shortcut.

MOVING AND ARRANGING ICONS

In Windows, you can arrange icons using any of several methods. In Explorer, Control Panel, and many other windows, you can move or arrange icons using the selections in the View menu:

Large Icons   Displays the files and folders as larger-sized icons.

Small Icons   Displays the files and folders as smaller-sized icons.

List   Displays small icons alongside the names of the files and folders.

Details   Displays files and folders in the List style and adds columns for the size of file, date last modified, and type of file. To sort entries within these columns, simply click the column heading. Click once for an ascending sort (A to Z and 0 to 9); click a second time for a descending sort.

Line Up Icons   Rearranges icons into straight vertical and horizontal lines.

TIP

To rearrange icons on the Desktop, simply drag them to their new location. To tidy up the Desktop quickly, right-click an area of free space, and choose Arrange Icons.

By clicking the Views button on the Explorer toolbar, you can cycle the display through the four presentations of Large Icons, Small Icons, List, and Details; each time you click the button, the display changes to the next format.

MULTIMEDIA

Establishes the default settings for multimedia devices connected to your computer; its contents depend on which multimedia devices you have installed.

Choose Start ➤ Settings ➤ Control Panel ➤ Multimedia to open the Multimedia Properties dialog box, containing tabs appropriate to the hardware installed on your computer. You might see the following tabs:

Audio Sets playback and recording controls.

Video Specifies the size of the video playback window.

MIDI Sets Musical Instruments Digital Interface controls and adds new instruments.

CD Music Sets the drive letter and head phone volume defaults.

Devices Lists the multimedia hardware connected to your computer and allows you to set or change properties for any of the hardware listed. Select the hardware component you want to configure, and then click Properties to open the related dialog box.

➡*See* Chapter 9 to learn more about multimedia in Windows 98.

MY COMPUTER

One of the file-management tools available with Windows. You can use My Computer to locate folders, files, and disks or printers on your computer or on mapped drives on other computers connected to the network.

My Computer Folder

Click the My Computer icon on the Desktop to open the My Computer folder, showing an icon for each drive and drive-level folder on your computer. Click an icon to display the contents of one of these folders or drives in a separate window.

Finding a File or Folder with My Computer

When you open My Computer, the My Computer folder displays all the disks and folders on your computer. Follow these steps to find the file or folder you want:

1. Click the down arrow at the end of the Address toolbar to find the device or folder you want. You will see all the shared disks on your network, important folders such as Control Panel, Printers, and Dial-Up Networking, and other Windows elements, such as Internet Explorer, Network Neighborhood, Recycle Bin, and My Briefcase.

2. Click a disk or a folder to see its contents in the window.

3. Once you find the file or folder (which may be several levels down), click it to open it.

MY DOCUMENTS

A Desktop folder that provides a convenient place to store graphics, documents, or any other files you might want to access quickly. When you save a file in programs such as Paint or Word-Pad, the file is automatically saved in My Documents unless you specify a different destination folder.

To specify a different destination folder, right-click My Documents and select Properties. Type the name of the new folder in the Target field and click OK. Changing to a different folder does not move existing files stored in My Documents.

NAMING DISKS

You can give a hard or a floppy disk a name that can be a maximum of 11 characters. To name or rename a disk, follow these steps:

1. Open My Computer or Explorer.

2. Right-click the disk you want to name, and select Properties to open the Properties dialog box.

3. Select the General tab, and type the name you want to use for this disk in the Label field. Click OK.

NAMING FILES AND FOLDERS

The first time you save a file using the Save or Save As command, you are asked to provide a name for the file. When you create a new folder, it is always called New Folder until you change the name. Names for files and folders can contain a maximum of 255 characters, including spaces, but cannot contain any of these special characters: / \ ? : * " < > |

You can rename both files and folders in Explorer or My Computer. Follow these steps:

1. Open Explorer or My Computer and find the file or folder you want to rename.

2. Click the name once, pause, and then click it again. A box will enclose the name, and the name will be selected. If you move the mouse inside the box, the pointer will become an I-beam.

3. Type the new name or edit the existing name and press Enter.

NETMEETING

A conferencing application that allows people working in different locations to collaborate simultaneously on the same project, sharing Microsoft applications to edit documents. NetMeeting also supports audio and video conferencing over the Internet (as long as you have the appropriate hardware such as a video camera or microphone attached to your computer system), as well as a file-transfer function.

Choose Start ➤ Programs ➤ Internet Explorer ➤ Microsoft NetMeeting to open NetMeeting.

ONLINE SERVICES

Allows you to access several popular online services such as AOL and the Microsoft Network. Before you can use any of these services, you must first register with it. You can do this using the items in the Online Services menu; each item connects you to a specific service. You can also use the Online Services folder on the Desktop.

Before you start, connect your modem to the phone line, and close any other open applications.

Outlook Express

 Windows application used to send and receive e-mail and read and post messages to Internet news groups. To start Outlook Express, click the Outlook Express Desktop icon, or choose Start ➤ Programs ➤ Internet Explorer ➤ Outlook Express. You can also click the Launch Outlook Express button on the Quick Launch toolbar, or use the Mail menu from within Internet Explorer.

Chapter 16 shows how to use Outlook Express for basic operations such as sending and receiving e-mail, as well as managing address books and mail folders. Following are additional highlights.

Reading the News

Outlook Express is also a newsreader, that you can use to access the thousands of specific-subject newsgroups on the Internet.

WARNING

Anything goes in many of these Internet newsgroups. There is absolutely no censorship, and if you are easily offended (and even if you are not), you might want to stay with the more mainstream Web pages.

In the same way that you set up an e-mail account with an ISP, you must also set up a newsgroup account, complete with password, before you can use Outlook Express as a newsreader.

Configuring Outlook Express

Configuration options for Outlook Express are quite extensive. You can customize the toolbar and add buttons for the tasks you perform most often, and you can define the rules you want Outlook Express to follow when you are creating, sending, and receiving e-mail. Choose Tools ➤ Options to open the Options dialog box. It has the following tabs:

General   Contains general-purpose settings for Outlook Express.

Send   Specifies the format for sending mail and articles to news-groups, as well as several other mail-related options, such as whether to include the text of the original message in any reply.

Read   Specifies options used when displaying articles from newsgroups.

Security   Establishes security zones and specifies how Outlook Express manages digital certificates (also known as digital IDs).

Dial Up   Specifies the options used when connecting to your ISP by dial-up connection.

Advanced   Specifies options only of interest to system administrators.

You can also choose View ➤ Layout to open the Layout Properties dialog box. Click Customize Toolbar to add or remove buttons from the Outlook Express toolbar. To return the toolbar to its original layout, click Customize Toolbar again, and then click Reset followed by Close in the Customize Toolbar dialog box.

PAINT

 A program with which you can create lines and shapes, with or without color, and place text within graphics. You can also use it to create backgrounds for the Desktop. Choose Start ➤ Programs ➤ Accessories ➤ Paint to open the main Paint window.

Paint Toolbar

Provides tools for drawing and working with color and text. Below the toolbar is an area containing optional choices depending on the type of tool you chose. For example, if you choose the Brush tool, a selection of brush edges is displayed. If you choose Magnifier, a selection of magnifying strengths is displayed. At the bottom of the main window, the Color Palette displays a series of colored squares.

The toolbox contains the following buttons for drawing lines and shapes and for working with color:

Free-Form Select   Selects an irregularly shaped area of the image to move, copy, or edit.

Select   Selects a rectangular area of the image to move, copy, or edit.

Eraser/Color Eraser   Erases an area of the image as you move the eraser tool over it.

Fill with Color   Fills an enclosed area with the currently selected color.

Pick Color   Selects the color of any object you click. It is for use with the tool that you chose immediately before you selected Pick Color.

Magnifier   Enlarges the selected area.

Pencil   Draws a free-hand line one pixel wide.

Brush   Draws lines of different shapes and widths.

Airbrush   Draws using an airbrush of the selected size.

Text   Inserts text onto the drawing. Click Text, click the color you want for the text, and then drag a text box to the location where you want to insert the text. In the font window that appears, click the font, size, and style (Bold, Italic, Underline) you want. Click inside the text box, and begin typing your text.

Line   Draws a straight line. After dragging the tool to create a line segment, click once to anchor the line before continuing in a different direction, or click twice to end the line.

Curve   Draws a curved line where one segment ends and another begins. After dragging the tool to create a line segment, click once to anchor the line before continuing. To create a curve, click anywhere on the line and then drag it. Click twice to end the line.

Rectangle   Creates a rectangle. Select the fill style from the toolbar below the main Paint window.

Polygon   Creates a polygon, or figure consisting of straight lines connecting at any angle. After dragging the first line segment, release the mouse, place the pointer where the second line segment is to end, click the mouse button, and repeat until the drawing is complete. Click twice to end the drawing.

Ellipse   Draws an ellipse. Select the fill style from the Color Palette below the main Paint window.

Rounded Rectangle   Creates a rectangle with curved corners. Select the fill style from the Color Palette below the main Paint window.

When you create an image in Paint, first select the tool, then select the tool shape, if applicable, and then click the color you want to use from the Color Palette at the bottom of the Paint window. The currently active color is displayed in the top square on the left of the palette. To change the background color, click Pick Color, and then click the color you want. The next image you create will use the new background color.

Paint Menus

Contain many of the standard Windows options. In addition, you can set a saved paint File to be used as wallpaper, zoom in various ways, flip or rotate an image, invert its colors, define custom colors, and set various image attributes.

PASSWORDS

Allows you to specify a logon password. Windows maintains a set of user profiles, each containing a different user name, password, Desktop preferences, and accessibility options. When you log on to Windows, your profile ensures that your Desktop settings, including elements such as your own Desktop icons, background image, and other settings, are automatically available to you.

Enabling User Profiles

To enable user profiles, follow these steps:

1. Choose Start ➤ Settings ➤ Control Panel ➤ Passwords to open the Passwords Properties dialog box.

2. Select *Users can customize their preferences and Desktop settings.*

3. In the User Profile Settings box; you can select one option or both:

   ➤ Include Desktop icons and Network Neighborhood content in user settings.

   ➤ Include Start menu and Program groups in user settings.

4. You'll have to use Shut Down to restart your computer for these changes to be applied.

Specifying a Password

When you start Windows 98 for the first time, you are prompted to enter a user name and password and then to confirm that password. If you are connected to a network, you may also be asked to enter a network password. On all subsequent startups, this series of dialog boxes will be slightly different. You will only be asked to enter the password; you will not have to confirm it.

Changing a Password

To change a password, follow these steps:

NOTE
You must know the current password in order to change it.

1. Choose Start ➤ Settings ➤ Control Panel ➤ Passwords to open the Passwords Properties dialog box.

2. Select the Change Passwords tab, and then click the Change Windows Password button to open the Change Windows Password dialog box.

3. Type the old password (asterisks will appear as you type), and enter the new password; you will have to retype the new password to confirm it. Click OK to close the Change Windows Password dialog box.

4. Click OK to close the Passwords Properties dialog box and finalize your new password. Next time you log on to Windows, remember to use your new password.

In addition to your logon password, you can establish a password for the following resources:

Dial-Up Connections   To change passwords, click My Computer, click the Dial-Up Networking icon, and select Connections ➢ Dial-Up Server. Click Allow Caller Access to enable the Change Password button.

Disks   To set and change passwords, right-click the disk in the Explorer window and select Sharing from the pop-up menu.

Folders   To change the password or sharing status, open Explorer or My Computer, select the folder, choose File ➢ Properties, and then click the Sharing tab.

Printers   To change the password or sharing status, open the Printers folder from either Explorer, My Computer, or Control Panel. Right-click the printer and select Sharing from the pop-up menu.

Network Administration   Set password access to shared devices from the Access Control tab in the Network applet in the Control Panel.

Screen Savers   You can use a password to prevent others from gaining access to your files when a screen saver is active. To change a password, choose Start ➢ Settings ➢ Control Panel ➢ Display to open the Display Properties dialog box. Select the Screen Saver tab and click Password Protected, and then click the Change button.

Shared Resources   To change the password or sharing status, open Explorer or My Computer, select the resource, choose File ➢ Properties to open the Properties dialog box, and select the Sharing tab. If the resource is shared, you can change the password. You can also change the sharing status from the Access Control tab in the Network applet in the Control Panel.

Click the Change Other Passwords button in the Passwords Properties dialog box to work with these other passwords.

Allowing Remote Administration

You can specify whether a system administrator can create shared folders and shared printers on your computer, and see the user names of anyone who connects to them by using the options on the Remote Administration tab in the Passwords Properties dialog box.

PASTE COMMAND

Copies the contents of the Clipboard into the current document. It is available from the Edit menu and some pop-up menus that are displayed when you right-click a file or a folder.

PLUG AND PLAY

A Windows feature that automatically detects hardware installed in your computer system. Today, most hardware is specifically designed with Plug and Play in mind. You just install the hardware, and Windows takes care of the details, loading the appropriate device drivers and other related software automatically.

Plug and Play adapters contain configuration information stored in permanent memory on the board, including vendor information, serial number, and other configuration data. The Plug and Play hardware allows each adapter to be isolated, one at a time, until Windows identifies all the cards installed in your computer. Once this task is complete, Windows can load and configure the appropriate device drivers. After installing a new Plug and Play adapter in your computer system, Windows will often ask you to restart the system. This is so the new device drivers can be loaded into the correct part of system memory.

PRINTERS

Manages all functions related to printers and printing. From here you can add a new printer, check on a job in the print queue, change the active printer, or modify a printer's properties. ➡️*See* Chapter 8 for a complete discussion of printers and printing in Windows 98.

PROGRAMS

Lists the programs available in Windows, either as stand-alone applications or as collections of applications located in submenus or program groups. Any selection that has an arrow pointer to the right of the name is not a single program but a program group. Choosing one of these groups opens another menu listing the items in the group.

Follow these steps to start a program from the Programs menu:

1. Choose Start ➤ Programs to display the current list of program groups.

2. Select a program group to display a list of the programs it contains.

3. Click an application name to start it.

Adding a New Submenu to the Programs Menu

Most Windows programs are added to the Programs menu automatically as they are installed—you are generally asked to verify in which folder or program group any new program should be placed—and the Setup program takes care of the rest. However, you can create a new submenu manually if you wish. Follow these steps:

1. Right-click the Start button and choose Open to open the Start Menu folder.

2. Select the Programs folder, and then choose File ➤ New ➤ Folder. This creates an empty folder in the Program group with the name New Folder.

3. Enter the name you want to use for the submenu as the name of this new folder, press Enter, and then open the folder you just created.

4. Choose File ➤ New ➤ Shortcut to start the Create Shortcut Wizard, which guides you through the process of adding applications to your new folder.

5. Enter the path and file name for the application in the Command Line box, or click the Browse button to locate the file.

6. Type a shortcut name for the program and click Finish.

The next time you open the Programs menu, you will see the entry you just created, and when you select that entry, you will see the list of items that it contains.

PROPERTIES

Characteristics of something in Windows—a computer, a peripheral such as a printer or modem, a file, or a folder—are displayed in the Properties dialog box. The properties for any item depend on what it is. To open any Properties dialog box, follow these steps:

1. Select the item in the Explorer.

2. Choose File ➤ Properties.

You can also open the Properties dialog box by right-clicking an object and then selecting Properties from the pop-up menu.

RECYCLE BIN

 A folder that stores deleted files until they are finally removed from your hard disk. The Recycle Bin is represented on the Desktop by a wastebasket icon. Files are copied to the Recycle Bin both directly and indirectly; you can simply drag a file there, or you can send a file to the Recycle Bin by choosing Delete from a pop-up menu. When you empty the Recycle Bin, the files it contains are permanently removed from your hard disk; once you empty the bin, anything it contained is gone for good.

 TIP
If the Recycle Bin contains deleted files, you will see paper protruding from the top of the wastebasket icon.

➡ *See* Chapter 5 for instructions on using the Recycle Bin.

REGIONAL SETTINGS

Sets the system-wide defaults for country (and therefore language), number, currency, time, and date formatting. If you are using English in the United States, you will probably never need Regional

Settings; if you want to use a different language, this is the place to start. Choose Start ➤ Settings ➤ Control Panel ➤ Regional Settings to open the Regional Settings Properties dialog box.

Regional Tab

On the Regional Settings tab, click the down arrow and select a language and a country.

Number Tab

Sets the defaults for how positive and negative numbers are displayed, the number of decimal places, the separator between groups of numbers, and so on. This tab contains the following options:

Decimal Symbol   Establishes which symbol will be used as a decimal point. The default in the United States is a period.

No. of Digits after Decimal   Specifies how many numbers will be placed to the right of the decimal point. The default is 2.

Digit Grouping Symbol   Determines the symbol that will group digits into a larger number, such as the comma in 999,999. The default is a comma.

No. of Digits in Group   Specifies how many numbers will be grouped together into larger numbers. The default is 3, as in 9,999,999.

Negative Sign Symbol   Establishes which symbol is used to show a negative number. The default is a minus sign.

Negative Number Format   Establishes how a negative number will be displayed. The default is to display the negative sign in front of the number, such as −24.5.

Display Leading Zeroes   Determines whether a zero is shown in front of a decimal number. The default is yes, as in 0.952.

Measurement System   Determines whether the system of measurement will be U.S. or metric. The default is U.S.

List Separator   Specifies which symbol will separate items in a list or series. The default is a comma.

If you make any changes in this tab, click Apply and then OK.

Currency Tab

Determines the format for displaying currency. For example, you might want to vary the number of decimal points or the presentation of negative numbers. This tab contains the following options:

Currency Symbol   Displays the symbol of the currency, such as the dollar sign.

Position of Currency Symbol   Shows where the currency symbol is displayed in the number—usually in front of a number.

Negative Number Format   Specifies how negative numbers are displayed.

Decimal Symbol   Determines which symbol separates the whole from the fractional parts of a number, such as a period or a comma.

No. of Digits after Decimal   Specifies how many digits are shown by default after the decimal—usually two.

Digit Grouping Symbol   Shows which symbol—usually a comma—separates the number groups, such as thousands, millions, and so on.

Number of Digits in Group   Specifies how many digits determine a number group, such as 3 for thousands, millions, and so on.

Click Apply and then OK to put any changes you make into effect.

Time Tab

Establishes the default formatting for the time. The Time tab has the following options:

Time Style   Determines how the time will be formatted.

Time Separator   Determines which symbol separates the hours from the minutes and seconds; the default is a colon.

AM Symbol   Specifies the default for the morning symbol.

PM symbol   Specifies the default for the afternoon symbol.

Click Apply and then OK to activate any changes you make.

Date Tab

Establishes the default formatting for the date. The Date tab has the following options:

Calendar Type   Displays the types of calendars that you can choose from.

Short Date Style   Lists the formats available for displaying the date.

Date Separator   Lists the symbols that can be used to separate the month, day, and year.

Long Date Style   Lists the formats available for displaying a formal date notation.

Click Apply and then OK to activate any changes you make.

RESTORE

Restores an archive copy of one or more files and folders to your hard disk after a disk or controller failure or some other unforeseen event. To start the Windows 98 backup and restore program, choose Start ➤ Programs ➤ Accessories ➤ System Tools ➤ Backup. The first time you start the program, a dialog box welcomes you to Microsoft Backup and leads directly into the Restore Wizard.

Using the Restore Wizard

Using the Restore Wizard is a quick and easy way to learn about restoring backups; it gets you going quickly with a minimum of technical knowledge. Check Restore Backed up Files, and then click OK in this opening dialog box to start the Wizard. If you would rather not use the Wizard, click Close; you can always restart it from the toolbar inside the Backup program if you change your mind.

The Wizard walks you through the following sequence of dialog boxes. Click the Next button when you have made your choice to advance to the next dialog box; click Back to retrace your steps, and click Cancel if you change your mind about using the Wizard.

Restore From   Specify the type and location of the backup you want to restore.

Select Backup Sets   Select a backup set for the restore.

What to Restore   You can restore all files and folders in the backup set, or you can restore selected files and folders.

Where to Restore   Specify the target of the restore; most of the time selecting Original Location to put the file back where it came from makes the most sense.

How to Restore   Specify whether existing files on your hard disk should be overwritten during the restore.

Click the Start button to begin the restore; a small progress indicator tracks the restore as it proceeds.

Using the Restore Tab

Using the Restore tab in the Backup program involves essentially the same tasks that the Restore Wizard does for you—selecting the files, deciding where to put them, and specifying how the restore should actually be made.

NOTE

A check mark in a gray check box means that only some of the files in a folder have been selected. A check mark in a white box means that all files in a folder have been selected.

Run

Starts a program or opens a folder when you type its path and name. You often use Run with a Setup program or installation programs or to run a program such as Scanreg that does not have a Windows shortcut. Follow these steps:

1. Choose Start ➤ Run to open the Run dialog box.

2. If you have run this program recently, you may find its name already entered in the Open list box. Click the down arrow, select it by name, and then click OK.

3. If you have not run this program recently or if the Open box is blank, type the full path and program name, such as C:*Folder**Program*.

4. If you are not sure of the path or program name, click Browse to find and select the program. Then click OK to load and run the program.

SCANDISK

Checks a disk for certain common errors. Once ScanDisk detects these errors, it can fix them and recover any data in corrupted areas. Windows 98 runs ScanDisk automatically if the operating system is shut down improperly, as might happen during a power outage.

Choose Start ➤ Programs ➤ Accessories ➤ System Tools ➤ ScanDisk to open the ScanDisk dialog box. ➤*See* Chapter 11 for instructions on using ScanDisk.

SCREEN SAVER

Displays an image on the screen after a fixed period of inactivity. The screen saver hides the normal information displayed by the application you are using and replaces it with another image.

You can change or select a screen saver using the Display applet in the Control Panel. You can set the speed, shape, density, and color of the screen saver, and you can set a password to get back to your work and other settings. You can also use certain active channels as screen savers.

SEND TO

Send To ▸ Sends items to common destinations, such as floppy disk drives, a fax, an e-mail, or My Briefcase. You can send a file quickly to a destination by following these steps:

1. Right-click the file or folder to open the pop-up menu.

2. Select Send To.

3. Click the appropriate destination.

SETTINGS

 Choose Start ➤ Settings to access all the Windows 98 configuration tools, including the Control Panel, Printers, Taskbar & Start Menu, Folder Options, and the Active Desktop controls.

SHORTCUTS

Quick ways to open an application or access a disk, file, folder, printer, or computer without going to its permanent location using the Windows Explorer. Shortcuts are useful for applications that you use frequently; when you access a shortcut, the file, folder, printer, computer, or program is opened for you. You can create a shortcut using the File menu, pop-up menus, or drag-and-copy. ➥*See* Chapter 4 for complete instructions on creating and using shortcuts.

SHUT DOWN

The procedure for closing Windows. You must always follow the Shut Down procedure before turning your computer off or restarting your system; if you don't, you run the risk of losing data. Follow these steps to shut down:

1. When you are ready to turn off your computer, choose Start ➤ Shut Down to open the Shut Down Windows dialog box. It contains the following options:

    Shut Down   Prepares the computer to be turned off.

    Restart   Prepares the computer for shut down and then automatically starts it again.

    Restart in MS-DOS Mode   Closes Windows and restarts the computer in MS-DOS mode.

2. Select the option you want, and then click OK.

3. Respond to any other questions that Windows displays, such as whether it is OK to disconnect network users.

When Windows 98 has finished saving data to your hard disk, it displays a final message telling you that it is now safe to turn off your computer.

SOUNDS

Assigns sounds to certain system events, such as warning dialog boxes, and to more common events such as opening or closing windows or receiving an e-mail message. Choose Start ➤ Settings ➤ Control Panel ➤ Sounds to open the Sounds Properties dialog box. ➙*See* Chapter 9 for instructions on assigning sounds and working with sound schemes.

START

The primary way to access files, folders, and programs on your computer. Initially, the Start button is on the bottom left of your screen at the left end of the Taskbar. Click Start to display the Start menu. Some of the options on this menu are standard with Windows 98, but you can add others to give you fast access to your favorite applications.

The Start menu contains the following options:

Shut Down   Prepares the computer to be shut down or restarted.

Log Off   Logs off the system quickly so that you can log back on with a different user profile or so that another user can log on.

Run   Opens the Run dialog box so that you can run a program or open a folder by typing its path and name.

Help   Opens the extensive Windows 98 Help system.

Find   Searches for a file, folder, device, or computer. You can also search the Internet and look for personal contact information.

Settings   Accesses the Control Panel, Printers, Taskbar & Start Menu, Folder Options, and Active Desktop controls so that you can configure the way Windows operates.

Documents   Gives you access to the last 15 documents you opened.

Favorites   Gives you access to Channels, Links, and Software Updates.

Programs   Gives you access to the program groups and files on your computer.

Windows Update   Automatically connects to the Microsoft Web site to check for updates to the Windows 98 operating system.

> **TIP**
>
> To add a program or a shortcut to the Start menu, simply drag its icon to the Start button.

STARTUP

An application that is activated automatically each time you start Windows. If you use certain applications frequently and do not want the bother of starting them manually every time you start Windows, simply put them in your Startup folder. Follow these steps:

1. Choose Start ➣ Settings ➣ Taskbar & Start Menu to open the Taskbar Properties dialog box.

2. Select the Start Menu Programs tab.

3. Click Add, and type the name of the path to the program you want, or click Browse to find it. Click Next.

4. Find the StartUp folder in the list of Start Menu folders, and select it. Click Next.

5. If you don't like the default, type the shortcut name that you want to appear in the StartUp folder, and click Finish.

6. If you are prompted to choose an icon, click one, and then click Finish.

7. To verify that the program you selected is now in the StartUp menu, choose Start ➣ Programs ➣ StartUp.

The next time you start Windows 98, the program you just added to the StartUp folder will be automatically loaded.

TASKBAR

Launches programs and is the primary tool for switching from one application to another. The Taskbar contains several types of icons:

▸ The Start button at the left end of the Taskbar is responsible for launching applications, opening documents, and adjusting settings.

▸ The Quick Launch toolbar contains buttons you can use to do the following:

   ▸ Open Internet Explorer

   ▸ Open Outlook Express

   ▸ Open TV Viewer

   ▸ Bring the Desktop to the front

   ▸ View channels

▸ Any shortcut buttons to the right of the Quick Launch toolbar represent the applications currently active in memory or open folders. You can use these icons to switch between the running applications.

▸ The system clock at the right end of the Taskbar displays the current time.

The Taskbar may also show other icons from time to time, indicating that an e-mail message is waiting, that you are printing a document, or the battery condition on a laptop computer.

Switching with the Taskbar

When you open a new application, the Taskbar gets another button, and by clicking that button, you can switch to the new application or folder.

Switching with Alt+Tab

You can also use the Alt+Tab key combination to switch between running applications. Press and hold down the Alt key and press the Tab key once to open a dialog box that contains an icon for each application running on your system. Each time you press the Tab key, the outline box moves one icon to the right until it wraps all the way round and reappears on the left side of the box. This outline box indicates the application that will run when you release the Alt key.

TASKBAR & START MENU

 The Taskbar is the main way that you switch from one application to another in Windows 98. The default Taskbar contains two types of buttons: the Start button, and any number of shortcut buttons for the applications currently active in memory.

To change how the Taskbar looks and works, choose Start ➤ Settings ➤ Taskbar & Start Menu to open the Taskbar Properties dialog box. You can also choose a toolbar from a set of default toolbars and add it to your Taskbar; you can even create your own custom toolbar.

TIP

You don't have to leave the Windows Taskbar at the bottom of the screen; you can place it along any of the four edges. To move it, simply drag it to its new location.

Modifying the Taskbar Display

The Taskbar is usually at the bottom of the screen and is always displayed on top of other windows so that you can get to it quickly and easily. To change how the Taskbar is displayed, follow these steps:

1. Choose Start ➤ Settings ➤ Taskbar & Start Menu to open the Taskbar Properties dialog box. You can also simply right-click an empty spot on the Taskbar and select Properties from the pop-up menu.

2. Place a check mark in the box next to the options you want:

   Always on Top   Forces the Taskbar to remain on top of other windows, ensuring that it is always visible to you.

   Auto Hide   Displays the Taskbar as a small thin line on the bottom of the screen. To also display the thin line when a full-screen window is displayed, select both Always on Top and Auto Hide.

   Show Small Icons in Start Menu   Displays a small Start menu with smaller icons.

Show Clock   Displays the time in the left of the Taskbar. By double-clicking the clock, you can reset the time or date.

3.   Click Apply to make the changes final, and then click OK.

Adding Toolbars

Windows 98 includes a default set of toolbars that you can add to your Taskbar if you wish:

Address   Allows you to open an Internet address without first opening Internet Explorer.

Links   Contains a set of Internet addresses.

Desktop   Contains all your Desktop icons. Because this toolbar is longer than the screen is wide, you can use the small arrows to see the other icons.

Quick Launch   Contains buttons you can use to do the following:

- ▶ Open Internet Explorer
- ▶ Open Outlook Express
- ▶ Open TV Viewer
- ▶ Bring the Desktop to the front
- ▶ View channels

To add one of these toolbars to your Taskbar, right-click an empty spot on the Taskbar, choose Toolbars from the pop-up menu, and then select the toolbar you want to add to your Taskbar.

TIP

You can also add your own shortcut to the Quick Launch toolbar. Open My Computer or Explorer, select the application you want to add, and drag it to the Quick Launch part of the Windows Taskbar. You will see that program's icon appear next to the other icons on the Quick Launch toolbar. To remove an icon from the Quick Launch toolbar, right-click it and choose Delete.

Creating a Custom Toolbar

If the default set of toolbars don't meet your needs, you can always create your own. Follow these steps:

1. Right-click an empty part of the Taskbar to open the pop-up menu.

2. Choose Toolbars ➤ New Toolbar to open the New Toolbar dialog box.

3. Select a folder from the list or type an Internet address that you want to appear as a toolbar.

Another way to build a custom toolbar is to create a new folder, add all your favorite shortcuts to it, and then choose Toolbars ➤ New Toolbar to turn it into a toolbar.

TASK SCHEDULER

A program you can use to run selected applications at specific times—daily, weekly or even monthly—without any input from you or involvement on your part. The Task Scheduler starts running in the background every time you start Windows 98; it just sits there until it is time to run one of your selected tasks, and then it moves into action. ➙*See* Chapter 11 for instructions about using Task Scheduler.

UNDELETING FILES

When you delete a file or a folder, it is stored in the Recycle Bin, but until you actually empty the Recycle Bin, you can still retrieve any files you deleted. To recover a file from the Recycle Bin and return it to its original location, follow these steps:

1. Click the Recycle Bin on the Desktop.

2. Select the file or files you want to restore.

3. Right-click and choose Restore, or choose File ➤ Restore.

If you have chosen to display the contents of the Recycle Bin as a Web page, you can also click Restore All to return multiple files to their original locations.

TIP
To select multiple files, hold down Ctrl while you click.

UNINSTALLING APPLICATIONS

The Uninstall program removes all traces that an application was ever installed. It removes all references to the program from the Windows directories and subdirectories and from the Windows Registry.

The Uninstall feature is found in the Add/Remove Program Properties dialog box. Follow these steps to uninstall a program:

1. Choose Start ➤ Settings ➤ Control Panel ➤ Add/Remove Programs to open the Add/Remove Programs Properties dialog box.

2. If necessary, select the Install/Uninstall tab.

3. Select the software you want to remove from the list and click Add/Remove.

USERS

Windows 98 maintains a set of user profiles each containing a different user name, password, Desktop preferences, and accessibility options. When you log on to Windows 98, your profile ensures that your Desktop settings—including elements such as your own Desktop icons, background image, and other settings—are automatically available to you.

To set up a new user profile, follow these steps:

1. Choose Start ➤ Settings ➤ Control Panel ➤ Users to open the Enable Multi-User Settings dialog box.

2. Click the Next button.

3. In the Add User dialog box, enter your user name and click Next.

4. In the Enter New Password dialog box, type your password. Type it again in the Confirm Password field and click Next.

5. In the Personalized Items Settings dialog box, select the items from the list that you want to personalize, and then choose whether you want to create copies of these items or create new items in order to save hard-disk space. Click the Next button.

6. Click the Finish button to complete the creation of this new user profile and to close the Wizard.

VOLUME CONTROL

An accessory you can use to control the volume of your sound card and speakers. If you have more than one multimedia capability installed, for example, MIDI or Wave-handling capability, you can control the volume and balance for each device separately. Follow these steps to access the Volume Control:

1. Choose Start ➤ Programs ➤ Accessories ➤ Entertainment ➤ Volume Control to open the Volume Control dialog box. It contains separate features to balance volume for the devices on your computer. Depending on the hardware installed on your computer, the following features may or may not appear:

    Volume Control   Controls volume and balance for sounds coming out of your computer. This is the "master" control.

    Line-In   Controls the volume and balance for an external device that feeds sound into your computer, such as audio tape or an FM tuner.

    Wave Out   Controls the volume and balance for playing .wav files as they come into the computer.

    MIDI   Controls the volume and balance for incoming sounds from MIDI files.

    Audio-CD   Controls the volume and balance for CD-ROM audio files as they come into the computer.

    Microphone   Controls the volume and balance for sound coming in via a microphone.

2. To control the volume of the components, move the vertical slider labeled Volume up or down to increase or decrease volume.

3. To control the balance between two speakers, move the horizontal slider labeled Balance to the left or right to move the emphasis to the left or right speaker.

4. Click Mute All or Mute to silence all components' or one component's contribution to the sound.

Varying the Recording Volume

To vary the volume and balance when you are recording, follow these steps:

1. From the Volume Control dialog box, choose Options ➤ Properties to open the Properties dialog box.

2. Select Recording to display a list of devices that apply to the recording task.

3. If it is not already checked, click the check box to select the device you want.

4. Click OK to open the Recording Control dialog box for the selected device.

5. Move the Balance and Volume sliders to adjust the volume and balance of the sound.

WELCOME TO WINDOWS

Opens an interactive guide to Windows 98. Choose Start ➤ Programs ➤ Accessories ➤ System Tools ➤ Welcome to Windows. The Welcome screen contains the following options:

Register Now Runs the Windows 98 Registration Wizard so that you can register your copy of Windows 98. In the Welcome screen, click Next to proceed with online registration, or click Register Later if you don't want to register right now.

Discover Windows 98 Starts a three-part Windows 98 tutorial consisting of Computing Essentials, Windows 98 Overview, and What's New.

Tune Up Your Computer   Runs Windows Tune-Up on your system.

Release Notes   Opens WordPad on the Windows 98 Release Notes file. You should check the information in this file as it may contain late-breaking information that didn't make it into the Windows Help system.

WHAT'S THIS

What's This?   Provides context-sensitive help in some dialog boxes. If you right-click an item in a dialog box, a small menu opens containing the single selection What's This. Click What's This to display help text for that specific item.

Other dialog boxes have a Help button in the upper-right corner (look for the button with a question mark on it) next to the Close button. When you click this Help button, the question mark jumps onto the cursor; move the cursor to the entry on the dialog box that you want help with and click again. A small window containing the help text opens; click the mouse to close this window when you are done.

WINDOWS TUNE-UP

Optimizes your system for best performance. The Windows Tune-Up Wizard can help make your programs run faster, free up precious hard-disk space, and optimize system performance.

The Wizard actually does its work by running three other Windows system utilities—Disk Defragmenter, ScanDisk, and Disk Cleanup—in concert with Task Scheduler, which controls when the other utilities run on your system. To run Windows Tune-Up, follow these steps:

1. Choose Start ➤ Programs ➤ Accessories ➤ System Tools ➤ Windows Tune-Up to start the Windows Tune-Up Wizard. The Wizard welcome screen gives you two choices:

    Express   Uses the most common optimization settings.

    Custom   Allows you to select the tune-up settings.

2. Choose Express and click Next.

The next screen lets you schedule when the Tune-Up Wizard will run on your system. Select a time when your computer will be switched on but you won't be using it, such as in the middle of the night, very early in the morning, or during your lunch break.

3. In the final screen, you will see a list of the optimizations that the Wizard plans to execute on your system. Check the box at the bottom of the screen to run these optimizations when the Wizard closes.

4. Click Finish to close the Wizard.

If you choose Custom in the Wizard welcome screen, you can also specify in more detail how Disk Defragmenter, ScanDisk, and Disk Cleanup will operate on your system.

WINDOWS UPDATE

Connects to the Windows Update Web site and keeps your system up-to-date by automatically downloading new device drivers and Windows system updates as they are needed. Choose Start ➢ Windows Update, or choose Start ➢ Settings ➢ Windows Update. Internet Explorer opens and connects to the Web site. The Wizard scans your system looking for items that could be updated. It makes a list of any new device drivers or system patches that you need and then downloads and installs the files for any items you want to update.

You will also find current information on using Windows 98 on the Windows Update Web site as well as a set of answers to frequently asked questions about Windows. Simply follow the instructions on the screen.

Appendix B

WINDOWS 98
USER'S GLOSSARY

Adapted from *PC User's Essential
Accessible Pocket Dictionary*,
by Peter Dyson (ISBN 0-7821-1684-1
240 pages $14.99), and *The Internet
Dictionary*, by Christian Crumlish
(ISBN 0-7821-1675-2   656 pages $14.99)

32-bit computer   Any computer that deals with information 32 bits at a time. This description can be applied to:

▶ The *word* size of the *microprocessor* used in the computer. A 32-bit computer works with 4 bytes at a time.

▶ The width of the computer's data *bus*. A 32-bit data bus has 32 separate data lines.

A: In DOS and Windows, the identifier used for the first floppy disk drive. Unless instructed differently in the ROM-BIOS settings, the operating system always checks drive A: for startup (or *bootstrap*) instructions before checking the hard disk, drive C:.

access   1. A connection to the Internet. 2. A type of Internet connection (network access, dial-up access, etc.). 3. The degree of ability to perform certain activities or read privileged information.

access provider   An institution providing Internet access, such as a commercial service provider, university, or employer. ➡ *See also* **online service**.

account   A form of access to a computer or network for a specific username and password, usually with a home directory, an e-mail inbox, and a set of access privileges. Accounts are usually kept for administrative or security reasons, although in communications and online services, accounts are used as a method of identifying a subscriber for billing purposes.

active window   In an operating system or application program capable of displaying multiple windows on the screen at the same time, the active window is the window that contains the cursor. If a window is active, its title bar changes color to differentiate it from all the inactive windows. Only one window can be active at a time. ➡ *See also* **cascade, graphical user interface, tile**.

address   1. The precise location in memory or on disk where a piece of information is stored. Every byte in memory and every sector on a disk have their own unique addresses. 2. A unique identifier for a computer or site on the Internet—this can be a numerical IP address (logical address) or a textual domain-name address (physical address). 3. A fully specified e-mail address (of the form *username@host.domain*).

address book   In Netscape's Communicator and Microsoft Outlook Express, a list of abbreviations for e-mail addresses. ➡ *See also* **alias**.

alias   1. An abbreviation for an e-mail address stored in a mail program, allowing the user to type or select a shorter alias instead of the full address. 2. An alternate name for an Internet address.

alt.   A hierarchy of newsgroups in the Usenet mold but outside of Usenet proper, devoted to "alternative" topics. These newsgroups were originally created to avoid the rigorous process required to create a normal Usenet newsgroup.

analog-to-digital converter   Abbreviated ADC or A–D converter. A device that converts continuously varying *analog* signals into discrete *digital* signals or numbers. Once analog signals have been converted into digital form, they can be processed, analyzed, stored, displayed, and transmitted by computer. ➞ *See also* **digital-to-analog converter**.

anchor   An HTML tag that indicates a hypertext link or the destination of such a link.

anonymous FTP   The most common use of FTP, the Internet file transfer protocol. FTP sites that allow anonymous FTP don't require a password for access—you only have to log in as *anonymous* and enter your e-mail address as a password (for their records).

applet   A small *application* program, limited in scope to a single small but useful task. A calculator program or a card game might be called an applet.

application   Abbreviated as "app." A computer program designed to perform a specific task, such as accounting, scientific analysis, word processing, or desktop publishing.

application key   Also called the "right-click key." The key marked with a menu symbol on 104-key enhanced keyboards; it is used in some Windows 9*x* applications to display the same menu as right-clicking in the same context.

application window   A window that contains the work area and menu bar for a running application program. An application window may contain one or more document windows within it.

archive   1. On the *Internet*, a site containing a collection of files available via *anonymous FTP*. 2. A collection of related files all stored under one file name; the files may also have been compressed to save hard-disk space.

article   An e-mail message posted to one of the Usenet newsgroups, accessible by anyone with a newsreader and a connection to the Internet.

ASCII   The abbreviation for *American standard code for information inter-change.* (Pronounced "as-kee.") ASCII is a standard character set that's been adopted by most computer systems around the world (usually extended for foreign alphabets and diacriticals).

asynchronous transmission   In communications, a method of transmission that uses start and stop bits to coordinate the flow of data so that the time intervals between individual characters do not have to be equal. Parity may also be used to check the accuracy of the data received. → *See also* **synchronous transmission**.

attach   To send a document along with an e-mail message.

attribute   1. A file attribute is a characteristic that indicates whether the file is a read-only file, a hidden file, a system file, or has changed in some way since it was last backed up. 2. A screen attribute controls a character's background and foreground colors, as well as other characteristics such as underline, reverse video, or blinking. 3. In a database, the name or the structure of a field is considered to be an attribute of a record.

authentication   Verification of the identity of the sender of a message.

backbone   A large, fast network connecting other networks. The National Science Foundation maintains one of the largest backbones in the United States, NSFnet. Other Backbone providers include UUNet and MCI.

backup   An up-to-date copy of all your files that you can use to reload your hard disk in case of an accident. It is an insurance against disk failure affecting the hundreds or possibly thousands of files you might have on your system hard disk, or on your local area network hard disk.

backward-compatible   Fully compatible with earlier versions of the same application program or computer system.

baud rate   In communications equipment, a measurement of the number of state changes (from 0 to 1 or vice-versa) per second on an *asynchronous* communications channel. Baud rate is often mistakenly assumed to correspond to the number of bits transmitted per second, but because in modern high-speed digital communications systems one state change can be made to represent more than 1 data bit, baud rate and bits per second are not always the same. → *See also* **asynchronous transmission**.

BBS   The abbreviation for *bulletin board system*. A computer system, equipped with one or more modems, acting as a message-passing system or centralized information source, usually for a particular special interest group. Bulletin board systems are often established by software vendors and by different PC user groups. → *See also* **online service**.

BIOS   The acronym for *basic input/output system* (pronounced "bye-os"). In the PC, a set of instructions, stored in read-only memory (ROM), that let your computer's hardware and operating system communicate with application programs and peripheral devices such as hard disks, printers and video adapters.

bit   A contraction of *BInary digiT*. A bit is the basic unit of information in the binary numbering system, representing either 0 (for off) or 1 (for on). Bits can be grouped together to make up larger storage units, the most common being the 8-bit *byte*. A byte can represent all kinds of information including the letters of the alphabet, the numbers 0 through 9, and common punctuation symbols.

bits per second   Abbreviated *bps*. The number of binary digits, or bits, transmitted every second during a data transfer. A measurement of the speed of operation of equipment such as a computer's data bus or a modem connecting a computer to a transmission line.

bookmark   In Web browsers, a reference to a page to which you might want to return later.

bounce   E-mail that fails to reach its destination and returns to the sender is said to have bounced.

browse   To skim an information resource on the Net, such as Usenet, gopherspace, or the Web.

browser   A client program used to read the Web. → *See also* **Web browser**.

bug   A logical or programming error in hardware or software that causes a malfunction of some sort.

button   1. A dialog-box element that lets the user select an option. In addition to application-specific buttons, almost all dialog boxes contain a Cancel button that allows you to abort the current operation, as well as the OK button, used to confirm a selection. 2. One of the keys on a mouse. → *See also* **dialog box**.

byte   A contraction of *BinarY digiT Eight*. A group of 8 bits that in computer storage terms usually holds a single character, such as a number, letter, or other symbol. Because bytes represent a very small amount of storage, they are usually grouped into *kilobytes* (1,024 bytes), *megabytes* (1,048,576 bytes), or even *gigabytes* (1,073,741,824 bytes) for convenience when describing hard disk capacity or computer memory size.

cache   (Pronounced "cash.") A special area of memory, managed by a *cache controller*, that improves performance by storing the contents of frequently accessed memory locations and their addresses. When the processor references a memory address, the cache checks to see if it holds that address. If it does, the information is passed directly to the processor; if not, a normal memory access takes place instead.

cache memory   (Pronounced "cash memory.") A relatively small section of very fast memory (often *static RAM*) reserved for the temporary storage of the data or instructions likely to be needed next by the processor.

capture   To save text as it scrolls across the screen. Captured text can be read while the user is offline.

cascade   In a windowed environment, the arrangement of several overlapping windows so that their title bars are always visible. The windows appear to be stacked, one behind the other. ➝ *See also* **tile**.

cascading menu   A menu selection that leads to one or more further menus; usually indicated by a right-pointing triangle.

case-insensitive   Not distinguishing between upper- and lowercase characters. In a case-insensitive search, *Internet, internet,* and *INTERNET* all match the same key word. The DOS operating system underlying Windows 98 is case-insensitive, as are e-mail addresses.

case-sensitive   Distinguishing between upper- and lowercase characters. To a case-sensitive program, *Peter, PETER, peter,* and *PeTeR* all mean different things.

cc: A list of additional recipients for an e-mail message listed in the header of the message (from *carbon copy*, a carryover from office-memo shorthand). Most e-mail programs enable the sender to add addresses to the cc: list.

CD-ROM   The abbreviation for *Compact Disc/Read-Only Memory*, a format for storing data on compact discs.

CD-ROM Extended Architecture   Abbreviated *CD-ROM/XA*. An extension to the CD-ROM format, developed by Microsoft, Phillips, and Sony, that allows for the storage of audio and visual information on compact disc, so that you can play the audio at the same time you view the visual data.

central processing unit   Abbreviated *CPU*. The computing and control part of the computer. The Intel Pentium is a CPU.

channel   1. A special Web site that uses push technologies to deliver information to the client software. (➡ *See also* **Dynamic HTML**.) 2. Any connecting path that carries information from a sending device to a receiving device. A channel may refer to a physical medium, like *coaxial cable*, or to a specific frequency within a larger channel. 3. An IRC topic area.

character   A letter, number, space, punctuation mark, or symbol—any piece of information that can be stored in one byte.

check box   In Windows dialog boxes, a small square box you toggle on or off to make nonexclusive choices.

circuit   A communications channel or path between two devices capable of carrying electrical current. Also used to describe a set of components connected together to perform a specific task.

circuit board   A computer card holding printed circuits.

clipboard   An area of memory reserved by Windows for temporary storage of text or graphics being transferred within the same file, between files in the same application program, or between applications. Material placed on the clipboard remains there until it is replaced by another selection, or the computer is turned off or restarted. ➡ *See also* **cut, Dynamic Data Exchange**.

clock   An electronic circuit that generates regularly spaced timing pulses at speeds of up to millions of cycles per second. These pulses are used to synchronize the flow of information through the computer's internal communications channels. ➡ *See also* **clock speed**.

clock speed   Also known as *clock rate*. The internal speed of a computer or processor, normally expressed in MHz. The faster the clock speed, the faster the computer will perform a specific operation, assuming the other components in the system, such as disk drives, can keep up with the increased speed.

close   1. To remove a file from memory and return it to disk (with or without saving any changes), at the same time removing its window from the screen. 2. To terminate an application program in an orderly fashion and remove its window from the screen. 3. To remove any window from the screen; also, to remove a dialog box from the screen.

.com   The Internet domain dedicated to commercial entities, generally in the United States.

command line   Any interface between the user and the command processor that allows the user to enter commands from the keyboard for execution by the operating system. In Windows, the DOS command line is accessible via Start ≻ Programs ≻ MS_DOS Prompt.

command prompt   A character or group of characters on the screen that lets you know that the operating system is available and ready to receive input.

commercial access provider   A service provider that charges for access to the Internet, as opposed to employers, universities, and free-nets, which provide access for free. Commonly referred to as an Internet service provider, or ISP.

common carrier   A communications company, such as AT&T, MCI, or ITT, that provides telecommunication services to the general public.

compatibility   The extent to which a given piece of hardware or software conforms to an accepted standard, regardless of the original manufacturer.

compressed file   A file that has been processed by a special utility program so that it occupies as little hard-disk space as possible. When the file is needed, the same program decompresses the file back into its original form so that it can be read by the computer.

computer system   Any complete collection of hardware, software, and peripherals, designed to work together. In the PC world, a computer system comprises at least the following: a system unit that houses hard- and floppy disk drives, memory, the motherboard, and any required expansion boards; a keyboard; a mouse; and a monitor.

connect time   The amount of time a user spends connected to a service provider. Many providers charge a fee based on connect time. Others are flat-rate providers.

context menu   The menu displayed in Windows 9*x* and many applications when the user right-clicks; the options offered depend on the application context—what you are doing at the time.

Control Panel   In Windows, a selection that contains settings to control hardware options such as the mouse, display, and keyboard.

cookie   A very small text file that many Internet sites use to track visitors. A cookie can contain information as basic as an identification number to count visits from a single person or as detailed as a complete user profile.

copy   To duplicate part of a document and reproduce it elsewhere. The material copied can range from a single character to pages of text and graphics. A copy operation leaves the original in place and unchanged.
→*See also* **clipboard, cut, cut-and-paste**.

corrupted   Term used to describe a file, block of data, or other communication, damaged in transmission.

Ctrl+Alt+Del   A three-key combination used in IBM-compatible computers to restart or reboot the machine and reload the operating system. By pressing Ctrl+Alt+Del, you initiate a warm boot, which restarts the computer without going through the power-on self test normally run if the computer goes through a cold boot when power is first applied.

cursor   A special character on a display screen that indicates where the next character will appear when it is typed. The cursor can take many shapes, depending on the current operation, and may also change shape as it moves to different parts of the screen. In Windows, a vertical I-beam cursor indicates the point at which text or graphics will be inserted.

cut   To remove a marked portion of a document into a temporary storage area such as the *clipboard*. This material can then be pasted from the clipboard into a different place in the original document or even into an entirely different document. →*See also* **cut-and-paste**.

cut-and-paste   To remove a marked portion of a document into temporary storage (such as the *clipboard*), and then insert it either into a different document or into a new place in the original document. Cut-and-paste allows compatible application programs to share text and graphics.
→*See also* **cut**.

cyberspace   A descriptive term for the virtual geography of the online world. This term first appeared in print in William Gibson's novel *Neuromancer,* published in 1984. The book describes the online world of computers and the elements of society that use these computers.

data   Information in a form suitable for processing by a computer, such as the digital representation of text, numbers, graphic images, or sounds.

default   A standard setting, used in the absence of any user-specified alternative.

default action   Any action performed when you press Enter in response to a dialog box without first changing anything; usually chosen because it is the action you would most likely want in any given circumstance.

delete   To remove a file from a disk, or to remove an item of information from a file. Files can be erased using operating system commands or directly from an application program. ➡ *See* also **file recovery, undelete program**.

deselect   The process of removing the highlighting from one or more choices or options. ➡ *See also* **select**.

desktop   Broadly, any on-screen version of a traditional desktop containing windows, icons, and dialog boxes that represent application programs, files, and other desktop accessories. As the user works, they open files, then put them away again, move items around on the desktop, and perform other day-to-day tasks. When capitalized, refers to the Windows 98 Desktop.

device   A general term used to describe any computer peripheral or hardware element that can send or receive data. For example, modems, printers, serial ports, disk drives, and monitors are all referred to as devices. Some devices may require special software, known as a *device driver*, to control or manage them.

device driver   A small program that allows a computer to communicate with and control a *device*. Each operating system contains a standard set of device drivers for the keyboard, the monitor, and so on, but if specialized *peripherals* are added, the user will probably have to add the appropriate device driver so that the operating system knows how to manage the device.

diagnostic program   A program that tests computer hardware and *peripherals* for correct operation.

dialog box   A dialog box always opens when the user chooses a menu selection followed by an ellipsis; that is, when more information is needed from the user before the program can continue. A dialog box may contain several different elements, including text boxes, list boxes, command buttons, and drop-down list boxes, depending on the purpose of the dialog box, but it does not have to contain all these elements at the same time.

dial-up account   An Internet account on a host machine that the user must dial up with a modem to use.

digital-to-analog converter   Abbreviated DAC or D-A converter. A device that converts discrete digital information into a continuously varying *analog* signal. Many modern sound boards can sample and play back at up to 44.1 kHz using a 16-bit digital-to-analog converter that produces spectacular stereo sound. Compact disc players use a digital-to-analog converter to convert the digital signals read from the disc to the analog signal that you hear as music. ➡ *See also* **analog-to-digital converter**.

dimmed command   Also known as a *grayed command*. A command that is not currently available is displayed in light gray rather than the usual black.

directory   In a hierarchical file system, a convenient way of organizing and grouping files and other directories on a disk. The beginning directory is known as the root directory from which all other directories must branch; directories inside another directory are often called subdirectories. In Windows 98, directories are called folders.

directory tree   A visual representation of the branching structure of all the directories, subdirectories, and files on a disk. Directories, subdirectories, and files may be shown by name or represented by icons.

disable   To turn off a function or prevent something from happening. In a graphical user interface, disabled menu commands are often shown in gray to indicate that they are not available. ➡ *See also* **dimmed command, enable**.

disk drive   A peripheral storage device that reads and writes magnetic or optical disks. When more than one disk drive is installed on a computer, the operating system assigns each drive a unique name—for example A: and C: in DOS and Windows.

DNS   A collection of distributed databases (*domain name servers*) that maintain the correlations between domain name addresses and numerical IP addresses, for example, the domain name address `ruby.ora.com` gets resolved into the numeric Internet address `134.65.87.3`, and vice versa. DNS allows human beings to use the Internet without remembering long lists of numbers.

domain   The general category that a computer on the Internet belongs to. The most common high-level domains are:

▶ **.com**: a commercial organization

▶ **.edu**: an educational establishment

▶ **.gov**: a branch of the U.S. government

▶ **.int**: an international organization

▶ **.mil**: a branch of the U.S. military

▶ **.net**: a network

▶ **.org**: a nonprofit organization

Most countries also have unique domains named after their international abbreviation. For example, .UK for the United Kingdom and .CA for Canada. ↦ *See also* **DNS, domain name, e-mail address**.

domain name   The easy-to-understand name given to an Internet host computer, as opposed to the numerical IP address. ↦ *See also* **DNS**.

DOS   The acronym for *Disk Operating System,* an operating system originally developed by Microsoft for the IBM PC.

DOS prompt   A visual confirmation that the DOS operating system is ready to receive input from the keyboard. The default prompt includes the current drive letter followed by a greater-than symbol; for example, C>. Even in Windows 98, the DOS prompt can be the most efficient way to perform some operations, particularly those where wildcard characters can represent large groups of files or folders. ↦ *See also* **command line, command prompt**.

dot   The separator character for domain names, newsgroup names, and other UNIX-oriented files. Dots should only be used to separate hierarchical levels in newsgroup names, not to split compound names.

double-click   To press and release the mouse button rapidly, twice in quick succession, without moving the mouse. Double-clicking is used to select an object as well as to initiate an action. For example, if you double-click a program icon, you select that program, and also start the application running. ➡ *See also* **click**.

download   To transfer a file over a modem from a remote computer to a desktop computer. (Technically, to transfer a file from a larger computer to a smaller computer.)

drag   To move a selected object using the mouse. The user places the mouse cursor on the selected object, and holds down the mouse button while moving the mouse to the new location. When the mouse button is released, and the object is inserted.

drag-and-drop   To move a selected object onto another object with the mouse to initiate a process. For example, if the user drags a document icon and then drops it onto a word processor's icon, the program will run and the document will be opened.

drop-down list box   A dialog box element that helps the user choose one item from a list of possible alternatives.

dump   To send the contents of a file (or other data) to a device or another file in order to print, display, or store the data.

dynamic data exchange   Abbreviated *DDE*. A method of communication between programs available in Windows and other environments. When two (or more) programs that both support dynamic data exchange are running at the same time, they can exchange *data* and commands, by means of "conversations." A DDE conversation is a two-way connection between two different application programs, used to transmit data by each program alternately. DDE has largely been superseded by a more complex but more capable mechanism known as Object Linking and Embedding (OLE).

dynamic HTML   Also referred to as *DHTML*. A more recent version of the HyperText Markup Language. it facilitates greater control over the placement of objects on a Web page, and the use of layering and style sheets.

dynamic RAM   Abbreviated DRAM (pronounced "dee-ram"). A common type of computer memory that uses capacitors and transistors storing electrical charges to represent memory states. These capacitors lose their electrical charge, and so need to be refreshed every millisecond, during which time they cannot be read by the processor.

edit   To make any change to the contents of a file.

e-mail   Also *email*, short for *electronic mail*, one of the most popular features of networks, online services, and the Internet in general. The term *e-mail* is used to describe both the overall process and the messages carried electronically from computer to computer.

e-mail address   1. An Internet mail address of the form *username@host .domain*. 2. The username portion of a mail account on a network.

enable   To turn on a function or allow something to happen. When a function is enabled, it is available. In a graphical user interface, enabled menu commands are often shown in black type to indicate that they are available. ➞ *See also* **disable**.

environment   Also called *operating environment,* a front end for an operating system. A set of tools and a consistent "look and feel" that allow the user to interact with the computer. Windows is an environment that runs on top of the MS-DOS operating system.

error message   A message from the program or the operating system, informing the user of a condition that requires some human intervention to resolve.

Eudora   An e-mail program for Windows or the Macintosh that can use the Post Office Protocol and function as an offline mail reader. Available via anonymous FTP from ftp.qualcomm.com.

event-driven program   Any program designed to react to a keystroke or a mouse click, rather than forcing a user to go through traditional menu selections and on-screen prompts. Microsoft Windows and the Macintosh operating system both use this design approach.

expand   1. To show all the subdirectories in a graphical display of a directory tree. 2. To decompress a *compressed file.* ➞ *See also* **directory tree**.

expandability   The ability of a system to accommodate expansion. In hardware, this may include the addition of more memory, more or larger disk drives, and new adapters. In software, it may include the ability of a network to add users, nodes, or connections to other networks.

export   To save a file in a different format (that of another program).

extension   The portion of a file name after the last dot, often used to indicate the type of file. DOS extensions have a three-character maximum length.

extranet   An enterprise's private intranet that relies on secure use of the public Internet to connect disparate locations.

FAQ   (Pronounced "fack.") 1. A *frequently asked question.* 2. A file containing frequently asked questions and their answers, sometimes called a FAQL (*frequently asked question list*). To find FAQs, look in the *.answers newsgroups or the FTP archive at rtfm.mit.edu. Many mailing lists and Usenet newsgroups maintain FAQs so that participants won't have to spend lots of time answering the same set of questions.

fax modem   An adapter that fits into a PC expansion slot and provides many of the capabilities of a full-sized fax machine, but at a fraction of the cost.

56K   Used to describe a telephone circuit with a 64-Kbps bandwidth that uses 8K for signaling and the remaining 56K for traffic. Also refers to the fastest available analog modems, of which there are two distinctive technologies: x2 and K56Flex.

file   A named collection of data stored on disk, appearing to the user as a single entity. A file can contain a program or part of a program, can be a data file, or can contain a user-created document.

file format   The structure in a file that defines the way information is stored in the file and how the file appears on the screen or on the printer.

file name   The name of a file on a disk used so that both you and the operating system can find the file again. Every file in a directory must have a unique name, but files in different directories can share the same name.

file recovery   The process of recovering deleted or damaged files from a disk. In many operating systems, a deleted file still exists on disk until the space it occupies is overwritten with something else.

file system   In an operating system, the structure by which files are organized, stored, and named.

filter   1. Any command that reads an input, processes or transforms that information, and writes the result out to a designated output device. 2. In e-mail, a program that allows certain messages to reach the user while eliminating other messages.

firewall   A security measure on the Internet, protecting information, pre-venting access, or ensuring that users cannot do any harm to underlying systems. Some networks are connected to the Internet via a firewall machine.

flame   An insulting e-mail or Usenet post. Flames are often ill-considered knee-jerk expressions of anger, but they can also be cruelly detailed and intended for the amusement of the general audience at the expense of the "flamee."

floppy disk   A flat, round, magnetically coated, plastic disk enclosed in a protective jacket. Data is written on to the floppy disk by the disk drive's read/write heads as the disk rotates inside the jacket.

folder   In Windows 98, a collection of programs and files stored on disk, symbolized by a graphical icon representing a file folder. A folder can con-tain other folders, in which case they are said to be nested. In DOS and earlier Windows versions, a subdirectory was the equivalent of a folder.
→ *See also* **directory**.

foreground   In an operating system, a process that runs in the foreground is running at a higher level of priority than a background task.

forum   A feature of online services and bulletin boards that allows sub-scribers to post messages for others to read, and to reply to messages posted by other users.

forward   To send received e-mail along to another address, either manually or automatically.

freeware   A form of software distribution where the author retains copy-right of the software, but makes the program available to others at no cost. Freeware is often distributed on the Internet, on bulletin boards, or through user groups. The program may not be resold or distributed by others for profit. → *See also* **public-domain software, shareware**.

FTP   Internet *file transfer protocol,* the standard TCP/IP protocol for trans-ferring files over the Internet, across any platform.

FTP server   An FTP file server, a computer serving files from an FTP archive.

FTP site   A host on the Internet containing archives and set up for FTP.

fully qualified domain name   Abbreviated as FQDN. The complete domain name that identifies a specific computer (or host network, at the very least) on the Internet, including a host name, a subdomain name, and a domain name. Also called *domain name address*.

gigabyte   (Pronounced "gig-a-bite.") Strictly speaking, a gigabyte is one billion bytes; however, bytes are most often counted in powers of 2, and so a gigabyte becomes 2^{30}, or 1,073,741,824 bytes.

gopher   A client/server application that allows you to browse huge amounts of information by performing FTP transfers, remote logins, and so on, presenting everything to the end-user in the form of menus. With the explosion of easy-to-access information on the Web, gopher has lost some of its appeal for users.

graphical user interface   Abbreviated *GUI* (pronounced "gooey"). A graphics-based user interface like that used in Windows 98, previous Windows versions, and the Macintosh, which allows users to select files, programs, or commands by pointing to pictorial representations on the screen rather than by typing long, complex commands from a *command prompt*. Application programs execute in windows, using a consistent set of pulldown menus, dialog boxes, and other graphical elements such as scroll bars and icons.

hacker   In the programming community, where the term originated, *hacker* describes a person who pursues knowledge about computer systems for its own sake—someone willing to "hack through" the steps of putting together a working program. More recently, in popular culture at large, it has come to mean a person who breaks into other people's computers with malicious intent (what programmers call a *cracker*). ➜ *See also* **firewall**.

hard disk drive   A storage device that uses a set of rotating, magnetically coated disks called *platters* to store data or programs. In everyday use, the terms *hard disk, hard disk drive,* and *hard drive* are all used interchangeably, because the disk and the drive mechanism are a single unit.

header   1. One or more lines at the top of a page in a printed document. 2. The rows of information at the top of an e-mail message that include who the message is from, who it's to, when it was sent, and what it's about. 3. Information preceding the data in a packet, specifying the addresses of the source and the destination as well as error-checking information.

hertz   Abbreviated Hz. A unit of frequency measurement; 1 hertz equals one cycle per second.

high-level format   The process of preparing a floppy disk or a hard disk partition for use by the operating system.

history   1. A list of a user's recent actions or commands. 2. A list of the gopher menus a user has passed through. 3. A list of the hypertext links a Web browser has followed.

hit   1. A connection made to a Web server. (⟶ *See also* **impression**.) 2. A successful match in a database search. (In some searches, you can specify a maximum number of hits.)

home page   On the World Wide Web, an initial starting page. A home page may have information about a single person, a specific subject, or a corporation, and is a convenient jumping-off point to other pages or resources. ⟶ *See also* **browser, HTML, URL**.

host   The central or controlling computer in a networked or distributed processing environment, providing services that other computers or terminals can access via the network. Computers connected to the Internet are also described as hosts, and can be accessed using FTP, telnet, gopher, or a World Wide Web browser.

hotlist   A list of frequent Internet destinations, or sites, arranged on a menu, such as a list of Web pages.

HTML   The acronym for *Hypertext Markup Language*, the hypertext language used in Web pages. It consists of regular text and tags that tell the browser what to do when a link is activated. It is a subset of SGML, a preexisting markup language. ⟶ *See also* **Dynamic HTML**.

HTTP   The acronym for *Hypertext Transport Protocol*. The Internet protocol that defines how a Web server responds to requests for files, made via anchors and URLs.

hyperlink   A hypertext link or a hypermedia link.

hypermedia   An extension of the concept of hypertext to include pictures, sounds, movies, and so on, along with text and links to other documents.

hypertext   Text that contains links to other text documents, allowing the reader to skip around and read the documents in various order.

IAB   Abbreviation for *Internet Architecture Board.* The coordinating committee for the management of the Internet.

IBM-compatible computer   Originally, any personal computer compatible with the IBM line of personal computers. Now it is becoming more common to use the term "Wintel computer" to describe any PC that runs Windows and DOS and is based on one of the *Intel* family of chips.

icon   A small screen image representing a specific element that the user can manipulate in some way. You select the icon by clicking a mouse or other pointing device. An icon may represent an application program, a document, embedded and linked objects, a hard disk drive, or several programs collected together in a group icon. ⟶ *See also* **graphical user interface**.

impression   A Web server's record of a browser's visit to a single page of a Web site. (The term is used to distinguish from a hit, in that a single impression may register as several hits—one on the HTML document, one for each graphic on the page, and so on.)

inbox   Also *in box, in-box.* A file in which a mail program stores incoming e-mail messages.

infection   The presence of a computer *virus.*

initialization files   In Microsoft Windows, files with the file-name extension INI that contain information about an individual Windows configuration. Windows and certain application programs use the settings stored in these files. ⟶ *See also* **SYSTEM.INI, WIN.INI**.

inline graphic   An illustration on a Web page (as opposed to a linked graphic). Can be either a GIF or JPEG graphic file, the two formats native to the World Wide Web.

input/output   Abbreviated *I/O.* The transfer of data between the computer and its peripheral devices, disk drives, terminals and printers.

install   To configure and prepare hardware or software for operation. Many application packages have their own install programs, programs that copy all the required files from the original distribution floppy disks or CD into appropriate directories on your hard disk, and then help you to configure the program to your own operating requirements. Microsoft Windows programs are usually installed by a program called SETUP.

internal modem   A modem that plugs into the expansion bus of a personal computer. ➝ *See also* **external modem**.

Internet   An international network of well over 10,000 networks linked using the TCP/IP protocols. Also used more loosely to mean either the worldwide information net or the conglomeration of all computers and networks that can be reached via an Internet e-mail address.

Internet Explorer   Microsoft's Web browser, which is rapidly changing, version to version, into the basic Windows desktop interface. (It is available for downloading from http://www.microsoft.com/ie/.)

Internet Protocol (IP)   The protocol that handles routing of datagrams from one Internet host to another. It works along with the Transmission Control Protocol (TCP) to ensure that data is transmitted accurately across the Internet. ➝ See *also* **TCP/IP**.

Internet service provider (ISP)   A company or enterprise that provides Internet access.

InterNIC   Short for the Internet Network Information Center, a service of the National Science Foundation. It provides information about the Internet and registers domain names, available via e-mail at info@internic.net or on the Web at http://www.internic.net/.

intranet   A private network that uses the standard Internet protocols.

intruder   An unauthorized user of a computer system, usually a person with malicious intent. ➝ *See also* **firewall, hacker**.

IP address   Also called a *dotted quad*, the numerical Internet Protocol address that uniquely identifies each computer on the Internet, made up of four numbers separated by dots.

ISDN   The acronym for *Integrated Services Digital Network*. A worldwide digital communications network emerging from existing telephone services, intended to replace all current systems with a completely digital transmission system.

Java   A programming language for making software that can be run on any type of computer over an Internet connection.

JavaScript   A scripting language developed by Netscape Communications Corp. to add dynamic (interactive) capabilities to Web pages.

Kbps   An abbreviation for *kilobits per second,* a measurement of transmission speed (such as modem speed or network speed).

kill   1. To delete a post (mark it as having been read). 2. To delete posts automatically, using a kill file. 3. To stop a process. 4. To erase a file.

kill file   Also a *killfile,* a file containing search instructions for automatically killing or autoselecting Usenet posts. Sometimes called a bozo filter, a kill file can be used to screen out annoying posters and avoid uninteresting threads.

kilobit   Abbreviated *Kb* or *Kbit.* It equals 1,024 *bits* (binary digits). ➞ *See also* **megabit, gigabit**.

kilobyte   Abbreviated *K, KB,* or *Kbyte.* It equals 1,024 *bytes.* ➞ *See also* **megabyte, gigabyte, terabyte**.

laptop computer   A small portable computer light enough to carry comfortably, with a flat screen and keyboard that fold together. Laptop computers are battery-operated, often have a thin, backlit or sidelit LCD display screen, and some models can even mate with a docking station to perform as a full-sized desktop system back at the office. Advances in battery technology allow laptop computers to run for many hours between charges.

launch   To start an application program running, usually by double-clicking on its icon with the mouse.

line length   The number of characters that fit on a line—fixed on some systems, changeable on others. The standard line length on the Internet is 80 characters; e-mail or Usenet posts produced with software using longer line lengths will wrap irregularly and appear awkward to users with 80-character lines.

link   In a hypertext document, an element (a word, phrase, graphic, or video clip) that is connected to another element in the same or a different hypertext document. ➞ *See also* **hypertext**.

list box   A dialog box element that helps the user make one choice from a list of possible alternatives.

listserver   An automatic mailing system on the Internet. Rather than sending e-mail on a particular topic to a long list of people, you send it instead to a special e-mail address, where a program automatically distributes the e-mail to all the people who subscribe to the mailing list. ➞ *See also* **newsgroup, Usenet**.

local   Said of a computer to which a user is connected directly or of a device (such as a printer) or process under the user's direct control, as contrasted with remote hosts, devices, and processes.

locked file   A file that you can open and read, but not write to, delete, or change in any way.

login   Also known as *logon*. To establish a connection to a computer system or online service before using it. Many systems require the entry of an identification number or a password before the system can be accessed. → *See also* **logout, password**.

login script   A small program or *macro* that executes the same set of instructions every time a user logs in to a computer system. A communications script may send the user-identification information to an online service each time a subscriber dials up the service. → *See also* **script**.

logout   Also known as *logoff*. To relinquish a session and sign off a computer system by sending a terminating message. The computer may respond with its own message, indicating the resources consumed during the session, or the period between login and logout. Logging out is not the same as shutting down or turning off the computer. → *See also* **login**.

long file name   Any file name that goes beyond the DOS "8.3" file-naming convention of eight characters before a period and three more optional characters forming the filename extension. Windows 98 and several other operating systems are not limited to the 8.3 naming convention; these systems can all manage long file names, even those containing spaces, more than one period, and mixed upper- and lowercase letters.

lurk   To read a mailing list or newsgroup without posting to it. Every new user should lurk for a while before posting to get a feel for what the group is all about and how others in the group behave.

mailbox   A file, directory, or area of hard disk space used to store e-mail messages.

mailing list   A discussion group, commonly referred to on the Internet simply as a *list*, consisting of people with a common interest, all of whom receive all the mail sent, or posted, to the list. Mailing lists are often more specialized than Usenet newsgroups. Lists can be moderated or unmoderated. → *See also* **moderated**.

MAPI The acronym for *Microsoft Application Program Interface.* An API used to add messaging capabilities to any Microsoft Windows application. MAPI handles the details of message storage and forwarding and directory services.

maximize To increase a window to its maximum size. To maximize a window, click the mouse on the button pointing upwards in the upper-right corner of the window, or use the Maximize command from the Control menu. ➞*See also* **minimize.**

MBONE The *multicast backbone,* an experimental, high-speed virtual network that can send packets simultaneously to a large number of Internet sites, suitable for audio and visual transmission. In 1994, a Rolling Stones concert was multicast to workstations around the world via the MBONE.

megabit Abbreviated *Mbit.* Usually 1,048,576 binary digits or bits of data. Often used as equivalent to 1 million bits. ➞*See also* **bit, megabits per second.**

megabits per second Abbreviated *Mbps.* A measurement of the amount of information moving across a network or communications link in one second, measured in multiples of 1,048,576 bits.

megabyte Abbreviated *MB.* Usually 1,048,576 bytes. Megabytes are a common way of representing computer memory or hard-disk capacity.

megahertz Abbreviated *MHz.* One million cycles per second. A processor's clock speed is often expressed in MHz. The original IBM PC operated an 8088 running at 4.77 MHz, the more modern Pentium II processor runs at speeds of up to 333 MHz.

memory The primary random-access memory (RAM) installed in the computer. The operating system copies application programs from disk into memory, where all program execution and data processing takes place; results are written back out to disk again. The amount of memory installed in the computer can determine the size and number of programs that it can run, as well as the size of the largest data file.

memory cache An area of high-speed memory on the processor that stores commonly used code or data obtained from slower memory, replacing the need to access the system's main memory to fetch instructions. The Intel 82385 cache controller chip was used with fast static RAM on some systems to increase performance, but more modern processors include cache management functions on the main processor. The Pentium II contains two separate 16K caches, one each for data and instructions.

memory chip   A chip that holds data or program instructions. A memory chip may hold its contents temporarily, as in the case of RAM, or permanently, as in the case of ROM.

memory map   The organization and allocation of memory in a computer. A memory map will give an indication of the amount of memory used by the operating system, and the amount remaining for use by applications.

menu   A list of the commands or options available in the program displayed on the screen. A menu item is selected by typing a letter or number corresponding to the item, by clicking it with the mouse, or by highlighting it and pressing Enter. ➞ *See also* **pull-down menu**.

menu bar   A row of pull-down menu names, usually displayed in a line across the top of the screen or window, just below the title bar. ➞ *See* also **task bar**.

microprocessor   Also called simply "processor." A CPU on a single chip. The first microprocessor was developed by Intel in 1969. The microprocessors most often used in PCs are the Motorola PowerPC RISC series used in the Apple Macintosh computers, and the Intel Pentium family used in IBM and IBM-compatible computers.

Microsoft Network   An online service from Microsoft, access to which comes built-in with Windows 98.

millisecond   Abbreviated *ms* or *msec*. A unit of measurement equal to one thousandth of a second. In computing, hard disk and CD-ROM drive access times are often described in terms of milliseconds; the higher the number the slower the disk system.

MIME   *Multipurpose Internet Mail Extensions*, a protocol that allows e-mail to contain simple text plus color pictures, video, sound, and binary data. Both the sender and the receiver need MIME-aware mail programs to use it.

minimize   To reduce the active window to an icon. To minimize a window, the user clicks on the button pointing downwards in the top right corner of the window, or uses the Minimize command from the Control menu.

mirror site   An archive site (generally **FTP**) containing an exact copy of the files at another site.

modem   Short for *modulator/demodulator*, a device that connects your computer to a phone jack and, through the phone lines, to another modem and computer. It transmits data by converting the computer's digital signal into the telephone's analog carrier signal, and vice versa.

moderated   Term used to describe lists and newsgroups whose posts must pass muster with a moderator before appearing.

moderator   The volunteer who decides which submissions to a moderated list or newsgroup will be posted.

modulation   In communications, the process used by a modem to add the digital signal onto the carrier signal, so that the signal can be transmitted over a telephone line. The frequency, amplitude, or phase of a signal may be modulated to represent a digital or analog signal. ➥ *See also* **modem**.

Mosaic   The first graphical Web browser, developed by National Center for Supercomputing Applications. It greatly popularized the Web in its first few years, and by extension the Internet, as it made the multimedia capabilities of the Net accessible via mouse-clicks.

Mozilla   A slang name for the Netscape Web browser.

MS-DOS   Acronym for *Microsoft Disk Operating System* (pronounced "emm-ess-dos"). MS-DOS, like other operating systems, allocates system resources such as hard and floppy disks, the monitor and the printer to the applications programs that need them. MS-DOS, or simply DOS, is the operating system underlying Windows.

multimedia   A computer technology that displays information using a combination of full-motion video, animation, sound, graphics and text with a high degree of user interaction. ➥ *See also* **hypermedia, hypertext**.

multitasking   The simultaneous execution of two or more programs in one computer. Windows 98 multitasks natively, unlike Windows 3.*x*.

name server   1. Also domain name server, an application that maintains a table of domain names and corresponding IP addresses in order to resolve the domain names of messages. 2. Also *CSO name server*, a searchable white pages listing of real names and associated e-mail addresses, usually reached via gopher.

navigate   Computer jargon meaning to get around a program, find commands, move through a document, or hunt around the Internet.

.net   An Internet domain, corresponding to constituent networks.

Net   Also *net* and *'net*, often used as an abbreviation for the Internet or for Usenet, really a more general term for the lump sum of interconnected computers on the planet.

net address   An Internet address. Can fall under any of the common internet address types (i.e., HTTP, FTP, NNTP, or *username@subdomain.domain*).

netiquette   Accepted proper behavior on the Net, especially in regard to e-mail and Usenet. Violate netiquette at your peril. Although the Internet and Usenet are effectively anarchies, they still have strong social cultures, and most of the rules and regulations of the Net are enforced by peer pressure. ➞ *See also* **lurking**.

netnews   Also *net news*, another name for Usenet.

network address   1. The unique name of a node on a network; 2. An e-mail address. ➞ *See also* **Internet address**.

network news   A synonym for Usenet.

Network News Transfer Protocol (NNTP)   The protocol used to distribute Usenet newsgroups.

newsfeed   The packet of news articles passed along from one computer to the next on Usenet.

newsgroup   A Usenet discussion group.

newsreader   A program used to read Usenet articles, and usually also to save, respond to, and post follow-ups to articles, as well as to post new articles.

NSFNET   Abbreviation for *National Science Foundation Network*. The NSFNET is not the *Internet* in itself, but it is a part of the Internet.

offline   A mode of Internet Explorer that does not connect to the Internet. Also describes the state of a printer or other peripheral that is not currently in ready mode and is therefore unavailable for use. ➞ *See also* **online**.

offline reader   An application that lets you read postings to Usenet newsgroups without having to stay connected to the Internet.

online   1. Most broadly, describes any capability available directly on a computer, as in "online help system," or any work done on a computer instead of by more traditional means. 2. Describes a peripheral such as a printer or modem when it is directly connected to a computer and ready to operate. 3. In communications, describes a computer connected to another, remote, computer over a network or a modem link; especially, currently connected to the Net.

online community   Also *virtual community*, a group of people with shared interests who meet, communicate, and interact via a network, BBS, Internet discussion group, or any other form of electronic common space. Online communities have many of the properties of real-world communities. ➡ *See also* **BBS**.

online service   A company that maintains a proprietary network and provides e-mail, forums, chats, games, databases of information, downloadable files, and information services (stocks, airlines, and so on), such as America Online, CompuServe, Delphi, eWorld, GEnie, Prodigy, Microsoft Network, and so on.

Most online services have e-mail connections to the Internet (though some charge extra for that e-mail). More and more are adding other Internet facilities, such as FTP, gopher, and the Web, blurring the distinction further between online services and Internet service providers. ➡ *See also* **Internet service provider**.

operating environment   A front end for an operating system. A set of tools and a consistent look and feel that allow the user to interact with the computer. For instance, Microsoft Windows is an operating environment that runs on top of the MS-DOS operating system.

operating system   Abbreviated *OS*. The software responsible for allocating system resources, including memory, processor time, disk space, and peripheral devices such as printers, modems, and the monitor. All application programs use the operating system to gain access to these system resources as they are needed. The operating system is the first program loaded into the computer as it boots, and it remains in memory at all times thereafter.

option button   Also known as a *radio button*. A small round button used to make an exclusive choice in a dialog box where only one option can be in effect at a time, like baud rate, or to choose between an ascending or a descending sort, for example.

.org   An Internet domain corresponding to (nonprofit) organizations.

packet   Any block of data sent over a network. Each packet contains information about the sender and the receiver, and error-control information, in addition to the actual message. Packets may be fixed- or variable-length, and they will be reassembled if necessary when they reach their destination.

partition   A portion of a hard disk that the operating system treats as if it were a separate drive. Very large hard drives can be partitioned into smaller, logical drives for more efficient use of space. It is not recommended to partition a drive that is smaller than 4 gigabytes in original size.

password   A secret code used to restrict access to an account, channel, file, and so on, only to authorized users who know the code.

path   The complete description of the location of a file or directory in the file system. The path consists of all the directory names that must be accessed in order to get to a specific file.

Pentium   A 32-bit microprocessor introduced by Intel in 1993. After losing a courtroom battle to maintain control of the *x*86 designation, Intel named this member of its family the Pentium rather than the 80586 or the 586. The Pentium represents the continuing evolution of the 80486 family of microprocessors, and adds several notable features, including 16K instruction code and data caches, built-in floating-point processor and memory management unit, as well as a superscalar design and dual pipelining that allow the Pentium to execute more than one instruction per clock cycle.

Available in a whole range of models (Pentium, Mobile Pentium, Pentium Pro, and Pentium II) and clock speeds (from 133 MHz all the way up to 333 MHz), the Pentium is equivalent to an astonishing 7.5 million *transistors*, more than twice that of the original Pentium!

peripheral   Any hardware device attached to and controlled by a computer, such as a monitor, keyboard, hard-disk, floppy-disk, and CD-ROM drives, printer, mouse, tape drive and joystick.

Plug-and-Play   Abbreviated *PnP*. A standard from Compaq, Microsoft, Intel, and Phoenix that defines automatic techniques designed to make PC configuration simple and straightforward.

PnP adapters contain configuration information stored in nonvolatile memory, which includes vendor information, and serial number and checksum information. The PnP chipset allows each adapter to be isolated, one at a time, until all cards have been properly identified by the operating system.

point of presence (POP)   A local phone number connected to a modem connected to the network of a service provider, to enable users to log in to the network without paying long distance charges.

Point-to-Point Protocol (PPP)   A TCP/IP protocol, similar to SLIP, for transmitting IP datagrams over serial lines such as phone lines. With PPP, PC users can connect to the Internet and still function in their native environment (instead of having to deal with a character-based UNIX environment).

pop-up menu   A menu displayed next to the element with which it is associated. A pop-up menu is usually only displayed on request; in other words, it is only displayed when you specifically ask for it.

port   1. A physical connection, such as a serial port or a parallel port. 2. To move a program or operating system from one hardware platform to another. 3. A number used to identify a specific Internet application (location).

post   An individual article or e-mail message sent to a Usenet newsgroup or to a mailing list, rather than to a specific individual. Post can also refer to the process of sending the article to the newsgroup.

Post Office Protocol (POP)   A protocol that specifies how a personal computer can connect to a mail server on the Internet and download e-mail.

program   A sequence of instructions that a computer can execute. Synonymous with software.

program information file   Abbreviated *PIF.* A file of specifications that defines how a non-Windows application programs runs from inside Windows. PIF files are short files, usually located in the same directory as the application program they relate to, and they contain information including:

> ▶ the file name and directory

> ▶ the directory used when an application starts running

> ▶ conventional and expanded or extended memory usage

> ▶ video adapter modes

> ▶ multitasking priority levels

If Windows does not find a PIF for a non-Windows application, it uses default settings instead.

prompt   Also *command-line prompt,* a string of text that a character-based operating system displays on the screen to tell a user that it is ready to accept input (such as a command or the name of a program to run).

Properties sheet   Summary information about a file or program, displayed by selecting Properties from the object's context ("right-click") menu.

proprietary software   Software developed in-house by a particular business or government agency, and never made available commercially to the outside world. ➡ *See also* **public-domain software, shareware.**

protocol   In networking and communications, the specification that defines the procedures to follow when transmitting and receiving data. Protocols define the format, timing, sequence, and error checking systems used. ➡ *See also* **protocol stack.**

proxy server   A security measure that enables users behind a firewall to browse the Web (visited resources are actually downloaded by the intervening proxy server and then viewed internally from there) without exposing the contents of the intranet to public scrutiny. A proxy server may render some Web services inaccessible to the user.

public-domain software   Software that is freely distributed to anyone who wants to use, copy, or distribute it. ➡ *See also* **proprietary software, shareware.**

pull-down menu   A vertical menu that you pull down from a set of menu names arranged in a menu bar across the top of the screen or the top of the window. To make a selection from a pull-down menu, you click on the item with the mouse, or use the cursor-movement keys to position the highlight over the item and press Enter, or type a special key combination.

push   A method of distributing information over the Web, by which updates are (scheduled and then) automatically sent to the user's screen or window, as if the content were being "broadcast" to a receiver (hence the synonymous terms *netcast* and *webcast*).

quit   To exit the current application program in an orderly way, and return control to the operating system.

quoting   To include a relevant portion of someone else's article when posting a follow-up to a Usenet newsgroup or online forum. It is considered to be very poor netiquette to quote more of the original post than is absolutely necessary to make your point.

RAM   The acronym for *random access memory*. The main system memory in a computer, used for the operating system, application programs, and data. → *See also* **dynamic RAM, static RAM**.

RAM chip   A semiconductor storage device, either dynamic RAM or static RAM.

random access   Describes the ability of a storage device to go directly to the required memory address without having to read from the beginning every time data is requested.

read   To copy program or data files from a floppy or a hard disk into computer memory, to run the program or process the data in some way. The computer may also read your commands and data input from the keyboard. → *See also* **write**.

README file   A text file placed on a set of distribution disks by the manufacturer at the last minute that may contain important information not contained in the program manuals or online help system. Users should always look for a README file when installing a new program on a system; it may contain information pertinent to their specific configuration. The file name may vary slightly; READ.ME, README.TXT, and README.DOC are all used. README files do not contain any formatting commands, so the user can look at them using any word processor.

read-only   Term used to describe a file that can be read but not altered.

real time   Also *realtime*, the time used for synchronous communication, in which both participants must be available (as in a telephone conversation). Also, taking place at the present time, live, not delayed or recorded.

reboot   To restart the computer and reload the operating system, usually after a crash.

rec.   A Usenet hierarchy devoted to recreation.

remote access   The process of accessing another computer's resources, such as files or printers. Dial-up accounts and telnet are both forms of remote access.

reply   1. A message sent in response to a previous message or post. 2. An e-mail command that takes the return path from the current message and makes that address the recipient of a new message, possibly quoting the previous message as well.

restore To return a window to its original size after it has been maximized. To restore a window, the user clicks on the downward-pointing part of the double arrow in the top right corner of the window, or uses the Restore command from the Control menu. ➞*See also* **maximize, minimize**.

ROM The acronym for *read-only memory.* A semiconductor-based memory system that stores information permanently and does not lose its contents when power is switched off. ROMs are used for firmware such as the BIOS used in the PC. In some portable computers, the application programs and even the operating system are being stored in ROM.

root directory In a hierarchical directory structure, the directory from which all other directories must branch.

run-time version A special, limited-capability release of software bundled with a single product, that allows that product to run, but does not support any of the other applications capable of running in that same environment. In other words, the run-time version provides some but not all the features of the full product.

save To transfer information from the computer's memory to a more permanent storage medium such as a hard disk.

screen-saver program A utility program that blanks the computer screen after a period of inactivity. If one image is displayed on the screen for a long period of time, it is possible to burn in a ghost image on the screen.

script A small program or macro invoked at a particular time. For example, a login script may execute the same specific set of instructions every time a user logs onto a computer system. A communications script may send the user-identification information to an online service each time a subscriber dials up the service.

scroll To move a window up, down, left, or right, in order to see information that was previously out of sight. ➞*See also* **scroll bar, scroll box**.

scroll bar A vertical or horizontal bar at the right or across the bottom of a window that is too small to show all the necessary information at the same time. At each end of the scroll bar, small arrows indicate the scrolling direction.

scroll box A small movable box located on one of the scroll bars. The scroll box indicates the user's relative position in the data shown in the window, and the user can drag the scroll box along the scroll bar to display a different part of the document. This is usually faster than repeatedly clicking on the arrows at the ends of the scroll bars.

SCSI (Pronounced "scuzzy.") Stands for *Small Computer Systems Interface*, a standard for connecting personal computers to some peripheral devices, including CD-ROM drives and external hard drives.

search engine Database software, usually fronted by a Web site for searching the Internet, the Web, or some other computer domain, such as AltaVista (at http://altavista.digital.com). Most search engines feature, at a minimum, a text box for typing key words and a Search (or Go or Do it Now! or whatever) button.

search string One or more characters to be matched in a search operation.

select The act of choosing a menu item or highlighting an option. When you make a selection, you expect a specific action to result. ➡ *See also* **deselect**.

session 1. The time during which a program is running on either a local or a remote computer. 2. A DOS or Windows program run as a separate protected task under certain multitasking operating systems, such as OS/2 and Windows NT. 3. In communications, the name for the active connection between a mainframe terminal (or a personal computer emulating a terminal), and the computer itself. Many different transactions or message exchanges may take place during a single session. ➡ *See also* **thread**.

SGML Abbreviation for *Standard Generalized Markup Language*. A standard (ISO 8879) for defining the structure and managing the contents of any digital document. HTML, used in many World Wide Web documents on the Internet, is a part of SGML. ➡ *See also* **HTML**.

shareware A form of software distribution that makes copyrighted programs freely available on a trial basis; if you like the program and use it, you are expected to register your copy and send a small fee to the program's creator.

shortcut In Windows 9*x*, an icon you can place on the Desktop for quick access to a file, program, or other resource.

shortcut key Any key or key combination that you can press to carry out a command or action. Some menu commands list shortcut keys immediately to the right of the menu item, and these keystrokes can be used directly from the keyboard, instead of first opening the menu and then choosing that command.

signature file   A short text file which is automatically added to the end of any e-mail message or Usenet post. A signature file usually contains the sender's name (or alias) and e-mail address, and some people like to add pithy quotes. Netiquette dictates that a signature file should always be short, between one and five lines long; anything longer will invite flames.

single in-line memory module   Abbreviated *SIMM*. Individual RAM chips are soldered or surface mounted onto small narrow circuit boards called *carrier modules,* which can be plugged into sockets on the mother-board. These carrier modules are simple to install and occupy less space than conventional memory modules.

SLIP   Abbreviation for *Serial Line Internet Protocol.* A communications proto-col used over serial lines or dial-up connections. Along with PPP, SLIP is one of the most popular protocols used when connecting a PC to the Internet.

smiley   A group of text characters used in e-mail and Usenet posts to indi-cate humor or other emotions. Turn a smiley on its side to read it. There are hundreds of different smileys in common use and new ones appear all the time. Two favorites are :-) for smiling, and ;-) to indicate winking or flirting.

snail mail   Internet slang for mail sent using the U.S. Postal Service, so called for its relative slowness compared to electronic mail.

sneakernet   An informal method of file sharing in which a user copies files onto a floppy disk and then carries them to a coworker to use in a com-puter in the next office.

spam   To post (or *robopost*) huge amounts of material to Usenet, or to post one article to huge numbers of inappropriate groups. (The term comes from the commercial meat product Spam and the Monty Python routine in which rowdy Vikings in a diner chant "Spam, Spam, Spam, Spam, Spam, Spam, Spam, Spam, wonderful Spam, marvelous Spam," and so on, *ad nauseam.*)

standalone   Describes a system designed to meet specific individual needs and that does not rely on or assume the presence of any other components to complete the assigned task.

standard disclaimer   A disclaimer attached to the end of a Usenet or mailing list post, usually to the effect that the user is not speaking in an official capacity for the user's employer or access provider.

static RAM   Abbreviated SRAM (pronounced "ess-ram"). A type of computer memory that retains its contents as long as power is applied; it does not need constant refreshment like dynamic RAM chips. A static RAM chip can only store about one-fourth of the information that a dynamic RAM chip of the same complexity can hold.

streaming   Term used to describe a media format that enables a player program to begin playing back or displaying the media content quite soon after the data starts flowing (in a *stream*) from the server (as opposed to formats that require that the browser download an entire, possibly huge, file before playing anything).

subdirectory   A *directory* (or *folder*) within another directory. The root directory is the top-level directory, from which all other directories must branch. In common use, subdirectory is synonymous with directory.

submenu   A menu invoked by selecting from a previous menu.

subscribe   To join a mailing list or start reading a newsgroup.

surf   To browse through different Internet resources. When a user surfs, they take tangents whenever they feel like it. Sometimes known as *net surfing*.

synchronous transmission   In communications, a transmission method that uses a clock signal to regulate data flow. Synchronous transmissions do not use start and stop bits. ➞ *See also* **asynchronous transmissions**.

sysop   Abbreviation of *system operator* (pronounced "siss-op"). The manager of a multiuser computer system or a bulletin board.

system   1. A program that supervises a computer and coordinates all its functions, also called an operating system. 2. An entire computer taken together with all its devices. 3. A large program.

system date   The date and time as maintained by the computer's internal clock. You should always make sure that the system clock is accurate, because the operating system notes the time that files were created; this can be important if you are trying to find the most recent version of a document or spreadsheet.

SYSTEM.INI   In Microsoft Windows, an initialization file that contains information on your hardware and the internal Windows operating environment. ➞ *See also* **WIN.INI**.

system time   The time and date maintained by the internal clock inside the computer.

T1   A long-distance, point-to-point 1.544-megabit-per-second communications channel that can be used for both digitized voice and data transmission; T1 lines are usually divided into 24 channels, each transmitting at 64 kilobits per second. ➞ *See also* **backbone, T3**.

T3   A long-distance point-to-point 44.736-megabit-per-second communications service that can provide up to 28 T1 channels. A T3 channel can carry 672 voice conversations and is usually available over fiber-optic cable.

task   Any independent running program, and the set of system resources that it uses. A task may be an operating system process or may be a part of an application program. ➞ *See also* **multitasking**.

TCP   Abbreviation for *Transmission Control Protocol.* The connection-oriented, transport-level protocol used in the TCP/IP suite of communications protocols. ➞ *See also* **IP**.

TCP/IP   The acronym for *Transmission Control Protocol/Internet Protocol.* A set of computer-to-computer communications protocols first developed for the Defense Advanced Research Projects Agency (DARPA) in the late 1970s. The set of TCP/IP protocols encompass media access, packet transport, session communications, file transfer, e-mail, and terminal emulation. ➞ *See also* **FTP, IP, TCP, telnet**.

telnet   That part of the TCP/IP suite of protocols used for remote login and terminal emulation; also the name of the program used to connect to Internet host systems. Originally a UNIX utility, telnet is available these days for almost all popular operating systems. You will find that most versions of telnet are character-based applications, although some contain the text inside a windowed system. ➞ *See also* **FTP**.

terabyte   Abbreviated TB. In computing, usually 2^{40}, or 1,099,511,627,776 bytes. A terabyte is equivalent to 1,000 gigabytes, and usually refers to extremely large hard-disk capacities.

text box   A dialog box element that accepts text as input. Sometimes a text box will already contain a default entry that you can accept or edit; at other times it will be empty, ready to receive your input.

text editor   Software used to work with ASCII text files, which contain none of the formatting information used by word processors. WordPad is the built-in, simple word processor supplied with Windows 98; it does insert formatting, but it can export a text file in ASCII-only format.

text file   A file that consists of text characters without any formatting information. Also known as an ASCII file, a text file can be read by any word processor. The *README* file, containing late-breaking news about an application, is always a text file.

thread   A connected set of postings to a Usenet newsgroup or to an online forum. Many newsreaders present postings as threads rather than in strict chronological sequence. ➞ *See also* **session**.

throughput   A measure of the rate of data transmitted, expressed as bits per second.

tile   To arrange all the open windows so that they do not overlap. To make sure that all the open windows will fit, some of them will have their position and size changed. ➞ *See also* **cascade**.

time out   To fail, as a network process, because the remote server or computer has not responded in time, to close a connection after waiting too long for acknowledgment.

title bar   A thin horizontal bar across the top of a window that contains the name of the window, as well as the maximize and minimize buttons. An application window's title bar will also contain the name of the file or document you are working on.

toggle   A command or selection that is alternately turned on and off again each time you select it. If the command or item is selected, an X or check mark is shown in the check box or next to the menu command; if the item is not selected, this visual indicator is missing.

toolbar   A convenient feature that represents commonly used commands in the form of icons or command buttons in a row across the screen.

undelete   To recover an accidentally deleted file. ➞ *See also* **file recovery**.

undelete program   A utility program that recovers deleted or damaged files from a disk. A file can be deleted accidentally, or can become inaccessible when part of the file's control information is lost. ➝ *See also* **backup, file recovery**.

unmoderated   Used to describe lists and newsgroups whose posts are not vetted by a moderator.

unread   Newsgroup articles that the user has not yet read or has marked as such. Unread articles will show up again the next time the user returns to the newsgroup.

unsubscribe   1. To remove one's name from a mailing list. 2. To remove the name of a newsgroup from the list of subscribed groups.

upgrade   1. The process of installing a newer and more powerful version; for example, to upgrade to a newer and more capable version of a software package, or to upgrade from your current hard disk to one that is twice the size. In the case of hardware, an upgrade is often called an upgrade kit. 2. A new and more powerful version of an existing system, either hardware or software, is also known as an upgrade.

upload   To transfer a file over a modem from a desktop computer to a remote computer.

URL   (Pronounced "you-are-ell.") Acronym for *uniform resource locator*, a Web address. It consists of a protocol, a host name, a port (optional), a directory (optional), and a file name (optional). In the URL `http://enterzone.berkeley.edu/enterzone.html`, the protocol is HTTP, the host name is `enterzone.berkeley.edu`, and the file name is `enterzone.html`. URLs can be used to address other Internet resources besides Web pages, such as FTP sites, gopher servers, telnet addresses, and so on.

Usenet   1. From *User's Network* and often written USENET, the collection of computers and networks that share news articles. Usenet is not the Internet (though it overlaps pretty well). It's sometimes called the world's largest electronic bulletin board. 2. The newsgroups in the traditional newsgroup hierarchies. ➝ See *also* **newsgroup**.

Usenet newsgroups   The individual discussion groups within Usenet. Newsgroups contain articles posted by other Internet and Usenet subscribers; very few of them contain actual hard news. Most newsgroups are concerned with a single subject; there are over 10,000 different newsgroups from which to choose.

user interface   That part of a program with which the user interacts. When a program responds only to typed commands, it is said to have a *command-line interface.* A program that receives commands through the use of menus is said to be *menu driven.* A program that presents the elements of the user interface on the screen using regular letters and numbers is called a *character-based interface,* and a program that uses graphical elements with a mouse—like Windows 98—is said to have a *graphical user interface.*

username   A login, the name a user logs in with. Also, the first part of an Internet e-mail address (up to the @).Choose your username well. In many ways it is more important (on the Net) than your real name. It's the name people see most often.

version number   A method of identifying a particular software or hardware release. The version number is assigned by the software developer, and often includes numbers before and after a decimal point; the higher the number, the more recent the release.

Video CD   A compact disc format standard developed by Sony, Phillips, JVC, and Matsushita that allows up to 74 minutes of video to be stored on one compact disc. Compact discs recorded in Video CD format can be played on CD-I, Video CD, and CD-ROM drives, and on CD players that have digital output and an add-on video adapter.

videodisc   An optical disk used for storing video images and sound. A videodisc player can play back the contents of the videodisc on a computer or onto a standard television set. One videodisc can contain up to 55,000 still images, or up to 2 hours worth of full-frame video. ➞ *See also* **CD-ROM**.

video RAM   Abbreviated *VRAM* (pronounced "vee-ram.") Special-purpose RAM with two data paths for access, rather than just one as in conventional RAM. These two paths let a VRAM board manage two functions at once—refreshing the display and communicating with the processor. VRAM doesn't require the system to complete one function before starting the other, so it allows faster operation for the whole video system.

virtual   Said of something that exists only in software, not physically.

virus   A program that deliberately does damage to the computer it's on. Viruses are often hidden inside an apparently benign program.

Visual Basic   A popular Basic language compiler from Microsoft, available for Windows. The language has been continually improved and now is often used for fast, vertical application development. Visual Basic also manages the creation of the user interface automatically, including menus, dialog boxes, and other interface elements; the Windows version also supports DDE (a precursor to OLE), OLE, and OLE2. There are also subsets of Visual Basic for Applications (VBA) and for ActiveX (VB Control Creation Edition).

WAIS   Abbreviation for *Wide Area Information Service* (pronounced "ways"). A service used to access text databases or libraries on the Internet. ➡ *See also* **Gopher**.

wallpaper   In Microsoft Windows, the graphical pattern on the Desktop used as a backdrop for windows, icons, and dialog boxes.

Web browser   A World Wide Web client application that lets you look at hypertext documents and follow links to other HTML documents on the Web. When you find something that interests you as you browse through a hypertext document, you can click your mouse on that object, and the system automatically takes care of accessing the Internet host that holds the document you requested; you don't need to know the IP address, the name of the host system, or any other details. ➡ *See also* **URL**.

Web page   An HTML document on the World Wide Web, usually containing hypertext links to other documents on the Web, often on other Web servers entirely. Surfing the Web consists of following links from page to page.

Web server   An application that stores Web pages and associated files, databases, and scripts, and serves up the pages to Web browsers, using HTTP.

Web site   A site on the Internet that hosts a Web server.

window   A rectangular portion of the screen that acts as a viewing area for application programs. Windows can be tiled or cascaded, and can be individually moved and sized on the screen. Some programs can open multiple document windows inside their application window to display several word processing or spreadsheet data files at the same time.

Windows application   Any *application* program that runs within the *Microsoft Windows environment* and cannot run without Windows. All Windows applications follow certain conventions in their arrangement of menus, the use and style of *dialog boxes*, as well as keyboard and mouse use.

Windows key   Either of two keys on the 104-key enhanced keyboard, marked with the Windows logo, that allow the user to display the Start menu.

Windows 9x   Shorthand used in this book for Windows 98 and its predecessor Windows 95, when referring to features common to both versions. Windows 9x is a *32-bit* system that supports true *multitasking* and *long file names*.

Windows NT   A 32-bit multitasking portable operating system developed by Microsoft, and first released in 1993.

Windows 3.x   Refers to versions 3.0 and 3.1; the first widely used editions of the Windows graphical user interface. Unlike Windows *9x*, versions 3.*x* were 16-bit systems that could not use long file names and did not support true multitasking.

WinFax   A family of best-selling fax modem-management applications from Delrina. WinFax runs under Microsoft Windows and manages all fax-related functions, including sending, receiving, and filing faxes.

WIN.INI   In Microsoft Windows, an initialization file that contains information to help customize your copy of Windows. When Windows starts, the contents of WIN.INI are read from the hard disk into memory so that they are immediately available. WIN.INI contains sections that define the use of colors, fonts, country-specific information, the Desktop, and many other settings. ➡ *See also* **SYSTEM.INI**.

wizard   1. A technique used by some applications to guide the inexperienced or infrequent user through a complex set of steps by asking questions about the document they are in the process of creating as they are actually creating it. A wizard may also be called an expert in some applications. 2. On the Internet, someone who really understands how a piece of hardware or software works and is willing to help newcomers ("newbies").

World Wide Web   Also called the *Web, WWW, W3,* and *w³,* an interlinked collected of hypertext documents (Web pages) residing on Web servers and other documents, menus, and databases, available via URLs (uniform resource locators). Web documents are marked for formatting and linking with HTML (hypertext markup language), and Web servers use HTTP (hypertext transport protocol) to deliver Web pages. The Web was invented as an online documentation resource by physicists at the CERN European Particle Physics Laboratory in Switzerland.

zip disk   A removable media storage disk, roughly the same size and thickness as a floppy disk, that can hold 100 megabytes of data, as opposed to a floppy disk's very limited 1.44 megabytes.

Appendix C

VENDOR'S GUIDE

The vendor listing that follows is divided into the following categories:

- ▶ Manufacturers of Computers, Peripherals, and Components
- ▶ Data Recovery Vendors
- ▶ Memory Vendors
- ▶ Storage Device Vendors
- ▶ Miscellaneous Computer Products Vendors
- ▶ Older PC Repair and Exchange
- ▶ Computer Recycling Centers

Wherever possible, I have included non-800 numbers for readers outside North America. Products, prices, and addresses change, so you may find some vendors listed here no longer exist or cannot be reached given the information below. I am not endorsing any particular vendors.

Adapted from *The Complete PC Upgrade and Maintenance Guide*, by Mark Minasi

ISBN 0-7821-2151-9   1,520 pages $59.99

Manufacturers of Computers, Peripherals, and Components

The following are names, addresses, and phone numbers of various manufacturers of computers, peripherals, and components:

1st Tech Corporation
12201 Technology Boulevard,
Suite 160
Austin, TX 78727
(800) 533-1744
Memory products

3Com Corporation
5400 Bayfront Plaza
Santa Clara, CA 95052-8145
(800) 638-3266, (408) 764-5000
http://www.3com.com

3DTV Corporation
1863 Pioneer Parkway East #303
Springfield, OR 97477
Voicemail/Fax (415) 680-1678
http://www.stereospace.com
Hardware and software for 3D
(stereoscopic) video, computer
graphics, and virtual reality

4Q Technologies
18563 Gale Avenue, Unit A
City of Industry, CA 91748
(818) 935-1999
Speakers

A4 Tech Corporation
20256 Paseo Robles
Walnut, CA 91789
(909) 468-0071
Scanners

ABS Computer Technologies, Inc.
1295 Johnson Drive
City of Industry, CA 91745
(800) 876-8088, (800) 685-3471,
(818) 937-2300
Fax (818) 937-2322
http://www.abscomputers.com

Absolute Battery Co.
50 Tannery Road, Suite 2
Somerville, NJ 08876
(800) 653-8294
Laptop/notebook computer batteries and charging systems

Abstract R&D, Inc.
120 Village Sq., Suite 37
Orinda, CA 94563
(925) 253-9588
Palmtop PCs

Acecad, Inc.
2600 Garden Road, Suite 121
Monterey, CA 93940
(408) 655-1900
Acecat III mouse replacement

Acer America Corporation
2641 Orchard Parkway
San Jose, CA 95134
(800) 848-3927, (408) 432-6200
http://www.adi-online.com

Acer Sertek Inc.
926 Thompson Pl.
Sunnyvale, CA 94086
(408) 733-3174
CD-ROMs, MPEG cards, sound cards

Achme Computer Inc., A Micro-Star Co.
4059 Clipper Ct.
Fremont, CA 94538
(510) 623-8818
http://www.achme.com
PC-based mainboards, Ethernet
cards, and video accelerators

ACL/Staticide
1960 E. Devon Avenue
Elk Grove Village, IL 60007
(708) 981-9212
http://www.aclstaticide.com
Anti-static equipment and cleaning kits

Acom Inc.
46600 Landing Pky.
Fremont, CA 94538
(510) 353-1600
Patriot multimedia notebooks

Action Electronics Co., Ltd.
198, Chung Yuan Road
Chung Li, Taiwan, ROC
(886) 3-4515494
Axion monitors

Action Well Development Ltd.
Rm. 1101, 1103 and 4 Star Center
443-451 Castle Peak Road
Kwai Chung, NT, Hong Kong
(852) 2422-0010
Fax modems, sound products,
controller and VGA cards, and
computer cases

ActionTec Electronics, Inc.
1269 Innsbruck Drive
Sunnyvale, CA
(408) 752-7700
Fax (408) 541-9003
http://www.actiontec.com
PC card (PCMCIA) products

Actix Systems, Inc.
3350 Scott Boulevard, Building 9
Santa Clara, CA 95054
(408) 986-1625
Advanced video/graphics
accelerators

Actown Corporation
8F, 527, Chung Cheng Road
Hsin Tien, Taipei, Taiwan ROC
(886) 2-218-4612
Opto-electronic products, including
handheld scanners, flatbeds, and
sheet-fed scanners

ACT-RX Technology Corporation
10F, 525, Chung Cheng Road
Hsin Tien, Taipei, Taiwan ROC
(886) 2-218-8000
CPU coolers

Adaptec, Inc.
691 S. Milpitas Boulevard
Milpitas, CA 95035
(800) 934-2766, (408) 945-8600
http://www.adaptec.com

Addonics Technologies
48434 Milmont Drive
Fremont, CA 94538
(510) 438-6530
http://www.addonics.com

Addonix Systems, Inc.
46723 Fremont Boulevard
Fremont, CA 94538
(800) 995-8828, (510) 440-7288
Fax (510) 440-7289
E-mail: qpinfo@quickpath.com
http://www.quickpath.com/

Addtronics Enterprise Co.
No. 66, Chen-Teh Road
Taipei, Taiwan ROC
(886) 2-5591122
An integrated computer case
manufacturer

ADI Systems, Inc.
2115 Ringwood Avenue
San Jose, CA 95131
(800) 228-0530, (408) 944-0100
Fax (408) 944-0300
http://www.adiusa.com/
Multi-scanning color monitors

Adobe Systems Inc.
1585 Charleston Road
Mountain View, CA 94043
(415) 961-4400
http://www.adobe.com

ADPI (Analog and Digital Peripherals, Inc.)
P.O. Box 499
Troy, OH 45373
(800) 758-1041
Backup devices

Adroit Systems, Inc.
9225 Chesapeake Drive, Suite G
San Diego, CA 92123
(619) 627-1888
CCD color video cameras,
including OmniCam

Advanced Digital Systems
13909 Bettencourt Street
Cerritos, CA 90703
(800) 888-5244
http://www.ads-mm.com
Multimedia specialty audio/video
hardware

Advanced Gravis Computer Technology Ltd.
101-3750 N. Fraser Way
Burnaby, BC V5J 5E9, Canada
(604) 431-5020
http://www.gravis.com
PC game interfaces

Advanced Integration Research, Inc.
2188 Del Franco Street
San Jose, CA 95131
(408) 428-0800
Fax (408) 428-0950
http://www.airwebs.com
486 and Pentium system boards
based on ISA, EISA, PCI, and
VL-bus architectures

Advanced Matrix Technology, Inc.
747 Calle Plano
Camarillo, CA 93012-8598
(805) 388-5799
Dot matrix, laser, and inkjet printers
and plotters

Advantage Memory
25A Technology Drive, building 2
Irvine, CA 92718
(800) 266-0488
http://www.advantagememory.com

Agfa (Bayer Corporation)
200 Ballardvale Street
Wilmington, MA 01887
(508) 658-5600
http://www.agfa.com
Scanners, film recorders, color
management software, digital
cameras

Ahead Systems, Inc.
44244 Fremont Boulevard
Fremont, CA 94538
(510) 623-0900
3D multimedia surround-sound,
accelerator, and 3D stereo vision
products

AITech International Corporation
47971 Fremont Boulevard
Fremont, CA 94538
(510) 226-8960
http://www.aitech.com
Multimedia and desktop video
products

Aiwa America, Inc.
800 Corporate Drive
Mahwah, NJ 07430
(800) 920-2673
http://www.aiwa.com
Tape backup products

Alaris Inc.
47338 Fremont Boulevard
Fremont, CA 94538
(510) 770-5700
http://www.alaris.com
Graphics acceleration and
scalable full-motion video
playback products

Alfa Infotech Co.
46600 Landing Pky.
Fremont, CA 94538
(510) 252-9300
Multimedia and communication
products

ALI (Acer Laboratories Inc.)
4701 Patrick Henry Drive, Suite 2101
Santa Clara, CA 95054
(408) 764-0644
ICs for personal computers and
embedded systems

Alpha & Omega Computer
101 S. Kraemer Boulevard, Suite 116
Placentia, CA 92670
(714) 577-7688
486/Pentium CPU coolers

Alphacom Enterprise Inc.
1407 Englewood Street
Philadelphia, PA 19111
(215) 722-6133
Joysticks, mice, trackballs, CPU
cooling fans with built-in heat sink,
and removable hard disk drive kits

ALPS
3553 N. First Street
San Jose, CA 95134
(408) 432-6000
http://www.alpsusa.com
GlidePoint input devices, drive
products

AMCC (Applied Micro Circuits Corporation)
6195 Lusk Boulevard
San Diego, CA 92121
http://www.amcc.com
(800) 755-2622

AMD (Advanced Micro Devices)
1 AMD Place
Sunnyvale, CA 94086
(800) 222-9323, (408) 732-2400
http://www.amd.com
CPUs

American Cover, Inc.
102 W. 12200 S
Draper, UT 84092
(801) 553-0600
Computer accessory products

AMI (American Megatrends, Inc.)
6145F Northbelt Parkway
Norcross, GA 30071
(770) 263-8181
Motherboards

Amptron International, Inc.
1028 Lawson Street
City of Industry, CA 91748
(818) 912-5789
http://users.deltanet.com/
users/amptron/
System boards

Amrel Technology Inc.
11801 Goldring Road
Arcadia, CA 91006
(800) 882-6735
http://www.amrel.com
Modular notebook computers

AMS, Inc.
12881 Ramona Boulevard
Irwindale, CA 91706
(800) 886-2671

Ana Precision Co., Ltd.
Suite 694, Kumjung-Dong,
Kunp'O-shi
Kyunggi-Do, 435-050, Korea
(0343) 53-0813
Inkjet and dot matrix printers

Angia Communications
441 East Bay Boulevard
Provo, UT 84606
(800) 877-9159
Fax (801) 373-9847
PCMCIA Fax modem

AOC International
311 Sinclair Frontage Road
Milpitas, CA 95035
(408) 956-1070
Sales (816) 891-0050
http://www.aocltd.com
Visual display products

APC (American Power Conversion)
132 Fairgrounds Road
West Kingdom, RI 02892
(800) 800-4APC
Fax (401) 788-2797
UPSs, phone line surge protectors

Apex Data, Inc. /SMART Modular Technologies, Inc.
4305 Cushing Parkway
Fremont, CA 94538
(800) 841-APEX, tech support (510) 249-1605
Fax : (510) 249-1600, tech support
Fax (510) 249-1604
E-mail: sales@smartm.com,
support@smartm.com
BBS: (510) 249-1601 (81N)
http://www.apexdata.com

Apple Computer, Inc.
1 Infinite Loop
Cupertino, CA 95014
(408) 996-1010
http://www.apple.com

APS Technologies
6131 Deramus, Suite 4967
Kansas City, MO 64120
(800) 235-2753, (816) 483-1600
Fax (816) 483-3077

Archtek America Corporation
18549 Gale Avenue
City of Industry, CA 91748-1338
(818) 912-9800
(626) 912-9700 Fax 24-hours
http://www.archtek.com
Voice/data communications and
network products

Arco Computer Products, Inc.
2750 N. 29th Avenue, Suite 316
Hollywood, FL 33020
(305) 925-2688
http://www.arcoide.com
IDE busless, slotless, operating
system- independent mirroring
adapter

Arkenstone, Inc.
1390 Borregas Avenue
Sunnyvale, CA 94089
(800) 444-4443
http://www.arkenstone.org/
Products to aid individuals who are
blind, visually impaired, or learning
disabled to better access written
information

Artek (Asicom, Inc.)
46716 Fremont Boulevard
Fremont, CA 94538
(510) 354-0900
High-end PC subsystems

Artisoft, Inc.
2202 N. Forbes Boulevard
Tucson, AZ 85745
(520) 670-7100
http://www.artisoft.com
Networking products suited to small
businesses and workgroups

ArtMedia
2050 Ringwood Ave.
San Jose, CA 95131
(408) 980-8988
http://www.artmedia.com

ASK LCD, Inc.
1099 Wall Street W, Suite 396
Lyndhurst, NJ 07071
(201) 896-8888
Fax (201 896-0012
E-mail: asklcd@aol.com
LCD presentation products

Ask Technology Ltd.
Unit 1, 4/F., Henley Ind. Ctr.,
9-15 Bute Street
Mongkok, Kowloon, Hong Kong
(852) 2398-3223
System boards, VGA cards, and
sound cards

Askey Communications USA

162 Atlantic Street
Pomona, CA 91768
(800) 890-2027 (24hr Voice Mail)
(909) 444-2167
http://www.askey.com
PCMCIA, external, and internal
modem cards and pocket models

Asolid Computer Supply, Inc.

4044 Clipper Court
Fremont, CA 94538
(510) 226-6678
Motherboards

Aspen Systems Inc.

4026 Youngfield Street
Wheat Ridge, CO 80033-3862
(303) 431-4606
RISC systems

Aspen Technologies

400 Rogers Street
Princeton, WV 24740
(304) 425-1111
http://www.aspentek.com
Internal, external, and PCMCIA fax
modems

Assmann Data Products

1849 W. Drake Drive, Suite 101
Tempe, AZ 85283
(602) 897-7001
http://www.pagelink.com/afm/a
ssman.html
Ergonomic mice

AST Computer

16215 Alton Pky.
Irvine, CA 92718
(714) 727-4141
http://www.ast.com

ATI Technologies

33 Commerce Valley Drive East
Thornhill, Ontario L3T 7N6, Canada
(905) 882-2600
Fax (905) 882-2620
http://www.atitech.com
Graphics accelerators

Atlantic Technology

343 Vanderbilt Avenue
Norwood, MA 02062
(781) 762-6300
http://www.atlantictechnology.com
Speakers

ATronics International, Inc.

45635 Northport Loop E
Fremont, CA 94538-6415
(510) 656-8400
http://www.atronicsintl.com
Advanced external storage products

ATTO Technology, Inc.

40 Hazelwood Drive, Suite 106
Amherst, NY 14228
(716) 691-1999
http://www.attotech.com
VantagePCI-Multi Channel SCSI
accelerator card

AuraVision Corporation

47865 Fremont Boulevard
Fremont, CA 94538
(510) 252-6800
http://www.metl.com/aura.htm
Multimedia IC devices

AVerMedia, Inc.

47923A Warm Springs Boulevard
Fremont, CA 94538
(510) 770-9899
http://www.aver.com
PC-Video multimedia hardware

AVM Technology, Inc.
9774 S. 700 East
Sandy, UT 84070
(801) 571-0967
Professional MIDI wavetable
modules

Avnet Technology Co., Ltd.
6F-1, No. 102, Sung Lung Road
Taipei, Taiwan ROC
(886) 2-7607603
Audio-Visual Network Card

Award Software International
777 E. Middlefield Road
Mountain View, CA 94043
(650) 237-6800
http://www.award.com
Desktop plug-and-play BIOS for
486, 586, Pentium, and P6-based PC
platforms

Axonix Corporation
844 S. 200 East
Salt Lake City, UT 84111
(801) 521-9797
CD-ROMs

Axxon Computer Corporation
3979 Tecumseh Road E
Windsor, ON N8W 1J5, Canada
(519) 974-0163
http://www.softio.com/
Jumperless I/O cards

Aztech Labs, Inc.
47811 Warm Springs Boulevard
Fremont, CA 94539
(510) 623-8988
http://www.aztechca.com
6× CD-ROM drive

Belkin Components
1303 Walnut Pky.
Compton, CA 90220
(310) 898-1100
http://www.belkin.com
Standard and custom computer cables,
printer sharing devices, surge protectors, and LAN cabling-related products

Benwin Inc.
345 Cloverleaf Drive, Suite B
Baldwin Park, CA 91706
(626) 336-8779
Multimedia products, specializing in
speakers

Best Data Products
21800 Nordhoff Street
Chatsworth, CA 91311
(818) 773-9600

Best Power
General Signal
P.O. Box 280
Necedah, WI 54646
(800) 356-5794
http://www.bestpower.com
UPSs and shutdown software

BIS Technology
13111 Brooks Drive, Suite A
Baldwin Park, CA 91706
(909) 305-8800
High-speed voice/Fax/data modems

Boca Research
1377 Clint Moore Road
Boca Raton, FL 33478
(407) 997-6227
Fax (407) 994-5848
http://www.bocaresearch.com

Borland International
100 Borland Way
Scotts Valley, CA 95066
(408) 431-1000
http://www.borland.com
Products and services for software
developers

Bose Corporation
The Mountain
Framingham, MA 01701
(800) 444-BOSE

Brooks Power Systems Inc.
1400 Adams Road
Bensalem, PA 19020
(800) 523-1551
SurgeStopper surge and noise
suppressors

Brother International Corporation
200 Cottontail Lane
Somerset, NJ 08875
(908) 356-8880
Multi-function products and laser
printers

BRYSiS Data, Inc.
17431 Gale Ave.
City of Industry, CA 91748
(818) 810-0355
Touch-screen monitors
http://www.pcdirect.com

CalComp Corporation
2411 West La Palma Avenue
Anaheim, CA 92801
(800) 225-6670, (714) 821-2000
Fax (714) 821-2832-1329
http://www.calcomp.com

California PC Products
205 Apollo Way
Hollister, CA 95023
(408) 638-9460
Computer chassis and power supplies

Calluna Technology Ltd.
1 Blackwood Road
Eastfield, Glenrothes
Fife KY7 4NP, Scotland, UK
(44) 1592-630-810
PC card hard disk drives

Canon Computer Systems
2995 Redhill Avenue
Costa Mesa, CA 92626
(800) 848-4123, (714) 438-3000
http://www.ccsi.canon.com

Canon U.S.A., Inc.
1 Canon Plaza
Lake Success, NY 11042-1113
(516) 488-6700
http://www.usa.canon.com
Bubblejet CJ10 desktop color copier,
scanner, and printer

Casco Products, Inc.
375 Collins Rd. NE, Ste. 115
Cedar Rapids, IA 52402
(319) 393-6960, (800) 793-6960
http://www.casco.com
LightLink infrared, cordless keyboard

CD Technology, Inc.
766 San Aleso Avenue
Sunnyvale, CA 94086
(408) 863-4800
Fax (408) 863-4801
http://www.cdtechnology.com
E-mail: cdtechnology@
compuserve.com
CD-ROMs

Centon Electronics, Inc.
20 Morgan
Irvine, CA 92718
(714) 855-9111, (800) 234-9292
http://www.centon.com
Memory upgrades for desktops,
workstations, laptops, notebooks,
portables, and printers

Cerwin-Vega, Inc.
555 E. Easy Street
Simi Valley, CA 93065
(805) 584-9332
Digital audio-quality multimedia
speaker systems
http://www.cerwin-vega.com

CH Products
970 Park Center Drive
Vista, CA 92083
(760) 598-2518
http://www.chproducts.com
Joysticks, F-16 sticks, throttles, rud-
der pedals, flight yokes, trackballs,
and gamecards

Chaintech Computer U.S. Inc.
509 Valley Way
Milpitas, CA 95035
(408) 935-6988
http://www.chaintech.com.tw
Mainboards, VGA cards, multi I/O
cards, SCSI interfaces, and sound cards

Chaplet Systems USA, Inc.
252 N. Wolfe Road
Sunnyvale, CA 94086
(408) 732-7950
Notebook computers

Chase Advanced Technologies
500 Main Street
Deep River, CT 06417
(860) 526-2400, (800) 526-3898
Computer peripheral products

Cirque Corporation
433 W. Lawndale Drive
Salt Lake City, UT 84115
(800) 454-3375, (801) 467-1100
http://www.cirque.com
GlidePoint trackpad

Cirrus Logic, Inc.
3100 W. Warren Avenue
Fremont, CA 94538
(510) 623-8300
http://www.cirrus.com

Citizen America Corporation
2450 Broadway, Suite 600
Santa Monica, CA 90404
(310) 453-0614
http://www.citizen-
america.com/
Printiva 1700 near-photo-quality
color printer

Clary Corporation
1960 S. Walker Avenue
Monrovia, CA 91016
(800) 442-5279
http://www.clary.com/onguard/
UPSs

CMD Technology, Inc.
1 Vanderbilt
Irvine, CA 92718
(714) 454-0800
http://www.cmd.com
SCSI RAID and PC host adapters

Colorgraphic
5980 Peachtree Road
Atlanta, GA 30341
(770) 455-3921
http://www.colorgfx.com

COM2001 Corporation
2035 Corte Del Nogal, Ste. 200
Carlsbad, CA 92009
(760) 431-3133, (888) COM-2001
http://www.com2001.com
Video and audio conferencing
software

Comdial Corp.
1180 Seminole Trail
Charlottesville, VA 22906-7266
(800) 347-1432, (804) 978-2200
http://www.comdial.com
PC and telephone interfaces

Command Software Systems
1061 E. Indiantown Road, Suite 500
Jupiter, FL 33477
(800) 423-9147
http://commandcom.com
F-Prot Professional anti-virus
software

Compaq Computer Corporation
P.O. Box 69200
Houston, TX 77269
(800) 345-1518
http://www.compaq.com

Computer Connections America
19A Crosby Drive
Bedford, MA 01730
(781) 271-0444, (800) 438-5336
http://www.storagecompany.com
Peripheral equipment for backup
and data storage

Computer Fun
8250 Valdosta Avenue
San Diego, CA 92126-2130
(619) 271-9090
E-mail: garyo@computerfun.com
http://www.computerfun.com/
Mouse pads and computer toys

Connectix Corporation
2655 Campus Drive
San Mateo, CA 94403
(800) 950-5880, (650) 571-5100
Fax (650) 571-5195
http://www.connectix.com
QuickCam video camera

Cornerstone Imaging, Inc.
1710 Fortune Drive
San Jose, CA 95131
(408) 435-8900, (800) 562-2552
http://www.corimage.com

Creative Labs, Inc.
1901 McCarthy Boulevard
Milpitas, CA 95035
(800) 998-1000, (408) 428-6600
Fax (408) 428-6631
http://www.creativelabs.com

CTX International, Inc.
748 Epperson Drive
City of Industry, CA. 91748
(626) 839-0500, (800) 888-9052
Monitors, desktops, and laptops
http://www.ctxintl.com

CyberMax Computer, Inc.
133 North 5th Street
Allentown, PA 18102
(800) 443-9868, from Canada (800)
695-4991, (610) 770-1808
http://www.cybmax.com

Cyrix Corporation
P.O. Box 853923
Richardson, TX 75085-3923
(800) 462-9749, (800) 340-7971
E-mail: tech_support@cyrix.com
BBS: (214) 968-8610
http://www.cyrix.com

Daewoo Electronics
120 Chubb Ave.
Lyndhurst, NJ 07071
(201) 460-2000
http://www.dwe.daewoo.co.kr
Monitors

Data Depot Inc.
1710 Drew Street, Suite 1
Clearwater, FL 34615
(813) 446-3402
PC diagnostic test products, including hardware and software products

DataLux Corp.
155 Aviation Dr.
Winchester, VA 22602
(800) DATALUX
Fax (540) 662-1682
E-mail: info@datalux.com
http://www.datalux.com
Space-saving PC hardware

Dell Computer Corporation
2112 Kramer Lane
Austin, TX 78758
(800) 545-7141, (512) 728-3431
http://www.dell.com

Delta Products Corporation
3225 Laurelview Ct.
Fremont, CA 94538
(510) 770-0660
Video display products

Denon Electronics
222 New Road
Parsippany, NJ 07054
(973) 575-7810
CD-ROM jukebox that houses
200 discs

DFI (Diamond Flower, Inc.)
135 Main Avenue
Sacramento, CA 95838
(916) 568-1234
http://www.dfiusa.com
Motherboards, video cards, notebooks, desktop systems, and multimedia components

Diamond Multimedia Systems, Inc.
2880 Junction Avenue
San Jose, CA 95134-1922
(408) 325-7000
Fax (408) 325-7070
http://www.diamondmm.com

Digital Equipment Corporation (DEC)
Computer Systems Div.
111 Powdermill Road
Maynard, MA 01754-1499
(800) DIGITAL
http://www.digital.com
PCs, servers, and workstations for 32- and 64-bit computing

Disctec
925 S. Semoran Boulevard, Suite 114
Winter Park, FL 32792
(407) 671-5500
http://disctec.com/
Parallel port products including CD-ROM drives, hard drives, floppy drives, and rewriteable optical drives

DPT-Distributed Processing Technology

140 Candace Drive
Maitland, FL 32751
(407) 830-5522
http://www.dpt.com
SmartCache SCSI host adapters

DTC Data Technology, Inc.

1515 Centre Pointe Drive
Milpitas, CA 95035
(408) 942-4000, technical support
(408) 262-7700
Fax (408) 942-4027
BBS: (408) 942-4010
http://www.datatechnology.com
Drives and SCSI devices

DTK Computer Inc.

770 Epperson Drive
City of Industry, CA 91748
(626) 810-0098
Pentium-based systems

Edek Technologies, Inc.

1212 John Reed Ct.
City of Industry, CA 91745
(626) 855-5700
Computer mainboard and VGA card
products

Enhance 3000 Memory Products, Inc.

18730 Oxnard Street, Suite 201
Tarzana, CA 91356
(818) 343-3066
Memory systems

Ensoniq

155 Great Valley Parkway
Malvern, PA 19355
(610) 647-3930

EPS Technologies

10069 Dakota Avenue
Jefferson, SD 57038
(800) 447-0921, (800) 526-4258,
(605) 966-5586
Fax (605) 966-5482
http://www.epstech.com

Epson America, Inc.

20770 Madrona Avenue
Torrance, CA 90509
(800) 463-7766, (310) 782-0770
http://www.epson.com

ESS Technology, Inc.

46107 Landing Pky.
Fremont, CA 94538
(510) 226-1088
ES689 Wavetable Music Synthesizer,
ES938 3D Audio Effects Processor

Exabyte Corporation

1685 38th St.
Boulder, CO 80301
(800) 445-7736, (303) 417-7511,
(303) 417-7792
Fax (303) 417-7890
E-mail: support@exabyte.com
http://www.exabyte.com

Exide Electronics

2727 Kurtz Street
San Diego, CA 92110
(619) 291-4211
http://www.deltecpower.com
Uninterruptible power systems and
power management software

EXP Computer Inc.
141 Eileen Way
Syosset, NY 11791
(516) 496-3703
Memory and PCMCIA products for
notebooks and palmtops

Expert Computer International, Inc.
129 166th St.
Cerritos, CA 90703
(562) 407-1740
Generic and name-brand VGA cards
in DRAM/VRAM ISA, VL-bus, and
PCI configurations

Fast Electronic U.S., Inc.
393 Vintage Park Drive
Foster City, CA 94404
(650) 345-3400
FPS60 video compression board for
multi- media production

Focus Electronic Corporation
21078 Commerce Pointe Drive
Walnut, CA 91789
(909) 468-5533
Signature Series keyboards

Fujitsu
Fujitsu Personal Systems, Inc.
5200 Patrick Henry Drive
Santa Clara, CA 95054
(408) 982-9500

**Fujitsu Computer Products
of America**
2904 Orchard Parkway
San Jose, CA 95134
(800) 626-4686
http://www.fujitsu.com,
http://www.fcpa.com

Peripherals including hard disk
drives, optical disk drives, tape drives,
laser and dot matrix printers, document imaging scanners

Gateway2000
610 Gateway Dive
N. Sioux City, SD 57049-2000
(888) 888-0244, from Canada
(800) 846-3609, (605) 232-2000
Fax (605) 232-2023
http://www.gw2k.com

**Hayes Microcomputer
Products, Inc.**
P.O. Box 105203
Atlanta, GA 30348-5203
(800) 377-4377, (770) 840-9200
Fax (770) 441-1213
http://www.hayes.com
Modems

Hercules Computer Technology, Inc.
3839 Spinnaker Court
Fremont, CA 94538
(800) 323-0601, (510) 623-6030,
(510) 623-6050
Fax (510) 623-1112
Tech support Fax (510) 490-6745
E-mail: support@hercules.com
CompuServe: GO HERCULES,
71333,2532
BBS: (510) 623-7449
http://www.hercules.com

Hewlett-Packard
5301 Stevens Creek Boulevard
Santa Clara, CA 95052
(800) 752-0900
http://www.hp.com

Hilgraeve Inc.
111 Conant Avenue, Suite A
Monroe, MI 48161
(313) 243-0576
http://www.hilgraeve.com
32-bit communications software,
including HyperTerminal

Hitachi America, Ltd.
50 Prospect Avenue
Tarrytown, NY 10591-4698
(800) 448-2244
Computer peripherals and components, including storage products

Hyundai Electronics America
510 Cottonwood Drive
Milpitas, CA 95035
(408) 232-8000
http://www.hea.com
Components including memory
devices for DRAM, SRAM

I/OMagic Corporation
9272 Jeronimo Street, Bldg. 122
Irvine, CA 92718
(714) 727-7466

IBM PC Co.
1 Orchard Road
Armonk, NY 10504
(800) 772-2227, (914) 766-1900
Fax (800) 426-4323
http://www.pc.ibm.com

Iiyama North America, Inc.
650 Louis Drive, Suite 120
Warminster, PA 18974
(215) 957-6543
http://www.iiyama.com

Intel Corporation
2111 N.E. 25th Avenue
Hillsboro, OR 97124-5961
(800) 628-8686
http://www.intel.com

Interact Accessories, Inc.
10945 McCormick Road
Hunt Valley, MD 21031
(410) 785-5661
Multimedia gaming products such
as joysticks, control pads, game
cards, speakers, woofers, mice,
storage cases, and cleaning kits

Iomega Corporation
1821 West Iomega Way
Roy, UT 84067
(800) MY-STUFF
http://www.iomega.com

Jazz Speakers
1217 John Reed Ct.
Industry, CA 91745
(626) 336-2689

JBL Consumer Products Inc.
Harmon Consumer Group
80 Crossways Pk. W
Woodbury, NY 11797
(800) 645-7484
Multimedia speakers, both satellites
and subwoofers

Joss Technology Ltd.
No. 20, Lane 84, San Min Road
Hsin Tien City
Taipei Hsien, Taiwan ROC
(886) 2-9102050
Motherboards, 4MB/16MB 72-pin
SIMM modules

JVC Information Products of America

17811 Mitchell Avenue
Irvine, CA 92714
(800) 252-5722
http://www.jvcdiscusa.com
CD-ROM products and software

KeySonic Technology Inc.

1040A S. Melrose Street
Placentia, CA 92670-7119
(714) 632-8887
MPEG video and audio decoding cards

Kinesis Corporation

22121 17th Avenue SE, Suite 107
Bothell, WA 98021-7404
(425) 402-8100
Fax (425) 402-8181
http://www.kinesis-ergo.com/
Ergonomic keyboards

Kingston Technology Corporation

17600 Newhope Street
Fountain Valley, CA 92708
(800) 259-9370, (714) 437-3334
Fax (714) 435-2699
http://www.kingston.com/b.htm

Konica Business Machines U.S.A., Inc.

500 Day Hill Road
Windsor, CT 06095
(203) 683-2222
http://www.konica.com
Multifunctional printers

Koss Corporation

4129 N. Port Washington Boulevard
Milwaukee, WI 53212
(800) USA-KOSS, (414) 964-5000
Stereo audio accessories for computers

Labtec Enterprises, Inc.

3801 109th Ave., Suite J
Vancouver, WA 98682
(360) 896-2000
http://www.labtec.com

Lava Computer Mfg. Inc.

LSMI Division
28A Dansk Ct.
Rexdale, ON M9W 5V8, Canada
(800) 241-5282
High-speed I/O boards

Leverage International, Inc.

46704 Fremont Boulevard
Fremont, CA 94538
(510) 657-6750
Memory modules and other semi-conductor products for IBM, Compaq, PC compatibles and other computers

Lexmark International, Inc.

2275 Research Boulevard
Rockville, MD 20850
(301) 212-5900
http://www.lexmark.com

LG Electronics

1000 Sylvan Avenue
Englewood Cliffs, NJ 95131
(201) 816-2000
Goldstar monitors

Liberty Systems, Inc.
120 Saratoga Avenue, Suite 82
Santa Clara, CA 95051
(408) 983-1127
http://www.libertyinc.com
CD-ROMs, hard drives, backup
devices

Logicode Technology, Inc.
1380 Flynn Road
Camarillo, CA 93012
(800) 735-6442, (805) 388-9000

Logitech, Inc.
6505 Kaiser Drive
Fremont, CA 94555
(510) 795-8500
http://www.logitech.com
Pointing devices

MAG InnoVision Co., Inc
2801 South Yale Street
Santa Ana, CA 92704
(800) 827-3998, (714) 751-2008
Fax (714) 751-5522
http://www.maginnovision.com
Monitors

Magnavox
Philips Consumer Electronics
Company
One Philips Drive
Knoxville, Tennessee 37914-1810
(800) 531-0039, (423) 521-4316
http://www.magnavox.com

Matrox Graphics, Inc.
1025 St-Regis Boulevard
Dorval, Quebec H9P 2T4, Canada
(514) 969-6320
Video boards

Maxell Corporation of America
Multi-Media Division
22-08 Rt. 208
Fair Lawn, NJ 07410
(800) 533-2836
Data storage media

Maximus Computers
710 East Cypress Avenue, Unit-A
Monrovia, CA 91016
(800) 888-6294, (818) 305-5925
Fax (818) 357-9140
http://www.maximuspc.com

Maxi-Switch
2901 East Elvira Road
Tucson, AZ 85706
(520) 294-5450
Keyboards

Maxtor Corporation
510 Cottonwood Dr.
Milpitas, CA 95135
(800) 2-MAXTOR, (408) 432-1700
Fax (408) 922-2050
Tech Support Fax (303) 678-2260
http://www.maxtor.com

Media Vision
47900 Bayside Pky.
Fremont, CA 94538
(510) 770-8600
http://www.mediavis.com
Semiconductor products, audio
products

Mediatrix Peripherals Inc.
4229 Garlock Street
Sherbrooke, PQ J1L 2C8, Canada
(819) 829-8749
http://www.fmmo.ca/mediatrix
Audiotrix Pro 16-bit sound board

Megahertz Corporation
605 North 5600 West
Salt Lake City, UT 84116
(800) 517-8677

Micro 2000, Inc.
1100 E. Broadway, Suite 301
Glendale, CA 91205
(818) 547-0125
http://www.micro2000.com
Universal Diagnostics Toolkit

Micro Accessories, Inc.
6086 Stewart Avenue
Fremont, CA 94538
(510) 226-6310
Computer interface cables and
terminators

Micro Solutions
132 West Lincoln Hwy
DeKalb, IL 60115
(815) 754-4500
Fax (815) 756-4986
BBS: (815) 756-9100
http://www.micro-
solutions.com

MicroClean, Inc.
2050 S. Tenth Street
San Jose, CA 95112
(408) 995-5062
Computer care cleaning products

MicroData Corp.
3001 Exec. Dr.
Clearwater, FL 34622
(813) 573-5900
PC diagnostic hardware and software products for technicians, system integrators, and computer
service professionals

Microlabs
204 Lost Canyon Court
Richardson, TX 75080
(972) 234-5842

Micron Electronics, Inc.
900 East Karcher Road
Nampa, ID 83687
(800) 214-6674, from Canada
(800) 708-1758, (208) 893-3434
Fax (208) 893-3424
http://www.mei.micron.com
Computer systems, WinBook notebook computers

Micronics Computers
221 Warren Avenue
Fremont, CA 94539
(800) 767-2443(800), 577-0977,
(510) 651-2300, (510) 661-3000
Fax (510) 651-6692
BBS: (510) 651-6837
CompuServe: GO ORCHID
http://www.orchid.com
Orchid series graphics accelerators

Microsoft Corporation
One Microsoft Way
Redmond, WA 98052-6399
(425) 882-8080
http://www.microsoft.com

Microtek Lab, Inc.
3715 Doolittle Drive
Redondo Beach, CA 90278
(800) 654-4160, (310) 297-5000,
Tech support (310) 297-5100
Fax (310) 297-5050
BBS: (310) 297-5102
CompuServe: GO GRAPHSUP,
library 6
http://www.mteklab.com

Minolta Corporation
101 Williams Drive
Ramsey, NJ 07446
(201) 825-4000
Graphics-specific input and output
devices

Mita Copystar America, Inc.
225 Sand Road
P.O. Box 40008
Fairfield, NJ 07004-0008
(800) ABC-MITA
Multifunctional printers

Mitsuba Corporation
1925 Wright Avenue
Laverne, CA 91750
(800) 648-7822
http://www.mitsuba.com:81/
Custom file servers, PCs, and
notebooks

Mitsubishi Chemical America
Optical Storage & Software
Systems Group
99 W. Tasman Drive, Suite 200
San Jose, CA 95134-1712
(408) 954-8484
Magneto-optical storage technologies

Mitsubishi Electronics America
5665 Plaza Drive
Cypress, CA 90630
(714) 220-2500
http://www.mela-itg.com

Mitsumi Electronics Corporation
6210 N. Beltline Road, Suite 170
Irving, TX 75063
(800) 648-7864, (800) 801-7927,
(214) 550-7300

BBS: (415) 691-4469
http://www.mitsumi.com
Keyboards, mice, floppy disk drives,
and CD-ROM drives

Motorola ISG
5000 Bradford Dr.
Huntsville, AL 35805
(205) 430-8000
http://www.mot.com/mims/isg/
Modems

Motorola PCMCIA Products Division
50 East Commerce Drive
Shaumburg, IL 60173
(800) 4A-PCMCIA

MTC America, Inc.
2500 Westchester Avenue, Suite 110
Purchase, NY 10577
(800) MTC-CDRS
Mitsui Gold CD-R device

Multi-Tech Systems, Inc.
2205 Woodale Drive
Mounds View, MN 55112
(800) 328-9717
Fax (612) 785-9874
http://www.multitech.com

Multiwave Technology, Inc.
15318 Valley Boulevard
City of Industry, CA 91746
(800) 234-3358, (800) 587-1730,
(626) 330-7030
Fax (818) 333-4609
http://www.mwave.com

Mustek, Inc.
1702 McGaw Avenue
Irvine, CA 92714
(800) 468-7835, (714) 247-1300
BBS: (714) 247-1330
http://www.mustek.com
Scanners

Mylex Corp.
4151 Burton Drive
Santa Clara, CA 95054
(510) 796-6100
Fax (510) 745-8016
http://www.mylex.com
SCSI host adapters

National Semiconductor
Personal Systems Div.
2900 Semiconductor Drive
Santa Clara, CA 95052
(408) 721-5000
Silicon products and systems for
personal computers and peripherals

NCE Storage Solutions
9717 Pacific Heights Blvd.
San Diego, CA 92121
(619) 658-9720
Emerald System backup devices

NCR Corp.
(800) 774-7406
Fax (803) 939-7824
http://www.ncr.com

NEC Corporation
12450 Fair Lakes Circle, Suite
FairFax, VA 22033
(703) 818-1218
http://www.nec.com
Desktops and wireless technology

NEC Technologies, Inc.
1414 Massachusetts Avenue
Boxborough, MA 01719
(978) 264-8000
http://www.nec.com

NEC Technologies, Inc.
NEC RISC Systems
339 N. Bernardo Avenue
Mountain View, CA 94043
(650) 528-6000
RISC-based servers

Network Associates (formerly McAfee Associates)
2710 Walsh Avenue
Santa Clara, CA
(408) 988-3832
http://www.macafee.com
VirusScan anti-virus software

New Media Corporation
One Technology Park, bldg. A
Irvine, CA 92718
(714) 453-0100
Fax (714) 453-0114
http://www.newmediacorp.com

NewCom, Inc.
31166 Via Colinas
Westlake Village, CA 91362
(818) 597-3200
http://www.newcominc.com/
Internal and external Fax modems,
high-fidelity stereo sound cards, and
multimedia kits

Nokia Display Products
1505 Bridgeway Boulevard
Sausalito, CA 94965
(415) 331-0322
http://www.nokia.com

NSA/Hitachi
100 Lowder Brook Drive
Westwood, MA 02090
(800) 441-4832, (617) 461-8300

**Ocean Information Systems Inc.
(Octek)**
688 Arrow Grand Circle,
Covina, California 91722, USA
(626) 339-8888
Fax (818) 859-7668
http://www.ocean-usa.com/ocean
http://www.oceanhk.com
PC computer systems, motherboards, cases, power supplies, multimedia products, and peripherals

Okidata Corporation
532 Fellowship Road
Mt. Laurel, NJ 08054
(609) 235-2600
http://www.okidata.com

Olivetti Office USA
765 US Highway 202
Bridgewater, NJ 08807
(908) 526-8200

Orchestra MultiSystems, Inc.
12300 Edison Way
Garden Grove, CA 92841
(800) 237-9988, (714) 891-3861
Fax (714) 891-2661
http://www.orchestra.com

Orevox USA Corporation
248 N. Puente Avenue
P.O. Box 2655
City of Industry, CA 91746
(626) 333-6803
Computer cases and multimedia
speakers

Padix Co. Ltd.
18F-3, No. 75, Sec. 1,
Hsin Tai Wu Road
Hsih-Chih, Taipei, Taiwan ROC
(886) 2-6981478
PC-compatible game controllers
and joysticks

**Panasonic Communications &
Systems Co.**
2 Panasonic Way
Secaucus, NJ 07094
(201) 348-7000
http://www.panasonic.com

Pantex Computer Inc.
10301 Harwin Drive
Houston, TX 77036
(713) 988-1688
Motherboards, bare-bones systems

Pathlight Technology Inc.
767 Warren Road
Ithaca, NY 14850
(607) 266-4000
http://www.pathlight.com
Storage I/O and networking interface technologies and products

PC Concepts, Inc.
10318 Norris Avenue
Pacoima, CA 91331
(800) 735-6071
Computer accessories including color-
coded cables, manual and auto data
switches, printer network devices,
surge protectors, and multimedia
products

PC Power & Cooling, Inc.
5995 Avenida Encinas
Carlsbad, CA 92008
(760) 931-5700
CPU cooler for Intel's P6 processor

PCMCIA (Personal Computer Memory Card Int'l. Association)
4529 Lillian Ct.
La Canada, CA 91011
(408) 433-2273

Pengo Computer Accessories
15612 First Street
Irwindale, CA 91706
(800) 447-3646
http://www.pengo.com
Floppy diskettes, dust covers, keyboard drawers, diskette file boxes, tool kits, and various work station accessories

Phillips Consumer Electronics Co.
1 Phillips Drive
Knoxville, TN 37914
(423) 521-4316
http://www.phillips.com

Pioneer New Media Technologies, Inc.
Multimedia & Mass Storage
2265 E. 220th Street
Long Beach, CA 90810
(800) 444-6784
CD-ROM and CD-R products for multimedia and mass storage applications

Pionex Technologies, Inc.
3 Riverview Dr.
Somerset, NJ 08873
(732) 563-9809

Pixie Technologies
46771 Fremont Boulevard
Fremont, CA 94538
(510) 440-9721
Monitors

PKWare, Inc.
9025 N. Deerwood Drive
Brown Deer, WI 53223
(414) 354-8699
http://www.pkware.com
PKZIP compression utilities

Play Inc.
2890 Kilgore Road
Rancho Cordova, CA 95670-6133
(916) 851-0800
Snappy Video Snapshot software

Plextor USA
4255 Burton Drive
Santa Clara, CA 95054
(800) 886-3935, (408) 980-1838
http://www.plextor.com
CD-ROM drives

Portrait Display Labs
6665 Owens Drive
Pleasanton, CA 94588
(510) 227-2700
http://www.portrait.com
Monitors

Powercom America, Inc.
1040A S. Melrose Street
Placentia, CA 92670-7119
(714) 632-8889
Modems and UPSs

PowerQuest Corporation

1083 North State Street
Orem, UT 84057
(800) 379-2566
http://www.powerquest.com
Manufacturer of Partition Magic,
software utility for creating and
managing disk partitions

Practical Peripherals

P.O. Box 921789
Norcross, GA 30092-7789
(770) 840-9966
http://www.practinet.com

Princeton Graphic Systems

2801 South Yale Street
Santa Ana, CA 92704
(800) 747-6249, (714) 751-8405
Fax (714) 751-5736
http://www.prgr.com
Monitors

Procom Technology

2181 Dupont Drive
Irvine, CA 92715
(714) 852-1000
Hard drives, backup devices

Professional Technologies

21038 Commerce Pointe Drive
Walnut, CA 91789
(800) 949-5018, (909) 468-3730
Fax (909) 468-1372
Computer systems

ProLink Computer

2530 Corporate Place, Suite A-100
Monterey Park, CA 91754
(213) 780-7978

QLogic Corporation

Costa Mesa, CA
(800) 867-7274, (714) 438-2200
Fax (714) 668-6950
http://www.qlc.com

Quadrant International, Inc.

269 Great Valley Parkway
Malvern, PA 19355 USA
(800) 700-0362, (610) 251-9999
Tech support (610) 251-9999
Fax (610) 695-2592
E-mail: qi-tech@quadrant.com
http://www.quadrant.com
Video editing and capture products

Quantex Microsystems, Inc.

400B Pierce Street
Somerset, NJ 08873
(800) 836-0566
http://www.quantex.com

Quantum Corporation

500 McCarthy Boulevard
Milpitas, CA 95053
(800) 624-5545, (408) 894-4000
http://www.qntm.com

Quarterdeck Select

5770 Roosevelt Boulevard #400
Clearwater, FL 34620
(800) 683-6696
Fax (813) 523-2391
Troubleshooting tools

Quatech, Inc.

662 Wolf Ledges Pky.
Akron, OH 44311
(800) 553-1170
Communication, data acquisition,
industrial I/O, and PCMCIA products

QuickShot Technology, Inc.
Milpitas, CA
(408) 263-4163
Fax (408) 263-4005
http://www.quickshot.com

QVS, Inc.
2731 Crimson Canyon Drive
Las Vegas, NV 89128
(800) 344-3371
Computer cables, computer electronic products

Regal Electronics, Inc.
4251 Burton Drive
Santa Clara, CA 95054
(408) 988-2288
Plug-and-play CD-ROM changers
and multimedia speakers

Relisys (Teco)
320 S. Milpitas Boulevard
Milpitas, CA 95035
(408) 945-9000
http://www.relisys.com
Video monitors, scanners, and multifunctional facsimile products

Rockwell Telecommunications
Multimedia Communications
Division
4311 Jamboree Road
Newport Beach, CA 92658
(714) 222-9119
http://www.nb.rockwell.com
Modems

Roland Corporation U.S.
Desktop Media Production
7200 Dominion Cir.
Los Angeles, CA 90040
(213) 685-5141
http://www.rolandus.com
Sound cards, PCMCIA cards, MIDI
keyboards, powered speakers, and
music software

S & S Software International
17 New England Executive Park
Burlington, MA 01803
(781) 273-7400
http://www.drsolomon.com
Dr. Solomon's Anti-Virus Toolkit

S. T. Research Corp.
8419 Terminal Rd.
Newington, VA 22122
(703) 550-7000
Palm top computers

S3, Inc.
2770 San Tomas Expy.
Santa Clara, CA 95051
(408) 980-5400
http://www.s3.com
Graphics acceleration products

Sager Computer
18005 Cortney Court
City of Industry, CA 91748
(800) 669-1624, (818) 964-8682
Fax (818) 964-2381
http://www.sager-midern.com
Notebook computers

Sampo Technology, Inc.
5550 Peachtree Ind. Boulevard
Norcross, GA 30071
(770) 449-6220
http://www.sampotech.com
Monitors

Samsung America, Inc.
14251 E. Firestone Boulevard
La Mirada, CA 90638
(562) 802-2211
CPU cooler for the Pentium and P6

Samsung Electronics America, Inc.
Information Systems Div.
105 Challenger Road
Ridgefield Park, NJ 07660
(800) 933-4110, (201) 229-4000
http://www.samsung.com
Notebook PCs, color monitors, hard
disk drives, and laser printers

Samtron
A Div. of Samsung Electronics
America
18600 Broadwick Street
Rancho Dominguez, CA 90220
(310) 537-7000
Monitors

Sanyo Energy (U.S.A.) Corporation
2001 Sanyo Avenue
San Diego, CA 92173
(619) 661-6620
Batteries and amorphous solar cells

Sanyo Fisher (USA) Corporation
Office Automation Products
21350 Lassen Street
Chatsworth, CA 91311
(818) 998-7322
Multifunctional Fax machines,
CD-ROM drives, notebooks, desk-
top personal computers, monitors

Seagate Software
920 Disc Drive
Scotts Valley, CA 95067
(408) 438-6550
Fax (408) 438-7612
http://www.arcada.com
Data protection and storage management software products

Seagate Technology
920 Disc Drive
Scotts Valley, CA 95066-6550
(408) 438-6550
http://www.seagate.com
Hard drives

Seattle Telecom & Data, Inc.
18005 N.E. 68th, Suite A115
Redmond, WA 98052
(425) 883-8440
Manufacturer of PS/2-compatible
accelerator boards for most Micro
Channel models

Sharp Electronics Corporation
Sharp Plaza
Mahwah, NJ 07430
(201) 529-8200
http://www.sharp-usa.com
LCDs and LCD-based products

Shining Technology, Inc.
10533 Progress Way, Suite C
Cypress, CA 90630
(714) 761-9598
Parallel I/O products to EIDE (supporting HDD and CD-ROMs)

Shuttle Computer International Inc.
1161 Cadillac Ct.
Milpitas, CA 95035
(408) 945-1480
Pentium 75-180MHz PCI motherboards with pipeline SRAM, EDO, and DRAM support

Shuttle Technology
43218 Christy Street
Fremont, CA 94538
(510) 656-0180
Parallel port interfacing technology

Sigma Interactive Solutions Corporation
46515 Landing Parkway
Fremont, CA 94538
(510) 770-0100

Simple Technology
3001 Daimler Street
Santa Ana, CA 92705
(714) 476-1180
Memory and PC card products

SL Waber
520 Fellowship Road
Mount Laurel, NJ 08054
(800) 634-1485, (609) 866-8888
Uninterruptible power supplies

Smart and Friendly
20520 Nordhoff Street
Chatsworth, CA 91311
(800) 542-8838, (818) 772-8001
Fax (818) 772-2888
http://www.smartandfriendly.com/
CD recording devices

SMART Modular Technologies, Inc.
45531 Northport Loop W
Fremont, CA 94538
(510) 623-1231
DRAM, SRAM, and Flash memory modules and upgrade cards

Smile International, Inc.
175 Sunflower Avenue
Costa Mesa, CA 92626
(714) 546-0336

Sony Corporation
1 Sony Drive
Park Ridge, NJ 07645
(201) 930-1000
http://www.sony.com
Digital technologies for computers, communications, audio, and video

SRS Labs, Inc.
2909 Daimler Street
Santa Ana, CA 92705
(714) 442-1070
http://www.srslabs.com
3D sound technology

Stac Electronics
12636 High Bluff Drive
San Diego, CA 92130-2093
(619) 794-4300
Backup and disaster recovery products

STB Systems, Inc.
1651 North Glenville, Suite 210
Richardson, TX 75085
(972) 234-8750, (972) 669-0989
Fax (214) 234-1306
Tech support fax (972) 669-1326
E-mail: support@stb.com
BBS: (972) 437-9615
http://www.stb.com

Storage Technology Corporation
2270 S. 88th Street
Louisville, CO 80028-4341
(303) 673-5151
http://www.stortek.com
StorageTek storage products

Stracon, Inc.
1672 Kaiser Avenue
Irvine, CA 92714
(714) 851-2288
http://www.superpc.com
Memory upgrades for PCs, laptops,
and workstations

Supra Corporation
7101 Supra Drive
Albany, OR 97321
(800) 727-8772
http://www.supra.com
Modems

Swan Instruments
Drive Div.
3000 Olcott
Santa Clara, CA 95054
(408) 574-7800
Ultra High-Capacity (UHC) Flexible
Disk Drives

Symantec Corporation
10201 Torre Avenue
Cupertino, CA 95014-2132
(408) 253-9600
http://www.symantec.com
Norton Utilities, Norton Anti-Virus
software

Synnex Information Technologies, Inc.
3797 Spinnaker Court
Fremont, CA 94538
(510) 656-3333
http://www.synnex.com

SyQuest Technology
47071 Bayside Pky.
Fremont, CA 94538
(800) 245-2278, (510) 226-4137
Removable storage products

Tagram System Corporation
1451-B Edinger Avenue
Tustin, CA 92680
(800) TAGRAMS, (714) 979-8900
Fax (714) 979-8970
http://www.tagram.com

Tahoe Peripherals
999 Tahoe Boulevard
Incline Village, NV 89451
(800) 288-6040
http:www.tahoeperipherals.com
Fax (702) 823-2200

Tandberg Data
2685-A Park Center Drive
Simi Valley, CA 93065
(805) 579-1000
SCSI QIC tape backup drives and kits

TDK Electronics Corporation
12 Harbor Park Drive
Port Washington, NY 11050
(800) TDK-TAPE
Optical and magnetic recording media

TEAC America, Inc.
Data Storage Products Div.
7733 Telegraph Road
Montebello, CA 90640
(213) 726-0303
http://www.teac.com
CD-ROM, tape, and floppy drives

Techmedia Computer Systems Corporation
7345 Orangewood Avenue
Garden Grove, CA 92641
(800) 379-0077, (714) 379-6677
Fax (714) 379-6688
Monitors

Tektronix, Inc.
P.O. Box 7000 MS 63-580
Wilsonville, OR 97070
(800) 835-6100, (503) 682-7377
Fax (503) 682-2980
http://www.tek.com

Tempest Micro
375 N. Citrus Avenue #611
Azusa, CA 91704
(800) 818-5163, (800) 848-5167,
(909) 595-0550
Fax (909) 595-5025

Texas Instruments, Inc.
P.O. Box 650311
M/S 3914
Dallas, TX 75265
(800) 336-5236, (972) 917-6278
http://www.ti.com

ThrustMaster, Inc.
7175 NW Evergreen Parkway, #400
Hillsboro, OR 97124
(503) 615-3200
Fax (503) 615-3300
http://www.thrustmaster.com

Thunder Max Corporation
15011 Parkway Loop, Suite A
Tustin, CA 92680
(888) 852-8898, (714) 259-8800
http://www.thundermax.com

TMC Research Corporation
631 S. Milpitas Boulevard
Milpitas, CA 95035
(510) 440-0888
Windows 95-compatible motherboards and SCSI host adapters

Toshiba America Information Systems, Inc.
9740 Irvine Boulevard
Irvine, CA 92718
(800) 457-7777, (714) 583-3000
CD-ROMs, hard drives

TouchStone Software Corporation
2124 Main Street
Huntington Beach, CA 92648
(714) 969-7746
http://www.checkit.com
CheckIt Pro, WinCheckIt 4.0 diagnostic software

Trend Micro Devices
20245 Stevens Creek Boulevard
Cupertino, CA 95014
(800) 228-5651, (408) 257-1500
http://www.trendmicro.com
PC-cillin anti-virus software

Trident Microsystems, Inc.

189 N. Bernardo Avenue
Mountain View, CA 94043
(650) 691-9211
http://www.trid.com
32- and 64-bit integrated graphics
and multimedia video processing
controllers for PC compatibles

Truevision, Inc.

2500 Walsh Avenue
Santa Clara, CA 95051
(800) 522-TRUE, (408) 562-4200
Fax (408) 562-4200
Tech support fax (317) 576-7770
E-mail: support@truevision.com
CompuServe: GO TRUEVISION
BBS: (317) 577-8777
http://www.truevision.com

Tyan Computer

1645 S. Main Street
Milpitas, CA 95035
(408) 956-8000
http://www.tyan.com
High-end motherboards and add-on
cards

U.S. Robotics Corp.

8100 North McCormick Boulevard
Skokie, IL 60076-2999
(800) DIAL-USR, (800) USR-CORP,
(708) 982-5001
http://www.usr.com
Modems

UMAX Technologies

3353 Gateway Boulevard
Fremont, CA 94538
(800) 562-0031, (510) 651-9488
Fax (510) 651-8834

Unisys Corporation

Personal Computer Div.
2700 N. First Street
San Jose, CA 95134-2028
(800) 448-1424
http://www.unisys.com
Notebook and desktop systems

Valitek

100 University Drive
Amherst, MA 01102
(413) 549-2700
Backup devices

Verbatim Corporation

1200 W.T. Harris Boulevard
Charlotte, NC 28262
(704) 547-6500
http://www.verbatimcorp.com
Optical discs, tape products, floppy
disks, CD-R and CD-ROM, and
imaging products

Video Electronics Standards Association (VESA)

2150 N. First Street, Suite 440
San Jose, CA 95131
(408) 435-0333

ViewSonic Corporation

20480 East Business Parkway
Walnut, CA 91789
(800) 888-8583, (909) 869-7976
http://www.viewsonic.com
ViewSonic and Optiquest monitors

VLSI Technology, Inc.

8375 S. River Pky.
Tempe, AZ 85284
http://www.vlsi.com
(602) 752-8574
64-bit+graphics controller supporting SGRAM

Voyetra Technologies and Turtle Beach Systems
5 Odell Plaza
Yonkers NY 10701-1406
914-966-2150, 914-966-1102
E-mail: support@tbeach.com
CompuServe: GO TURTLE,
GO TBMIDI
http://www.tbeach.com

WACOM Technology Corporation
501 S.E. Columbia Shores Blvd.,
Suite 300
Vancouver, WA 98661
(800) 922-9348, (360) 750-8882
Fax (360) 750-8924
BBS: (360) 750-0638 (300 to 14400
baud, 8N1)
E-mail: sales@wacom.com,
support@wacom.com
http://www.wacom.com
Pen tablets

Weitek Corporation
1060 E Arques Avenue
Sunnyvale, CA 94086
(408) 738-8400
http://www.weitek.com
Processors

Western Digital
8105 Irvine Center Drive
Costa Mesa, CA 92718
(714) 932-5000
http://www.wdc.com
IDE hard drives, integrated circuits,
and board-level products for the
microcomputer industry

Willow Peripherals
(800) 444-1585, (516) 432902-4222
Fax (718) 402-9603
BBS: (718) 402-1443
E-mail: peripherals@willow.com
http://willow.com
Manufacturer of video output and
video capture products

Winner Products (U.S.A.) Inc.
21128 Commerce Pointe Drive
Walnut, CA 91789
(909) 595-2490
http://www.joystick.com
Joysticks and other peripherals

Wyse Technology
3471 N. First Street
San Jose, CA 95134
(408) 473-1200
http://www.wyse.com
Advanced video display terminals

Xerox Corporation
80 Linden Oaks Pky.
Rochester, NY 14625
(800) 349-3769
http://www.xerox.com
Printers

Xircom
2300 Corporate Center Drive
Thousand Oaks, CA 91320-1420
(800) 438-4526
Fax (805) 376-9311
http://www.xircom.com

Yamaha Sys of America
Systems Technology Group
100 Century Center Court, Suite 800
San Jose, CA 95112
(408) 467-2300
Fax (408) 437-8791
http://www.yamahayst.com
Computer sound products

Zoom Telephonics
207 South Street
Boston, MA 02111
(800) 631-3116
Fax (617) 423-3923
http://www.zoomtel.com

DATA RECOVERY VENDORS

The following vendors specialize in products for recovering data from damaged hard drives:

AA Computech
28170 Avenue Crocker #105
Valencia, CA 91355
(800) 360-6801, (805) 257-6801
Fax (805) 257-6805
http://www.scvnet.com/~bobs

Data Recovery Labs, Inc.
24705 US 19 North Suite 312
Clearwater, Florida 34623
(813) 725-3818
Fax (813) 712-0800
http://www.webcoast.com/drl/

Express Point Technologies Electronics
1101 National Drive
Sacramento, CA 95834
(800) 767-9281, (916) 928-1107
Fax (916) 928-1006
E-mail: sacrepair@aur.com

Data Retrieval Services
1040 Capp Drive
Clearwater, FL 33765
(813) 461-5900
Fax (813) 461-5668

Data Recovery Labs
1315 Lawrence Avenue East, Unit 502-503
Don Mills, Ontario, Canada M3A 3R3
(800) 563-1167, (416) 510-6990
Fax (416) 510-6992
E-mail: admin@datarec.com
http://www.datarec.com

Disk Drive Repair, Inc.
863 Industry Drive, Bldg. 23
Seattle, WA 98188
(206) 575-3181
Fax (206) 575-1811
http://www.members.aol.com/ddrinc/

Disktec
5875 W. 34th Street
Houston, TX 77092
(713) 681-4691
Fax (713) 681-5851

Drive Service Company
3303 Harbor Blvd. Suite E-7
Costa Mesa, CA 92626
(714) 549-DISK (714-549-3475)
Fax (714) 549-9752
E-mail: jimc@driveservice.com
http://www.driveservice.com

DriveSavers Data Recovery
400 Bel Marin Keys Blvd.
Novato, CA 94949
(800) 440-1904, (415) 382-2000
Fax (415) 883-0780
E-mail: recovery@drivesavers.com
http://www.drivesavers.com

Electric Renaissance
105 Newfield Avenue
Edison, NJ 08837
(800) 724-6339, (732) 417-9090
Fax (732) 417-9099
E-mail: ercorp@compuserve.com

Excalibur Data Recovery, Inc.
101 Billerica Avenue, Bldg. #5
N. Billerica, MA 01862-1256
(800) 466-0893, (508) 663-1700
Fax (508) 670-5901
E-mail: brnonteer@excalibur
.ultranet.com
http://www.excaliburdr.com

Micro Com
19011 Ventura Boulevard
Tarzana, CA 91356
(800) 469-2549, (818) 881-7417
Fax (818) 881-8015

OnTrack Data Recovery, Inc.
6321 Bury Drive
Eden Prairie, MN 55346
(800) 872-2599, (612) 937-5161
Fax (612) 937-5750
http://www.ontrack.com

Total Peripheral Repair
(a division of Technical Parts, Inc.)
4204 Sorrento Valley Blvd., Suite A
San Diego, CA 92121-1412
(800) 890-0880, (619) 552-2288
Fax (619) 552-2290
E-mail: sales@recoverdata.com,
service@recoverdata.com
http://www.recoverdata.com/

Valtron Technologies, Inc.
28309 Avenue Crocker
Valencia, CA 91355
(800) 2VALTRON, (805) 257-0333
Fax (805) 257-0113

VANTAGE Technologies, Inc.
4 John Tyler Street, PO Box 1570
Merrimack, NH 03054
(800) ITS-LOST (800-487-5678),
(603) 429-3019, (603) 883-6249
Fax (603) 883-1973
E-mail: recovery@vantagetech.com
http://www.vantagetech.com

MEMORY VENDORS

Here are a number of computer memory dealers. Many will also buy your old memory; however, call and check first before sending anything.

DMS (Data Memory Systems)
24 Keewaydin Drive
Salem, NH 03079
(800) 662-7466, (603) 898-7750
Fax (603) 898-6585
E-mail: datamem@aol.com
http://www.datamem.com

H&J Electronics International, Inc.
2700 West Cypress Creek Road
Ft. Lauderdale, FL 33309
(800) 275-2447, (954) 971-7750
Fax (954) 979-9028
http://www.askchip.com
Laptop, printer, and PC memory for name-brand computers

McDonald and Associates:
The Memory Place
2544 South 156th Circle
Omaha, NE 68130
(800) 694-1307, (800) 306-8901,
(402) 691-8548
Fax (402) 691-8548
E-mail: buymemory@aol.com
http://www.buymemory.com

Memory 4 Less
2622 West Lincoln, Suite 104
Anaheim, CA 92801
(800) 821-3354, (714) 821-3354
Fax (714) 821-3361

The Memory Man
7225 NW 25th Street
Miami, FL 33166
(800) 854-0067, (305) 418-4149
Fax (305) 418-4277
http://www.memory-man.com

Worldwide Technologies
437 Chestnut Street
Philadelphia, PA 19106
(800) 457-6937, (215) 922-0050
Fax (215) 922-0116
http://www.worldwide-
technologies.com
They carry motherboards and drives, too.

BIOS UPGRADE VENDORS

These are vendors who sell upgrade BIOS ROMs to support new hard and floppy drive types, solve some compatibility problem, or add a new feature (such as built-in SETUP):

Alltech Electronics Co.
1300 E. Edinger Avenue, Suite D
Santa Ana, CA 92705
(714) 543-5011
Fax (714) 543-0553
E-mail: allelec.com
http://www.allelec.com

Unicore Software
1538 Turnpike Street
N. Andover, MA 01845
(800) 800-2467, (978) 686-6468
Fax (978) 683-1630
http://www.unicore.com

STORAGE DEVICE VENDORS

In case you're looking specifically for a new hard drive or tape drive, here are a few vendors who specialize in storage devices:

AA Computech
28170 Avenue Crocker #105
Valencia, CA 91355
(800) 360-6801, (805) 257-6801
Fax (805) 257-6805
http://felix.scvnet.com/~bobs/
Hard drives and data recovery

Ashtek, Inc.
2600-B Walnut Avenue
Tustin, CA 92680
(800) 801-9400
Fax (714) 505-2693
Buy and sell hard drives and memory SIMMs

Bason Hard Drive Warehouse
(800) 238-4453, (818) 727-9054
Fax (818) 727-9066
http://www.basoncomputer.com

MegaHaus Hard Drives
2201 Pine Drive
Dickinson, TX 77539
(800) 786-1185, (713) 534-3919
Fax (713) 534-6580
Drives, controller cards, drive accessories

Storage USA
101 Reighard Avenue
Williamsport, PA 17701
(800) 538-DISK, (717) 327-9200
Fax (717) 327-1217
http://www.storageusa.com

MISCELLANEOUS COMPUTER PRODUCTS VENDORS

Many manufacturers also sell their own products. Here, however, are the dealers who sell a wide range of useful computer parts and peripherals:

1st Compu Choice
740 Beta Drive - Unit G
Cleveland, OH 44143
(800) 345-8880, (216) 460-1002
Fax (216) 460-1066

A2Z Computers
701 Beta Drive, Unit 19
Mayfield Village, OH 44142
(800) 983-8889, (216) 442-9028
Fax (216) 442-8891
http://www.a2zcomp.com
Computer components and
peripherals

ABC Drives
8717 Darby Ave.
Northridge, CA 91325
(818) 885-7157
http://www.abcdrives.com
Specializes in the sale and service of
most major storage devices, including hard-to-find or obsolete drives

Allsop Computer Accessories
4201 Meridian
Bellingham, WA 98226
(800) 426-4303
http://www.allsop.com
Ergonomic enhancements (drawers
and glare filters)

Alpha Systems, Inc.
47000 Warm Springs Blvd, #455
Fremont, CA 94539-7467
(510) 249-9280
Fax (510) 259-9288
E-mail: compu@alphasys.com
http://www.alphasys.com

American Computer Products (ACP)
(503) 697-9777
Fax (503) 697-4889
http://www.acp1.com

American Computer Resources, Inc.
155 Research Drive
Stratford, CT 06497
(203) 380-4600

American Ribbon and Toner Co.
2895 West Prospect Road
Ft. Lauderdale, FL 33309
(800) 327-1013
Printer ribbons, toner cartridges, etc.

AMP Tech (American Micro Products Technology)
5351 Naiman Parkway
Solon, OH 44139
(800) 619-0508, (216) 498-9499
Fax (216) 349-6170
E-mail: amptech@icgroup.net
http://www.amptech.com
Computers, motherboards, cases,
drives, memory

Arlington Computer Products
851 Commerce Court
Buffalo Grove, IL 60089
(800) 548-5105, (847) 541-6583
Fax (847) 541-6881

ARM Computer Inc.
1637 South Main Street
Milpitas, CA 95035
(800) 765-1767, (408) 935-9800
Fax (408) 935-9192
E-mail: arm@armcomputer.com
http://www.armcomputer.com

ASI
48289 Fremont Boulevard
Fremont, CA 94538
(510) 226-8000
Distributor of computer hardware,
peripherals, and private-label
Nspire personal computers and
multimedia kits

Aspen Imaging International, Inc.
1500 Cherry Street, Suite B
Louisville, CO 80027-3036
(800) 955-5555(303) 666-5750
Fax (303) 665-2972
Computer printer supplies including
printer ribbons, printbands, and
laser toner and inkjet supplies

**Associates Computer
Supply Co., Inc.**
275 West 231st Street
Riverdale, NY 10463
(718) 543-8686
Fax (718) 548-0343
http://www.associa
comp.com
Motherboards, cases, vi
drives, keyboards, memo   ROMs

Atlantic Logic
41 Canfield Road
Cedar Grove, NJ 07009
(973) 857-7878

ATronics International Inc.
44700-B Industrial Drive
Fremont, CA 94538
(800) 488-7776, (510) 656-8400
Fax (510) 656-8560
http://www.atronicsintl.com
Parallel port CD-ROM adapter, BIOS
enhancement card for IDE hard
drive controllers

Automated Tech Tools
851B Freeway Drive
Macedonia, OH 44056
(800) 413-0767

Autotime Corporation
6605 S.W. Macadam Avenue
Portland, OR 97201
(888) MEMORYS, (503) 452-8577
(503) 452-8495
http://www.memorytime.com
Memory recycling services and
products

Barnett's Computers
417 Fifth Avenue
York, NY 10017
) 696-4777

y Network
nnery Road
, North Branch, NJ 08876
653-8294
//www.batnetwest.com
.bly, sales, and service of
rechargeable batteries

Battery Technology Inc.
5700 Bandini Boulevard
Commerce, CA 90040
(213) 728-7874
http://www.batterytech.com
Battery products for laptop computers and portable peripherals

Battery-Biz Inc.
31352 Via Colinas Ste. 104
Westlake Village, CA 91362
(800) 848-6782, (818) 706-2767,
(818) 706-3234
http://www.battery-biz/
battyer-biz/
Distributes batteries for desktops,
laptops, and notebooks, as well as
for UPS systems and utility meters

Black Box Corporation
1000 Park Drive
Lawrence, PA 15055
(724)746-5500
http://www.blackbox.com
Networking and data communication products

BNF Enterprises
134R Rt.1 South Newbury St.
Peabody, MA 01960
(978) 536-2000
Fax (978) 536-7400
http://www.bnfe.com

Cable Connection
102 Cooper Ct.
Los Gatos, CA 95030
(408) 395-6700, (408) 354-3980
http://www.cable-connection.com
Manufacturer of cable products and
interconnect accessories

Cables America
(800) 348-USA4
Fax (800) FAX-USA4

Cables To Go
1501 Webster Street
Dayton, OH 45404
(800) 225-8646, (800) 826-7904
Cables, test equipment, toolkits

CAD & Graphics Warehouse
8515-D Freeway Drive
Macedonia, OH 44056
(330) 468-1468

Century Microelectronics, Inc.
4800 Great America Parkway,
Suite 308
Santa Clara, CA 95054
(408) 748-7788
http://www.century-micro.com/
Memory upgrades, with products
ranging from industry-standard
SIMMs and DIMMs to proprietary
modules and memory cards

Chemtronics
8125 Cobb Centre Drive
Kennesaw, GA 30144
(800) 645-5244, (404) 424-4888
Fax (800) 243-6003, (404) 423-0748
Ozone-safe compressed gas for
cleaning inside PCs

CIRCO Technology Corporation
222 South 5th Avenue
City of Industry, CA 91746
(800) 678-1688
Fax (626) 369-2769
http://www.circotech.com
Cases, power supplies, removeable
hard drive kits, motherboards

CMO Corporation
101 Reighard Avenue
Williamsport, PA 17701
(800) 417-4580, (717) 327-9200
Fax (717) 327-1217
http://www.cmo.newmii.com

Compaq DirectPlus
P.O. Box 692000
Houston, TX 77269-2000
(800) 332-8683

CompUSA Direct
15167 Business Avenue
Addison, TX 75244
(800) COMP-USA

ComputAbility
P.O. Box 17882
Milwaukee, WI 53217
(800) 554-9950, (414) 357-8182
Fax (414) 357-7814
http://www.computability.com

Computer City
P.O. Box 2526
Tempe, AZ 85280-2526
(800) THE-CITY

Computer Discount Warehouse (CDW)
1020 East Lake Cook Road
Buffalo Grove, IL 60089
(800) 726-4239
Fax (847) 465-6800
http://www.cdw.com
Computers, parts, memory, monitors, printers

Computer Gate International
2960 Gordon Avenue
Santa Clara, CA 95051
(408) 730-0673
Fax (408) 730-0735
E-mail: cgate@aimnet.com
http://www.computergate.com
Testers, cleaning products, cables, switches, computer assembly products

Computer Parts Outlet, Inc.
33 S.E. First Avenue
Delray Beach, FL 33444
(800) 475-1655
Buys all types of memory, including large or small quantities of working or non-working modules

Computer Products Corporation
1431 South Cherryvale Road
Boulder, CO 80303

Computer Things
2608 Mountain Road, Suite #2
Pasadena, MD 21122
(410) 661-8613
http://www.computerthings.com
Inkjet printer supplies

Computers Direct
3613 Lafayette Road
Portsmouth, NH 03801

CompuWorld
24441 Miles Road
Cleveland, OH 44128
(800) 666-6294, (216) 595-6500
Fax (216) 595-6565

Core Components

9728 Alburtis Avenue
Santa Fe Springs, CA 90670
(888) 267-3266, (310) 654-2866
Fax (310) 801-5630
Motherboards, controllers, video
boards, memory

Dalco Electronics

275 S. Pioneer Boulevard
Springboro, OH 45066
(800) 445-5342, (513) 743-8042
Fax (513) 743-9251
BBS: (513) 743-2244
CompuServe: GO DA
http://www.dalco.com

DataVision

445 Fifth Avenue
New York, NY 10016
(800) 771-7466, (212) 689-1111
Fax (212) 689-1743
http://www.datavis.com
Computers and multimedia
components

DC Drives

1110 NASA Road One, Suite 304
Nassau Bay, TX 77058
(800) 473-0960, (281) 534-6292

DellWare Direct

2214 West Baker Lane, Building 3
Austin, TX 78758-4053

Digital Micro, Inc.

901 S. Fremont Avenue, Suite 118
Alhambra, CA 91803

Diskette Connection

P.O. Box 1674
Bethany, OK 73008
(800) 654-4058, (405) 789-0888
Fax (405) 495-4598
Diskettes, tapes, drive cleaning kits

Diskettes Unlimited

6206 Long Drive
Houston, TX 77087
(713) 643-9939
Fax (713) 643-2722
Diskettes

Edmund Scientific Corporation

101 E. Gloucester Pike
Barrington, NJ 08007
(609) 573-6250
Fax (609) 573-6295
Dual Function Digital Lab Ther-
mometer

ELEK-TEK

7350 North Linder Avenue
Skokie, IL 60077
(800) 395-1000, (708) 677-7660

Envisions Solutions Technology, Inc.

47400 Seabridge Drive
Fremont, CA 94538
(800) 365-SCAN
http://www.envisions.com
Scanners, printers, graphics/OCR
software

Expert Computers

2495 Walden Avenue
Buffalo, NY 14225
(716) 681-8612

FairFax
145 West 45th Street, Suite 1010
New York, NY 10036
(800) 932-4732, (212) 768-8300

First Computer Systems, Inc.
6000 Live Oak Parkway, Suite 107
Norcross, GA 30093
(800) 325-1911, (770) 441-1911
Fax (770) 441-1856
E-mail: sales@fcsnet.com
http://www.fcsnet.com
Motherboards, computers, peripherals

First Source International
7 Journey
Aliso Viejo, CA 92656
(800) 348-9866, (714) 448-7750
Fax (714) 448-7760
E-mail: sales@firstsource.com
http://www.firstsource.com

Global Computer Supplies
2318 East Del Amo Boulevard,
Dept. 73
Compton, CA 90220
(800) 829-0785, (800) 227-1246,
(630) 357-4441
Fax (630) 357-2345

Global MicroXperts
6230 Cochran Road
Solon, OH 44139
(800) 676-0311, (216) 498-3330
http://www.microx.com

Graphics Warehouse
8515 Freeway Drive, Unit C & D
Macedonia, OH 44087
(330) 468-1468

Harmony Computers
1801 Flatbush Avenue
Brooklyn, NY 11210
(800) 441-1144, (718) 692-3232
http://www.gcsnet.com.harmony

Hartford Computer Group, Inc.
1610 Colonial Parkway
Inverness, IL 60067
(800) 617-4424, (847) 934-3380
Fax (847) 934-9724
http://www.awa.com/hartford

HDSS Computer Products
2225 El Camino Real
Santa Clara, CA 95050

Hi Tech USA
1562 Centre Point Drive
Milpitas, CA 95035
(800) 831-2888, (408) 262-8688

**Hi-Tech Component
Distributers, Inc.**
59 S. La Patera Lane
Goleta, CA 93117
(800) 406-1275, (805) 967-7971
Fax (805) 681-9971

Hi-Tech USA
1582 Centre Pointe Drive
Milpitas, CA 95035
(800) 831-2888, (408) 262-8688,
(408) 956-8285
Fax (408) 262-8772
BBS: (408) 956-8243

HyperData Direct
809 South Lemon Avenue
Walnut, CA 91789
(800) 786-3343, (800) 380-1899,
(909) 468-2933
Fax (909) 468-2954
BBS: (909) 594-3645
http://www.hyperbook.com
Laptops, accessories

InterPro Microsystems, Inc.
46560 Fremont Boulevard, Suite 417
Fremont, CA 94538
(800) 226-7216, (510) 226-7226
Fax (510) 226-7219
http://www.interpromicro.com

Jade Computer
18503 Hawthorne Boulevard
Torrance, CA 90504
(800) 421-5500, (310) 370-7474
Fax (310) 371-4288
http://www.jadecomputer.com/mail
Parts and peripherals

Jinco Computers
5122 Walnut Grove Avenue
San Gabriel, CA 91776
(800) 253-2531, (818) 309-1108
Fax (818) 309-1107
E-mail: jinco@wavenet.com
http://www.jinco.com
Cases and power supplies

Kahlon, Inc.
22699 Old Canal Road
Yorba Linda, CA 92687
(800) 317-9989, (714) 637-5060
Fax (714) 637-5597
E-mail: kahlonmem@aol.com
IBM and Compaq parts and memory

Kenosha Computer Center
2133 91st Street
Kenosha, WI 53143
(800) 255-2989, (414) 697-9595
Fax (414) 697-0620

KREX Computers
9320 Waukegan Road
Morton Grove, IL 60053
(800) 222-KREX, (847) 967-0200
Fax (847) 967-0276
http://www.trcone.com/
krexcom.html

Legend Micro
5590 Lauby Road, Suite 70B
N. Canton, OH 44720
(800) 366-6333, (330) 644-7955
Fax (330) 644-7960
Motherboards and components

Macro Tech Inc.
23151 Verdugo Drive, Suite 102
Laguna Hills, CA 92653
(714) 580-1822
http://www.macropc.com

Magic PC
5400 Brookpark Road
Cleveland, OH 44129
(800) 762-4426, (216) 661-7218
Fax (216) 661-2454
http://www.magicpc.com
Motherboards, systems, components

Megacomp International, Inc.
261 N.E. 1st Street, #200
Miami, FL 33132
(888) 463-4226, (305) 372-0222
Fax (305) 374-5040

Megatech Inc.
3070 Bristol Pike
Bensalem, PA 19020

Merritt Computer Products, Inc.
5565 Red Bird Center Drive,
Suite 150
Dallas, TX 75237
(800) 627-7752, (214) 339-0753
Fax (214) 339-1313
SafeSkin keyboard cover

Micro Pro, Inc.
5400 Brookpark Road
Cleveland, OH 44129
(800) 353-3003, (216) 661-7218
Fax (216) 661-2454
BBS: (216) 661-7431
http://www.magicpc.com
Computers, parts, accessories,
motherboards

Micro Time, Inc.
35375 Vokes Drive, Suite 106
Eastlake, OH 44095
(800) 834-0000, (216) 954-9640
Fax (216) 954-9648
CPUs, memory, motherboards,
peripherals

Micro X-Press
5646-48 West 73rd Street
Indianapolis, IN 46278
(800) 875-9737, (317) 328-5780
Fax (328) 5782

MicroniX USA, Inc.
23050 Miles Road
Cleveland, OH 44128
(800) 580-0505, (216) 475-9300
Fax (216) 475-6610
Motherboards, memory, and other
hardware

MicroSense, Inc.
370 Andrew Avenue
Leucadia, CA 92024
(800) 544-4252, (800) 246-7729,
(909) 688-2735
Fax (619) 753-6133
E-mail: docdrive@microsense.com
http://www.microsense.com

MicroSupply, Inc.
(800) 535-2092
http://www.microsupply.com

Midland ComputerMart
5699 West Howard
Niles, IL 60714
(800) 407-0700, (847) 967-0700
Fax (847) 967-0710
E-mail: sales@midlandcmart.com
CompuServe: 102404,327

Midwest Computer Works
180 Lexington Drive
Buffalo Grove, IL 60089
(800) 86-WORKS, (847) 367-4700
Fax (847) 367-8540
http://www.mcworks.com

Midwest Micro
6910 US Route 36 East
Fletcher, OH 45326
(800) 537-1426, (513) 368-2309
Fax (513) 368-2306
http://www.mwmicro.com

Midwestern Diskette
509 West Taylor
Creston, IA 50801
(800) 221-6332
Fax (515) 782-4166
E-mail: salesinfo@mddc.com
http://www.mddc.com
Bulk diskettes

Millenium Technologies
35 Cherry Hill Drive
Danvers, MA 01923
(800) 251-3448
Motherboards, additional
components

MMI Corporation
2400 Reach Road
Williamsport, PA 17701

Motherboard Discount Center
1035 N. McQueen, Suite 123
Gilbert, AZ 85233
(800) 486-2026, (602) 955-3837
Fax (602) 955-3997
http://www.motherboardsolutions.com
Motherboards, video boards, other
hardware

Motherboard Express
333-B West State Road
Island Lake, IL 60042
(800) 560-1195, (847) 487-4639
Fax (847) 487-4637
http://www.motherboardx.com
Motherboards and drives

Nationwide Computers Direct (NWCD)
110A McGaw Drive
Edison, NJ 08837
(800) 747-NWCD, (732) 417-4455
Fax (800) 329-6923
Notebook computers, PCMCIA
cards, printers, modems, scanners

NCA Computer Products
1202 Kifer Road
Sunnyvale, CA 94086
(800) NCA-1115, (408) 522-5066
Fax (800) NCA-1666
http://www.mediacity.com./nca

NECX Direct
4 Technology Drive
Peabody, MA 01960
(800) 961-9208
http://www.necx.com

Network Express
1720 Oak Street
P.O. Box 301
Lakewood, NJ 08701-9885
(800) 333-9899, (732) 370-3801
Fax (732) 905-5731
E-mail: netexp@netline.net
http://www.whse.com
Computers, peripherals, and test
equipment

Next International
13622 Neutron Road
Dallas, TX 75244
(800) 730-NEXT, (972) 481-1113
Fax (972) 481-1508
E-mail: next@fastlane.net

North American CAD Company
4A Hillview Drive
Barrington, IL 60010
(800) 619-2199, (847) 381-8834
Fax (847) 381-7374
http://www.nacad.com
Graphics-related peripherals, including printers, monitors, video boards,
digitizers, and scanners.

Odyssey Technology
5590 Lauby Road, Suite 70B
Canton, OH 44720
(800) 683-2808, (330) 497-2444
Fax (330) 497-3156

PC Importers
290 Lena Drive
Aurora, OH 44202
(800) 458-3133
Fax (216) 487-5242
Parts, systems, and components

PC Universe
2302 North Dixie Highway
Boca Raton, FL 33431
(800) 728-6483, (407) 447-0050
Fax (407) 447-7549
E-mail: sales@pcuniverse.com
http://www.pcuniverse.com
Computers, peripherals, accessories

PCL Computer Inc.
636 Lincoln Highway
Fairless Hills, PA 19030
(215) 736-2986
Cases

PCComputer Solutions
130 West 32nd Street
New York, NY 10001
(212) 629-8300

PCs Compleat (CompUSA Direct)
34 St. Martin Drive
Marlborough, MA 01752-3021
(800) 210-8323, (508) 624-6400
E-mail: sales@pcscompleat.com
http://www.pcscompleat.com

Peripherals Unlimited, Inc.
1500 Kansas Avenue, Suite 4C
Longmont, CO 80501
(303) 772-1482
http://www.peripherals.com/
peripherals
Computer-related hardware and software products, specializing in mass storage and connectivity

Power Pros, Inc.
105 Cromwell Court
Raleigh, NC 27614
(800) 788-0070, (919) 782-9210
(919) 782-1904
http://www.powerpros.com
Power protectors, UPSs

Price Pointe
3 Pointe Drive
Brea, CA 92621
(800) 840-7860
Fax (800) 840-7861
Computers, peripherals, and software

Publishing Perfection
P.O. Box 307, dept. CS9608
Menomonee Falls, WI 53052-0307
(800) 716-5000, (414) 252-5000
Fax (414) 252-2502
http://www.publishingperfection.com
E-mail: cs9608@perfection.com
Digital cameras, scanners, multimedia hardware

Quark Technology
5275 Naiman Parkway
Solon, OH 44139
(800) 443-8807, (216) 498-7387
Fax (216) 498-8857

Quick-Line Distribution
26001 Miles Road, Unit 8
Warrensville Heights, OH 44128
(800) 808-3606, (216) 514-9800
Fax (216) 514-9805

Royal Computer
1208 John Reed Court
Industry, CA 91745
(800) 486-0008, (818) 855-5077
Fax (818) 330-2717
http://www.royalpcs.com
Multimedia/graphics monitors

Seattle Data Systems
746 Industry Drive
Seattle, WA 98188
(206) 575-8123
Fax (206) 575-8870
E-mail: sdsinc@seadat.com
http://www.seadat.com

Starquest Computers
4491 Mayfield Road
Cleveland, OH 44121
(800) 945-0202, (216) 691-9966
Systems, parts, peripherals

Sunway Inc.
(715) 483-1179
Fax (715) 483-1757
Ergonomically designed computer
accessories

Swan Technologies
3075 Research Drive
State College, MA 01680

TC Computers
P.O. Box 10428
New Orleans, LA 70181-0428
(800) 723-8282, (504) 733-2527
http://www.tccomputers.com
Motherboards, cases, peripherals

TDN Inc.
1000 Young Street, Suite 270
Tonawanda, NY 14150

BigCity Express
Parsippany, NJ
(800) 882-8682
http://www.bigcityexpress.com

Technology Distribution Network
1000 Young Street, Suite 270
Tonawanda, NY 14150
(800) 420-3636, (716) 743-0195
Fax (716) 743-0198
Motherboards and components

The PC Zone
15815 SE 37th Street
Bellevue, WA 98006-1800
(800) 258-2088

Tiger Software
800 Douglas, Executive Tower
Coral Gables, FL 33134

North American Computer
574 Wedell Drive, #5
Sunnydale, CA 94089
(800) 888-3318, (408) 734-9100
http://www.nacom.com

Tri-State Computers
650 6th Avenue
New York, NY 10011
(800) 433-5199, (212) 633-2530
Fax (212) 633-7718

USA Flex
444 Scott Drive
Bloomingdale, IL 60108
(800) 944-5599, (708) 582-6206
Fax (708) 351-7204

Vektron
2100 N. Highway 360, Suite 1904
Grand Prairie, TX 75050
(800) 725-0009
http://www.vektron.com

OLDER PC REPAIR AND EXCHANGE

For those of you with older PCs, there are vendors who will repair and/or exchange parts for these PCs. Many vendors will not service all brands, so call to confirm that the vendor actually services your specific model of hard drive, motherboard, floppy drive, etc., before sending it off. Typically, vendors will not exchange damaged parts (i.e., the board is in two pieces or is water or fire damaged).

Computer Recycle Center, Inc.
303 East Pipeline
Bedford, TX 76022
(817) 282-1622
Fax (817) 282-5944
E-mail: recycles@spindle.net
http://www.recycles.com
A world wide trading site and recycling center for used and surplus computer equipment and materials; provides upgrades for users of older equipment

Computer Recycler
670 West 17th Street
Costa Mesa, CA
(714) 645-4022
E-mail: maurer44@wdc.net
http://www.computerrecycler.com
Buyer, seller and trader of new and preowned Mac and PC equipment

Computer Recyclers
4119 Lindberg Road
Addison, TX 75244
(972) 245-3008
Fax (214) 774-1161
http://www.comp-recycle.com

CPAC (Computers, Parts, and Commodities)
22349 La Palma Ave, #114
Yorba Linda, CA 92687
(800)778-2722, (714)692-5044
Fax (714)692-6680
E-mail: cpac@wavenet.com
http://remarketing.com/
broker_html/cpac/

Crocodile Computers

240 West 73rd Street
New York, NY 10021
(212) 769-3400
(212) 724-3501
http://www.crocs.com/

DakTech

4025 9th Ave. SW
Fargo, ND 58103
(800) 325-3238, (701) 282-6686
Fax (701) 282-9690
E-mail: daktech@ix.netcom.com
http://www.daktech.com
Specializing in IBM and COMPAQ
parts

Data Exchange Corporation

3600 Via Pescador
Camarillo, California 93012, USA
(800) 237-7911, (805) 388-1711
Fax (805) 482-4856
http://www.dex.com/dexhome/
A leading full-service company specializing in contract manufacturing,
end-of-life support, depot repair, logis-
tics services and worldwide inventory
management services for all high-
technology industries; has an extensive inventory of spare parts for sale.

Eritech International, Inc.

(888) 808-6242, (818) 244-6242
Fax (818) 500-7699
Buyers of old CPUs and memory

NIE International

3000 E. Chambers
Phoenix, AZ 85040
(602) 470-1500
Fax (602) 470-1540
E-mail: nie@nieint.com
http://www.onsale.com/
vendors/nie.htm
A leading supplier of microcomputer
parts and systems to companies that
maintain and support PC installations.

Northstar

7101 31st Avenue North
Minneapolis, Mn 55427
(800) 969-0009, (612) 591-0009
Fax (612)591-0029
http://www.northstar-mn.com/
A complete PC repair service

Oak Park Personal Computers

130 South Oak Park Avenue,
Suite #2
Oak Park, IL. 60302
(708) 848-1553
Fax (708) 524-9791
E-mail: mlund@oppc.com
http://www.oppc.com/

OnLine Computing

3550-L SW 34th Street
Gainesville, FL 32608
(352) 372-1712
Fax (352) 335-8192
E-mail: online@gnv.fdt.net
http://www.ftd.net/~online

The Used Computer Marketplace

http://www.remarketing.com
A place where you can list for-sale or wanted items for free in their confidential classifieds, which are then accessed by subscribing dealers.

United Computer Exchange

2110 Powers Ferry Road, Suite 307
Atlanta, GA 30339
(800) 755-3033, (770) 612-1205
Fax (770) 612-1239
E-mail: united@uce.com
CompuServe: 73312,1224
America Online: UnCoEx
A global clearinghouse for buyers and sellers of new and used microcomputer equipment.

COMPUTER RECYCLING CENTERS

After upgrading your PC, you might prefer to donate the older parts to needy organizations rather than sell them. Here are some organizations that help with the redistribution:

Computer Re-use Network (CoRN)

P.O. Box 1078
Hollywood, SC 29449
(803) 889-8247
E-mail: jas@awod.com
http://www.awod.com/gallery/probono/corn/

Computer Recycling Project, Inc.

www.wco.com/~dale/list.html
E-mail: dale@wco.com
A listing of additional organizations that deal with accepting old computers and funnelling them to nonprofit groups/individuals in need.

Lazarus Foundation, Inc.

10378 Eclipse Way
Columbia, MD 21044
(410) 740-0735
E-mail: Ebard@aol.com
http://www.lazarus.org
A computer recycling center that accepts donated computers which they in turn refurbish. These computers are then provided to educational institutions and other nonprofit organizations.

Appendix D

FINDING AND DOWNLOADING WINDOWS SOFTWARE ONLINE

O nce you've had the chance to explore the Web a bit, you may start wondering how you're ever going to *find* anything there. As easy as it is to follow tangents and get lost wandering from interesting site to interesting site, there's no clear path through the Web and no obvious way to find a destination if you don't know its address.

Adapted from *The Internet: No Experience Required*, by Christian Crumlish

ISBN 0-7821-2168-3   528 pp. $24.99

That's not a problem as long as you're content to browse and surf. But for most users, it doesn't take long before we are looking for something in particular. It might be information—job opportunities in Vancouver, for example, or the natural history of the bluebelly lizard, or pictures from Mars—or it might be software. Suppose you've heard that there's a demo version of a great new program available for downloading from the Web. It's free, for thirty days. You know the name of the program, approximately, but not the software publisher. And, of course, you didn't get the URL. Or maybe, after reading about hardware upgrading earlier in this book, you've decided to see if there's a new driver for your printer or video adapter. In any of these cases, you've got some Web-searching to do.

Fortunately, various clever individuals and companies have set up sites to help you find information on the Web. While there's no single, definitive location for searching, there are, in fact, quite a few ways to search the Web (and more coming on line all the time), and the Net is changing so rapidly that any central listing of sites presented in a book would be out of date almost before it was published. Still, the process of "mapping the Net" is going on all the time, and the work in progress is usually useful enough to help you find what you're looking for.

Because there's no single, definitive way to search the Web, it's sometimes best to try several different approaches. This appendix will introduce you to a few different ways to search (by subject, keyword, date, or language) and different search tools, such as AltaVista and Yahoo!.

Later, you'll see how to download (save) files from the Web to your own computer and how to buy stuff online.

WHAT'S NEW WITH SEARCHING?

With Microsoft Internet Explorer, you can type search terms directly into the address box and get results back from your default search page (which you can change if you prefer a different place to search from). As the Net continues to grow exponentially and becomes more complicated along the way (as if it weren't chaotic and confusing enough!), you can be sure that new, sophisticated search mechanisms will appear on the market, helping you zero in on the information or resources you need.

SEARCHING THE WEB

Most of the search tools on the Web offer two models for finding specific information. One model is that of a directory, organized by topic and subtopic, something like a yellow pages phone book. The other model is that of a searchable index, where you enter a keyword to search for, and the search page gives you a list of suggested sites that seem to match what you're searching for. You'll see an example of each approach.

Searching through a Directory

One of the best directories on the Web is the Yahoo! site. To see it for yourself, type **http://www.yahoo.com** into the address box at the top of your Web browser, or click on Search and then choose Yahoo from the list of search services that appears. Figure D.1 shows how Yahoo! looks as I'm writing this. Remember, most Web sites update their design and layout from time to time, so the site may look slightly different to you today.

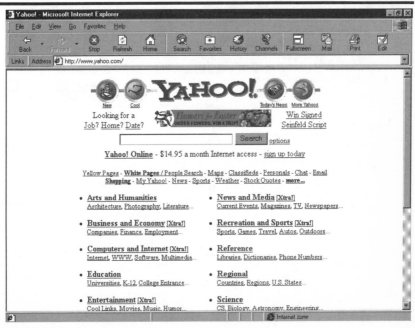

FIGURE D.1: The popular Yahoo! directory site

TIP

Make a Favorites listing in Internet Explorer (or bookmark in Navigator) for Yahoo!, as discussed in Chapter 17 (or 19), so you can come back here easily any time you want to start looking around.

Searching by Topic

Yahoo! is organized hierarchically, which means that you can start with a general topic area and then narrow it down to more specific topics as you go. Some of the major subtopics are listed under each topic as well, so you can skip one step, if you like.

Let's say you're interested in finding some Windows programs on the Internet. You could start by choosing the Computers and Internet link on Yahoo!'s main search page.

This will take you to Yahoo!'s Computers and Internet page (see Figure D.2).

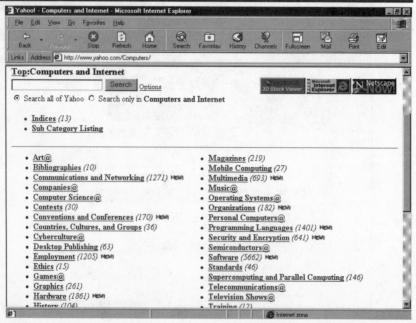

FIGURE D.2: You can get to the Computers and Internet page by clicking on the Media link in Yahoo!'s main search page.

As you can see, one of the sub-subtopics is Software. (An @ sign after a listing means that topic appears in several different places in Yahoo!'s listings—this means you can reach topics of interest by more than one route, without having to read the minds of the people who set up the site.) Click on Software to go to the list of pages on that subject (see Figure D.3).

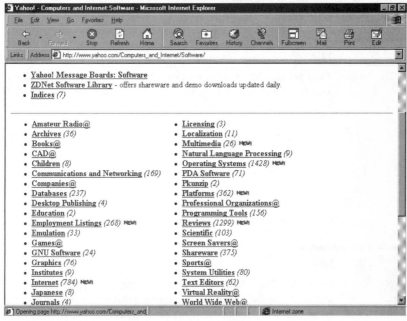

FIGURE D.3:   The Computers and Internet: Software page at Yahoo!

Remember to use the Back button if you want to return to a previous topic in Yahoo!'s hierarchies.

Needless to say, there's plenty on this page that sounds interesting. If you'd like to look for general-purpose Windows programs, simply click on the link to the Shareware page to jump to it. From here you'll be able to access sites that offer tens of thousands of Windows programs.

Searching by Keyword

Of course, it's not always easy to guess where a page or topic might be listed in an organized structure such as Yahoo!'s. Fortunately, the site also includes a search feature at the top of each page.

To perform a search, type a word (or a few words, to make the search more specific) in the box near the top of the page and then click the Search button.

TIP

If you perform your search from any of the pages besides the home page, you have the choice of searching the entire Yahoo! directory (Search All of Yahoo!) or just the items in the current category (Search Only in *Topic*).

So, let's say you're interested in a Windows 98 system monitoring program and want to see if there are any such programs available on the Net. Type the phrase **Windows system monitor** into the search box and click on the Search button. Yahoo! quickly returns a list of categories relating in some way or another to your keywords (in fact, the word will appear in bold type in a blurb for each category).

NOTE

Keep in mind that the speed of your connection to the Internet—for most home and small-business users, that's the rate at which your computer's modem communicates with your Internet Service Provider—is what ultimately determines the speed of category searches and other Web interactions. If you have a fast modem, be sure your ISP account allows it to run at full speed; there is no advantage in owning a 56K modem if it's running at 33K. A direct network connection to the Internet, typically found in larger organizations, is much faster than a modem connection; and delays are unlikely in search operations.

Note that there are some programs listed, but there are many extraneous entries listed too because each of those pages contains the words **Windows** and **system** and **monitor**. To search for an exact phrase, simply enclose your phrase in quotes. The **"Windows system monitor"** search turns up only the programs you're looking for, as shown in Figure D.4.

From there, all you have to do is start clicking on the most promising looking files or sites.

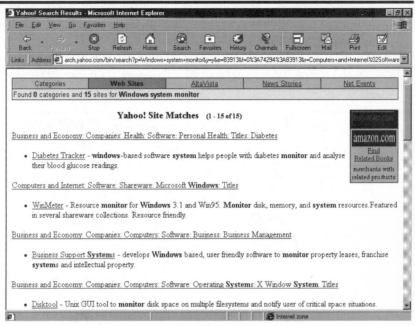

FIGURE D.4:   Some of the Windows system monitoring-related pages listed as the result of a Yahoo! search

Searching with a Search Engine

Now that you know how to search the contents of a directory hierarchically, it's easy to perform a search of the entire Net. Most search engines allow you to enter very specific, even complicated, search queries, much like ones you would submit to a database program. Fortunately, for your everyday searches you shouldn't need those advanced features. Instead, a single keyword—or a couple, for a narrower search (such as *Windows screen saver or Windows animated cursors*)—will usually do the job.

One of the more popular search engines is AltaVista at `http://www.altavista.digital.com` (see Figure D.5).

TIP
Make a Favorites listing (or bookmark) for the AltaVista site as well.

As with the search feature in Yahoo!, just type a keyword (or several words) into the box and click on the Search button. AltaVista will return a list of sites, ranked in order of their likeliness to match your keywords (this is especially useful when you've entered more than one word). Figure D.6 shows the results of an AltaVista search on the phrase *Windows screen saver*.

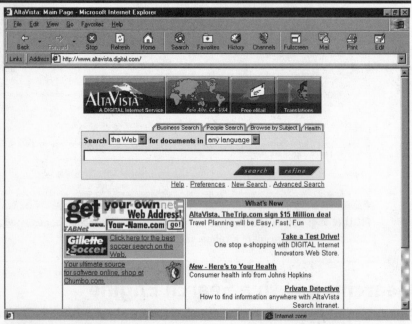

FIGURE D.5: The AltaVista search engine is powerful and easy to use.

Click on any of the hyperlinked listings to visit the listed site.

One important piece of advice: use quotation marks to make your searches more precise. The phrase *Windows screen saver* finds almost four hundred thousand sites that contain all three words! However, when you add quotes to the beginning and end of the phrase, you are telling the program to look only for the exact phrase, and you will find a much more manageable number of targeted sites. These are listed with the best possible matches first, as illustrated in Figure D.7.

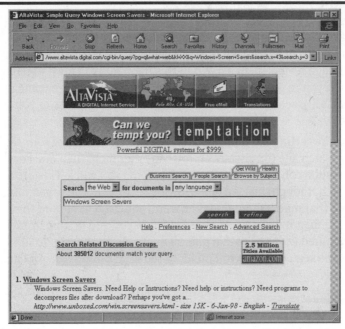

FIGURE D.6:   Web sites turned up by AltaVista in a search using the phrase *Windows screen saver*

FIGURE D.7:   Putting the search phrase in quotation marks turns up a much more manageable list of relevant sites.

Refining Your Search

Sometimes your first attempt to search for a topic will fail. You won't find what you're looking for or you'll get so many results that you won't have time to review them all. When this happens, you need to refine your search. If you're getting no results or too few, you'll have to come up with an alternative search term that's more general than whatever you tried at first.

If you're getting too many results, you can try to narrow your search. At any search site (or directory), you can enter more than one keyword to get results containing any one of the words you enter. This broadens the search, though, instead of narrowing it. To limit the pages you find to those that match more than one word, you need to require that *each* word match, not just *any*. At most search pages, you do this by preceding each required keyword with a plus sign, but check the help or hints section of the search engine you prefer to see what options are available to you there.

NOTE

At some search sites, you can also narrow your search by date (type in a very recent range to get only the sites that were updated a short time ago), by language (English is a good place to start), or by stringing together search words with the *logical operator* "AND" (*screen saver AND fish*, for example, will match sites that have both of these phrases). AltaVista's Advanced Search feature at http://www.altavista.digital.com can narrow searches with these methods. HotBot is another site that offers this capability.

Visiting a Central Search Page

Most of the popular Web browsers have a shortcut to one or more directory or search pages built into the program.

Microsoft Internet Explorer has a built-in search page that you can activate by pressing the Search button in Internet Explorer. You can also change your preferences to specify a different default search page, if you have a favorite.

Some Search Addresses

Here are the Web addresses of a bunch of other good directories and
search pages:

Resource	Web Address
AltaVista	`http://www.altavista.digital.com`
Electric Library	`http://www.elibrary.com/id/2525/`
Excite	`http://www.excite.com`
HotBot	`http://www.hotbot.com`
Infoseek	`http://www.infoseek.com`
Lycos	`http://www.lycos.com`
Magellan	`http://www.mckinley.com`
Yahoo!	`http://www.yahoo.com`

TIP

In Windows 98 you can also use the Find menu (choose Start ➢ Find, or in Windows Explorer choose Tools ➢ Find) to see a central search page. The option On
the Internet uses Internet Explorer to connect you to a Microsoft site that gives
you access to some of the most powerful and popular search engines on the
Internet, including Infoseek, AOL NetFind, Lycos, Excite, and Yahoo!.

DOWNLOADING AND
DECOMPRESSING FILES

Sometimes when you search the Net you're looking for information, but
often you're looking for files to download from the Internet to your computer. For example, there's a lot of software out there available either for
free or as *shareware* (meaning you're expected to pay for it after evaluat-
ing it, if you decide to keep using it). Also, a lot of programs, especially
Internet-related software programs, are updated from time to time, with
newer versions being available for downloading from the Net.

NOTE

Coming soon are programs that can update themselves whenever the developer adds a new feature. This may lead to more programs being sold on a subscription basis instead of as a one-time license. There are already programs, such as online service interfaces, that you can upgrade by choosing commands within the program itself. Internet Explorer 4.0 offers a foretaste of this self-updating capability; it asks you if you want to update the Search bar when you first use it. The modifications are minor, but they happen online and in real time.

Once you start using Internet software (such as Web browsers, news readers, mail programs, and so on), you have to get used to the idea that if you want to have the latest version of the program, you occasionally have to check the software manufacturer's Web site to download the latest update.

No matter what your reason for downloading a file, the procedure with most Web browsers is pretty much the same. It generally involves finding your way to the appropriate site, working your way through a few links, and ultimately clicking on a link that connects directly to the file in question. When you do this, your browser will realize that you've requested something that can't be displayed in a browser window, and it will offer to download or even try to run the file for you.

TIP

The file you're downloading may be a compressed file. See *Compression Programs*, later in this section, for tips on how to "unsquish" files.

Figure D.8 shows the dialog box that Internet Explorer displays when you click on a link to download a file.

Be sure to select *Save this program to disk*. After you click on OK, the Save As dialog box appears; here you should select a folder where you want to save the file. Usually a Temp folder is best, since most of the time you'll be unpacking a compressed file or running an installation program to actually set up the software you're downloading.

TIP

If you need to create a Temp folder, just switch to Windows Explorer. Once you're ready, click on the browser's icon in the Taskbar to resume downloading.

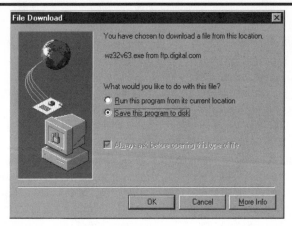

FIGURE D.8: Internet Explorer gives you choices when you download a file.

Your browser will then download the file, showing you its progress either in a special dialog box or in the bottom-right corner of the browser window.

WARNING

Be careful when downloading files from the Internet. Only take files from reputable sources. If you download a file from some unofficial archive, it could easily contain a virus or other software designed to damage your computer. If you're downloading from a well-established company site, though, you usually have nothing to worry about.

DOWNLOADING AND VIRUS PROTECTION

Viruses are prankish computer programs written by renegade programmers to play tricks on your files and your system. Most viruses enter your system from files downloaded from the Internet, although some viruses can be picked up from contaminated files sent to you via e-mail or on a floppy disk or other storage media. (You cannot "infect" your system with a virus simply by reading an e-mail message; but you can do so by running an infected executable file attached to a message.)

CONTINUED ➡

An entire software industry has sprung up to deliver products to protect computers, programs, and company networks from viruses. These programs can scan files for viruses, remove the viruses, and notify you if you are about to download a file containing a virus. Antivirus software is often bundled with new computers; if you already have such a program, you'll probably see its "splash" screen as part of the startup sequence.

If you don't have an antivirus program yet, you can download one from the Internet. The guide to vendors in Appendix C lists URL addresses for some of the antivirus publishers, or you can use the search tools described earlier to find a site. In Yahoo, for example, try the following sequence of categories: Business and Economy: Companies: Computers: Software: System Utilities: Utilities: Virus Protection.

Once you have an antivirus program, get in the habit of using it. With a Windows 9x virus scanner installed, you can simply right-click on an executable file in Windows Explorer, and Scan for Viruses will appear as one of the context-menu options.

See Chapter 18 to learn about related security features in Internet Explorer.

COMPRESSION PROGRAMS

Files archived for downloading are usually stored in a compressed format. Each of the major platforms (Windows, Macintosh, and Unix) has its own compression standards. Fortunately, files intended for a specific platform are invariably compressed in a format favored on that platform. Compressed Windows (or DOS) files usually end in .zip, .arc, or .lhz, with zip being by far the most common. If you're a Windows user, get yourself an up-to-date copy of WinZip (and pay for it—it's shareware and a bargain at the price). It "speaks" all the major PC compression formats and is easy to use. Compressed files that end in .exe are self-extracting. Just double-click the icon when it's finished downloading.

Downloading WinZip

If you do happen to download a file ending in .zip instead of .exe, you have obtained a zip *archive*, or a file that contains many other files in compressed format. You need to unzip this archive with the WinZip program (or another unzipping program) before you can use the files inside it. The following steps will take you through the process to download WinZip:

1. Open your browser and log on to your Internet service. In the browser Address window, type **http://www.winzip.com**. WinZip's home page (sponsored by WinZip's owner, Niko Mak Computing, Inc.) is shown in Figure D.9.

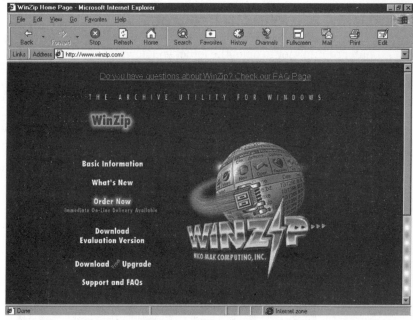

FIGURE D.9:   Download an evaluation copy of WinZip from http://www .winzip.com by clicking on Download Evaluation Version and then choosing the correct version of the program.

2. Click on Download Evaluation Version. Instruct your browser where on your hard drive you want the file downloaded.

3. When the file is finished downloading, you will have WinZip in an .exe (self-extracting) archive called winzip95.exe or

something similar, depending on which version you downloaded. (A version specifically for Windows 98 may be available by the time you read this, but the current version 6.3 for Windows 95 works without any problems under Windows 98.)

4. Exit from your Web browser and disconnect from the Internet.

NOTE

WinZip is a shareware program. It's OK to evaluate it for 30 days, but after that, you should pay Niko Mak Computing for an official copy. The WinZip Web site has information on online ordering of an official copy at http://www.winzip.com.

Using the WinZip Program

After you download WinZip and exit from your browser, use My Computer or Explorer to open the folder you downloaded WinZip into. When you find the .exe file, such as winzip95.exe, follow these directions:

1. Double-click on winzip95.exe to begin installing WinZip. Then click on the Setup button in the WinZip Setup dialog box. In the second WinZip Setup box, type in a different directory name in the Install To text box if you prefer something other than C:\WinZip, then click OK.

2. You will see the first WinZip Wizard screen, extolling the virtues of WinZip. Click on Next when you are finished reading.

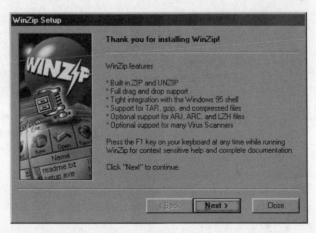

3. Click on View License Agreement in the License Agreement and Warranty Disclaimer dialog box. You can print out the agreement or just read it on the screen. Click Close when you are finished and click Yes if you agree to the agreement's terms.

4. In the second WinZip Wizard screen, you have two choices:

   ▶ Select Start with the WinZip Wizard option if you are new to this program and would like to be guided through its basic features.

   ▶ Select the Start with WinZip Classic to use all of WinZip's features with less wizard help.

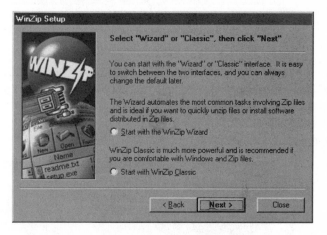

5. In the next screen, select either of these setup options:

   ▶ The Express option creates a program group for WinZip, along with Desktop and Start menu icons, and associates the program with archive files. *Association* means that double-clicking on a .zip file in Windows Explorer will launch WinZip to open the archive. You'll probably want to have all of these convenience features.

   ▶ The Custom option allows you to specify which of the Express features will be installed.

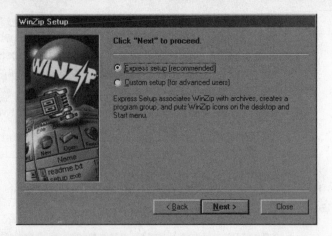

6. The setup is complete and you can click Next to start the program or Close to exit from Setup.

It's easy to switch back and forth between the WinZip Wizard, which guides you through the entire zipping process, and WinZip Classic, which just brings up the standard program. If you selected Start with the WinZip Wizard during the installation, you will be greeted by the Wizard screen shown here each time you start the program.

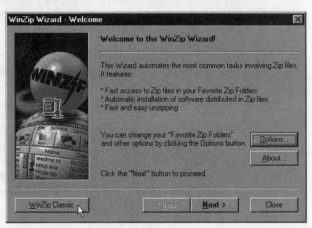

Click on the Options button to specify how your zip folders will be handled, or select Next to proceed with the Wizard, which will assist you in unzipping archives and installing programs from zipped archives you may have already downloaded, such as the antivirus programs discussed earlier. You can also click on the WinZip Classic button in the WinZip Wizard to close the Wizard and proceed with the basic program, shown next.

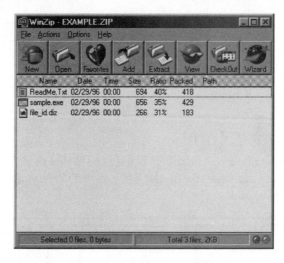

WinZip's interface is very simple and you can learn more about it by using the WinZip Wizard or by selecting Help ➤ Brief Tutorial, or Help ➤ Hints and Tips. You can activate the WinZip Wizard at any time by clicking on the Wizard button at the far right end of the WinZip toolbar.

TIP

If you use the WinZip Wizard to open your archive and extract files, it will also activate the Setup program if there happens to be one in the zip archive you obtained or downloaded.

To open a zip archive and unzip, or *extract*, the files inside of it, use these steps in WinZip Classic:

1. Double-click on the WinZip desktop shortcut, or select Start ➤ Programs ➤ WinZip ➤ WinZip 6.3 32-bit (or whichever version you have).

2. Click the Open button in the WinZip Classic toolbar, or select File ➤ Open Archive.

3. Browse through your hard drive in the Open Archive dialog box until you find the zip archive, then highlight it and click the Open button.

4. Highlight all of the files in the archive by clicking on the top one and then pointing to the last file and shift-clicking on it. Then select the Extract button or Actions ➤ Extract.

5. Browse through your folders in the Extract dialog box to specify where the unzipped files should be placed, then click Extract.

6. Select File ➤ Close Archive, and then File ➤ Exit to leave WinZip.

Shareware.com

A good "one-stop-shopping" place to go to download the latest version of software available free on the Net is c|net's Shareware.com site (see Figure D.10).

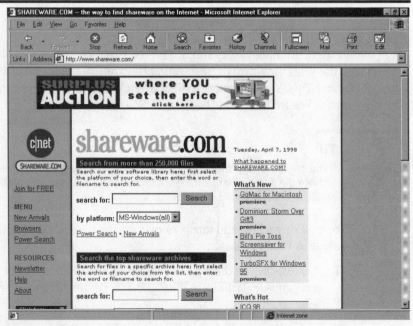

FIGURE D.10: Finding software is a breeze at Shareware.com.

The Shareware.com site will offer automatic links to recent arrivals and popular downloads, but you can search for any program by name. Just type the name (or part of it) in the search box, specify Windows as your operating system, and click the Search button. Shareware.com result pages contain links to various files (including duplicates at different sites) matching your search terms. Click on a file name to download a file.

HOW SHAREWARE WORKS

Shareware is software that's distributed for free (sometimes in a limited or *lite* format) on a trial basis. If you like the software and want to continue to use it beyond its trial period, it is your responsibility to register and pay for it. Sometimes you will gain access to additional features (or prevent the program from expiring entirely), printed documentation, or technical support.

Software distributed absolutely free is called *freeware*. Although the software is given away, the programmer retains all rights to it and does not put it into the public domain. In practice, this usually means that other programmers are expressly forbidden to incorporate the freeware into for-profit software of their own, unless they have written permission. Programmers who make freeware either derive personal satisfaction from the adoption and use of their handiwork, or they benefit financially from the reputation that accrues to the developer of a popular program. Software that periodically reminds you to register is often called "nagware."

A good shareware site for owners of Windows computers is http://www.tucows.com (the name is an acronym for The Ultimate Collection of Winsock Software).

BUYING THINGS ONLINE

As electronic commerce becomes more and more commonplace, you may find yourself searching for and purchasing products online. While software can be sent electronically over the Internet, other purchases are "fulfilled" in traditional ways (by mail, courier, and so on), much like catalog sales.

Perhaps the biggest remaining bugaboo holding back the inevitable tide of online commerce is the question of security. How can you safely transmit something delicate like your credit-card information over an open, public network such as the Internet? There are several different answers to this question, but no single universal model yet for online credit purchases.

TIP

See Chapter 18 for a complete discussion of Web security issues and Internet Explorer's tools for dealing with them.

One way to look at it is to compare it to handing your credit card to a waiter without worrying that someone in the kitchen might jot down your number and expiration date. The difference is that data transmitted over the Internet could lie around on drives and backup disks indefinitely, and individuals so inclined could probably hunt for likely information long after the fact.

Some online businesses have invested in secure Web servers that, when coupled with savvy Web browsers, initiate an encrypted "secure" connection, thereby preserving the secrecy of your private information. For that matter, most browsers will inform you *any* time you send information on a form to a nonsecure server, just in case the information in the form might be sensitive.

Other companies skirt the entire issue for now, offering alternative verification methods using 800 numbers or the like. This is an adequate approach for the time being, because it relies on more dependable existing methods of checking credit-card info, but it takes away a good deal of the convenience of shopping online by adding those extra steps. Another approach some businesses take is to have you set up an account (and choose from various payment methods) the first time you make a purchase.

WARNING

Just as a general matter of common sense, do not send private information, such as credit-card numbers via regular, unencrypted e-mail, and be suspicious of any messages you receive suggesting that you do so. Beware of official-looking Web pages that turn out to be fronts for people who just want your credit card number for their own nefarious purposes.

In addition to the matter of security, you may also have legitimate concerns about your privacy. Of course, these issues are not limited to the Internet. Any time you use a credit card or automatic-teller (debit) card you are leaving an electronic "paper trail" tracking your spending habits. The issue is similar on the Net. Beyond the basic transaction information any store would naturally expect to track, some online businesses will also request or require that you fill out a questionnaire before completing your purchase. Your answers on such a form will become part of a customer database that may then find its way into the hands of other businesses.

If you're concerned about limiting your exposure when spending money on the Net, refuse to fill out such questionnaires whenever possible and refuse to be put on mailing lists or to have your registration information "made available" to other entities, again, whenever possible.

Having addressed all the potential negatives of online shopping, I'd like to avoid giving too negative or scary an impression. I've bought a number of real-world objects and services online and have not had a problem yet.

At most "store" sites, such as Columbia House CD-ROM (`http://www.columbiahouse.com`), you can search or browse your way to the merchandise you want and then add it to a shopping basket (essentially a list of items you wish to buy), to be "rung up" all at once when you're finished shopping. You repeat this process as often as you wish, and then proceed to an Order page or area where you can buy the items you selected (see Figure D.11).

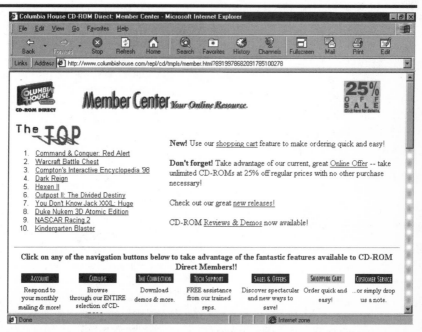

FIGURE D.11: Buying some Windows games at Columbia House CD-ROM, a typical online "store" site.

Index

Note to the reader: Page numbers in *italics* refer to figures; page numbers in **bold** refer to primary discussions of the topic.

Symbols & Numbers

& (ampersand), in FrontPage Express, 562

#pre, in LMHOSTS file, 348

+ (plus sign), in Explorer folders, 73

< (less-than symbol), in FrontPage Express, 562

> (greater-than symbol), in FrontPage Express, 562

1K Xmodem protocol, 378

1st Compu Choice, 868

1st Tech Corporation, 834

3Com Corporation, 834

3DTV Corporation, 834

4Q Technologies, 834

32-bit computer, 792

32-bit operating system, 15

56K, 805

56K modem, 706–707

403 Forbidden error message, 551

404 Not Found error message, 551

8514/A display, resolution for, 52

16550 UART (Universal Asynchronous Receiver/Transmitter), 644, 706–707

A

A: identifier, 792

\<A\> tag (HTML), NAME attribute, 590

A2Z Computers, 868

A4 Tech Corporation, 834

AA Computech, 864, 867

ABC Drives, 868

ABCs of Microsoft Internet Explorer 4 (Ross), 443

The ABCs of Windows 98 (Crawford and Salkind), 37, 57, 277, 363

ABS Computer Technologies, 834

Absolute Battery Co., 834

Abstract R&D, Inc., 834

Accelerated Graphics Port (AGP) graphics cards, 14

access, 792

access provider, 792

access speed, of memory, 673, 682

Accessibility applet, 113, **116–125**, *117*

   display settings, *120*, **120–121**

   General tab, *124*, **124–125**

   keyboard settings, *117*, **117–119**

   mouse settings, **121–124**, *122*

   sound settings, *119*, *119*

Accessories

   ➤ Calculator, 373

   ➤ Communications

      ➤ HyperTerminal, 375

      ➤ Phone Dialer, 370

   ➤ Entertainment, 731

      ➤ CD Player, 234

      ➤ DVD Player, 217

      ➤ Media Player, 226

      ➤ Sound Recorder, 229

      ➤ TV Viewer, 243

      ➤ Volume Control, 222, 786–787

   ➤ Fax

      ➤ Compose New Fax, 737

      ➤ Request a Fax, 740

   ➤ Multimedia, 213

      ➤ CD Player, 721

   ➤ Notepad, 364

   ➤ Paint, 368, 765

   ➤ System Tools

      ➤ Backup, 298

➤ Character Map, 369
➤ Clipboard Viewer, 367
➤ Disk Cleanup, 283, 729
➤ Disk Defragmenter, 281
➤ DriveSpace, 294, 296
➤ Maintenance Wizard, 286
➤ ScanDisk, 278
➤ System File Checker, 312
➤ System Information, 310, 311
➤ System Monitor, 313
➤ WordPad, 365
account, 792
Acecad, Inc., 834
Acer America Corporation, 639, 834
Acer Sertek Inc., 835
Achme Computer Inc., 835
ACL/Staticide, 835
Acom Inc., 835
ACT-RX Technology Corporation, 835
Action Electronics Co., Ltd., 835
Action Well Development Ltd., 835
ActionTec Electronics, Inc., 835
active button, on Taskbar, 41
Active Channels, 455. *See also* channels
active content, and security, 507
Active Desktop, **13**, 39, **714–715**
    Channel bar on, **624**
    channels on, **627–629**
    Control Panel on, *725*
    and Desktop icons, 51
    subscriptions, 11
active window, 792
    copying to Clipboard, 68
    refreshing, 68
ActiveX applets
    folder of downloaded, 517
    and security, 507
activity indicator, for Internet Explorer, 445, *445*
Actix Systems, Inc., 835
Actown Corporation, 835
Adaptec, Inc, 835
Add a New Address dialog box, 492, *492*

Add a Printer Wizard, 174–175
Add Favorite dialog box (Internet Explorer),
    447, *448*, *602*, 737
Add New Hardware Wizard, 75, 113, **125–134**,
    715–716
    Have Disk option, 133
    telling wizard what you have, **129–132**
    when item isn't on list, **133–134**
Add Printer Wizard, 262, 263
    for local printer, *183*, **183–185**
    for network printer, **178–182**
    port selection, 183, *184*
    for printer not in list, **186–187**
Add/Remove Programs applet, **99–100**,
    134–136, *135*, **716–718**
    Install/Uninstall tab, 30, *102*, **716**, 785
    Network Install tab, **718**
    Startup Disk tab, **717–718**
    Windows Setup tab, *325*, **717**
Addonics Systems, Inc., 836
Addonics Technologies, 835
Address Book, **438–440**, **718–720**, 792
    creating entry, **719**
    and Microsoft Wallet, 492
Address style, in FrontPage Express, 581
Address toolbar, 5, 9, **44**, **720**, 783
    in Explorer, 735
    opening drop-down list, 68
addresses, 792. *See also* e-mail addresses
    Internet, **399–400**
    in Microsoft Wallet, *491*, **491–493**
Addtronics Enterprise Co., 836
ADI Systems, Inc, 836
Adobe fonts, 745
Adobe Systems Inc., 836
ADPI (Analog and Digital Peripherals Inc.), 836
Adroit Systems, Inc., 836
Advanced Connection Settings dialog box,
    258, *259*
Advanced Digital Systems, 836
Advanced Download Options dialog box,
    612–613, *613*
Advanced Gravis Computer Technology Ltd., 836

Advanced Integration Research, Inc., 836

Advanced Matrix Technology, Inc., 836

Advantage Memory, 836

Agfa (Bayer Corporation), 837

AGP (Accelerated Graphics Port) graphics
   cards, 14

Ahead Systems, Inc., 837

Airbrush button, in Paint, 766

airport metal detectors, 656

AITech International Corporation, 837

Aiwa America, Inc., 837

AJR NewsLink directory, 465

Alaris Inc., 837

Alfa Infotech Co., 837

ALI (Acer Laboratories Inc.), 837

alias, 438, 793

alignment
   of horizontal line, in Web pages, 573
   of inline images, **595–596**
   of paragraphs in Web page, 581–582

Allsop Computer Accessories, 868

Alltech Electronics Co., 867

Alpha & Omega Computer, 837

Alpha Systems, Inc., 868

Alphacom Enterprise Inc., 837

ALPS, 837

alt., 793

Alt key, as StickyKey, 117, 118

Alt+Tab key, to switch running applications, 781

AltaVista, 889, *890*, *891*, 893

Always on Top option for Taskbar, 42, 782

AM radio, to monitor RFI field strength, 660

AMCC (Applied Micro Circuits Corporation), 837

AMD (Advanced Micro Devices), 838

America Online, 11

American Computer Products (ACP), 868

American Computer Resources, Inc., 868

American Cover, Inc., 838

American Ribbon and Toner Co., 868

AMI (American Megatrends, Inc.), 838

AMP Tech (American Micro Products
   Technology), 868

ampersand (&), in FrontPage Express, 562

Amptron International, Inc., 838

Amrel Technology Inc., 838

AMS, Inc., 838

Ana Precision Co., Ltd., 838

analog-to-digital converter, 793

anchor tag (HTML), 793
   NAME attribute, 590

Andy's Art Attack, 592

Angia Communications, 838

animated cursor, 165

animated GIF files, 593

animated graphics, Media Player for, 226

animation, in menus, 154

anonymous FTP, 793

anti-static spray, 665

antivirus programs, 403, 515, 896

AOC International, 838

APC (American Power Conversion), 838

Apex Data, Inc./SMART Modular Technologies,
   Inc., 838

APIs, multimedia, 208

Apple Computer, Inc., 839, 640

applets, 113–116, 363, 793. *See also* Accessories

application key, 793

application window, 793
   size of, 757

applications, 95, 793
   adding to Send To menu, 84–85
   adjustments during Windows 98 install, 27
   Alt+Esc to switch, 68
   Alt+F4 to close, 68
   deleting, **136**
   Dial-up networking and, **331–332**
   downloading certificated, **516–517**
   file deletion by, 88
   finding, **103–105**
   finding online & downloading, **883–905**
   improving access to, **105–108**
   installing, **96–100**, **134–136**, 755. *See also*
      Add/Remove Programs applet
   with Internet features, 394
   keyboard shortcuts to start, **66**
   memory requirements, 676

open, icon on Taskbar, 41
printing documents from, **192–196**
property sheets for, 48
running from CD, **97–98**
self-updating, 894
starting at Windows startup, **65–66**
switching with Alt+Tab, 781
switching with Taskbar, 781
uninstalling, **101–103**, 716, 785
APS Technologies, 839
archive, 793
    for e-mail, 435
    restoring copies, 775–776
Archtek America Corporation, 839
Arco Computer Products, Inc., 839
Aritsoft, Inc., 839
Arkenstone, Inc., 839
Arlington Computer Products, 869
ARM Computer Inc., 869
arranging icons, **760–761**
arrow keys, for mouse pointer control, 121
Artek, 839
article, 793
ArtMedia, 839
ASCII, 794
    LMHOSTS file as, 347
    printing file as, 204
Ashtek, Inc., 867
ASI, 869
ASK LCD, Inc., 839
Ask Technology Ltd., 839
Askey Communications USA, 840
Asolid Computer Supply, Inc., 840
Aspen Imaging International Inc., 869
Aspen Systems Inc., 840
Aspen Technologies, 840
Assmann Data Products, 840
Associates Computer Supply Co., Inc., 869
associating file with application, 744–745
    checking for, 195
AST Computer, 840
asynchronous transmission, 794

ATI Technologies, 840
    All-In Wonder card, 697
Atlantic Logic, 869
Atlantic Technology, 840
ATronics International Inc., 840, 869
AT&T, 11
attaching file to e-mail, **422–425**, 794
ATTO Technology Inc., 840
attribute, 794
audio CDs. *See also* CD Player
    recording sound from, 222
AuraVision Corporation, 840
authenticating server
    and error message when changing
        password, 345
authentication, 794
Authenticode technology, 515
authors, xxxi
Auto Hide for Taskbar, 42, 782
AutoComplete, in Internet Explorer, 450
Automated Tech Tools, 869
AutoPlay, 211
AutoScan command, in Internet Explorer,
    450–451
AutoSignature, in Outlook Express, 431
Autotime Corporation, 869
AVerMedia, Inc., 840
AVM Technology Inc., 841
Avnet Technology Co., Ltd., 841
Award Software International, 841
Axonix Corporation, 841
Axxon Computer Corporation, 841
Aztech Labs, Inc., 841

B

Back button
    in Explorer, 733
    in Netscape Navigator, 525, 543–544
Back command, in Internet Explorer, 458
backbone, 794
background
    for Desktop, 50, **139–142**, 714–715

graphic for Web page, 583, **584**
setting color in Navigator, 536, *537*
backorder, 646
Backup, **298–307**, *299*, 720
creating, **301–305**
deciding on files for, **300–301**
defining file set for, **301**
drag and drop for, **305–306**
options for, **305–306**
restoring files, **306–307**, 775–776
types of, **299–300**
Backup Wizard, *302*
backups, 794
before Windows install, 21
backward-compatibility, 794
bank of RAM, 681
bar charts, from System Monitor, *314*
Barnett's Computers, 869
Bason Hard Drive Warehouse, 867
Battery-Biz Inc., 870
Battery Network, 869
Battery Technology Inc., 870
baud rate, 794
BBS (bulletin board system), 795
Belkin Components, 841
Benwin Inc., 841
Best Data Products, 841
Best of the Web Quick Link, 447
Best Power, 841
bidirectional parallel ports, 645
BigCity Express, 878
Bigfoot, 743
binary files, sending in HyperTerminal, **378**
binary numbers, 15
BIOS (Basic Input/Output System), 795
error message after memory upgrade, 683
vendors for upgrade, 867
BIS Technology, 841
bit, 795
bit-blitting, 643
bit-block transfer, 643
bitmap editor, for Desktop pattern, 141–142
bitmaps, for Desktop, 50

bits per second, 795
Black Box Corporation, 870
.BMP files, Paint to edit, 369
BNF Enterprises, 870
Boca Research, 841
<BODY> tag (HTML), 583
MARGINS attribute, 584
bold type, in Web pages, 579
bookmarks, 795. *See also* Favorites list
changing name, 590
creating, **589–590**
jumping to, 590
links to, **588**
boot process, memory check, 677
bootable floppy disks, 83. *See also* emergency
startup disk
BootCom, 28
borderless frames, 545
borders
for inline images, 596
of windows, size of, 150
Borland International, 842
Bose Corporation, 842
bounce, 795
Briefcases, **381**
Broadcast Architecture, 248–249
Broken Pipe error message, 551
Brooks Power Systems Inc., 842
Brother International Corporation, 842
brownouts, 663
browse, 795
Browse for Printer dialog box, *263*
browsers, 795
browsing, **720–721**
to find setup file, 99, *100*
for network printer, 180, *180*
offline in Internet Explorer, 603–604, 754
updated subscriptions, **603–604**
Brush button, in Paint, 766
BRYSiS Data, Inc., 842
bug, 795
Windows Update for fixes, 288
bulleted lists, in FrontPage Express, **575–577**

bulletin boards, 388
bus, **642**
buttons, 795
byte, 796

C

Cable Connection, 870
cable, for direct connection, **359–360**
Cables America, 870
Cables To Go, 870
cache, 796
    cleanup of, **283–285**, *284*
    for Web pages in Navigator, **547–550**
cache memory, 796
CAD & Graphics Warehouse, 870
CalComp Corporation, 842
Calculator, *373*, **373–375**
California PC Products, 842
call preferences, for modem settings, 258
call waiting, disabling, 328, 708
Calluna Technology Ltd., 842
cameras, **261**
canceling
    all print jobs, **199**
    subscriptions, **604–605**
Canon Computer Systems, 842
Canon U.S.A. Inc., 842
Caps Lock key, sound for, 117, 118
capture, 796
career information, on Internet, 392
cascade, 796
cascading menu, 796
Casco Products, Inc., 842
case for computer, 636–637
    design and heat problems, **651**
    opening, **678**, *679*
case-insensitivity, 796
case sensitivity, 796
    of URLs, 531
cataloging disc
    in CD Player, 238–239
Cc line, in e-mail, 422, 796

CD Player, 213–214, **233–240**, *234*, 721
    basic controls, **235–236**
    cataloging disc, 238–239
    display options for, **236–237**
    play list creation in, 239–240
CD-Quality sound scheme, 231
CD-R (recordable CDs), DVD drives and, 216
CD-ROM, 796
    installing applications from, **96–97**
    installing Windows 98 from, 22
    running applications from, **97–98**
    vs. DVD disks, 214
    Windows 98 support, 212
CD-ROM drive
    minimum recommended for multimedia,
    692–693
CD-ROM Extended Architecture, 797
CD-RW (recordable/erasable CD), 694
    DVD drives and, 216
CD Technology, Inc., 842
CD Writer, recommendations for, **693–694**
CDF (Channel Definition Format), 621, 626
centering, wallpaper, 140
Centon Electronics, Inc., 843
central processing unit (CPU), **641–642**, 797
    heat from, 650
Century Microelectronics, Inc., 870
certificated applications, downloading, **516–517**
certificates, **514–519**, 719, 751–752
    for Netscape Communicator, 534
    setting security options, **517–518**
Cerwin-Vega, Inc., 843
CH Products, 843
Chaintech Computer U.S. Inc., 843
challenge code, 357
Challenge Handshake Authentication Protocol
    (CHAP), 334, 357
Channel bar, 455–457, *456*, 621
    adding Active Channel to, 457
    viewing channels from, **624**
channel content providers, 456
Channel Definition Format (CDF), 621, 626
Channel Guide, 622

Channel screen saver, 627

Channel Viewer, **622–624**, *623*

channels, **621–630**, 797

adding to TV Viewer toolbar, **246–247**

icon on Quick Launch toolbar, *43*, 43, 108

options for, **629–630**

and setup, 25, *25*

subscriptions to, **11–12**, 606, **624–627**

for TV Viewer, **245**, *246*

viewing in Internet Explorer, **622**

CHAP (Challenge Handshake Authentication Protocol), 334, 357

Chaplet Systems USA Inc., 843

chapters, on DVD disks, 219–220

Character Map, **369–370**, *370*

characters, 797

properties, in FrontPage Express, **577–580**

Chase Advanced Technologies, 843

chat rooms, 402

check boxes, 797

Chemtronics, 870

children, preventing access to Web sites, **495–506**

CHKDSK utility, 278

CIRCO Technology Corporation, 870

circuit, 797

circuit board, 797

handling, 668

Cirque Corporation, 843

Cirrus Logic, Inc., 843

Citizen America Corporation, 843

Clary Corporation, 843

Classic style, 47, 743

cleaning fluids, 668

clearing, Documents menu entries, 39

client computer, installing dial-up networking on, **327–332**

Client for Microsoft Networks, 76

properties, 345

Client for NetWare Networks, 76

client-server, 400

client software, 76

for Dial-up networking, 324

configuring connection, *332*, **332–334**

Clipboard, 721, 797

calculator and, 374–375

copying active window to, 68

copying screen to, 69

saving contents, **368**

Clipboard Viewer, 69, **367–368**, *368*

clock, 43, 727, 797

clock speed, 797

clone-makers, 641

close, 798

closed captioning, 119

closing, windows, **721–722**

.CLP extension, 368

CMD Technology, Inc., 843

CMO Corporation, 871

CMOS (Complementary Metal Oxide Semiconductor), static electricity and, 664–665

color

customizing, **151–152**

of horizontal line, in Web pages, 573

for hyperlinks, 529–530, 583–584

number for screen display, 51

and resolution, 52

of text, in Netscape Navigator, **534–537**, *537*

for web page background, 583

for Web pages, 750

color-coding, HTML window in FrontPage Express, 564

color depth, 155

and Web page preview, 565

Color dialog box, 151, *151*

color profiles, 261

color schemes

creating, **149–151**

for Desktop, 50

loading, **147–148**

in themes, 138

Colorgraphic, 844

Columbia House CDROM, 905, *905*

.com domain, 400, 798, 802

COM port, 185, 700

COM2001 Corporation, 844

Comdial Corp., 844

cometizing, 522

command line, 39, 798

command prompt, 798
    for WINS connection, 349, *350*

Command Software Systems, 844

comments, in FrontPage Express, **563**

commercial access provider, 798

common carrier, 798

communications. *See also* Dial-up networking
    HyperTerminal for, *375*, **375–380**
    infrared devices for, **267–268**

Compaq Computer Corporation, 639, 844

Compaq DirectPlus, 871

compatibility, 798
    of printers, 186
    and proprietary designs, 638

*The Complete PC Upgrade and Maintenance
    Guide* (Minasi), 635, 649, 833

component bar, in Netscape Navigator,
    525, 528

components
    precautions when handling, 666
    system information on, 310

Compose New Fax Wizard, **738–739**

compound device, 227

compressed air, 655

compressed drives, installing Windows 98
    on, **32–34**

compressed files, 798

compressing
    before data transmission, 334
    hard drive, **293–296**
    how it works, **295–296**
    JPEG file, 594–595

CompUSA Direct, 871, 877

CompuServe, 11

ComputAbility, 871

Computer City, 871

Computer Connections America, 844

computer dealers, categories, **639–641**

Computer Discount Warehouse (CDW), 871

Computer Fun, 844

Computer Gate International, 871

Computer Parts Outlet, Inc., 871

Computer Products Corporation, 871

Computer Re-use Network, 881

Computer Recycle Center, Inc., 879

Computer Recycler, 879

Computer Recyclers, 879

Computer Recycling Project Inc., 881

computer system, 798

Computer Things, 871

computer viruses, 403

computers
    Find command for, 742
    minimum recommended for multimedia,
        692
    power to, 661–662
    safe temperature ranges, **652–653**
    vendors, 881

Computers Direct, 871

CompuWorld, 871

Confirmation Form template, in FrontPage
    Express, 568

confirmation notice, of file deletion, 91

conflict troubleshooter, 131

conflicts, between hardware components,
    131, *132*

connect time, 798

Connect To dialog box, for HyperTerminal, *376*

Connected To... dialog box, 338

Connection Refused error message, 551

Connection Wizard, **722–724**

connections
    with Dial-up networking
        creating, **328**, *329*
        testing, **337–338**
    to Internet. *See also* Internet Connection
        Wizard
        changing, **341–342**
    to network printers, **190–191**

Connectix Corporation, 844

Content Advisor, 751
    adding another rating system, **504–506**

enabling, **499–501**

to filter Web sites, **495–506**

setting ratings criteria for, **501–502**

what to do when page is disallowed, **502–504**

context menu, 799

context-sensitive help, 788

for printer properties, 176

continuous play, for CD Player, 237

contrast of display, *120*, **120–121**

Control menu, opening, 68

Control Panel, 39, *724*, **724–725**, 799. *See also* Properties sheets

Accessibility applet, 113, **116–125**, *117*

Add New Hardware Wizard, 113, **125–134**

Add/Remove Programs applet, **134–136**, *135*

adjustments during install, 27

applets on, 113–116

Date/Time, 113, **137–138**, 727

Desktop Themes, 113, **138**

Display, 113, **138–146**, 270, 271, 730

Fonts, 113

game controllers, 113

Infrared communications applet, 114, 268

installing applications from, **99–100**

Internet, 114, 722

Keyboard, 114, 755

Mail, 114

Microsoft Mail Postoffice, 114

Modems, 114

Mouse, 114, **163–168**

Multimedia, 114, 761

Network, 114

opening, *112*, **112–116**

Passwords, 115, 344, 345, 767, 768

PCMCIA applet, 115

Power Management applet, 115

Printers folder, 115

Regional Settings applet, 115, 727

Registry and, 112

to remove programs, 136

Sounds, 115, **221–226**, 223–225, *224*, 779

System applet, 115

Telephony, 115

Users, 116, 785

cookies, 799

passwords in, 486

privacy on the Web and, **487**

Cool Edit, 213

Copy button, in Explorer, 733

copy command (DOS), for print file, 203

copy stands, magnets in, 657

copying, 799

e-mail between word processor and e-mail program, 428

files and folders, **725–726**

floppy disks, **82**

keyboard shortcuts for, 68

Core Components, 872

Cornerstone Imaging, Inc., 844

corrosion, **668**

heat and, 653

corrupted, 799

cover page, for fax, 739

Cowart, Robert, *Mastering Windows 98*, 19, 111, 171, 207, 687

CPAC (Computers, Parts, and Commodities), 879

CPU (central processing unit), **641–642**

heat from, 650

Crawford, Sharon

The ABCs of Windows 98, 37, 57, 277, 363

Windows 98: No Experience Required, 71, 95, 253, 277, 309

Creative Labs, Inc., 844

credit card, for computer purchase, 645–646

credit card information

Microsoft Wallet to manage, **490–494**, *494*

for telephone, 377

Crocodile Computers, 880

cross-linked files, ScanDisk to fix, 280

crosstalk, **658**

Crumlish, Christian

The Internet Dictionary, 791

The Internet: No Experience Required, 385, 407, 408, 883

CSLIP, 333-334

Ctrl key, as StickyKey, 117, 118

Ctrl+Alt+Del, 799

CTX International, Inc., 844

currency, format for displaying, 774

cursor blink rate, 756

cursors, 799

   in themes, 138

Curve button, in Paint, 766

Custom Schedule dialog box, *619*, 619-620

Cut button, in Explorer, 733

cutting, 799

cutting and pasting, 799

   keyboard shortcuts for, 68

Cyber Patrol filtering software, 498

CyberMax Computer, Inc., 844

CyberNOT Block List, 498

cyberspace, 800

CyberYES Allowed Sites List, 498

Cyrix Corporation, 845

D

Daewoo Electronics, 845

DakTech, 880

Dalco Electronics, 872

data, 800

Data Depot Inc., 845

Data Exchange Corporation, 880

Data Recovery Labs, 864

data recovery, vendors, 864-865

Data Retrieval Services, 864

DataLux Corporation, 845

DataVision, 872

Date/Time Properties dialog box, 113,
   137-138, **727-728**

dates

   default formatting for, 775

   and Find command, 741

   system settings for, 137

DC Drives, 872

decimal symbol, 773

   for currency, 774

decoder card, in DVD drive, 216-217

decompressing files, **896-901**

default action, 800

default HTML editor, FrontPage Express as, 558

default printer, 181-182, **192-193**

   drag and drop and, 196

   icon for, 182, *182*

default settings, 800

   font in Internet Explorer, 578

   Windows 98 maintenance of, 4

default Web browser, **479-480**

Delete button, in Explorer, 733

deleted files, recovering, **88-90**, 728, 784

deleting, 800

   applications, **136**

   beginning or end of sound file, 232

   by bypassing Recycle Bin, **87**, 92

   channel from Channel bar, 457

   Client for NetWare Networks, 76

   color schemes, 149

   e-mail, **416**

   e-mail in Outlook Express, 419

   file in print queue, **198-199**

   files and folders, **728**

   in FrontPage Express, 560

   hyperlinks, 589

   items in Favorites list, 472-473

   keyboard shortcuts, 66

   messages in Netscape, 421

   modems, **256**

   printers from Printers folder, **191**

   and Recycle Bin, 47

   shortcuts, 58

   sound schemes, 226

Dell Computer Corporation, 645-646, 845

DellWare Direct, 872

Delta Products Corporation, 845

Denon Electronics, 845

depth of color, 155

   and Web page preview, 565

depth, of downloading subscription links,
   611-612

deselecting, 800

Desktop, 5, *38*, **729**, 800. *See also* Active Desktop;
 Display Properties dialog box; Recycle Bin
  Backup icon on, 306
  change in, 7
  icon on Quick Launch toolbar, 43, *43*, 108
  icons on, 38
  My Computer, **46–47**
  Online services folder, 11
  placing Start menu item on, **63**
  properties, **138–146**
    background and wallpaper, **139–142**
    screen savers, **143–146**
  setup, **48–52**
  shortcuts for applications on, **106**
  Start button, **38–41**
  taskbars, **41–46**
  themes, 14, 113, **138**, 152
  Web browsers as, 392
Desktop toolbar, **44**, 783
destination directory, for Windows 98 install, 28
Details view, 89, *89*, 733, 760
device drivers, 800
  finding, 133
  installing, 27, **129–132**
  master database of, 13
  for modems, 709
  for mouse, 168, 265
  for multimedia, 214, **249–250**
  for printers, **177–178**
    printer removal and, 191
  System applet to remove, 126
  for video cards, 269
  Windows Update for, 288
device-independent bitmap format (.DIB), 50
devices, 800
  property sheets for, 48
DFI (Diamond Flower, Inc.), 845
diagnostic program, 800
dial-up account, 801
dial-up adapter, binding protocols to, 327
dial-up connection
  installing Windows 98 from, 22
  unattended for subscriptions, **617–618**

Dial-up networking
  advantages, 319–320
  configuring network connection, **326–327**
  Connection dialog box, *332*, **332–334**
    General tab, 334, *335*
    Multilink tab, 334, *336*
    Scripting tab, 334, *336*
  creating new connection, **328**, *329*
  for data access, not applications, **331–332**
  installing, **325–334**
    on client machine, **327–332**
    on networks, **325–326**
  for Internet Explorer, 444
  for Netscape Communicator, 523
  password for, 769
  protocols supported, **323–324**
  remote access with, **357–359**
  security concerns, **355–360**
  setup options for, **322–324**
  testing connection, **337–338**
  vs. WINS or PPTP, **350**
Dial-Up Server
  installing, **351–355**
  selecting for Dial-up networking client,
   332, *333*
Dial-Up Server dialog box
  Allow caller access, 352, *352*
dialing properties
  for fax, 739
  for modems, **259**, *260*
dialog boxes, 801
  browsing from, **720–721**
  font for, 150
  help for, 749
Diamond Multimedia Systems, Inc., 845
.DIB files, 50
  Paint to edit, 369
digit grouping symbol, 773
digital cameras, 692–693
Digital Equipment Corporation (DEC), 845
digital IDs, 719
Digital Micro, Inc., 872
digital signature, 516

digital temperature probe, 653
digital-to-analog converter, 801
digitized sounds, Media Player for, 226
DIMM (dual inline memory module), 675
    locating, 679
dimmed command, 801
DIP (dual inline package) switches
    on modem, 701
DIPs (dual inline chips), 674
direct cable connections, **359–360**
    with Dial-up networking, 322
direct sunlight, heat from, 654
directories. *See* folders
directory tree, 801
DirectShow, 211–212, 241
DirectX API, 14, 211
disabling, 801
Disc Settings dialog box for CD Player, *239*
disclaimer, in signature block, 430
Disctec, 845
discussion groups, **387**, 388, 401
disk cache, size for Netscape Navigator,
    548–550
Disk Cleanup, **283–285**, *284*, 729
    scheduling, 286–287, 788
Disk Defragmenter, **281–283**, *282*
    for FAT32 drive, 293
    scheduling, 286–287, 788
Disk Drive Repair, Inc., 864
disk drives, 801. *See also* floppy disks; hard
    drive
    I/O board for, 637
    shortcuts to, **67**
disk space, **289–296**, **729**
    application install options and, 98
    freeing up, 33
    for installing Windows 98, 21, 22
    for Recycle Bin, 90
    removing uninstall files to gain, **32**
    for sound recording, 231
    for Temporary Internet files, 452
Diskette Connection, 872
Diskettes Unlimited, 872

DiskTec, 865
Disney, channel from, 12
display adapters. *See* video display adapters
display monitors, 644
    changing, 273
    Energy Star, 143, 144, 146, 162
    magnetism from, 656
    optimizing settings, **271–274**
    Properties sheet, *159*, **159–163**
        Monitor tab, **161–162**, *162*
        Performance tab, **163**
    purchasing decision, 160
    recommendations for, **696–697**
    settings for accessibility, *120*, **120–121**
    TV as, 162
Display Properties dialog box, 113
    Appearance tab, **50**, **147–152**, *148*
    Background tab, *49*, **50**, *140*, 140–141,
        714–715
    Color Management, 274
    Effects tab, **51**, **152–154**, *153*
    font settings in, 745
    Performance tab, 274
    Screen Saver tab, **50**, 144–146, *145*
    Settings tab, **51–52**, **154–163**, *155*, *272*
        Advanced properties, **158–163**
        color palette, **155**
        Desktop Area, **156–157**, *157*
        font size and, **157–158**
    Web tab, **51**, **154**, 624, *625*, 715
DMS (Data Memory Systems), 866
DNS (domain name service), 802
docked Taskbar, 528
Document Contains No Data error message,
    551
documents
    printing in Navigator, **552–553**
    recently edited, 730
Documents in Start menu, 39
domain, 802
    in Internet address, 399
domain name, 400, 802
DOS, 802

DOS programs
  removing, **103**
  shortcuts to, **67**
DOS prompt, 39, 802
  installing Windows 98 from, 23
dot pattern adjustments, 802
dot pitch of monitor, 697
double-clicking, 4, 802–803
  speed of, 165, 758
DoubleSpace, **33**
downloaded program files, cleanup of, 284
downloading, 803
  certificated applications, **516–517**
  files from Internet, **402–403**, **893–895**
  preventing for graphics, 755
  software, *902*, 902–903
  subscribed Web sites, 602, 607
    limits for, **610–613**, *611*
  Web sites, 11
  WinZip, **897–898**
DPT-Distributed Processing Technology, 846
Dr. Watson, **311**, *312*
drag and drop, **730**, 803
  for backup, **305–306**
  to copy file or folder, 725–726
  to create hyperlink, 587
  to move files and folders, 759
  to print file, **194–196**
dragging, 803
DRAM (dynamic random access memory), 673
Drive Converter, 291–293, *292*
Drive Service Company, 865
drives
  disconnecting from mapped, **81**
  mapping, **79–80**, *81*
  selecting in Explorer, **736**
  sharing, **78–79**
DriveSavers Data Recovery, 865
DriveSpace, 32, **33**, 289, **293–296**
drop-down list box, 803
DTC Data Technology, Inc., 846
DTK Computer Inc., 846
dual inline chips (DIPs), 674

dual inline memory module (DIMM), 675
  locating, 679
dual inline package (DIP) switches, on modem, 701
dump, 803
dust, **654–655**
duty cycles, **653**
DVD (Digital Versatile Disk) disks, capacity, 215
DVD (Digital Versatile Disk) drives, 14, **694–695**
  purchasing decision, **216–217**
DVD (Digital Versatile Disk) player, 212, **214–221**
  running, **217–221**
  specifics, **215–216**
dynamic content, and security, 507
dynamic data exchange, 803
dynamic HTML, 803
dynamic RAM (DRAM), 673, 803
Dyson, Peter
  *PC User's Essential Accessible Pocket
    Dictionary* (Dyson), 791
  Windows 98 Instant Reference, 713

E

e-mail, **10–11**, **387**, 395, **407–441**, 804. *See also* Outlook Express
  advantages, **407–408**
  attaching file to, **422–425**
  deleting, **416**
  exiting program, **418**
  filing, **432–434**
  filtering, 413, **434–437**
  forwarding, **425–426**
  free Internet accounts for, 409
  HTML formatting to enhance, **426–427**
  from multiple accounts, **437–438**
  netiquette, **416–417**
  Netscape Messenger for, **419–421**, *420*
  in Outlook Express, **418–419**
  reading, *413*, *414*
  replies to, 410, **414–415**
  running program, **409**

sending, **409–413**

sending to multiple addresses, 411, **421–422**

signatures for, **430–432**

spelling check, **429–430**

for Web site change notice, 608–609

word processor to write, **427–429**

e-mail addresses, 399, 410, 804

aliases for, 438

common, 411

finding, **440–441**

from receiving mail, 440–441

Edek Technologies, Inc., 846

Edit menu

to copy file or folder, 726

in Explorer, 732

to move files and folders, 759

editing, 804

in FrontPage Express, **560–566**

Edmund Scientific Corporation, 872

EDO RAM (extended data out random access memory), 674, 682–683

.edu domain, 400, 802

EIDE connector, for DVD drive, 216

Eject button

in CD Player, 236

in Media Player, 227

Electric Library, 893

electric motors, radio frequency interference (RFI) from, 659

Electric Renaissance, 865

electromagnetic interference, **657–660**

electromagnetism, **657–666**

electronic commerce, **903–905**

electronic components, precautions when handling, 666

Electronic Frontier Foundation, 403

electronic packaging, 516

electrostatic discharge, **663–666**

ELEK-TEK, 872

Ellipse button, in Paint, 767

emergency startup disk, 26, **717–718**

from Backup, 298

booting from, 28

using, 31

employers, Internet-usage monitoring by, 395

empty folders, deleting, 86

emptying, Recycle Bin, **92**

enabling, 804

encapsulated PostScript files, printing, 204

Encarta World Atlas, 98

encoding attached files, 423

encryption, of file transfers, **512–514**

Energy Star Monitors, 143, 144, 146, 162

Enhance 3000 Memory Products, Inc., 846

Enhanced Parallel Port (EPP), 645

enhanced TV viewer, 242

Ensoniq, 846

Entertainment, 731. *See also* Accessories ➤ Entertainment

Enterzone, 399

environment, 804

Envisions Solutions Technology, Inc., 872

EPP (Enhanced Parallel Port), 645

EPS Technologies, 846

Epson, 644

Epson America, Inc., 846

Eraser button, in Paint, 766

Eritech International Inc., 880

error checking, by modem or software, **709**

error messages, 804

in Netscape Navigator, **550–551**

ESS Technology, Inc., 846

Eudora, 804

event-driven program, 804

Exabyte Corporation, 846

Excalibur Data Recovery, Inc., 865

Exchange/Windows Messaging system, 10

fax capability of, 11

Excite, 893

excluding files, from backup, 305

.exe file extension, 106

Exide Electronics, 846

exiting

e-mail program, **418**

Netscape Navigator, **553–554**

EXP Computer Inc., 847

expandability, 804

expanding, 804

expansion card, 700

expansion slots, 637

   for modem, 703–704

   plugging unused, 660

Expert Computer International Inc., 847

Expert Computers, 872

The Expert Guide to Windows 98 (Minasi), 319

Explorer. *See* Internet Explorer; Windows Explorer

Explorer bars, *9*, 9–10, **453–457**, *454*, 622

   in Channel Viewer, 623

   Channels bar, 455–457, *456*, 621

   Favorites bar, 454, *454*, *467*, 467

   History bar, 455, *455*

   Search bar, 454, 462–463, *463*

export laws, Internet Explorer encryption levels and, 513

exporting, 804

Express Point Technologies Electronics, 864

Extended Attributes dialog box, for Web pages, 573

extended data out random access memory (EDO RAM), 674, 682–683

extension, 805

   viewing, **73–74**, *74*

external modem, 700

   installing, **701–703**

extracting files with WinZip, 901

extranets, 805

F

FairFax, 873

fan in computer, **650–652**, **651–652**

FAQ (frequently asked question), 401, 805

Fast Electronic U.S., Inc., 847

FAT16 file system, converting FAT32 to, 293

FAT32 file system, 14, 289, **290–291**

   converting to, 291–293

Favorites bar, *454*, 454, *467*, 467

Favorites list

   adding Hot List page to, 473

   adding other items, **470**

adding Web pages to, **467–468**

cleaning out, **472–473**

default browser to open pages on, 479

in Internet Explorer, **464–473**

   viewing list, **466–467**

moving items in, 471

organizing, **468–469**

subfolders for, **470–472**, *471*

Favorites menu, **736–737**

   in Explorer, 733

   in Internet Explorer, 466, *466*

   in Start menu, 39

fax, **737–740**

   Exchange for, 11

fax/modems, 700, 805

fiber optic cable, 658

File and Print Services for Microsoft Networks, 78

file extensions, viewing, **73–74**, *74*

file format, 805

   for e-mail attachments, 423

file fragments, **281–283**, *282*

   ScanDisk to fix, 280

File Manager (Windows 3.x), to run setup, 23

File menu, in Explorer, 731–732

File menu (Windows 3.1), Run, 23

file names, 805

file recovery, 805

file set

   backing up existing, **304–305**

   defining for Backup, **301**

file system, 805

File Transfer Protocol (FTP), 402, 806

files, 805. *See also* Backup

   arranging in Details view, 89

   attaching to e-mail, **422–425**

   backing up specific, **302–303**

   Briefcase to synchronize, **381**

   copying, **725–726**

   decompressing, **896–901**

   deleting, **728**

   downloading from Internet, **402–403**, **893–895**

finding, **740–742**
finding with My Computer, 762
fragmented, **281–283**, *282*
Internet Explorer to display local, 468
moving, 759–760
names for, 763
opening local in Internet Explorer, 451
printing to, 185, **201–204**
property sheets for, 48
recovering deleted, **88–90**
searching for, 40
selecting in Explorer, **736**
sending to Recycle Bin, **86–87**
undeleting, 784
filing, e-mail, **432–434**
Fill with Color button, in Paint, 766
filter, 805
filtering
   e-mail, 413, **434–437**
   Web sites, Content Advisor for, **495–506**
FilterKeys, 117, 118
Find: All Files dialog box, *40*, 741–742
Find command in Start menu, 40, **740–743**
Find: Files dialog box, *104*
finding
   applications, **103–105**
   computers, 742
   device drivers, 133
   e-mail addresses, **440–441**
   files or folders, **740–742**
     with My Computer, 762
   help topic, 748
   on Internet, **884**. *See also* Web searches
   people, 743
finding and replacing text, in FrontPage
   Express, **562–563**
firewalls, 344, 806
First Computer Systems, Inc., 873
First Source International, 873
fixed font, in Netscape Navigator, 535, 536
flame, 417, 806
flickering, 158, 159–160, 697
floating toolbars, *528*, 528

flooding, 667
floppy disks, 643, 806
   for Backup, 299
   copying, **82**
   in Explorer, **81–83**
   formatting, **82–83**, 746
   heat from, 650
   installing from, 22
   naming, 762–763
   password for, 769
   sending files to Recycle Bin, **87**
floppy drive, dust in, 655
fluorescent lights, and crosstalk, 658
Focus Electronic Corporation, 847
Folder Options dialog box, 39, **743–745**
   File Types tab, 744–745
   General tab, 46–47, 743–744
   View tab, 73, 744
folders, 7–8, 806
   backing up specific, **302–303**
   copying, **725–726**
   creating, **727**
   customizing in Explorer, **735–736**
   deleting, **728**
   deleting empty, 86
   finding, **740–742**
   finding with My Computer, 762
   for installing Windows 98, 20
   installing Windows 98 to new, **28–29**
   moving, 759–760
   names for, 763
   Online services, 11
   opening, 5
   password for, 769
   searching for, 40
   selecting in Explorer, **736**
   sharing, **78–79**
   for sounds, 224
   for Web shortcuts, **476–477**
Font dialog box, in FrontPage Express,
   577–580, *578*
font size, on screen display, **157–158**
font smoothing, 152, 154

‹FONT› tag (HTML), 579

fonts, **745–746**

  for Desktop, 50

  for display elements, 150

  installing, 746

  printer removal and, 191

  printing samples, 746

  for Web pages, 750

Fonts applet, 113

Fonts folder, 745

foreground, 806

Formatted paragraph style, in FrontPage
  Express, 581

formatting

  disks, 746

  e-mail with HTML, **426–427**

  floppy disks, **82–83**

  tools in WordPad, 366, *366*

  Web pages, in FrontPage Express, **577–585**

forms, on Web pages, 538

forums, 388, 806

Forward button

  in Explorer, 733

  in Netscape Navigator, 525, 543–544

Forward command, in Internet Explorer, 458

forwarding e-mail, **425–426**, 806

  automatic, 438

Four11, 440, 743

FQDN (fully qualified domain name), 807

fragmented files, **281–283**, *282*

frames

  printing in Navigator, **552–553**

  in Web pages, **545–546**

framesets, 587

Free-Form Select button, in Paint, 765

freeware, 403, 806, 903

Frequently Asked Questions, 401, 805

FrontPage Express, 13, 557–597, *559*, 747

  bookmark creation, **589–590**

  bulleted and numbered lists, **575–577**

  comments in, **563**

  creating new page, **567–569**

  editing in, **560–566**

  finding and replacing text, **562–563**

  graphics, **591–597**

  headings, **575**

  horizontal line insertion, **572–574**

  HTML source code in, **563–564**, *564*

  inline images creation, **592–593**

  line breaks, **561–562**

  link creation, **586–588**

  meta page information, **585–586**

  navigating in, **559–560**

  opening existing page, **569–570**

  page formatting, **577–585**

  page properties, **582–584**

  page structure in, **572–577**

  paragraph properties, **580–582**

  previewing work in Internet Explorer, **565**

  printing, **565–566**

  saving work, **571**

  special characters, **561–562**

  starting, **558–559**

FrontPage Server Extensions, 568

FrontPage98, 558

FTP (File Transfer Protocol), 402, 806

FTP servers, 806

FTP sites, 806

  URL (Uniform Resource Locator) for, 451

Fujitsu, 847

Fujitsu Computer Products of America, 847

Full format, 83

Full System Backup, 300

full-window drag, 152

fully qualified domain name (FQDN), 807

function keys, 68

  F1 for help, 54

  F3 for search, 40

G

game controllers, 113, **266**

games, 747

  hard drive vs. CD, 98

gateway, 387, 395, 411

Gateway Destination entertainment system, 247

Gateway2000, 847

generic PC, parts, **636-637**

Generic text-only printer driver, 187, 204

GIF file format, 591, 594

    for wallpaper, 142

gigabyte, 807

Global Computer Supplies, 873

Global MicroXperts, 873

GNN, Whole Internet Catalog, 460

Go menu

    in Explorer, 733

    in Internet Explorer, 458

gopher, 807

.gov domain, 400, 802

graphical user interface (GUI), 4, 807

graphical Web browsers, development of, 390

graphics. *See also* inline images

    in FrontPage Express, **591-597**

    for horizontal line in Web page, **574**

    Paint to create, **369**

    preventing Internet downloading, 755

    saving in Navigator, 541

    in signature, 431

    for Web pages

        background, 583, **584**

        hyperlinks, 530, 588

        saving, 571

        sources for, 591-592

    when opening file in FrontPage, 570

graphics programs, arrow keys for mouse pointer control, 121

Graphics Warehouse, 873

greater-than symbol (>), in FrontPage Express, 562

ground strap, 666

groups, in Address Book, 720

guest book, on Web pages, 538

GUI (graphical user interface), 4, 807

Guide button, in Netscape Navigator, 526

H

<H1> tag (HTML), **575**

hacker, 807

hard drive, 643, 807

    compressing, **293-296**

    heat from, 650

    installing Windows 98 to new, **28-29**

    naming, 762-763

    password for, 769

    problems during Windows 98 install, **29-30**

    Recycle Bin on each, 86

hardware, 46. *See also* printers

    bus, **642**

    cameras, **261**

    choosing PC parts, **641-645**

    conflicts between components, 131, *132*

    display adapters, **268-274**. *See also* video display adapters

    game controllers, **266**

    generic PC parts, **636-637**

    icons on Taskbar, 43

    infrared devices, **267-268**

    memory, **642**

    modems, **254-261**

    multimedia upgrade, **688-691**

    requirements for TV Viewer, 241

    scanners, **261**

    setup check for, 24

    types of sellers, **645-646**

hardware buying guide, market niche, **639-641**

hardware drivers. *See also* device drivers

    installing, 27

Hardware Installation Wizard, **126-132**, *127*

Harmony Computers, 873

Hartford Computer Group, Inc., 873

Hayes Microcomputer Products, Inc., 847

HDSS Computer Products, 873

<HEAD> tag (HTML), 582

header, 807

headings, in FrontPage Express, **575**

heat sensor devices, **652**

height of horizontal line, in Web pages, 573

help, *53*, **53-55**, **747-749**
    adjustments during install, 27
    context-sensitive, 788
        for printer properties, 176
    Index tab for, 55
    printing topic, 55
    for scientific calculator, 374
    Search tab, 55
    in Start menu, 41

Help menu
    in Explorer, 733
    in Internet Explorer, 753-754

Hercules Computer Technology, Inc., 847

hertz, 808

Hewlett-Packard, 847

Hi-Tech Component Distributors, Inc., 873

Hi-Tech USA, 873

hiding, Taskbar, **42**

High Color (16 bit), themes in, 138

High Contrast, 120

high-level format, 808

high-speed modems, **706-709**

Hilgraeve Inc, 848

history, 808

History bar, *455*, 455

History folder
    default browser to open pages on, 479
    settings for, 750

Hitachi America Ltd., 848

hits, 808

H&J Electronics International, Inc., 866

.hlp file extension, 105

Home button, in Netscape Navigator, 526

home, Internet access at, **395-398**

home pages, **459-461**, 808
    changing, **460-461**
    choosing, **459-460**, 749

horizontal line
    graphics for, **574**
    inserting in FrontPage, **572-574**

host, 808

host-controlled modem, 709

host drive, ScanDisk check of, 281

hostname, in Internet address, 399

hot links. *See* hyperlinks

Hot List page, creating, **473-474**, *474*

HotBot, 893

hotlist, 808

HotMail, 409

hover option, 451

HP laser printers, 644

<HR> tag (HTML), 572, 573

.HTM files, program associated with, 479

HTML editor. *See also* FrontPage Express
    setting default, 558

HTML files. *See also* FrontPage Express;
        Web pages
    creating or editing, 735-736
    as Desktop background, 714-715
    program associated with, 479
    as wallpaper, 142

HTML (Hypertext Markup Language), 13, 808
    to enhance e-mail formatting, **426-427**

HTML layer, as Active Desktop, 13

HTML source code
    in FrontPage Express, **563-564**, *564*
    viewing, 558

HTML tags, inserting attributes for, **573**

HTTP (Hypertext Transfer Protocol), 808

HTTPS, in URL, 512

hue, 151

humidity, and static electricity, 665

HyperData Direct, 874

hyperlinks, 808
    color for, 529-530, 583-584
    creating in FrontPage Express, **586-588**
    deleting, 589
    in e-mail, 415
    navigating inside FrontPage, 570
    in Netscape Navigator, **529-531**
    speed of response to clicking, 530
    for Web navigation, **451-452**

hypermedia, 808. *See also* multimedia

HyperTerminal, *375*, **375-380**

how to use it, **376–377**
receiving files, **379**, *379*
sending files, **378–379**
to test modem, 706
using connection, **380**
hypertext, 390, 808. *See also* hyperlinks
Hypertext Markup Language (HTML), 808
Hypertext Transfer Protocol (HTTP), 808
Hyundai Electronics America, 848

I

I/O board, 637
I/OMagic Corporation, 848
IAB (Internet Activities Board), 809
IBM-compatible computer, 809
IBM Corporation, 639, 640
IBM PC Co., 848
icons, 809
    for default printer, 182, *182*
    on Desktop, 38
    for folders, 477
    Internet as source, 153
    libraries for, 63
    moving and arranging, **760–761**
    for new Web site content, 609
    screen resolution and arrangement, 52
    for shared printers, 190
    for shortcuts, 58, *58*, **62–63**
    size on toolbars, 46
    sources for, 475
    in themes, 152
    for Windows 98, 153
idle time, for screen saver activation, 146
Iiyama North America, Inc., 848
image maps, 595
Image Properties sheet (FrontPage)
    Appearance tab, 597
images. *See* graphics
Images button, in Netscape Navigator, 526
<IMG> tag (HTML), 593
importing, Address Book, **718–719**
impression, 809

inbox, 809
index for help, 747
infection, 809
Infoseek, 893
Infrared communications applet, 114
infrared devices, **267–268**
Infrared Monitor dialog box, *268*
infrared printing port, 185
initialization files, 809
inline images, 809
    alignment of, **595–596**
    alternatives to, **595**
    borders for, 596
    creating in FrontPage Express, **592–593**
    properties, **593–597**, *594*
    specifying size, 596–597
input/output, 809
installing, 809. *See also* memory installation
    applications, **134–136**, 755. *See also*
        Add/Remove Programs applet
    Dial-up networking, **325–334**
        on client machine, **327–332**
        on networks, **325–326**
    Dial-up server, **351–355**
    fonts, 746
    local printers, **183–185**
    modems, **254–255**, *256*
        external, **701–703**
        internal, **703–706**, *705*
    network printers, **178–182**, *179*
    off-brand printers, 186
    printers, **174–187**
    replacement modem, 257
    TV Viewer, 241
installing applications, **96–100**
    from CD-ROM, **96–97**
    from Control Panel, **99–100**
installing Windows 98, **19–35**
    on compressed drive, **32–34**
    to fresh disk or directory, **28–29**
    full upgrade from previous version, **22–27**
    hard drive problems during, **29–30**
    to machine running Windows NT, **34–35**

rebooting after, 26–27

reverting to previous operating system, **30–32**

.int domain, 802

Integrated Services Digital Network (ISDN), 322

Intel Corporation, 848

Intellimouse, 123

Interact Accessories, Inc., 848

interactive media. *See* multimedia

interactivity, 209

interface, World Wide Web as, 389

interlaced GIF image, 594

interlaced or noninterlaced video, 644

internal modem, 700, 810

connecting to phone line, **705–706**, *706*

installing, **703–706**, *705*

Internet, 5, **386–404**, *388*, 810. *See also* privacy on the Web

accessing, **394–400**

changes in, 390

Chat, 402

discussion groups, **387**

downloading files from, **402–403**

e-mail, **387**

error messages, **550–551**

features in applications, 394

Find command for, **742**

FTP (File Transfer Protocol), 402

as icon source, 153

installing programs downloaded from, 100

latest developments, **392–394**

multiple platforms on, 400

new developments, 554

search engines for, 401, **461–464**

Usenet, 401

vs. World Wide Web, **388–392**

Web sites about, **403–404**

Internet Activities Board (IAB), 809

Internet addresses, **399–400**

Internet applet, 114

Internet connection

altering, **341–342**

modifying, **723–724**

to NT domain using WINS, **343–350**

setup, **722–724**

Web help through, 53–54

Internet Connection Wizard, **339–343**, *340*

The Internet Dictionary (Crumlish), 791

Internet Explorer, 5, **753–755**, 810

browsing offline, 754

configuring, 754

default font in, 578

encryption levels, and export laws, 513

Favorite Web pages, **464–473**

home page loading by, 459

icon on Quick Launch toolbar, 43, *43*, 108

increasing speed of, 754–755

multiple open windows, **458–459**

previewing FrontPage work in, **565**

Quick Links creation, **447–448**

saving image in, 591

screen display, **444–446**, *445*

starting, **444**

subscribing to site in, 601

toolbar appearance, **446**

viewing channels in, **622**

Internet newsgroups, 10–11

The Internet: No Experience Required (Crumlish), 385, 407, 408, 883

Internet Options dialog box, **749–753**

Advanced tab, 753

Connection tab, 752

Content tab, 751–752

for personal profile, 489

General tab, *460*, 749–750

Programs tab, 752–753

Security tab, 508–509, *509*, 750–751

to add sites to zone, 510–511

Internet Properties dialog box, 722

Internet protocol (IP), 810

Internet Relay Chat (IRC), 402

Internet security zone, 507, 750

Internet service provider (ISP), 396, *397*, 810

connecting to, 320

list of local, 339

sample information, **343**
   types of accounts, **396–398**
Internet Society, 403
InterNIC, 400, 810
InterPro Microsystems, Inc., 874
interrupt request line (IRQ), for modem,
   700–701
intranet, 810
intro play, for CD Player, 237
intruder, 810
Iomega Corporation, 848
IP addresses, 810
IP (Internet protocol), 810
IPX/SPX protocol, 75
IRC (Internet Relay Chat), 402
IRQ (interrupt request line), for modem,
   700–701
ISDN (Integrated Services Digital Network),
   322, 810
ISP (Internet service provider), 810. *See also*
   Internet service provider (ISP)
italics type, in Web pages, 579

J

Jade Computer, 874
Java, 810
   and security, 507
JavaScript, 810
Jazz Speakers, 848
JBL Consumer Products Inc., 848
Jinco Computers, 874
Joss Technology Ltd., 848
joysticks, **266**
JPEG file format, 591, 594–595
   for wallpaper, 142
jumpers, for hardware, 130, *131*
Juno.com, 409
JVC Information Products of America, 849

K

Kahlon, Inc., 874
Kbps, 811

Kenosha Computer Center, 874
Kermit protocol, 378
keyboard
   accessibility settings, *117*, **117–119**
   arrow keys for mouse pointer control, 121
   cover for, 667
Keyboard applet, 114, **755–756**
keyboard shortcuts, **67–69**
   to open Web page, 477
   to start programs, **66**
KeySonic Technology Inc., 849
kill, 811
kill file, 811
kilobit, 811
kilobyte, 811
Kinesis Corporation, 849
Kingston Technology Corporation, 849
kit in box, 690
Kodak photo format, 692, 693
Konica Business Machines U.S.A., Inc., 849
Koss Corporation, 849
KREX Computers, 874

L

L2 cache, 642
labels, for floppy disks, 83
Labtec Enterprises, Inc., 849
language
   and DVD disks, 220–221
   and keyboard layout, 756
   RSACi rating standard for, 501–502
laptop computers, 811
   CD drive for, 692
   mouse trails on, 168
   thermal shock and, 654
Large Icons view, *88*, 154, 733, 760
   for high screen resolution, 273
launching, 811
Lava Computer Mfg. Inc., 849
Lazarus Foundation, Inc., 881
LCD screens, High-Contrast White color
   scheme for, 148

leading zeros, displaying, 773
left-handed mouse settings, 164–165
Legend Micro, 874
less-than symbol (<), in FrontPage Express, 562
Leverage International Inc., 849
Lexmark International, Inc., 849
LG Electronics, 849
Liberty Systems, Inc., 850
line breaks, in FrontPage Express, **561–562**
Line button, in Paint, 766
line length, 811
links, 400, 811. *See also* hyperlinks
Links bar, in Explorer, 735
Links toolbar, **44–45**, 783
    in Internet Explorer, **447–448**
liquid, as computer hazard, **667–668**
list boxes, 811
list separator, 773
List view, 733, 760
listserver, 811
LMHOSTS file, 344
    creating, **347–348**
local, 812
local area network (LAN), 74
    installing Windows 98 from, 22
local bus video card, 696
local computer vendors, 645
Local Intranet security zone, 507, 750
local printers, 178
    adding, **262**
    installing, **183–185**
    sharing on network, **189–190**
local Web pages, creating, **473–474**
Location toolbar, in Netscape Navigator, *525*, 527
    entering URL in, 532
The Location (URL) is Not Recognized error
    message, 551
locked file, 812
log
    from HyperTerminal, 380
    for modem connection, 258
    from ScanDisk, 280
    telephone, 371, **372–373**

Log Off from Start menu, 41, **756–757**
log on, 757
Logicode Technology, Inc., 850
login, 812
login script, 812
Logitech,Inc., 850
logon dialog box, for DVD player, 218
logout, 812
long filenames, 16, 812
low-resolution image, as alternative, 595
LPT ports, 183, 185
luminosity, 151
Luminosity bar, in Color dialog box, *151*
lurking, 812
Lycos, 893
Lynx, 390

M

Macro Tech Inc., 874
MAG Innovision Co., Inc., 850
Magellan, 893
Magic PC, 874
Magnavox, 850
magnetic shielding, in speakers, 695
magnetism, **656–657**
Magnifier button, in Paint, 766
Mail applet, 114
mail order, 645–646
mailboxes, to store e-mail, 432, 812
mailing list, 812
main window, for Internet Explorer, 445, *445*
Maintenance Wizard, *286*, **286–287**
manufacturers list, 834–864
MAPI (Messaging Application Programming
    Interface), 813
mapped drive, **79–80**, *81*
    disconnecting from, **81**
margins, in FrontPage Express, **584**
Mastering Microsoft Internet Explorer 4
    (Weisskopf), 483, 557, 599
Mastering Windows 98 (Cowart), 19, 111, 171,
    207, 687

Matrox Graphics, Inc., 850

Maxell Corporation of America, 850

Maxi-Switch, 850

Maximize button, for application window, 757

Maximized option, for automatic program startup, 66

maximizing, 813

Maximus Computers, 850

Maxtor Corporation, 850

MBONE (multicast backbone), 813

McAfee Associates, 853

McDonald and Associates: The Memory Place, 866

MCI (Media Control Interface), 249

measuring systems, 773

Media Control Interface (MCI) devices, 249

Media Player, 213, **226–228**, *227*, 757

Media Vision, 850

Mediatrix Peripherals Inc., 850

megabit, 813

megabits per second, 813

megabyte, 813

Megacomp International, Inc., 874

MegaHaus Hard Drives, 867

megahertz, 813

Megahertz Corporation, 851

Megatech Inc., 875

mem command (DOS), 677

memory, **642**, 813

    32-bit addressing, 15

    access speed of, 673, 682

    bank of, 681

    characteristics, **682–683**

    determining current amount, 677–678

    limits to improvement from upgrade, 678

    pins on, 681

    reasons to upgrade, 676–677

    software loaded in, 311

    space for, **681–682**

    types of chips, **674–675**

    on video adapter, 159

    Windows 98 requirements, **672**

Memory 4 Less, 866

memory cache, 813

    for Netscape Navigator, 549

memory chip, 814

memory installation, **671–684**

    choosing modules, **673–674**

    locating existing, **679–681**

    opening case, **678**, *679*

    planning, **675–676**

    steps, **683–684**, *684*

The Memory Man, 866

memory map, 814

menu bar, 814

    focus on, 68

    for Internet Explorer, 444, *445*

    in Netscape Navigator, 524, *525*

menus, 4, 814

    font for, 150

Merritt Computer Products Inc., 875

message format, for fax, 738–739

Messenger. *See* Netscape Messenger

<META> tag (HTML), **585–586**

Mickeys, 166–167

Micro 2000 Inc., 851

Micro Accessories, Inc., 851

Micro Com, 865

Micro Pro, Inc., 875

Micro Solutions, 851

Micro Time, Inc., 875

Micro X-Press, 875

MicroClean Inc., 851

MicroData Corporation, 851

Microlabs, 851

Micron, 639

Micron Electronics, Inc., 851

Micronics Computers, 851

MicroniX USA, Inc., 875

microphone, 228

microprocessor, **641–642**, 814

    heat from, 650

    System Monitor to track usage, 313

MicroSense, Inc., 875

Microsoft Corporation, 851

Microsoft Fax, and WordPad, 365

Microsoft Mail Postoffice, 114

Microsoft Network, 11, 814

Microsoft Office, and Disk Defragmenter, 282

Microsoft Quick Link, 447

Microsoft Wallet, **490–494**

Microsoft Web Gallery, 591–592

   for line images, 574

Microsoft Web site

   accessibility support, 116

   for Broadcast Architecture, 241

   Channel Guide, 12, *12*

   for printer drivers, 186

   Windows 98 driver library, 13, 126

MicroSupply, Inc., 875

Microtek Lab, Inc., 851

MIDI (Musical Instrument Digital Interface)

   Media Player for, 226

Midland ComputerMart, 875

Midwest Computer Works, 875

Midwest Micro, 875

Midwestern Diskette, 875

.mil domain, 400, 802

Millenium Technologies, 876

millisecond, 814

MIME (Multipurpose Internet Mail

   Extensions), 423, 814

Minasi, Mark

   *The Complete PC Upgrade and Maintenance
   Guide*, 635, 649, 833

   The Expert Guide to Windows 98, 319

Minimize button, for application window, 757

Minimized option, for automatic program

   startup, 66

minimizing, 814

Minolta Corporation, 852

minus sign (-), in Explorer folders, 73

mirror site, 814

Mita Copystar America Inc., 852

Mitsuba Corporation, 852

Mitsubishi Chemical America, 852

Mitsubishi Electronics America, 852

Mitsumi Electronics Corporation, 852

mix and match components, 691

mixing sounds, 231, 233

MMI Corporation, 876

modems, **254–261**, 758, 814. *See also*

   Properties sheets, for modems

   basics, **700–701**

   configuring, **707–708**

   deleting, **256**

   for Dial-up networking, 322

   dialing properties for, **259**, *260*

   error checking by, **709**

   high-speed, **706–709**

   installing, **254–255**, *256*

   installing replacement, 257

   multiple for connection speed, 334

   speed and Internet connection, 398

   troubleshooting problems, **259–261**, 708

Modems applet, 114

moderated, 815

moderator, 815

modulation, 815

monitors. *See* display monitors

More Info... dialog box, for modem, 260, *261*

Mosaic, 815

motherboard, 637, 643

   proprietary, 637

Motherboard Discount Center, 876

Motherboard Express, 876

Motorola ISG, 852

Motorola PCMCIA Products Division, 852

mouse, 644

   accessibility options, **121–124**, *122*

   changing, **265–266**

   left-handed settings, 164–165

Mouse applet, 114

mouse pointer, 4, 758

   customizing, **165–166**, *166*

   speed, 166

Mouse Properties dialog box, 758. *See also*

   Properties sheets, for mouse

movies, DVD for, 215

moving

   files and folders, 759–760

   icons, **760–761**

Mozilla, 815
MPC (multimedia PC), 687–688
MS-DOS, 815
　FAT (file allocation table) for, 290
　multiboot with Windows NT, 35
MS-DOS applications
　adjustments during install, 27
　printer driver for, 177
　printer setup for, 180–181
　spooled printing from, 172
MS-DOS mode, name length error report from
　ScanDisk, 281
MSCDEX, 212
MTC America Inc., 852
multi-session Kodak photo format, 692, 693
Multi-Tech Systems, Inc., 852
multiboot options, 35
multicast backbone (MBONE), 813
multimedia, 761, 815
　CD Player, 213–214, **233–240**, *234*
　Cool Edit, 213
　device drivers for, 214, **249–250**
　DVD (Digital Versatile Disk) player, 214,
　214–221
　Media Player, **226–228**, *227*
　new features in Windows 98, **211–212**
　Sound Recorder, 213, **228–233**
　Sound Settings applet, 213, **221–226**
　TV Viewer, **240–249**, *244*
　uses for, 208–209, 210–211
　WaveWorks, 213
　what it is, **209–211**
Multimedia applet, 114
multimedia PC (MPC), 208, 687–688
multimedia upgrade
　features to look for, **691–696**
　options, **688–691**
multiple files
　recovering from Recycle Bin, 89
　selecting, 89–90
Multipurpose Internet Mail Extensions
　(MIME), 423, 814
multitasking, 7, 15–16, 815

multithreading, and print process, 173
Multiwave Technology, Inc., 852
Mustek, Inc., 853
My Computer, **46–47**, **761–762**
　mapped drive in, 80
My Documents, 8, 762
Mylex Corporation, 853

N

N icon, 522
nagware, 903
name server, 815
names
　for drives, 762–763
　for files or folders, 763
　for local printer, 184
　for network printer, 181, *181*
　for shared resources, 78
　for shortcuts, **61**
nanoseconds, 673, 682
narrowing Web searches, 892
National Geographic, channel from, 12
National Science Foundation (NSFNET), 816
National Semiconductor, 853
Nationwide Computers Direct, 876
navigating, 815
Navigation toolbar, in Netscape Navigator,
　524–526, *525*
NCA Computer Products, 876
NCE Storage Solutions, 853
NCR Corporation, 853
NCSA Mosaic, 390
NEC Corporation, 853
NEC Technologies, Inc., 853
NECX Direct, 876
negative sign symbol, 773
Net, 816. *See* Internet
net address, 816
.net domain, 400, 802, 815
net use command, 349
net view command, 349
NetBEUI protocol, 75

NetBIOS name, 348

netcasting software, 393

netiquette, 401, **416–417**, 816

 and signature, 432

NetMeeting, 763

 information in Address Book, 719

netnews, 816

Netscape Communicator

 online documentation, 529

 security in, 533–534

Netscape, dedicated FTP sites, 522

Netscape is Out of Memory error message, 551

Netscape Messenger, **419–421**, *420*

 address book, **439–440**

 attaching file to e-mail, **425**

 creating folders for filing e-mail, 433–434

 e-mail replies in, 415

 filing messages in folders, 434

 filtering e-mail, *436*, **436–437**

 Forward command, 425

 HTML to format e-mail in, **427**

 and mail from multiple accounts, 437

 signature file in, 431–432

 spelling check, 430

 Web addresses as links, 421

 word wrap in e-mail, 412

Netscape Navigator, 5, *391*, **521–554**

 caching and reloading, **547–550**

 error messages, **550–551**

 image autoloading in, 526

 interface, **524–528**, *525*

 launching, **522–524**

 moving backward and forward, **543–544**

 Navigation toolbar, 523

 opening first document, **529–533**

 opening multiple windows, 533

 printing, **552–553**

 quitting, **553–554**

 saving files in, **538–542**

 saving items not in view, **541–542**

 size and color of text, **534–537**

 troubleshooting pages loading, 544

 viewing saved documents, **542–543**

NetShepherd content-filtering software, 495

NetShow Player, 212

NetWare Connect, 323

NetWare Connect server, connections to, 333

network. *See also* client software

 installing applications from, 718

 installing Dial-up networking on, **325–326**

 quick guide to setup, **75–78**

 refreshing print queue, **198**

 searching for computer on, 40

 shortcuts to dial, 338–339

network adapters, adding to system, 75

network address, 816

network administration, password for, 769

Network applet, 114

Network Associates, 853

Network dialog box

 Configuration tab, *346*

network drive, mapping, **79–80**, *81*

A Network Error Occurred Unable to Connect

 error message, 551

Network Express, 876

network identification, 345

Network Neighborhood, 74

 network with WINS connection in, 348

 shared resources, **78–79**

network news, 816

Network News Transfer Protocol (NNTP), 816

network printers

 adding, **263–264**

 connecting to, **190–191**

 installing, **178–182**, *179*

 offline, 198

Network Wizard, 76

 Configuration tab, *76*

new computer, as upgrade option, 689–690

New Media Corporation, 853

New Toolbar dialog box, *45*

The New York Times, channel from, 12

newbies, 387

NewCom, Inc., 853

newsfeed, 816

newsgroups, 388, 401, 816

newspapers, online, 465, 600

newsreader, 816

   Outlook Express as, 764

Next International, 876

nicknames, for e-mail address, 438

NIE International, 880

NNTP (Network News Transfer Protocol), 816

Nokia Display Products, 853

Normal style, in FrontPage Express, 580

Normal Windows option, for automatic program startup, 66

North American CAD Company, 876

North American Computer, 878

Northstar, 880

Norton Disk Utilities, 85

   for file recovery, 88

Notepad, **364**

NSA/Hitachi, 854

NSFNET (National Science Foundation), 816

NT Domain, WINS to connect using Internet, **343–350**

Nudity, RSACi rating standard for, 501–502

Num Lock key, sound for, 117, 118

numbered lists, in FrontPage Express, **575–577**

numbers, settings for display, 773

O

Oak Park Personal Computers, 880

objects

   changing properties in FrontPage Express, 561

   creating shortcut for visible, **60**

Ocean Information Systems Inc., 854

Odyssey Technology, 877

off-brand printers, installing, 186

Office 95, My Document folder for, 8

Office 97, My Document folder for, 8

Office Properties sheet, Sharing tab, 79

offline, 816

offline browsing, of updated Web sites, 11, 603–604, 754

offline help, 53

   using, 54, **54–55**

offline network printer, 180, 198

Okidata Corporation, 854

<OL> tag (HTML), 575

Olivetti Office USA, 854

online, 816–817

online community, 817

OnLine Computing, 880

online newspapers, 465, 600

online services, 339, 387, 396, 397, 763–764, 817

Online Services folder, 11, 339

OnTrack Data Recovery, Inc., 865

Open Page dialog box, 542

Open Profiling Standard (OPS), 488–489

operating environment, 817

operating system, 817

   and FAT32, 290–291

   reverting to previous after Windows 98 install, **30–32**

option buttons, 817

Orchestra MultiSystems, Inc., 854

Orevox USA Corporation, 854

.org domain, 400, 802, 817

Organize Favorites dialog box (Internet Explorer), 448, 449, 469, 469, 737

   canceling subscriptions in, 604–605

OS/2, and Windows 98 setup, 35

Outlook Express, 10, **10–11**, **418–419**, 764–765

   address book, **439**

   attaching file to e-mail, 424, **424**

   correcting spelling, **429–430**

   creating message folders in, 433

   e-mail replies in, 415

   e-mail signatures in, 431

   Forward command, 425

   HTML to format e-mail in, **427**

   icon on Quick Launch toolbar, 43, 43, 108

   new message windows in, 409, 410

   sorting messages with filters, 435, 436

   word wrap in e-mail, 412

overvoltage, **662–663**

owner, of print job, 197

P

‹P› tag (HTML), 580

packet, 818

Padix Co. Ltd., 854

Page Display Area, in Netscape Navigator, *525*, 527

page layout, for printing in FrontPage Express, 566

Page Properties dialog box (FrontPage Express)
Background tab, **583–584**
Custom tab, 585
General tab, 582, *583*
Margins tab, 584

page setup, in WordPad, **367**

pages. *See* Web pages

Paint, **368–369, 765–767**

Paint Shop Pro, 369

Panasonic Communications & Systems Co., 854

panning mode, 123

Pantex Computer Inc., 854

PAP (Password Authentication protocol), **355–356**

paragraph text, properties in FrontPage Express, **580–582**

parallel ports, 645

parity RAM, 677

PartitionMagic, 28, 293

partitions, 290, 818

Password Authentication protocol (PAP), **355–356**

passwords, **767–770**, 818
for backup, 305
changing, 768–769
for credit card information, 493, 494
in Dial-up networking, 334
for Dial-up server, 352, *353*
for DVD player, 218
during install, 27
for NT domain using WINS connection, 344
for printers, 190
and privacy on the Web, **485–487**
for screen saver, 144, 145–146
for shared resources, 79
for supervisor in Content Advisor, 499–500, 503
synchronizing Windows and Networking, 327
troubleshooting problems changing network, 345

Passwords applet, 115

Paste button, in Explorer, 733

Paste command, 770

path of target, for shortcuts, 62

Pathlight Technology Inc., 854

paths, 818

patterns on Desktop, 141
editing, 141–142

pause
in CD Player, 235
in printing, **200–201**

PC compatible, 640

PC/Computing Web Map, 460

PC Concepts Inc., 854

PC friendly environment, 668–669

PC Importers, 877

PC Power & Cooling, Inc., 855

PC Power and Cooling Systems, 652

PC Universe, 877

PC Upgrading & Maintenance: No Experience Required, 671, 699

PC User's Essential Accessible Pocket Dictionary (Dyson), 791

The PC Zone, 878

PCComputer Solutions, 877

PCI (Peripheral Connection Interface), 642, 696

PCL Computer Inc., 877

PCMCIA applet, 115

PCMCIA (Personal Computer Memory Card International Association), 855

PCs. *See also* computers

PCs Compleat, 877

PCT (Private Communications Technology), 512

.PCX files, Paint to edit, 369

Pencil button, in Paint, 766

Pengo Computer Accessories, 855

Pentium, 818

Pentium chip, 641
memory banks for, 682

people, finding, 743
peripheral devices, 818
 buses for, 14
Peripherals Unlimited, Inc., 877
permanent swap file, size of, 33
personal certificates, 515, **519**
Personal Computer Memory Card International
 Association (PCMCIA), 855
Personal Home Page Wizard, 568, *569*
personal information, 752
personal profile, for Profile Assistant, 488
Personal toolbar, in Netscape Navigator, *525*, 527
Phillips Consumer Electronics Co., 855
Phone Dialer, **370–373**, *371*
 telephone log, **372–373**
phone line
 connecting internal modem to, **705–706**, *706*
 connecting modem to, 702
photos, and Windows 98, 692–693
phrase, Web search by, 888
physically challenged user, Accessibility options
 for, **116–125**, *117*
Pick Color button, in Paint, 766
PICS standard, 497
 Web page without, 501
PIF (program information file), 819
pins on memory module, 681
 tin or gold, 683
Pioneer New Media Technologies, Inc., 855
Pionex Technologies, Inc., 855
pixels, relationship of Mickeys to, 167
Pixie Technologies, 855
PKWare, Inc., 855
Play Inc., 855
play list, creating in CD Player, 239–240
Please Enter Username and Password error
 message, 551
Plextor USA, 855
plug and play, 125, 254, 642, 770, 818
 display monitors as, 162
 installing devices, 27
 for multimedia, 208
 printers as, 171, 177

Plus! program, 152
plus sign (+), in Explorer folders, 73
point of presence (POP), 819
Point-to-Point protocol (PPP), 323, 333, 819
 and Internet account, *398*, 398
Point-to-Point Tunneling protocol (PPTP), 323
 connection setup, **329–331**, *330*
 Microsoft Virtual Private Networking
  Adapter for, 327
 vs. Dial-up networking or WINS, **350**
point-to-select, 4
PointCast, 393, *393*
 channel from, 12
pointers, shortcuts as, 8
Polygon button, in Paint, 766–767
POP (point of presence), 819
POP (Post Office Protocol), 819
pop-up menus, 819
 for channels, Refresh command, 630
 to copy file or folder, 726
 Create Shortcut, 59, *59*
 for Desktop
  New, Shortcut, 60
 Disconnect, 81, *81*
 to move files and folders, 760
 in Netscape Navigator, 543
  to recent History list, 544
 Print, **196**, *196*
 Restore, 89
 Send To, **84–85**, 777
  adding shortcuts to, **64–65**
  Desktop As Shortcut, 106
  shortcuts, **108**, *109*
 Sharing, 78
 for Taskbar
  Toolbars, New Toolbar, 45
Portrait Display Labs, 855
ports, 819
 application access to, 172
 for printers, 183, 185
post, 819
Post Office Protocol (POP), 819
postmaster@address, 441

PostScript printers
 deleting file from print queue, 198
PostScript printing, 187
power management, 14, 115, 146
power noise, **660–663**
Power Pros, Inc., 877
power supply, 637
power surges, user-induced, **661–662**
Powercom America Inc., 855
PowerQuest Corporation, 856
PPP (Point-to-Point protocol), 323, 333, 819
 and Internet account, 398, *398*
PPTP (Point-to-Point Tunneling protocol), 323
 connection setup, **329–331**, *330*
 Microsoft Virtual Private Networking
  Adapter for, 327
 vs. Dial-up networking or WINS, **350**
Practical Peripherals, 856
#pre, in LMHOSTS file, 348
<PRE> tag (HTML), 581
Preferences dialog box (Netscape Navigator),
 535
 cache settings, 547–548, *549*
 colors settings, 536, *537*
preventive maintenance, **649–669**
 dust, **654–655**
 electromagnetism, **657–666**
 heat, **650–653**
 magnetism, **656–657**
 precautions when handling electronic components, 666
 thermal shock, **654**
 water and liquids, **667–668**
preview
 of FrontPage work in Internet Explorer, **565**
 pane in Outlook Express, 418
 of printed Web page, 566
price/performance, and proprietary designs,
 638
Price Pointe, 877
Princeton Graphic Systems, 856
Print button, in Netscape Navigator, 526
Print dialog box, *193*

print jobs, canceling all, **199**
Print Manager (Windows 3.x), 172
Print Manager (Windows 98), **173–174**
print queue, 172, *197*, **197–201**, *200*
 deleting file from, **198–199**
 order of, 174
 rearranging, 200, **201**, *202*
 refreshing from network, **198**
printers, 644. *See also* Properties sheets, for
  printers
 adding and configuring, **261–264**
 deleting from Printers folder, **191**
 device drivers for, **177–178**
 dust in, 655
 installing, **174–187**
 managing, 191
 multiple definitions for, 176
 options for customizing, 175
 password for, 769
 ports for, 183, 185
 setting for shared network use, **189–190**
 shortcut in Send To, 64
 troubleshooting problems, **264**
 uninstalling, **264**
Printers folder, 39, 115, 172–173, 770
 deleting printers from, **191**
 opening, 178
printing
 from applications, **192–196**
 drag and drop for, **194–196**
 encapsulated PostScript files, 204
 to file, 185, **201–204**
 font samples, 746
 in FrontPage Express, **565–566**
 help topic, 55
 in Netscape Navigator, **552–553**
 pausing and resuming, **200–201**
 right-clicking to begin, **196**
 test page, 182, 185
 in WordPad, **367**
privacy on the Web, **484–494**
 and cookies, **487**
 Microsoft Wallet, **490–494**

passwords and, **485–487**

Profile Assistant for, **488–489**

Private Communications Technology (PCT), 512

processor, **641–642**

heat from, 650

System Monitor to track usage, 313

processor cache, 642

Procom Technology, 856

Prodigy Internet, 11

Product News Quick Link, 447

Professional Technologies, 856

Profile Assistant, **488–489**

Program Guide data, Web connection for, 243, *244*

program information file (PIF), 819

program patches, Windows Update for, 288

programs, 819. *See also* applications

Programs in Start menu, 39, 771–772

ProLink Computer, 856

prompts, 820

properties, 772

right-clicking to view, 47–48

Properties button, in Explorer, 733

Properties sheets, **47–48**, *48*, 820

Alt+Enter to open, 188

for channel subscriptions, 630

Receiving tab, 630

Subscription tab, *630*

for Favorites, 607

for game controllers, 266

for horizontal line in Web page, 572

for host drive, 296

for inline images, **593–597**, *594*

for modem

Connection tab, 258, *258*

Diagnostics tab, 260

General tab, **256–257**, *257*

for mouse, 758

Buttons tab, *164*, 164–165

General tab, 168

Motion tab, 166–167, *167*

Pointers tab, 165–166, *166*

for My Computer, 677

for personal profile, 488–489, *490*

for printers, **187–189**, *188*, 264

for Recycle Bin, 90–91

Global tab, *91*

for screen saver, *628*

for shortcuts, 61–62, *62*, 65–66

Shortcut tab, 66

for subscriptions

Receiving tab, 609, *609*, 612

Schedule tab, *614*, 618, *618*

for video adapter, Adapter tab, *270*

for Web shortcuts

Internet Shortcut tab, 477, *478*

Subscription tab, 607–608, *608*

proportional font, in Netscape Navigator, 535, 536

proprietary PCs, problems with, **637–638**

proprietary software, 820

protocols, 820

binding to dial-up adapter, 327

Dial-up networking support for, **323–324**

for file transfer in HyperTerminal, 378

for Internet, 386

proxy server, 752, 820

public domain software, 820

publisher certificates, 514, **515–518**

Publishing Perfection, 877

pull-down menu, 820

punctuation, in URLs, 531

purchasing decision, online, **903–905**

push, 820

Q

QLogic Corporation, 856

Quadrant International Inc., 856

Quantex, 639

Quantext Microsystems, Inc., 856

Quantum Corporation, 856

Quark Technology, 877

Quarterdeck Select, 856

Quatech, Inc., 856

queue. *See also* print queue

of outgoing e-mail, 412

Quick format, 83
Quick Launch toolbar, 42, **43–44**, 781, 783
   adding shortcuts to, **107–108**
   Explorer icon on, 444
   Outlook Express icon on, 418
   TV set icon, 243
   View Channels button, 622
Quick-Line Distribution, 878
Quick Links, default in Internet Explorer, 447
QuickShot Technology, Inc., 857
quit, 820
quitting, Netscape Navigator, **553–554**
quoting, 820
QVS, Inc., 857

R

radio frequency interference (RFI), **658–660**
Radio Sound Quality, 231
RAM chip, 821
RAM (random access memory), 821.
   See memory
random access, 821
random access memory (RAM), 821
random order, for CD Player, 237
RAS (Remote Access Service), 322, 324
   dialing into, 333
Rating Systems dialog box, 506, *506*
ratings system for children, 497
   Web page authors and, **497–498**
read, 821
read-only, 821
Read only access, 79
read-only memory (ROM), 822
reading, e-mail, **413**, *414*
README file, 821
readme.txt file, 23
real time, 821
reboot, 821
   after install, 26–27
rec., 821
receiving files, in HyperTerminal, *379*, **379**
recordable CDs (CD-R), DVD drives and, 216

recordable/erasable CD (CD-RW), DVD drives
   and, 216
recording volume, 787
recovery, of deleted files, **88–90**, 728, 784
Recreational Software Advisory Council
   (RSAC), 497
Rectangle button, in Paint, 766
Recycle Bin, **47**, **85–92**, **772**
   bypassing, **87**, **92**
   and disk cleanup, 285
   emptying, **92**
   Properties sheets of, 90–91, *91*
   recovering files from, **88–90**, 728, 784
   sending files to, **86–87**
   sending floppy disk files to, **87**
   settings adjustment for, **90–92**
   what it is, **85–86**
recycling centers, for computers, 881
refresh rate, 158, 159–160, 697
Regal Electronics, Inc., 857
Regional Settings applet, 115, **772–775**
registered file types, 73–74
   displaying list, 744
Registry
   backup of, 305
   and Control Panel, 112
   removing printer setup from, 191
   setup initialization of, 24
   updating for new hardware, 127
relative font size, on Web pages, 580
Relisys (Teco), 857
Reload button
   in Netscape Navigator, 526, 544
   to replace cached Web page, 547
remote access, **319–360**, 821
   with Dial-up networking, **357–359**
   requirements for, 321
   what it is, **321–322**
Remote Access Service (RAS), 322, 324
remote administration, 320, 770
remote control, 322
   for TV Viewer, **247–248**
repeat delay, for keyboard, 755

repeat rate, for keyboard, 755

repeated keystrokes, filtering out, 117

replies to e-mail, 410, **414–415**

reply, 821

reply separator, 425

Reply to All option, for e-mail, 422

Reply To Sender option, for e-mail, 422

Request a Fax dialog box, **740**

resolution of screen display, 51–52, 696–697

Resource Monitor, *315*, **315–316**

resources, system information on, 310

Restart in MS-DOS mode, 778

restoring files, 775–776, 822

    after Backup, **306–307**

Restricted Sites security zone, 507, 750

retail computer stores, 645

Rich Text Format (RTF), 478

right-clicking

    to copy file or folder, 726

    to move files and folders, 760

    to print, **196**

    for properties, 47–48

rocker DIP switches, 701

Rockwell Telecommunications, 857

Roland Corporation U.S., 857

ROM (read-only memory), 643, 822

root directory, 822

Ross, John, *ABCs of Microsoft Internet Explorer 4*, 443

Rounded Rectangle button, in Paint, 767

Royal Computer, 878

RSAC (Recreational Software Advisory Council), 497

rules. *See* horizontal line

Run from Start menu, 41, 776–777

Run Installation Program dialog box, *100, 101*

run-time version, 822

Russel, Charlie, *Upgrading to Windows 98*, 3

S

S & S Software International, 857

S3, Inc., 857

Sager Computer, 857

sags, 662

Sampo Technology, Inc., 858

Samsung America, Inc., 858

Samsung Electronics America, Inc., 858

Samtron, 858

Sanyo Energy (U.S.A.) Corporation, 858

Sanyo Fisher (USA) Corporation, 858

satellite TV, 241

saturation, 152

Save As dialog box, in Netscape Navigator, *540*

saving, 822

    Clipboard contents, **368**

    e-mail as word processing files, 433

    in FrontPage Express, **571**

    in Netscape Navigator, **538–542**

    sound schemes, **225–226**

    system files in Windows 95 before upgrade, 20–21

ScanDisk, **278–281**, *279*, 777

    approaches to running, 29–30

    automatically running, 280

    deleting file fragments after, 284

    scheduling, 286–287, 788

    when running Setup from DOS, 28

scanners, **261**

scheduling

    for checking Web sites for new content, 602, 607, **613–615**

        customizing, **616–620**, *619*

    sending fax, 738

schemes

    for mouse pointer, 166

    for sounds, 222

scientific calculator, 374

screen display, **138–146**

    copying to Clipboard, 69

screen resolution, 51–52, 156, 696–697

    changing, 272

    and Web page preview, 565

Screen Saver Properties dialog box, *628*

screen savers, **50**, **143–146**, 777, 822

    channels as, 457, 627–628

conflict with Power Management, 274

loading, **144–146**

password for, 769

in themes, 138

scripts, 822

for log on, 356

scroll bars, 822

in Netscape Navigator, *525*, 528

scroll box, 822–823

Scroll Lock key, sound for, 117, 118

scrolling, 822

with wheel mouse, 123

SCSI (Small Computer Systems Interface), 688, 823

for CD-Rs, 694

Seagate Software, 858

Seagate Technology, 858

Search bar, 454, 462–463, *463*

Search button, in Netscape Navigator, 526

search engines, 823, **889–890**, *890*, *891*

AltaVista, 889, *890*, *891*

for e-mail addresses, 440

Find command to access, 742

focusing searches in, **464**

for Internet, 401

variations in results, 462

search string, 823

searching. *See also* finding; Web searches

Seattle Data Systems, 878

Seattle Telecom & Data, Inc., 858

Secure Password Authentication (SPA), 341

Secured Sockets Layer (SSL), 512

security. *See also* certificates

for Dial-up networking, **355–360**

for Dial-up server, 352, *353*

encrypting transfers, **512–514**

for fax, 739

on Internet, 527, 750–751

in Netscape Communicator, 533–534

for online purchases, 903–905

Windows Update and, 289

Security button, in Netscape Navigator, 526

Security Settings dialog box, *510*

security zones, **507–511**

and active content download, 517–518

assigning Web site to, **510–511**

changing security level for, **508–510**

for Internet Explorer, *445*, 446

types, **507–508**

Select button, in Paint, 766

Select Network adapters dialog box, *328*

Select Network Client dialog box, 77

Select Network Component Type dialog box, *77*, *327*

selected files, backup of, 300–301

selecting, 823

Ctrl+A for, 68

drives in Explorer, **736**

in FrontPage Express, 561

multiple files, 89–90

Send To command, 777

adding shortcut to menu, **64–65**

in pop-up menus, **84–85**

Send To folder, finding, 85

sending

e-mail, **409–413**

e-mail to multiple addresses, **421–422**

files with HyperTerminal, **378–379**

shortcuts to Web pages, **478–479**

separator file, for print jobs, 175

Serial Line Internet Protocol (SLIP), 324, 333, 824

and Internet account, *398*, *398*

serial ports, 644

The Server Does Not have a DNS entry error message, 551

servers, for Dial-up networking, 324

serviceability, and proprietary designs, 638

sessions, 823

Settings, 778. *See* Start menu, ➢ Settings

Settings dialog box (Internet Explorer)

and temporary Internet files, *452*, 452–453

setup files, cleanup of, 285

Setup Wizard, 21

setup.txt file, 23, 30

Sex, RSACi rating standard for, 501–502

SGML (Standard Generalized Markup
Language), 823

shadow effect, for horizontal line in Web
page, 573

share-level security, 357–358

share name, for printers, 189

shared resources

drives as, 74

drives or folders, **78–79**

FAT32 file system and, 291

password for, 769

printer as, 173, **189–190**

shareware, 823, 893, 903

Shareware.com, *902*, **902–903**

Sharp Electronics Corporation, 858

shell account, 398

shielded cable, 658

Shift key, as StickyKey, 117, 118

Shining Technology, Inc, 859

shipping, 646

Shiva Password Authentication Protocol
(SPAP), 357

shopping basket in Web site, 487

shortcut keys, 823–824

shortcuts, **8**, **57–69**, 778, 823

adding to toolbar, **107–108**

and application location, 103

creating, **59–60**

to dial multiple networks, 338–339

to disk drives, **67**

to DOS programs, **67**

icons for, *58*, 58, **62–63**

locations for, **63–64**

names for, **61**

in Send To menu, **108**, *109*

settings, 61–62, *62*

to shortcuts, 106

in Startup folder, 65

for Web pages, **474–477**

creating for current, 475

folder for, **476–477**

icon for, 475–476

sending, **478–479**

subscription settings, **607–608**

to Windows Explorer, 72–73

Show Desktop icon, on Quick Launch toolbar,
108

Show Sounds setting, 119

Shut Down, 778

Alt+F4 for, 68

and print queue, 199

from Start menu, 41

Shuttle Computer International Inc., 859

Shuttle Technology, 859

Sigma Interactive Solutions Corporation, 859

signature file, 824

signatures

digital, 516

for e-mail, **430–432**

SIMM (single in-line memory module),
674–675, 824

locating, 679–680, *680*

Simple Technology, 859

single-clicking, 4

single in-line memory module (SIMM),
674–675, 824

locating, 679–680, *680*

single-session Kodak photo format, 693

site certificates, 515, **518**

size of fonts

in Netscape Navigator, **534–537**

on Web pages, **579–580**

SL Waber, 859

slide DIP switches, 701

SLIP (Serial Line Internet Protocol), 324, 333,
824

and Internet account, 398, *398*

Small Computer Systems Interface (SCSI), 823

Small Icons view, 733, 760

Smart and Friendly, 859

SMART Modular Technologies, Inc., 859

Smile International Inc., 859

smiley, 824

smoking, and computer maintenance, 655

snail mail, 824
    address in e-mail signature, 430
sneakernet, 824
software publisher certificates, 514, **515-518**
solid colors, 152
Sony Corporation, 639, 859
sorting e-mail, 413
    in Outlook with filters, **435**, *436*
sound card, 222, **696**
    recording quality from, 233
Sound Recorder, 213, **228-233**, *229*
    editing, **232-233**
    playing sound file, **229-230**
    recording sound, *230*, **230-231**
sound recording, from audio CD, 222
sound schemes, 138, 231
    loading and saving, **225-226**
Sound Sentry, 119
SoundBlaster, 208
sounds
    assigning to Windows events, 223, 779
    maximum file size, 232
    sources for, 222, 223
    troubleshooting, 223
    on Web pages, 582
Sounds applet, 115, 223-225, *224*
SPA (Secure Password Authentication), 341
spam, 824
speakers
    magnets in, 657
    recommendations for, **695**
special characters, **369-370**, *370*
    in FrontPage Express, **561-562**
speed
    of Internet response to clicking hyperlink,
        530
    of memory, 673
speed dial, 371-372
spooled print jobs, 172
SRAM (static random access memory), 673
SRS Labs, Inc., 859
SSL (Secured Sockets Layer), 512
S.T. Research Corporation, 857

Stac Electronics, 859
Stacker, 32, **33**
stand-alone, 824
standard disclaimer, 825
Standard Generalized Markup Language
    (SGML), 823
Starquest Computers, 878
Start button, *38*, **38-41**
Start menu, 779-780
    adding program to, **64**
    adjustments during install, 27
    closing, 38-39
    ➤ Documents, 39, 730
    ➤ Favorites, 39
    ➤ Find, 40
        ➤ Computer, 349
        ➤ Files or Folders, 104
    ➤ Help, 41, *53*, **53-55**
    ➤ Log Off, 41
    placing item on Desktop, **63**
    ➤ Programs, 39, 103, 771-772
        shortcuts on, **106-107**, *107*
    ➤ Run, 23, 41, 776
    ➤ Settings, 39, 778
        ➤ Active Desktop, 714
        ➤ Control Panel, *112*, *724*, **724-725**.
            See also Control Panel
        ➤ Printers, 178
        ➤ Taskbar & Start Menu, 42, 780,
            782-784
    ➤ Shut Down, 41, 280
startup disks, for Windows 98, 21. *See also*
    emergency startup disk
Startup folder, 65, 780
static electricity, **663-666**
    and memory chips, 675
static RAM, 825
static random access memory (SRAM), 673
status bar
    in FrontPage Express, 560
    for Internet Explorer, *445*, 446
        padlock icon, 514
    in Netscape Navigator, *525*, 527-528

STB Systems, Inc., 860

StickyKeys, 117, 118

Stop button, in Netscape Navigator, 526

storage devices, vendors, 867

Storage Technology Corporation, 860

Storage USA, 867

Stracon, Inc., 860

streaming, 825

stretching, wallpaper, 140

subdirectory, 825

subdomain, in Internet address, 399

subfolders

    for Favorites list, **470–472**, *471*

    including in Find, 741

submenu, 825

    adding to Programs menu, 771–772

Subscribe Favorite dialog box, 603

Subscribe Wizard, 626

subscribing, 825

subscriptions, **600–605**, 737

    browsing updated, **603–604**

    canceling, **604–605**

    to channels, **11–12**, 621, **624–627**

    custom schedule, **616–620**

    defining, **606–616**

    downloading contents, limits for, **610–613**, *611*

    frequency of updating, 616

    means of notification, **608–609**

    scheduling check for content change, **613–615**

    signing up for, **600–601**

    unattended dial-up connections for, **617–618**

    updating manually, **615–616**

    viewing current, *605*, **605–606**

Subscriptions folder, 606

subtitles, and DVD disks, 220–221

summary

    after formatting floppy, 83

    displaying for ScanDisk, 279, *279*

sunlight, heat from, 654

Sunway Inc., 878

SuperStor, 32, **33**

supervisor in Content Advisor, passwords for, 499–500

Supra Corporation, 860

surf, 825

Surfing the Internet with Netscape Communicator 4 (Tauber, et al.), 521

surge protection, 662

Surround Video, 212

Survey Form template, in FrontPage Express, 568

suspend mode, and monitor display, 162

SVGA display, 644

    resolution for, 52

Swan Instruments, 860

Swan Technologies, 878

swap file, 672

    size of permanent, 33

switches, for hardware, 130, *131*

Sybex, web site, xxxv

Symantec Corporation, 860

Symbol dialog box (FrontPage Express), 561–562

sync link, 381

synchronizing files, Briefcase for, **381**

synchronous transmission, 825

Synnex Information Technologies, Inc., 860

SyQuest Technology, 860

sysop, 825

system, 825

System applet, 115

    to remove drivers, 126

system board. *See* motherboard

System Commander, 291

system data, 825

system events, assigning sounds to, **221–226**

System File Checker, 14, *312*, **312–313**

system files

    copying to formatted floppy, 83

    limits on options to save, 31

    saving before upgrade, 20–21, 24, *25*

System Information utility, **310–311**, *311*

System Monitor, **313**

System Properties dialog box
Device Manager, *266*
system resources, 15
system time, 826
SYSTEM.INI file, 826

T

T1 line, 826
T3 line, 826
Tagram System Corporation, 860
Tahoe Peripherals, 860
Tandberg Data, 860
tape drive, for Backup, 299
target object
for hyperlinks, 588
creating, 589–590
for shortcuts, 62
Task Scheduler, **287**, 784
Taskbar, **41–46**, 780–781. *See also* toolbars
Display icon on, 273
Display Settings icon on, 158
hardware icons on, 43
hiding, **42**
icons for StickyKeys or Filterkeys, 118
location and size, **42**
printer icon on, 194
Quick Launch toolbar, 42, **43–44**
Resource Monitor icon on, 315
sizing, 45
Task Scheduler on, 287
Taskbar & Start Menu, 782–784
Start Menu Programs tab, 39
tasks, 826
Tauber, Daniel, et al., *Surfing the Internet with Netscape Communicator 4*, 521
TC Computers, 878
TCP/IP Properties dialog box, WINS Configuration tab, *347*
TCP/IP (Transmission Control Protocol/Internet Protocol), 826
settings for DUN connection, *335*
TCP (Transmission Control Protocol), 826

TDK Electronics Corporation, 861
TDN Inc., 878
TEAC America, Inc., 861
Techmedia Computer Systems Corporation, 861
Technology Distribution Network, 878
Tektronix Inc., 861
telecommuting, 320
telephone log, 371, **372–373**
Telephone Sound Quality, 231
telnet, 826
Telphony applet, 115
temperature, safe ranges for computers,
652–653
Tempest Micro, 861
templates, in FrontPage Express, **567–568**
temporary files, cleanup of, **283–285**, *284*, 285
temporary Internet files, 749
disk space for, 452
and encrypted pages, 512
terabyte, 826
test page, printing, 182, 185
testing, Dial-up networking connection,
337–338
Texas Instruments, Inc., 861
text
finding file containing specific, 741
size and color in Netscape Navigator,
534–537
text alternative, for inline images, 595
text boxes, 827
Text button, in Paint, 766
text editor, 827
text files, 827
sending in HyperTerminal, **379**
themes for Desktop, 14, 113, **138**, 152
thermal shock, **654**
threads, 415, 827
throughput, 827
ThrustMaster, Inc., 861
Thunder Max Corporation, 861
Tiger Software, 878
tiling, 827
wallpaper, 140

time
    default formatting for, 774
    system settings for, 137
time out, 827
time zones, 138
title bar, 827
    font for, 150
    in FrontPage Express, 559
    for Internet Explorer, 444, *445*
    in Netscape Navigator, 524, *525*
<TITLE tag (HTML), 582
titles
    on DVD disks, 219–220
    of Web pages, 582
TLS (Transport Layer Security), 513
TMC Research Corporation, 861
Today's Links Quick Link, 447
toggle, 827
ToggleKeys, 117, 118
Too Many Users error message, 551
toolbars, 4, **43–46**, 783, 827
    adding shortcuts to, **107–108**
    Address toolbar, **44**
    in CD Player, 236, *236*
    in Channel Viewer mode, 623
    configuring, **46**
    creating, **45**, 784
    Desktop toolbar, **44**
    in Explorer, 733–735
    in FrontPage Express, 560
    for Internet Explorer, 444–445, *445*
        appearance of, **446**
    Links toolbar, **44–45**
    in Netscape Navigator, 524–528, *525*
    for Paint, 765–767
    space for, **45**
Tools menu, in Explorer, 733
topology of network, 75
Toshiba America Information Systems, Inc.,
    861
Total Peripheral Repair, 865
TouchStone Software Corporation, 861
Track display, in Media Player, 228

trails, for mouse pointer, 167–168, 758
transients, **662**
Transmission Control Protocol/Internet
    Protocol (TCP/IP), 826
Transmission Control Protocol (TCP), 826
Transport Layer Security (TLS), 513
Trend Micro Devices, 861
Tri-State Computers, 879
Trident Microsystems, Inc., 862
troubleshooters, 748
troubleshooting problems, **309–316**
    changing network passwords, 345
    Dr. Watson, **311**, *312*
    external modem install, 702–703
    modems, **259–261**, 708
    page loading in Navigator, 544
    printers, **264**
    Resource Monitor, *315*, **315–316**
    System File Checker, *312*, **312–313**
    System Information utility for, **310–311**,
        311
    System Monitor, **313**
    with Windows 98 tools, **316**, *317*
    WINS connection, **348–349**
TrueType fonts, 745
Truevision, Inc., 862
Trusted Sites security zone, 507, 750
TTL (Transistor-Transistor Logic) chips
    static electricity and, 664–665
TV set, as monitor, 162
TV Viewer, **240–249**, *244*
    adding channels to toolbar, **246–247**
    channels for, **245**, *246*
    how it works, 242–243
    remote control and special keys, **247–248**
twisted-pair cable, 658
Tyan Computer, 862

U

UDF (Universal Disk Format), 215–216
<UL> tag (HTML), 575
UMAX Technologies, 862

UNC (Universal Naming Convention), 338

undeleting, 827

   files, 784

   program for, 828

undervoltage, 662, **663**

Undo button, in Explorer, 733

undo feature

   in FrontPage Express, 561

   keyboard shortcuts for, 68

upgradability, 638

Unicore Software, 867

Uniform Resource Locator (URL), 5, 828. *See also* URL (Uniform Resource Locator)

Uninstal.exe, 31–32

Uninstaller, 102, 136

uninstalling

   applications, **101–103**, 716, 785

   DOS programs, **103**

   printers, **264**

   removing files to gain disk space, **32**

   Windows 3.1 programs, **102–103**

   Windows 98, emergency startup disk for, 26

Unisys Corporation, 862

United Computer Exchange, 881

Universal Disk Format (UDF), 215–216

Universal Naming Convention (UNC), 338

Universal Serial Bus (USB) devices, 14

Unix shell account, 398

unmoderated, 828

unread, 828

unsubscribe, 828

unverifiable transactions, restricting, 488

unvisited links, setting color in Navigator, 536, *537*

Up button, in Explorer, 733

Update Device Driver Wizard, 265, *267*, 270–271, *271*

Update Wizard, *288*, 288–289

upgrade, 828

Upgrading to Windows 98 (Russel and Crawford), 3

uploading, 828

URL (Uniform Resource Locator), 5, 399, 828

   creating link from, 587

   for FTP site, 451

   to open document in Netscape Navigator, **531–533**

   for page in FrontPage, 569, 582

U.S. Robotics Corporation, 862

USA Flex, 879

The Used Computer Marketplace, 881

Usenet, 828

Usenet newsgroups, 828

user interface, 829

user-level permissions, 358

user-level security, for Dial-up server, 352, *353*

user profiles, 756, 767–768, 785–786

usernames, 829

   in e-mail address, 399

   entering during install, 27

Users applet, 116

V

Valitek, 862

Valtron Technologies, Inc., 865

VANTAGE Technologies, Inc., 865

variable-width font, in Netscape Navigator, 535, 536

variables, for <META> tag, 585

Vektron, 879

vendors

   BIOS upgrade, 867

   data recovery, 864–865

   manufacturers, 834–864

   older PC repair & exchange, 879–881

   parts and component dealers, 868–878

   recycling centers, 881

   storage devices, 867

Verbatim Corporation, 862

VeriSign, Inc., 519

version number, 829

VESA Display Power Management Signaling (DPMS), 144

VGA display, 644
  resolution for, 52
video capture cards, 241
Video CD, 829
video device drivers, 269
  changing, **270–271**
  settings for, 154–163, *155*
video display adapters, **268–274**, 637, 643–644
  changing, **269**
  color options, 155
  memory on, 159
  new driver for, 159
  purchasing decision, 160
  recommendations for, **696–697**
  and resolution options, 52
Video Electronics Standards Association, 862
video monitors. *See* display monitors
video, playback, 211
video RAM, 829
video random access memory (VRAM), 674
video standards, 641
videodisc, 829
View menu
  in Explorer, 732
  to open Explorer bars, 9, *9*
viewing
  channels from Channel bar, **624**
  channels in Internet Explorer, **622**
  current subscriptions, *605*, **605–606**
  local documents in Navigator, **542–543**
Views button, in Explorer, 733
ViewSonic Corporation, 862
Violence, RSACi rating standard for, 501–502
virtual, 829
Virtual Private Network (VPN), 326, 327
viruses, 403, 829, 895–896
visited links, 531
  setting color in Navigator, 536, *537*
Visual Basic, 830
VLB bus, 696
VLSI Technology, Inc., 862
Vmu.exe, 34
Volume Control, 222, 786–787

Voxware plug-in, 233
Voyetra Technologies and Turtle Beach
  Systems, 863
VPN (Virtual Private Network), 326
  for PPTP connection, 327
VRAM (video random access memory), 674

W

WACOM Technology Corporation, 863
WAIS (Wide Area Information Service), 830
wall socket, problems from, **660–663**
wallpaper, 830
  for Desktop, 50, **139–142**
  help screen as, 55
  loading, **142**
water, as computer hazard, **667–668**
Watermark option, for background image on
  Web page, 584
.wav files, 222
  creating, **228–233**
  sources for, 223
Wavetable cards, 696
WaveWorks, 213
Web addresses
  Address toolbar to enter, **44**
  typing to navigate Web, **450–451**
Web browsers, 390, 830
  choosing, 539
  default, **479–480**
  Netscape Navigator, *391*
  and page appearance, 577
  Windows 98 interface functioning as, 5, *6*
Web Gallery Quick Link, 447
Web help, **55**, 749
Web page authors, page rating determination
  by, **498**
Web pages, 830. *See also* shortcuts, for Web
  pages
  creating. *See also* FrontPage Express
  creating local, **473–474**
  Desktop as, 714
  formatting in FrontPage, **577–585**
  frames in, **545–546**

properties in FrontPage Express, **582–584**
saving in Navigator, **539–541**
  missing graphics after, 542
without PICS standard, 501
Web searches, **885–893**. *See also* search
  engines
  central page for, 892
  directories for, **885**, *885*, *886*
  by keyword, **888**
  refining, **892**
  search pages for, 893
  by topic, **886–887**
Web server, 830
Web sites, 830
  about Internet, **403–404**
  AltaVista, 889, *890*, *891*
  assigning to security zone, **510–511**
  creating Hot List for, **473–474**, *474*
  downloading, 11
  for graphics, 591–592
  for icons, 475
  Netscape Communicator online documenta-
    tion, 529
  NetShepherd content-filtering software, 495
  Netsite Commerce Servers, directory of sites
    using, 534
  for newspapers online, 465
  RSACi rating standard, 498
  for searches, 893
  for shareware, 903
  shortcuts for, **474–477**
  for specialized directories, 463
  subscribing to, **601–603**
  Sybex, xxxv
  VeriSign, Inc., 519
  for WinZip, 897, *897*
Web style, 47, 743
WebBots (bots), 563, 568
Webcast receiver, 248–249
Webcasting, 599
Weisskopf, Gene, *Mastering Microsoft Internet
  Explorer 4*, 483, 557, 599
Weitek Corporation, 863

Welcome to Netscape home page, 523–524
Welcome to Windows, 787–788
Western Digital, 863
Western encoding set, in Netscape Navigator,
  535
What's This?, 788
wheel mouse support, 123
Whole Internet Catalog (GNN), 460
WhoWhere?, 440, 743
Wide Area Information Service (WAIS), 830
width of horizontal line, in Web pages,
  572–573
wildcard characters, in URL for security zone
  assignment, 511
Willow Peripherals, 863
WinDelete, 102
windows, 830
  closing, **721–722**
Windows 3.x, 831
  printer driver for, 186
Windows 3.1
  removing programs, **102–103**
Windows 3.1 users
  shortcuts description for, 8
  Windows 95 improvements, **15–16**
Windows 9x, 831
Windows 95, vs. Windows 98, 7
Windows 98, 1
  changes, **4–7**
  deleting uninstall information, 285
  as dial-up server, **351–355**
  fonts used in, 745
  installing, **19–35**
  license for logo, 101
  memory requirements, **672**
  new features, **3–4**, **14**
  Web browser functions in interface, 5, *6*
Windows 98 CD
  extracting system file from, 313
  information about printers, 174
Windows 98 Driver Library Disk, 186
Windows 98 Instant Reference (Dyson), 713

Windows 98: No Experience Required
   (Crawford), 71, 95, 253, 277, 309
Windows 98 Registration Wizard, 787
Windows 98 setup
   disk space for, 21
   options maintained by, 4
   welcome screen, *24*
Windows 98 startup, starting program at,
   65–66
Windows application, 830
Windows events, assigning sounds to, 223
Windows Explorer, 5, *72*, **72–74**
   to create folder, 727
   customizing folder, **735–736**
   file extension display in, **73–74**, *74*
   to find files, 104–105, *105*
   floppy disks in, **81–83**
   to format floppies, **82–83**
   mapped drive in, 80, *81*
   menus in, 731–733
   to open Control Panel, 112
   to run setup, 23
   selecting drive in, **736**
   toolbars in, 733–735
Windows, installing Windows 98 from
   within, 20
Windows key, 830
Windows NT, 831
   multiboot with MS-DOS, 35
   RAS (Remote Access Service), vs. Win-
      dows 98 dial-up server, **351–355**
   and Windows 98, 21
   and Windows 98 install, **34–35**
Windows resources, 15
Windows tour, 210
Windows Tune-Up, 14, **788–789**
Windows Update, **13**, **287–289**, *288*, 789
Windows\Downloaded directory, 517
Windows\Media directory, 224
WINDOWS\MORICONS.DLL file, 62
WinFax, 831
WIN.INI file, 831
winipcfg, 348–349, *349*

Winner Products (U.S.A.) Inc., 863
WINS address for TCP/IP adapter, 345
WINS (Windows Internet Name Service)
   for NT domain connection over Internet,
      343–350
   troubleshooting connection problems,
      348–349
   vs. Dial-up networking or PPTP, **350**
WinZip, 897
   downloading, **897–898**
   using, **898–902**
wireless communication, infrared devices for,
   267–268
wizards, 831
   to create Web page in FrontPage Express,
      568–569
Word for Windows, WordMail for, 429
word processor
   saving e-mail as files for, 433
   to write e-mail, **427–429**
word wrap, in e-mail, 412
WordMail, 429
WordPad, **364–367**, *365*
   document creation and formatting, **366**
   opening, **365**
   page setup and printing, **367**
work, Internet access at, **394–395**
workstations, services to share resources, 77–78
World Wide Web, 5, 831. *See also* privacy on
   the Web
   Content Advisor to filter access, **495–506**
   error messages, **550–551**
   seamless connections, **9–10**
   subscriptions to, **600–605**
   vs. Internet, **388–392**
World Wide Web Consortium, 404
   Platform for Internet Content Selection, 497
World Wide Web navigation, **449–459**
   Explorer bars, **453–457**, *454*
   hot links for, **451–452**
   moving backward and forward, **457–458**
   for recently visited sites, **452–453**
   typing address, **450–451**

WorldPerfect, running from CD, 97, 97
Worldwide Technologies, 866
write cache, turning off for XtraDrive, 34
writeable DVD, 216
Wyse Technology, 863

X

X-ray machines, 656
Xerox Corporation, 863
XGA display, resolution for, 52
Xircom, 863
Xmodem protocol, 378
XtraDrive, **34**

Y

Yahoo!, **885**, 885, *886*, 893
    for graphics, 592
Yamaha Sys of America, 864
Ymodem-G protocol, 378
Ymodem protocol, 378

Z

zeros, displaying leading, 773
zip disk, 831
Zip drive, deleting files to Recycle Bin from, 87
Zmodem protocol, 378
Zmodem with Crash Recovery protocol, 378
Zoom Telephonics, 864

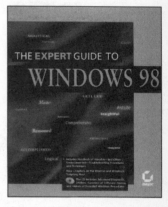

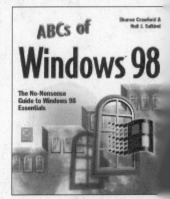

About the Contributors

S ome of the best—and best-selling—Sybex authors have contributed chapters from their current books to *Windows 98 Complete*.

Sharon Crawford   contributed chapters from *Windows 98: No experience required.* as well as *Upgrading to Windows 98* (coauthored with Charlie Russel) and *ABCs of Windows 98* (coauthored with Neil J. Salkind).

Ms. Crawford has written many successful books designed to make computers more accessible to professionals and consumers. Her recent titles include *The ABCs of Windows 95, Upgrading to Windows 95*, and *Your First Modem*. She is also an advisor to the Windows User Group Network (WUGNET).

Charlie Russel   contributed a chapter from *Upgrading to Windows 98* (coauthored with Sharon Crawford).

Mr. Russel has shared authorship of many successful books on Windows and personal computers with Sharon Crawford and is also the author of *The ABCs of Windows NT Workstation 4*.

Neil J. Salkind   contributed chapters from *ABCs of Windows 98* (coauthored with Sharon Crawford).

Mr. Salkind teaches at the University of Kansas and is the author of a number of books about Windows and the Macintosh.

Robert Cowart   contributed chapters from *Mastering Windows 98* and *Mastering Windows 98, Premium Edition*.

Mr. Cowart is one of the most well-known Windows authors in the world. He has written over thirty books on computer programming and applications, with twelve books on Windows, including *Windows 3.1 Quick and Easy, Windows 95 Quick and Easy, Windows NT Server 4: No Experience Required*, and the best-selling *Mastering Windows 95*, all from Sybex. His articles have appeared in *PC Week, PC World, PC*, and *Microsoft Systems Journal*.

Mark Minasi   contributed chapters and appendices from *Expert Guide to Windows 98* and *The Complete PC Upgrade and Maintenance Guide*.

Mr. Minasi is a noted lecturer and writer in the fields of PC computing, data communications, and operating systems. His best-selling books include *Mastering Windows NT Server 4, Mastering Windows NT 4 Workstation, Mastering TCP/IP for NT, The Hard Disk Survival Guide*, and *Troubleshooting Windows*, all from Sybex.

Gene Weisskopf   contributed chapters from *Mastering Internet Explorer 4* (coauthored with Pat Coleman).

Mr. Weisskopf has been involved in the PC revolution since the early 1980s. He has developed software applications for business and science and has taught a variety of classes and training sessions. His articles have appeared in a number of computer magazines, and he has written several books for Sybex, including *The ABCs of Excel 97*, *Mastering Quattro Pro 6*, and *Murphy's Laws of PCs*.

Pat Coleman   contributed chapters from *Mastering Internet Explorer 4* (coauthored with Gene Weisskopf).

Ms. Coleman is the co-author of *Mastering Intranets, Windows 95/NT Edition*, as well as many other Sybex books.

Peter Dyson   contributed material from *The PC User's Essential Accessible Pocket Dictionary* and *Windows 98 Instant Reference*.

Mr. Dyson is a writer and consultant software engineer with more than twenty years of experience in engineering, software development, and technical support. His computer-related publications include numerous technical research papers and over two dozen books. Among his recent Sybex titles are *ABCs of Intranets* and *Mastering Microsoft Internet Information Server*.

Christian Crumlish   contributed material from *The Internet: No Experience Required* and *The Internet Dictionary*.

Mr. Crumlish is co-owner of an Internet and network consulting firm. He has written several books on the Internet, including *A Guided Tour of the Internet*, *The Internet Dictionary*, and *The ABCs of the Internet*, all from Sybex. Crumlish is known for his easy, witty writing style and ability to simplify difficult topics.

Daniel A. Tauber and Brenda Kienan   contributed material from *Surfing the Internet with Netscape Communicator 4*.

Mr. Tauber has led technical development of Web sites for Fortune 500 companies and holds a degree in Computer Science. Ms. Kienan produces Web content for the publishing and search engine industries. Their other books include *Mosaic Access to the Internet*, *The Complete Linux Kit*, and the best-selling *SimCity 2000 Strategies and Secrets*, all from Sybex.

John Ross   contributed chapters from *ABCs of Internet Explorer 4*.

Mr. Ross has been writing about computers and telecommunications for more than fifteen years. He has written award-winning user's manuals and articles for AT&T, Motorola, and many other communication equipment manufacturers. His other books include *Connecting with Windows 95* and *All About WinFax PRO 7 for Windows 95*, both from Sybex.

Windows 98:
No experience required.
Sharon Crawford

608pp; 7 1/2" x 9"
ISBN:0-7821-2128-4
$24.99 US

Every user who's new to Windows 98 needs this book. This no-nonsense guide teaches the essential skills necessary for readers to use Microsoft's newest operating system effectively at home or at the office. Each chapter presents hundreds of real-world examples that let readers learn the practical skills they need to succeed in today's marketplace. Not only is Windows 98 completely explained, but so is Microsoft's Internet Explorer browser, which now built into the operating system. When you learn Web View, the wide world of the Web is as close as your Windows 98 desktop— and this book shows you how to take advantage of both!

PC Upgrading & Maintenance:
No experience required.
PC Novice/Smart Computing

544pp; 7 1/2" x 9"
ISBN:0-7821-2137-3
$24.99 US

Of the more than 200 million computers in use today, nearl 75 percent are obsolete according to today's fast Pentiur standards. If your machine is more than a year old, you nee this book. The clear, step-by-step explanations in this boo allow even complete computer novices to make all of th important software and hardware upgrades necessary t keep their computers running trouble-free. Tutorials, phc tos, and illustrations show you how to install memory, har drives, CD players, and scores of other peripherals. A glo. sary of terminology rounds out this essential book for begir ning and intermediate computer users.

UPGRADING TO WINDOWS 98

CHARLIE RUSSEL AND SHARON CRAWFORD

448pp; 7 1/2" x 9"
ISBN:0-7821-2190-X
$19.99 US

This easy-to-use guide gives current users of Windows 95 and 3.1 all the information they need to upgrade to Microsoft's revolutionary new Windows 98. Step-by-step instructions tell the reader how to prepare a PC for installing the new operating system without losing their current settings or data. The book gives users all the tips and tricks they need to get the most out of Windows 98—easy networking, troubleshooting, hardware upgrading, Internet tips, and important connectivity advice. This invaluable information will save readers countless hours of frustration and confusion.

EXPERT GUIDE TO WINDOWS 98

MARK MINASI, ERIC CHRISTIANSEN, AND KRISTINA SHAPAR

1CD
944pp; 7 1/2" x 9"
ISBN:0-7821-1974-3
$49.99 US

Based on Mark Minasi's $800 seminar, this book is the MIS, consultant, and power user's troubleshooting bible to the new version of Windows. Technically precise, yet enjoyable to read, this is the most accessible guide to networking, installing, and supporting Windows 98. The new Explorer/ Web View shell, which integrates the Internet with the operating system and local network, is also covered in great detail. The companion CD includes animations of the book's procedures, and several commercial Windows antivirus, diagnostic, and troubleshooting utilities.